What in the World is Music?

What in the World is Music? Second Edition is an undergraduate, interactive e-textbook that explores the shared ways people engage with music and how humans organize and experience sound. It adopts a global approach, featuring more than 300 streaming videos and 50 streaming audio tracks of music from around the world. Drawing from both musicological and ethnomusicological modes of inquiry, the authors explain the nature and meaning of music as a universal human practice, making no distinction between Western and non-Western repertoires while providing students with strong points of connection to the ways it affects their own lives.

The *What in the World is Music?* curriculum is divided into five parts, with a fully integrated multimedia program linked directly to the chapters:

- **The Foundations of Music I** proposes a working definition of "music" and considers inquiry-guided approaches to its study: Why do humans have innate musical perception? How does this ability manifest itself in the human voice? A catalog of musical instruments showcases global diversity and human ingenuity.
- **The Foundations of Music II** continues the inquiry-guided approach, recognizing the principles by which musical sound is organized while discussing elements such as rhythm, melody, harmony, texture, form, genre, and style. Where did music come from? What is it for?
- **Music and Identity** examines how music operates in shaping, negotiating, and expressing human identity and is organized around three broad conceptual frames: the group, hybridity, and conflict.
- **Music and the Sacred** addresses how music is used in religious practices throughout the world: chanting sacred texts and singing devotional verses, inspiring religious experience such as ecstasy and trance, and marking and shaping ritual space and time.
- **Music and Social Life** analyzes the uses of music in storytelling, theater, and film. It delves into the contributions of sound technologies, while looking at the many ways music enhances nightlife, public ceremonies, and festivals.

Alison E. Arnold, Ph.D., is Lecturer in the Music Department and Assistant Teaching Professor in the Arts Studies program at North Carolina State University. She edited the South Asia Volume of the *Garland Encyclopedia of World Music*. She performs Celtic Music on Irish flute and whistles, and is Director of the Irish Music Session at North Carolina State University.

Jonathan C. Kramer, Ph.D., was Teaching Professor of Music and Arts Studies, North Carolina State University and Adjunct Professor of Ethnomusicology, Duke University until retirement. He is a two-time Fulbright Fellow (India and South Korea) and former cellist with the San Francisco Opera and Ballet Orchestras and the North Carolina Symphony.

What in the World is Music?

SECOND EDITION

Alison E. Arnold
NORTH CAROLINA STATE UNIVERSITY

Jonathan C. Kramer
NORTH CAROLINA STATE UNIVERSITY

Routledge
Taylor & Francis Group

NEW YORK AND LONDON

Second edition published 2023
by Routledge
605 Third Avenue, New York, NY 10158

and by Routledge
4 Park Square, Milton Park, Abingdon, Oxon, OX14 4RN

Routledge is an imprint of the Taylor & Francis Group, an informa business

First edition published by Routledge 2016

ISBN: 978-1-032-43284-7 (ebk+)
ISBN: 978-1-032-34149-1 (pbk & ebk+ pack)

Typeset in Berling and Futura
by codeMantra

Access the instructor resources at www.routledge.com/9781032341491.

To our teachers, with gratitude:

Gordon Epperson (1921–2006)
David McAllester (1916–2006)
Bruno Nettl (1930–2020)

"When you pray … you thank God, you thank your ancestors, and you thank your teachers, whether they are alive or not alive."—Henk Tjon (1948–2009), "The Griot of Suriname"

Thanks, Henk. This is for you, too.

Contents

Figures

Maps

Preface

What in the World is Music? is an exploration of music's materials, contexts, and purposes. The textbook approaches music as a global phenomenon and a fundamental mode of expression of all people, as basic as language. *What in the World is Music?* considers the nature of musical sound, and examines the shared ways people engage with music: in worship, courtship, entertainment, etc. This textbook describes on the one hand the enormous variety and ingenuity of human musical invention, and on the other, the similarities in the ways people use music to express their emotions and organize their social interactions.

What in the World is Music? is written for undergraduate courses in Music Appreciation and World Music. This Second Edition emphasizes more a World Music curriculum, yet it differs from conventional approaches in the ways information is organized and delivered. This textbook explores the many roles music plays in human life, and the situations, both live and mediated, in which music takes place. Genres, styles, performance contexts, and artists from all parts of the world and various time periods exemplify fundamental patterns of musical engagement.

This curriculum grew out of a Music Appreciation course called "Understanding Music," which was originally taught as a chronological survey of Western art music. It gradually became more and more a hybrid, more and more like a World Music course as the authors/ instructors grappled with the question, "What does it mean to understand *all* music?" Western art music constitutes only a very small percentage of human musical engagements. Music is an extraordinarily diverse and complex universal category of human expression that has neurological, psychological, mythological, metaphysical, acoustical, social, and cultural dimensions and ramifications. Neither the regional survey of World Music nor the historical and chronological survey of Western art music was adequate to address these larger questions: What is music for? When does music happen? Who are the music makers? What else is going on when people make and listen to music? How and why is musical skill taught and learned? Furthermore, the material in existing textbooks was insufficient for considering these questions.

These larger questions, perhaps, need to be considered before asking students to differentiate between North Indian *bhajan* and *ghazal* for example, before asking detailed questions on world music forms and styles. This kind of factual knowledge, easy to test and grade, becomes more relevant in the context of a broader inquiry into the nature of music as a fundamental form of human expression and a commonality of human social life. To deepen student understanding, the case studies in this textbook demonstrate humanity's extraordinary musical diversity and creativity. Distinctions between Western and non-Western music are no longer relevant. Western music is a World Music. Juxtaposing

Gregorian plainchant with Buddhist chant sheds greater light on forms of sacred music than considering plainchant in Western music history and Buddhist chant in Asian studies. Similarly, juxtaposing Bollywood with Hollywood both accentuates our common humanity and liberates music from the boxes and categories of time and place, and even academic disciplines.

THE CURRICULUM

What in the World is Music? is a curriculum designed for undergraduate music students who will benefit from the global perspectives that this textbook offers. It is presented in an online eText format, and a print book is available as an ancillary to the eTextbook, for the convenience of re-reading and studying offline. Central to the organization of the text is a fully integrated multimedia program that includes over 380 video clips and audio tracks directly linked to the chapters. This rich multimedia program is an essential feature that allows students to understand performances, styles, and traditions as expressions of human engagement with music, as well as the social occasions and contexts in which these engagements take place.

The curriculum consists of fifteen chapters divided into five parts.

The Foundations of Music I

Part I deals with two fundamental questions for musical understanding. Chapter 1 asks the question "What is Music?" and presents definitions from a variety of cultures, as well as ways for engaging with musical sound. This Second Edition adds discussions of music and the natural world, the field of Ethnomusicology, and the preservation of musical sound. Chapter 2 discusses the human voice in all of its variety and diversity. The text highlights significant singers who have made a singular impact on their societies. Chapter 3 is a catalog of musical instruments from throughout the world, organized by the Sachs-Hornbostel classification system. Chapters 2 and 3 together consider the fundamental question, "What is Music Made Of?" If music is made of sound, what is making the sound? More than 100 videos from around the world present students with a rich experience of people engaged with musical artistry.

The Foundations of Music II

Part II continues the quest for musical understanding. Chapter 4 explores the ways musical sound is organized, in terms of melody, harmony, rhythm, etc. Examples are drawn from many of the world's music traditions. Chapter 5 uses origin myths from around the world and origin theories from the scientific and anthropological literature to explore possible reasons for music's existence. Finally, in Chapter 6, the text presents functions of music and the different ways people use music in their lives. These chapters have been enriched by additional examples in the Second Edition.

The rest of the curriculum considers in depth three fundamental ways in which people engage with music: to project their identities, respond to the sacred, and enhance their social lives. These three themes, taken together, provide a comprehensive view of the world's music and how it is used in these important areas of people's lives. Other themes such as music and film, theater, concerts, technology, song, and dance are subsumed within these three broad themes.

Music and Identity

Part III explores the concept of identity using three broad conceptual frames: the group, hybridity, and conflict. Chapter 7 discusses musical instruments and forms of song, dance, and composition as expressions of national, regional, ethnic, and cultural identity. Case studies include Argentine tango, Portuguese fado, nationalist composers, and music in multi-cultural Suriname. Chapter 8 explores how migration, trade, conquest, and the sharing of cultural forms can result in hybridized musical styles. Cajun culture in Louisiana, the Mon-tagnard refugee community in North Carolina, and Indo-Trinidadian music are among the case studies presented. In Chapter 9, Latin American protest songs (*Nueva Canción*), musicians resisting and opposing South African Apartheid, and Global Hip-Hop are among the case studies that exemplify music serving as a primary expression of defiance.

Music and the Sacred

Part IV explores sacred music in Hindu, Buddhist, Jewish, Christian, and Islamic contexts as well as in folk and syncretic traditions. Chapter 10 deals with forms of sacred chant including Vedic, Plainchant, and Qur'anic recitation; and with singing devotional forms such as Sufi *qawwali* and Christian hymns. Chapter 11 discusses the roles music plays in inspiring religious experience such as ecstasy and trance, and in conveying religious expressions through dance and drama. The chapter draws from traditions in China, Zimbabwe, Côte d'Ivoire, Japan, Bali, and India. In Chapter 12, case studies examine life-cycle and calendrical rituals, pilgrimages and processions, and the demarcation of sacred locales in Myanmar, Cape Verde, Ethiopia, and elsewhere.

Music and Social Life

Part V begins with an exploration of music in narrative traditions: bardic, theatrical, and operatic. Chapter 13 includes epic narration from the Balkans and West Africa, storytelling from Korea and China, puppet theater from Japan and Java, and Western and Chinese opera. Music in urban nightlife, sporting events, ceremonies, and festivals constitutes the subject matter of Chapter 14. Examples are drawn from Brazil, Canada, Mexico, Nigeria, Trinidad, the United States, and elsewhere. The final Chapter 15 discusses cultural tourism and presents a history of sound technologies and film music (Hollywood and Bollywood), topics specifically relevant to the world today.

SPECIAL FEATURES

- Unique thematic organization designed for both World Music and Music Appreciation curricula.
- Case studies drawn from nearly forty countries representing every continent except Antarctica.
- Over 300 videos linked directly to the chapter texts.
- Over sixty audio files accessed through Spotify and CREM (Centre for Research in Ethnomusicology, Paris), integrated into the chapters.
- Over 250 illustrations, in color.

- Key terms and concepts at the end of each chapter for study purposes.
- "Thinking About Music" questions that tie chapter material to students' own musical experiences.
- Endnotes containing bibliographic information.
- Glossary with over 300 words.
- Quiz questions for the use of instructors.
- Over twenty-five maps showing geographical locations for the traditions that the chapters present.

NEW IN THE SECOND EDITION

- Chapters reorganized into five parts of three chapters each that more closely match standard academic calendars.
- Around twenty-five new case studies, including Notational Systems, The Black Atlantic, Carifesta (Caribbean Arts Festival), *Jingju* (Chinese Opera), and Cultural Tourism.
- Case studies updated to include such current topics as "Black Lives Matter" and the impact of COVID-19.
- Sixty-six new videos linked to the eText.
- Media links bolded in blue, leading directly to streamed audio and video.
- A Media Index listing video and audio files by chapter and by geographic region.
- Eighty-eight new images.
- "Further Resources" section of selected readings listed by chapter.
- Additional maps.

TO THE INSTRUCTOR

What in the World is Music? can be used as a self-sufficient curriculum for either World Music or Music Appreciation in the classroom or online. The eTextbook contains everything needed for teaching such courses, including all video and audio examples linked directly to the chapter texts. In the traditional classroom setting, instructors may use this curriculum in a variety of ways. Students can read the chapters in preparation for classroom discussion, or video and audio recordings may be presented in lectures and discussions before the students read the chapters, which are then assigned through the online platform for out-of-class study and review. Instructor's resources are located at the Instructor Resources Download Hub, https://routledgetextbooks.com/textbooks/instructor_downloads/.

Instructors using *What in the World is Music?* for either World Music or Music Appreciation courses may wish to supplement or modify the material based on their individual areas of interest, expertise, or specialization. For example, an instructor with expertise in African percussion might engage students in a drumming practicum in order to deepen their understanding of polyrhythm, or other relevant topics relating to African music. The extensive media resources can be used as a media library. An instructor might illustrate a general discussion of India, for example, with some of the more than twenty-five videos related to the music of South Asia, using the Media Index "By Geographical Region."

TO THE STUDENT

This textbook is designed to encourage you to develop a deeper appreciation of why music is important in your life and in the life of humanity. Understanding music from a global perspective, critically engaging with its many and intricate inner workings and connections to the wider world, shows how essential it is. The late Ernest Boyer, former President of the Carnegie Foundation for the Advancement of Teaching, urged students to engage thoughtfully with those aspects of human experience that are shared throughout the world. He called these aspects "core commonalities"—"those universal experiences that are shared by all people and all cultures on the planet and make us truly human."[1] Making and responding to music is one of Boyer's core commonalities. A primary objective of this music curriculum is to provide a deep engagement with music as a universal human activity and communicative code. While forms of musical expression around the world can be radically different from each other, there are fascinating and important areas of convergence, which constitute the foundation of this curriculum. What people everywhere *do* with music is not so different from what *you* do with music, and this course provides the means for you to explore both the diversity of musical expressions and the similarity of musical functions. This is a curriculum that requires your active engagement. *What in the World is Music?* is not a traditional textbook. Text, videos, maps, pictures, and audio files all work together to constitute a complete platform for learning that you access through the internet. There is a famous quote, variously attributed: "Talking (or writing) about music is like dancing about architecture." Reading about music without hearing it, seeing its context, and engaging with its multiple meanings is inadequate. Music must be experienced in all its complexity for it to be understood as a living force in our lives. By accessing the eTextbook, you will see, hear, and read about musicians, dancers, actors, worshipers, audience members, and even boxers: a world of human expressive culture.

THE AUTHORS

In developing *What in the World is Music?* we draw from decades of experience performing, researching, and writing about music, and teaching college-level music courses. We are both professors of Music and Arts Studies at North Carolina State University. We have traveled extensively and have carried out music research in diverse regions of the world. We have significant backgrounds in Western and non-Western music as performers and scholars, and continue professional lives as instrumentalists outside the university.

ALISON E. ARNOLD

From my earliest memories in Yorkshire, England, music has always been a significant part of my life. My siblings and I took piano lessons from age five, my parents enjoyed opera and symphony concerts, and our home had an old wind-up gramophone and a stack of 78 rpm records. I went on to pursue a BA degree in music at the University of Liverpool. I sang with the Liverpool University Singers, and studied flute with the principal flautist of the Royal Liverpool Philharmonic Orchestra, Atarah Ben-Tovim (1940–2022). My first formal introduction to non-Western music was in London, working as an editorial assistant in the area of

Ethnomusicology for *The New Grove Dictionary of Music and Musicians* (6th ed.). In 1978, I moved to the United States for graduate study in Musicology and Ethnomusicology at the University of Illinois at Urbana-Champaign. Guided by my dissertation advisor, Professor Bruno Nettl (1930–2020), I carried out field research in India on Hindi Film Song ("Bollywood"). Teaching positions in subsequent years took me to Colorado, Pennsylvania, and North Carolina, and in 2000, I joined the Music Faculty of North Carolina State University. Over the past twenty years I have taught courses in World Music, Music of Asia, Celtic Music, and Arts Studies. Research and conference travel have taken me to Japan, China (the Silk Road), Malaysia, Cambodia, Laos, Vietnam, Trinidad, France, Ireland, Cape Breton, and Newfoundland. In the late 1990s I edited the South Asia volume of *The Garland Encyclopedia of World Music* (©2000). Further publications include journal and encyclopedia articles on Indian and Indian American music, and the first edition of this World Music textbook in 2016. Since moving to North Carolina, I have played traditional Irish and Scottish music on wooden flute and whistles, and now perform with several bands as well as leading a local Irish music session.

JONATHAN C. KRAMER

I grew up in a musical family in Hartford, Connecticut. My six brothers and sisters all sang and played instruments, and I began the study of the cello at age eight. I discovered the field of Ethnomusicology at Wesleyan University, where I studied "Native American Dance and Vocal Techniques" with David McAllester (1916–2006) and South Indian *veena* with Sri Kalyanakrishna Bhagavatar (1913–1979), while continuing the study of the cello at Yale with Aldo Parisot (1918–2018). Ethnomusicology and Cello Performance would continue as professional interests throughout my career. Later, I attended the University of Arizona where I worked with cello mentor and aesthetician Dr. Gordon Epperson (1921–2006). While performing with the San Francisco Opera Orchestra, I attended the class of Ali Akbar Khan (1922–2009) in San Raphael. I was awarded a Fulbright to study *dhrupad* at Banaras-Hindu University with Dr. Ritwik Sanyal (b. 1949). I served a second Fulbright in South Korea after completing a Ph.D. in Ethnomusicology and Performance Studies at the Union Institute with a dissertation on "bi-musicality." I joined the Music Faculty of North Carolina State University in 1985, after performing for two seasons with the NC Symphony. Over 35 years there, I taught courses in Western Music History, World Music, and Arts Studies. I also taught as adjunct professor of Ethnomusicology at Duke University, with courses in both South Asian and East Asian music cultures. My primary interest in the cello has shifted from performer to teacher, and my former students have attended many of America's major music conservatories including Juilliard, Manhattan, New England, Boston, Cincinnati, Peabody, and the UNC School of the Arts. Ethnomusicological research has taken me to India, Korea, China (particularly the Tibetan regions), Suriname, Uganda, and Ethiopia.

Alison E. Arnold
Jonathan C. Kramer

NOTE

1 Ernest Boyer, *Selected Speeches 1979–1995* (Princeton, NJ: Carnegie Foundation for the Advancement of Teaching, 1997), 109.

Acknowledgments

First Edition

In developing materials for this eTextbook, we have relied on the research and writing of many scholars, both of the present and past, known to us personally or by reputation. We do not claim global expertise, but readily acknowledge that we draw on a wide range of texts and other media in order to discuss music as a truly universal human phenomenon. We have corresponded with literally hundreds of musicians, scholars, filmmakers, writers, photographers, and publishers from around the world, and are indebted to the many contributors without whom this project would have been inconceivable. In this Acknowledgments section, we would like to express our enormous gratitude to all those who have supported the project and contributed to making this curriculum available to general students.

During the nearly twenty years of our collaboration on *What in the World is Music?* we have taught at North Carolina State University and are most grateful for the generosity and friendship of our colleagues there. In particular, we would like to thank our colleagues in the Music Department, and former chair, J. Mark Scearce; our invaluable Teaching Assistant, friend, and associate Elizabeth Holt; the Caldwell Fellows Program Director Janice Odom; Lavon Page and Donna Petherbridge of the LITRE grant program; Melissa Williford, former director of Distance Education; the D.H. Hill Library staff; Professor Emeritus David B. Greene; and the Hewlett Initiative. We have been fortunate to receive travel funds on a number of occasions, notably from the NCSU Division of Academic and Student Affairs, the College of Humanities and Social Sciences, the Music Department, and the NCSU Confucius Institute. Many of our travel arrangements were made with the capable assistance of Music Program Manager Kathleen Laudate. This project could not have been undertaken without the continuing support of our home institution.

We have received generous support and encouragement from a number of colleagues at regional academic institutions. At Duke University, Louise Meintjes and Paul Berliner provided much appreciated wise counsel. Also at Duke, Hsiao-Mei Ku and the Ciompi String Quartet; the late Benjamin Ward; Miriam Cook, Leo Ching, and Eunyoung Kim of the Asian and Middle Eastern Studies Department; and Ingrid Byerly in the Cultural Anthropology Department—all made invaluable contributions. From the University of North Carolina system, we greatly appreciate the help of David Garcia and Juan Alamo at UNC-Chapel Hill, and Gavin Douglas at UNC-Greensboro.

Other academics in ethnomusicology and related fields have given indispensable assistance: Juliana Azoubel (UFMG, Escola de Belas Artes, Brazil); Birgitt Drüppel (International School of Düsseldorf); John Baily (Goldsmiths, University of London, Emeritus); Tingting Chen,

Alessandra Ciucci (Northeastern University); the late Marnie Dilling (UC Berkeley); Ellen Dissanayake, Ter Ellingson (University of Washington); Peter Manuel (CUNY); Helen Myers, Don Niles (Institute of Papua New Guinea Studies, PNG); Dale Olsen (FSU, Emeritus); Cathy Ragland (University of North Texas); Ann Rasmussen (College of William and Mary); Tim Rice (UCLA, Emeritus); George Sawa, János Sipos (Hungarian Academy of Sciences); Beth Szczepanski (Lewis and Clark College); and Holly Wissler (Texas State University).

During the course of our research and writing for this project, we have each traveled extensively and would like to express our enormous appreciation to the many scholars, musicians, institutions, and travel organizers for welcoming us into their communities and sharing with us their expertise and firsthand knowledge.

- In Cape Breton, Canada: Paul Cranford, David ("Papper") Papazian, Otis A. Tomas, Mario Colosimo, Brenda Stubbert;
- In China: Frank Kouwenhoven, the late Antoinet Schimmelpennink, and CHIME (European Foundation for Chinese Music Research); Gerald Roche, Tsering Samdrup, Dawa Drolma of the Plateau Music Project; Hsiao Mei and Xiaolin Dai of the Shanghai Conservatory; Wen Xiangcheng, Acko Choedrag, and Xiao Wenli; Steven Zhang of Xinjiang Western International Travel Service, and Baiwei, Liang, Vicky, Jimmy, Jack, YaFan;
- In Ethiopia: Lidetu Shambal, Azmari Gezate, and Imagine Ethiopia Tours;
- In India: American Institute of Indian Studies (AIIS), Shubha Chaudhuri and Saraswati Swaminathan of the Archives and Research Center for Ethnomusicology (ARCE), Pandit Ritwik Sanyal, Shanti Shivani, Raju Bharatan, Adrit Joseph, and Holiday India;
- In Korea: Korean-American Educational Commission (Fulbright Korea), Baewon Lee of the National Gugak Center; Shim im Taek, Byon Kyong Hyuk, Jocelyn Clark, Joseph Celli, Lee Byon Won;
- In North Carolina, USA: the Irish community in the Triangle region, especially Julie Gorka and Tim Smith; the Montagnard community of Raleigh and Greensboro, especially Hip Ksor, Mondega (Bom Siu), Dock Rmah, Y Dha Eban;
- In Suriname: Cyriel Eersteling, the late Henk Tjon, the late President Elfriede Baarn-Dijksteel of NAKS (Na Afrikan Kulturu fu Sranan), the American Embassy in Suriname and former Ambassador Lisa Bobby Schreiber-Hughes; the late Granman Belfon Aboikoni of Djoemoe; Ricardo van Varsseveld, Rakieb Waggidhossain, Roy Raghu, Narider Singh, Hilary de Bruin of the Department of Culture Studies, Paramuru Native American Culture Society, Marlene Lie A. Ling of Marlene Dance Company, Wilgo Baarn and Alakondre Dron, and the late Director Herman Snijders of the Volksmuziekschool;
- In Trinidad: Marilyn Rousseau, Mungal Patasar and Pantar, Wendell Manwaran and 3Canal band;
- In Uganda: Nicholas Sempijje (Makarere University), James Isabirye (Kyambogo University), Nile Beat Artists Troupe, Larry Council of Teaching and Travel Sojourners (TATS); Zziwa Annet and the staff at Adonai House;
- In Vietnam: Dam Thi Thao of Handspan Adventure Travel, Hanoi.

In addition to the musicians and dancers we encountered on our travels, we are indebted to many more we have met via the internet, who have generously shared their artistry and recordings with us in support of World Music education.

Armour Hill Singers (Canada); Ayan Basi Adeleke (Nigeria and USA); Sergio and Odair Assad (Brazil); Maya Beiser (Israel, and New York, USA); Diali Cissokho, Will Ridenhour, and

Kaira Ba (Senegal, and North Carolina, USA); Nana Kimati Dinizulu and the Dinizulu Archives (USA, Ghana); Duo Agua Y Vino—Barbara Hennerfeind and Erik Weisenberger (Germany); Karlheinz Essl (Germany); Carolina Eyck (Germany); Bela Fleck (USA); Steve and Kate Fowler (California, USA); Imamyar Hasamov (Azerbaijan); Dan Heymann (South Africa); Naji Hilal (Lebanon and USA); Jorge Choquehuillca Huallpa (Peru); Louis-Daniel Joli (Canada); Kamal Kant (North India); Soheil Kaspar (Lebanon and USA); Areti Ketime (Greece); the late Ali Akbar Khan (North India); Ivan Kovachev (Bulgaria); Ladysmith Black Mambazo (South Africa); Michael Levy (USA); Cosmas Magaya (Zimbabwe); Wu Man (China and USA); Gilbert Mandere (Zimbabwe); Koji Matsunobo (Japan); Randy Max (UK); Nusaiba Mohammad (UK); Sahba Motallebi (Iran and USA); Mauricio Murcia (Colombia); Nuuk Posse (Greenland); Ricky Olombelo and Salala (Madagascar); Luca Paciaroni (Italy); Karen Panigoniak (Canadian Inuit); Wes Parker and Carolina Brass Band, music director Brian Meixner (North Carolina, USA); Steve Riley (Louisiana, USA); Rabbi Rodriguez Sabino (Israel); Mohammed Reza Shahjarian (Iran); Durian Songbird (USA); Vijayalakshmi Subramaniam (South India); Kayohito Takenaka (Japan); Victoria and Jussef Vasquez (Chile); Glen Velez (USA); Aishu Venkataraman (South India); Wolf's Robe (Native American, USA); and Darlene Zschech (Australia).

We are also grateful to the many music and film producers and organizations for sharing with us materials they have developed.

Swami Arun (Balinese Calonarang); *Centre National de la Recherche Scientifique* (CNRS) and the *Département d'ethnomusicologie* at *Musée de l'Homme*, Paris (CREM Archive recordings); Cat Celebrezze (Ravi Shankar's Raga); Jeremy Chevrier (Mali wedding party); Martin Cradick (Baka pygmies); Banning Eyre at Afropop Worldwide; the late Howard Gardner (*Altar of Fire*); Michal Goldman (Umm Kulthum); Harvard Archive (Avdo Međedović); Paul Hodge (Argentine tango, Brazilian carnival); Nic Hofmeyr (Weeping Music Video); International Olympic Committee (Seoul Olympic Ceremonies); Ulf Jägfors (Gambian *akonting*); Susan Levitas ("Shout Bands" in *The Music District*); Antonio Lino (*mbira* musicians); Hari Madathipparambil and Invis.org (*Kathakali*); Manohar Lalas (Epic of Pabuji); Lomax Foundation (*Cajun Country; Jazz Parades*); Jeremy Marre and Harcourt Films (*Konkombe; Rhythm of Resistance*); Peter Miller (*The Internationale*); Bruno Monsaingeon (*Nadia Boulanger*); Shauna Murray and Playing for Change; George T. Nierenberg (*Say Amen, Somebody*); Nobel Prize Committee; Michael Y. Parker and Leda Scearce (Laryngoscopy videos); Fraser Pennebaker (*Monterey Pop*); Marcia Rego (Cape Verde footage); Thomas Roebers and Floris Leeuwenberg ("Foli: There is no Movement without Rhythm"); Chris Simon and Sageland Media (*Oil Barrels, Steel Drums: Pan in Trinidad and Tobago*); Im Kwan Tek (*Sopyonje*); and UNESCO (Intangible Cultural Heritage of Humanity films).

We give special thanks to Yoko Ono Lennon for generously granting us permission to include the video of her late husband John Lennon performing "Mother" in concert; Coleman Barks for translations of Jalaluddin Rumi's poetry; the Venkateswara Temple of Cary, NC; and the great friend of music, the late Pete Seeger, with whom we spoke at length in November 2013 regarding his 1966 documentary *Afro-American Work Songs in a Texas Prison*, and whose hope for a world reconciled through music permeates this work.

A number of individuals at Routledge have guided this project. We would especially like to thank Music Editor Constance Ditzel for believing in our project from the very beginning, and shepherding this complex work through two editions. Assistants Denny Tek and Aurora Montgomery, and Editors Mhairi Bennett and Ruth Jeavons at Taylor & Francis in the United Kingdom. We also appreciate the assistance of the Design Staff at Routledge and the Technical Support staff at Vital Source.

Second Edition

We are most grateful to the following musicians who have shared videos of their artistry:

Eimear Arkins (Ireland); Talat Aziz (India); Zdravko Beshendzhiev (Bulgaria); Caroline Ní Chonaire (Ireland); Xiao Chu (China); Caitríona Ní Churraoin (Ireland); Matthew Detrick and the Apollo Chamber Players (USA); Wirruungga Dunnggiirr (Australia); Ann Marie Ní Fhatharta (Ireland); Darragh O Heiligh (Ireland); Maria Magdalena Kaczor (Poland); Yvonne Ní Loideáin (Ireland); Bao Narisu (China/Mongolia); Arsen Petrosyan (Armenica); Jhonathan "PUKA" Simon (Peru); Bom Siu (USA/Vietnam); Kim Seonghoon (Republic of Korea); Elijah Stevens (USA); Sanjay Subrahmanyan (India); and Joseph Torobeka (Burundi).

Performance videos were generously provided by the following individuals:

Robert Louis Baghdasaryan (Armenia); M. Jill Barone (USA); James DeWeaver (USA); Jean During (France/Uzbekistan); Esmail Gholamreza (Iran); James Isabirye (Uganda); Stephen Jones (England/China); Fran Kodra (Albania); Joshua Maroof (USA); Olympe Niragira (Rwanda/Burundi); Desiree Sampson (Trinidad and Tobago); Alexandra Sfintesco (Netherlands); Xiaofei Song (China); Reinhold Spatz/mickspatz (Germany/Thailand); Valdas Steponavicius (Lithuania); and Dai Xiaolin (China).

We gratefully acknowledge contributions by the following artists for providing demonstration videos:

Mairead Brady (USA/Ireland); John Caldwell (USA/Java); Xiao Chu (China); Jocelyn Clark and Choi Jinsook (Republic of Korea); Silvain Guignard (Japan); Naji Hilal (USA); Karen Panigoniak and Ida Kolola (Inuit); Smriti Sridharan, Kapil Ramanarayanan, and Samarth Rao (USA/South India).

Music and film producers and organizations who graciously contributed video material:

James Allen, The Singing Wells Project (Uganda); April Centrone, NY Arabic Orchestra (USA/Arabia); Rupin Dang, Wilderness Films India, Ltd. (India); Frances M. Dunlop, Sgioba Luaidh Inbhirchluaidh ("Waulking Song Group"); Deepa Dutta Chaudhuri, WheelsOnOurFeet (India); Cleon D. Frazier, Fairfield Baptist Church, Lithonia, GA (USA); Phil Hart, Dataforge (USA); Haruko Komoda, Todo Music Preservation Association (*Todo Ongaku Hozankai*) (Japan); Lillis Ó Laoire, Roinn na Gaeilge/Discipline of Irish, the National University of Galway (Ireland); Helen Lauder, Kalulu Ukulele Band (Australia); Mestre Fabio Melo, Acervo da capoeira Angola (Brazil); Adiyabold Namkhai, New Milestone Tours (Mongolia); Michael Ney, Eagle Spirit Media (Australia); Valerie Polk, Great Smoky Mountains Association (USA); Dessi Stefanova, London Bulgarian Choir and Wellcome Institute (UK/Bulgaria); Ciarán Ó Súilleabháin, Tuairisc (Ireland); Deepti Suridhingra, Radha Madhav Society (India); Todo Music Preservation Association (*Todo Ongaku Hozankai*) (Japan); Dan Torigoe, Dolceola Recordings, Antioch Old Regular Baptist Church, KY (USA); Tsoggy, Mongolian Ways—Mongolian Tours and Travel (Mongolia); UNESCO Intangible Cultural Heritage of Humanity (Korea, Japan, Uganda); Nikki Wanting, African Frenzy agency (South African); Joshua Weber (Israel); Robert L. Weitzner, RLWProductions (Armenia); and Nabil Zorkot, ProFoto Productions (Côte d'Ivoire).

We would like to express our gratitude to the following individuals for:

Text translations:
Emebet Hailu and Caleb Kebede (Ethiopia); Maryam Mohaghegh (USA/Iran); Ravi Mulukutla (USA/South India).

Images:
Stuart Carter (USA); University of Arkansas Special Collections.

Assistance with chapter case studies:
Margaret H. Beissinger (Croatia); Tang Cai (China); Jonathan Henderson (USA); Doryl Jensen (USA); Mark Katz (USA); Cherif Keita (USA/Mali); Ben Koen (Hong Kong); Kenny Rodriguez (USA); Chris Syren (Mali).

Finally, throughout the many years of our collaborative work we have enjoyed the love, comfort, and patience of our families. On the Arnold side, sons Adam and Nathan, granddaughter Ember, brother Nick and sister Gill and her family, and my late mother and father, Cathy and Jim. I owe an enormous debt of gratitude to my closest friend and life partner, husband Gordon, for his unfailing love and support, and for his invaluable assistance in editing and processing all of the new videos for our Second Edition. My sincerest thanks. On the Kramer side, beloved wife Lisa; children, their spouses, and grandchildren: Vieve Radha, Jamie P., Kahlila, Anthony, Matthias, Andreas, and Stella. Special thanks to my six brothers and sisters who taught me nearly everything I know—Stephen, David, Katherine, Susan, Christina, and Paul, and their families (especially sister Christina who maintained enthusiasm for the project when my own flagged, and brother Paul whose wizardry with photo editing saved many of our field photographs). Finally, my parents Herbert and Karyl, now deceased, who raised their unruly brood to be lovers of music, and of the life of the mind and the spirit.

For the second edition, we are extremely grateful to the following individuals at Code-Mantra and Routledge/Taylor & Francis for their hard work and expertise: Assunta Petrone (Production Manager), Peter Sheehy (Assistant Editor), Christopher Taylor (Production Editor), Christina Edwards (Copy Editor), Rejena James (Proofreader), Jo Steer (Cover Design)

A Visual Tour of the Enhanced eTextbook, *What in the World is Music?* Second Edition

This Second Edition offers a variety of features that help students identify and understand World Musics and cultures in all their diversity.

Table of Contents presents the thematic organization of the book.

Contents

Outline at the beginning of each chapter lists its main headings, which identify the principal topics discussed. These main headings are hyperlinked to their respective topic in the chapter. Each chapter includes an **Introduction.**

CHAPTER 1

What Is Music?

Introduction
A Working Definition
Music and the Natural World
The Field of Ethnomusicology
Four Approaches to Musical Understanding
What Is Sound?
What Is Hearing?
The Preservation of Music
Conclusion

Glossary Terms are **bolded in black** throughout the text, and definitions appear in pop-ups when the user hovers the cursor over the term. For example:

general terms music and musician require long and awkward

[explana

> **Classical Greek term for the arts that fall under the influence of the nine muses.**

Indeed, in _____, music and dance—sounds and the movements t_____ a single, indivisible category.
Some lang_____ term but with a broader meaning. The ancient Greek **musiki** included all the arts under the influence of the nine Muses. Thus, the words of a song along with its melody and rhythm were considered part of this single concept. In ancient India, the **Sanskrit** term *sangīta* "is the closest equivalent to the Western concept of music, although the inclusion of dance as one of the three main compartments suggests that in early

Media links are bolded in blue, and lead directly to streamed audio and video examples. For example:

Societies tend to favor higher or lower pitches within the normal range of the human voice. In the Andes Mountains in Peru, Quechua women (2.4) sing at the top of their vocal range. The video shows a family of musicians dedicated to preserving the traditional culture of the Andean region, in a performance that also features traditional dress, instruments, songs, and dances. The Sioux grass dance songs (2.5) heard in Native American powwows are sung by *men* with high-pitched voices in a register that elsewhere would be considered normal for women. Sometimes the voice is stretched beyond its normal range. Tibetan Buddhist monks (2.6) perform exercises as a religious practice that over years deepen their vocal range. It is with these specially cultivated voices that they recite their sacred scriptures.

Key Terms and Concepts are provided at the end of each chapter to identify important words and phrases for student review. These terms and concepts are searchable using the magnifying glass icon in the top navigation bar.

KEY TERMS AND CONCEPTS

Aerophone
Chordophone
Circular Breathing
Electrophone
Hocket
Idiophone

Thinking about Music questions appear at the culmination of each chapter. These are open-ended questions to encourage thought and discussion.

THINKING ABOUT MUSIC

1. How would you describe a familiar instrument in terms of the concerns Jan Mrázek expresses and the things this writer finds most important?

2. What does Jan Mrázek find limiting about the ways that instruments are described and classified by scholars?

3. Consider the violin, the guitar, and the accordion. These instruments are found throughout the world and have been adapted to many different cultural and social situations. How have each of these instruments been adapted to suit various musical contexts?

4. What does this mean: The lute family represents "the most dramatic example of the diffusion of a musical technology" (p. 56)?

5. How has the Chinese "free reed" technology contributed to World Music culture?

6. The sound of an aerophone comes from a vibrating column of air. What are some of the ways used to set the air vibrating?

7. What did the film composer Vangelis do to send "shockwaves through the entire music industry" (p. 89)?

Media Index lists all of the video and audio titles by reference number and clicking each one leads the reader back to the page where used, so that specific media links can be easily located in class or on a course syllabus. The Media Index by Chapter lists media in the order in which they appear in the book. The Media Index by Geographical Region organizes media by world region and country, for the benefit of instructors who wish to employ a geographical approach in addition to a topical one.

Media Index

By Chapter

CHAPTER 1

1.1 Audio: Albanian funeral song

1.2 Audio: Swiss cowherds

1.3 Audio: Yodeling song

1.4 Audio: Tuvan singers

1.5 Video: Competing Amazonian songbirds

1.6 Audio: *Cantus Arcticus (Concerto for Birds and Orchestra)*

1.7 Audio: *Lullaby from the Great Mother Whale for the Baby Seal Pups*

1.8 Video: Buzzing of a beetle

1.9 Video: Albanian funeral ritual

1.10 Video: Shape note singing

1.11 Video: *Biwa* notation

By Geographical Region

AFRICA

General Index includes all significant locales, genres, instruments, musicians, etc., and refers the reader to the page(s) where used. Each page reference is hyperlinked to the page on which the term occurs.

Index

Note: *Italic* page numbers refer to figures.

For instructors, additional materials are available online at https://routledgetextbooks. com/textbooks/instructor_downloads/.

Instructors will set up a passcode for access to an instructor's manual and quizzes from the authors.

PART I

The Foundations of Music I

INTRODUCTION

There has never been a time in history when music was more available, more portable, and more pervasive than today. People of the industrial and post-industrial world wake to music from their mobile phones. They go about their day accompanied by music delivered directly into their brains by earbuds connected to digital devices. They play video games, they shop in **Muzak**-saturated malls, and watch movies where a background music track calibrates their emotional responses. Before the early experiments with sound recording in the late 19th century, people had to be present where music was made in order to hear it. The technologies of sound recording, amplification, transmission, and broadcast that began around the beginning of the 20th century have radically altered the way people make and listen to music. These transformational technologies have reached even the remotest corners of the globe. Inuit of the Arctic listen to playlist songs while riding on their snowmobiles. Tibetans post yak-herding songs on YouTube. The roofs of shanties and shacks that line the banks of the Mekong Delta sprout a forest of wire TV antennas and satellite dishes (Figure 1.0). As radio, television, laptops, and cellphones become ever more accessible, the environment is increasingly saturated with recorded and broadcast music. Never before have so many different kinds of music been available on such a wide scale. The internet is a crossroads of World Music; and song files and music videos from all continents and centuries flash across information superhighways.

This textbook concerns music as a commonality of human experience, made and listened to by people in every society. Humans are born with innate and inherited musical competence, to which particular domains within the brain are assigned. Music, like language, is an inherited capacity that then develops after birth in culturally determined ways. While humans are born with the ability to acquire language, they don't grow up speaking language

FIGURE 1.0 Antennae rising from shanties along the Mekong Delta, southeast Vietnam

as such, but specific languages like French, Swahili, or Korean. Similarly, human groups have created distinctive musical languages that are constantly evolving. As the circumstances in which people live their lives change, they share, transform, and adapt tunes, instruments, and dance rhythms to new purposes. Songs are forgotten, instruments become obsolete, and musical fashions change with changing times.

Why do humans have musical perception and skill "hard-wired" into their neural circuitry? And how do humans use this innate ability to create and respond to the infinitely diverse musical experiences that shape and enhance their lives? Whether by nature or nurture, most have an appreciation for music, but why this is so is a great mystery. Through this textbook, students may come to appreciate a wider variety of music than they do now, but more importantly, they will have a deeper understanding of the role music plays in human life. These chapters aim to explore the mysterious power of music to move the heart along with music's many less lofty purposes.

The first part is divided into three chapters. Chapter 1 proposes a working definition of "music." It further examines some of the questions presented above and considers approaches to the study of music. Chapter 2 explores the production of musical sound by the human voice; and Chapter 3 is a catalogue of musical instruments, both chapters highlighting global diversity and human ingenuity.

What Is Music?

INTRODUCTION

This textbook begins with the question "What IS music?" From a global perspective, the term "music" may refer to a single universal category or many categories, each culturally determined. Not all languages have a single term to encompass all the meanings and associations the English word usually carries. Some languages have no equivalent term, although they may have many words to describe associated activities and concepts. Author Charles Keil noted that many West African languages,

> do not yield a word for 'music' gracefully. It is easy to talk about song and dance, singers and drummers, blowing a flute, beating a bell but the general terms 'music' and 'musician' require long and awkward [explanations] that still fall short.[1]

Indeed, in certain African languages, music and dance—sounds and the movements that accompany them—form a single, indivisible category.

Some languages have an equivalent term but with a broader meaning. The ancient Greek **musiki** included all the arts under the influence of the nine Muses. Thus, the words of a song along with its melody and rhythm were considered part of this single concept. In ancient India, the **Sanskrit** term *sangita* "is the closest equivalent to the Western concept of music, although the inclusion of dance as one of the three main compartments suggests that in early Indian thought sangita was regarded as a composite art."[2] Melody, rhythm, and bodily movement in the forms of dance and theatrical mime were all considered components of this single broad concept. The Inuit of the Arctic region, prior to their encounter with

English-speaking people in the 19th century, did not have a specific word for music. "The closest word in Inuktitut is 'nipi'—which includes music, the sounds of speech, wild animals, the forces of nature and noise."[3]

Even in English there is disagreement over how to define music. Proposing a suitable definition that is broad enough to encompass all the world's music yet narrow enough to be workable and precise proves to be a challenge. Music surely has something to do with sound, but not all sound is music. Ethnomusicologist John Blacking's famous definition of music was "humanly organized sound."[4] A problem with Blacking's definition is that it is too broad. Language is humanly organized sound, yet an adequate definition of music must differentiate between spoken language and song. The definition needs to be limited further because speech as well as car horns, ringtones, shouts, murmurs, and other human-made sounds would be included in this definition and would make it too large and unwieldy. The exact quantifiable moment when "singsong" speech becomes "monotone" or "tuneless" singing is ambiguous. Perhaps what identifies a given sound as *music* lies in the intention of the person making it. This point can be clarified by considering a car horn. When used politely to invite a driver, who is distracted, to move when a traffic light has turned green, the horn serves as a substitute for the word "Move!" The horn is therefore not music. If, however, the driver is traveling along a boring stretch of interstate, beeping the horn perhaps in accompaniment to a tune on the radio, it IS music because the car horn is being used AS music. Similarly, if a percussionist in an orchestra accidentally drops the cymbals on the floor, it is not music. When she crashes her cymbals at the appropriate moment in the performance, it IS music because of the musician's *intention* that the sound be music. Thus, it is the *purposes* of humanly organized sounds that are decisive. Accidental sounds may be intentionally incorporated into music, but music itself is not accidental.

A WORKING DEFINITION

In this textbook, a working definition of music is: "*Sounds organized by humans and intended for musical purposes.*" While this definition is problematic because it includes a form of the word being defined, it is nevertheless broad enough to encompass the enormous diversity of all human musical expression. It focuses our attention on musical sounds themselves as well as what is most revealing about them: the purposes they serve and the meanings they convey. After all, in the examples of the car horn and the cymbals, it is not the quality of the sound itself that makes it music, but human intention.

The following three examples allow consideration of music's conceptual limits. First is the famous "**composition**" by the American **avant-garde** composer John Cage (1912–1992) titled 4'33" (Figure 1.1). The work consists of four minutes and thirty-three seconds of silence. Is this music? Critic Peter Gutmann describes the work as follows:

> 4'33" was Cage's favorite work. Written in 1952, it came at the exact mid-point of his 80-year life of discovery and culminated his exploration of indeterminacy, music in which some elements are carefully scripted with others left to chance... Here's how one performance went: A tuxedoed performer came on stage, sat at a grand piano, opened the lid, occasionally turned some music pages but otherwise sat as quietly as possible for 4 minutes and 33 seconds, then rose, bowed and left. And that was it.

FIGURE 1.1 John Cage (1912–1992)

Although often described as a silent piece, 4'33" isn't silent at all. While the performer makes as little sound as possible, Cage breaks traditional boundaries by shifting attention from the stage to the audience and even beyond the concert hall. You soon become aware of a huge amount of sound, ranging from the mundane to the profound, from the expected to the surprising, from the intimate to the cosmic—shifting in seats, riffling programs to see what in the world is going on, breathing, the air conditioning, a creaking door, passing traffic, an airplane, ringing in your ears, a recaptured memory. This is a deeply personal music, which each witness creates to his/her own reactions to life. Concerts and records standardize our responses, but no two people will ever hear 4'33" the same way. It's the ultimate singalong: the audience (and the world) becomes the performer.[5]

Does 4'33" satisfy the working definition of music: "*sounds organized by humans and intended for musical purposes*"? The composer invites the audience to listen to the *sounds* around them the way they listen to music. Specifying the time interval and the performance space constitutes "*organization*"; and Cage's *intention* that engaged listening will transpire in a public venue designed for such a purpose meets (perhaps just barely!) the definitional requirements: *sound, organization,* and *human intention.*

A second example is an Albanian funeral song (1.1) on a CD collection titled "*Voices of the World*."[6] On first listening, the voices may seem random and disorganized, like the hubbub in an athletic stadium. The sound lacks those "ingredients" that are usually associated with music—pitch, melody, beat, instruments, etc. Yet after listening several times, one may notice that the sonic events follow a predictable pattern. A solo male calls out; he is joined by a group of men shouting an elongated cry; and then a clamoring chorus of individual voices gradually descends in pitch and intensity, finally dissipating. The sequence begins again with the call of the leader. These events repeat in the same order two more times forming the sonic pattern. Is it music? It is certainly produced by humans and has some degree of organization. The question is whether the men *intend* their cries to be music. Crowd noise in a football stadium, which this resembles sonically, is produced by humans but is *not* intended as musical expression. The world over, rites for the dead have been accompanied by singing, chanting, and other forms of expressive sound intended as public outpourings of grief. The scholar Hugo Zemp, who made the Albanian funeral song recording, described it in musical terms as "song." How do the participants at the funeral experience these sounds? They may have a category of their own, like "organized wailing," which is separate from other forms of music making in their society. Do they decide or do scholars like Zemp? Or do listeners decide, who hear this recording far removed from the funeral in time and space? Perhaps the question cannot ultimately be answered. Nevertheless, is this suitable material for an investigation of the world's music? Based on the working definition, the Albanian funeral song IS music (Figure 1.2).

The third example, also from *"Voices of the World,"* is a recording of Swiss cowherds (1.2) leading their cattle home from an upland pasture for the evening milking. A striking feature is the sound of cowbells that provides a steady accompaniment to the shouts and calls of the cowherd—a repeating sequence of shouted syllables, vocal warbling, and **falsetto** singing. Without the herders' voices, would the cowbells alone be music? It is true that the cows moving along the mountain trail have no musical intention, just as the wind has no musical intention when it causes wind chimes to sound. The cowbells ring with the random movements of the animals (Figure 1.3). However, the cowherds hung the bells around the necks of the animals in the first place. Was the intention of the herders to use the sound of the bells only to locate cows that have strayed? Such a utilitarian purpose is akin to an automobile horn or a fire alarm—an auditory signal substituting for a speech act: in the case of the car horn, "Move out of the way!"; in the case of the fire alarm, "Get out of the building!"; and

FIGURE 1.2 *Gjama* funeral ritual in Theth, Albania, 1937

in the case of the cowbell, "Here I am!" Might there be an additional musical purpose: to beautify the Swiss mountain air with music? Is it possible that the jangling bells, in addition to locating strays, give aesthetic, musical pleasure to the human listener? Perhaps in this sense the sound of the cowbells can be considered music, as can the sound of wind chimes. No intention is ascribed to the wind and yet there IS intention on the part of the chimes' designer and the human hand that hung them in a windy spot. As to the voice, the liner notes for the recording explain that the herder is saying in Swiss dialect "Come on, little cow, come on"—surely a speech act. Yet the "**yodeling**" falsetto portions, in addition to encouraging the cows, no doubt entertain the herder and his human companions. In mountainous regions of the world, people have developed highly specialized forms of vocalizing that make use of the acoustical properties of thin atmosphere and narrow valleys. Providing aesthetic musical pleasure for oneself and one's companions IS a musical purpose. If the sounds of the Swiss cowherds are marginally music, this kind of cattle calling furnished the raw material for an international singing style, as in Frank Ifield's yodeling song (1.3), "She Taught Me How To Yodel." Here the intentions of the songwriter and performers are unambiguous. The song, with its yodeling, serves to entertain, communicate a story, and symbolize the Swiss Alps—all musical purposes.

FIGURE 1.3 Cowbell

MUSIC AND THE NATURAL WORLD

What of the sounds of nature? Are the "songs" of birds and whales music? These and other natural sounds, such as pounding surf, whistling wind, and dripping water, have features that resemble many kinds of human music: pitch, rhythmic regularity, etc. Indeed, it has been suggested that bird song and other natural sounds were a source of musical inspiration among early humans. Two of the primary reasons birds "sing"—to mark territory and attract mates—are important in *human* music making as well, evidenced by the sheer number and universality of national anthems, fight songs, and love ballads. However, the sounds of nature lack *human* intention, although they can be considered music under certain circumstances. There are many examples of music around the world imitating the sounds of nature. Tuvan singers (1.4), who live on the steppes of Central Asia, manipulate their vocal cords and mouth cavities in ingenious ways to imitate the natural sounds of their environment: wind, mosquitoes, horses, etc. Compositions for Chinese *guzheng* (21-string long zither) often have evocative titles such as "Autumn Moon Above Calm Lake" and "Fighting the Typhoon," as do Japanese *shakuhachi* (bamboo flute) solos with names like "Bell Ringing in the Misty Ocean." In the Western symphonic repertoire, there are such works as Vivaldi's *Four Seasons* and Beethoven's *Pastoral Symphony*.

There are also examples of natural sounds themselves being incorporated into human music making. In Afghanistan, before the Taliban banned public performances, musicians brought caged birds with them to musical gatherings in order that the singing of the birds in response to the instrumental music became a part of the total musical sound. In Beijing, hobbyists bring their caged birds to public parks so that the birds can learn new songs from each other. In Suriname in South America, birdsong is competitive and prizes are awarded to owners of the most active songbirds. In the capital, Paramaribo, two judges score competing Amazonian songbirds (1.5) to determine which bird sings the most times in a fifteen-minute interval. Competition is fierce, and championship birds are sold for thousands of dollars. The Finnish composer Einojuhani Rautavaara (1928–2016) journeyed to the Arctic and recorded colonies of nesting birds, and in 1972 composed his *Cantus Arcticus (Concerto for Birds and Orchestra)* (1.6) around these haunting sounds. Similarly, American composer and musician Paul Winter (b. 1939) used recorded whale "songs" in his *Lullaby from the Great Mother Whale for the Baby Seal Pups* (1.7) (on his 1980 album *Callings*). A final example comes from a recording in which the buzzing of a beetle (1.8) in Papua New Guinea is "turned into" music by a child who holds the insect, tied to a twig, between his lips. By changing the shape of his mouth cavity, he can "play" melodies on the insect.

Some scholars are deeply involved with the study of non-human sound-making. A developing field since the 1990s called **Biomusicology** has raised important questions about the behavior of animals and the sounds they make. So it is an open question whether animal sounds are within the definition of music and thus in the purview of its study. The examples above demonstrate the close connections between music and the natural world. However, this textbook primarily concerns the human dimensions of musical sounds: how and why they are made, and what the study of them reveals about humans, human relationships, and values.

THE FIELD OF ETHNOMUSICOLOGY

The material in this textbook comes primarily out of the academic discipline of **Ethnomusicology**. The term, coined by Jaap Kunst in 1950,[7] referred to the study of non-Western music and European folk music previously called Comparative Musicology. Its parent discipline, **Musicology**, claimed as its area of investigation the history and analysis of Western art music. Much of the material that musicologists studied was based on music preserved through notation. Ethnomusicologists, on the other hand, investigated musics of the rest of the world that were primarily based on oral traditions. The invention of sound recording technology and film made possible the study of ephemeral performances, and in turn allowed for archiving, deep description, and comparative analysis.

Early ethnomusicologists who encountered music outside of Europe found the theories and methods of musicologists inadequate to account for the ways in which music was incorporated into people's lives. They turned to the disciplines of Folklore and Anthropology for more relevant approaches to researching musics of other cultures. Fieldwork became a central focus, beginning in the early 20th century with the new technology of sound recording. A generation of researchers brought the cumbersome new equipment into the field and became self-styled "song-catchers." The Hungarian composers Béla Bartók (1881–1945) and Zoltán Kodály (1882–1967) found new musical resources among the rural "folk" of Eastern Europe to incorporate into their "classical" compositions, thereby creating a new kind of musical nationalism. The famous image from 1908 shown in Figure 1.4 depicts the young Béla Bartók collecting folk songs from volunteer singers in Slovakia on an Edison "wax disc" machine. Anthropologist Frances Densmore (1867–1957) grew up in rural Minnesota and heard the singing of the Dakota Sioux as a child. At a time when U.S. government policy discouraged Native Americans from using their own languages and other native forms of expression, Densmore sought to preserve their culture. In 1907, just one year before Bartók undertook his travels through Hungary, Romania, Bulgaria, Slovakia, and Albania, Densmore began traveling in North America, recording the songs of Native Americans for the Smithsonian Institution (Figure 1.5).

Ethnomusicologists studied music not only in terms of performance and theory but as an essential component of culture. Culture can be defined as the sum total of all aspects of human behavior that are not instinctual, such as "knowledge, belief, art, morals, law, [and] custom."[8] These continually change and evolve, yet give groups and individuals their social identity. Two important American scholars framed the discipline of modern ethnomusicology in the 1960s. Cultural anthropologist Alan Merriam (1923–1980), studying the Flathead Native Americans of Western Montana, noted the importance of music in their daily lives. Merriam observed that music, as well as dance and ritual, were not separate from but rather embedded in their social and spiritual lives.[9] Having first described music as a part of culture ("music in culture"), he later coined the phrase "music *as* culture." Ethnomusicologist Mantle Hood (1918–2005) was trained as a composer of Western music, then studied Javanese music in Indonesia. Based on his experience learning from master musicians while living there, Hood invented the term "bi-musicality" to describe his method of entering and understanding the music culture he was studying as an "insider."[10] Thus, two distinct approaches to the study of non-Western music emerged: the anthropologist's objective stance observing human behavior from the outside and the musician's participation in musical events from the inside.

FIGURE 1.4 Béla Bartók recording Slovak folk songs, 1908

By mid-century, a new generation of ethnomusicologists became participant-observers of the musical cultures they studied.

Along with other disciplines in the humanities, great changes took place at the end of the 20th century. With advanced communication and technology, **globalization** was affecting every corner of the world. Ethnomusicologist Jo Miller writes that in the 1980s, "ethnomusicologists were increasingly investigating not only music from far-flung parts, but also starting to conduct fieldwork 'at home'—in one's own culture," using the research methods of the discipline.[11]

Students from these same "far-flung parts"—from Africa, Asia, and elsewhere—were also acquiring degrees in ethnomusicology from Western institutions, and taking these same research methods "home." In some cases, these returning scholars have started ethnomusicology programs in their own countries and academic institutions.

The notion of "authenticity" or "a pure culture" was rejected in favor of a more complex picture of global processes. Scholars in the 21st century are wrestling with permeable boundaries and how to account for such phenomena as the popularity of Dolly Parton in Zimbabwe, or the global success of Korean boy band BTS. Ethnomusicologists have come to critique the gross inequalities between those doing the studying and those being studied. They are concerned that other peoples and cultures have been treated in the past as "exotic" specimens. Many of the societies under investigation continue to be deeply affected by the history of European colonization despite achieving independence in the mid-20th century. Issues of colonialism and postcolonialism, as well as women and gender studies, LGBTQ+

FIGURE 1.5 Frances Densmore recording Blackfoot Mountain Chief, 1916

studies, and activism for social justice feature prominently in the work and scholarship of contemporary ethnomusicologists. In addition, an important sense of social responsibility has emerged in the field, whereby recordings, instruments, and other aspects of musical culture deposited in Western museums, collections, and archives are now being repatriated to their original creators. Finally, ethnomusicologists continue the mission of making important contributions to general education, by helping students gain a deeper understanding of the world that they share with others.

FOUR APPROACHES TO MUSICAL UNDERSTANDING

Considering "What Is Music?", four approaches are helpful in understanding human musical behaviors and products, whether a Super Bowl half-time show or a boy playing on a beetle. The kinds of questions that ethnomusicologists ask when confronting musical phenomena lead them to search for connections between musical sound and the ways that humans live and organize their lives. They do this in order to understand the meanings, values, structures, beliefs, and goals that people encode in their music.

The first approach is *analytical*. **Analysis** initiates a process of investigation that deals with the component elements of musical sound and their interrelationships: the instruments or voices that produce the sound, and such organizing principles as melody, harmony, rhythm, and form. Further analytical questions might include: How do these elements relate to each other? How do they produce such aesthetic qualities as unity, variety, and expressive power?

Does a musical style have grammar like a language? If so, what are the structuring principles that make it recognizable and meaningful? Analysis, however, is limited for it requires isolating music from the human environment and separating out components that musicians and listeners experience holistically. Music does not exist apart from the people who create, perform, record, experience, and subsidize it. For a full understanding of music, it needs to be considered in its human environment.

The second approach is *contextual*. The Albanian funeral ritual (1.9), *gjama*, was only "heard" earlier in this chapter. How much more is learned from watching people in the act of mourning than simply listening to disembodied voices? Exploring the *context* of *gjama* connects the practice to its world. *Gjama* dates back at least to the 15th century, to descriptions of the funeral rites for Albanian military hero Skander Beg (1405–1468). The practice of public mourning in this region may even have been described by Homer in the *Iliad*. *Contextual* questions would include: Under what circumstances do people sing or play musical instruments or listen to the radio? Who makes music, who listens to it, who pays for it? How and why is it produced and reproduced, taught, remembered, learned, preserved, marketed, etc.? What goes on while music is playing: dancing, eating, exercising, acting, lovemaking, studying, sleeping, or simply listening? The word "**context**" refers to all these non-musical, social factors that surround musical performance and musical experience.

Analytical and contextual approaches are powerful tools for understanding music, but are insufficient; at least two others are needed. Because the working definition—*sounds organized by humans and intended for musical purposes*—emphasizes "intention," musical study continues with an inquiry into *why* people make music. Like other products of the human will and imagination such as poems, pictures, stories, and dramas, music is made specifically for the purpose of carrying and conveying meaning between and among people.

The third approach is **semiotic**, a term scholars use to explain how musical meaning is created and communicated. In seeking to understand a song, "Amazing Grace" for instance, a semiotic approach would investigate what feelings, ideas, and values the song communicates. What did it mean to the songwriter, John Newton? What does it mean to those who sing and respond to its powerful lyrics and stirring melody? How has it functioned as a mode of communication? What messages does it convey? What occasions does it mark? How does "Amazing Grace" motivate actions, move the body and the emotions, transform consciousness? How does musical meaning change over time and circumstance? It is through questions like these that ethnomusicologists seek to "unpack" a musical event to reveal both personal and collective histories, value systems, modes of livelihood, and social structures, in short, meanings.

The fourth approach to understanding music deals with *performative* questions: How do people do it? How and why do they sing songs, play the guitar, or create beats using digital software? The New Zealand-born musicologist and educator Christopher Small proposed replacing the word music with the verb, "to music," or simply "**musicking**," suggesting that music should be viewed as an act instead of a thing. He explains:

> To music is to take part, in any capacity, in a musical performance, whether by performing, by listening, by rehearsing or practicing, by providing material for performance (what is called composing), or by dancing. We might at times even extend its meaning to … the roadies who set up the instruments and carry out the sound checks or the cleaners who clean up after everyone else has gone. They, too, are all contributing to the nature of the event that is a musical performance.[12]

In Christopher Small's view, guitarists are musicking, as are their listeners. So too are the shopper in the department store, and the janitor in the stadium sweeping up after the concert. For Dr. Small, any involvement with music, active or passive, is a kind of performance. In his view, to understand music fully is to take into account the "doing" of it. What human actions bring about, sustain, conclude, and evaluate music? What teaching, learning, composing, rehearsing, and organizing precede any music activity? Is music preserved for future performances? How is it preserved, and how does it change as it is notated, recorded, engineered, marketed, sampled, compressed, stored, played back, and streamed? What constitutes a good rendition? What is the relationship of a performance or recording to a musical score, template, or ideal? What social relationships are enacted, celebrated, contested, and supported in the processes of performance?

These four approaches—analytical, contextual, semiotic, and performative—lead to a more profound understanding of music. The questions generated by these approaches are open-ended and theoretically infinite. Understanding is never a goal that is ultimately accomplished, but rather a relationship that, once established, may grow over a lifetime. It is the hope that this textbook will encourage or deepen an already established love of music, one of humanity's most intimate as well as most essential forms of expression and pleasure.

WHAT IS SOUND?

At its most basic level, music is sound. In our working definition, *sounds organized by humans and intended for musical purposes*, sound is the fundamental element. Therefore, it is important to understand what sound is and how humans perceive and respond to it. All music is sound, but all sound is not music. Sound is vibrations that pass through a medium such as air or water and are received and perceived by a human or animal. Reception and perception are part of the definition. Thus, if a tree falls in the forest and no one—human or animal—is there to hear it, there is no sound (although there is, of course, vibratory disturbance of the atmosphere). Sound is a psychological result of a physical phenomenon. A singer on a stage provides a simple example of sound production. Her chest and abdominal muscles and her breath power provide the *energy*, which causes her vocal cords, the *object*, to vibrate. The vibrations travel through the *environment*, the atmosphere, and reach the *receiver*, the ears of the audience members. The vibrations are then channeled through the hearing system to the brain, where they are recognized and interpreted as musical sounds.

For *sound* to be present, four conditions are required:

> *Energy* that activates an object
> *Object* that vibrates in an environment
> *Environment* that conducts vibrations to a receiver
> *Receiver* that collects and interprets the vibrations

WHAT IS HEARING?

The ear/brain system is our primary receiver. Sound waves or vibrations travel into the outer ear, along the ear canal, and hit the tympanic membrane (ear drum), causing it to vibrate

sympathetically. Vibrations are transmitted into the middle ear. There, three tiny, connected bones—the malleus (hammer), incus (anvil), and stapes (stirrup)—amplify the force of the vibrations in order for them to pass through the oval window membrane into the more dense fluid in the spiral-shaped cochlea (inner ear). The oval window moves in and out, creating pressure waves that cause hair fibers along the inner ear to vibrate. The vibrating hair fiber cells trigger electrical nerve impulses that then travel along the auditory nerves to the cerebral cortex of the brain (Figure 1.6).

There are four important characteristics of musical sound that our brain distinguishes: volume, pitch, timbre, and duration. The **volume** (amplitude) of sound can be described subjectively using terms such as "loud" and "soft"; and measured objectively by calculating the physical pressure of the sound waves. The volume of a sound wave is measured scientifically in decibels (dB). A normal speaking voice is approximately 60 dB, while a loud orchestra measures 90–100 dB, and the threshold of human pain is 120–130 dB. Rock concerts can reach a level of 135–140 dB. Long-term exposure to this **decibel** level may cause permanent and irreversible hearing loss.

Pitch too can be described subjectively with terms such as "high" and "low"; and measured objectively by calculating how many times per second an object vibrates through a complete wave cycle. Frequency is measured in cycles per second (cps) or Hertz (Hz): the greater the frequency, the higher the pitch. Humans distinguish sounds between approximately 16 cps and 20,000 cps. Animals can hear sounds well beyond 20,000 cps. Most sounds of the world, like water flowing or thunder, are composites of multiple frequencies. Sounds of a single, measurable frequency—called pitches or tones—are somewhat rare in nature. The sounds many bird species produce, unlike those of most other animals, consist of clear, recognizable pitches. These special sounds, which humans also produce and respond to in many complex ways, are the building blocks of much of the world's music. This is why humans attribute "song" to songbirds.

Timbre refers to the tone quality or tone color of a sound. When two sounds of exactly the same volume and pitch are produced, as on a flute and a violin, the difference between the sounds is a difference in *timbre*. As the object vibrates, it does so as a whole, producing a fundamental tone that the ear hears. The object also vibrates in sections, as two halves, as three thirds, as four quarters, etc. Each of these further vibrations simultaneously produces **overtones**, which are higher and softer than the fundamental tone and are not heard as

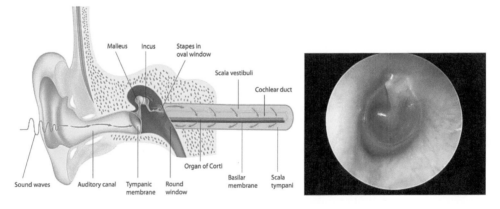

FIGURE 1.6 Diagram of the anatomy of the ear (L), and the human eardrum (R)

distinct sounds by the ear.[13] However, the brain interprets these overtones as part of a composite sound with a particular tone quality or timbre. Different sizes, shapes, and materials of musical instruments favor different sets of overtones. The relative strengths and proportions of the overtones in a flute sound, for example, are what determine its characteristic flute timbre. Likewise, a variety of anatomical differences contribute to the uniqueness of each human voice.

Like volume and pitch, the **duration** of a sound can also be described subjectively as in a long or short sound; and objectively as a sonic event measured in beats, or even in minutes and seconds. Duration may be represented in note values such as quarter notes or whole notes in Western music notation. Another aspect of duration is the decay of a musical tone. A musical sound may be sustained then abruptly stopped or gradually allowed to decay and dissipate.

The real mystery of hearing begins not in the domain of mechanics but in the domains of perception and consciousness. It is in the brain that the impulses are interpreted as sounds, and where sound now changes from physical vibrations to psychological information. The manner in which the auditory nerve connects to the brain is much more complicated than the manner in which the eye's optic nerve connects to the brain's frontal lobes. The auditory nerve branches into complex networks of neurons that stimulate the limbic system, balance, the ways we interpret language, fight-and-flight responses, and emotions. Sound provides humans with their most complex channel for communication and interaction with their social and natural environments. Because hearing is such a complicated process and carries so much vital information, it is no wonder that music as an expressive code is such a fundamental aspect of being human.

The involvement of multiple designated sites in the brain suggests that humans have musical perception and skill "hard-wired" into their neurophysiology as a genetic inheritance. Why this is so remains a mystery. The phenomenon has nevertheless been studied by those whose research is involved with humans at the very dawn of evolutionary history. Modern neuroscience has reached the conclusion that, as the late Oliver Sacks (1933–2015), former Professor of Clinical Neurology and Psychiatry at Columbia University, writes:

> We humans are a musical species no less than a linguistic one. This takes many different forms. All of us (with very few exceptions) can perceive music, perceive tones, timbre, pitch intervals, melodic contours, harmony, and (perhaps most elementally of all) rhythm. We integrate all of these and "construct" music in our minds using many parts of the brain. And to this largely unconscious structural appreciation of music is added an often intense and profound emotional reaction to music.[14]

THE PRESERVATION OF MUSIC

It is the nature of music to be ephemeral. A song once sung disappears into thin air. Sound lingers only until its vibrations die away. Of the ancient Greeks, a great deal is known about their art and architecture but very little about what their music sounded like. For most of human history, music had to be memorized to be preserved, and communicated orally across generations. Music served as a powerful **mnemonic** device for retaining and retelling stories, myths, beliefs, prayers; all things that are required to maintain the stability and continuity of a culture. Thus, musical memory was fundamental to survival. With the aid of music, adolescents were able to memorize long passages of instruction on the responsibilities of adulthood during tribal initiation. Priests and elders performed sacred chants that were a central component of ritual. What was not memorized and passed down was forgotten and lost. Therefore, notational systems were developed in a number of parts of the world to aid the preservation of music.

Two different kinds of notational systems have been invented. One uses symbols to represent musical notes—their pitch and duration; and the other, called **tablature**, uses symbols that represent *how* music is executed on an instrument. The earliest form of musical notation unearthed by archeologists dates from around 1400 BCE in Babylonia (present-day Iraq). Figure 1.7 shows a baked clay tablet on which symbols are etched. Above the double line, the cuneiform script presents hymn lyrics, dedicated to Nikkal, a Sumerian goddess of orchards. Below are the pitches indicated by the nine string names of the **lyre**. The five-line notational system commonly used today was developed in Europe around 900 CE and was continuously refined over the next 1,000 years. It had a profound impact on the development of music in the Western world. Wherever European powers colonized and missionaries spread Christianity, this staff notation system was used to teach Christian hymns to the colonized. Staff notation was the most important development in sound preservation technology until the invention of sound recording at the end of the 19th century.

In staff notation, the position of a note head on a line or space indicates pitch, and the shape of the note head and the stem indicates duration. A simplified system of notation was developed during a period of religious revival in late 19th- and early 20th-century America.

FIGURE 1.7 Cuneiform tablet (L), and handwritten staff notation by J.S. Bach (1685–1750) (R)

Singing schools were established to introduce this simplified notation system called shape note singing (1.10). Shapes were assigned to the note heads for ease of hymn singing in Sunday morning church services. The practice of using **shape notes** continues in rural Appalachia to this day.

The Russian *stolp* ("hook and banner") notation, a refinement of Byzantine musical notation, is a specialized system for Znamenny Orthodox chant, representing the shape of chant melodies along with the moods in which they should be sung, such as forcefulness or meekness. Students of Indian classical music utilize a notation system called *sargam* to study what is otherwise an oral tradition. In the early 20th century, Vishnu Narayan Bhatkhande (1860–1936) classified and notated classical melodies (***ragas***) using traditional pitch names (*sa-re-ga-ma*)—equivalent to do-re-mi-fa etc.—along with rhythms and other aspects of performance (Figure 1.8).

The second notation system, tablature, illustrates visually *how* musical sound is produced on an instrument. Players of fretted stringed instruments, such as the guitar, commonly use this form of notation. Guitar tablature consists of six lines representing the instrument's six strings. A number placed on one of the six lines indicates the fret number on which the player's finger should stop that particular string. A vertical arrangement of numbers on several lines graphically represents a chord, as seen in Figure 1.9 (L). The illustration shows a measure of guitar music in standard five-line staff notation with the same music in tablature below. Guitarists today also use fretbox diagrams known as "chord tabs" (the word "tab" short for "tablature"). These diagrams represent the guitar's fretboard precisely, with the strings and frets shown on the grid. Dots indicate where to place the fingers on each string to produce a single chord, as shown in Figure 1.9 (R). Another instrument that used tablature is the *vihuela* (Figure 1.10), the ancestor of the modern Spanish guitar. Figure 1.11 shows a

FIGURE 1.8 Russian *stolp* notation, 19th century (L), and North Indian *sargam* (R)

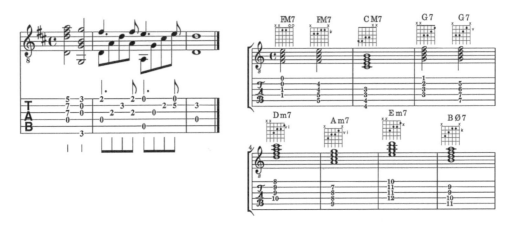

FIGURE 1.9 Guitar tablature (L), and guitar chord tab (R)

FIGURE 1.10 *Vihuela*, illustration in *Libro de Musica de Vihuela* by Luis de Milan, 1536

16th-century *vihuela* tablature. The black numbers indicate the particular fret where the fingers should be placed on the string. Rhythmic values are indicated above the system, and red pitches indicate the notes of a vocal line that the *vihuela* accompanies. Tablatures, of course, are specific to the instrument that the music is written for. There were tablatures from the 14th to the 18th centuries, now obsolete, for violin, keyboard, and wind instruments in addition to fretted ones.

In East Asia, several tablature systems dating back more than 1,500 years are still in use today. The Japanese *biwa* accompanies epic narration and uses one of the world's most complex tablature systems. Professor Silvain Guignard is a Swiss scholar who has lived, studied, and taught in Japan for more than thirty years. In the linked video, Dr. Guignard first narrates a battle scene from *"The Tale of the Heike,"* which concerns a civil war that took place in 12th-century Japan. He then explains the *biwa* notation (1.11) system by which the performance tradition is preserved. A feature that makes this system unique in the world is that it requires two texts, one for the vocal part that includes the words of the tale, and the other for the instrumental accompaniment. In performance, only the vocal notation is used by the narrator-*biwa* player. All the instrumental accompaniments have to be memorized. It should be noted that Dr. Guignard plays the *chikuzen biwa*, a modern version of the traditional *heike biwa*.

While forms of notation preserve music in written symbolic form, they are always mere approximations of the dynamic processes that take place in learning and performance. The

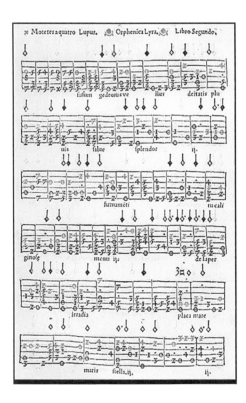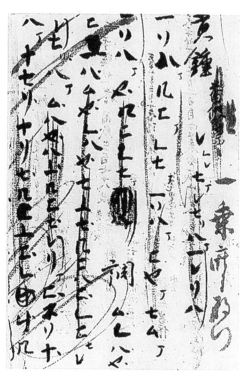

FIGURE 1.11 *Vihuela* tablature from *Orphenica Lyra*, 1554 (L), and *biwa* tablature, Shosoin Imperial Storehouse at Nara, ca. 738 (R)

survival of musical practices depends on human transmission. Throughout history old forms have died out while new ones have emerged. These are natural processes of cultural change. However, there are counterforces within societies that act to preserve and revitalize older forms of expression in order to maintain important links with the past. Several musical traditions described in this textbook are in danger of disappearing or have already become extinct. Many artistic forms are passed from generation to generation through oral transmission, and skipping a generation due to war, environmental cataclysms, or the social disruptions of modernity breaks the chain. The United Nations Education, Scientific, and Cultural Organization (UNESCO) supports and funds efforts to counter trends of cultural loss. A number of case studies in the following chapters describe endangered forms of cultural expression, preserved through programs such as those of UNESCO's Representative List of Intangible Cultural Heritage of Humanity. With the belief that preserving cultural diversity is a human value, UNESCO, founded in 1945 in the aftermath of World War II, seeks through global cooperation in education, science, and culture, to recognize the world's intangible resources of human artistry and to provide funding and support to maintain them.

CONCLUSION

This chapter has provided a definition of music and ways of understanding it. Emphasis has been placed on music's human and social dimensions, highlighting the reasons why people engage with music around the world. The chapter has also provided an introduction to the field of ethnomusicology and suggests four approaches to musical understanding. It has presented the physics of sound, and the biology and psychology of hearing. Finally, Chapter 1 has discussed the preservation of musical sound through notational systems. Chapters 2 and 3 further investigate the nature of musical sound with the study of the human voice and musical instruments respectively.

KEY TERMS AND CONCEPTS

Analysis

Conditions of Sound

Context

Defining Music Cross-Culturally

Duration

Ear/Brain System

Ethnomusicology

Globalization

Mnemonic

"Music-like" Sounds of Nature

"Musicking"

Musicology

Notation

Performance

Pitch

Russian *stolp* Notation

Semiotics

Shape Notes

Tablature

Timbre

UNESCO

Volume

Yodeling

THINKING ABOUT MUSIC

1 Why is music difficult to define? How would you define it? What are the strengths and weaknesses of the definition provided by the authors?
2 Consider the example of the Swiss cowherds. Why is it music, by the textbook definition? Why isn't it music, by this definition?
3 Why did ethnomusicologists reject the notion of "authenticity" or "pure culture" in favor of a more complex picture of global processes in the late 1980s and 1990s?
4 Choose a selection of music that you like and try considering it from each of the four perspectives: Analysis, Context, Semiotics, and Performance. Write a few descriptive sentences from each perspective (you may need to do a bit of research). Does this exercise deepen your understanding and appreciation of your selection? How? And if not, why not?
5 Composer Igor Stravinsky said that the sounds of nature are not music, although they are "music-like." What do you think he means by that? Based on the definition of music in Chapter 1, why are the bird songs in Einojuhani Rautavaara's composition *Cantus Arcticus* music and not merely "music-like"?
6 Consider Christopher Small's concept of "musicking." Does Small's idea change the way you think of music?
7 Explain the difference between notation and tablature. Why, in Silvain Guignard's *biwa* tradition, are there two notational systems in two volumes? And why must one be memorized in order to perform the music and sing the story?

NOTES

1 Charles Keil, *Tiv Song: The Sociology of Art in a Classless Society* (Chicago, IL: University of Chicago Press, 1979), 27.
2 Lewis Rowell, *Music and Musical Thought in Early India* (Chicago, IL: University of Chicago Press, 1998), 9.
3 "Music and Performance Art," *Travel Nunavut*, https://travelnunavut.ca/things-to-see-do/music-performance-art/.
4 John Blacking, *How Musical Is Man* (Seattle: University of Washington Press, 1973), Ch. 1.
5 Peter Gutmann, "John Cage and the Avant-Garde: The Sounds of Silence," *Classical Notes* (1999), http://www.classicalnotes.net/columns/silence.html.
6 Hugo Zemp, ed., *Voix du Monde - Voices of the World* (Paris: Centre National de la Recherche Scientifique et Musée de l'Homme, 1995), 3 CD compilation, includes 187-page booklet in French and English, https://archives.crem-cnrs.fr/archives/collections/CNRSMH_E_1996_013_001/.
7 Jaap Kunst, *Musicologica: A Study of the Nature of Ethno-Musicology, Its Problems, Methods, and Representative Personalities* (Amsterdam: Indisch Instituut, 1950).
8 Edward Tylor, *Primitive Culture*, Vol. 1 (New York: J.P. Putnam's Sons, 1920 [1871]).
9 Alan Merriam, *Ethnomusicology of the Flathead Indians* (Chicago, IL: Aldine, 1967).

10 Mantle Hood, *The Ethnomusicologist* (Kent, OH: Kent State University Press, 1971).

11 Jo Miller, "The Contributions of My Mentor, Ethnomusicologist Peter Cooke (1930–2020)," *Folklife*, September 24, 2021, https://folklife.si.edu/magazine/peter-cooke-ethnomusicologist-tribute.

12 Christopher Small, *Musicking: The Meanings of Performing and Listening* (Middletown, CT: Wesleyan University Press, 1999), 9.

13 Leonard Bernstein, "The Greatest Five Minutes of Music Education," Norton Lecture series, "The Unanswered Question" (lecture 1 of 6, Harvard University, 1973), https://www.youtube.com/watch?v=Gt2zubHcER4&ab_channel=paxwallacejazz.

14 Oliver W. Sacks, *Musicophilia: Tales of Music and the Brain* (New York: Alfred A. Knopf, 2007), xi.

CHAPTER 2

What Is Music Made Of? The Human Voice

Introduction
Human Vocal Apparatus
Human Vocal Diversity and Expression
Choral Singing
Specialized Singers
Four Voices of Renown
Conclusion

INTRODUCTION

The voice is a primary organ of human communication, and the singing voice is a primary faculty for self-expression. In some parts of the world, public singing is an intensely social custom. At a dinner party following a music conference in Central China, scholars, students, and local officials share a final meal at a hotel restaurant, and after toasts and speeches the singing begins. One by one, in no particular order, each participant comes up to a micro-phone in the front of the banquet hall and shares a song of her or his choosing. Because the conference includes international participants, there is quite a variety of singing styles, languages, and levels of confidence and competence. The Chinese participants, used to this custom, are ready to belt out a folk song at the drop of a hat. The Americans seem a bit more self-conscious, although Sam, a university student from New York, has no trouble finding his voice with an old Elvis Presley ballad that everyone enjoys. Strangers become friends, as each in turn takes the microphone and performs a song that serves as an introduction, an auditory calling card. One of the members of the party, Wangmo, is a nineteen-year-old Tibetan music researcher. She grew up in a nomadic family that followed a herd of sheep, yak, and horses across the Central Asian Plateau, one of the highest, coldest, and most isolated regions of the world (Figure 2.1). At the hotel party, she sings a song addressed to the "Sky Mother." She later explains that in her early life she spent many hours alone with the herds. Singing was both a way to pass the time and to communicate with other herders, out with their own animals a long distance away. Wangmo's song (2.1) carries to the dinner guests something of the wide vistas, isolation, and emptiness of her childhood world. The New York singer of the Elvis song also communicates something of who he is and what his life and his world are

FIGURE 2.1 Yak herd on the Tibetan Plateau

like. Because the singing voice is so much a part of human identity, both Wangmo and Sam convey in a few moments an intensely felt impression of who they are.

Chapter 2 describes the anatomy of the human vocal apparatus and surveys the diversity of musical sounds that humans produce vocally. A wide variety of biologically and culturally conditioned vocal timbres are discussed, as well as their social contexts. The chapter ends with the specialization of the professional singer and considers several individuals from various parts of the world whose distinctive vocal creativity is recognized as exceptional within their societies.

HUMAN VOCAL APPARATUS

The primary organ of the human voice is the vocal folds (or cords) located in the larynx or "voice box," which men and some women feel externally as the Adam's apple (Figure 2.2). Humans have voluntary control over whether these elastic folds are open or closed. When the folds are open, exhalation does not produce a sound. When they are closed and air is forced between them, a sound is produced in the same way that blowing air between two blades of grass produces a buzz. The vocal folds (2.2) are seen in this video vibrating during singing. The amount of air forced through the folds determines the volume of the voice. There is also control over the pitch by means of a complex neuromuscular mechanism. The sound produced within the larynx is the raw material for both speech and song. Within the

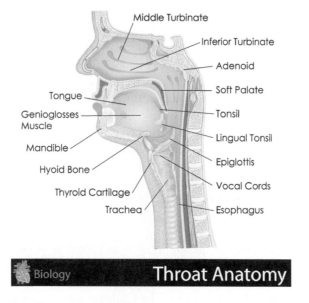

Middle Turbinate
Inferior Turbinate
Adenoid
Soft Palate
Tongue
Genioglosses Muscle
Tonsil
Lingual Tonsil
Mandible
Hyoid Bone
Epiglottis
Thyroid Cartilage
Vocal Cords
Trachea
Esophagus

Biology   **Throat Anatomy**

FIGURE 2.2 Anatomy of the human vocal apparatus

mouth the buzzing sound produced by the vocal folds is manipulated and shaped into spo-ken and musical languages. The sound is then amplified when the vibrations resonate within the nasal and sinus cavities, the mouth itself, and the chest cavity. Thus, the human voice con-sists of an energy source (breath), a vibrating object (vocal folds), and a resonator to amplify the vibrations (the oral and chest cavities and sinuses). All normally abled humans share this physiology, but there is a great deal of variation in the sounds produced by this apparatus, due both to biological and cultural diversity.

HUMAN VOCAL DIVERSITY AND EXPRESSION

The voice changes as humans grow and develop. There is little difference between the voices of young boys and girls. However, the voices of children are easily differentiated from those of adults, because smaller vocal folds and resonating chambers produce the timbres or sound qualities associated with young voices (2.3). The video presents children singing in Ethiopia and the People's Republic of China. Although these children are widely separated geograph-ically, the timbre of their voices is similar.

The development of the larynx at puberty produces one of the most important human secondary sex characteristics: the differentiated voice. Mature male voices are approximately an octave lower than those of females, because the longer and thicker vocal folds of the male have a lower fundamental frequency. As humans grow older, their vocal folds lose flexibility causing the timbre of their voices to change yet again, into the vocal sounds characteristic of the elderly. Aside from age and gender differences, there is also a great deal of diversity in terms of human anatomical features that affect sound production, such as size and thickness of the skull and vocal tissues, overall stature, lung capacity, etc.

Characteristic vocal norms are a complex interaction of biological tendencies and socially constructed preferences. While nothing is as personal and self-identifying as one's voice, vocal timbre, volume, speed, contour, range, and expressive gesture are all learned from family and community. These aspects of the voice develop along with language acquisition in childhood. Habits of language and voice learned in childhood last a lifetime.

However, the human voice is extremely adaptable. Both the speaking and singing voice can be changed, even radically, through imitation, training, and practice. A case in point is the alteration of the singing voice among evangelical Christians in South Korea. The traditional Korean singing voice may be described as "rough and husky," with deep pitch fluctuations suited for expressing intense emotions of sorrow, anguish, and bitterness. Korean evangelicals believe that since this form of Christianity arrived in Korea in the mid-1960s, the sorrows of the past are gone. They believe that only the trained Western "operatic" voice is capable of expressing the joy of Christian redemption. Hundreds of South Korean Christians attend music conservatories each year in Europe and North America to, as they say, "clean up" their Korean voices.

> Vocal "cleanliness" refers to the suppression and removal of two types of unwanted sounds: the 'fuzz' caused by pressed vocal chords … and the "wobble" … [and] "shakiness" from habituated muscle tension…. Such "unclean" sounds are associated with the voices of the past…. As a key part of the Christian soundscape, the clean voice is an emblem of personal and national advancement.[1]

The sounds produced by the vocal cords serve as raw material for the qualities of speaking and singing that children learn by listening and imitating. Anthropologists call this process of learning, "**enculturation**." People use their voices in ways that are considered socially acceptable and "normal" within their families and communities, modifying them according to circumstance or context. For example, a very different voice is used in a classroom than at a football game. What is considered normal for speaking and singing differs widely among social groups. Yet, like athletic ability, vocal skill may be developed through training and practice. Some individuals come from "musical families," and their children develop singing expertise from childhood. This raises the question of whether specialized aptitude rests on genetic inheritance or on musical training, or both. All fans at a sporting event are encouraged to participate in singing the national anthem, for it is assumed that this level of competence is universally shared. However, often a professional, trained "singer," who has been chosen for her outstanding vocal skill, leads the singing with her amplified voice. It should be noted that throughout the world there are singers who, without any specialized training, pursue successful careers. Some become world-famous superstars, such as Dolly Parton and Nobel prizewinner, Bob Dylan.

Societies tend to favor higher or lower pitches within the normal range of the human voice. In the Andes Mountains in Peru, Quechua women (2.4) sing at the top of their vocal range. The video shows a family of musicians dedicated to preserving the traditional culture of the Andean region, in a performance that also features traditional dress, instruments, songs, and dances. The Sioux grass dance songs (2.5) heard in Native American powwows are sung by *men* with high-pitched voices in a register that elsewhere would be considered normal for women. Sometimes the voice is stretched beyond its normal range. Tibetan Buddhist monks (2.6) perform exercises as a religious practice that over years deepen their vocal range. It is with these specially cultivated voices that they recite their sacred scriptures.

Humans have learned to produce a surprising variety of sounds that are expressive of their cultural identities. Inuit women living near the Arctic Circle make the unique vocal sounds of *katajjaq* (2.7) or **throat singing**, as a form of entertainment. In this follow-the-leader game of endurance, the first to laugh or quit is the loser. The sounds the women make imitate those of their natural environment: birds, mosquitoes, wind, and ocean waves. This game has been played by Inuit women since before European missionaries arrived in the Arctic in the early 19th century. In Video 2.7, Karen Panigoniak and her singing partner, Ida Kolola, throat sing in Arviat, Nunavut, northern Canada. Their throat songs are "*Qimiruluapik*" (Dogteam Puppy), "*Amma Ullu Aa*" (Inuktitut Syllabics), and a "Competition" song.

An example of the way people use the voice for celebratory purposes is a type of vocalization known by scholars as **ululation**. Ululation is a high-pitched warble involving the rapid flipping of the tongue back and forth. It is a vocal sound characteristic of women and found in many parts of the world. It can be heard as a congratulatory exclamation in wedding ceremonies from Tunisia to Bangladesh. For example, a bride in West Bengal performs a ritual blessing to the accompaniment of joyful ululation (2.8) by the women in her party. This is followed by ceremonial feeding of her groom.

In some vocal traditions, singing is extraordinarily loud, while in others, the singing is barely audible. The male Spanish flamenco voice is nearly a shout since it must convey the character of "*machismo*," or exaggerated masculinity, and "*duende*," or deep sentiment and heightened emotion. A farmer who is also a professional folk singer in north central China demonstrates his loud "outdoor" voice (2.9) at the top end of his vocal range. Similarly, an anonymous shepherdess in Tibet sings a love song in a forceful voice (2.10) that was developed out-of-doors on the high plateau of Central Asia, like Wangmo's voice in Video 2.1. Here, singers use this vocal style for courtship across miles of endless grassland. In contrast, the Central African nation of Burundi is known for its "*inanga* whisper singing." At the turn of the 20th century nearly all Burundian men could play the *inanga* (trough zither), since most Burundian men raised cows. The instrument was used to pacify cattle at night while keeping the cowherds awake. It also accompanied "whisper singing" (2.11) to entertain the kings (*mwamis*) of Burundi as they slept. The video features Mr. Joseph Torobeka, one of the last surviving whisper singers.

CHORAL SINGING

People singing together in organized groups has been part of human social and ritual life since ancient times. Indeed, the bonding enacted in human choral singing may have been essential to the survival of early humans. In the ancient Greek theatre, the chorus took part in the action and provided sung commentary on the unfolding drama. The early Church Father, St. Basil of Caesarea (330–379 CE), encouraged choral singing of the Psalms among worshippers:

> Who indeed can still consider him an enemy with whom he has uttered the same prayer to God? So that psalmody, bringing about choral singing, a bond, as it were, toward unity, and joining the people into a harmonious union of one choir, produces also the greatest of blessings, charity.[2]

From the early days of Christianity, churches employed professional choirs to sing the liturgy of the Mass. There were, however, opportunities for the general congregation to sing various portions of the service. The music was divided into parts for high voices and low voices. Further subdivision led to the four standard vocal parts: soprano, alto, tenor, and bass. In the professional church choirs of Medieval and Renaissance Europe, women were not permitted to sing. Therefore, male voices had to cover the entire range of the human voice, from treble to bass. Boys sang the two upper parts, soprano and alto, and men the two lower parts, tenor and bass. In the 17th and 18th centuries, pre-pubescent boys who were recognized for outstanding vocal ability were castrated to preserve the upper (or soprano) range of their voices. These *castrati*, as they were called, sang in the great chapel choirs of the Vatican in Rome as well as for church choirs and courts in France and Germany. In 18th-century Spain, the **castrato** voice was highly prized and leading roles in operas of the time were performed by these singers. Women sang along with men in the general congregation, and beginning in the mid-1700s, women were permitted to join church choirs in Germany and elsewhere. Church choirs are often accompanied by the organ, or by contrast they some-times sing **a cappella** (unaccompanied). Christian missionaries brought the practice of hymn singing, with its emphasis on congregational participation and SATB harmony, to many areas of the globe. An example is gospel singing in Malawi (2.12), southeastern Africa. Local musicians have created a style that is unique to that regional culture by blending multipart vocal harmony with a call-and-response song structure and choreography characteristic of local custom.

Today **amateur** singers participate in both secular and church choirs. A unique form of choral singing has developed over generations in Bulgaria (see Map 9.1), featuring a vocal technique called (in English) the "twang." The London Bulgarian Choir (2.13) led by Dessi Stefanova consists of both Bulgarians and English singers who have learned the style. In the video, Stefanova describes this style in detail, both anatomically and aesthetically. Bulgarian choral singing has been imitated by amateur choirs in Europe and North America.

Choral singing is one of the most powerful collective expressions of group solidarity. In many parts of the world, children participate in choral activities in schools, in religious institutions, at athletic events, and in their homes. Choir is a pedagogical tool for educating children in the values of their communities. Patriotic anthems bridge generations with shared expressions of national pride.

The small Baltic nation of Estonia (Map 2.1) provides a dramatic example of mass choirs expressing national pride and solidarity. Throughout its history, Estonia had been conquered repeatedly by its larger, more powerful neighbors: Sweden, Denmark, Poland, and Russia. From the mid-19th century, Estonians sought to assert the Estonian language and customs that had been suppressed for centuries. While still under Russian occupation, the first Esto-nian Song Festival was held in 1869, celebrating this nationalist movement. Nearly every five years thereafter the festival has been held with ever-increasing numbers of singers and dancers. Estonia enjoyed a brief period of independence in 1918, following World War I. This period abruptly ended with the invasion by Nazi Germany. After World War II and its devastations, Estonia was taken over by, and absorbed into Stalin's Soviet Union. All aspects of Estonian language and cultural identity were brutally repressed, with hundreds of patriots sent to labor camps in Siberia. Estonians only achieved independence with the thawing of the Cold War in 1991, which saw the breakup of the Soviet Union. For four years leading up to Independence, Estonia and the other Baltic nations of Latvia and Lithuania took part in what became known as the "Singing Revolution." Thousands gathered spontaneously to sing patriotic songs together. In 1989, a human chain of 2 million people, spanning 370 miles between the capitals of Estonia and Lithuania, held hands and sang songs of freedom. Song festivals have brought together tens of thousands of participating singers and dancers. About

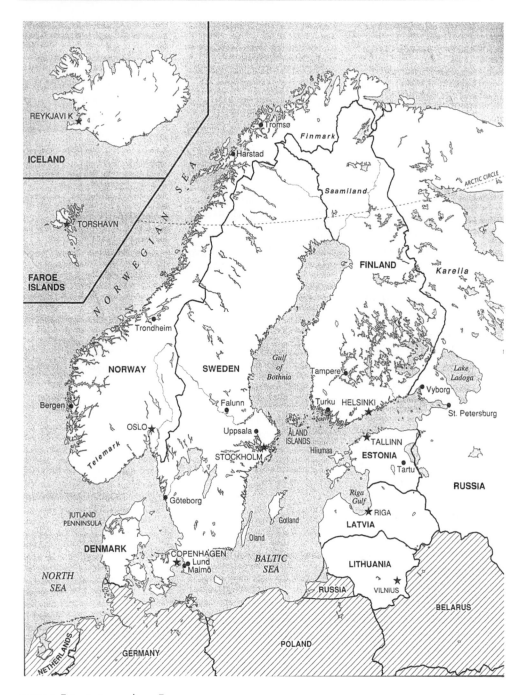

MAP 2.1 Estonia in northern Europe

Source: Garland Encyclopedia of World Music, Vol. 8, Europe

these festivals, Estonian composer and conductor Roman Toi has remarked: "It was 1869, we gathered in the city of Tartu for our first Song Festival, and ever since, the song festival has been a beautiful way to express: 'Please, Dear Lord, help us to keep our country and our language'."[3] Estonian Song Festival XXVII (2.14) was held in 2019 with more than 33,000 choral participants performing for an audience of 60,000.

SPECIALIZED SINGERS

At the banquet described in the chapter introduction above, the Chinese hosts assume that everyone can sing. There are no exceptions. The ability to sing is as universal as the ability to speak. However musical ability is unevenly distributed throughout the general population. Some people possess exceptional aptitude, and they may cultivate a specialized singing voice that exhibits, to a high degree, characteristics such as volume, range, flexibility, projection, and expressive power. Such singers serve important social roles in theatrical, entertainment, and/or ritual events. At Mount Carmel Baptist Church, Atlanta, Georgia, Reverend Timothy Flemming Sr. (b. 1950) leads his congregation in an old time camp meeting song (2.15). This mode of group singing is known as "**call and response**," and metaphorically enacts the role of the preacher as the shepherd leading his flock. Rev. Flemming began his career as a preacher at the age of eleven. Known for his singing ability as well as his powerful preaching, Flemming became famous throughout Georgia as "The Singing Preacher." He founded his own record label in the 1990s, "God's Strength Records," and has preached and sung internationally.

A singing voice, unlike a musical instrument, can effectively convey words. In the following examples, the verbal skill of the singers—conveying a dramatic narrative or performing an operatic role—is paramount. In each case a special vocal timbre or color is cultivated to add expression to the verbal delivery. Opera singers like the great Italian tenor Enrico Caruso (1873–1921) are the inheritors of a sophisticated pedagogy, hundreds of years old, that is characterized by the use of both chest and facial resonance, and a vocal technique called **vibrato**. They are trained in the careful enunciation of vowels and consonants in order to portray a dramatic character through the singing voice, and to project the voice into large auditoriums without electronic amplification. Enrico Caruso (2.16) sings the aria "*Vesti la Giubba*" ("Put on the costume") from Ruggiero Leoncavallo's early 20th-century opera *I Pagliacci* ("The Clowns"). The character Canio, leader of a circus troupe, has just learned that his wife has been unfaithful. He must now prepare for the afternoon's performance by putting on his clown's makeup and costume. While seated before his mirror, he weeps in anguish, crying "*Ridi, Pagliaccio!*" ("Laugh, Clown, Laugh!"). The audio recording was made in 1902 at the very outset of the commercial phonograph industry. The session was held in a hotel in Milan, where Caruso recorded several arias including this one (Figure 2.3). The young tenor was paid 100 pounds sterling for the session. Caruso's recording of "*Vesti la Giubba*" was the first gramophone record to sell 1 million copies, making Caruso a world-renowned artist and a very wealthy man. The Gramophone Company earned twice what Caruso received in profits. Thus began one of the most lucrative new consumer industries of the 20th century. In 1987, the Recording Academy, which gives out the Grammys, recognized Enrico Caruso posthumously with a Lifetime Achievement Award.

One of the most famous forms of world vocal music that is associated with a specific location and environment is the throat singing of the Gobi Desert regions of Mongolia and Tuva (Map 2.2). **Khoomei** involves a singer producing a very low fundamental pitch and manipulating the oral cavity to produce upper overtones so that two or more pitches are sounded at once. Throat singer Bao Narisu grew up in Inner Mongolia, a province of China, where his father and uncle were both music teachers. He did not hear *khoomei* until he

FIGURE 2.3 Enrico Caruso (1873–1921), in the role of Canio in *I Pagliacci*, 1908

attended university. For most of his childhood, cultural contact between Inner Mongolia and the country of Mongolia was prohibited by the Chinese government. Only in the 1990s were exchanges between the two regions permitted and encouraged. Bao Narisu explains:

> After that time, it was possible for Inner Mongolian students to study in the country of Mongolia, and outstanding *Khoomei* teachers were invited to teach in Inner Mongolia.
>
> After I graduated from college in 2006, the Inner Mongolia Broadcasting Art Troupe invited Mongolian *Khoomei* Master Aode Su Rong to set up a *Khoomei* class. I received *Khoomei* training for the first time in this class, and then I went to the country of Mongolia to continue my study of *Khoomei* as a graduate student in Ulaanbaatar. After I returned from Mongolia, I began to work at the School of Music of the Inner Mongolia University for the Nationalities in 2009 where I started teaching *Khoomei*.[4]

Bao Narisu, now full professor at the School of Music, demonstrates throat singing (2.17) (*khoomei*) accompanying himself on the *tobuxiur* (two-string Mongolian lute). The song he sings is titled "Praise for the Black Horse." It describes the magnificent animal given to a young man by a rich merchant long ago. The horse galloped unimpeded in snowstorms and ran like water through the scorching sun. The epitome of speed and strength, the black horse symbolizes the Ye people of this region and their music.

Not all forms of vocal music contain lyrics. Some English songs dating back at least as far as the late 16th century, to the time of Shakespeare, used words like "fa-la-la" and "hey nonny no." These nonsense words often suggested intimate situations that could not be described

MAP 2.2 Mongolia and China

Source: Garland Encyclopedia of World Music, Vol. 7, East Asia: China, Japan, and Korea

verbally. An example is Thomas Morley's famous ballad, "Now is the Month of Maying" (1595).

> Now is the month of maying,
> When merry lads are playing,
> Fa la la la la la la la la,
> Fa la la la la la la la lah.
> Each with his bonny lass
> Upon the greeny grass.
> Fa la la la la la la la la, etc…

North American jazz singers in the 1920s developed a kind of performance art called **scat singing** that used **non-lexical vocables** (syllables without meaning) to swing a tune vocally. American jazz singer Ella Fitzgerald (2.18) made scat singing a hallmark of her career, as demonstrated by this recording of "Air Mail Special," which she famously sang at the 1957 Newport Jazz Festival.

In Ireland, for many generations musicians have used a vocal form similar to scat singing called **lilting** in order to remember and teach tunes that are orally transmitted, and to accompany dancing. Singer, multi-instrumentalist, and dancer Eimear Arkins from County Clare, Ireland, is an expert. She writes:

> I heard someone lilting (2.19) at a festival when I was about 11 and I thought "I think I can do that." So I practiced a couple of tunes and entered a lilting competition and the

rest is history. I was always lilting to myself anyway - I just didn't realize that people did it publicly or for performance/competition. It is a fun, creative way to express oneself and I often use it as a tool when I'm teaching. It is the perfect combination of singing and playing music![5]

FOUR VOICES OF RENOWN

There are individual singers throughout the world whose voices have so captured the imagination of their audiences that their vocal timbre, expression, and persona have become iconic. The four vocalists featured below are each identified as "the voice of the people."

Jimmie Rodgers

Chapter 1 presented the Swiss cattle herders singing in a highly specialized way called yodeling, taking advantage of the acoustical properties of their alpine environment. This technique, by which the voice fluctuates between registers, was a popular feature in American country music of the 1930s, particularly recognizable in the songs of Jimmie Rodgers (Figure 2.4).

Jimmie Rodgers (1897–1933) was born in Meridian, Mississippi. His father worked for the railroad and wanted his son Jimmie to follow in his footsteps. By the age of thirteen he was working with his father as a water boy, although even then he had ambitions to be a singer. He received great inspiration from African American railroad workers (sometimes referred to as "gandy dancers") through their field hollers and work chants. Stricken by tuberculosis at the age of twenty-four, he left the railroad permanently and set out to make a career as an entertainer. He developed his own particular style that combined early African American blues with an emerging form called "hillbilly music." Jimmie Rodgers was discovered by Ralph Peer, a record producer working for RCA Victor who was touring the southern United States looking for talent. At the famous Bristol Sessions in Tennessee, Rodgers recorded two

FIGURE 2.4 Jimmie Rodgers, "The Singing Brakeman," 1931

songs then went north to the Victor Studios in Camden, New Jersey, for further recording with Peer. At this session, the songs included "Blue Yodel" (also known as "T for Texas"), which became one of Rodger's biggest hits. This song introduced his signature yodel, which Rodgers claimed to have learned from Swiss visitors he heard in a church. Under the nicknames "The Singing Brakeman" and "The Blue Yodeler," he became one of country music's first and most successful stars. He died of the tuberculosis that he had contracted in his twenties, recording songs right up to the end of his short life. By the year of his death in 1933, as the record industry faltered during the Great Depression, fully 10% of RCA Victor's sales were Jimmie Rodgers' songs.

He was one of the first inductees to the Country Music Hall of Fame and Museum in Nashville, Tennessee, in 1961, at which time he was honored with the title, "The Father of American Country Music." Among later performers who "covered" his songs are Bob Dylan, Bono, Alison Krauss & Union Station, Jerry Garcia, Aaron Neville, John Mellencamp, Willie Nelson, and others. Fifty-six years later, in 2017, he received the Grammys Recording Academy's Lifetime Achievement Award. A short documentary created for the event used a film clip from *The Singing Brakeman*, a movie short that Jimmie Rodgers (2.20) made for Columbia Pictures in 1929. The song he sings is his famous "Blue Yodel" (later "Blue Yodel #1"), also known as "T for Texas."

Inscribed on his memorial statue in Meridian, Mississippi, are these words:

> His is the music of America. He sang the songs of the people he loved, of a young nation growing strong. His was an America of glistening rails, thundering boxcars, and rain-swept night, of lonesome prairies, great mountains and a high blue sky.

Not only the songs he sang, but the quality of his voice, high and lonely, resonated with millions of rural Americans and echoed back to them a sound both authentic and familiar.

Umm Kulthum

Umm Kulthum (1904–1975) is known as "The Voice of Egypt" (Figure 2.5). Her voice came to represent an entire nation, and her rise to iconic status coincided with the development of the **mass media**. Her career exemplified the unifying power of a popular singer in the new technological era. Umm Kulthum was raised in a small village in the Nile Delta (Map 2.3) where her father was the *imam* (prayer leader) and a singer of traditional wedding songs. Because the practice of Islam rests upon the recitation of the Qur'an in classical Arabic, correct enunciation of the language is highly prized in Egyptian culture. Her career began by joining her father at wedding performances dressed as a boy to avoid the social censure of women singing in public. As a singer, her exquisite pronunciation that she learned from her father along with her melodic art was a primary attribute of her performance style to be praised. Her singing became more renowned and her travels with her father extended to the large cities of Cairo and Alexandria. She became a master of *maqam*, the melodic system of classical Arabic modes that forms the basis of both composition and improvisation. Like her, much of the Egyptian population had moved from the countryside to the cities in the great 20th-century urban migrations, marking the end of traditional agrarian ways that had lasted for millennia. Thus, her life embodied both the humble roots of the millions in her audience as well as the highest values of their artistic traditions and faith. In her concerts, songs went on for hours. Audiences demanded that she repeat certain lines over and over, each time

FIGURE 2.5 Umm Kulthum singing at The Olympia, Paris, 1967

with different melodic improvisation and emphasis, as shown in Umm Kulthum (2.21). She understood the media and music industry, and managed her career impeccably. But beyond any power of analysis, she conveyed a sense of authenticity, of genuine "Egypt-ness"; and could generate through her singing an environment of **tarab**, enchantment.

Ethnomusicologist Scott Marcus writes:

> With her ever-rising fame and the growth of the new radio medium, Umm Kulthum was given an unprecedented honor: on January 7, 1937, she began giving live-radio-broadcast concerts on the first Thursday of each month from November or December to June, a practice that continued throughout the rest of her life and, with recordings, even after her death. When Gamal Abdel Nasser came to power in Egypt after the 1952 revolution against the Egyptian monarchy, he understood the potential of the voice and persona of Umm Kulthum for promoting Egyptian and indeed pan-Arab unity. Thus, one of his first acts was to dramatically strengthen the broadcasting power of the Egyptian national radio so that the signal could be received throughout the Arab world, as far north as Lebanon and Syria. There are countless stories of how the streets would empty as the time for her Thursday concerts approached and people took their seats in front of a radio. I have heard such stories from Israelis, Lebanese, and Moroccans. In the 1960s, Nasser created the "Umm Kulthum" radio station, an all-music station that still features broadcasts of Umm Kulthum songs twice a day …Umm Kulthum not only became "The Voice of Egypt" to the people of the Arab world, but they also embraced her as their own. Thus she became a part of Arab individual and collective identity.[6]

Her career to an exceptional degree was shaped by, and to an extent shaped, the turbulent times in which she lived. Of the millions of Egyptians and thousands of Egyptian singers, why did Umm Kulthum attain the unique status of culture bearer? She came of age with the rise

MAP 2.3 Egypt and the Near East

Source: Garland Encyclopedia of World Music, Vol. 6, The Middle East

of recording, broadcast, and cinema technologies that made possible the phenomenon of the national or international "superstar." Her appearance in early motion pictures such as *Weddad* (1936) by Fritz Kramp solidified her status as Egypt's reigning diva. Through these technologies, her voice and image were projected upon the national and pan-Arab consciousness, and millions saw in her image and heard in her voice something utterly authentic, something of their deepest sense of self and the lives they were living.

In the Lebanese novel, *The Hakawati* (2008), by Rabih Alameddine, a young boy recalls drinking tea in a Beirut cafe while listening to the Thursday evening Umm Kulthum radio broadcast with his uncle and friends:

> Applause could be heard on the radio. "She's onstage," Uncle Jihad whispered. "She has arrived." Silence … Her voice came on, clear, strong, powerful. The room sighed in unison at her first utterance, then quieted again. A man wearing dark eyeglasses held together with a gray piece of tape leaned back in his chair as if he were about to be showered with rose petals. Another man conducted an imaginary orchestra with both

hands … Umm Kulthoum carried the melody, sang of love in Egyptian dialect, and the words of longing made sense….She repeated each line, once, twice, three times, more, until it vibrated within me….When she finished the melody, the room shook. Men applauded, stood up, yelled at the radio. "Long may you live!" … "May God keep you!" "It didn't happen," one man said to the radio. "You have to do it again."

    She did…When she finished the melody the second time, the audience erupted…A short man stood on a table and shouted "Allah-u-akbar [God is great]." … She began the same melody again. I was in ecstasy. The room shook in delight…By the time she was done, a full hour into the song, the room was utterly exhausted and hoarse…" Umm Kulthoum is the quintessential Arab," Uncle Jihad said [as we drove home together]. "She's probably the one person whom all Arabs agree to love."[7]

Four million people attended Umm Kulthum's funeral in Cairo in 1975, one of the largest gatherings in human history (Figure 2.6).

FIGURE 2.6 Statue of Umm Kulthum in a square named after her, on the site where her home once stood in Cairo

Salif Keita

Salif Keita (b. 1949) is one of West Africa's most famous and influential singers, songwriters, and producers. He was born in the former colony of French Sudan, now the Republic of Mali (Map 2.4), and is a direct descendant of Sunjata Keita, who founded the Malian Empire in the 13th century. Among the Mande-speaking peoples of Mali, occupations are hereditary and are identified by family names. The surname Keita indicates the ruling aristocracy. In traditional Mande society, a musician (*jali*, also known by the French term *griot*) had important roles as oral historian, orator, genealogist, and praise singer. For a member of the aristocratic Keita family to become a musician was unheard of. Being born albino, he was consequently ostracized by both his family and community. He turned to performing music in Bamako, the capital city, after poor eyesight eliminated teaching as a career option. He said in a 1992 interview with Banning Eyre of Afropop Worldwide Radio,

> There were two ways I could go. I could become a delinquent and practice banditry or I could play music. There was no other way. Because I was a noble, it seemed better to play music than become a crook. So I chose music.[8]

He was soon recognized for having an unusually powerful and expressive singing voice, and at the age of nineteen he joined first the Rail Band and then *Les Ambassadeurs*, the two most popular local bands of the day in Bamako. Political repression led him to emigrate to neighboring Côte d'Ivoire, and then in 1984 to Paris where he became an international celebrity (Figure 2.7).

In the 1980s, worldwide interest in African-based popular music (known in the recording and broadcasting industries as "**Afropop**") reached its peak. From Mali and other countries

FIGURE 2.7 Salif Keita (1949–) at the Festival Internacional Cervantino, Mexico, 2015

of the region—Senegal, Guinea, Gambia—came a number of prominent musicians, mostly from *jali* families, who pursued highly successful careers in Europe and North America. Salif Keita became known as "The Golden Voice of Africa." He was known for his fusion of *jali*-inspired roots singing in his native language of Wolof, and electronic and synthesizer-backed accompaniments. Yet by the 1990s he was frequently criticized for pandering to the tastes of the primarily European public with overly produced, slickly packaged recordings. In 1995 he recorded his song *"Africa"* (2.22) on the Paris-produced album *Folon* for Mango Records. In this song, African traditional instruments join with electric guitars, bass, synthesizer, and keyboards to produce African-flavored music with a techno beat. Keita sings this song in French, the language of Mali's European colonizers.

Keita's title song *"Folon"* (2.23) on the same 1995 album, "marks his growing desire to create a music that would more truthfully reflect his personal lyricism and inner space. In this song," writes author Cherif Keita,

> Salif asserts that in the past, individuals and their needs were neglected for the sake of collective harmony … [whereas in the present] he can finally use his music to sing about his own outlook on life's tragedies and denounce the oppression inflicted on him by ignorance and intolerance.[9]

MAP 2.4 West Africa showing Mali and Côte d'Ivoire

Source: Garland Encyclopedia of World Music, Vol. 1, Africa

Around the year 2000, Salif Keita returned to Africa to live. Keita built a studio in Bamako where he produced acoustic music rooted in the traditions of his native land, collaborating with musicians he had played with for decades. In 2002, on his album titled *Moffou*, he produced an acoustic remake of his song *"Ana Na Ming"*[10] that first appeared with more elaborate accompaniment on his 1995 album *Papa*. His simpler, more personal and direct musical idiom reveals a different side of Keita's musical identity.

With his move back to Mali, Salif Keita came home to himself. Having once sought to compose pop songs that everyone sings, he returned to his own authentic voice. Through this voice, he could express aspects of his identity that he had moved to the background—a West African man, a Wolof-speaking Mande, a Muslim, a blind albino, and thus from a group that has historically been outcast in his native land. He himself chose early in life to take on the identity of a musician while rejecting his aristocratic family status and identity. Yet, despite his continuing success in his homeland, some members of Keita's own family have never forgiven this betrayal of his ancestry. In 2019, Keita retired from performing and recording in order to dedicate his efforts to his charitable organization, the "Salif Keita Global Foundation" for the fair treatment and social integration of persons with albinism (salifkeita.us). His final concert and album were titled *Un Autre Blanc* ("Another White").

> For more than half a century, the political force of Salif Keita's music has been intimately bound up with the distinctive grain of his voice, its embodied resonance. That voice is gritty, but pitch-perfect. And it is loud. It wells up from the core of his body, takes shape in his chest, gathering texture in his throat before projecting from his mouth. At its most intense, when Keita's voice cries out (often at the outset of a song, and again at its climax), his body is still, but tense and reverberant, every inch devoted to the act of voicing. When Keita sings, his body is an instrument. And when he cries, Salif Keita *is* his voice.[11]

Mohammad Reza Shajarian

On October 8, 2020, internationally renowned Iranian vocalist Mohammad Reza Shajarian's death created headlines throughout the world. As Farnaz Fassihi wrote in the *New York Times* obituary:

> The Persian classical music singer Mohammad Reza Shajarian, a towering figure to Iranians for both his artistry and his public stand with protesters against the government, died on Thursday at a hospital in Tehran. He was 80 and had battled kidney cancer for more than a decade.
>
> His son Homayoun Shajarian, also a classical singer, announced the news on his Instagram page with one line that captured the singular place Mr. Shajarian held in the hearts of Iranians, as well as his humility: "The dust beneath the feet of the people flew home to meet his true love."
>
> Mr. Shajarian's appeal crossed generations and political factions, and the news of his death spurred an outpouring of grief from Iranians the world over. In Tehran, thousands of fans packed the streets outside the hospital where he died — people of all ages, wearing masks because of the pandemic, weeping openly and singing some of his most famous songs, derived from Persian poetry and cloaked in political metaphor.
>
> "Bird of freedom sing for me, renew my grief," the crowd sang in unison. "Oh God, oh sky, oh nature, turn our night of darkness into dawn."…

The internationally renowned artist Shirin Neshat said in a statement to The New York Times, "The voice of Iran has died, a man who didn't only touch the hearts of every Iranian with the power of his music but became the healing force in a country drowned in political injustice."[12]

Mohammad Reza Shajarian (1940–2020), the son of a *qari* (expert reciter of the Qur'an), was born in Mashhad, Iran (Map 2.5). He would have listened to his father's voice from a young age. He began studying Qur'anic recitation with his father at the age of five. However, his father did not approve of his son's studying the vocal art music of Iran (***avaz***) on religious grounds. So at the age of twelve, Shajarian began the study of the *radif* in secret. The **radif** is a repertoire of melodies that forms the basis of Iranian classical music. Shajarian began his career performing for Radio Khorasan at the age of nineteen, and on stage in his early twenties (Figure 2.8). By the age of forty, he had become the most famous Iranian classical vocalist. For decades his singing of the prayer "*Rabbana*" ("Oh God") was broadcast nationally on the Iranian Islamic broadcasting service during the holy month of Ramadan, to prepare Muslim listeners for breaking the daily fast at sunset. Following the Iranian Revolution

FIGURE 2.8 Mohammad Reza Shajarian

MAP 2.5 Azerbaijan, Iran, and Turkey in West Asia

Source: Garland Encyclopedia of World Music, Vol. 6, The Middle East

in 1979, his voice became one of protest, with such song lyrics as "a once beautiful country being reduced to shambles and bloodshed." He was silenced permanently in 2009 by the government for outspoken public opposition to a contested presidential election. When President Mahmoud Ahmadinejad referred to protesters as "dust and trash," Shajarian referred to himself as the *voice* of dust and trash, taking on the role of spokesperson for the oppressed.

In a Masters of Persian Music concert in New York City, 2002, Mohammad Reza Shajarian (2.24) sings *avaz* accompanied by master musicians Kayhan Kalhor on *kamanche* (spike fiddle) and Hossein Alizadeh on *tar* (long-necked lute). Iranian vocal music is a vehicle for the artful presentation of sacred poetry, and Shajarian was the undisputed master of *avaz* in the 20th century.

In the documentary *The Voice of Dust and Ash* on the life of Mohammad Reza Shajarian, he states the following in Farsi, translated in English subtitles:

> I am Mohammad Reza Shajarian. Son of Iran. My voice is among the ancient voices of Iran that wants to be remembered as the type of people we were. People of humanity, love, peace and purity. We have no other message for the world than that of friendship, love, life and happiness. And if we complain it is to rid ourselves of societal problems so our people can live.[13]

CONCLUSION

Chapter 2 has presented the human voice as the most ancient, the most versatile, and the most natural instrument of musical expression. The chapter began with an explanation of the vocal apparatus that all normally abled people are endowed with, for speaking and singing. Chapter 2 then discussed issues of nature versus nurture in the cultivation of vocal timbre. Vocal norms are a complex interaction of biological tendencies and socially constructed preferences. The chapter has explored the diversity of the human singing voice globally, and its extraordinary flexibility to express the full range of the human experience. Chapter 3 presents a catalogue of musical instruments from all parts of the world that reveals the ingenuity of human inventiveness. Chapters 2 and 3 emphasize that vocal and instrumental sound production are the raw material of music making.

KEY TERMS AND CONCEPTS

Anatomy of the Human Voice	Call and Response
Vocal Timbre	*Khoomei*
Human Vocal Differentiation: Biological	Non-Lexical Vocable
Human Vocal Differentiation: Cultural	Lilting
Enculturation	Mass Media
Katajjaq	Afropop
Ululation	*Radif*
Amateur Singers	

THINKING ABOUT MUSIC

1   Is there such a thing as a "natural" human singing voice? Or are all voice types conditioned by culture and social expectations? Discuss several examples from the chapter.
2   What is a "specialized singer"?
3   Listen to the video recording of Jimmie Rodgers again. What, in the quality of his voice, made it so emblematic of rural America in the early 20th century?
4   Do you consider yourself a "singer"? If not, do you know others who consider themselves singers? What factors contribute to this self-identification? Is it the sheer enjoyment of singing? Success in a school or church choral program? Peer or family recognition of a particular talent?
5   How would you describe the traditional Bulgarian vocal style, both anatomically and aesthetically?
6   Why has Umm Kulthum been called "The Voice of Egypt"?
7   How would you describe the extraordinary transformation of Salif Keita's musical style at the age of fifty?

NOTES

1 Nicholas Harkness, *Songs of Seoul: An Ethnography of Voice and Voicing in Christian South Korea* (Berkeley: University of California Press, 2013), 9.
2 St. Basil, Exegetic Homilies, in *Pierro Weiss and Richard Taruskin, Music in the Western World: A History in Documents* (New York: Schirmer, 1984), 21.

3 Remarks quoted in "Let Freedom Sing: the Laulupidu Song Festival," Bill Frakes photographer and videographer, YouTube video posted by Nikon Europe, July 2014, https://www.youtube.com/watch?v=aCDsPbUORtc&ab_channel=NikonEurope.

4 Bao Narisu, email to author, October 5, 2021.

5 Eimear Arkins, email to author, February 13, 2021.

6 Scott L. Marcus, *Music in Egypt: Experiencing Music, Expressing Culture* (Oxford and New York: Oxford University Press, 2006), 118–119.

7 Rabih Alameddine, *The Hakawati* (New York: Anchor Books, 2009), 166–167.

8 Banning Eyre, *In Griot Time* (Philadelphia, PA: Temple University Press, 2000), 91.

9 Cheick M. Cherif Keita, *Outcast to Ambassador: The Musical Odyssey of Salif Keita* (St. Paul, MN: Mogoya Books, 2011), 149.

10 Salif Keita, "Ana Na Ming," on *Moffou* (2002), YouTube video, uploaded by Ina Music Live, February 17, 2016, https://www.youtube.com/watch?v=gXaJbu6M5e0&ab_channel=InaMusicLive%2FInaMusiqueLive.

11 Ryan Skinner, "Salif Keita's Incomparable Call," *Africa Is A Country*, https://africasacountry.com/2019/08/salif-keitas-incomparable-call.

12 Farnaz Fassihi, "Mohammad Reza Shajarian, Iranian Master Singer and Dissident, Dies at 80," *New York Times* Obituary, Oct. 8, 2020, updated October 10, 2020.

13 From *The Voice of Dust and Ash* (trailer), Matilda Productions, 2022.

CHAPTER 3

What Is Music Made Of? Musical Instruments

INTRODUCTION

A musical instrument is an object that, combined with the skill and knowledge of a human player, becomes almost a living thing, a voice, a culture bearer, a purveyor of meaning and value, a source of fascination … some would say an extension of the human soul. Many objects can produce sound, but not all are musical instruments. Some objects, such as household pots and pans, may be used to make music but music making is not their primary function. Musical instruments are devices created *intentionally* to produce musical sounds, and *The New Grove Dictionary of Musical Instruments* catalogues more than 12,000 varieties of them. All instruments, like the human voice, require a minimum of three components: a power source, something that vibrates, and something to increase the resonance of the vibrations. This chapter highlights both their extraordinary diversity and how few fundamental ways there are for producing musical sound: a vibrating string, a vibrating air column, a vibrating skin, or a vibrating shaped piece of metal, wood, or gourd.

People have spread musical instrument technologies around the world through exploration, trade, conquest, and the global sharing of cultural resources. In new locations, these resources have been adapted to new purposes and contexts. Sometimes the same instrument goes by different names and is put to very different uses in different cultural settings. An example of this would be the Italian violin and the Irish **fiddle**. Sometimes the opposite is true. The Indonesian *rebab* and the Afghani *rubab* share the same name but are very different instruments—a bowed fiddle and a plucked lute respectively. In the late 20th and early 21st centuries, there has been a revolution in the development of new musical instruments based on electronic and digital technologies, which has affected music making across the entire globe.

What follows is the longest chapter in the textbook, with the most video examples. This extensive examination of musical instruments may be approached in a number of ways. The chapter may be read straight from beginning to end. Other approaches include studying one or two instruments in each category or subcategory, and investigating instruments from particular geographical regions using the video index. This catalogue presents instruments from many cultures played by musicians who have devoted years to acquiring mastery. It is a true aural introduction to the music of the world.

CLASSIFICATION

Classification systems provide order to the enormous variety of musical instruments that exist in the world. Instrument collectors, museum curators, organologists (musical instrument scholars), musicologists, ethnomusicologists, and anthropologists employ such organizational systems to make comparisons across time and across cultures, and for a variety of other purposes specific to their disciplines.

A familiar system is the way instruments of the Western symphony orchestra are grouped into four categories (Figure 3.1):
Woodwinds
piccolo, flute, clarinet, oboe, bassoon
Brass
trumpet, trombone, French horn, tuba
Strings (bowed/plucked)

FIGURE 3.1 Western symphony orchestra

violin, viola, cello, double bass

Percussion (pitched/unpitched)

cymbals, triangle, timpani, bass drum

In ancient China, musical instruments were classified into eight groups according to the material of which they were made (Figure 3.2):

Metal

bronze bell, gong

Stone

stone chime

Silk

long zither (with silk strings), bowed fiddle

Bamboo

flute, panpipe

Gourd

mouth organ (bamboo pipes inserted in gourd chamber)

Leather

drum

Clay

ocarina (globular flute), clay pot

Wood

tiger-shaped wooden scraper, woodblock

The impressive sets of tuned stone and bell chimes that were once part of the ancient Chinese court ensemble are no longer played in China (except at tourist venues on modern reproductions), but they are still heard in Korea. The National *Gugak* Center for Traditional Music in Seoul houses a traditional Korean court ensemble (3.1). In the ancient Chinese and Korean courts, the belief was held that when instruments constructed from this variety of materials played together harmoniously in court rituals, their music harmonized the ruling family with the cosmos and the common people.

In the early 20th century, two German scholars, Curt Sachs and Erich Moritz von Hornbostel, developed an elaborate instrument classification system based upon a 2,000-year old Indian treatise on drama, music, and dance, the **Natya Shastra**. The **Sachs-Hornbostel system** is based on the means by which musical instruments produce sound, and has four major categories, each of which is further subdivided into many subcategories. It has since been widely adopted by organologists, ethnomusicologists, and others.

FIGURE 3.2 Ancient Chinese bronze bell chime of the Marquis Yi of Zeng (L), and Korean traditional orchestra with flutes and stone chime (R)

Chordophones
sound produced by a vibrating string
Aerophones
sound produced by a vibrating column of air
Membranophones
sound produced by a vibrating drum head
Idiophones
sound produced by the material itself vibrating
In 1940 Curt Sachs added a fifth category:
Electrophones
sound produced electronically, and now digitally

Classifying instruments into categories and subcategories has been useful to scholars interested in their historical development, diffusion, adaptation, and structure. However, such analytical methods may take away from what musicians find most significant about musical instruments. Jan Mrázek, a Czech musicologist, wrote of his instrumental studies in Thailand and Indonesia:

> I realized that the "standard" scholarly descriptions and classifications of musical instruments—which I learnt first as a teenager studying violin at the Prague Conservatory, and then again a number of times later—are not just unsatisfactory for my purposes, but are in direct conflict with my own experience of what are musical instruments: in separating the instruments from human experience, human bodies, feelings, imaginations, worlds, and applying "universal" methods of "identifying" them, all that I feel is important is methodically ignored. Where are the joy and pain of learning to play an instrument; the feel of the instrument in my hand, as it gives me a magical power to enter the realm of music and opens up for me a whole field of possibilities; the intimate, physical, life-long bond between the musician and his instrument; the respect and gratitude for my teacher for making me suffer through learning; the atmosphere, excitement, magic of being part of a performance? Each kind of instrument is different, not primarily because of what vibrates in or on the instrument (as the standard classification would lead us to believe), but because each grows from and into human lives and worlds differently. Where are these differences between instruments, the different experiences they make possible, the different ways in which they extend and empower human bodies, the different feelings they evoke, the different roles they play in people's lives and in their world, the different associations they accumulate?[1]

The following catalogue of world instruments attempts to strike a balance between descriptions of the physical objects themselves, and how and why they are played. It employs a modified form of the Sachs-Hornbostel classification system.

CHORDOPHONES

Chordophones are musical instruments in which sound is produced by one or more vibrating strings under tension. Types of **chordophone** include **musical bows**, harps, zithers, lutes, and fiddles. There were no **indigenous** chordophones used by the native peoples of the Western

Hemisphere or Australia. This suggests that of the four categories of acoustic instruments, these developed last. One can imagine the discovery of the sound possibilities of a string under tension coming from the twang of the hunting bow. Perhaps around a campfire at night, hunter-ancestors related stories of how game was brought down, accompanying themselves by plucking on the bowstring used to shoot the killing arrow. Hunters may have discovered that placing the end of the bow frame against their teeth greatly amplified the sound of the instrument, the mouth serving as a resonating chamber. A hole in the ground, a gourd, or a clay pot attached to the bow served the same function. The!Kung of the Kalahari Desert in southwest Africa used a resonator made from an ostrich egg. In modern-day Zambia, Chris Haambwiila plays a musical bow known as *kalumbu* (3.2), accompanying a traditional song.

During the Atlantic slave trade, captive Africans from what is now Angola brought the musical bow to Brazil, where it is known as the *berimbau* (3.3). It became incorporated into a popular Afro-Brazilian martial art called *capoeira*, providing the beat patterns that coordinate the moves of the martial artists. Slave owners confused the moves of *capoeira* for a dance or entertainment, while in fact the slaves were training for defense and revolt. Today *capoeira* is a worldwide martial art phenomenon, always accompanied by the *berimbau*, the *pandeiro* (frame drum), the *atabaque* (tall hand drum), the *agogo* (metal bell), and the *reco-reco* (scraper). Video 3.3 shows the musicians of the *Grupo Capoeira Angola Zimba* accompanying Mestre Cobra Mansa and CM Jorge, who demonstrate the art in Salvador, Bahia, the center of Afro-Brazilian culture in Brazil.

Harps and Lyres

Harps and **lyres** have strings stretched perpendicular to the soundboard that are plucked with the fingers. Two or three strings of different lengths added to the frame of a hunting bow produced the first harps. In the development of the harp, more strings were added, increasing the range and versatility of the instrument. Harps are depicted on the walls of ancient Egyptian tombs, as in Figure 3.3 showing a mural of a blind musician dated from ca. 1400 to 1390 BCE.

A defining feature of the original harps is that each string produced a single pitch. Over the centuries, the instruments became more versatile by the addition of mechanisms to change the tuning of individual strings. Harps today exist in a proliferation of forms. The Celtic harp (3.4), played by Julie Gorka, has a lever system to alter the pitch of each string by half a step. The concert grand harp of the Western symphony orchestra has an elaborate pedal mechanism for changing the pitches. The Spanish brought harps to South America where they became popular among the indigenous peoples of the Andes regions and elsewhere, as shown in Figure 3.4(L). The *arpa* (3.5), played by Silvio Solis, is the national instrument of Paraguay, as seen in Figure 3.4(R), and of Venezuela. In Asia, the largest and most populous continent, all indigenous harps have fallen into disuse, except in Myanmar. There the Burmese *saung gauk* (3.6), an arched harp, is played solo and sometimes accompanies refined and courtly forms of sung poetry (Figure 3.5).

Harps are abundant throughout Africa. The *kora* of Mali, Senegal, and Gambia (Figure 3.6) and the *seperewa* (3.7) of Ghana are hybrid harp-lutes that combine the "one string per pitch" characteristic of the harp with the long neck of a lute from which the strings are suspended. Toward the end of the 20th century when African traditional music became popular

FIGURE 3.3 Ancient Egyptian harp

FIGURE 3.4 Harps (*arpa*) from Cusco, Peru (L), and Paraguay (R)

throughout the world, touring *kora* artists popularized the instrument to a wide audience. Unlike the *kora*, writes Osei Korankye of the University of Ghana's Department of Music,

> the *seperewa* has largely fallen out of use over the past century due to the popularity of the guitar, one of many European instruments that came to the coast through colonial contact. Now it seems the once ubiquitous guitar has been replaced by MCs and producers with laptops.[2]

FIGURE 3.5 Myanmar *saung gauk*

The lyre (3.8) is made by attaching strings to a yoke—two arms and a crossbar—above a resonating chamber.[3] The ancient Greeks associated the instrument with the god Apollo and the mythical singer Orpheus. This video shows representations of the lyre in pottery and sculpture, and demonstrates the sound of a modern replica. Instruments like the ancient Greek lyre are rare today except in northeastern Africa, and an example of an African lyre is the Ethiopian *krar* (3.9). An electronically amplified *krar* is heard in a band that plays nightly in a tourist restaurant in the Ethiopian capital, Addis Ababa.

Lutes

Instruments of the **lute** family have strings stretched along a neck and along the surface of a resonating chamber. The performer plucks the strings with a pick or with the fingers of one hand, and stops the strings by pressing them against the fingerboard with the fingers of the other hand. The word "lute" derives from the Arabic word *al ud* (literally, "wood"). It is the name of an instrument popular in the Middle East, known to virtuoso players as "The King of Musical Instruments." The modern *ud* has a smooth, unfretted fingerboard like the violin. This allows the player to bend pitches and glide continuously from one pitch to another. Lebanese musician Naji Hilal demonstrates the Arabic *ud* (3.10). Many types of lute, however, are fitted with raised frets or bars on the fingerboard that mark the location of specific pitches. Instruments of this type are called *tar* (3.11), *dotar* (3.12), and *setar* (3.13) in Iran, *sitar* in India, and guitar in Spain—names indicating a common ancestry by the final syllable *tar*, meaning "string" in Farsi. Sahba Motallebi plays the *tar* and *setar* in videos 3.11 and 3.13. The *dotar* ("two strings") is played throughout Central Asia, following the Silk Road trade routes that extended all the way from the Mediterranean Sea to Xian, the ancient capital of China (Figure 3.7). Video 3.12 features Abdurahim Hamidov (1952–2013) who was the greatest *dotar* player of his generation. He plays two characteristic dance tunes, "*As bolaman,*

FIGURE 3.6 Senegalese *kora*

mas bolaman" ("I'm drunk") and "*Chupon*" ("Shepherd"). In "*As bolaman*," Hamidov uses his right hand both to strum the strings and produce a fast percussive rhythmic pattern. This rhythm is popular in Iran and other countries in the region, including Azerbaijan, Tajikistan, and Uzbekistan.

The *sitar* (3.14), played in the video by Harihar Sharan Bhatt, became an international icon of Indian culture. The *sitar* (Figure 3.8) along with other plucked lutes of North India has **sympathetic strings** for increased resonance. Sympathetic strings are a secondary set that lie between the main playing strings and the soundboard, and vibrate "in sympathy" with the primary strings. It was featured in several songs of the Beatles in the 1960s, played by George Harrison who had studied with the legendary virtuoso sitarist Ravi Shankar (1920–2012). The *sarod* is a plucked lute of similar prominence in North Indian classical music, also having sympathetic strings but no frets. The *sarod*, meaning "beautiful sound" in Farsi, is related to the Afghan *rabab* (see Video 4.42) and other Central Asian lutes. A foremost *sarod* player of his generation, Ali Akbar Khan (1922–2009), is seen performing with Ravi Shankar in Video 4.56.

FIGURE 3.7 Uighur *dotar*

The principal long-necked lute of South India is the *veena*, or *Saraswati veena* (Figure 3.9), named after the goddess of music, art, and learning. This revered instrument dates back at least to 1000 BCE. Unlike the North Indian *sitar* with its large, lower gourd, the *veena* has a pear-shaped wooden bowl. The *veena* also differs from the *sitar* in having fixed, raised metal frets over which its four main playing strings are stretched. It does not have sympathetic strings.

In China, at the eastern end of the Silk Road, an instrument of the lute family known as the *pipa* dates back more than 2,000 years. Pictures of it appear in cave paintings along the Silk Road. Over the centuries, the angle at which the instrument was held changed from horizontal to vertical. In the 20th century, the number of frets increased from four to thirty, extending the range of the instrument and making it much more versatile. In the linked video, *pipa* (3.15) virtuoso Wu Man (b. 1963) plays her original composition, "Collage." The *pipa* was exported to Japan in the 8th century where, as the *biwa*, it was used for a number of purposes. It was particularly important in **gagaku** court music as well as providing accompaniment to storytellers (Figure 3.10).

The Spanish conquistadors brought fretted lutes to the New World where they were adapted by colonists and indigenous peoples. In the Andes of Bolivia and Peru, a small hybrid instrument called the *charango* (3.16) was developed. Its body was traditionally made from the hard shell of the armadillo, although more recently most are carved from wood. The ten-string *charango* is portable, versatile, and for its size, loud. *Charanguistas*, as players of the instrument are called, have developed extraordinary feats of virtuosity. The song, "*Adios, Puebla de Ayacucho*," is popular in Peru and has been recorded many times, here in

FIGURE 3.8 North Indian *sitar* played by Anoushka Shankar (1981–)

FIGURE 3.9 South Indian *Saraswati veena*

an instrumental version by Puka (Jhonattan Simon). For Peruvians, the song transmits a deep feeling, a transcendental theme. It tells the story of an unattainable dream, an inconfessable secret.

> A Priest, who falls in love with a sweet young woman named Perla;
> an impossible love; as day and night are always close but never together....
> A relationship like a labyrinth with no way out,

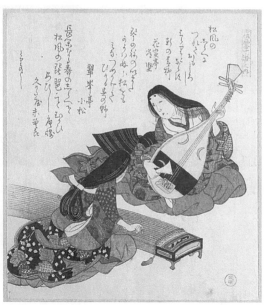

FIGURE 3.10 Chinese *pipa*, Tang Dynasty silk painting, 897 CE (L), and Japanese *biwa*, "Two Ladies; One is Playing the *Biwa* (Japanese Lute) and the Other, the *Koto* (Japanese Harp)," print by Kubo Shunman, 18th century (R)

like a night without stars, like a sea without its waves,
like sand without its footprints.
And feeling that illusion far away, loving the one he should not love …
he decides to leave Ayacucho, composing this beautiful melody.
[English translation by www.DeepL.com/Translator]

In the words of *charanguista* José Prudencio Bustillo, "The strings of my *charango* translate my feelings: when I'm happy they laugh, when I'm in pain they cry" (Figure 3.11).

Other small guitar-like instruments, notably the *machête* and *rajão*, were brought to Hawaii by Portuguese indentured workers from Madeira, who were recruited to work on the sugar cane plantations in the late 1870s. Laborers played the instruments in night-time street concerts to the delight of the native Hawaiians. When their indentureship periods ended in the 1880s, three former Madeiran cabinet makers—Manuel Nunes, José do Espírito Santo, and Augusto Dias—found work in the furniture industry. They adapted the Portuguese instruments to make the first ukuleles to accompany Hawaiian songs and hula dances. The name "ukulele" means "leaping flea," referring to the natives' observation that the fingers of the musicians jumped like insects. In the linked video, Herb Ohta, Sr. plays the tune "Hawaii" on the ukulele (3.17).

Some lutes utilize animal skin to increase their resonance. In West Africa, a number of lutes including the *akonting* (3.18) and *ngoni* are made out of gourd covered with skin (Figure 3.12). Instruments like these, especially the *akonting* (played by Remi Diatta in Video 3.18), were brought by slaves to the New World. Over several centuries the banjo (3.19) evolved into its present form with a flat neck, frets, tuning pegs, and a skin resonator. The

FIGURE 3.11 Peruvian *charango* made from an armadillo shell

FIGURE 3.12 Senegalese *akonting* played by Daniel Laemouahuma Jatta (L), and Senegalese *ngoni* played by Bassekou Kouyate (R)

banjo was adapted for multiple uses in all genres of American popular music from the mid-1800s, and was iconic in minstrel shows and vaudevilles. It continues to be popular in old time, bluegrass, and other American roots genres. In Video 3.19, banjo player Chuck Levy plays the American folk ballad "Little Sadie," along with several variations of the tune.

In China, the *sanxian*, a long-necked, three-string fretless lute, has python skin covering the resonating chamber. This instrument is popular with blind storytellers. Its derivative in Japan, the three-string *shamisen*, has delicate cat skin for resonance in the finest models (Figure 3.13).

The lute family of chordophones is perhaps the most dramatic example of the diffusion of a musical technology, and the guitar is the most widespread lute within this family. The acoustic classical guitar (3.20), played here by Brazilian-born brothers Sérgio and Odair Assad, was developed in mid-19th-century Spain. The guitar has proven to be one of the world's most versatile instruments, used to accompany dances, serenades, church services, and campfire sing-alongs, as well as a solo repertoire of its own. Like the harp and the piano,

FIGURE 3.13 Blind Chinese storyteller with *sanxian* (L) and Japanese *shamisen* (R)

it is able to sound multiple simultaneous pitches for accompanying melodies, but is more portable than either. The guitar owes much of its adaptability to the spread of chordal harmony and popular song styles. Efforts to produce instruments loud enough to compete with the saxophones and horns of the dance band led to experimental models of the modern electric guitar, developed in the 1920s. The first successful solid-body model to be put on the market was designed in 1950 by Leo Fender, whose name is still associated with the instrument. It has become a staple of popular music the world over. Jimi Hendrix, one of the great innovators on the electric guitar, made use not only of amplification of the strings via electronic pickups but also pedal-controlled distortion and feedback effects. Thus, his guitar became a hybrid chordophone-electrophone. Popular genres that grew out of African American song and dance forms of the early 20th century, like blues and jazz, influenced a worldwide renaissance of electric guitar playing in the late 20th century with rock and heavy metal.

Fiddles

The **fiddle** family of chordophones refers to bowed lutes. The horsehair bow was an invention of the horsemen of the Central Asian steppes. Fiddles spread west through Arabic lands to Europe by the 8th century CE and east to China around the same time. Unlike plucked chordophones, fiddles are capable of imitating the human voice because the bow can sustain a sound. The Chinese named the class of bowed fiddles *huqin*, literally "barbarian instrument," referring to its origin outside of China. The most popular Chinese variety of *huqin* today is the *erhu*, played with the bow threaded between the two strings of the instrument (Figure 3.14). Like the three-string Chinese lute, *sanxian*, the *erhu's* octagonal sound box is covered with python skin. In Iran, the *kamanche* (3.21) has a spike attached to its lower end, which supports the instrument on the player's knee as demonstrated by Imamyar Hasanov. Often the *kamanche* is used to accompany the voice in storytelling and religious poetry recitation.

FIGURE 3.14 Chinese *erhu*

The modern violin reached its present form in Renaissance Italy in the mid-16th century. Instrument families at that time were made with a single basic design but of different sizes to match and support the full range of human singing voices. The string quartet (3.22)—two violins, a viola, and a cello—has inspired many European composers to write music for this ensemble. The violin, often called a "fiddle" when used to play folk or popular music, has spread throughout the world. It is the dominant instrument of the Western symphony orchestra, a leading instrument in Irish and Scottish dance music, and the most important accompanying instrument in **Carnatic** classical vocal music in South India. "Violinists" in a symphony orchestra hold their instrument under the chin; "fiddlers" hold their instrument in a number of different ways, perhaps resting on the arm in an Appalachian old time gathering, or against the rib cage in Louisiana **zydeco** or in a Cape Breton dance band (Figure 3.15L). The violinist in South India supports the top of the neck (the scroll) on her foot as she sits cross-legged on the floor, and the Moroccan musician holds the instrument vertically by the neck (Figure 3.15R). In Video 3.23, this Moroccan wedding musician plays a viola, known there as a *kamanja* (3.23) or *jemanja*. He performs with the Ouled Ben Aguida wedding ensemble.

The Indian *sarangi* (3.24), its name meaning "one hundred colors," is carved from a single piece of wood and the body is covered by a skin or parchment membrane (Figure 3.16). It has three thick melody strings that are bowed, and forty sympathetic strings positioned beneath the playing strings. The sympathetic strings enrich the overall sound when set in motion by the bowed strings above. The playing technique is extremely difficult to acquire and takes years to master. The left hand stops the melody strings not with the fingertips but the cuticles, sliding the fingernails along the strings to produce nuances that imitate the

FIGURE 3.15 Cape Breton fiddle in dance band (L); Moroccan street musician playing *jemanja* (R)

FIGURE 3.16 North Indian *sarangi*

human voice. Throughout its history, the *sarangi* has been played to accompany Indian vocal music, although in the 20th century it was popularized by Pandit Ram Narayan (b. 1927) as a solo concert instrument. Like the *sarangi*, the two-string Mongolian *morin khuur* (horsehead fiddle) is also played by stopping the strings with the cuticles. It is the national instrument of Mongolia. Mongolian musician Daxi Jiapu performs on the *morin khuur* (3.25) in a musical show for tourists at "Heavenly Lake" in Xinjiang, northwestern China, showing various playing techniques for a group of visitors. The demonstration took place in a hall beside the sound stage (Figure 3.17).

FIGURE 3.17 Mongolian *morin khuur* ensemble including bass version

Zithers

Zithers are chordophones whose strings are stretched across the top of the resonating chamber. They are found in various forms throughout the world. Box zithers originated in ancient Persia, spread east and west along trade routes, and today are widely distributed. They have been adopted into the art music of Iran (Figure 3.18L) and North India (*santur*), and in folk traditions in Greece (*santouri*) and Hungary (*cimbalom*). The Greek *santouri* (3.26) in this video is played by Areti Ketime. During the Ming Dynasty (1368–1644) the instrument entered China, where it is called *yangqin* or "foreign instrument." The 'hammered dulcimer' is a box zither popular in Appalachian regions of North America. All these examples are trapezoidal in shape and have multiple strings that players strike with small hammers. In Egypt and Turkey, another trapezoidal box zither, the *qanun* (3.27) (played in this video by George Sawa), is plucked with the fingers. In Europe, keyboard mechanisms were added to zithers by the late 1300s. During the Renaissance (ca. 1400–1600), the harpsichord (3.28) became an important solo and ensemble instrument played in the courts of Europe. It worked by means of a feather quill or leather pick plucking the string when a key was depressed. The video shows Rafael Puyana playing a sonata by Domenico Scarlatti. Bartolomeo Cristofiori (1655–1732), an instrument master for the Medici family in Florence, Italy, invented the piano (an abbreviation of "pianoforte") around 1700. His hammer mechanism resulted in a revolutionary instrument whose most innovative features were its ability to play both loud

FIGURE 3.18 Iranian *santur* (L), and Vietnamese *dan tranh* (R)

(forte) and soft (piano) sounds, depending on the force with which the keys were pressed, and its ability to sustain notes by means of foot pedals. More pianos are now made in China than anywhere else in the world, indicating the global diffusion of this instrument.

The most common form of zither in East Asia is the long board zither, which is not indigenous to any other world region. China had board zithers by at least 1500 BCE. The *guqin* (3.29), a board zither without bridges, was played by gentlemen scholars and government officials as a form of meditation and inner refinement—seldom for an audience. It was suppressed during the Chinese **Cultural Revolution** (1966–1976) because of this association with the feudal aristocracy, but is now making a comeback. Xiaolin Dai, professor of *guqin* at Shanghai University, demonstrates this ancient instrument in the video. Another Chinese board zither, the *guzheng* (3.30), on which the strings are stretched over bridges, was associated with female entertainers, as was the Korean *gayageum* (3.31) and Japanese *koto*. The Vietnamese *dan tranh*, played with finger picks, is used to accompany dramas and poetry recitals as well as in chamber groups and orchestras (Figure 3.18R). Throughout East Asia, these instruments are associated with tradition and elegance; one often hears them today played in theaters and teahouses for locals and tourists alike.

Two unique examples of the board zither are the Vietnamese *dan bau* (3.32) and the Korean *ajaeng*. The *dan bau* is constructed of a soundboard, a flexible rod, a single string, and a coconut shell resonator. The player's right hand plucks the string while the left hand gently moves the flexible rod, to change the tension of the string. The video shows the *dan bau* as part of an instrumental ensemble accompanying a water puppet show in Hanoi, northern Vietnam. The Korean *ajaeng* is the only board zither played with a bow, and performs in numerous Korean instrumental ensembles including those that accompany shamanic rituals (see Video 4.27).

AEROPHONES

Free Aerophones

The simplest **aerophone**s are those that produce sounds in air unconfined by a chamber, such as sirens and bullroarers. The bullroarer is a thin elliptical piece of wood, or less commonly bone or stone, attached to a string. When swung around in the air, it produces a distinct humming sound. Prehistoric cave paintings in Africa depict rituals involving the use of bull-roarers. In France, bullroarers made of reindeer antlers are believed to be more than 12,000 years old. The bullroarer is now most often associated with Aboriginal Australians who use it in funerals and initiation ceremonies. In the linked video, Wiruungga Dunggiirr demonstrates the bullroarer (3.33) for videographer Michael Ney.

Unlike the bullroarer, however, most aerophones consist of a tube or vessel in which the air is caused to vibrate by various means. This category includes flutes, panpipes and ocarinas, oboes and bagpipes, clarinets, free reeds, and trumpets and horns.

Flutes

Flutes made of bone, tusk, and antler are among the most ancient of all musical instruments for which there exists archeological evidence. A 9,000-year-old flute made of a bird bone found in a cave in China is fully playable, its pitches corresponding to the familiar "do-re-mi" of the Western major scale. Of course, the kind of music that musicians played on these instruments can only be imagined.

When the flow of air is directed against the edge of a surface splitting the air current, it produces a whistling sound. This is why the wind whistles as it blows against the corner of a building. Blowing on the edge of a soda bottle produces sound in this manner. A **flute** works by a player directing the air current across an edge at or near the end of a tube. Covering and uncovering holes drilled into the tube changes the pitch of the instrument by changing the length of the vibrating air column.

Worldwide, there are currently thousands of varieties of flutes. Musicians and scholars categorize flutes by the way in which they are held and played, horizontally, vertically, or obliquely. Flutes are also categorized by the material from which they are made: bamboo, wood, metal, bone, glass, ivory, and cane. The Hindu God Krishna is often depicted in religious art playing the horizontally held bamboo flute (*bansuri*). The beauty of the flute music symbolizes the spellbinding attraction Krishna exerts upon his devotees (Figure 3.19). The obliquely held, end-blown *ney* (3.34) of Turkey, Iran, and the Arabic world has a recorded history of more than 7,000 years, making it one of the world's oldest instruments in continuous use. Its simple construction, made from hollow cane with finger holes drilled into it, belies the complexity and sophistication of the music that is played on it. In the religious poetry of mystical Islam, its sound is a metaphor for the cry of the human soul longing to be reunited with the divine. Bassam Saba plays the *ney* with the New York Arabic Orchestra in Video 3.34 (Figures 3.20 and 3.21).

The Japanese bamboo *shakuhachi* is an end-blown, vertical flute. Buddhist monks have used the instrument to develop breath control and endurance while meditating upon its sound. In the 17th century, many samurai became masterless *ronin* and joined the Fuke Buddhist sect that used the practice of playing *shakuhachi* as a meditation technique. These itinerant monks wandered the countryside incognito with baskets on their heads, begging and in some cases carrying out acts of espionage for their former employers (Figure 3.22L).

Fipple flutes are found throughout the world and are one of the oldest forms of the instrument. The **fipple flute**, like the police whistle, has a duct at the mouth end that directs the air current against a sharp edge. The indigenous peoples of North America played fipple flutes for courtship and ceremonies (Figure 3.22R). Since the 1990s, Native American music has enjoyed a revival, such as that played on a wooden fipple flute (3.35) by Wolf's Robe in Sedona, Arizona. He performs for tourists in many locales in the southwestern U.S., and makes and sells handmade flutes of his own design as well as his own recordings.

The pennywhistle is a fipple flute indigenous to the British Isles, whose forebears date back to European **recorders** of the Middle Ages. The six-hole "tin whistle," as it was also called, was a factory-produced instrument marketed from the 1840s as the Clarke London Flageolet after Robert Clarke, the factory owner. There are two stories as to why the instrument is called a "pennywhistle." One is that the instrument was cheap, as cheap as a penny.

FIGURE 3.19 Krishna playing his flute under the sacred Kadamba tree. Illustrated page from *Gita Govinda* manuscript, India, 1790

FIGURE 3.20 North Indian side-blown *bansuri* (L), and Lebanese oblique-blown *ney* (R)

FIGURE 3.21 Female *ney* player, from a 19th-century Iranian ceramic tile

FIGURE 3.22 Japanese *shakuhachi* played by a mendicant Buddhist monk at Kita-kamakura temple near Tokyo (L); Cipriano Garcia playing a flute of the Tohono O'odham people of the southwestern U.S. and northern Mexico (R)

The other is that children played it on street corners expecting passers-by to put a penny in their hats. By the early 20th century, it had spread throughout the British Isles and North America, and by the 1950s, it had caught on in the Black townships of Apartheid South Africa. Because the instrument was cheap and affordable, more than a million instruments, called "jive flutes," were sold, and a genre of popular street music, *kwela*, developed from the craze. It was jazzy and fun dance music, and hit records of *kwela* were sold throughout South Africa. In this video, Nelson Makoka plays pennywhistle (3.36) with the late Solomon Sibiya accompanying him on guitar. The duo was known as The Sophia Town Stars. The name comes from a famous township suburb of Johannesburg in which there occurred an artistic renaissance famous for its musicians, writers, and visual artists. In 1955, the population was driven out under draconian segregation laws, and Sophiatown was bulldozed, displacing nearly 60,000 people. How is it that the world's happiest music sometimes comes from the world's saddest circumstances?

There are also double and triple flutes, with one or more tubes producing a **drone** pitch, such as the Bulgarian *dvoyanka*. This instrument is a double flute, usually carved from a single piece of wood. Zdravko Beshendzhiev demonstrates a *dvoyanka* (3.37) of his own making. In the Rhodope Mountains in southwest Bulgaria, solitary shepherds played the *dvoyanka* to entertain themselves.

Like lutes, flutes are found throughout the world; but unlike lutes, their universal diffusion is due as much to independent invention as to cultural dissemination.

Panpipes and Ocarinas

Greek myth tells of the god Pan's love for the nymph Syrinx, who captivated him by the beauty of her singing. To avoid his advances, she sought protection from the river nymphs who transformed her into a hollow reed. Yet when the wind blew across the river, Pan could still hear her voice now emanating from the reeds. Distraught by his loss, Pan cut the reeds into descending lengths and tied them together to make an instrument that was thereafter associated with him: the **panpipes**, known as syrinx by the Greeks. In modern-day central Europe, including Romania, Moldova, and Ukraine, the panpipe is known as the *nai* where it has been played at least since the 17th century. The twenty-pipe instrument (Figure 3.23) was taken up by an extraordinary Romanian musical personality, Gheorghe Zamfir (b. 1941). He popularized the instrument around the world and more than doubled the number of pipes to forty-two. In the course of a five-decade career, he sold more than a hundred million recordings, and invented various sizes of the instrument including in 1982 the contrabass pan flute. He performed in many different genres including folk, jazz, popular, sacred, and Western classical. Zamfir played on the soundtracks of a number of feature films, including *Picnic at Hanging Rock* (3.38). He has been called "The Master of the Pan Flute."

FIGURE 3.23 Gheorghe Zamfir (1941–) playing panpipes

In Uganda, panpipes form part of instrumental ensembles, playing short repeating melodic-rhythmic phrases. In the linked video, Haruna Walusimbi, a master of Ugandan traditional music, tunes *enkwanzi* (3.39) panpipes by moving a wax plug up or down inside the tubes. He then joins his bandmates who are playing the lamellophone (*endongo*) and the single string fiddle (*endingidi*).

Globular flutes, popularly known as **ocarinas**, are made of clay, pottery, or other materials, and have been in existence for at least 12,000 years in South America. They were found in the New World by Hernando Cortés during his conquest of Mexico in 1521 and brought back to Europe. The Chinese ocarina (*xun*) was used in court rituals more than 2,000 years ago. These court rituals required the harmonious sounds of instruments made from a variety of materials, the *xun* representing the instrument category of earth or pottery. The modern globular flute was invented by a seventeen-year-old Italian brickmaker named Guiseppe Donati in 1853. He took the idea of the Aztec globular flute and reworked the design to increase the number of holes to eight. His final version looked to him like a little goose, so he called his instrument "ocarina" (3.40) ("little goose" in Italian). In this video, the ocarina is played by Durian Songbird. During World War I American troops carried these instruments overseas and named Donati's model "the sweet potato" because of its shape (Figure 3.24).

FIGURE 3.24 *Suonatore di ocarina* ("Ocarina player"), Attilio Polato, ca. 1930

In 1998, Nintendo released its fifth video game in the *Legend of Zelda* series. According to a 1999 article in the *New York Times*:

> The new Nintendo video game, Legend of Zelda: Ocarina of Time, is on pace to become one of the best-selling video games ever. And its popularity seems to have spawned another craze—demand for real ocarinas, those flute-like musical instruments that look like sweet potatoes with finger holes.[4]

Oboes and Bagpipes

Many people are familiar with the sounds that can be made by blowing on a blade of grass or a leaf held between the thumbs and fingers. This demonstrates the basic principle of the type of aerophone that uses one or two thin pieces of reed mounted at the end of a tube to produce vibrations, as in the **clarinet** (single reed) or **oboe** (double reed). Among the Hmong of Southeast Asia, a banana leaf becomes a sophisticated instrument called the *nplooj* (3.41), which is capable of being heard over long distances. Because the Hmong language is tonal, the *nplooj* can be used to send verbal messages both of courtship and war. Double-reed instruments spread along the Silk Road overland and via ocean trade routes by Arab traders. These instruments reached as far afield as China, Korea, and Japan, as well as Thailand, Vietnam, Myanmar, and Indonesia (Figure 3.25). The English word "shawm" is often used to denote double-reed aerophones, and the term is related etymologically to the Turkish *zurna* (Figure 3.26L), the Chinese *suona*, and the Indian *shehnai*, demonstrating how widely dispersed these instruments are. The *nadaswaram* (Figure 3.26R) accompanies many Hindu temple rituals and is a ubiquitous sound throughout South India. In central and western China, where the *suona* (3.42) accompanies festive celebrations as well as funeral processions, the players use a technique called **circular breathing** to sustain the airflow through the instrument while taking in air, using the cheeks to store a constant air supply. The tubular body of many instruments of this family ends with what is called a flaring bell. In Korea, the short wooden *taepyeongso* (3.43) has a brass bell at the end of its tube, and a short double reed held in the mouth of the performer. It is the loudest of Korean instruments and, prior to the Japanese occupation in the early 20th century, it was played in military processions. Today it is used in sporting events, dances, and many other outdoor occasions.

The double-reed *duduk* (3.44) is a symbol of Armenian national identity and is the only indigenous instrument that has survived Armenia's long history. Armenians date its music to more than 2,000 years ago and the reign of King Tigran the Great (95–55 BC). The *duduk* has a sound unlike any other double-reed instrument in the world and is still played today for weddings, funerals, and to accompany Armenian traditional dance. Like the panpipes, it is widely used in feature films as a sound that represents "the exotic." It is also featured in the soundtracks for a number of popular video games including *World of Warcraft* and *The Elder Scrolls* series.

Bagpipes are found throughout the Mediterranean region from the British Isles across Northern Africa to the Persian Gulf. The bags made of sheepskin or pig bladder make circular breathing unnecessary. Two methods were developed in Europe to keep the bag filled with air. For the earliest and most common bagpipes, the player blows into a pipe to maintain sufficient air pressure while squeezing a bag to provide a constant airflow. Mouth blown bagpipes date back at least to the 13th century. In the second method, players pump air into

FIGURE 3.25 Conical wooden shawms played in Bac Ha market in northern Vietnam

FIGURE 3.26 Turkish *zurna* with *bendir* (frame drum) (L), and South Indian *nadaswaram* (R)

the bag with their arm using a bellows system. This method dates from the 16th century, and is utilized in the Irish *uilleann pipes* (3.45) and the Northumbrian smallpipes. In both systems, the air is forced from the bag through at least two pipes that are fitted with either

FIGURE 3.27 *The Peasant Dance* (1567), Pieter Bruegel the Elder (ca.1525–1569), Kunsthis-
torisches Museum, Vienna

single or double reeds. One is the chanter pipe that has finger holes for changing pitches and
playing melodies. The other pipe (or pipes) provides a steady drone accompaniment. The
medieval *cornamusa* (3.46) (Italian bagpipe) had a single drone. The video shows a replica
played by its maker Luca Paciaroni. Bagpipes were made in many regional styles during the
Middle Ages, and were the party instruments of choice, as seen in this famous 16th-century
painting by Pieter Bruegel the Elder. They were loud enough to keep a whole field full of
revelers dancing (Figure 3.27).

The Great Highland bagpipes (3.47) were played as "weapons of war" by the British army
during Britain's colonial expansion and right up until World War II. The sound of a massed
regiment of pipers is deafening. Bagpipers have marched with military regiments in Scotland
at least since the Battle of the North Inch of Perth in 1396. The last use of British regimental
bagpipes was in Aden in 1967. Now the Great Scottish bagpipes are played at Highland
games, military tattoos, royal processions, and other ceremonial events. Video 3.47 shows
the massed bagpipes and drums of the Royal Military Tattoo as they march into the parade
grounds at Edinburgh Castle in Scotland.

Clarinets

Clarinets are aerophones with a single reed mounted in a mouthpiece. In Sardinia, triple-
pipe clarinets (*launeddas*) have been played for more than 2,000 years. The *pungi* (3.48), a
double-pipe clarinet with gourd resonator, is used in India to captivate cobras and tourists
alike (Figure 3.28). Video 3.48 shows a snake charmer in Cochin, South India, pursuing his

trade. The *pungi* music, however, is strictly for the human listeners. Ryan Bradley writes in *Popular Science*, in answer to the question, "Can snakes really be charmed by music?":

> The charm has nothing to do with the music and everything to do with the charmer waving a *pungi*, a reed instrument carved out of a gourd, in the snake's face. Snakes don't have external ears and can perceive little more than low-frequency rumbles. But when they see something threatening, they rise up in a defensive pose. "The movement of the snake is completely keyed in on the guy playing the toodley thing," says Robert Drewes, chairman of the department of herpetology (the study of amphibians and reptiles) at the California Academy of Sciences in San Francisco. "He sways, the snake sways."[5]

The reed in most ancient varieties of clarinet, including the *launeddas* (3.49) and *pungi*, is made of the same material as the pipe, whether wood, bamboo, or river reed (Figure 3.29L). Instruments of this kind were played by pre-Columbian indigenous peoples of South America. Throughout northwest Africa, single-reed aerophones are made from a hollowed-out stalk of sorghum inserted into a gourd resonator. The hornpipe of the British Isles has a body of cow horn to which a mouthpiece holding the reed is attached (Figure 3.30). A French single-reed instrument with a straight, cylindrical tube, the *chalumeau*, was the predecessor of the European clarinet (3:50). During the 18th century the clarinet was fitted with metal keys to increase the range and ease of playing, and this version of the family has had widespread adaptations (Figure 3.29R). In Video 3.50, Mauricio Murcia Bedoya plays

FIGURE 3.28 Snake charmer playing *pungi* in Kerala, southwest India

FIGURE 3.29 Sardinian *launeddas* (L), and Eastern European Roma clarinet (R)

FIGURE 3.30 Huw Roberts playing Welsh *pibgorn* (hornpipe)

Jean Françaix's Clarinet Concerto, 4th movement (1967) with the Orquesta Filarmónica de Bogotá, Colombia. Particularly in Eastern Europe and the Middle East, it often plays a predominant role in wedding and dance bands, as in the klezmer (3.51) ensemble associated with Jews of Southeastern Europe. Video 3.51 shows the Budapest Klezmer Band.

The modern church organ is perhaps the world's most complex form of aerophone, using electric bellows to force air through a variety of pipes, each set of pipes producing a characteristic and consistent timbre. The Wanamaker Organ (3.52) in Philadelphia was made originally for the 1904 St. Louis World's Fair. It was then permanently installed in Wanamaker's Department Store, now owned by Macy's. Twice a day, Monday through Saturday, the instrument is played for shoppers, and special concerts are held throughout the year. It is the largest pipe organ in the world with 28,750 pipes, and after 120 years it can still hold a crowd spellbound. Video 3.52 shows the great American organist Virgil Fox (1912–1980) playing the six keyboards of this great organ.

Free Reeds

The free reed, or flexible metal tongue, was a musical technology indigenous to East Asia, and developed more than 3,000 years ago in China. Mouth organs consist of a set of bamboo "pipes" of varying lengths each fitted with a metal reed and all secured together in a gourd or hardwood wind chest. In most East Asian mouth organs, the wind chest sits at the base of the instruments; in southeast Asia the wind chest is in the middle and the pipes extend both above and below. The free reeds vibrate when a player inhales or exhales air through a mouth hole in the wind chest and simultaneously covers the finger hole of each pipe that the player wishes to sound. If a hole is left open, no sound is produced. In China, the *sheng* has a documented history dating back to 1100 BCE, and has been used both in instrumental ensembles and to accompany Chinese opera. In the modern Chinese orchestra, the *sheng* comes in a variety of sizes including a contrabass version that utilizes a keyboard (Figure 3.31).

In the highlands of Laos and northern Thailand, the *khaen* (3.53) is used for social functions and also in healing rituals for inducing trance in spirit mediums. Among the Lao people in these highland regions, the *khaen* is virtually ubiquitous. It serves similar functions in Laos as the guitar in America: accompanying family gatherings, political rallies, religious rituals, songs, and dances. Like many traditional folk instruments of the world, the *khaen* has been brought into the 21st century through electronic amplification and its use in rock bands and other forms of popular music. Video 3.53 shows the legendary blind master musician Sombat Simlah in the Thai province of Maha Sarakham. An article in the *Bangkok Times* states that Sombat Simlah can "mimic horns, ambulances and police cars, disco beats and synth drums, and the sound of heavy traffic. But his tour de force ... is the sound of a train journey, complete with traffic crossings and the calls of barbecue chicken vendors."[6]

After the Chinese *sheng* was first introduced to Europe in the 1770s by a French missionary, free reed technology led to the development of the accordion, the concertina, the pump organ (harmonium), and the harmonica (Figure 3.32). A prototype accordion was invented in Germany in the 1820s and two basic forms were developed, the button accordion and the piano accordion, both operated by pulling and pushing bellows. By the 1840s the accordion was being mass produced in Russia, and within thirty years, more than 700,000 instruments were being made annually in the industrial city of Tula alone. During World War II,

FIGURE 3.31 Chinese *sheng* (mouth organ) (L), and contrabass *sheng* (with keyboard) (R)

FIGURE 3.32 Harmonica and diatonic accordion, Japanese self-study book, 1899

60,000 accordions were sent from Tula to the Western Front, since boosting soldier morale with the instruments was considered essential to the Russian war effort. As the accordion spread around the world, it became known as the "instrument of the people." From Russia the instrument spread to China. During the Cultural Revolution (1966–1976) it provided accompaniment to mass political rallies and revolutionary marches. Today there are more accordions in China than in the rest of the world combined. In Madagascar, the instrument provides the musical stimulus for spirit possession in the *tromba* ceremony. In Mexico, the

FIGURE 3.33 South Asian harmonium (L); Roma piano accordion player in Italy (C); Cajun button accordion (R)

FIGURE 3.34 Pump organ (harmonium made by Mason and Hamlin)

accordion is an indispensable member of the *Norteño* ensemble that plays for dance parties; it is also a favorite of Cajun musicians in Louisiana. In Irish sessions, musicians play both the button accordion and the concertina. The English concertina (3.54), played in the video by Tim Smith, is typically octagonal in shape, and sounds the same pitches whether the bellows are pushed or pulled. On the German or Anglo concertina, the direction of the air pressure changes the pitches, like on a harmonica. In our current age of globalization, music unites the ancient and the modern in this concert of free-reed aerophones, the ancient *sheng* with the accordion (3.55).

Harmonium reed organs were once very popular in Europe and its colonies, and in North America. They were smaller and lighter than the piano and more durable in tropical weather. Two foot-pedals activated the bellows that kept the air stream flowing. Before the development of today's electric organs, harmonium reed organs were often used in small rural churches that couldn't afford a pipe organ (Figure 3.34). In India, European missionaries introduced small, portable, hand-pumped harmoniums in the mid-19th century (Figure 3.33L). There they became the most popular accompanying instrument for vocal music (see Video 3.72).

Trumpets and Horns

Trumpets are aerophones in which the buzzing of the performer's lips causes the air column enclosed in a chamber or tube to vibrate. In many parts of the world, the end of a conch shell is cut off and the hole is placed against the lips to create a conch **trumpet**. These instruments are among the oldest that archeologists have discovered, one in southwestern France dating from ca. 15,000 BCE. In Tibet, far from the ocean in the center of the high Asian Plateau, conch shells (*dung-dkar*) have been used for both ritual purposes and signaling (Figure 3.36L). Buddhist monks play conch shells in pairs from the tops of monasteries or nearby hillsides to invite the public to religious ceremonies. The sound symbolizes the proclamation of Buddhist law to the world as the players face each of the four directions in turn. Ritual use of the *dung-dkar* in Tibet predates the introduction of Buddhism, for **shamans** in the indigenous Bon religion used conch shells to summon spirits "to help grow cattle or food and even banish evil spirits that caused illness and destruction."[7]

The Australian didgeridoo is a natural wooden trumpet made of a trunk or limb of eucalyptus wood that has been hollowed out by termites (Figure 3.35). It is the most important instrument of the indigenous peoples of northern Australia. The name "didgeridoo" (3.56) was first seen in print in a 1908 Hamilton, Victoria, newspaper article. The author coined the onomatopoeic term to imitate the sounds produced by this tubular instrument, which has many names among the various linguistic groups. In Video 3.56, Wiruungga Dunggiirr plays the *yidaki*, the instrument's name among the Yolŋu-speaking Aboriginal peoples of northeast Arnhem Land. Because it is so simple in its construction, the didgeridoo has become an instrument of choice for street musicians and buskers around the world, raising concerns of cultural appropriation.

The long telescopic metal trumpet *dung-chen* serves ritual purposes and accompanies ceremonial dances in Tibet and Ladakh (northern India) and in the Himalayan Kingdom of Bhutan. It is the most widely used instrument in Tibetan Buddhism. In this video, Buddhist monks play a pair of *dung-chen* (3.57) (Figure 3.36R) joined by a Tibetan double-reed *gyaling*.

The bugle, a valveless trumpet, serves important military functions as it has for centuries. Soldiers have known bugle calls from camp life, signaling "wake up," "chow time," etc. These calls could be heard above the fray on the battlefield announcing "advance" and "retreat." The bugle is only capable of playing the notes of a single overtone series, which gives their melodies a characteristic sound. At military funerals, the sound of the bugle honors the fallen. U.S. Army bandsman Keith C. Clark played the bugle (3.58) at Arlington National Cemetery on November 25, 1963 for the funeral of President John F. Kennedy, who had been assassinated

FIGURE 3.35 didgeridoo, Queensland, Australia

FIGURE 3.36 Tibetan trumpets: conch *dung-dkar* (L), and metal *dung-chen* (R)

three days earlier in Dallas, Texas. The day was bitter cold, and Clark missed the sixth note of the famous bugle call, "Taps." Some journalists have speculated that he missed the note purposely, to symbolize the grief of the nation.

Beginning in the 18th century, military units began to enlist and support ensembles of wind and percussion instruments to play for formation drills and ceremonial events. Napoleon believed that martial music was extremely important in maintaining the morale of his troops. In the 19th century, piston and rotary valves were fitted onto brass instruments. These valves opened the airstream to additional lengths of tubing, further increasing the number of pitches the instruments could produce. Governments around the world have since encouraged the establishment of military bands, modeled after those used by the colonial powers, to play for state occasions. In New Orleans, brass instruments from Navy bands were taken up by street entertainers and in the early 20th century became the instruments associated with Dixieland jazz. Louis Armstrong, the father of jazz improvisation, developed his signature style on the trumpet. The symphony orchestra today has a full complement of trumpets, trombones, French horns, and a tuba. Other brass aerophones—cornet, baritone, flugelhorn, and euphonium—may be heard in this video of the North Carolina Brass Band (3.59). The timbre of brass instruments is affected by the shape of the tubing (or "bore"). Conical bore instruments gradually widen between the mouthpiece and bell, whereas in cylindrical bore instruments the tube is the same diameter for most of its length, except for the flaring bell. Conical bore instruments (cornet, flugelhorn, euphonium, and tuba) have a softer sound that blends more easily with other instruments. Orchestral brass instruments besides the tuba—trumpet, trombone, and French horn—use cylindrical bore tubing that gives these instruments a more focused, directional sound.

MEMBRANOPHONES

The term "**membranophone**" describes instruments on which musical sound is produced by striking or rubbing a stretched membrane. Generically called "drums," these instruments are distributed worldwide and are classified by the number of membranes (single- or double-headed) and by the shape of the resonating body (goblet, cylindrical, conical, barrel, hour-glass, frame, etc.). Most drums do not produce specific pitches, although some, like the *tabla* and *mridangam* of India, are tunable.

In North Indian classical music, the word *tabla* refers to a pair of instruments, a small barrel-shaped drum for the right hand and a kettledrum for the left (Figure 3.37L). They are tuned with leather thongs to match the fundamental pitch of the instrumental or vocal soloist they are accompanying. They also have a characteristic black circle on each drum head made of flour paste and iron filings, which allows the drum head to ring with overtones. The playing technique is among the most complex in the world. In South India, the *mridangam*, a double-headed barrel drum, plays a similar accompanying role. A barrel-shaped drum called the *dholak* is used in sacred and popular music in North India as well as in Suriname, Guyana, the Caribbean, and elsewhere following the Indian diaspora. The two drum heads are of different sizes, producing both high and low sounds.

In Myanmar, the *pat waing* (3.60) (literally, "drum circle") is a set of twenty-one tuned barrel drums, adopted from the Indian *tabla*. These drums hang inside a circular frame in which a performer sits, and are fine-tuned with the same tuning paste that is used in India, here called *pat sa* (literally, "drum food"). This may be added or removed to raise or lower the drum's pitch for playing melodies in different modes or scales. The *pat waing* is the lead instrument of the *hsaing waing* ensemble. This is a traditional orchestra that dates back at least to the 1600s and it serves many functions including weddings, funerals, Buddhist ordinations, dances, theatrical works, and puppet plays. Video 3.60 features a student group from Yangon University of Culture.

Goblet-shaped hand drums are found throughout North Africa and the Near East, and are now played in many other parts of the world, due to the widespread interest in World Music and dance. The performer in this video, Jussef Bichara, who teaches at a dance school in Chile, is playing the North African *derbake* (3.61). The West African *djembe* is also enjoying worldwide popularity (Figure 3.37C). It is used as the lead drum in an ensemble that includes at least three cylindrical or barrel drums of varying sizes. These drums set up repeating rhythmic patterns while the lead *djembe* drummer plays intricate improvised variations, frequently responding to the movements of dancers.

Hourglass drums (double-headed drums with a narrow waist) are found in many parts of the world, including West Africa, India, East Asia, and Papua New Guinea. In Japan, two sizes of hourglass drum, the larger *otsuzumi* and the smaller *kotsuzumi*, accompany theatrical performances. The *janggu* arrived in Korea as part of a large gift of instruments to the Korean court from the Emperor of China ca. 1110 (Figure 3.37R). Today, this large hourglass drum is used in nearly every form of Korean musical performance: court and religious rituals, folk song accompaniment, even during student demonstrations. In Korean court music, a delicate strip of bamboo taps the outer rim of the right drumhead, traditionally made of dog skin or horsehide, while the open left hand taps the thicker left drumhead made of cow skin. Many styles of folk song and dance use the *janggu* as rhythmic accompaniment, much as the guitar provides harmonic accompaniment in the West; without either, the music sounds incomplete. A smaller "folk" *janggu* plays a dominant role in farmers' band festivals *(pungmul)* as part of an ensemble consisting also of large and small gongs (*jing* and *kkwaenggwari*, respectively) and a large barrel drum (*buk*). The folk *janggu* is played with the bamboo strip in the right hand and a wooden mallet in the left. The culminating event of a festival is the virtuosic dance called *seoljanggu* (3.62). The video depicts Kim Seonghoon playing and dancing gracefully with his drum tied to his body. While *seoljanggu* is traditionally performed outdoors, this performance takes place on a stage with the rest of the accompanying *pungmul* ensemble off to the side.

Hourglass "talking drums" (3.63) are played throughout West Africa where they go by many names: *dondo* in Akan languages, *gangan* in Yoruba, *kalangu* in Hausa, etc. There is considerable variety in the shape and size of the instrument's wooden body. The two drum heads are tied onto the drum's body with rope thongs. The player supports the drum under the left arm and strikes one head with a curved stick held in the right hand. Applying pressure to the

FIGURE 3.37 Indian *tabla* drum pair (L); West African *djembe* (C); and Korean *janggu* (R)

strings with the left elbow stretches and loosens the drumhead, producing varying pitches as it is struck. These pitch variations mimic the inflections of spoken language (Figure 3.38).

Ethnomusicologist John Miller Chernoff studied talking drums in Ghana in 1970 and 1971 and wrote about his experiences in *African Rhythm and African Sensibility:*

> While in Western music, certain kinds of musical themes may suggest images or feelings, the astounding fact is that in traditional African music, the rhythms themselves are a specific text. When the earliest European travelers described drum-signaling between villages, they assumed that the beating was a kind of code. In reality, the drums actually speak the language of the tribe. During my first day practicing with Gideon [my teacher], I was following him well until he suddenly performed a rather complicated series of rhythms and then went back to the basic rhythm he was showing me. A few minutes later a man who had passed at that moment returned with two bottles of beer.[8]

Cylindrical drums are played throughout the world. They were and continue to be the most important instruments of the native peoples of North America. At powwow (3.64) ceremonies, large double-headed cylindrical drums are set on the ground and played communally by groups of men, often as accompaniment to dance (Figure 3.39L). The video features the Armour Hill Singers performing at the Las Vegas powwow. The Turkish *daul* or *davul* has two heads strung together with zigzag lacing, like similar bass drums in Greece, Albania, and several Middle Eastern countries. When played for outdoor dancing and in processions, the

FIGURE 3.38 Yoruba drummers playing talking drums in Ijomu Oro, Nigeria, 2004

FIGURE 3.39 Native American powwow drum (L), and Inuit frame drum (R)

daul is almost always paired with the double-reed aerophone, the *zurna*. Cylindrical drums are particularly widespread in Western music, ranging from the bass drum of classical symphony orchestras and marching bands to the drum kit in rock bands.

Frame drums have a single membrane stretched over a shallow wooden rim. The frame is usually made of thin wood that provides little resonance when the membrane is struck. Frame drums are used in religious rituals by Shiite Muslims in Iran and Afghanistan, by the Inuit of northern Alaska, and by shamans in Siberia (Figure 3.39R). The great percussionist Glen Velez (3.65) demonstrates what is possible on this simple instrument. The tambourine, such as the Brazilian *pandeiro* (3.66), is a composite instrument: a frame drum combined with metal discs or jingles, which are idiophones. In the linked video, Louis-Daniel Joly shows off his virtuosic technique at a Canadian nightclub.

"In many parts of the Middle East frame drums are strongly associated with women," writes ethnomusicologist Veronica Doubleday.[9] This situation is remarkable because in many other regions—Europe and sub-Saharan Africa, for instance—drumming is traditionally performed by men, not women. Miniature paintings and palace wall frescos in Iran document women playing frame drums with jingles in court settings to entertain royalty and accompany dancers. Figure 3.40 shows a fresco on the walls of the 17th-century Chehel Sotoun Palace in Isfahan. In more recent times, male dominance in Islamic religious and political life has restricted women's traditional music making to all-female gatherings. Nevertheless in weddings and other life-cycle and festive events, women have continued to play frame drums in private domestic spaces as an essential component of these rituals. The frame drum, Doubleday continues, "accompanies songs of blessing whose verses give emotional support to the bride and her close relatives"; it "promotes bonding between the bride and groom's families,"[10] and provides an exhilarating atmosphere conducive to birth and marriage celebrations.

Nowhere on earth is the variety of membranophones greater than in Africa, where they form an integral accompaniment to many social and religious occasions. Because the same or similar drums can have different names in different tribal languages, classification can be quite bewildering. The world-renowned African ethnomusicologist Kwabena Nketia (1921–2019) notes:

> There are bottle-shaped, cylindrical, conical, and goblet or hourglass drums. There are single- and double-headed drums; closed and open; tuned and untuned drums. There are those drums that are covered by ox hide and others covered by lizard, calf, or apron

FIGURE 3.40 Persian woman playing *daf*, from painting on the walls of the Chehel Sotoun Palace, Isfahan, 17th century

skins. Some are played with sticks and others with bare hands. There are drums with and without jingles and buzzers attached to the membrane. There are small, medium-sized, and very big drums. The diversity of tribes, languages, and musical systems is enormous; each tribe, each language group has a name for every instrument.[11]

In many parts of sub-Saharan Africa, social and ritual occasions without drums are inconceivable. The African diaspora brought the richness of African percussion to the New World. While in most of North America, the drumming culture of the West African slaves was suppressed, in much of the Caribbean and South America, African percussion-based music was free to develop.

In Africa, barrel-shaped drums were fashioned out of logs, but in the New World they were made from barrel staves. Barrel drums called congas (3.67), derived from West African models, are the heart of Puerto Rican salsa and Cuban rumba dance rhythms. Many forms of popular music that developed during the 20th century in the Americas and spread throughout the world are based on this rich rhythmic heritage. The congas in Video 3.67 are played by Juan Alamo.

IDIOPHONES

The fourth Sachs-Hornbostel instrument category, idiophones, is the most diverse. The word literally means "self-sounding"; an **idiophone** is a musical instrument whose material itself vibrates. The instrument's shape and the material from which it is made contribute to its resonance and amplification when played. This category comprises instruments that produce a fixed pitch: bells, chimes, xylophones, metallophones, lamellophones, gongs, etc.; and instruments that produce indefinite pitch: cymbals, woodblocks, scrapers, shakers, castanets, maracas, rattles, etc.

Bells

Bells throughout the world are often used for signaling or other purposes that could be characterized as "music" or not. The cowbells in Chapter 1 are an example of this ambiguity: a herder hangs the bell on a cow's neck to keep track of the animal, and also to enjoy its beautiful sound. In Buddhist temples throughout East Asia, a large hanging bell (3.68) is rung for ceremonial purposes, while small hand bells announce the end of meditation sessions. Video 3.68 shows a Buddhist monk at the Sudeok-sa temple in South Korea swinging the large suspended log that strikes the great bell. In Japan, *suzu* bells filled with pellets are hung at the entrances to Shinto shrines (Figure 3.41). Visitors pull on thick ropes to shake the bells and thereby honor the *kami* spirits. European church bells (3.69) are constructed with clappers on the inside, such as those in the video recorded in Seville, Spain. In African and Latin American drum ensembles, single or double iron bells such as the *agogo* (3.70) are often used to hold a steady pattern that serves as a sonic nucleus for complex and improvised drum patterns. Its high metallic pitch is always audible to drummers and dancers and so acts as the ensemble's timekeeper or conductor.

FIGURE 3.41 Visitors at Yasaka Shinto Shrine in Kyoto ring *suzu* bells to call *kami* spirits, 2009

Time Keepers

Like the iron bells of Africa and Latin America, a number of wooden and gourd instruments also serve the purpose of keeping time in percussion ensembles. The West African *sekere*, a beadnet-covered gourd, and the Zimbabwean *hosho*, a seed-filled gourd rattle, fulfill this function. Joining the drums and cowbell in Cuban dance bands, the *guiro*, a notched gourd scraper, adds to the rhythmic accompaniment with its distinctive raspy sound (Figure 3.42). One of the most basic methods of producing rhythmic accompaniment is clapping together two similar objects. At the heart of Afro-Cuban music is the repeating pattern played on the *claves*, two thick wooden sticks struck together. In Spain, flamenco dancers often play wooden castanets (3.71) to accentuate their dance rhythms, like Barbara Hennerfeind in the video.

Ordinary household objects, farming implements, vessels, and weapons have been used to produce musical sounds and rhythms for festivals, rituals, and other occasions. In these special circumstances such objects become idiophones; however, this is not their primary function. In South India (Figure 3.43L), a *ghatam* (clay pot) is struck and slapped by the bare hands of the performer, producing an amazing variety of sounds (see Video 4.15). Brake

FIGURE 3.42 Cuban *guiro*

FIGURE 3.43 South Indian *ghatam* (L), and North Indian *jaltarang* (R)

drums are used as timekeepers in Trinidad's steel drum ensembles. **Indentured** laborers of India, transported to Trinidad and Suriname by British and Dutch plantation owners, adapted a simple iron rod into a complex percussion instrument called *dhantal*. Players strike the rod with an iron stirrup (formerly a horseshoe), and provide rhythmic accompaniment for ensembles such as the Surinamese *baithak gana* (3.72) (literally, "seated singing"). In this genre, the vocalist and harmonium player (in the video, Rakieb Waggidhossain) is accompanied by the *dhantal* and *dholak* (double-headed barrel drum), played by Narinder Singh and Roy Raghu, respectively. African American slaves in Protestant North America were not allowed to play drums on plantations. They became experts in playing washboards, spoons, and other household implements. The washboard became a popular rhythm instrument in Louisiana *zydeco* and other folk and popular genres.

Xylophones

The word "**xylophone**" derives from the Greek words *xylon* for wood and *phōnē* for sound. Instruments made from tuned wooden bars or keys are found in many parts of the world. Known as the marimba, it is the national instrument of Guatemala. Xylophones are also featured in a number of Southeast Asian ensembles. In Thailand and Cambodia, the *ranat ek* is an important member of the classical *pi phat* ensemble, the most highly regarded and prestigious instrumental ensemble in Thailand.

Wooden xylophones are popular throughout equatorial Africa. In Uganda, the xylophone has many names (*amadinda, akadinda, embaire,* etc.). It also varies by size, number of keys, and tuning system, according to ethnic group. All are constructed from hardwood logs that are carefully selected and shaped into slabs. The performance technique for the *embaire* requires two or more musicians to sit on opposite sides of the instrument, and by alternating mallet strokes they create rapid interlocking patterns. The *embaire* of the Basoga people has large wooden slabs placed over a pit dug in the ground for greater resonance. A minimum of six musicians sit around the instrument, and play highly coordinated interlocking melodies.

This video depicts a large Basoga *embaire* (3.73) in the village of Nakibembe. According to Ugandan ethnomusicologist James Isabirye, these xylophones are used for social gatherings rather than for ritual or religious practice. Young boys often gather in the evening after finishing school and chores, and play for fun before dark. There are no formal meeting times or lessons. Older children teach the younger ones during these spontaneous informal gatherings. Adult performers grew up in the tradition of collective music making from childhood. The dancer performing the *nalufuka* dance in the video is a man wearing a traditional dress for women called a *gomesi*. Before the 1970s, this dance was performed by women. However, because of the strenuous, athletic nature of the dance, men started dancing dressed as women in the *gomesi* dress. At times the performance leaves audiences wondering whether they are watching a woman or a man.

Metallophones

Keyed instruments with metal bars are found in many parts of the world, perhaps most famously in Indonesia in the forms of the *saron* and *gender*. These two families of instruments differ in that each metal key of the *gender* is placed over a bamboo or metal resonating tube, whereas the keys of the *saron* are all placed over a single "trough" resonator. The keys of these instruments are struck with hammers made of metal, wood, or other material. The keys of the *saron peking*, the smallest member of the *saron* family, for example, are struck with a mallet made of water buffalo horn. In the Javanese **gamelan** ensemble, the role of the *saron* is to play a fixed melody while other instruments play elaborations of the melody and provide rhythmic accompaniment.

The Indian *jaltarang* (3.74) consists of a set of up to twenty-two metal or ceramic bowls filled with water to varying levels and struck with wooden beaters (Figure 3.43R). The differing bowl sizes and water levels produce the instrument's range of pitches. The instrument is of ancient origin, mentioned in the *Kama Sutra* from approximately 100 CE. Today it is rarely played, and when it is, the preferred material is almost always ceramic. In Video 3.74, Ranjana Pradhan plays the *jaltarang* in Sydney, Australia.

Lamellophones

Metal tongues of different lengths attached to a lateral bar and placed over a wooden board or box resonator constitute the **lamellophone** or "thumb piano," so called because the tongues are plucked primarily with the thumbs. Often these instruments are placed inside large gourds or, more recently, cut-off plastic jugs to give further resonance for outdoor performances. Lamellophones are indigenous to Africa, where they occur in many sizes and shapes, and go by many names such as *sanza*, *kalimba*, and *mbira* (Figure 3.44L). Among the Busoga people of Uganda, it is called the *endongo* (3.75) and is often played in pairs. Here, James Isabirye and Haruna Walusimbi play *endongos* in Jinja, the town situated at the source of the Nile. The *mbira dzavadzimu* is the national instrument of Zimbabwe and is one of the largest and most developed lamellophones in Africa. Its name means "instrument of the ancestors," both because it is of ancient origin and because it is used by the Shona people to connect the living with the spirit world.

FIGURE 3.44 Zimbabwean *mbira* (L), and West African *balafon* (R)

Cymbals

Cymbals, thin round concave discs of metal, are either crashed together or suspended and struck. In Turkey, dancers use small brass finger cymbals (*zil*) to perform an especially energetic style of belly dancing. As belly dance (known as **raqs sharqi** in Egypt) spread throughout the world, particularly in the late 20th century, finger cymbals also spread. In the linked video, a belly dancer in New York (whose stage name is "Willow") uses *zil* (3.76) to accompany the dance rhythms. The global center of the cymbals industry is in Turkey. The Zildjian Company of Istanbul has been manufacturing cymbals for over 400 years, and their instruments are used in Western orchestras and popular music ensembles. An informational video shows percussionist Brook Alexander demonstrating the variety of cymbals (3.77) produced by the Turkish Soultone company. Buddhist monks throughout Asia have used cymbals such as the Tibetan *rolmo* (3.78) to accompany chanting and ceremonial events, played in the video by the monks of Labrang Monastery. These instruments differ from Turkish cymbals in that they have a deeply concave center. In temple rituals, their crashing sounds ward off "wrathful" spirits.

Gongs

Gongs, which originated in East and Southeast Asia, are circular metal discs struck with a mallet. The onomatopoeic word "**gong**" comes from the Javanese language. Another metal instrument in the Javanese *gamelan* is the *bonang* (gong chime), consisting of a number of upturned, knobbed kettle gongs that rest on strings in a wooden rack. The knobs of the kettles are struck with two padded wooden sticks, one in each hand. In China and Korea, gongs are flat and do not have knobs like the Javanese ones. Two professional folk singers in southeast China accompany themselves with small flat, hand-held gongs (3.79). A similar small gong is used to accompany singing and acrobatics in *jingju* (Beijing opera), and has a characteristic rise in pitch when it is struck (see Video 13.17). In the Philippines and Vietnam, ensembles of tuned gongs (3.80) accompany dances and celebrations. The players perform alternating strokes that create melodies, much like hand-bell ensembles in America. These interlocking patterns reinforce community cohesion and interdependence. Video 3.80 shows villagers playing tuned gongs and dancing in Guilguila, the Philippines. The Chinese *yunluo* (a rack of

FIGURE 3.45 Chinese *yunluo* (hanging gong chime)

small disc-shaped tuned gongs) has been played in Daoist and Confucian rituals at least since the 14th century (Figure 3.45). More recently the *yunluo* has been played in private family rituals like weddings and funerals, and in contemporary Chinese orchestras. Large gongs are typically hung from a frame, as is the Chinese tam tam that has been incorporated into the Western symphony orchestra. Percussionist David Skidmore demonstrates two playing techniques on the Chinese tam tam (3.81): the strike and the roll.

ELECTROPHONES

In 1940, Curt Sachs added the **Electrophone** category to the Sachs-Hornbostel classification system to describe instruments whose sound is produced using electricity. The first completely electronic musical instrument was the theremin (3.82), invented in 1919 by Russian physicist Leon Theremin and demonstrated here in this documentary by world-renowned performer and teacher, Carolina Eyck (Figure 3.46). The theremin produces its unearthly sound quality because the vibrations it emits have no overtones. In the mid-20th century, early experiments with synthesizing sound included computer punch cards and vacuum

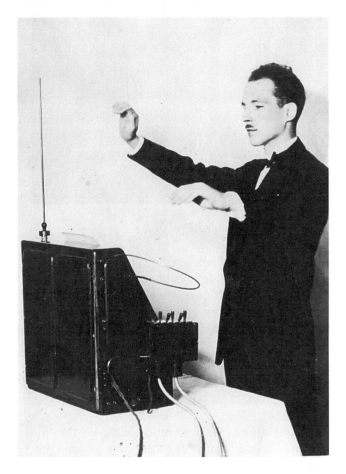

FIGURE 3.46 Leon Theremin (1896–1993) playing his theremin

tubes to manipulate the shape of soundwaves. At the same time, competing technologies for making music included the sampling of sound by recording and replaying slices of magnetic tape. An early synthesizer invented and popularized by Dr. Robert Moog in 1964 made use of electric keyboards and transistor circuitry (Figure 3.47). A single musician could simulate an entire orchestra with this new device. In 1981, the **film score** of the British movie *Chariots of Fire* (3.83) was composed primarily on synthesizer by the composer Vangelis (Evángelos Odysséas Papathanassíou, 1943–) sending shockwaves through the entire music industry. While some big budget Hollywood films continue to use symphony orchestras, a great deal of contemporary film and popular music is now put together entirely through digital means.

By the 1980s, computer programs were sophisticated enough to manipulate sound, but the requisite computer equipment was unaffordable for a majority of people. Also, in addition to the prohibitive cost, music production was complex; it could take weeks to produce ten minutes of music. Furthermore, music could not be produced digitally in real time. Any elaborate sound manipulation had to be pre-recorded rather than created during live performance. Since the late 20th century, computer technology has made enormous advances and

FIGURE 3.47 Robert Moog and his synthesizer, 1970s

the ability to digitally manipulate and produce sound has increased exponentially. This digital revolution has allowed individual musicians and bands to produce in real time what would have previously taken a 20+ piece band and multiple hours and days to produce. Today, DAWS (digital audio workstations) have become the norm in music production throughout the world. A British music publication in 2016 stated, "The synthesizer is as important, and as ubiquitous, in modern music today as the human voice."[12]

ENSEMBLES

While people play musical instruments alone, or to accompany their own or others' singing, they also play in ensembles. In a Scottish Highland bagpipe band, for example, marching pipers play the melody and drone while drummers provide the rhythmic accompaniment. In other cases, instruments of different timbres play together creating an enriched sound because of the contrast in sound "colors," as in the Korean *shinawi* (3.84) ensemble. This traditional group consists of a bowed board zither (*ajaeng*), fiddle (*haegeum*), bamboo flute (*taegum*), and oboe (*piri*). These instruments all play the same melody but each one adds its own unique timbre. The hourglass drum (*janggu*) and the large barrel drum (*jwago*) play accompanying rhythmic patterns known as **jangdan**. The overall effect is a dense and complex sound structure. The *shinawi* ensemble in the video is from the National Gugak Center in Seoul.

In another combination, a chordophone and/or aerophone provide a melodic line while a membranophone and/or idiophone provide a rhythmic substructure. Much of the traditional music of the Middle East and South Asia is organized this way. In this video of a South Indian Carnatic ensemble (3.85), violinist Aishu Venkataraman performs the lead melodic line, accompanied by a double-headed barrel drum (*mridangam*) and a small tambourine (*kanjira*). In music cultures that utilize a system of harmony, lutes, accordions, or keyboard instruments often provide that function. Some societies have developed large ensembles, such as the military brass band; in others, small groups are favored. In dance music, combinations of membranophones and idiophones are common, as in the drum kit of the swing band with its cylindrical drums and suspended cymbals.

FIGURE 3.48 Javanese *gamelan*

Two music ensembles made up primarily of idiophones are the Javanese *gamelan* and the Trinidadian steel band. The Javanese *gamelan* (Figure 3.48) is composed of tuned, knobbed gongs (*bonang, kenong, kethuk, kempyang*), metallophones (*gender, saron*), wooden-keyed xylophones (*gambang*), suspended gongs of various sizes (*kempul, siyem, ageng*), and drums (*kendang*). In the video, the Javanese *gamelan* (3.86) plays music for a wedding party. Similar ensembles are also used throughout the Indonesian islands to accompany dance and theatrical performances.

The former Dutch colony of Suriname in South America has a substantial population of Javanese, descendants of indentured servants brought over from Southeast Asia in the early 20th century. As the original laborers did not bring musical instruments with them, they had to forge the Surinamese *gamelan* (3.87) from scrap iron and melted-down farming implements. They meticulously tuned them by ear based on their memory of the Old-World tuning system.

In Trinidad, the steel pan is made from the hammered-out bottom of a 55-gallon oil drum. Each dimple sounds a different pitch, struck with beaters. It was invented in the 1930s to replace the drums that had been outlawed by the colonial British authorities during Carnival. Over time the tuning system became more and more precise, and different size instruments were developed to cover the whole range of an orchestra. The family of steel pans includes tenor or lead pans (soprano), double seconds (alto), double guitars (tenor), triple guitars and cellos (baritones), and tenor bass pans (bass). Its development as an ensemble instrument played in steel bands throughout the Caribbean and elsewhere is a marvel of human ingenuity (Figures 3.49 and 3.50). This video features the Starlift Junior Steel Orchestra (3.88) directed by Barry Mannette, who founded the band in 2005. They are rehearsing for an upcoming award ceremony to celebrate placing fourth in the Trinidad Junior Panorama Competition in their very first year of competing.

FIGURE 3.49 Caribbean Airlines Invaders steelband perform in 2011 Panorama competition, St. Clair, Trinidad

FIGURE 3.50 Rising Stars Youth Orchestra plays steel pans in downtown parade, Frederiksted, U.S. Virgin Islands, 2020

The Quechua and Aymara people of the Andes Mountains developed ensembles of variously tuned wooden pipes (*sikus*). In Peru,

> While modern panpipes … may offer a complete scale allowing solo performance, traditional models are played in pairs, as described by sixteenth-century chroniclers. The pipes share the melody, each with alternate notes of a whole scale so that two or more players are needed to pick out a single tune using a **hocket** technique. Usually one player leads and the other follows. While symbolically this demonstrates reciprocity within the community, practically it enables players to play for a long time without getting too 'high' from dizziness caused by over-breathing.[13]

In this video, a traditional Peruvian *sikuri* panpipe band (3.89) plays for the celebration of the anniversary of Aguas Calientes, a town near Machu Picchu, a famous archeological site.

CONCLUSION

Some musical instruments are simple and require little time and practice to gain proficiency. Others require years of intense labor and observation of elders, or formal study under a master teacher. The videos in this chapter depict instruments that are testaments to the creativity and craftsmanship of their designers and makers. They are also testaments to the men and women who have given so much pleasure to so many by devoting their lives to the mastery of them. Chapter 3 features renowned artists as well as amateur players and folk musicians. They are all continuing traditions that extend back for generations. Some travel internationally performing in concert halls throughout the world. Others serve their local communities by providing music for dancing, worship, celebrating, and lamenting. Human life would be so much the duller without musicians and their music. The next part considers principles by which musical sound is organized, as well as the origins of music and its many uses.

KEY TERMS AND CONCEPTS

Aerophone	Idiophone
Chordophone	Instrument Classification Systems
Circular Breathing	Membranophone
Electrophone	Sachs-Hornbostel System
Hocket	Time Keepers

THINKING ABOUT MUSIC

1   How would you describe a familiar instrument in terms of the concerns Jan Mrázek expresses and the things this writer finds most important?
2   What does Jan Mrázek find limiting about the ways that instruments are described and classified by scholars?
3   Consider the violin, the guitar, and the accordion. These instruments are found throughout the world and have been adapted to many different cultural and social situations. How have each of these instruments been adapted to suit various musical contexts?
4   What does this mean: The lute family represents "the most dramatic example of the diffusion of a musical technology" (p. 56)?
5   How has the Chinese "free reed" technology contributed to World Music culture?
6   The sound of an aerophone comes from a vibrating column of air. What are some of the ways used to set the air vibrating?
7   What did the film composer Vangelis do to send "shockwaves through the entire music industry" (p. 89)?

NOTES

1   Jan Mrázek, "Xylophones in Thailand and Java: A Comparative Phenomenology of Musical Instruments," *Asian Music* 39/2 (2008), 59.
2   Colter Harper and Osei Korankye, "A Song of and about Time: Osei Korankye and the Seperewa Harp," April 26, 2017, https://medium.com/recital/a-song-of-and-about-time-osei-korankye-and-the-seperewa-harp-478c9e112b7f.
3   The Sachs-Hornbostel classification system places the lyre in the "Lute" category, but in this chapter it is placed with "Harps" because of a closer physical resemblance.
4   Sharon R. King, "Compressed Data; Can You Play 'Feelings' on the Ocarina?" *New York Times*, February 15, 1999, http://www.nytimes.com/1999/02/15/business/compressed-data-can-you-play-feelings-on-the-ocarina.html.
5   Ryan Bradley, "FYI: Can Snakes Really Be Charmed by Music?" *Popular Science*, September 11, 2013, https://www.popsci.com/science/article/2011-11/fyi-can-snakes-really-be-charmed-music/.
6   John Clewely, "Stunning Chorus of Molam Sounds," *Bangkok Post*, March 31, 2015, https://www.bangkokpost.com/life/arts-and-entertainment/513335/stunning-chorus-of-molam-sounds.
7   Clay Irving, "Eight Auspicious Symbols of Bhutan," last updated January 17, 2010, http://www.panix.com/~clay/currency/Bhutan-8-symbols.html.
8   John Miller Chernoff, *African Rhythm and African Sensibility: Aesthetics and Social Action in African Musical Idioms* (Chicago, IL: University of Chicago Press, 1979), 75.
9   Veronica Doubleday, "The Frame Drum in the Middle East: Women, Musical Instruments and Power," *Ethnomusicology* 43/1 (1999), 101.
10 Veronica Doubleday, "The Frame Drum," 117.

11 J. H. Kwabena Nketia, "The Musical Languages of Subsaharan Africa," report prepared at the request of UNESCO for presentation to the Meeting on Musical Traditions in Africa, held in Yaounde, Cameroon, February 23–27, 1970. Quoted in Ashenafi Kebede, "The Music of Ethiopia: Its Development and Cultural Setting" (PhD diss., Wesleyan University, 1971), 158.

12 "The 14 Most Important Synths in Electronic Music History – and the Musicians Who Use Them," *FACT Magazine; Music News, New Music,* 15 September, 2016, https://www.factmag.com/2016/09/15/14-most-important-synths/.

13 "Peruvian Traditional Music," *Peru Gateway Travel,* edition 2014, http://www.peru-explorer.com/traditional_music.htm.

PART II

The Foundations of Music II

INTRODUCTION

Part II continues with the question "What is Music Made Of?" and examines the principles by which musical sound is organized. Chapter 4 discusses the elements of music—rhythm, melody, harmony, texture, form, genre, and style—presenting examples from all over the world. There is a methodological problem, however, with using English terms and concepts to describe aspects of music that are based on non-Western principles. The use of native terms for analyzing indigenous musics would be more relevant and preferable to scholars, but this approach would require a poly-linguistic textbook.

Chapter 5 considers the question "Where does music come from?" The simple answer is no one knows when, where, or how music originated. Indeed, no one knows where language, religion, or visual representation of the observable world—what is called "art"—originated. But it is precisely these developments that made our distant ancestors distinctly and recognizably human. This chapter introduces thirteen myths from various cultures around the world that provide an explanation to the mystery of where music came from. These myths give an indication of how music was valued within these societies. Chapter 5 continues with five explanatory theories based on evidence provided by scientists from different disciplines such as paleontology, primatology, anthropology, and neuroscience.

The working definition of music introduced in Chapter 1 is "sounds organized by humans and intended for musical purposes." Throughout history, these sounds have constituted a complex and diverse realm of human engagement and creativity. Music integrates the individual and social dimensions of experience in ways that are difficult to define, but may nonetheless be indispensable. Chapter 6 explores the question "What is music for?" and proposes ten functions of music. Six of these are drawn from anthropologist Alan Merriam's landmark study, *The Anthropology of Music*. Taken together, the ten functions attempt to explain why music is a universal form of human expression.

What Is Music Made Of?
Elements of Music

INTRODUCTION

When most people listen to music on their smartphone or computer, or experience it in the context of a concert, movie, or religious ritual, they usually do not concern themselves with the ways musical sound is organized. Often music moves in and out of their attention, serving as a stimulus for physical movement, mood, or a succession of memories, associations, and fantasies. Music is frequently connected with other forms of expression such as song, dance, and theater, and one may focus attention on lyrics, dance movements, or plot. However, music can be contemplated as the coordinated interaction of a number of elements such as rhythm, melody, and harmony, each of which contributes to an overall expressive purpose. This could be compared to a wristwatch that contains hidden inner workings directing moment by moment the digital numbers or position of the hands. One normally looks at a watch to tell the time, not to ponder its electronic or mechanical movements, but people who design, market, repair, or write books about watches are very much concerned with these internal parts and functions. Similarly, professional musicians—performers, composers, teachers, and scholars—consider music in terms of its elements in order to understand how music is created, remembered, taught, incorporated into wider social contexts, and connected to socially held meanings and values. Analytical understanding can focus attention on musical sound and help one to engage more fully with the richness and diversity of music throughout the world. Musical systems, along with the purposes they serve, vary widely; yet by paying attention to their inner structural workings, one may observe broad areas of convergence.

One such area of convergence relates to the ways music is generated, by means of a contrast or tension between fixed, pre-composed elements and those that are produced spontaneously in performance. The terms "composition" and "improvisation" refer to these complementary tendencies. Many performances present existing compositions—musical structures that have been prepared and preserved either through memory, notation, or sound recording technology. Others are generated at the time of performance through processes of spontaneous musical creativity, based upon pre-existing patterns and norms. Most common is a combination of the two. In traditional Irish music, for example, musicians memorize a large corpus of tunes (reels, jigs, hornpipes, polkas, etc.) that are passed on orally from one player to another and from one generation to the next. They play this repertoire in group sessions, dances, and concerts. Yet performance is not simply the precise repetition of tunes; musicians embellish the melodies using learned techniques of **ornamentation**. They string together melodies in new tune medleys, and vary the numbers and types of tunes depending on the social context. In addition, sometimes they compose new tunes, adding to the ever-growing corpus that constitutes the tradition.

Another area of convergence that is particularly useful when examining music across a wide cultural and historical spectrum is ***periodicity*** and *contrast*. "Periodicity" is a word that composer and theorist Michael Tenzer borrows from physics referring to the regular recurrence of phenomena like wave forms, life-cycle stages, lunar phases, the turning of the seasons, and the alternation of day and night. People experience the world as ordered and predictable by the cycles experienced in time. As with periodicity in the physical world, the repetition of melodic and rhythmic patterns in music creates a sense of stability "through return or constancy, and such stability will always be in dynamic dialog with change."[1] From the verse-refrain structures of songs to the "one-two one-two" drumbeats of a march, patterns of recurrence and their potential for near infinite variation underpin much of the world's music. Yet with the exception of certain styles of religious chant or modern "electronica" dance beat patterns, repetition and return is only half the story. In a march, while the drumbeats are the same throughout the event, melodies above the drumbeats change and provide contrast. In the verse-refrain form, the melody remains constant and the song lyrics change from verse to verse. Musical structures such as these often provide a balance between stability and novelty.

Chapter 4 presents a discussion of each of the elements of music: rhythm, melody, harmony, texture, form, genre, and style. One further element of music is timbre, which has been discussed in the two previous chapters on voices and instruments.

RHYTHM

Music is fundamentally an expression of the experience of time, as the visual arts and architecture are expressions of the experience of space. The understanding of time is based in part on patterns of motion, many of which are rooted in biological make-up. From the human heartbeat, respiratory cycle of breathing in and out, and two-legged means of locomotion, to the alternation of sleeping and waking, the rhythms of sexuality, birth, aging, and death— these regularities structure the shape of human life. Repeating patterns, or periodicities, are also found in the natural world, such as the rise and fall of the tides. They provide a sense of time passing and its continuous renewal. Perhaps the most basic element of music is rhythm, defined as the organization or grouping of musical sounds in time. It is the element that is most dynamically felt at a physical and visceral level. Music may have a heavy rhythmic emphasis as in dance music, or little rhythmic stress as in soft ballads and lullabies. Different musical cultures have different ways of organizing musical time, and worldwide there is great variety. The following examples illustrate some of the ways in which musical time may be structured and experienced in different parts of the world.

Regular Rhythm

Much of the world's music is organized around more or less regular time units, like the duration separated by two successive handclaps or beats on a drum. Beats in turn are organized into repeating groups of two, three, or more, often with an emphasis on the first beat of each group. Like footsteps and heartbeats, rhythmic patterns may range from very slow and languid to very fast and peppy, with all gradations in between. The University of Michigan football marching band (4.1) plays the "Stars and Stripes Forever" by John Philip Sousa, written to coordinate the movements of a parade of soldiers. The drums and cymbals mark the steady "left right, left right" two-beat pattern that drives the marchers into the formation of the American flag, as the drill team interweaves red, white, and blue banners to complete the effect. If the drummers were to speed up the pattern, the marchers would move around the field faster. The word "**meter**" is used to describe the beat pattern (one-two, one-two, for example), and "**tempo**" describes the speed.

In contrast, some genres of music such as jazz and swing derive their vitality and energy from rhythmic irregularity and syncopation (accenting offbeats). The great jazz diva Ella Fitzgerald (1917–1996) here performs Duke Ellington's jazz standard, "It Don't Mean a Thing (If It Ain't Got That Swing)" (4.2). She sings "doo wop doo wop doo wop" against the regular beats of the piano, upright bass, and drums (called the "rhythm section" in a jazz combo). This kind of exchange between the steady beat of the rhythm section and the "off the beat" **syncopation** of the melody is what is meant by the word "swing" (Figure 4.1).

Other musical systems organize rhythm into longer periods, with greater numbers of beats, such as the Arabic *iqa'*, the Korean *jangdan*, and the Indian *tala*. These patterns, referred to as **rhythmic modes**, are often expressed by the alternation of different sounds that are produced on a drum. Smaller, faster-moving divisions typically fill in the time between larger temporal units. The goblet-shaped hand drum of Egypt, *dumbek*, produces two basic sounds: a deep resonant one when the hand hits the drum head in the center (referred to by the onomatopoeic syllable *dumm*), and a high-pitched crisp one (*takk*) when the head is struck on the rim. Lebanese percussionist Souhail Kaspar demonstrates the ten-beat rhythmic cycle (4.3) *sama'i thaqil*: *dumm – – takk – dumm dumm takk – –*. The video shows how the drummer improvises complex and varied "fills" within the underlying structure of the ten-beat cycle. This Middle Eastern practice exemplifies both the composed/improvised dichotomy, and the periodicity of the repeating pattern offset by the ever-changing variations. Indeed, these basic recurrent phrases are subject to near-infinite elaboration and embellishment. When used to accompany belly dance (4.4) (*raqs sharqi*), the two tones *dumm* and *takk* correspond to movements made by the feet and hips of the dancer, who skillfully responds to the drummer's spontaneous creativity.

In South Indian Carnatic music, rhythm is organized in time cycles (*talam*), each one having a specific number of beats. Players of the *mridangam* (double-headed barrel drum) and *kanjira* (frame drum with jingles) learn to play rhythmic patterns by reciting syllables

FIGURE 4.1 Ella Fitzgerald

that correspond with beats and subdivisions of beats (Figure 4.2). The eight-beat *adi talam* is the most basic and fundamental rhythmic cycle in Carnatic music. Indeed, in Sanskrit the term *adi talam* literally means "primary rhythm." Kapil Ramanarayanan (*mridangam*) and Samarth Rao (*kanjira*) here perform intricate and virtuosic unison patterns in *adi talam* (4.5). They first speak the drum syllables (**solkattu**) that they then play on their instruments, demonstrating this ancient practice of reciting drum syllables (*konnakol*). The *veena* and violin players are keeping track of the *talam* with hand claps, waves, and finger counts.

Free Rhythm

Music without a regular pulse is said to be in free rhythm. Religious texts in various parts of the world are recited to the natural flow of speech rhythms. Some forms of instrumental music are unstructured by a strong pulse or meter. Japanese *shakuhachi* (4.6) flute players shape melodic phrases to coincide with their natural breathing, here demonstrated by Koji Matsunobu. Thus, the music seems to float freely and spontaneously, unbound by metrical control. This style of music lends itself to contemplation because it does not stimulate the kind of bodily involvement that strong rhythmic pulse and pattern do.

A distinctive genre of unaccompanied Irish singing in free rhythm is **sean-nós**. The term means "in the old way," and refers to a form of solo singing usually in the Irish Gaelic language, although sometimes in English. *Sean-nós* singers focus on expressing the emotion of the song lyrics by following the pulse of the poetic meter rather than a regular beat. Singers freely lengthen or shorten words and phrases to emphasize their meaning, and often ornament the melody line. Three regional styles and song repertoires exist. These correspond with

FIGURE 4.2 *Mridangam* players in Koodalmanikyam Temple, Irinjalakuda, Kerala

the dialects of three areas of western Ireland where Irish is still spoken by the local community: Donegal (north), Connemara (central), and Munster (south). Four *sean-nós* (4.7) singers—Caroline Ní Chonaire, Yvonne Ní Loideáin, Caitríona Ní Churraoin, and Ann Marie Ní Fhatharta—participate in a song session at The Crane Pub, Galway, in the Connemara region of Ireland. The teacher and mentor of three of the singers, Máire Uí Dhroighneáin, sits in the audience. Each in turn sings her song using long melodic phrases, **melismatic** singing, and subtle vocal ornamentation. During the singing, listeners remain respectfully quiet but may interject words of encouragement. Traditionally, an audience member might hold the singer's hand and turn it slowly in time with the song rhythm. As seen in this video, listeners show their appreciation as well as their knowledge of the Irish *sean-nós* tradition by joining in with the singers at the end of their vocal phrases.

Polyrhythm

When two or more rhythms are played simultaneously, the resulting sound is known as **polyrhythm** or rhythmic polyphony (from the Greek word for "many sounds"). In West African drumming, individual drummers within a group each play a different rhythmic pattern that interlocks with the others to create a dense and complex polyrhythmic texture. Often an idiophone such as a metal bell or shaker is used to keep time and orient the various parts to a common rhythmic framework. In this video, a *djembe* ensemble from Guinea, West Africa, demonstrates polyrhythm (4.8) and its relationship to spoken language. The video begins with the carving of the *djembe* drum and ends with its use in performance, accompanying dance. Each drummer performs a characteristic rhythmic phrase that fits with the others. The lead drummer on *djembe* is the last to start playing. The ensemble is coordinated by the metal bell (*agogo*).

In Rio de Janeiro, percussion bands called *batería* (4.9), derived from African drum ensembles, hammer out the rhythms of the famous Carnival street parades. Video 4.9, taken at a neighborhood **samba school**, shows the *batería*'s last rehearsal before Carnival. On drums, metal bells, and shakers of different sizes, musicians create a deafening sonic tapestry. These polyrhythms inspire Carnival dancers to move their bodies in sync with each other. In both West Africa and Brazil, music and dance are inseparably linked and are understood as a single category, one inconceivable without the other (Figure 4.3).

Work Rhythm

People around the world have long used music as a way of providing rhythmic accompaniment for repetitive work as well as a pleasant distraction from the drudgery of physical labor. In the past, prison work gangs (4.10) in the United States sang songs to synchronize their movements. "Afro-American Work Songs in a Texas Prison," a documentary film made by Pete Seeger in 1966, shows inmates from the Ellis unit of Huntsville Prison in Texas singing as they swing their axes to fell large trees. In the next video example from Ghana, West Africa, women are hoeing garden rows (4.11), the motions of their stoop labor coordinated by the rhythm of their singing. Their alternating call-and-response pattern is typical of much African and African American music.

A technique called "stimulus progression," developed during World War II, kept workers in weapons plants going at a steady pace throughout the day by controlling the speed and intensity of piped-in recorded music. Decades later, the same technology was used to coordinate the flow of customers through a shopping mall. A soundtrack broadcast through hidden speakers provided up-tempo music in the morning, slower music at lunchtime, and then more lively music again as the afternoon progressed.

In the Western Isles of Scotland, singing accompanied the domestic work of women fulling newly woven tweed cloth. This process of shrinking and softening the wool—now completed by commercial machinery—was carried out in Scottish homes until the mid-20th century, and was called "waulking the tweed." A group of women rhythmically beat the cloth against

FIGURE 4.3 *Engenho de Rhaina Batería,* Rio de Janeiro

a table or flat surface, passing it clockwise from one person to the next. **Waulking songs** sung in Scots Gaelic helped keep the rhythm, made the work more enjoyable, and served to bond the local community of women. The tradition is carried on in Scotland today as a celebration of cultural heritage. It is likewise performed by descendants of Scottish immigrants in Nova Scotia, Canada, where events are known as "milling frolics" and songs are sung by both women and men. A waulking song (4.12) session begins with one woman singing the verse of a song, and the other women joining in with a chorus of non-lexical syllables or Gaelic words after each verse or each song line. Song lengths vary depending on the time needed to work the cloth (Figure 4.4). Lead singers may add or eliminate verses, or even make up new ones referencing local people or events. Video 4.12 shows the Inverclyde Waulking Song Group, *Sgioba Luaidh Inbhirchluaidh*, which formed on the west coast of Scotland in Greenock in 2000.[2] The women demonstrate waulking the tweed as they sing a favorite song of theirs learned from Flora MacNeil of the Scottish island of Barra. The song is titled "*An cuala sibh mu 'n mhaighdean cheutach?*" ("Did you hear about the pretty girl?").

> Chorus:
> Haghaidh O Haghaidh O Ho
> Haghaidh O A Hi A Bho
> Haghaidh O Haghaidh O Ho
> Verse:
> Did you hear about the pretty girl
> whom Niall Ban took to his bed?
> O Lord, I wish it had been me.

FIGURE 4.4 Scottish women waulking cloth, ca. 1770 engraving

I would not have torn the breast of your shirt.
If I tore it, I myself would sew it
with a little needle and pure white thread.
I would wash it in the mountain stream.
I would dry it on top of the bushes.
I would then put the iron on it,
and I would give it folded into the hand of your page.
I wish you and I, darling, were
in the little island of the sea, with no ebb-tide,
with no ferry available to us,
until sunrise tomorrow.

[English translation by Sgioba Luaidh Inbhirchluaidh]

Grooves and Dance Rhythms

Dance forms throughout the world are defined by short, repeating rhythmic phrases, referred to as "**grooves.**" The term was coined by ethnomusicologists Charles Keil and Steven Feld.[3] The interaction between drummers and dancers is vividly displayed at a wedding party in Mali (4.13), West Africa. Dancers and members of the percussion ensemble connect and freely improvise in a dynamic and exciting rhythmic give-and-take.

Rhythmic patterns and the footwork that they motivate in dancers define the various forms of Western ballroom dance: the foxtrot, quickstep, and waltz, for example. Using digital and sampling technologies, DJs collect beats from many sources that they process into groove tracks to use at dance parties and to accompany rappers.

Rhythmic Virtuosity

"**Virtuosity**" is a term used to describe a high level of skill; a virtuoso is a musician who demonstrates great technical and artistic ability. In many cultures rhythmic virtuosity is highly valued as a source of aesthetic pleasure, apart from its role in coordinating the movements of marchers, laborers, and dancers. In this video, for example, the great African American drummer Nana Kimati Dinizulu (1956–2013) performs on the hand and foot drum (4.14) of the Ga people of Ghana. Dinizulu was born in New York City. His parents both worked on Broadway, his father a drummer, his mother a dancer. As a young man, he spent two years in Ghana studying with master drummers, and returned to Africa more than fifty times throughout his life to continue his learning. He also studied with drummers of the African diaspora, particularly in Haiti and Brazil. He was a culture-bearer and major force in promoting African performing arts on a global stage. In the video, the dense improvised "riffs" of Dinizulu are accompanied by the steady and continuous pattern of the iron bell (*agogo*), which plays in the background and serves as the timekeeper. In addition to virtuosity, this performance also exemplifies the creative tension between fixed and free elements found in many forms of music worldwide.

In a second example, Vikku Vinayakram, a virtuoso *ghatam* (4.15) (clay pot) player from South India, performs an impressive solo with the fusion band Mynta from Sweden. His solo contains rapid-fire strokes on the *ghatam* as his son recites syllables (*solkattu*) that represent, in classical Carnatic music, the rhythmic patterns he plays.

FIGURE 4.5 Tito Puente

A third example shows the incomparable "King of Latin Music," Tito Puente (1923–2000) playing *timbales* (4.16) in a recording studio. As a composer, arranger, and band leader, Tito Puente was one of the most important figures in American popular culture during the 1950s and 1960s, bringing to the mainstream such Latin and Caribbean dance rhythms as the cha-cha-cha, mambo, merengue, and salsa (Figure 4.5).

MELODY

"Melody" is a sequence or succession of pitches arranged in musical time. A melody has an identity, and often carries meanings, feelings, and associations. Palestinian musician Simon Shaheen defines a melody fancifully as "a group of notes that are in love with each other."[4] One can imagine a shepherd on a hill tending his sheep and playing idly on a wooden flute. He improvises, selecting pitches at will from those available on his instrument. It may be that a particularly serendipitous combination strikes his fancy and he plays it over and over, working with it, getting it "just right." It gradually becomes "a melody" that he can then play for, and teach to, his friends. The shepherd's melodic improvisations here are the raw material for his musical invention: his melody or tune. If he adds words to his melody, it becomes his song.

The following examples demonstrate the diversity of melody in our world from the perspective of pitch vocabulary, **melodic contour**, and ornamentation.

Pitch Vocabulary

The arrangement of a particular set of pitches in ascending or descending order is called a scale, the "distance" between one pitch and another being called an **interval**. From all possible pitches or tones, scales employ particular ones from which melodies are derived. Musical scales and melodies, like letters and words, are culturally determined. It is the difference between these scales that gives melodies from different parts of the world their distinctive character. Much Western music uses the pitches of major or minor scales, which are based on whole- and half-tone intervals. Each of these scales carries an association for listeners familiar with the tradition, the major scale often suggesting happier feelings than the minor scale. Whether these associations are based on inherent acoustical properties, or are learned through early childhood enculturation, is not well understood.

Javanese *gamelan* orchestras play music based on a five-tone scale (*slendro*) or a seven-tone scale (*pelog*), each having a different interval structure. Since most *gamelan* instruments are made of bronze or other metal and have fixed pitches that cannot easily be tuned, *gamelan* orchestras often consist of two sets of instruments, one for each scale system. Pairs of instruments are placed at right angles to each other so that the musicians all face one direction when performing music in the *pelog* scale, then turn ninety degrees to play their *slendro* instruments. In theatrical performances such as *wayang kulit* shadow puppet plays, where the *gamelan* serves an accompanying role, *pelog* instruments are played during the daytime and the *slendro* set is played at night. Dr. John Caldwell of the University of North Carolina at Chapel Hill here demonstrates the scale pitches of *slendro* and *pelog* (4.17) on *saron* metallophones.

Maqam is an Arabic term, originally meaning "place" or "location." It refers to a system of melodic modes central to musical practices from North Africa through Central Asia into China. A **melodic mode** consists of a set of pitches as well as melodies traditionally generated from them, conveying a mood or feeling. In Azerbaijan, *mugam* (4.18), a derivation of the term *maqam*, refers to the system of Azeri classical music. In Video 4.18, two of the greatest modern practitioners of the art, father and daughter Alim (1957–) and Fargana (1979–) Qasimov, demonstrate the deeply expressive and spiritual qualities of *mugam* (Figure 4.6).

In Xinjiang, an autonomous region of northwestern China, the predominant melodic system of the Uighur people consists of twelve modes called *muqam*. In the linked video, taken at a busy restaurant in Kashgar in 2008, the westernmost city in China, three Uighur musicians (4.19) perform traditional *muqam* melodies on *tambur* (five-string, long-necked lute), *ghichak* (spike fiddle), and *dutar* (two-string, long-necked lute).

In India, there are two systems of classical music, **Hindustani** in the north and **Carnatic** in the south. While they deviate in a number of features that give each a distinctive sound quality, the systems share root concepts such as **raga** and **tala** (known as *ragam* and *talam* in Carnatic music). The classical *raga* system encompasses hundreds of different scales—most of five, six, or seven pitches—that musicians use to compose and improvise melodies. "In its broadest sense," writes George Ruckert, Indian music scholar and performer on *sarod* (plucked lute), "the word [raga] refers to the 'color,' and more specifically the emotion or mood produced by a particular combination or sequence of pitches."[5] *Ragas* not only carry associations of feeling (**rasa**) but also are associated with times of day and seasons of the year. In this video, Smriti Sridharan demonstrates a Carnatic *ragam* (4.20) and performs a traditional *kriti* on the South Indian *veena* (long-necked lute).

Five-tone (**pentatonic**) scales characterize Chinese and other East Asian musics as well as many sub-Saharan African traditional melodies. *Erhu* player Xiao Chu from the Shanghai

FIGURE 4.6 Alim Qasimov at Eurovision Song Contest, 2012

Conservatory demonstrates a Chinese pentatonic scale (4.21), starting first on a higher pitch then on a lower pitch. In a Western scale, the pitches would be equivalent to: do-re-mi-sol-la. Xiao Chu then performs perhaps the most famous composition for her instrument, *Erquan Yingue* ("Moon Reflected in the Second Spring"). This pentatonic piece was composed by the blind musician Abing (Hua Yanjun, 1893–1950). Abing was a street musician who composed more than 600 pieces (Figure 4.7). He was discovered by two musicologists of the Beijing Central Conservatory who traveled to his home town to record some of his works both for *erhu* and *pipa*. At the recording session in 1950, they recorded six of his performances, yet three months later he died and the rest of his works died with him.[6] *Erquan Yingyue* became one of the most famous and often-played melodies of twentieth-century China.

Two distinguished artists demonstrate the three primary Korean modes (4.22). Choi Jinsook is a **kwangdae** who performs **pansori**, a genre of musical storytelling, and Dr. Jocelyn Clark performs on *gayageum* (plucked twelve-string board zither). As Choi and Clark explain, Korean musicians value timbre, articulation, phrasing, ornamentation, and flow. Thus, these primary modes are better described by their expressive function (like major = happy, minor = sad in Western music) than by their scale. The vocal fluctuations of the *kwangdae* and the use of the left hand on the *gayageum* strings add slides, shakes, and a deep characteristic vibrato. The Korean word commonly translated as "vibrato" is *nong*, which literally means, "to play around." The first mode, *ujo*, is described as grand or spacious and providing an uplifting sensibility. The second mode, *gyeumyeonjo*, is sad, having a sobbing tone and wide vibrato. The third, *pyeongjo*, is placid, having a peaceful tone and shallow vibrato. Choi Jinsook sings short excerpts from dramatic scenes that utilize these modes to capture the expressive moment in her story: *ujo* for the description of a vast landscape, *gyeumyeonjo* for bemoaning an absent

FIGURE 4.7 Abing

lover, and *pyeongjo* for a joyful outcome. Dr. Clark demonstrates these modes using sections from an instrumental genre called *sanjo* (literally, "an assortment of modes").

Melodic Contour

As contour lines are used to mark elevation levels on a geographical map, the term "contour" can also describe the rise and fall of pitches in a melody. Aboriginal Australians have depended on memorized melodies, shared and passed down for generations, to find their way across the trackless outback of Australia. They trace their inherited oral legacy of songs and knowledge back to a "dream time," during which primal ancestors traveled across the continent naming every geographical feature. The dream-time ancestors then invented melodies called (by the British colonizers) "**songlines**." These were long expanses of melody that matched the rising and falling contours of the land. The descendants memorized the melodies and passed them down to their children. Each hunting band "owned" the songlines that corresponded to its territory. While the song's words could be changed, the melody always remained the same. "By singing the landscape, [Aboriginal peoples] could navigate from one sacred location to the next, taking in waterholes, sheltering places and sources of food and materials," writes Lynn Kelly in *The Memory Code*.[7]

Melodies often follow the contours of natural speech, particularly when they are associated with texts. They are often divided into logical structural units called phrases, which correspond to the grammatical structures of language. In the popular hymn "Amazing Grace" (4.23) for example, each verse consists of two sentences separated by a period: "Amazing Grace, how sweet the sound, that saved a wretch like me. I once was lost but now am found, was blind but now I see." As heard in audio 4.23, sung by American singer-songwriter Judy Collins (b. 1939), the melody, in two phrases, mirrors this structure with a pause at the end of the first sentence where the singer takes a breath. The melody begins on the lowest pitch, and rises to its highest point at the end of the first sentence. The second line starts high and ends low again. This melodic contour is called "arch form."

Melodic contours not only distinguish one melody from another but can characterize entire music genres. Native American Plains Indian songs begin high in the falsetto range and descend through a terraced contour to a low ending pitch, as in the Sioux "Montana grass song" (4.24). In contrast to this long pulsating, descending line, Tibetan Buddhist chant (4.25) moves slowly around a few extremely low pitches. Some melodic contours seem to be as recognizable as human faces. The national anthem of the United Kingdom, "God Save the Queen," has a melody in which the notes move mostly in step (conjunct motion), up and down the scale encompassing a narrow range. The American national anthem, "The Star-Spangled Banner," on the other hand, has large skips (disjunct motion) and covers a much wider range. Periodically, bills have been introduced in Congress to change the national anthem to "America the Beautiful" because it is so much easier to sing.

Ornamentation

Ornamentation refers to the embellishing of melodic pitches. Techniques for embellishing melody such as vibrato, trills, shakes, and other types of inflection vary widely and are important in establishing the identity of a musical style. In many world cultures where melody is the primary vehicle for musical expression, ornamentation plays an especially important role. The Korean genre of sung poetry known as *sijo* (4.26) is characterized by the use of a deep pitch fluctuation, demonstrated in the video by singer Hong Changnam. *Sijo* melodies have few pitches and move very slowly, yet they still hold a fascination for the listener because of the complexity of the singer's ornamentation. Similarly, Korean instruments, like the bowed zither *ajaeng* (4.27), are constructed to produce ornaments that replicate vocal pitch fluctuations. This seven- or eight string instrument is bowed with the right hand; the left hand presses down on the flexible silk strings to the left of the bridges to produce the characteristic ornaments. In Video 4.27, Kim Young-gil demonstrates this technique.

Another highly ornate style comes from the South Indian Carnatic tradition, in which ornaments inflecting pitches are called **gamak**. An interesting feature of this classical music system is that the scale pitches themselves are sounded only with the ornaments. A proverb among musicians in this part of the world is: "a note without a *gamak* is like a night without stars." Here, Dr. Vijayalakshmi Subramaniam presents a highly ornamented performance of the **kriti** "*Shadanane*" (4.28) ("*The Six-Headed God*"), composed by Muthuswami Dikshitar (1775–1835).

The Mongolian long song (urtiin duu) (4.29) is one of the most highly ornamented vocal styles in the world. Literary descriptions of the practice date back at least to the 13th century. The long song remains a significant expression of nomadic identity among the herders of the Gobi Desert. The genre is called long song because not only are the songs long, but each syllable of text is greatly extended. It is on these extended syllables that singers place vocal ornaments. *Urtiin duu* songs are shared at many social gatherings, such as weddings, births, the branding of horses, and traditional festivals, which include competitive wrestling, archery, and horse racing. In Video 4.29, a singer in traditional costume auditions for a spot on Mongolian Radio. Mongolians believe that *urtiin duu* expresses the essential experience of nomads herding their animals across the vast, bare steppes.

The voice of Iranian classical singer Afsâne Ziâ'i produces the same intricate and subtle inflections as the accompanying *ney* (flute), which shadows her melodic improvisation. Throughout this excerpt, but particularly at 1' 20", the singer ornaments a single syllable in a manner characteristic of this tradition, using a technique called *tahrir* (4.30). This level of skill and deep emotional expression are not "natural," but rather require years of training.

In Middle Eastern music, elaboration of the Arabic *maqam* scale pitches is integral to the performance of both vocal and instrumental melodies. In Video 4.31, Lebanese musician Naji Hilal plays the ascending and descending scale pitches of *maqam nikriz* on the *ud* (Arabic lute). He then adds ornamentation to the scale pitches. The demonstration continues with melodic improvisation in free rhythm known as **taqsim**, based on *maqam nikriz*. The highly ornamented *taqsim* (4.31) typically precedes a musical composition, and in performance serves to introduce the *maqam* and its particular emotional content to its listeners.

Ornamentation is also an important feature of instrumental music composed for keyboard in 18th-century France, Italy, and Spain, exemplified by Pastór de Lasala playing a composition by François Couperin (4.32) (1668–1733) on the harpsichord. Since the harpsichord had no means of sustaining pitches, players used ornamentation to fill in gaps between the notes.

In traditional Irish music, ornamentation is fundamental to the way instrumentalists play tunes. Melody players not only embellish tunes using commonly known ornaments, such as cuts, taps, rolls, and crans, they also typically vary the ornamentation at will each time they repeat a tune. Embellishments are often specific to particular instruments. What is possible and easy to play on a fiddle, for example, may not be possible or may be challenging to play on an Irish flute. Mairead Brady here plays a medley of two hornpipes demonstrating the slides and rolls characteristic of Irish fiddle (4.33) playing technique.

If rhythm is the "bones" of music that gives it form and structure, melody is the "face" of music, which reveals its emotional content.

HARMONY

The term "harmony" is used to account for a number of features of musical sound. It refers to relationships between pitches played or sung either in succession or simultaneously. It also refers to the combining of notes to produce chords, and the way in which chords relate to each other to produce progressions that can propel musical motion. Because musical situations are often social and participatory, it is not surprising that numerous traditions have developed with music composed of multiple parts. In many regions of the world, depth is added to a melodic line by means of a drone: a single pitch or combination of pitches sustained through the entire performance. Bagpipes, for instance, are often fitted with drone pipes that sound a constant pitch to accompany the melody produced on the chanter pipe. The Bulgarian *gaida* (4.34) made from sheep or goat hide has a blowpipe for filling the bag with air, a chanter pipe on which the melody is played, and a single long drone pipe (Figure 4.8). The musical experience is based on the contrast between the stability of the drone pitch and the decorative complexity of a highly ornamented melody. In Video 4.34, master *gaida* player Dafo Trendafilov (1919–2010) plays music to welcome guests to his village in the Rhodope Mountains for an evening celebration. In Indian classical music, the *tambura* (long-necked lute) serves to provide an ambient drone that underpins melodic lines played or sung by a soloist. *Dhrupad* singer Shanti Shivani plucks the individual strings of the *tambura* (4.35) as she performs the North Indian *raga bhairavi* in this video. *Dhrupad* is a form of contemplative vocal music with a 500-year history.

FIGURE 4.8 Bulgarian *gaida*

Pitches produced by vibrating strings, which are related in length by simple ratios (1:2, 2:3, 3:4, 4:5), are consonant or harmonious when sounded together. The Pythagoreans of ancient Greece first demonstrated this phenomenon. The intervals of the octave, fifth, fourth, and third are described, respectively, by the ratios listed above. The discoveries of the Greeks became the basis for harmony as it developed in Europe. Triadic harmony, based on thirds, and chord progressions were in use by the time of the early Renaissance. Some famous works from the European art music tradition, like Beethoven's "Moonlight Sonata" (4.36) (Piano Sonata in C♯ Minor, Op.27, No.2) draw their primary source of inspiration and expression from **harmonic progressions**. Some genres of popular music are defined by a repeating sequence of chords, like the twelve-bar blues heard in the 1951 song "Honey Bee" (4.37) by Muddy Waters (1913–1983). A single bass line played on the guitar can also provide a strong harmonic accompaniment to a vocal melody, as illustrated in the song "I Walk the Line" (4.38) by Johnny Cash (1932–2003). The worldwide popularity of instruments like the guitar, accordion, and piano, which are capable of producing more than one pitch at the same time, suggests how the harmonic system based on chords has come to be accepted internationally as an important, even indispensable musical ingredient (Figure 4.9).

FIGURE 4.9 Muddy Waters (L) and Johnny Cash (R)

TEXTURE

In music, "texture" describes how simultaneous parts fit together to create a musical whole. Analysts use four terms to define different types of musical texture: monophony, polyphony, homophony, and heterophony.

Monophony

"**Monophony**" refers to a single melody line performed by one or more voices or instruments. A solo voice singing an unaccompanied melody provides a clear example of monophonic singing, as in the folk ballad "Lady Margaret and Sweet William" (4.39). A choir of voices singing the same melody in unison, that is, at the same pitch or in octaves, is also monophonic. Solo, monophonic instrumental music is found in many musical traditions. Three examples played by instrumentalists who are renowned in their own societies demonstrate monophony. The first example by Jalal Ahmad of Bangladesh playing the *bansuri* (4.40) (bamboo flute). His use of complex ornamentation adds musical interest where there is no accompaniment. In the second example, Ivan Kovachev plays the Bulgarian *gadulka* (4.41) (bowed fiddle). This instrument's sympathetic strings add resonance that makes up for the lack of harmony. Ustad Rahim Khushnawaz of Herat in Afghanistan playing the *rabab* (4.42) (plucked lute) provides the third example. Toward the end of the *rabab* video, Ustad Rahim is joined by Ustad Karim Herawi on the *tabla* drums, adding a rhythmic structure to what began as a melodic improvisation in free rhythm.

A single melody line accompanied by an unpitched rhythm instrument does not clearly match any of the four terms commonly used to describe musical texture. While melody alone is described as monophony, and melody with harmonic accompaniment is homophony, melody with purely rhythmic accompaniment falls between the two. An example of this texture is the piece "*Samai Nahawand*" (4.43), played by Simon Shaheen on Arabic *ud*, Maya Beiser on cello, and Glen Velez on frame drum. The *ud* and cello play the single melody with contrasting timbres between the plucked *ud* and the bowed cello, and the drum adds a strong and prominent rhythmic underpinning. There is no widely accepted analytical term for this common musical texture.

Polyphony

Polyphony consists of two or more independent melodies performed simultaneously. In Zimbabwe, the Shona people play the *mbira* (lamellophone) in pairs, the two instrumental lines woven together, mutually supporting each other. In this video, two of the great Shona *mbira* musicians of the 20th century, Cosmas Magaya (1953–2020) and Ambuya Beauler Dyoko (1944–2013), play "*Nhemamusasa*" (4.44) ("to build a shelter"). The leading part (*kushaura*), played by Beauler, introduces the basic melodic pattern. After approximately twenty seconds, Magaya joins in with the intertwining part (*kutsinhira*). Both rhythmically and melodically, the *kutsinhira* melody follows the *kushaura* creating a dense polyphonic tapestry of sound. At 0'42" Beauler starts to sing a third melody with lyrics that express Shona proverbs. Cosmas joins her around 1'05" singing a vocal bass line, for a total of four interlocking melodic lines.

Likewise, the simultaneous singing of different lines arranged for the four voice parts—soprano, alto, tenor, and bass—was the standard musical practice at the time of Shakespeare, when Thomas Morley (1557–1602) composed madrigals, setting to music the poems of the Bard and his contemporaries. In "April is in My Mistress' Face" (4.45) (1594), the two female vocal lines are paired, as are the two lower male lines. The female voices begin, the male voices follow, and for the most part the two pairs overlap throughout the performance. More recently, the simultaneous sounding of The Mamas and the Papas' male and female vocal lines similarly alternate to create a polyphonic texture in their 1965 hit single, "California Dreaming" (4.46).

Homophony

A homophonic texture is one in which a single melody is accompanied by supporting harmony. An example of **homophony** is the song "Paper Airplane" (4.47) by bluegrass-country artist Alison Krauss and her band Union Station. In this title track of the 2011 bluegrass album that won Alison Krauss (b.1971) her 27th Grammy Award, the singer's vocal melody is prominent above the accompanying instruments of mandolin, guitars, and string bass (Figure 4.10). Another example is the four-part vocal harmony of the unaccompanied, all-male barbershop quartet, made popular in the early 1930s by the Mills Brothers. Interest in this genre reached the level of a national fad in the United States after World War II. By the year

FIGURE 4.10 Alison Krauss

2000, there were more than 30,000 barbershop quartets as well as national associations and competitions. The genre is characterized by close harmony, hand gestures that coordinate the four voices, and a great deal of camaraderie. The primary melody is in the second to the top voice, with the other three harmonizing both below and above. "The Unlikely 4" met together literally in a barbershop in an Atlanta suburb. One day they spontaneously started to sing together, led by the barber Joey Turner. As journalist Meghan Overdeep relates the story for *Southern Living* magazine:

> Joey Turner was cutting Bobby Dwayne Robinson's hair when he heard him humming. "You must sing," he noted. Two other customers at Gary's Barber Shop in Canton, Georgia, happened to overhear them. It turns out they also sang. So, Turner suggested the four of them sing a song together. "They all kind of giggled, but I said, let's sing something" ... And that's when something beautiful happened. With their voices blending seamlessly for the first time ever, a true barbershop quartet was born...
>
> Turner shared a video of their impromptu collaboration on Facebook and the response was incredible. "First, it had a couple 'thousand views (online), then, I wake up the next day and it has 50,000 and then the next day it has a million! ... This day in age, with all the negativity going on in the world, I just like the content, it's so positive. And looking at the video, you see different colors, different ages, different backgrounds."[8]

Music may remain in one texture throughout a song or instrumental piece, or may move from one texture to another. For example, in the call-and-response form of South African *isicathamiya* (4.48), a solo lead singer alternates with group vocal harmony creating an unaccompanied choral music that moves back and forth between monophony and homophony. The group seen in the video, Ladysmith Black Mambazo, led by the group's founder Joseph Shabalala (1940–2020), has been one of the world's leading a cappella groups for more than fifty years (Figure 4.11).

FIGURE 4.11 Ladysmith Black Mambazo

Heterophony

A single melody performed slightly differently yet simultaneously by two or more musicians creates a heterophonic texture. In a number of music cultures, **heterophony** is the dominant form of musical organization. The Japanese *sankyoku* (4.49) ensemble ("music for three"), made up of three traditional instruments: *koto* (long zither), *shamisen* (three string lute), and *shakuhachi* (bamboo flute), exemplifies heterophony. In Video 4.49, "*Shojo No Tsuru*" ("A Crane in the Pines"), the three instrumentalists perform in unison a core melodic line yet with minute, simultaneous variations. The *shamisen* player adds a fourth part by also singing a poetic text to the core melody. These deviations from the vocal line as well as the contrast in instrumental timbres provide the kind of depth to the listening experience that other cultures satisfy with harmony or polyphony. The musicians in the video are Nakanoshima Keiko, Nakanoshima Kinichi, and Yamaguchi Goro.

In Dublin and many other parts of the world where Irish music is played, musicians gather at "sessions" in pubs and bars. They bring their instruments such as fiddles, flutes, whistles, button accordions, and guitars, and play together from memory a shared repertoire of Celtic dance tunes. Melody players typically join together three tunes and play each of them three times. They ornament and vary the tunes slightly according to the traditions and capabilities of their individual instruments as well as their level of skill and inspiration, producing a heterophonic texture. This mode of performance maximizes group participation without minimizing individuality, as in this typical Irish session (4.50). The video shows a group of amateur musicians at a sports bar in Pittsboro, North Carolina, making music for their own pleasure as well as that of the clientele.

In Shanghai teahouses, a similar tradition called jiangnan sizhu (4.51) is practiced. The name refers to the Jiangsu region south of the Yangtze River (*jiangnan*) and to the wind and stringed instruments that are made of bamboo and silk (*si-zhu*). The instruments are sometimes owned by the teahouse. Musicians come and go taking turns playing them, novices in the early afternoon and the most experienced closing the session. The repertoire of *jiangnan sizhu* pieces is relatively small and musicians typically play many repetitions of each tune. They gradually move from slow, heavily ornamented variations to quick versions of the basic melodies. They each vary the melody with ornamentation based on the idiomatic techniques and conventions of their instruments, as Irish musicians do at sessions. This creates the characteristic heterophonic texture. After playing a few pieces, *jiangnan sizhu* musicians may exchange instruments since they can often play several.

In both North and South Indian classical vocal music there is a technique called *sangat* (4.52). This involves accompaniment of the singer by a melodic instrument that follows or "shadows" the vocal line after a short time interval. The accompanying instrument is usually a *sarangi* or *harmonium* in the North Indian Hindustani tradition, and violin in the South Indian Carnatic style. While a number of ethnomusicologists and theorists have classified *sangat* as "heterophony," the solo and accompanying melody lines are not simultaneous as with other traditions described as heterophonic. In Video 4.52, Carnatic vocalist Sanjay Subrahmanyan interacts with his accompanist, violinist S. Varadarajan, through gestures and facial expressions; he is clearly in charge in this game of "follow the leader." This portion of the performance is called *alapana*, in which the *raga* is freely developed, and the *mridangam* player awaits his entrance.

It should be noted that there are often problems with applying Western technical terms and categories to aspects of non-Western musical systems and traditions. While cross-cultural analyses are necessary and important to understand the world's musics comparatively, a given musical system is always best understood in its own terms.

FORM

"Form" refers to the structure or internal organization of a musical composition or improvisation by identifying repetitions, contrasts, and variations of musical ideas or events. Scholars describe the form of music in terms of sections characterized by particular themes, melodies, rhythm patterns, etc. It can describe a short tune like "Twinkle, Twinkle, Little Star," for example, in terms of the relationship between its three musical phrases. The first and last lines of text, which are identical, share the same melodic contour, whereas the middle, contrasting line has its own contour. This form can be described as A-B-A or ternary form:

> A Twinkle twinkle little star, How I wonder what you are.
> B Up above the world so high, Like a diamond in the sky,
> A Twinkle twinkle little star, How I wonder what you are.

Form can also describe much longer and more complex musical constructs. A South Indian devotional song form (*kriti*), for example, has at least four parts. A *kriti* begins with *alapana* that introduces the *raga*. The following three parts coincide with the three sections of the poem upon which the performance is based: a refrain-like *pallavi* section, a secondary refrain section *anupallavi*, and verses (*charanam*). These three parts are expanded through repetitions, non-verbal elaborations, and improvised sections to produce a highly developed performance. It includes both pre-composed music and improvisation. The *kriti* is a flexible form that can last anywhere from five to twenty minutes or more depending on the occasion, the amount of improvisation, and the ingenuity of the artists. Video 4.24 above presents a *kriti* performed by Dr. Vijayalakshmi Subramanian.

Ghazal, like *kriti*, is both a poetic and a musical form. The poetic form has its origin in 7th-century Arabic rhyming poetry, which Sufis and Islamic courts spread to Iran and later to South Asia. *Ghazals*, written in Persian, Urdu, and other languages, consist of a number of rhyming couplets. The end rhyme of each line of the first couplet rhymes with the second line of every successive couplet, forming the pattern AA, BA, CA, etc. (as indicated in the poetry below). A further distinctive characteristic, called *takhallus*, is the inclusion of the poet's name in the final couplet. *Ghazal* poems always express the feelings of an unrequited lover for his "beloved." The beloved was traditionally a metaphor for the divine love of God or a spiritual master, but also often referenced human love. The practice of "singing" *ghazal* poetry in India was established by the Indo-Persian Sufi singer and musician Amir Khusrau (1253–1325). The musical structure has two parts, the *sthayi* and the *antara*, the latter melody sung in a higher register. In recent times, the *ghazal* has become popular as a light classical music genre and also through its use in Hindi and Urdu films. The next video presents renowned *ghazal* (4.53) singer Talat Aziz performing Urdu *ghazals* by the legendary Indian poet Mirza Ghalib (1797–1869). The vocalist begins by singing the first couplet of the Ghalib *ghazal* "Mehrban ho ke bula lo mujhe chaho jis vaqt" ("Be kind and call me whenever you want") in free rhythm. Accompanied by harmoniums, violin, bamboo flute, and *sarangi*, Aziz then presents a second *ghazal* in regular time when the *tabla* drums join in. He repeats each line several times, emphasizing and ornamenting particular words and phrases to enhance the subtle meanings of the poem.

> Hai bas-ki har ek un ke ishare men nishan aur
> karte hai mohabbat to guzarta hai guman aur
> Ya-rab von a samjhe hain na samjhenge miri baat
> De aur dil un ko jo na de mujh ko zaban aur
> In every gesture of hers, there are so many signals
> that when she expresses love, I suspect something else
> O Lord, she has not understood nor will she understand what I say
> Give her more heart if you won't give me a more effective tongue
> [English translation by Deewan][9]

A call-and-response pattern with a vocal leader and chorus is common in much sub-Saharan African music, as well as in African American R&B and gospel. Songs in many parts of the world consist of an alternating verse and refrain form, with the music mirroring the structure of the lyrics, as in Bob Dylan's song "Knockin' on Heaven's Door" (4.54). In this recording, it is sung by country superstar Dolly Parton and the South African *isicathamiya* group Ladysmith Black Mambazo. After a brief instrumental introduction, singer Dolly Parton performs the first verse, "Lord, take this badge off of me, I can't use it any more…" This is followed by the refrain, "Knock-knock-knockin' on heaven's door," in which she is joined by Ladysmith Black Mambazo in a call-and-response pattern. Then Parton sings the second verse, "Lord, take these guns away from me, I can't shoot them any more…" What makes the form of this performance interesting is its combination of verse and refrain with call and response.

Hip-hop producers create groove tracks, combinations of pre-recorded beats, that they loop to provide a repetitive structure over which rappers (4.55), beatboxers, and break dancers can perform for indefinite and flexible periods of time. The video is an educational production created by the administrators at CERN (the European Organization for Nuclear Research) near Geneva, Switzerland, in order to teach school children about the Large Hadron Collider and particle physics using a musical form with which the children are familiar. It is both ironic and humorous that a form associated with contemporary youth culture is performed by "nerdy" European physicists. The explanation is rapped in verse accompanied by a pre-recorded, repeating tape loop.

GENRE

The term "genre" derives from the Latin *genus*, a word familiar to students of biology as a type or category within a system of classification. Categories of music are created according to stylistic, contextual, and historical similarities. Recording companies and streaming services use computer-generated algorithms to market new artists by placing them in pre-existing categories of music with similar features. Rock, hip-hop, country, soul, jazz, classical, etc., are all genres. Wedding and funeral songs are genres defined by occasion. **Salsa**, **cumbia**, and **reggae** are genres based upon characteristic dance beats and place of origin: Puerto Rico, Colombia, and Jamaica, respectively. Often identification with a particular genre is related to and marks class or regional divisions within a society. American bluegrass is associated with the rural Appalachian Mountain region while hip-hop is considered an urban genre.

In Trinidad, among the descendants of East Indian indentured laborers, two types of wedding songs are performed by women at weddings: *byah ke geet* are old songs with deep roots in the ancestral home of North India, while *lachari* are contemporary songs, often comical and with sexual innuendos. Pop songs in China are called **tongsu**. These popular entertainments are composed and recorded by government-employed artists and receive government support and approval. In contrast, subversive Chinese rock songs (**yaogun yinyue**) often have lyrics that express individualistic and anti-establishment sentiments. Underground rock musicians in China are not supported by the state and are marginalized by the lack of radio play and popular venues in which to perform.

The use of the term "**World Music**" dates back to the late 1950s when one of the founders of the Society for Ethnomusicology, David McAllester, declared that the academic study of music should not be limited to Western classical music. The study of music, he claimed, should be of the whole world, "as a universal phenomenon beyond the confines of Western European tradition."[10] His colleague Robert Brown joined McAllester at Wesleyan University to start an academic program and develop courses in what they called World Music. College-level textbooks followed, with one of the first being *Musics of Many Cultures* (1980) edited by Elizabeth May, in which McAllester wrote the chapter on "North American Native Music." Other prominent volumes included the first editions of *Worlds of Music* (1984) by Jeff Todd Titon, and *Excursions in World Music* (1992) by Bruno Nettl.

One of the first "World Music" artists was Indian musician Ravi Shankar. His vast and diverse musical experiences redefined the role of the "musician" in the age of mass media and globalization. Shankar played a unique role as cultural ambassador for Indian music around the world. As the first Indian classical instrumentalist to gain an international reputation, he pioneered the role of musical advocate and mediator. In concert performances, his fluency in English enabled him to explain the complex melodic and rhythmic systems of Hindustani classical music to new audiences with clarity and charm. He frequently performed with other celebrity musicians. This video shows a 1973 concert featuring Ravi Shankar and Ali Akbar Khan (4.56), accompanied by *tabla* drummer Alla Rakha (1919–2000). The great *sarod* player, Ali Akbar Khan and Ravi Shankar both trained under Khan's father, Ustad Allauddin Khan (1862–1972). Shankar attained superstar status and performed at both the Monterey Pop Festival in 1967 and the Woodstock Rock Festival in 1969. He continued to perform concerts into his nineties. Until the end of his life, Pandit Ravi Shankar served as India's preeminent musical representative, bringing the music of India to the West and nurturing global audiences for Indian classical music. He also paved the way for artists from around the world to find and cultivate international audiences for their music in concert halls and on recordings.

As artists like Ravi Shankar began to reach international audiences, music producers sought new ways of selling records of their music. The use of the term "World Music" as a marketing category, rather than as an academic subject, began in the late 1980s in London; specifically, on June 29, 1987 at the Empress of Russia pub on St. James Street. From a series of meetings held at the pub that included record store owners, music producers, radio hosts, and other interested parties, World Music as a genre was born. It became a genre for the global record industry in the 1990s, adding to such marketing categories as classical, jazz, rock, and adult contemporary. "International" recordings were gaining popularity while multiculturalism and globalization grew in influence as social ideologies. Cities became more cosmopolitan, and interest in and enjoyment of music from diverse countries and cultures flourished. Ethnomusicologists and adventurers found a surprising new market for their field recordings among a segment of the general population. From around the beginning of the recording industry in the first decade of the 20th century, recordings were made of music from every part of the world, but records pressed from these recordings were marketed back to the country of origin for local consumption. It was nearly one hundred years later that a global market opened up for recordings of World Music.

STYLE

The term "style" refers to the sum total of the ways musicians combine the elements described in this chapter to create music. The term has many different uses and implications. It can refer broadly to *national* styles as in French style or Russian style. Music historians speak of *historical* "stylistic periods" such as Renaissance or Contemporary style. The term is applied to *regional* styles like New Orleans jazz or San Francisco jazz (4.57), here played by Steve and Kate Fowler. The term identifies *individual* styles, as in Elvis Presley and Lady Gaga each having "a style of their own." Genres such as hip-hop, country, rhythm and blues (R&B), or electronic dance music (EDM) have their own musical style. Musicians performing in these genres follow conventional ways of making music that meet and respond to the expectations of their audiences.

Within a particular genre, there may be *performance* styles differentiated by geographical location. *Pansori*, a genre of Korean musical storytelling, is performed in two ways: a Western style (*sopyonje*) and an Eastern style (*dongpyonje*). These styles are described by practitioners and audiences in contrasting terms—stories in *dongpyonje* are told in a heavy and vigorous manner, while those of *sopyonje* are presented in a sorrowful and tender manner.

Styles often follow teacher–pupil lines of transmission within musician families, across generations. In the classical Hindustani tradition of North India, the term **gharana** refers to such family lineages. *Gharanas* may be named for cities associated with these families, such as the Gwalior *gharana* or the Agra *gharana*, or named after instruments associated with its members, such as the *beenkar gharana* (*been*, stick zither). Within each *gharana*, musicians maintain and preserve a consistent style of performance, and in the past they closely guarded their treasure trove of melodies, improvisational strategies, and minute technical details. Asad Ali Khan (1937–2011) inherited the style of playing known as the *beenkar gharana* of Jaipur. He was one of the last surviving masters of this style, and referred to his instrument as the *rudra veena* (*rudra* being a name for Lord Shiva) (Figure 4.12).

The term style is also used to describe the role of the conductor in the Western symphony orchestra. In rehearsals and performances, the conductor makes *stylistic* decisions relating to speed, volume, and balance for a large group of instrumentalists. However, the conductor's decisions are highly determined by the musical score of the composer, who often is not present or even alive at the time of the performance. A conductor will often impose a *personal* style on a performance that contrasts with that of other conductors, who may interpret the same score quite differently.

Musical performances may be based upon the contextual demands of a particular occasion and location. For example, encountering the electric guitars, dance rhythms, light shows, and staging of some Christian rock bands in a high Anglican church would be strange indeed, whereas in many evangelical churches this style of performance is normal, indeed, expected.

Music styles are rarely static. As times change, so do fashions in clothing, hairstyles, automobile designs, and of course music. Some musicians work *against* traditional expectations, finding inspiration in new digital technologies, performance venues, and ever-evolving social

FIGURE 4.12 Asad Ali Khan playing the *rudra veena* (stick zither)

circumstances. An example of this is the prevalence of computer music (4.58) in many academic circles. This video shows Austrian composer Karlheinz Essl giving a live performance of his composition *"Sonnez la Cloche!"* based on the sound of a single church bell. Acoustic instrumentalists "go electric" to reach new audiences by developing more commercial, pop-oriented styles. Perhaps the most famous example of "electrification" occurred in 1965 when Bob Dylan showed up at the Newport Folk Festival with a newly acquired electric guitar and blasted the ears of audience members accustomed to acoustic "hootenanny" music. Irish rock bands like the Cranberries in the 1990s, used electric guitars, African-based rhythms, and ear-splitting amplification, to create a hybrid style based on traditional Irish music. Their performances and recordings, such as "Zombie" (4.59) (1994), may have made listeners with more traditional tastes cover their ears, while audiences accustomed to the high decibel level of rock, punk, and heavy metal were enthusiastic about the contemporary performance style.

CONCLUSION

This chapter has presented the elements by which musical sound may be analyzed: rhythm, melody, harmony, etc. While each music culture has musical concepts and terms in its own language by which its music is best understood, two fundamental principles of organization are found in most musical systems: composition and improvisation, and periodicity and contrast. Examples in this chapter were drawn from throughout the world in order to illustrate the universal applicability of these root concepts. The next two chapters consider music more holistically, and raise the questions, "where did music come from?" and "what is it for?"

KEY TERMS AND CONCEPTS

Composition and Improvisation	Monophony
Drone	Ornamentation
Elements of Music	Pentatonic
Form	Periodicity and Contrast
Free Rhythm	Polyphony
Genre	Polyrhythm
Grooves and Dance Rhythms	Rhythm
Harmonic Progression	Rhythmic Mode
Harmony	Rhythmic Virtuosity
Heterophony	Scale
Homophony	Style
Interval	*Taqsim*
Melismatic	Texture
Melodic Contour	Work Rhythm
Melody	World Music
Mode	

THINKING ABOUT MUSIC

1   Choose a recording of music that you are familiar with. As you listen to it, can you recognize the two "areas of convergence" discussed at the beginning of this chapter: Composition vs. Improvisation, and Periodicity vs. Contrast? Describe them in your own words. Now listen again to the selections in this chapter: "*Shadanane* (4.28)," "Moonlight Sonata (4.36)," and "I Walk the Line (4.38)." Try to do the same.

2   How would you describe in your own words the concepts of "rhythmic mode" and "melodic mode"?

3   What do *raga* (India), *mugam* (Azerbaijan), and *ujo* (Korea) have in common?

4   Listen to the following four selections (from "Texture"): Benedictine nuns, "California Dreaming," *isicathamiya*, and "*Shojo No Tsuru*." In each case, how would you describe the texture?

5   Choose two music videos in this chapter and describe their musical styles in terms of at least three musical elements discussed in the chapter. In what ways are the videos similar and different?

6   Think about the relationship between musical sound and context. How does the way music is used shape the way it sounds? Discuss this question in relation to the rhythmic demonstrations by *dumbek* player Soheil Kaspar (Videos 4.3 and 4.4).

7   How and why did "World Music" become a genre?

NOTES

1 Michael Tenzer, ed., *Analytical Studies in World Music* (Oxford and New York: Oxford University Press, 2006), 22.
2 Sgioba Luaidh Inbhirchluaidh, Waulking Song Group, http://www.waulk.org/index.asp.
3 Charles Keil and Steven Feld, *Music Grooves: Essays and Dialogues* (Tucson, AZ: Fenestra Books, 2005).
4 Interview with Simon Shaheen in the documentary film series, *Exploring the World of Music, VI: Melody*, Pacific Street Films and the Educational Film Center, 1999.
5 George Ruckert, "Hindustani Raga," in *The Garland Encyclopedia of World Music*, Vol. 5: *South Asia*, ed. Alison Arnold (New York: Garland Publishing, 2000), 64.
6 Jonathan Stock, *Musical Creativity in 20th-Century China: Abing, His Music, and Its Changing Meanings* (Rochester, NY: University of Rochester Press, 1996), 31–32.
7 Lynne Kelly, *The Memory Code: The Secrets of Stonehenge, Easter Island and Other Ancient Monuments* (Winnipeg, MB: Pegasus, 2017), 13.
8 Meghan Overdeep, "When These 4 Strangers Met at a Georgia Barbershop, a True Barbershop Quartet Was Born," *Southern Living*, January 16, 2020.
9 English translation of *ghazal* lyrics by Deewan, http://urdustuff.blogspot.com/2010/04/ghalib-hai-bas-ki-har-ek-un-ke-ishaare.html.
10 David McAllester, cited in "Guide to the Music Department Records, 1863–[ongoing]," Wesleyan Library, Special Collections and Archives, https://www.wesleyan.edu/libr/sca/FAs/mu1000-182.xml.

CHAPTER 5

Where Does Music Come From? Origins of Music

Introduction
Origin Myths
Origin Theories
Conclusion

INTRODUCTION

Music is a universal form of human expression whose roots reach back into the dim recesses of pre-history. Chapter 5 considers the question "Where does music come from?" The simple answer is "no one knows," as no one knows where, or when, language or religion or visual art originated. But it was perhaps the use of music as a code of communication, engagement, and relationship that made our distant ancestors distinctly and recognizably human.

With no definitive evidence of where music came from or when it began, humans over the centuries have created numerous myths and stories to explain its origins. This chapter presents a selection of myths as well as several more recent evolutionary theories relating to the origins of music. Together the myths and theories may shed light on why music is universal as well as the multiple functions it serves in human life.

ORIGIN MYTHS

The ancient Greeks believed that music pre-existed humanity and was part of the very order of the cosmos. The "Music of the Spheres," whose perfect harmonies were thought to permeate the universe, was inaudible because humans would have heard it continuously from birth, and so were insensitive to the sound. However, harmonious "human music," based on mathematical proportions, mirrored this perfect music of the spheres and allowed humans to participate in that perfection.

In an early Christian context, the 4th-century bishop St. Basil attributed the invention of music directly to God, saying:

> When, indeed, the Holy Spirit saw that the human race was guided only with difficulty toward virtue … what did He do? The delight of melody He mingled with the doctrines

so that by the pleasantness and softness of the sound heard, we might receive without perceiving it the benefit of the words.[1]

Visual artists from diverse religious traditions represent heavenly realms as places filled with divine music. The early 16th-century painting in Figure 5.1 by the Italian Renaissance artist Raphael (1483–1520) depicts the Patroness of Music, St. Cecilia, renouncing the pleasures of earthly music, represented by the scattered instruments at her feet, in exchange for the heavenly choirs above. As she contemplates eternity, she rejects even human-made sacred music, represented by the organ slipping out of her grasp.

Some myths are based on religious beliefs and teachings, in which the beginnings of sound and music are integrally linked to the creation of the world. Other myths place the origin of music in the spirit world or the realm of human ancestors. Yet others ascribe music's origin

FIGURE 5.1 St. Cecilia with Mary Magdalene, St. Augustine, John the Evangelist, and St. Paul

to human invention. All origin myths and narratives serve to satisfy basic human curiosity and desire to find answers to the as yet unanswered and perhaps unanswerable question, "where did music come from?" Through origin myths, people have also sought to account for its mysterious attractiveness.

> *In the first three origin myths from India, West Africa, and the Hopi Nation*
> *of the southwestern United States, music is the very force of creation.*

Shiva Nataraja (India)

The image of Shiva Nataraja, Lord of the Dance, is found in many temples in South India and reached its present form more than a 1,000 years ago (Figure 5.2L). The image depicts the god Shiva, one of the three great divinities of the Hindu Trinity (along with Brahma and Vishnu), dancing on the back of a dwarf who represents ignorance. In his upper right hand he holds a drum whose beat accompanies the god's ecstatic dance, through which the universe comes into being (Figure 5.2R). In one of his left hands he holds fire, the symbol of destructive forces that will one day bring the universe to an end. Thus, the image encompasses the entire span of time, and the god's music becomes not merely the symbol of creation but the creative power itself, which sustains the cosmos.

"The World Was Created to the Notes of a Sanza" (Bantu, West Africa)

In the beginning, there was nothing.
Neither light, nor darkness.
Nothing but boredom.

FIGURE 5.2 Shiva Nataraja (L), and Shiva's *damaru* drum (detail) (R)

FIGURE 5.3 African *sanza* (lamellophone)

> And Nyambé, creator of the Bantu, was bored to death.
> One day, he asked Imagination:
> "What's there to do?"
> Imagination answered:
> "Make a sanza! As soon as you start playing it,
> your boredom will go away."
> So Nyambé made himself a sanza, plucked a reed
> and the first sound of music was heard,
> from which emerged the sun.
> Another note of the sanza created man,
> soon joined by a wife and many children who very
> soon populated the earth. And so it is that all men,
> white and black, yellow and red, were born of the sanza.
> And even now as I speak, I am making a child…
> another child … many children, of all colors…This
> is why the Bantu love all men without distinction.[2]
> (See Figure 5.3)

The Myth of Spider Woman (Hopi Nation)

The Spider Woman myth of the Hopi people is also a story of the cosmos-creating power of music. In the beginning, Spider Woman, one of the co-creators of the world, made twin boys from earth and saliva. She brought them to life by singing the Creation Song over them. To the first twin she gave the duty of keeping the world in order. The second she instructed to "go about all the world and send out sound so that it may be heard throughout all the land." This twin would then be known as Echo, "for all sound echoes the Creator." When he did this,

> all the vibratory centers along the earth's axis from pole to pole resounded his call; the whole earth trembled; the universe quivered in tune. Thus Echo made the whole world

an instrument of sound, and sound an instrument for carrying messages, resounding praise to the Creator of all.[3]

Some myths link the origin of music with the origin of human beings, as in this Sufi narrative from Kashmir.

The Angels' Song (Sufis in Kashmir)

Sufis (Islamic mystics) in Kashmir, the northernmost state of the Indian Subcontinent, relate that Allah, the Creator and Protector, gave life to Adam by blowing the fire of the soul into the human body of clay, chanting the words "to be." The Lord commanded the soul into Adam's body but from fear the soul would not enter. "The angels then 'sang in' the melody: 'Into the body, into the body, get into the body.'"[4] The singing of the angels was thus the original act of creation, and their divine sound filled the human world. This sound was then ordered into eight musical pitches, and human music was born.

Music in some narratives is considered a gift from divine beings, as in the early Christian view of St. Basil referred to above, and in this story from ancient India.

A Gift from the Gods (Ancient India)

According to the *Natya Shastra*, a 2,000-year old Indian treatise on music, dance, and drama, music was originally a divine gift from the gods to humankind. In ancient times, the god Indra together with other gods, asked Brahma, the Creator, to give something to humans so that they would turn away from their evil ways, from their greed, lust, and anger. Brahma decided to give to humans the celestial art of music as a plaything and distraction. The Hindu heaven was filled with divine beings (*gandharvas* and *apsaras*) who were well versed in the musical arts. The gods sought a suitable human who was wise enough to receive from them this sacred gift. Music was thus conveyed to the world through a single sage known as Narada,[5] who had been a *gandharva* in a previous birth. Narada, in turn, taught this divine art to humanity (Figure 5.4).

Several myths place music in an ongoing relationship or connection between humans and spirit beings. In the following two examples, humans receive songs in dreams and visions as manifestations of sacred power.

Old Man Tulh (Australian Aboriginal Myth)

In Aboriginal mythology, songs come from ancestors and are transmitted to the world of the living through dreams. One of the myths of the Mari-ammu people of northwestern Australia involves the song-giving ancestor Old Man Tulh. He is one of many world-creating ancestors who were active at the beginning of time. Old Man Tulh appears in dreams to certain individuals called songmen and gives them *wangga* songs and dances that the songmen when awake must then perform in ceremonies. The success of a ritual depends on mingling songs of the living with songs that the long-ago dead bring to the dreaming songmen. The songmen must replicate not only the melody, rhythm, and words of the received song, but also must exactly imitate the voice of Old Man Tulh. It is the timbre of the ghostly voice that gives the singers their power, and it is through the living singers that the dead can participate in the ritual life of the people.[6]

FIGURE 5.4 Sage Narada with *veena*

Vision Quest (Native American Salish and Sioux Nations)

In the rite of passage known as the "Vision Quest," practiced in a number of Native American societies, songs were the primary evidence of divine contact and empowerment. Anthropologist Alan Merriam writes of the Native American Flathead people of western Montana:

> The most important single fact about music and its relationship to the total world is its origin in the supernatural sphere. While it is clearly recognized that some songs are individually composed by human beings, and that some other songs are borrowed from neighboring peoples, all true and proper songs … owe their origin to a variety of contacts experienced by humans with beings which, though a part of the world, are superhuman and the source of both individual and tribal powers and skills.[7]

In the following story, the Oglala Sioux prophet Black Elk (1863–1950) describes his encounter with supernatural beings from whom he learns a song:

> The grass was young and I was on horseback. A thunder storm was coming from where the sun goes down, and just as I was riding into the woods along a creek, there was a kingbird sitting on a limb. This was not a dream, it happened. And I was going to shoot

at the kingbird with the bow my Grandfather made, when the bird spoke and said: "The clouds all over are one-sided." Perhaps it meant that all the clouds were looking at me. And then it said: "Listen! A voice is calling you!" Then I looked up at the clouds, and two men were coming there, headfirst like arrows slanting down; and as they came, they sang a sacred song and the thunder was like drumming. I will sing it for you. The song and the drumming were like this:

> Behold, a sacred voice is calling you;
> All over the sky a sacred voice is calling.

I sat there gazing at them, and they were coming from the place where the giant lives (north). But when they were very close to me, they wheeled about toward where the sun goes down, and suddenly they were geese. Then they were gone, and the rain came with a big wind and a roaring.[8]

Several myths give musical instruments a divine origin—in some cases from a "trickster deity"—like the next three from ancient Greece, West Africa, and the Near East.

Invention of the Lyre (Ancient Greece)

Greek mythology attributes the invention of several musical instruments—the lyre, panpipes, and flute—to Hermes, the messenger of the gods and the son of Zeus and the nymph Maia.

A Homeric Hymn from between the 7th and 6th centuries BCE tells the story of Hermes who invented the lyre on the day he was born.[9] Hermes was the youngest and most cunning of the Olympian gods. On the morning of his birth, he escaped the swaddling bands his mother had wrapped him in as she slept in their cave on Mt. Cyllene. He then went out seeking food and adventure. As soon as he stepped over the threshold he was distracted by the sight of a tortoise waddling across his path and had a grand idea, to invent the lyre.

> He took up the tortoise in both hands and went back into the house carrying his charming toy. Then he cut off its limbs and scooped out the marrow of the mountain-tortoise with a scoop of grey iron…He cut stalks of reed to measure and fixed them, fastening their ends across the back and through the shell of the tortoise, and then stretched ox hide all over it by his skill. Also he put in the horns and fitted a cross-piece upon the two of them, and stretched seven strings of sheep-gut.
>
> [39–40, 43–48]

He plucked the strings one by one and each sounded marvelous. Accompanying himself on his new invention, he sang a glorious song about himself and his divine parentage. Then he hid the lyre in his cradle and went in search of his brother Apollo's sacred cows grazing on the mountains of Pieria. Finding them, he hastily invented fire, rubbing dry sticks together, and butchered and roasted two. He herded fifty more back to Mt. Cyllene and hid them in a grotto. Then the infant god huddled back into his swaddling bands beside his mother and pretended to sleep. It wasn't long before Apollo, the sun god who sees all, tracked the stolen cows to the cave and accused Hermes of the theft. "Child, lying in the cradle, make haste and tell me of my cattle, or we two will soon fall out angrily." [254–255] Hermes denied everything, asking how he, an infant, could steal cattle.

> This is no task for me: rather I care for other things: I care for sleep, and milk of my mother's breast, and wrappings round my shoulders, and warm baths…. Neither am I

guilty myself, neither have I seen any other who stole your cows—whatever cows may be; for I know them only by hearsay.

[266–268, 275–277]

The argument was interrupted by the arrival of Zeus, their father, who brought the two brothers before the council of the gods on Mt. Olympus to settle the dispute. When Hermes could no longer deny the theft, he took out the lyre he had fashioned and began to play. Hearing the beautiful notes,

> Phoebus Apollo laughed for joy; for the sweet throb of the marvelous music went to his heart, and a soft longing took hold on his soul as he listened. Then the son of Maia, harping sweetly upon his lyre, took courage and stood at the left hand of Phoebus Apollo; and soon, while he played shrilly on his lyre, he lifted up his voice and sang, and lovely was the sound of his voice that followed. He sang the story of the deathless gods and of the dark earth, how at the first they came to be, and how each one received his portion.

[420–429]

FIGURE 5.5 Apollo playing the lyre, ancient Greek jar (580–500 BCE)

And Apollo cried, "Slayer of oxen, trickster, busy one, comrade of the feast, this song of yours is worth fifty cows, and I believe that presently we shall settle our quarrel peacefully." [436–438] Thus the lyre became Apollo's own instrument (Figure 5.5), exchanged for the cattle, and thereafter he was known as the god of music. Hermes, for his part, invented the panpipes and flute, to play while looking after the cattle he had purchased with the lyre.

"How the Dan Got the Baa Drum" (West Africa)

A woman was sent by her husband to the forest to gather leaves for a sauce. She hears a strange and enchanting voice. Following the sound, she finds a genie sitting atop a termite mound in the middle of an empty field, beating a thing that people would later call the Baa Drum. The Genie spoke:

> "With us, we dance to this thing. If I beat it, you'll dance to its voice from here all the way down there…" The genie beat the drum and the woman began dancing.

When she did not return home, the husband sent their son, who also became entranced by the new sound and started to dance. The husband, looking for his family, followed them to the field. He too could not resist; first his neck began to shake, then his arms, then his whole body. The people of the village, missing the man and the woman, went looking for them in the forest. Before they heard the sound, the villagers saw them from afar. "Why are you moving about like that?" they shouted, for they had never seen dancing. But as they approached, the villagers heard the sound and they too were caught in the drum's spell. After a time, an elephant hunter, who had been following the trail of an elephant for seven days, came upon this scene. He saw men and women, children and old people all dancing in the field. He told the genie to stop the dance. And the genie stopped. "Where does this drum come from?" he asked.

> The genie said, "It comes from our village. It's to this rhythm that we dance in the evening. When there's a party, everyone without exception … they all come and line up and dance together."

The hunter asked, "How do you make the thing speak?" And the genie instructed him on the drum's construction from a hollow log and the skin of a dead animal (Figure 5.6).

> "When the skin dries, its voice becomes beautiful. Then you beat on it."
> "We will take this beautiful thing with us back to our village," said the hunter. The genie refused. So the hunter pointed his loaded rifle at the genie and fired. The drum rolled to the ground.
> Then the hunter said, "Pick up the drum and take it to the village. Instead of dancing here in the field, take this beautiful thing to the village so we can dance down there." They picked up the drum and they all went back to the village. Once they reached the village, they gave everyone this advice: "Anyone who wants to have a good party, let him do it with the drum. And we'll dance."
> So it was that we [humans] got the drum. Then we learned to make more. At festivals, we pick them up and dance.[10]

FIGURE 5.6 West African cylindrical drum, Accra, Ghana

Jubal and Lamech (Jewish and Islamic Myth)

According to the Old Testament book of Genesis, the invention of music in Jewish tradition is ascribed to Jubal: "the father of all who play the harp and flute" (Genesis 4:21). Later Jewish sources attributed to Jubal the origin of all musical instruments as well as singing. With the beginning of Islam in the 7th century, Muslim writers claimed music originated not with Jubal but his father Lamech, and not with the harp and flute but with the Arabic *ud*. A 9th-century Muslim text associates the origin of the *ud* with the human body, in the form of Lamech's son.[11]

Lamech had no children until old age, then finally having a son, the boy died at the age of five. Lamech grieved and hung his son's body on a tree until the flesh fell off the bones. Eventually only the thigh, leg, and foot remained. Lamech then made an instrument of wood to represent the thigh, leg, foot, and toes, with strings for the sinews, and he played on it and wept, becoming the first person to sing a lament (Figure 5.7).

In this Islamic tale from Kashmir in South Asia, it is the musical notes themselves, not instruments, that have a divine origin.

FIGURE 5.7 Egyptian *ud* player

Moses Strikes the Stone (Sufis in Kashmir)

A Kashmiri Sufi tale from the late 18th century attributes the origin of melody to Moses as he led the Israelites out of Egypt.

On seeing a stone in the middle of the Nile River, Moses wanted to return to pick it up but did not do so. Angel Gabriel appeared to Moses and told him to pick it up, saying some day he would find a use for the stone. Tired and thirsty after spending forty days in the desert with his tribe, Moses prayed to God. Angel Gabriel appeared again and told Moses to strike the stone with his staff. The stone cracked into twelve pieces and from each burst a spring, and the echoes of the springs blended together. As his tribe drank the water, Moses "departed into a flight of fancy in these sounds" … In his own tongue he read some verses in those melodies and gave them the names of the twelve *maqams* (melodic modes).[12]

> *Two final myths explain music as inherent in the very nature of existence. Like the ancient Greeks, the Chinese believed that through music, humans could participate in the perfection of the cosmos.*

Friction between Heaven and Earth (Ancient China)

In ancient Chinese thought, musical sound was believed to originate in the friction between heaven and earth, and between the *yin* (the passive female principle) and the *yang* (the active male principle). According to ancient Chinese thinkers, music was conceived as a natural force resulting from the dynamic interactions between these elements. *The Record of Ritual Music and Dance* from the late Zhou dynasty (ca. 6th–3rd centuries BCE) explains this concept:

> The *chhi* [vital force] of earth ascends above: the *chhi* of heaven descends from the height. The *yang* and the *yin* come into contact; heaven and earth shake together. Their

drumming is in the shock and rumble of thunder; their excited beating of wings is in wind and rain; their shifting round is in the four seasons; their warming is in the sun and moon. Thus the hundred species procreate and flourish. Thus it is that music is a bringing together of heaven and earth.[13]

Legend of the Yellow Bell (Ancient China)

Perhaps the most famous Chinese legend on the origin of music places it ca. 2700 BCE when the Chinese Emperor Huang Di sent his mathematician Ling Lun to the far western mountains of China to cut a set of twelve tuned bamboo pipes. These would be used to provide pitches for a set of bronze bells. The largest, producing the lowest pitch, was named the Yellow Bell, yellow being the imperial color. From this measurement, all the other pitches were derived, and the pitches became the tonal system for Chinese music. When the bells were played in rituals of state, the sound was so perfect that it united and harmonized the human realm with nature and the divine under the beneficent rule of the Chinese Emperor, the Son of Heaven.[14] In 1977, an entire set of sixty-four bronze bells was excavated from the tomb of the Marquis Yi in Hubei province, central China. Bells and other ritual objects were buried with rulers and military generals so they could have ceremonial music in the afterlife. Based on an inscription on one of the bells, the Marquis Yi of Zeng's set was dated to 433 BCE.

These myths and others like them do more than provide an explanation of music's origins. They also underscore music's importance to the living, and serve as a basis and justification for the ways people use music within their societies. Thus, in the case of the two West African myths, music is integral to socialization and group cohesion. In the story of Jubal, music's central role in funerals and mourning is legitimized. The ancient Chinese legend of the Yellow Bell points out the ways ritual music establishes the prestige of the emperor. With the Aboriginal Australians, song unites the living with the dead and the first ancestors in shared community. In every case, music is seen as a source of connection between people, and between the human and trans-human worlds: nature, the ancestors, and the gods.

ORIGIN THEORIES

Associations with dreams, the supernatural, and myth suggest human involvement with music at deep levels of consciousness. Many musicians have spoken of the mysterious sources of musical inspiration. Bassist Ed King of the southern rock band Lynyrd Skynyrd claims that the chord progression and guitar riffs of "Sweet Home Alabama" (1974) came to him, note for note, in a dream. Joseph Shabalala (1940–2020), founder of the popular South African *isicathamiya* group Ladysmith Black Mambazo, launched his career following a series of dreams. American composer Aaron Copland writes in his book *What to Listen for in Music*: "The composer starts with a theme; and the theme is a gift from Heaven. He doesn't know where it comes from—has no control over it. It comes almost like automatic handwriting."[15]

From a scientific point of view, the question "Where did music come from?" is a subject of intense interest and debate. Recent discoveries in neurophysiology, human paleontology, and infant psychology, among other fields, have brought music to the forefront of the study of human mind/brain relationships, evolution, and social integration. Nevertheless, as with many basic human behaviors such as tool use, upright locomotion, and language, music's origins may never be discovered or fully understood. Moreover, unlike tool use, music itself leaves little trace in the fossil record upon which to base or support an origin theory.

The capacities to make and respond to music are biologically supported by genetic makeup. From a Darwinian, evolutionary perspective, this suggests that musical "instincts" were selected and passed on to offspring because they gave some survival, adaptive, and/or reproductive advantage to our distant hominid ancestors. Relevant archeological findings, though small, are tantalizing in their implications. A 43,000-year-old flute made of vulture bone found in a cave in southwestern Germany, reported in the *New York Times* in 2012, is the world's oldest artifact that is without doubt a musical instrument.[16] In *National Geographic News* in 2009, James Owen states:

> The ancient flutes are evidence for an early musical tradition that likely helped biologically modern humans communicate and form tighter social bonds...Music may therefore have been important to maintaining and strengthening Stone Age social networks ... allowing for greater societal organization and strategizing.

Quoting archeologist Nicholas Conard of the University of Tübingen in Germany who studied these flutes, the article continues:

> Think how important music is for us. Whether it's at church, a party, or just for fun, you can see how powerful music can be. People often hear a song and cry, or feel great joy or sorrow. All of those kinds of emotions help bond people together.[17]

Before constructing instruments out of non-perishable materials, humans could have been producing proto-musical sounds for millennia, using their voices, bodies, and natural objects in the environment. These sounds would have accompanied dance movements and would have been incorporated into rituals and daily activities. This evidence suggests that humans have been making music for a very long time, and a number of theories propose that music, along with language, developed at that time when our earliest ancestors became recognizably human.

Why did humans evolve innate capacities for making and responding to music? An inherited trait, according to evolutionary theory, promotes either survival or reproductive advantage. Scholars and researchers disagree on what advantages our ancestors gained from their musical capacities. Unlike tool making, language, upright posture, and bipedal locomotion, it is not obvious what music did to promote survival and reproductive success. Even now, it seems to some like "mere entertainment" or a useless behavioral extravagance, despite the fact that all societies have music and that billions of dollars are spent on it annually. Below are five theories that scholars have put forward to explain or shed light on why humans are born with these innate capacities.[18]

Imitation of Sounds of the Natural World

By the working definition of music proposed in this textbook, sounds produced by animals and natural forces like wind and water are "music-like," but not music. However, many researchers have considered these to be important in several ways when thinking about music in human evolution. There are certainly sounds in the natural world that resemble human music making, and the imitation of these sounds by our ancestors could plausibly have influenced its development. Birdsong in particular is often cited as a source for human musical inspiration. It has also been noted that two of the primary reasons birds "sing"—to mark territory and attract mates—are important in human music making as well, as evidenced by the sheer number and universality of national anthems, fight songs, and love ballads. Yet despite the similarities between human music and birdsong, they evolved separately and have only coincidental resemblance.

Social Bonding Behaviors among Higher Mammals

Certain higher mammals exhibit behaviors that resemble human music making in more subtle and sophisticated ways. Researchers have observed humpback whales (5.1) "composing" their songs; that is, adding on new phrases to melodic contours "sung" in previous mating seasons, and repeating and altering musical units in highly creative ways. In other words, their songs are not simply instinctual, but are subject to creative processes. Some primates use vocalizations to acknowledge or strengthen social bonds. Gibbons (5.2), who are monogamous unlike most mammals, sing morning duets with their mates in one of the animal kingdom's most impressive sonic displays. The gelada baboons (5.3) of Ethiopia use coordinated group vocalizations to resolve conflicts and re-establish group harmony. Perhaps geladas experience "temporary physiological synchrony"—a state of mutual metabolic and emotional coordination—through group vocalizing. In much the same way, humans experience a feeling of solidarity and social cohesion from choral singing and at concerts and festivals. Primatologist Bruce Richman, who spent years studying the geladas, suggests that during the course of human evolution, the use of melody and rhythm developed as a specialized language of group emotional and physiological bonding, "a kind of vocal grooming." Indeed, Richman was struck by how human-like these vocalizations are both in sound and apparent function.[19]

Anthropologist John Blacking speculated that singing and dancing preceded by several hundred thousand years the development of spoken language, in which words are linked to meanings. "There is so much music in the world that it is reasonable to suppose that music, like language and possibly religion, is a species-specific trait of man."[20] Singing and dancing, like the grooming behaviors of the gelada baboons, contributed to the bonding of social groups upon which early human survival depended and continues to depend.

Psychiatrist and music commentator Anthony Storr (1920–2001) writes:

> The idea that music causes a general state of arousal rather than specific emotions partly explains why it has been used to accompany such a wide variety of human activities, including marching, serenading, worship, marriages, funerals, and manual work… By imposing order [in a group], music ensures that the emotions aroused by a particular event peak at the same moment…What matters is the general state of arousal and its simultaneity.[21]

Music as a Form of Courtship Display in the Attraction of Mates

Charles Darwin, in his study *The Descent of Man, and Selection in Relation to Sex*, wrote that it "appears probable that the progenitors of man, either the males or females or both sexes, before acquiring the power of expressing their mutual love in articulate language, endeavored to charm each other with musical notes and rhythm."[22] Darwin argued that music preceded speech in human evolution and was connected with courtship behaviors between the sexes. He had observed that birds, particularly males, sing much more often during the mating season to attract mates, defend territory, and repel rivals. These sounds, which convey emotion and intention, are describable in the terms we use for musical analysis such as pitch, rhythm, and timbre.

Darwin's position that music evolved in humans as a complex biological adaptation related to male courtship display has been defended by evolutionary biologist Geoffrey Miller. Along with artistic creativity, language, and fitness indicators like dance, Miller claims that musical competence in males signaled to prospective mates such desirable traits as endurance, intelligence, resourcefulness, coordination, and general health. According to Miller, musical creativity and complexity in humans may have been the result of a kind of "endless arms race" in which "our ancestral hominid-Hendrixes could never say, 'OK, our music's good enough, we can stop now,'" because they were competing with all the hominid-Eric Claptons, hominid-Jerry Garcias, and hominid-John Lennons."[23] The process that he calls the "runaway" theory of evolution led peacock males, for instance, to grow ever larger and more elaborate tail feathers, since the one with the largest had the best chance of attracting a mate and passing along the long-tail trait to the next generation. So human musicians would have developed ever more flashy and complex musical displays for the benefit of their prospective mates, and those who competed most successfully would have passed on their musical talent to the most offspring.

Evolutionary Models of Music and Language

Several origin theories underscore the fact that human communication by means of *spoken* language, as opposed to written language, conveys meaning not only through the grammatical sense of words, but in the sounds and inflections of speech. These elements include those that most resemble the qualities of musical sound: volume, pitch, speed, timbre, etc. Consider the sentence in English, "I love you." The range of possible meanings based on the stress used in spoken language render the sentence quite ambiguous in print. If, in spoken language, the first word is stressed: "*I* love you," the sentence implies that I, as opposed to the person over there, love you. If the third word is emphasized: "I love *you*," the meaning changes. I love you instead of the other person over there. If the emphasis is placed upon the verb: "I *love* you," the meaning emphasizes love as opposed to hate or indifference. And if the sentence is spoken ironically and as a question: "I … love you?" with a rise in pitch at the end, it can mean the exact opposite of its dictionary meaning as in, "you gotta be kidding!" If music developed in relation to language, as many scholars believe, it is the *intonational* aspects of spoken language that it most resembles, rather than the grammatical elements (sentence structure and literal meaning).

Neuroscientist Steven Brown believes the faculties of music and speech may have emerged from a stage of human development he calls "Musilanguage."[24] This combination of sounds and gestures (the rudiments of dance and theater) by which our ancestors communicated, would have contained elements of what would become language and music. Brown sees the various functions of language and music existing along a spectrum, rather than occupying mutually exclusive communication domains. According to his view, music and language differ mainly in their emphasis rather than in their fundamental nature. As the two ends of the spectrum became more specialized, they diverged into the two communicative modes of music and language, although each retained vestiges of the other. East Asian tonal languages such as Cantonese, and "sing-song" speech that characterizes spoken Welsh and Norwegian, contain aspects of music in spoken language. African drum languages work the opposite way, containing vestiges of spoken language in a system that is fundamentally musical.

Language and music are each able to express, through vocalized sound, two kinds of information: referential meaning and emotive meaning. The verbal sound-structure TREE, for example, refers to that big leafy thing growing in the yard (referential meaning). Excited speech, such as "HEY! THAT TREE IS ABOUT TO FALL ON YOUR HEAD!" conveys emotion (emotive meaning). Here, the words with dictionary meanings and their vocal delivery, loud and urgent, convey the emotional charge. To use a musical example, the Wedding March has referential meaning in conveying associations relevant to the occasion, as in "Here Comes the Bride," everyone stand up! The Wedding March also has emotive meaning, conveying powerful feelings appropriate to the solemnity and joy of the occasion through its stately rhythm and simple, memorable melodic contour.

Music's Evolution in Mother–Infant Bonding Behaviors

One of the most compelling theories of music's origins is that proposed by theorist Ellen Dissanayake in her book *Art and Intimacy: How the Arts Began* (2000). She argues persuasively that music began with the interactive sound sequences and give-and-take behaviors that characterize the bonding of mothers and their infants (Figure 5.8). These behaviors, in turn, were adaptations necessitated four million years ago by "the collision course between two incompatible anatomical trends": bipedal (two-legged) locomotion and greatly increased brain size and capacity. According to Dissanayake, for humans to gain the various survival advantages that standing and walking upright on two legs brought, a number of profound adaptations had to occur. Of course, these adaptations took place incrementally over many generations.

> Over four million years, hominid brains more than doubled in size.... Obviously there was a conflict at the time of childbirth between a large-brained infant and the narrow pelvis shape necessary to support an upright walker, requiring several other adaptations that would ease the risk to both mother and infant.[25]

One of the important adaptations that accommodated this change was human infants being born prematurely so that the head would fit through the narrow birth canal before it grew too large.

> If human infants were as mature at birth as infant apes are, [pregnancy] would last for twenty-one months and result in a twenty-five-pound baby.... A human infant's brain continues to grow and mature outside the womb: between birth and age four, its size triples.[26]

The result of these adaptations is a long period of infant helplessness.

> Because human infants were helpless for a far longer time after birth than any other species, they required prolonged attention and care. Mothers and infants who found

ways to develop and sustain intense affective bonds would have been at an advantage over mothers and infants who did not.[27]

The vocalizations of the mother, imitated by the infant with coos and squeals within a few months of birth, are "composed of elements that are literally, not metaphorically, musical."[28] These mother–infant interactions (5.4) are remarkably similar around the world, with infants responding to the pitch, contours, and rhythms of the mother's voice in addition to facial expressions, gestures, touching, and patting, and a whole repertoire of dynamic, interactive engagements. "Imitation and matching each other's vocalizations and facial expressions, both involuntary and deliberate, contribute to mutual enjoyment and attunement."[29]

Dissanayake maintains that these behaviors are innate; infants respond instinctively to these "motherese" sounds and gestures, and parents instinctively perform them for their babies. However, as with other innate behaviors like learning to speak or to swim, for which humans are also genetically prepared, mother-infant bonding behavior requires post-natal fostering to be activated and developed.

> A child who never hears language will not learn to speak; someone who lives in the desert will not learn to swim; women who have never been around babies will not instinctively know how to care for them [despite having the predisposition].[30]

It is this interaction between innate, inborn capacities and living "out in the world" that produces the nature/nurture dynamic that characterizes human experience. Through interactions with parents and other caregivers, infants learn to respond to and produce musical sounds that have pitch, rhythm, and melodic contour. They learn these behaviors from the very beginning of life in the context of intensely pleasurable social interactions, and they learn to experience human connectedness through these sounds. Humans maintain this capacity into adulthood, which enables them to replicate the behaviors with their own offspring.

FIGURE 5.8 Ellen Dissanayake, March 2008

CONCLUSION

Myths on the origin of music suggest its extraordinary, even transcendent power in human life. Many of these myths presented in this chapter attribute the origin to divine beings, further acknowledging this power. Chapter 5 has introduced five developmental theories, each of which presupposes that music served important functions in aiding the survival of our hominid ancestors. These include group cohesion, communication, reproductive advantage, and mother-infant intimacy. For whatever reason or reasons, the capacity to make and respond to music is part of the human genome. Human biology changes extremely slowly over many generations, but human technologies and expressive forms and behaviors—those aspects that constitute "culture"—can change dramatically within a single generation. While humans share fundamentally the same genetic code with their ancestors who hunted, gathered, and presumably "musicked" on the African Savannah 100,000 years ago, the music of today is quite different. The modern world of bluetooth earbuds and digital streaming services is far removed from the environment for which the human body was adapted. The fact that so much brain development occurs after birth means that while humans have few useful instincts compared to birds and other animals, they have an enormous capacity for learning. Musical instruments are fiddled and strummed with hands whose digits and opposable thumbs originally evolved to hold tree branches and then to make and use tools. Our ancestors built upon a repertoire of innate and inherited capacities and taught their innovations to their children. Just as weapons over the millennia have evolved from chipped flint arrowheads to missiles and smart bombs, and storage technologies have evolved from woven baskets to computer hard drives, so the proto-musical activities of our distant ancestors have developed over generations of cultural transmission into the spectacular range of sounds, instruments, and music technologies of today. The question then remains, "what do people do with music?" This is the subject of the next chapter.

KEY TERMS AND CONCEPTS

Ancestor or Spirit Realms

Courtship Display

Darwinian Evolutionary Perspective

Evolutionary Theories

Intonational Aspects of Speech

Mother–Infant Interaction

"Musilanguage"

Origin Myth

Origin Theory

Promotion of Survival

Referential and Emotive Meaning

Reproductive Advantage

"Runaway" Theory of Evolution

Shiva Nataraja

Social Bonding

St. Cecilia

Vision Quest

THINKING ABOUT MUSIC

1   Where do *you* think music comes from?

2   Why does St. Basil think that God invented music?

3   Choose three of the myths presented in this chapter. What does each tell us about the attitudes, beliefs, and values with regard to music that the myth in question expresses?

4   Explain in your own words the relationship between the grammatical and intonational aspects of spoken language. How do the intonational components of spoken language resemble music?

5   In what ways do you think music has contributed to the survival of our species?

6   Make up your own origin of music myth that has relevance to the way music functions in your own life. Does your myth relate to music's promotion of survival and reproductive advantage, and if so, how?

7   This chapter proposed four scientific theories that suggest a deep relationship between music and human codes of communication. Theorists have emphasized music's possible origins in the following human relationships: (a) the bonding of social groups, (b) courtship, (c) the grammatical and intonational aspects of speech, and (d) interactions between mother and child. Discuss each of these four relationships in terms of your own observations of music in human life today. How do your observations support one or more of these origin of music theories?

NOTES

1   Piero Weiss and Richard Taruskin, "The Church Fathers on Psalmody and on the Dangers of Unholy Music," in *Music in the Western World: A History in Documents* (New York: Schirmer, 1984), 25.

2   Francis Bebey, "The World Was Created to the Notes of a Sanza," in Leonardo D'Amico and Francesco Mizzau, ed., *Africa Folk Music Atlas* (Florence, Italy: Amharsi Edizioni Multimediali, 1997), 4.

3   Frank Waters, *Book of the Hopi* (New York: Penguin Books, 1977), 4–5.

4   Gordon Arnold, trans. "The Angels' Song," from Daya Ram Kachroo "Khushdil," *Taraana-e Saroor* ("On Music in Kashmir") (Srinagar: Jammu and Kashmir Government, Research and Publication Dept., 1962), 1.

5   David Courtney, "Mythological Origins of Sangeet" (1988), last updated February 5, 2012, http://chandrakantha.com/articles/indian_music/myth_origin.html.

6   Allan Marett, *Songs, Dreamings, and Ghosts: The Wangga of North Australia* (Middletown, CT: Wesleyan University Press, 2005), 16–17.

7   Alan P. Merriam, "The Importance of Song in the Flathead Indian Vision Quest," *Ethnomusicology* 9/2 (1965), 91.

8   John G. Neihardt, *Black Elk Speaks* (New York: Washington Square Press, 1972), 14–15.

9   Citations in this origin myth from "Hymn 4 to Hermes," *The Homeric Hymns and Homerica* with Eng.trans. by Hugh G. Evelyn-White (Cambridge, MA: Harvard University

Press; London, William Heinemann Ltd, 1914), public domain, http://www.perseus. tufts.edu/hopper/text?doc=Perseus%3Atext%3A1999.01.0138%3Ahymn%3D4.

10 Hugo Zemp, "The Origin of the Baa Drum," in Leonardo D'Amico and Francesco Mizzau, ed. *Africa Folk Music Atlas*, 58–62.

11 From al-Mufaddal ibn Salama, *Kitab al-malahi* ("The Book of Musical Instruments"), in Amnon Shiloah, *Music in the World of Islam* (Detroit, MI: Wayne State University Press, 1995), 36–37.

12 Gordon Arnold, trans., from Khushdil, *Taraana-e Saroor*, 16–17.

13 Joseph Needham, *Science and Civilisation in China*, Vol. 4, Pt. 1, Sec. 26 (Cambridge: Cambridge University Press, 1961), cited in Lewis Rowell, *Music and Musical Thought in Early India* (Chicago, IL: Chicago University Press, 1992), 54–55.

14 The Legend of the Yellow Bell is documented in many sources. See Jenny So, ed. *Music in the Age of Confucius* (Seattle: University of Washington Press, 2000), 29.

15 Aaron Copland, *What to Listen for in Music* (New York: McGraw Hill, 1957), 18.

16 John Noble Wilford, "Flute's Revised Age Dates the Sound of Music Earlier," *New York Times*, 2012.

17 James Owen, "Bone Flute Is Oldest Instrument, Study Says," *National Geographic News*, June 24, 2009, http://news.nationalgeographic.com/news/2009/06/090624-bone-flute-oldest-instrument.html.

18 Anthony Storr, "Origins and Collective Functions," in *Music and the Mind* (New York: Ballantine Books, 1992), 1–23.

19 Nils L. Wallin et al., eds., *The Origins of Music* (Cambridge: MIT Press, 2000), 301.

20 John Blacking, *How Musical Is Man?* (Seattle: University of Washington Press, 1973), 7.

21 Anthony Storr, *Music and the Mind*, 30–31.

22 Charles Darwin, *The Descent of Man, and Selection in Relation to Sex* (London: John Murray, 1871), 880.

23 Geoffrey Miller, "Evolution of Human Music through Sexual Selection," in Nils L. Wallin et al., ed., *The Origins of Music* (Cambridge, MA: MIT Press, 2000), 343.

24 Steven Brown, "The 'Musilanguage' Model of Music Evolution," in Nils L. Wallin et al., eds. *The Origins of Music* (Cambridge, MA: MIT Press, 2000), 272.

25 Ellen Dissanayake, *Art and Intimacy: How the Arts Began* (Seattle: University of Washington Press, 2000), 13.

26 Ellen Dissanayake, *Art and Intimacy*, 14.

27 Ellen Dissanayake, *Art and Intimacy*, 14.

28 Ellen Dissanayake, "Antecedents of the Temporal Arts in Early Mother–Infant Interaction," in Nils L. Wallin et al., eds. *The Origins of Music* (Cambridge, MA: MIT Press, 2000), 34.

29 Ellen Dissanayake, "Antecedents," 393.

30 Ellen Dissanayake, *Art and Intimacy*, 12.

CHAPTER 6

What Is Music For? Functions of Music

Introduction
Functions of Music
Conclusion

INTRODUCTION

This chapter concerns the uses that music has served over millennia. Having developed the aptitude for "music," our distant ancestors began the dynamic processes that now present an infinitely rich and complex expressive inheritance. They responded to the rhythms of their biology—bipedal locomotion, the respiratory cycle, the pumping heart—and imitated natural sounds from insects and birds to wind and water, and also the sounds of their natural emotional expressions like laughing, weeping, panting, sighing, and shouting. They may have become fascinated by echo phenomena and special timbres produced by vocalizing in caves and other resonant acoustical spaces. These became intentional and replicable utterances. Over thousands of generations, music changed in myriad ways along with all the other shared attitudes, values, goals, technologies, and practices that constitute, in sum, culture. Humans create music out of the sounds around them, and as the sounds of the human environment change, music likewise changes. As new technologies and modes of livelihood developed, the social soundscape of people's daily lives became filled with the sounds of pounding grain, churning butter, chipping flint, galloping horses; and, more recently, factories, trains, planes, and automobiles. Technological advances, from agriculture to the forging of metals, silk production, the electric turbine, audio recording, and the MP3 file, all contributed new possibilities for sound production and creativity. For millennia, each successive generation inherited from the previous generation a musical "language": a set of melodic and rhythmic patterns and ways of organizing them into songs, dances, and rituals. Either gradually or suddenly these forms of expression evolved as new purposes for music were found. Differences in environment, modes of livelihood, social structure, language, religion, and many other factors have resulted in the enormous and ever-changing diversity of musical styles and preferences among groups and individuals in the world today.

While many scholars conclude that music was of fundamental importance in the survival of our hominid ancestors, a number of cognitive psychologists and other scientists, most famously Steven Pinker of Harvard University, suggest that music really served no adaptive function. Pinker has called music "auditory cheesecake." He writes, "It just happens to tickle several important parts of the brain in a highly pleasurable way, as cheesecake tickles the palate." His controversial view is that spoken language did indeed evolve as an advantage-giving adaptation; and music developed as an accidental by-product, an "evolutionary parasite." Pinker states, "Compared with language, vision, social reasoning, and physical know-how, music could vanish from our species and the rest of our lifestyle would be virtually unchanged."[1] This chapter presents some of the ways that people use music today, as evidence that Pinker is wrong. For whatever reason or reasons, music has become an indispensable component of human social life. Music serves a number of purposes, beyond the merely hedonistic, upon which the viability of human social structures and indeed, human survival may depend.

FUNCTIONS OF MUSIC

In his classic study *The Anthropology of Music*, Alan P. Merriam (1923–1980) presented ten functions that music serves among nearly all peoples of the world. Merriam believed that there were many aspects of personal and social life that could not be performed as well, or at all, without music. Based on his research among the Basongye of the Democratic Republic of the Congo, Merriam described how essential music is for many aspects of their society, and, he believed, for all societies. Merriam wrote:

> A major funeral cannot take place among the Basongye without the presence of a professional musician and his music.... The professional musician makes his appearance after the body has been interred and performs a number of functions which he alone can contribute.... It is also the musician's role to help the mourners begin to forget the tragedy of death. Upon his appearance [during the fourth day of the funeral] ... people begin to smile and joke for the first time since the death.... The musician is a key figure in the funeral. He is similarly a key figure in other kinds of activities, including dancing, hunting, certain religious behavior, and other aspects of Basongye life as well. Indeed, without the musician, whose numerous roles have been barely touched upon here, the structure of much of Basongye behavior would be markedly changed.[2]

Merriam concludes, "There is probably no other human cultural activity which is so all-pervasive and which reaches into, shapes, and often controls so much of human behavior."[3] While music is not a "universal language"—its meanings do not cross cultural boundaries as readily as some have suggested—it is universally used within a great variety of social contexts.

Although music does not convey meaning in the same way as spoken language, it does seem to convey something, and to express aspects of our experience that language cannot. The working definition of music proposed in Chapter 1 placed a great emphasis on "purpose": it was the purposes certain sounds were used for that made them "music." This chapter delineates some of Merriam's musical purposes and adds several others. Any given musical example may serve multiple musical purposes, and this fact validates the enormous importance of music in the healthy functioning of humans both individually and in their societies. This claim cannot be made of Pinker's "Cheesecake" theory, which states that music is a superfluous indulgence.

Emotional Expression

Emotional expression is clearly one of music's most basic functions in human life. The ways musical sounds embody and convey human emotions is a complex question, and the precise nature of the relationship is not well understood. Nevertheless, the function of emotional expression was first on Merriam's list. He quotes anthropologist Edwin G. Burrows' description of the South Sea Tuamotu people in French Polynesia, among whom music is used for

> … stimulating and expressing emotion in the performers, and imparting it to the listeners. The emotion may be religious exaltation, as in the creation chant and song of the sacred red bird; grief, as in the laments; longing or passion, as in the love-songs; joy in motion; sexual excitement, and a variety of other emotions.… Underlying all of these in greater or less degree is the general function of stimulating, expressing, and sharing emotion.[4]

Ethnomusicologist David McAllester writes:

> With us a principal function of music seems to be as an aid in inducing attitude. We have songs to evoke moods of tranquility, nostalgia, sentiment, group rapport, religious feeling, party solidarity, and patriotism, to name a few. Thus we sing to put babies to sleep, to make work seem lighter, to make people buy certain kinds of breakfast foods, or to ridicule our enemies.[5]

In India, a theory of correspondence between melodic systems (*ragas*) and emotions was presented in the *Natya Shastra* nearly 2,000 years ago. Because the music described in the ancient treatise was used to accompany a drama, it was essential that the mood (*bhava*) conveyed by the music was appropriate to the situation it accompanied. A musical scale or melodic gesture was said to contain an emotional essence (*rasa*) that allowed all present, performers as well as listeners, to experience the same emotion at the same time. The treatise recognized eight basic emotions: love, joy, anger, compassion, disgust, fear, courage, and wonder, to which a ninth was later added, peace.

John Lennon (1940–1980) wrote the song "Mother" (6.1) in 1970 to describe his one-sided relationship with his parents. As the song progresses, the emotional torment expressed in his singing builds in intensity until the ending with its impassioned cry: "Mama don't go! Daddy come home!" After leaving the famous band The Beatles, John Lennon entered an intensive period of self-examination under the care of psychotherapists Arthur and Vivian Janov. Arthur Janov had written an influential book on the subject of a new form of therapy he had developed called "Primal Scream," based on the assumption that pent-up childhood trauma causes psychological pain in adults. Patients were encouraged to re-live vividly and express viscerally their suppressed childhood anguish. This technique inspired Lennon's writing of several songs in the early 1970s with his wife, artist Yoko Ono, including "Mother." Many people, whether performers or listeners, likewise find in music a cathartic outlet for relieving pain or suffering, for releasing otherwise inexpressible feelings, and for regaining psychological balance.

Portuguese *fado* ("destiny, fate") is a vocal genre whose lyrics and music embody deep feelings of longing and nostalgia (*saudade*). The genre arose in 19th-century Lisbon, although the style originated much earlier and is considered one of the world's oldest urban folk musics. For nearly two centuries, its lyrics and moods have expressed the cares and sorrows of the poor and working-class patrons of the taverns where *fado* performers sing long into the night. In her song *"Fado Loucura"* (6.2), internationally renowned *fado* singer Ana Moura (b. 1979) pours out her feelings, accompanied by the *guitarra* (twelve-string Portuguese guitar), the classical six-string guitar, and the *viola* (Portuguese bass guitar). She wears the traditional long black dress and shawl of the *fadista* (Figure 6.1).

"Fado Loucura" ("Fado Madness")

I belong to fado
The one I know
I live a sung poem
A fado that I invented
With words I can't express it
But when I let the soul sing
The soul knows how to listen
Cry, cry
Poets of my country
Trunks of the same root
The life that brought us together
And if you were not by my side
Then there would be no fado
Nor fadistas as I am

[English translation by Nat Dailey][6]

The next example shows Tito Puente's salsa band (6.3) playing at a South Bronx street party in the 1970s. This was a particularly violent time of rioting in the South Bronx. In this Latino community, Tito Puente and his band did more than anyone else to pacify the neighborhoods. Through their music, Puente and his band inspired feelings of ethnic pride, hope, and solidarity to replace feelings of anger and despair.

An announcement for an International Conference on Music and Emotion in the United Kingdom (2009) states that:

> Emotion's crucial role in musical experience has long been the object of philosophical reflection.... Contemporary work on music and emotion is happening in fields as diverse as aesthetics, psychology, sonic arts, evolutionary biology, anthropology, and neuroscience. Ironically, the subject is relatively neglected by music theory itself.[7]

Australian neuroscientist Manfred Clynes (1925–2020) carried out research into music's emotional language, as featured in a 1988 PBS Nova film titled, *What Is Music?* His research explored the relationship between physical gestures, such as those pianists use at the keyboard, and the resulting sonic "gestures" that emerge from the piano as music. On the basis of sophisticated psychological experiments on both American and Australian Aboriginal subjects, Clynes concluded that composers and musicians consciously or unconsciously use archetypal sound gestures—drooping ones for grief, bouncing ones for joy—to convert emotion into musical sound. These emotions are then transmitted through the music to the audience. Clynes' research suggested the existence of a universal emotional language that is found everywhere in music.

FIGURE 6.1 Portuguese *fado* singer, Ana Moura

However, there is evidence that unlike facial expressions such as smiles and frowns that *are* universal, much of the expressive power of music is culturally determined. In 1903, when the first European record company opened in China to produce recordings for local consumption, the foreign businessmen were baffled; the differences between the songs were too slight to detect. On one occasion, a local musician was singing and a company representative asked the Chinese go-between if it wasn't a love song. The reply was "No. He is singing about his grandmother."[8] Nevertheless, since the invention of the internet, popular songs circulating globally have crossed geographical, political, and cultural barriers that once rendered the expressive power of some musics unintelligible to outsiders. Even without understanding the language of the lyrics, people can often feel deep emotional expression from the music of a song. One does not need to understand Portuguese to weep over a *fado*.

Aesthetic Enjoyment

Merriam's second function, Aesthetic Enjoyment, refers to music when it is at the foreground of attention and appreciated for its inherent beauty or expressive power. Music fulfilling this function is not part of some entertainment activity or ritual event beyond itself. One often associates music fulfilling this function with classical traditions and concert situations where the experience is elevated above normal everyday life. In many parts of the world, some types of music have a status equivalent to art treasures found in museums or great literary texts, and these are often considered among the highest expressions of a civilization. In Japan and Korea, renowned musicians are given the status of "Living Cultural Treasures," and the music they perform, "Intangible Cultural Assets." Aesthetic experience presupposes deep listening. While aesthetic listening may occur in many settings, a concert auditorium epitomizes this function by providing a dedicated space where people gather specifically for the purpose of making and listening to music.

The following examples demonstrate a range of aesthetic musical experiences from a variety of cultures. In each case, the term "aesthetic" is applied because the music is meant to be savored like a fine wine, and enjoyed for its expressive beauty.

The first example is from a documentary film about French musician Nadia Boulanger (6.4) (1887–1979), known as the greatest composition teacher of the 20th century (Figure 6.2). In the first segment she comments on the mystery of musical "masterpieces." Certain compositions seem to have the uncanny power to move a listener to tears or raptures, or to provide the experience of beauty usually associated with the natural world: sunrises and seascapes, for instance. But exactly where that power resides, she cannot say. Then, in the documentary she and her students listen with profound attention to just such a masterpiece: an art song by the 19th-century German composer Johannes Brahms. It is precisely this kind of deep listening that characterizes the aesthetic experience,

The Japanese art song *"Kyo no shiki"* (6.5) ("Four Seasons of Kyoto") is sung and played on the *shamisen* (three-string plucked lute) by Satoyuki, accompanying a graceful dance performance of Naosuzu. Both artists are *geishas* (professional female entertainers) of the Kamishichiken district in northern Kyoto. In this performance, music and dance together constitute the aesthetic experience, rather than music alone. *Geishas* have traditionally

FIGURE 6.2 French composition teacher Nadia Boulanger in 1925

performed such songs and dances for a clientele of wealthy businessmen, merchants, and government officials. At exclusive tea houses and private clubs, men enjoy the company and the artistry of these highly educated professional female companions."

Bi Kidude (ca. 1910–2013) of Zanzibar (see Map 10.1) was perhaps the oldest performer in the world when she sang at the annual *Les Orientales Festival* in France in 2004 at the age of 94. She was accompanied by the "Culture Musical Club" *taarab* orchestra, founded in 1958. Since at least the 1920s, Bi Kidude had been the leading exponent of Zanzibari *taarab*, a genre whose name means "ecstasy" in Arabic. The term highlights the belief, held throughout the Middle East and East Africa, that this music is a source of intense delight bordering on "intoxication." Bi Kidude's role model and teacher was Siti binti Saad (1880– 1950), called "The Mother of *Taarab*" and one of the most popular recording artists of the early 20th century. While the average recording artist in the first decades of the commercial recording industry sold around 900 discs through their lifetime, Siti binti Saad sold more than 72,000 in 1931 alone. For a hundred years, these two women led the otherwise male-dominated field of *taarab*. Indeed, Bi Kidude (6.6) was known as "The Queen of *Taarab*." Music festivals like *Les Orientales* are important venues for experiencing music aesthetically (Figure 6.3).

In each of these examples, music is intended to serve as the center of attention for the listeners. The performers are all highly trained professionals whose artistry is prized by their

FIGURE 6.3 Bi Kidude performs at the Go Down Arts Center, Nairobi, Kenya, in 2006

respective societies. Where Aesthetic Enjoyment ends and the next function, Entertainment, begins is unclear. One can certainly attend a symphony concert to be entertained, and pay attention to music at an entertainment venue for its aesthetic appeal.

Entertainment

Almost as soon as children learn to walk and talk, they learn to dance and sing, "for the fun of it." Many people engage in music making and listening as a way of passing the time: students in their dorm rooms listening to hip-hop while doing their homework, girl scouts singing around a campfire, and the prisoner in the cell block blowing on a harmonica. In Tibet, yak herders spend long hours alone on the high plateau tending their animals and singing their songs to alleviate boredom and solitude. Children sing as they skip rope, commuters tap out rhythms on the steering wheels of their cars. Singer-songwriter Jimmy Buffet (b. 1946) might feel embarrassed if his song, "Cheeseburgers in Paradise" was categorized as "art" or "aesthetic expression." He might simply say that his music is supposed to be fun, and he hopes that people will dance to it.

Friends get together for evenings of communal music making in string bands, drum circles, a cappella groups, etc. In Kalista, a suburb of Melbourne, Australia, the Kalulu Ukulele Band (6.7) meets twice a month in a community hall for music and socializing. Their name, Kalulu, stands for Kooky And Luscious Ukulele Lovers United. All members of this group have taken up ukulele playing for their own enjoyment as amateurs. The word "amateur" derives from the Latin word *amare* meaning "to love," implying that amateurs do what they do solely for the love of it. Members of this group range from rank beginners to virtuosos. Ethnomusicologist Ter Ellingson writes: "Music enhances, intensifies, and … transforms almost any experience into something felt not only as different but also as somehow better."[9]

Music has an entertainment function in all societies. In the Republic of Georgia in the Western Caucasus, unaccompanied polyphonic singing (6.8) in the Georgian language is a popular pastime that dates back at least to the 9th century. The tradition is practiced throughout the country by families gathered around a dining table, farmers tending grape vines, and even young men "hanging out" on a street corner. All manner of everyday life is accompanied by polyphonic singing. The tradition has influenced the liturgical singing of the Georgian Orthodox Church to the extent that secular and sacred styles of song have become interchangeable. A standard quartet such as that in the video consists of two bass voices overlapping each other to sustain a continuous drone, while two lead singers exchange highly ornamented, partially improvised melodic lines. This ancient expression of Georgian culture was suppressed during the period of Soviet occupation (1921–1991) and practiced in secret, only to be revived following the fall of the Soviet bloc. At present, the popular practice of polyphonic singing in Georgia, according to UNESCO, is threatened by "the increasing success of pop music."[10]

Music as entertainment has become a multi-billion-dollar global industry supported by transnational corporations and digital media streaming services. Particularly with the development of sound recording and broadcast technologies in the early 20th century, music became a commodity to be bought, sold, and passively consumed. Many people now spend their entire days accompanied by a musical soundtrack while they drive, walk, exercise, work, shop, eat, and ride in elevators. They say that they simply cannot live without music.

Communication

"Music is not a universal language,"[11] as noted above. Music is used universally as a mode of communication, although it is within shared social contexts that performers and listeners shape and interpret its meanings. Music is often used by lovers to communicate their intimate messages of courtship. Music provides a specialized format for worshipers to offer up their prayers and devotions. In a more practical vein, advertising jingles communicate the messages of the marketplace. West African drumming has been used for many generations as a way of conveying messages over long distances. Drum languages imitate the sounds and intonations of spoken language using special drumming techniques. In the next video, tradition meets modernity among a group of master drummers in Nigeria. One member tries out an American-produced Remo talking drum (6.9), the body of which is made not of traditional wood but state-of-the-art "advanced acousticon," and the drumhead is made of Power-max Ultra White material. In syncretic religions of the New World that blend West African beliefs and Roman Catholicism, such as **Vodun** in Haiti and **Candomblé** in Brazil, worshipers play drum rhythms through which they communicate directly with African deities, inviting them to participate in rituals of celebration and healing. In Suriname, playwright Henk Tjon demonstrates the talking drum *apenti* (6.10). This drum "speaks" in the ceremonial Kumanti language, a ritual language of the Akan people of Ghana that was brought to the New World on slave ships more than 400 years ago. At the end of the video, a Saramaccan drummer uses an *apenti* drum to invite the African deities of his ancestors to participate in a ritual. The Saramaccan Maroons are descendants of slaves who escaped colonial plantation labor in the 17th and 18th centuries and re-established African village life deep in the Amazon rainforest of South America.

In some cases, music itself, without text or gesture, functions as a kind of language with specific, linguistic meanings. Among the Hmong in Laos, when a young man hopes to arrange a tryst with a young woman, he plays a bamboo jaw harp outside the walls of her bedroom. She knows immediately what the sound signifies! The soldier called to charge or retreat by a particular bugle melody relies similarly on its communicative function. While the lover and the soldier count on the power of music to convey important information, these codes of communication must be learned.

Music often provides a kind of envelope for lyrics, which communicate directly through words. When the melodies are played without the lyrics, the listeners can often recall them and understand the meaning by association. Yet, music functions as more than simply an envelope or delivery system. It adds a significant dimension, whereby a trite message like "a kiss is just a kiss, a sigh is just a sigh," when *sung*, becomes a sincere, heartfelt communication. This song sung by Dooley Wilson, "As Time Goes By" (6.11), comes from the movie *Casablanca* (1942).

Symbolic Representation

Music functions in all societies as a symbolic representation of objects, ideas, beliefs, and behaviors. Musicologist Christopher Small writes that music is *fundamentally* a symbolic activity wherein

> the act of musicking establishes in the place where it is happening a set of relationships, and it is in those relationships that the meaning of the act lies … relationships between

person and person, between individual and society, between humanity and the natural world and even perhaps the supernatural world. These are important matters, perhaps the most important in human life, and … we learn about [and celebrate these relationships] through musicking.[12]

Musical instruments represent nations, like the Irish harp and the Russian balalaika (Figure 6.4). Music symbolizes time periods and locales, as movie producers well know when they use bagpipes to accompany the title credits for a film set in Scotland, for example. One way that music symbolizes is through imitation or suggestion. Trumpet fanfares and drum cadences symbolically represent military life because their sounds are drawn directly *from* military life. In symphonic **program music**, composers attempt to depict non-musical situations, objects, or states of being, as in Debussy's *La Mer*, a musical portrait of the sea. *"Sai Ma"* ("Horse Race") (6.12) by Huang Haihuai is a popular piece for the Chinese two string fiddle *erhu* that evokes the excitement of a galloping stallion. Many cases of this kind of overt representation could be cited, yet there is some doubt whether what is being symbolized can be correctly identified without descriptive titles.

Another way that music symbolizes is through learned association. Musical instruments, genres, melodies, and other elements may be used to symbolize non-musical referents by juxtaposition or intentional pairing. For instance, a scrap of melody may symbolize a commercial product like a brand of coffee when the two are repeatedly joined in advertisements. In Rwanda, the drum is the symbol of political power, since ceremonial drummers always accompanied the king whenever he appeared before his people. Writing in the 1940s about

FIGURE 6.4 Men playing balalaikas of two sizes at a "City Day" parade in Staraja, Russia

music used in radio dramas, George Davis noted that, "serialized Radio-drama [composers] create musical themes by which characters will be identified.... These themes will announce the characters, suggest their influence, etc."[13] From the 1930s through the 1950s, a march from Gioachino Rossini's *William Tell Overture* (1829) was used as the theme music for the popular North American radio series and television show *The Lone Ranger* (6.13). For those who listened to and watched the program, Rossini's music was forever associated with the masked Texas ranger and his Native American friend, Tonto.

For many adults, nursery rhymes symbolize days of childhood. Similarly, songs of bygone years featured on radio stations and online music channels, geared toward the nostalgia of older listeners, symbolize youth and the days of courtship. For immigrant communities, music from the mother country serves as a powerful symbol of a distant homeland. The Caribbean island of Trinidad has a large population of East Indian descent. For them, *tassa* drumming (6.14) represents India, their ancestral home and place where this form of drumming originated. It is also a popular form of cultural expression that is associated with weddings and other festive occasions. *Tassa* drumming is symbolic both of the occasion and of the participants' roots in the traditions of their ancestors. Calendrical and important life-cycle events, festival days, and seasons are symbolized throughout the world by special musical styles and repertoires.

Physical Response

Music can have a profound effect on human physiology. The pace of music and its other features and associations may have a sedative or stimulative effect on the listener. Soft, gentle music relaxes patients in dentist chairs and lulls babies to sleep (6.15), while pep bands rouse the fans at basketball games. Music is used to pump up athletes before the big game, or whip warriors into an adrenaline frenzy before battle. American GIs on patrol in Iraq listened to heavy metal with its double-pedal bass drums and tremolo-style guitars. Musicologist Jonathan Pieslak notes that this is a good way to prepare mentally for a mission because it "sounds considerably like the consistent discharge of bullets fired from an automatic gun."[14] Rhythm patterns coordinate the steps of social dancing, from the chaste minuet to the highly erotic tango. Courtly dances in 17th-century France, like the gavotte, bourrée, and minuet (Figure 6.5), were defined by and inextricably linked to patterns of choreography performed by Lords and Ladies under the watchful eye of Louis XIV, The Sun King. The strong electric beats and thumping bass of hip-hop has inspired the erotic movements of "twerking" at dance parties since its origin in New Orleans in the 1980s.

At a New Orleans jazz funeral parade (6.16), on the other hand, the slow somber cadence accompanying the mourners to the gravesite changes at a certain point to lively jazz rhythms. Mourners now become dancers, joyfully celebrating the life of the deceased and their faith in salvation. For Charles Keil, the human response to rhythm is a mystery worth investigating. He proposed a "joyous science of groovology" with the central research question: "What do we [musicians] have to do with *our* bodies playing these instruments and singing in order to get *their* bodies [the folks in the crowd] moving, bobbing their heads, snapping their fingers, up from their tables and dancing?"[15] This mystery raises two further questions: How do musicians get the music inside the people and the people inside the music? And, how does musicking bring people together and inspire feelings of transcendence and community?

FIGURE 6.5 The minuet

Health and Healing

Music is widely used in medicine and in therapeutic situations. The Louis Armstrong Center for Music and Medicine at Mount Sinai Beth Israel Hospital in New York City does pioneering work in the therapeutic implications of music. Through both research and clinical practice, physicians and music therapists work together developing effective healing strategies. In this video, Dr. Joanne Loewy discusses the history of music therapy (6.17) as a branch of medicine and shows some applications in a modern hospital setting.

Traditional healers around the world have used music in a variety of ways to restore and maintain health and wellbeing. One of the most dramatic forms of traditional healing comes from the shamanic practices of Mongolia in North Central Asia. Indeed, the word *"shaman"* derives from the Mongolian language. The term refers to an individual who has the ability to communicate with the world of spirits and the unseen, often through a trance experience. In Mongolia, and Siberia to the north, shamanic healers, both male and female, specialize in curing diseases that have spiritual causes. In order to carry out healings, the shaman crosses the threshold between the world of the living (that of the patient) and the realm of various kinds of spirits, both beneficent and malevolent. While in a state of trance, the shaman encounters the spirits causing the patient's illness, and through various incantations and charms, frees the patient of the offending spirit's influence. The shaman puts on a special robe, headgear, and boots in order to enter the spirit world. However, of greatest importance to a successful trance is the shaman's drum. The Mongolian shamaness (6.18), shown in the video, enters and sustains her trance by rhythmically beating her drum. She experiences the drum as a horse and the drumstick as a whip; and the trance is a journey taken by flying horse to the world of spirits (Figure 6.6).

In rural communities of the northeastern Isan region of Thailand, shamans perform traditional healing rituals to the accompaniment of an indigenous bamboo mouth organ. The *khaen* (mouth organ) player produces continuous melody, which is possible because the

FIGURE 6.6 Shaman with frame drum, Tsaaten village, Mongolia

instrument makes sound during both exhalation and inhalation. In the Thai *Phi Faa* healing ritual, the *khaen*'s unbroken melodies serve to bridge the realms of spirits and humans, and are thus essential in helping the shamanic healer, typically a woman, enter and maintain a state of trance. The **Phi Faa** **ritual** is often performed for patients recovering from a serious illness. The ritual begins with an opening ceremony in which the shaman becomes possessed and is then called *Mor Lam*. She invites the heavenly spirit *Phi Faa* to enter her body. The *Mor Lam* then dances as she diagnoses the illness and its cause. She presents successive shamanic songs and dances to call the patient's guardian spirit, placate the spirit, heal the patient's ailments, and instruct both the patient and relatives on their proper conduct regarding the illness. The continuous *khaen* music, "harmonizes the patient's bodily systems back in proper function ... [and] also helps ease the pain and refresh the mind of the patient."[16] The shaman makes up the song verses during the ritual and varies them according to the patient's illness. The style of *Mor Lam* songs also differs from one shaman to another, and from one region of Isan to another. The linked video documents several sequences from a *Phi Faa* ritual (6.19) in Baan Nong Keng village, Isan, in 2009. Following the initial invitation to the spirit *Phi Faa*, the ritual participants decorate a sacrificial altar that they dance around through the night. The morning brings final prayers as the spirit leaves and the *khaen* player takes a rest. The gathering concludes with a *Baasii* ritual, held to propitiate guardian spirits with offerings of food, drink, and money. To ensure that the guardian spirits do not leave the human souls they protect, the shaman symbolically binds them, tying string to the wrists of ritual participants. The *khaen* playing resumes and the participants dance.

Music has also served as a vehicle for promoting public health by providing useful information on avoiding and preventing illness. In his 2006 study *Singing for Life: HIV/AIDS and Music in Uganda*, ethnomusicologist Gregory Barz writes that creative artists and musicians spread the message of how the AIDS epidemic and its ravages in Central Africa could be halted.[17] Healthcare workers and government officials failed to get this message across, and it was only through the power of musicians and their songs that behaviors were modified and infection rates reduced. Because music and dance play such a central role in the everyday lives of Ugandans, indeed of sub-Saharan Africans in general, music could successfully deliver this life-saving message.

More recently, in response to the worldwide COVID-19 pandemic, UNICEF (United Nations International Children's Emergency Relief Fund) produced a powerful "infomercial" featuring World Music superstar Angelique Kidjo of Benin. Kidjo re-worked her hit song "*Pata Pata*" ("Touch Touch"), originally composed and sung by South African singer Miriam Makeba, as "*No Pata Pata*," to encourage social distancing and personal hygiene. The infomercial video features people from all over the world, mainly children, dancing to her song while also observing hand washing and social distancing, thus staying safe and avoiding the virus' devastating consequences. This public service video was uploaded to YouTube in 2020, the year of the outbreak.[18]

Enhancement of Religious Rituals

In some religious traditions around the world the presence of music is controversial. However, nearly all religions have some form of sacred vocalization or instrumental music. Through collective music making, people validate shared belief systems and rituals. The mere presence of appropriate music at a sacred event makes that event special by separating it from ordinary time. When people at such an event participate together in singing, dancing, clapping, or simply listening attentively, they are mutually affirming their beliefs and values, while creating an atmosphere of devotion and sanctity.

One of the earliest surviving forms of Christian chant has roots in the Eastern Roman Empire. At the Kimisis Theotokou Greek Orthodox Church in Brooklyn, New York, the male choir performs at the altar a hymn composed in the 9th century by Saint Kassia (ca. 805–ca. 865). She is one of only two Byzantine women whose literary and liturgical works are known to have survived to the present. Some of the male choir (6.20) singers participate by intoning a drone on the first note of the scale. Being present at this traditional performance reaffirms for the congregation the reality of their faith, in which they experience the performance together as "an entering into the reality of the Kingdom of God, an ascent to an invisible reality."[19]

The South Indian *nadaswaram* (Figure 6.7) is played by ritual musician-specialists at weddings and temple festivals, usually accompanied by drums (*tavil*). Guest *nadaswaram* (6.21) players Kasim and Babu Kalaimamani from Chennai were invited to the Sri Venkateswara

FIGURE 6.7 South Indian *nadaswaram*

Temple in Cary, North Carolina in 2014. There they participated in the 5th Annual *Brahmotsavam*, a cleansing ceremony in honor of the Hindu God of Creation, Brahma. The festival also honors the wedding of the temple's presiding deity, Venkateswara (Vishnu) to his two consorts, Padmavathi and Goda Devi. The dancing priests in the video enact the exchange of flower garlands between the deities. As the priests dance, the worshipers sing a joyful ***bhajan*** (Hindu hymn).

> Flower garland put on his neck
> Kothai exchanged garland with him
> On him who is the spotless Ranga,
> The winsome lady,
> With her flower-like hands
> With love filling her heart

[English translation by Ravi Mulukutla]

Another Hindu ritual, in the small South American country of Suriname, includes the singing of *bhajans* (6.22). The worshipers are the descendants of indentured servants brought from India to replace newly emancipated African slaves on the sugar plantations. Unlike a comparable Hindu ritual in the Indian homeland, the worshippers in Suriname sit in pews, like in a Protestant Sunday service, rather than on the floor as would be typical in India. In the early 20th century, Protestant missionaries converted many of the Hindu workers to

Christianity. Hindu missionaries from India later in the century converted the Christians back to Hinduism. This re-conversion accounts for the unusual hybrid worship practice. Throughout the ritual, as women offer ceremonial fire and water to the deities and the seated priest, there is continuous singing of *bhajans* by the standing congregants, accompanied by harmonium and *dholak* drum.

Cohesion of Social Groups

"Music … provides a rallying point around which the members of society gather to engage in activities which require the cooperation and coordination of the group," according to Alan Merriam.[20] After the terrorist attacks of September 11th, 2001, songs like "God Bless America" became anthems that brought Americans together in an unprecedented expression of unity. Ethnomusicologist Kwabena Nketia wrote,

> For the Yoruba in Accra, performances of Yoruba music … bring both the satisfaction of participating in something familiar and the assurance of belonging to a group sharing similar values, similar ways of life, a group maintaining similar art forms. Music thus brings a renewal of tribal solidarity.[21]

Cultural anthropologist Victor Turner (1920–1983) coined the term "*communitas*" to describe the intense experience of merging one's individual identity with a group's identity during festivals, religious meetings, political rallies, and rock concerts. A live performance by the Madagascan a cappella trio *Salala* provides a vivid example of music contributing to *communitas*. The three male singers were all members of the Antandroy ethnic group from Madagascar's dry and impoverished south (see Map 9.3). The Antandroy faced prejudice from the peoples of the more developed north, and when they moved to the cities to escape the poverty of their region, they took jobs at the very bottom of the economic ladder, like night watchman and rickshaw driver. The vocal trio *Salala*, including their bass vocalist Sengemanana who died in 2001, became spokespersons for their ethnic group, drawing on traditional Antandroy songs for their material. In 1998 they released a CD self-titled *Salala*, from which the song "*Lanitra Manga Manga*" (6.23) ("Blue, Blue Sky") became a national hit broadcast frequently over the radio. A video of their 2005 live performance (6.24) in a huge outdoor soccer stadium in the capital Antananarivo reveals the extraordinary power of a song to unite people in a shared experience of deep emotion. Salala begins to sing the song "*Lanitra Manga Manga*" to enormous applause, and the entire audience then spontaneously unites in singing the lyrics, at which point the trio drops out. The song continues in a remarkable call and response between Salala and their fans, joining everyone present in this intense, joyful music making.

> Blue, blue sky
> Hidden by the clouds
> Is home for the saints
> Who doesn't wanna be there, my friend?
> Quarrels you had before
> Don't do it anymore
> The tree has lost some leaves,

But you have to grow the rest, my friend
You and I Are only pilgrims
Nobody's gonna stay here
So let's forgive each other, my friend
If you ever feel blue
Because some relatives left you
They're just a bit ahead
And we're gonna be too there, my friend
The blue sky Hidden by the clouds
Is home for the saints
Who doesn't wanna be there, my friend?

[English translation by Richard Nwamba]

Music also plays a role as a catalyst for social change, contributing to dis-continuity and in-stability. Because musical styles are so flexible and able to generate new meanings and associations rapidly, music frequently serves as a harbinger for new and revolutionary value systems, fashions, and changes in social mores. For instance, the 1960s in North America and Europe was a period in which young people sought to distinguish themselves from their parents' generation by growing their hair long, rejecting the materialistic values they attributed to their societies, and taking part in massive street protests against war and social injustice. The popular musicians of the time—The Beatles, Bob Dylan, Jimi Hendrix, the Grateful Dead—were leaders of this social revolution.

When conformity to officially sanctioned norms becomes odious or repressive, songs of protest provide a means of publicly expressing opposition. Collective singing of "We Shall Overcome," for example, solidified the group cohesiveness of civil rights activists during the Selma to Montgomery, Alabama, march for voting rights in March 1965. In situations of strict repression and censorship, song is often the only form of protest allowed. Indeed, musicians are often on the front lines of civil strife and silenced by empowered and armed authorities. From "Yankee Doodle" during the American Revolution to "The Patriot Game" during Ireland's struggle against British rule in the mid-20th century, these songs inspire people with the courage to act collectively in the interest of their side. The song "The Patriot Game" (6.25), performed by Liam Clancy (1935–2009), tells the story of Fergal O'Hanlon, an Irish Republican Army volunteer who was killed at the age of twenty while taking part in a raid on British police barracks on January 1, 1957. The composer of the song, Dominic Behan, imagines the thoughts of the young revolutionary as he lies dying of bullet wounds.

In many parts of the world, music exerts its disruptive power, affecting ways of life that had previously continued for millennia. Modern communication technologies have carried popular musical forms from urban centers to formerly isolated rural areas. Popular music has enticed the children of farmers and herders away from the agrarian countryside to the slums and shanty towns surrounding great megacities like Mumbai, Nairobi, and Rio de Janeiro, seeking, often in vain, a better life.

Enculturation and Education

Enculturation is the process by which children within a society learn the rules of membership: the language, values, behaviors, and the modes of livelihood. The oil painting *The Banjo*

Lesson (1893), by African American artist Henry O. Tanner, vividly captures the passing on of music and musical skills from one generation to the next; and by extension, a way of life and an inherited sense of self (Figure 6.8).

Music is transmitted orally from one generation to the next, from parent to child and from teacher to student. In Trinidad, acclaimed singer-songwriter Rakesh Yankarran teaches his daughter (6.26) to sing popular songs. After listening to her father repeat the song many times, the young girl has learned the words and the melody, and as seen in the video, proudly sings them back to him, accompanied by his harmonium playing. Similarly, Alim Qasimov, one of Azerbaijan's foremost singers of traditional *mugam* music, taught this vocal art to his daughter Fargana, and she now joins him on the international concert stage. Together, they pass on their songs to Fargana's daughter Fatima, continuing this family tradition. Believing in the importance of children learning songs by heart and of developing their talent at a young age, Alim gives his granddaughter the opportunity to perform, preparing her for a music career of her own one day. In the linked video, Fatima sings in a house concert (6.27) accompanied by her grandfather's musicians.

In Korea, the art of musical storytelling (*pansori*) has been passed down through the generations from teacher to student since the 1700s. In 1993, *pansori* became the subject of a

FIGURE 6.8 The *Banjo Lesson* (1893), Henry O. Tanner (1859–1937)

South Korean feature film, *Sopyonje*. A scene from the film shows a professional storyteller (*kwangdae*) teaching his stepson a basic twelve-beat drum pattern (6.28), *choongmoli*, so the boy can accompany his sister in storytelling performances. This scene illustrates how the art of *pansori* was passed on from one generation to the next. The *kwangdae*'s adopted son has no talent for singing. He is therefore learning to be a drummer. The boy, facing his father and following his instructions, plays the rhythmic pattern, calling out the stroke names as he goes. Each stroke on the barrel drum (*buk*) is designated by an onomatopoeic syllable. His sister has clear vocal talent and will inherit the *kwangdae*'s vocal art.

In various parts of sub-Saharan Africa, educational systems struggle to teach students the values and lifeways of their local communities. These systems strive to prepare children for a fast-approaching future in which European and American technologies are ubiquitous. As a result, foreign idioms have become more familiar to young people than their own native cultures. To further complicate the African situation, educational systems that were put in place during the colonial period by missionaries, served the interests of colonizing bureaucracies and not the needs of local communities. Few areas have been more negatively affected by these factors than music education. Between a colonial past and an unknown technological future that threatens to make the traditional ways irrelevant, indigenous scholars attempt to find a way to "Africanize" the classroom. Dr. Benon Kigozi, a music education professor from Uganda writes: "Africanisation is regarded as a regeneration of what was good and respected in the African culture, a rejection of subservience to foreign dominance and the assertion of the interests and rights of the African."[22] Prior to the arrival of European missionaries in the late 19th century, indigenous education of the young was guided by a principle known in Uganda as *okugunjala*, literally, "upbringing." The raising of children into mature, responsible adults prepared to play meaningful roles within their communities was the responsibility of the entire society. The enculturation process included acquisition of the heritage of the ancestors, "manifested in … music, poetry, art, drama, dance and stories."[23] Children learned by observation and imitation of their elders. Peers helped peers master the various art forms that enabled full participation in social and religious life. However, this lived, informal, communal process of *okugunjala* has run counter to the formal test-driven, teacher-centered, competitive "colonial model" already in place.

In many sub-Saharan African music classrooms, this colonial model for music study persists. It is based on Western music notation and European methods and repertoires, despite the fact that this music bears little resemblance to the musical experiences encountered by children in their home communities. In the festivals and rituals of African communal life, the musical arts are a multimedia conglomeration of artforms that cannot be comfortably separated. Ethnomusicologist Dr. Jean Ngoya Kidula, originally from Kenya, describes the indigenous musical arts as including "sound (vocal and otherwise), text (verbal and non-verbal), costume (including masks), décor, body movement, drama and related theatrical displays and material artefacts (including music instruments)."[24] Traditionally, children learned to participate through actively engaging in musical events, taking larger and more complex social roles as they grew and learned the ways of adulthood. Dr. Ifeoluwa A. O. Olorunsogo of Nigeria makes the simple suggestion, which would in fact be revolutionary, to incorporate, "indigenous songs into the elementary school system as a vehicle to transmit cultural values, oral history, epic poems, African belief systems and philosophy. Through this, children can be instructed, entertained and enlightened about the peculiar attributes of African cultures."[25]

A short documentary on a music school in Kirina (6.29), Mali, shows how music and dance traditions are passed on to children in the 21st century. The school is funded by the American "Playing for Change" Foundation. Kirina, a village just outside Bamako, Mali's capital, has a 700-year history of musician families living there. The school serves approximately 200 students and offers lessons in *kora*, *djembe*, *balafon* (West African xylophone), as well as in dance. Through the study of music, the children learn about their culture, society, and history, and keep alive the cultural traditions of their families and ancestors.

CONCLUSION

Music is involved in the most important circumstances in the lives of individuals and communities. It is integral to the *personal* realms of courtship and mating, child rearing and education, work and leisure, celebration and mourning; it marks holidays and can be heard *publicly* in coronations and inaugurations, sporting events, wartime muster, protest and rebellion. As demonstrated in Chapter 6, music has the power to express emotion; to enthrall us with beautiful sounds, rhythmic grooves, and sonic forms; to entertain us and communicate in ways that words cannot; to symbolize abstract concepts; to move us physically and affect us neurologically; to heal us in body and mind; to enhance sacred rituals; to bind us together into cohesive social groups; and to pass the values and ways of life on to the next generations. The remaining Parts III-V examine the near universal roles music plays in three human domains: the expression of identity, the observation of religious traditions, and various aspects of social life. Some of the examples introduced in the first six chapters of the textbook return in these later parts as detailed case studies.

KEY TERMS AND CONCEPTS

Amateur

Archetypal Sound Gestures

Bhajan

Biological Evolution vs Cultural and Social Evolution

Communitas

Fado

Function of Aesthetic Enjoyment

Function of Cohesion of Social Groups

Function of Communication

Function of Emotional Expression

Function of Enculturation and Education

Function of Enhancement of Religious Rituals

Function of Entertainment

Function of Health and Healing

Function of Physical Response

Function of Symbolic Representation

Manfred Clynes

Music as Evolutionary Parasite

Music Therapy

Natya Shastra

Pinker's "Cheesecake"

Playing for Change

Taarab

THINKING ABOUT MUSIC

1 Do you agree with Pinker's "Cheesecake" theory? Why or why not?
2 How would you explain the difference between the function of Aesthetic Enjoyment and the function of Entertainment? Think of music that you enjoy. Is there a difference in the way you experience it if you allow it to serve one or the other function, or both simultaneously?
3 Consider these four situations in which music symbolizes something: in advertising, in education, in sports, and in video games. Can you think of a specific example of each? What is the relationship between the music and what it symbolizes?
4 What kinds of music affect you physically? What music pumps you up? Chills you out? Puts you to sleep? Gets your toes tapping?
5 Watch again the Madagascan band Salala performing in front of the crowds in the Antananarivo soccer stadium. What functions of music is the song "Lanitra Manga Manga" serving?
6 Watch again Video 6.27 of the granddaughter of the great Azeri singer Alim Qasimov performing at a house party in Azerbaijan. In what ways is music functioning in this social gathering?
7 Define Victor Turner's concept of *communitas*. In what ways does music bring people together? In what ways does music pull people apart?

NOTES

1 Steven Pinker, *How the Mind Works* (New York: W. W. Norton, 1997), 528.
2 Alan P. Merriam, *The Anthropology of Music* (Evanston, IL: Northwestern University Press, 1964), 215–216.
3 Alan P. Merriam, *Anthropology of Music*, 218.
4 Alan P. Merriam, *Anthropology of Music*, 218.
5 David P. McAllester, "The Role of Music in Apache Culture" (1960), quoted in Merriam, *Anthropology of Music*, 220.
6 English translation of Ana Moura's "Loucura" song lyrics by Nat Dailey, https://lyricstranslate.com/en/loucura-madness.html-1.
7 International Conference on Music and Emotion, August 31–September 3, 2009, Durham University Music Department, UK, https://www.dur.ac.uk/ias/events/events_listings/?eventno=5756.
8 Richard C. Kraus, *Pianos and Politics in China* (New York: Oxford University Press, 1989), 35.
9 Ter Ellingson, "Music and Religion," in *The Encyclopedia of Religion*, ed. Mircea Eliade (New York: Macmillan, 1987), 168.
10 Alan P. Merriam, *Anthropology of Music*, 223.

11 "Georgian Polyphonic Singing," UNESCO Intangible Cultural Heritage website https://ich.unesco.org/en/RL/georgian-polyphonic-singing-00008.

12 Christopher Small, *Musicking: The Meanings of Performing and Listening* (Middletown, CT: Wesleyan University Press, 1998), 13.

13 George Davis, "Music-Cueing for Radio-Drama" (1947), quoted in Merriam, *Anthropology of Music*, 240.

14 Jonathan Pieslak, *Sound Targets: American Soldiers and Music in the Iraq War* (Bloomington: Indiana University Press, 2009), 150

15 Charles Keil, "Groovology and the Magic of Other People's Music," (2010), 1, www.musicgrooves.org/articles/GroovologyAndMagic.pdf.

16 Warawut Roengbuthra and Bussakorn Sumrongthong, "Phi Faa Ritual Music of the Northeastern Part of Thailand," *Voices: A World Form for Music Therapy* (2006), https://voices.no/index.php/voices/article/view/1694/1454.

17 Greg Barz, *Singing for Life: HIV/AIDS and Music in Uganda* (New York: Routledge, 2006).

18 "Pata pata by Angelique Kidjo" UNESCO public service video, https://www.youtube.com/watch?v=0xprciOSg4c.\.

19 "Byzantine Chant," accessed March 28, 2014, http://www.liturgica.com/html/Byzantine_Chant.jsp (website no longer available).

20 Alan P. Merriam, *Anthropology of Music*, 227.

21 J. H. Kwabena Nketia, "Yoruba Musicians in Accra," *Odu* 6 (1958), 43, quoted in Merriam, *Anthropology of Music*, 226.

22 Benon Kigozi, "Africanising the Music Classroom Through Technology," in *Music Education in Africa: Concept, Process, and Practice*, ed. Emily Achieng Akuno (New York: Routledge, 2019), 315.

23 Benon Kigozi, "Africanising the Music Classroom," 316.

24 Jean Ngoya Kidula, "Music and Musicking: Continental Africa's Junctures in Learning, Teaching and Research," in *Music Education in Africa*, 8.

25 Ifeoluwa A. O. Olorunsogo, "Incorporating Indigenous Songs into the Elementary School System in Nigeria," in *Music Education in Africa*, 164.

PART III

Music and Identity

INTRODUCTION

This part examines how music operates in shaping, exploring, and expressing identity. The term identity refers to the sum of those inherited and acquired factors that make up who we are. These factors include homeland, age, gender, profession, beliefs, and values. It is also those distinguishing characteristics by which one knows others, both as individuals and as members of groups. Between the poles of one's experience as an autonomous and unique individual and as a member of groups that temper individuality, one makes choices and compromises.

When you consider your own identity—how you understand yourself and project yourself to the world—imagine your reflection in many differently angled mirrors. In your family you are a brother or sister to your siblings, son or daughter to your parents, grandson or granddaughter to your grandparents. Each of these relationships defines different aspects of your personality. In different situations you may consider a primary aspect of your identity to be your gender, your nationality, your religion, your ethnicity or race, your generation or age group. In relation to the wider world, you are an American or member of another nationality, in which case you are, perhaps, an immigrant. You are marked by the region you grew up in: a Northerner, a Southerner, etc. You hold affiliations to political parties, to educational institutions, to social, civic, and religious organizations. Some aspects of your identity are yours by birth and are unchangeable; others you choose and can change at will. You are enmeshed in a web of relationships that gives your life the structure, meaning, and sense of belonging that constitute your identity. Many aspects of your identity you express by making or listening to the music that is associated with your region, religion, nationality, generation, etc. Like the clothes you wear, your playlists and the songs you sing present to others a sense of who you are. Music often serves as a rallying point and marker for subcultures to which you may belong. Popular music genres such as hip-hop, metal, emo, techno, alternative, R&B, and

FIGURE 7.0 Everyone dances; the music specialist becomes the drummer: Tsonga (Shangaan) women, South Africa

country bring together people who share common values. Through music, people project and receive impressions of identity at the level of feelings.

An aspect of identity may be the possession of exceptional musical ability, and some individuals self-identify as "musicians." They may come from "musical families." This raises the question of whether specialized aptitude rests on genetic inheritance or on musical training in early childhood, or both. In the social and ritual life of the Venda of southern Africa, for example, it is expected that everyone will participate in dancing, while the more accomplished musicians, by a combination of natural ability and applied effort, become drummers. Ethnomusicologist John Blacking writes, "The Venda may not consider the possibility of unmusical human beings, but they recognize that some people perform better than others." Why some people and not others become "musicians" is a combination of factors:

> The Venda may suggest that exceptional musical ability is biologically inherited, but in practice they recognize that social factors play the most important part in realizing or suppressing it. For instance, a boy of noble birth might show great talent, but as he grows up he will be expected to abandon regular musical performance for the more serious (for him) business of governing…. Conversely, a girl of noble birth has every encouragement to develop her musical capacities, so that as a woman she can play an active role in supervising the girls' initiation schools which are held in the homes of rulers.[1]

Chapters 7–9 examine in detail three manifestations of identity that illuminate how music functions in human life: Music and Group Identity; Music and Hybrid Identity; and Music and Oppositional Identity (Figure 7.0).

NOTE

1 John Blacking, *How Musical Is Man?* (Seattle: University of Washington Press, 1973), 46.

CHAPTER 7

Music and Group Identity

Introduction
Musical Instruments (Ireland, Argentina)
Dances (Argentina)
Singers (Argentina, Portugal, USA)
Composers (Bohemia/Czech Republic, USA, Tibet)
A Multicultural Society (Suriname)
Conclusion

INTRODUCTION

From school fight songs to national anthems, music is one of the fundamental ways in which people express their solidarity with other people as members of groups. At social rituals like sporting events, civic holidays, coronations, and state funerals, special music marks the occasion and establishes the proper mood: festive, celebratory, dignified, or solemn. Participatory group singing of anthems and patriotic songs encourages feelings of unity and public acknowledgment of shared history, values, and allegiances. Through music we celebrate our collective identities and project them *to* others; by their music, we know something of the feelings and values *of* others. Entering the airport in Fiji, for example, the traveler's first encounter with Fijian culture is a traditional song performed by two musicians playing ukuleles. Fijian music—friendly, laid-back, "Island Music"—establishes a sense of locale, a mood, a sonic threshold to the pleasures that the tourist is there to enjoy. Music conveys features that are familiar to most travelers—harmonies, rhythms, instruments—while at the same time conveying, through sound, markers of a particular locale, time, and history. Anthropologist Anthony Seeger states, "Music and food are two features of human culture that circulate most widely in the world today while maintaining elements of their origins."[1]

This chapter explores various aspects of the roles that musical instruments, dances, performers, and composers play in celebrating and projecting a group's identity.

MUSICAL INSTRUMENTS (IRELAND, ARGENTINA)

Musical instruments often serve as emblems or icons for groups: Great Highland pipes of Scotland, the ukulele of Hawaii and Fiji, and the didgeridoo of Australia. These are powerful symbols of identity and, by association, history and value. The commemorative quarters of both Tennessee and Louisiana are engraved with musical instruments, proclaiming to all Americans the importance of music to the identity (and tourist industry) of Nashville, Memphis, and New Orleans (Figure 7.1). Tourists leaving from Incheon International Airport in South Korea can pick up souvenir key chains attached to tiny *janggu* hourglass drums. Because this drum plays such an important role in most forms of traditional music in Korea, the chances are good that a tourist has heard one at a restaurant or cultural event and would therefore treasure the keepsake. Indian restaurants bearing the name and logo "*Sitar*" can be found in San Diego, Knoxville, Vancouver, Durham, Nashville, Tuscaloosa, Huntsville, New Haven, Hagerstown, and the list could go on and on. In the restaurant as patrons are eating, they hear either live or piped-in strains of the instrument. Its unique timbre and the style of music it plays suggest that here is an authentic experience of Indian culture. Often, an instrument takes on the iconic status of a nation or ethnic group because it is indigenous or unique to that place or people. The steel drums were invented in Trinidad but now project a pan-Caribbean identity. The *bandura* of Ukraine, the *cimbalom* of Hungary, and the *dan tranh* of Vietnam all serve as icons of their original home (Figure 7.2). In the video, street musician Stepan Shcherbak plays the *bandura* (7.1) (lute-zither) in Kyiv, while singing a traditional song. The instrument combines features of both the zither and the lute.

The Celtic harp has been an emblem of Irish identity since at least the 10th century. Traditionally, Irish harpers were highly skilled storytellers and **bards** who performed for the nobility and thus enjoyed prestige and royal protection. At the end of the 16th century, during Tyrone's Rebellion (1594–1603), a popular uprising against English rule, Elizabeth I outlawed the playing of the harp as an act of sedition against the crown. The English accused the Irish harpers of being spies, since they traveled freely between the courts of the rebellious chieftains. Harpers were hung and their instruments destroyed despite the fact that the English liked harp music. While traditional Irish music is played more often today on instruments such as the fiddle, the pennywhistle, the concertina, and the guitar, it is the harp that decorates the official Irish coat of arms. The Irish harp is also the trademark of Guinness stout, which, when combined with Harp lager, makes a drink called a "Black and Tan" in Dublin.

The violin, invented in the late 16th century in Italy, played a prominent role in Western classical music throughout its history, but as the "fiddle" it has been adopted into various traditional music contexts around the world. In Cape Breton in northeastern Canada, the

FIGURE 7.1 The U.S. Mint's State Quarters for Tennessee and Louisiana

FIGURE 7.2 Ukrainian *bandura* (L), and Hungarian *cimbalom* (R)

FIGURE 7.3 Huge statue of fiddle in Sydney harbor, Cape Breton

fiddle is ubiquitous in music sessions, performances, and dances, where musicians play and adapt Scottish and Irish tunes that their ancestors brought to the New World. A statue of the instrument stands sixty feet high on the Sydney waterfront, proclaiming to cruise ship passengers and island visitors alike the fiddle's singular importance as an expression of Cape Breton identity (Figure 7.3).

Accordions of all sorts took root in many parts of the world following the invention of the first "squeezebox" in early 19th-century Germany. Their presence in contexts as diverse as Argentina and Madagascar demonstrates the phenomenon known to ethnomusicologists as

FIGURE 7.4 The *bandoneon* (L), and monument to the *bandoneon* in Buenos Aires (R)

"**glocalization**": the adaptation of globally diffused technologies to particular local customs and purposes. The *bandoneon*, a type of button accordion invented in Germany around 1860, is the national instrument of Argentina (Figure 7.4). It was originally intended by its German manufacturers to be used by missionaries to play at services in churches without organs. However, when it arrived in the port of Buenos Aires at the end of the 19th century among the few possessions of German and Italian immigrants, it was found to be the perfect accompaniment to an urban dance form that was gaining popularity there: the tango. The prominent role of the *bandoneon* in Argentine dance orchestras (7.2) is shown in this video compilation. Because the instrument was so difficult to play, yet had the mournful, sentimental sound that fit the mood early pioneers of the genre were seeking, the tempo of the dance slowed to accommodate the *bandoneonistas*, allowing thereby more intimate and sensual moves by the dancers.

Through their association with place, the harp, violin, and accordion visually and aurally project group identity. Furthermore, these associations are deepened by the contexts in which they are used: parties, festivals, holidays, concerts. It is at events like these that people come together to express solidarity with each other and with the traditions they share.

DANCES (ARGENTINA)

In many parts of the world, national and ethnic identity and pride are also expressed through dance forms that carry strong associations with the history and traditions of a group. The "steps" of a dance are physical expressions of a rhythmic pattern that, like dress and food, mark the day-to-day realities that constitute a way of life. In the context of the dance, important aspects of social organization are publicly performed. Gender roles, courtship patterns, generational obligations, and rites of passage are all ritualized and also actualized through the dance. In the Caribbean and Latin America, many islands and nations are so closely identified with dances that it is difficult to think of one without the other. Columbia has *cumbia*, Brazil has *samba*, Jamaica has *reggae*, Dominican Republic has *merengue*, Puerto Rico has *bomba* and *plena*, and more recently a pan-Latino dance form, *salsa*, that is now performed throughout the world. In the United States, regions are deeply connected with genres of song and dance: *tejana* along the Rio Grande, polka in Milwaukee, and jazz in urban centers like New York, Chicago, Kansas City, and of course, New Orleans.

The tango (7.3), called "the vertical expression of a horizontal desire," has been associated worldwide with Uruguay, Argentina, and especially the city of Buenos Aires at least since the 1920s (Map 7.1). In 1921, Hollywood actor and matinee idol Rudolph Valentino danced the tango in the silent film *The Four Horsemen of the Apocalypse*, launching the

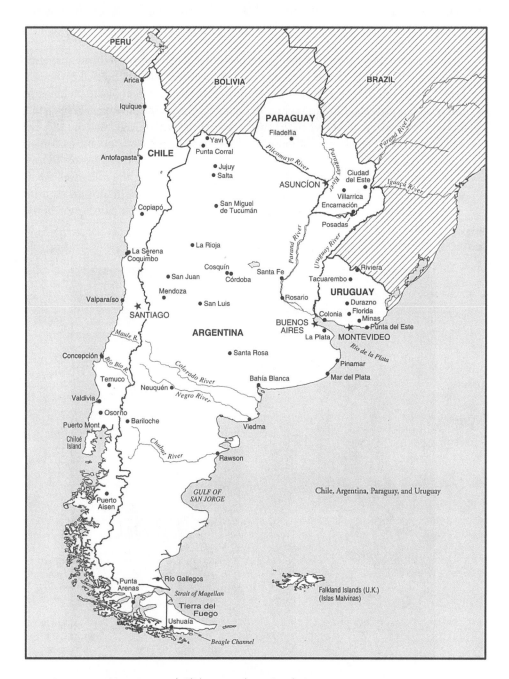

MAP 7.1 Argentina, Uruguay, and Chile in southern South America

Source: Garland Encyclopedia of World Music, Vol. 2, South America, Mexico, Central America, and the Caribbean

dance to international popularity. Musical soundtracks were provided at the time, either by live musicians or recordings provided by Metro Pictures film studio. Cinema and other new media of the time—radio and the phonograph—spread local styles around the globe. Within ten years people were dancing the tango in Shanghai.

Of the tango (Figure 7.5), Teddy Peiro and Jan Fairley write in *The Rough Guide to World Music*:

> Nobody can exactly pinpoint tango's birthplace, but it certainly developed amongst the porteños—the people of the port area of Buenos Aires—and its bordellos [houses of prostitution] and bars. It was a definitively urban music: a product of the melting pot of European immigrants, Criollos [people of mixed European and African ancestry], Blacks and natives, drawn together when the city became the capital of Argentina in 1880. Tango was thus forged from a range of musical influences that included Andalucian flamenco, southern Italian melodies, Cuban habanera, African candombé and percussion, European polkas and mazurkas, Spanish contradanse, and, closer to home, the milónga—the rural song of the Argentine gaucho [cowboy]. It was a music imbued with immigrant history.
>
> In this early form, tango became associated with the bohemian life of bordello brawls and compadrítos—knife-wielding, womanizing thugs. By 1914, there were

FIGURE 7.5 Argentine tango

over 100,000 more men than women in Buenos Aires, thus the high incidence of prostitution and the strong culture of bar-brothels. Machismo and violence were part of the culture and men would dance together in the low-life cafés and corner bars practicing new steps and keeping in shape while waiting for their women, the minas of the bordellos. Their dances tended to have a showy yet threatening, predatory quality, often revolving around a possessive relationship between two men and one woman. In such a culture, the compadrito danced the tango into existence.[2]

SINGERS (ARGENTINA, PORTUGAL, USA)

The electronic recording and broadcast technologies and industries of the early 20th century created the mass media, which revolutionized the ways people worldwide experienced and consumed music. This technological revolution began with Thomas Edison's "talking machine." It allowed musicians and singers to gain iconic status both within their home region and abroad. By 1930 a musical personality could reach not just hundreds or thousands in auditoriums and clubs, but millions. As the impact of the mass media became more and more all-pervasive, certain highly gifted and charismatic singers became symbols of their country, their ethnic group, their region, and their generation.

Carlos Gardel (1887–1935) was the most influential tango singer of his day, and in Argentina he continues to be revered (Figure 7.6). More than any other figure, he raised the

FIGURE 7.6 Carlos Gardel

music and dance of tango from the slums and bars of the Buenos Aires waterfront to the popular entertainments of the middle class and the glamorous nightclubs of the wealthy. Gardel's career entered a new phase with the advent of radio broadcasts and films. In more than a dozen movies, he sang of the loves, the losses, the loneliness, and the tragedy of a nation of immigrants. His death in a plane crash at the height of his career only solidified his position as the voice of his country. Gardel recorded his signature song *La Cumparsita* (7.4) on more than four separate occasions. The title means, "a little street party." The music was composed in 1916 by a young architecture student from Uruguay named Gerardo Matos Rodriguez. He wrote out a little tune and bass line for a student social club and gave the sheet music of the instrumental version to the band leader at a popular dance hall in Montevideo. Rodriguez casually sold the rights to a publisher for twenty pesos. Rodriguez moved to Paris in 1924. There he discovered that his little tune had become an enormous hit, with added lyrics by Pascual Contursi, a lyricist who composed words to more than thirty tangos. Rodriguez spent the following twenty years in law courts trying to secure royalties for the world's most popular tango.

Fado is a form of Portuguese urban folk music that was introduced in Chapter 6. *Fado* singer Amália Rodrigues (1920–1999) began her singing career as a child on the streets of Lisbon, and from the age of fifteen sang professionally in nightclubs. Immediately following World War II, her commercial recordings and films launched her career as an international celebrity. Her remarkable voice, deeply expressing the melancholy and longing of so many *fado* songs, earned her the title *"Rainha do Fado"* ("Queen of *Fado*"). When she died on October 6, 1999, tens of thousands attended her state funeral, and the BBC announced: "Portugal mourns the voice of its soul." Rodrigues recorded *"Tudo isto é fado"* (7.5) ("All of this is *fado*") in 1955. The melody and lyrics contain all the tragedy of life in the slums of Mouraria, wrapped up in a song.

> *Chorus:*
> Vanquished souls
> Lost nights
> Bizarre shadows
> In the Mouraria
> A pimp sings
> Guitars cry
> Jealous love
> Ashes and fire
> Pain and sin
> All of this exists
> All of this is sorrowful
> All of this is fado
>
> [English translation by Fernando Reis]

If the sound technologies of the early 20th century made possible the spectacular reach and influence of Carlos Gardel and Amália Rodrigues, it was the international recording industry later in the 20th century that made Bob Marley (1945–1981) a worldwide celebrity artist. The genre he performed called *reggae*, a derivative of Jamaican dancehall music, was one of the first popular styles with a truly global reach. Bob Marley was born in a small village, Rhoden Hall, on the island of Jamaica to a nineteen-year old Afro-Caribbean mother and an absentee fifty-year old English father. He came to represent a number of group identities:

FIGURE 7.7 Bob Marley, ca. 1970

those associated with a song and dance genre (*reggae*), a hairstyle (dreadlocks), a religion (Rastafarianism), a nation (Jamaica), a region (the Caribbean), a historically dispersed population (the African diaspora), and indeed, the poor and powerless everywhere. Bob Marley was one of the most influential musicians of the 20th century, for while rooted in the particulars of his *individual* identity, he aspired to universality (Figure 7.7).

A similar aspiration for universality comes from the multimedia music project Playing for Change, started in 2004 by producers Mark Johnson and Whitney Kroenke. These visionary music producers saw the possibility of music serving as an expressive medium that could truly unite the world. Their goal was to "inspire, connect, and bring peace to the world through music."[3] The pilot project was to record a local street musician, Roger Ridley in Santa Monica, California, playing a single song, "Stand by Me" (1961) by Ben E. King. They then traveled around the world to such places as India, South Africa, the Middle East, and Ireland to record musicians playing the same song each in their own style. Returning to the United States the producers mixed many different versions to create an edited performance that gave the illusion of a world of musicians playing together and, symbolically, "standing by" each other. Through the worldwide web and digital technology, Playing for Change gave Bob Marley's song "One Love" a similar treatment.

Since 1956, the "Eurovision Song Contest" has been held every year in the member countries of the European Broadcasting Union (EBU). The year 2020 was the only year that the event did not take place at all due to the COVID-19 pandemic. It is one of the oldest and most-watched, televised events in the world. Each country selects a song and an artist to represent it in the competition. Winners are chosen by a combination of call-in votes and a panel of judges who are music professionals. Fifty-two countries have participated at least once.

The event is held each year in the country of the previous year's winner and is an important tourist attraction, with young people from all over the EBU coverage area flocking to attend the event live. Furthermore, in 2021 the contest was viewed by 183 million online viewers in 234 countries.[4] The winners that year were the Italian alt-rock band Måneskin, whose success not only brought them enormous Italian recognition but made them overnight global superstars. In 2022, the winner was war-torn Ukraine.

COMPOSERS (BOHEMIA/CZECH REPUBLIC, USA, TIBET)

Songwriters and composers often create music that evokes unifying feelings in their listeners.

Following the tragic and shocking events of September 11, 2001, Americans found a renewed sense of solidarity through the song "God Bless America" (7.6). This popular anthem of American renewal, first featured in the Hollywood film *This is the Army* (1942), was composed by Irving Berlin (1888–1989), a Russian Jewish immigrant and son of a cantor (Jewish liturgical singer). During his extraordinary career that spanned more than six decades, Berlin wrote more than 1,500 songs, many of them iconic of the American experience (Figure 7.8). About him, composer Jerome Kern once said,

> Irving Berlin has no place in American music. He *is* American music. Emotionally, he honestly absorbs the vibrations emanating from the people, manners, and life of his time and, in turn, gives these impressions back to the world—simplified, clarified, and glorified.[5]

FIGURE 7.8 Irving Berlin

Bedřich Smetana

Bedřich Smetana (1824–1884), "the father of Czech national music," was a composer and pianist born in Bohemia, then part of the Austrian Empire (Figure 7.9). Using the expanded harmonic and orchestral resources pioneered by early 19th-century Romantic composers, Smetana and many of his contemporaries later in the century wrote richly evocative music incorporating folk elements to convey a sense of national identity, solidarity, and pride to middle class urban audiences. The ideal of the nation-state swept Europe in the second half of the 19th century, inspired by the democratic principles put forth in the American and French Revolutions and intensified by the failed uprisings of 1848 against the Austrian Empire. At that time, music rooted in folk traditions became a potent symbol of national identity, and Poland, Norway, Finland, Russia, Hungary, Romania, and Bohemia all produced composers of nationalist music who attained international stature. In each country, musicians evoked heroes and legends of the mythic past, folk tales and dances, scenes of the countryside and peasant life, in order to compose symphonic music that carried audible markers of a region and way of life. Smetana used all of these nationalistic themes in the six short symphonic pieces with descriptive titles (**tone poems**) that comprise *Má Vlast* ("My Fatherland," 1874–1879), a significant work to come out of the 19th-century Nationalist Movement. The six-tone poems are as follows:

> *Vyšehrad:* the castle in Prague that was the home of the original Czech kings
> *Vltava:* one of the main rivers that flows through Bohemia
> *Šárka:* a female warrior who is the main character in a folk legend
> *Zkeských luhu a háju:* "From Bohemia's meadows and forests"
> *Tábor:* a city in southern Bohemia that was the site of a famous 15th-century battle
> *Blaník:* a mountain in which a mythological army sleeps, waiting to awake and defend the country in a time of crisis.

FIGURE 7.9 Bedřich Smetana

MAP 7.2 The Czech Republic and the Vltava River in central Europe

Source: Garland Encyclopedia of World Music, Vol. 8, Europe

The second tone poem of the set, *"Vltava"* (7.7) (more commonly known by its German name, *Moldau*), is a musical depiction of a journey along the Vltava River as it flows from the mountains of southern Bohemia, first southeastward then north through Prague and merging into the Elbe River (Map 7.2). Smetana wrote the following paragraph explaining this composition, to be included in a concert program:

> The composition depicts the course of the river, beginning from its two small sources, one cold the other warm, the joining of both streams into one, then the flow of the Moldau through forests and across meadows, through the countryside where merry feasts are celebrated; water nymphs dance in the moonlight; on nearby rocks can be seen the outline of ruined castles, proudly soaring into the sky. The Moldau swirls through the St. John Rapids and flows in a broad stream toward Prague. It passes Vyšehrad [where an ancient royal castle once stood], and finally the river disappears in the distance as it flows majestically into the Elbe.

Each phrase in the composer's description is expressed in an episode in the music: two flutes evoke the streams flowing out of the mountain, horns evoke forest hunts, and folk dance tunes represent the peasant weddings performed on the banks of the great river. Muted strings create a dreamy, mystical sound for the water nymphs dancing in the moonlight. A great surge of orchestral excitement represents the St. John Rapids, and finally the main theme of the previous tone poem Vyšehrad is repeated to represent the river's arrival in the capital, Prague.

Aaron Copland

American composer Aaron Copland (1900–1990) sought to use the European conventions of the symphony orchestra and the genres associated with "high art" concert music—the symphony, opera, and ballet—to convey an American identity that draws from, but ultimately transcends, its European roots (Figure 7.10). Copland was born in Brooklyn to Russian-Jewish immigrant parents, and studied composition in France with Nadia Boulanger before returning to New York to pursue a career as a freelance composer. Like many artists of the 1920s, he was inspired to express through music the ideals and aspirations of American Democracy. Although his education had grounded him in the techniques of European modernism, he used this training to transform the music of America's people—jazz, folk songs, hymns, fiddle tunes, and spirituals—and bring it to the concert hall. In the early 1940s, Copland composed several ballet scores depicting the American Wild West (*Rodeo* and *Billy the Kid*) and early 19th-century rural Pennsylvania (*Appalachian Spring*). In these works he created a nationalist music that portrayed the lives of ordinary working Americans. In "Hoedown" (7.8), the final scene from his 1942 ballet *Rodeo*, Copland captures the exuberance of frontier social life: the square dance, the reel, the rip-snortin' buckaroo a-courtin'. He evokes the spirit of the West through quotations and re-workings of folk dance tunes: "Bonaparte's Retreat" and "Miss McLeod's Reel." His instrumental "Fanfare for the Common Man" (7.9)

FIGURE 7.10 Aaron Copland

FIGURE 7.11 Florence Price

has also come to evoke the spirit of the American pioneer, symbolizing in its wide intervals and strong brass harmonies the ambitious explorers of the American nation across land and sea. The kind of brass fanfare that had traditionally announced the arrival of a monarch receives a populist treatment: it is the ordinary citizen who is accorded this recognition and honor. Copland is remembered as the Dean of American Composers, whose influence would shape the history of American symphonic music, ballet, and Hollywood film scores.

Florence Price

Florence Beatrice Price (1887–1953) was the first African-American woman composer to have an important symphonic work performed by a major American symphony orchestra (Figure 7.11). She was born into an upper-class African-American family in Little Rock, Arkansas. Her father was a highly successful dentist, her mother was a schoolteacher and Florence's first piano teacher. As a child, Florence showed great talent on the piano and at the age of fifteen went to Boston to attend the New England Conservatory of Music. There, at the encouragement of her mother, she was listed as "Mexican" to avoid the persistent racism she would otherwise have encountered, despite Boston's far more liberal attitude toward race than Little Rock's.

After several teaching positions in the Jim Crow South, she found her way to Chicago. She joined a dynamic community of Black artists, poets, scholars, and musicians as well as women's organizations that fostered further opportunities. Florence Price was extremely prolific during her career. Her long list of compositions includes symphonies, concertos, string quartets, and more than a hundred songs with lyrics by such poets as Paul Lawrence Dunbar and Langston Hughes. Her style fully expressed her African-American identity. She infused in the classical idioms that America inherited from Europe the great legacy of melody and rhythm of her own African roots. Although she was painfully shy, Price knew the value of her accomplishments. She wrote repeatedly to Serge Koussevitzky, conductor of the Boston Symphony, pleading with him to give her work a public performance. Koussevitzky had been a strong champion of American composers including Aaron Copland. In 1943, she wrote to him:

> My Dear Dr. Koussevitzky,
> To begin with I have two handicaps – those of sex and race. I am a woman; and I have some Negro blood in my veins.

> Knowing the worst, then, would you be good enough to hold in check the possible inclination to regard a woman's composition as long on emotionalism but short on virility and thought content; -- until you shall have examined some of my work?

She received no answer. She then wrote the following:

> ...In keeping with one last promise to myself that I will no longer hang back, I am now being so bold as to address you. I ask no concessions because of race or sex, and am willing to abide by a decision based solely on the worth of my work.
> Will you be kind enough to examine a score of mine?[6]

Again, no answer.

Florence Price captured, magnified, and celebrated her American identity as much as did Aaron Copland, the child of Eastern European Jewish immigrants. Like Copland, she borrowed liberally from folk traditions: gospel, ragtime, spirituals, jazz, and the dances of the minstrel shows. She was able to capture in her own style the spirit of Black America. For example, her composition *"Fantasie Nègre"* (7.10) (1929) for solo piano, here played by Elijah Stevens, is based on the African American spiritual "Wade in the Water." Also, "Five Spirituals in Counterpoint" (7.11) for string quartet (1951), in this video played by the Apollo Chamber Players, includes variations on "Swing Low, Sweet Chariot."

Copland in his maturity reaped multiple honors as the "Dean of American Music" along with the Pulitzer Prize, the National Medal of Arts, the Presidential Medal of Freedom, and many others. His compositions remain squarely in the canon of works that appear year after year on concert programs throughout the world. However, Florence Price died in obscurity, except within her community of Black artists in Chicago. Almost her entire body of work was lost following her death, most of it never performed.

What happened then was nothing short of miraculous. Alex Ross of *The New Yorker* writes:

> In 2009, Vicki and Darrell Gatwood, of St. Anne, Illinois, were preparing to renovate an abandoned house on the outskirts of town. The structure was in poor condition: vandals had ransacked it, and a fallen tree had torn a hole in the roof. In a part of the house that had remained dry, the Gatwoods made a curious discovery: piles of musical manuscripts, books, personal papers, and other documents. The name that kept appearing in the materials was that of Florence Price.[7]

One of classical music's major publishers, G. Schirmer and Sons, has edited, printed, and made available her entire corpus. In the aftermath of the social upheavals of the #MeToo and Black Lives Matter Movements of the late 2010s, concert promoters have scrambled to add the music of Florence Price and other previously marginalized artists to their programs, and not just because of "sex and race" but because of the quality of the work.

Acko Choedrag

Acko Choedrag (b. 1976), a Tibetan Buddhist monk in China's western province of Qinghai, formerly the Tibetan province of Amdo, is a media producer and something of a regional pop star. In his monk's cell he has set up a sound and editing studio to produce the recordings on which his reputation and fame rest. A member of the self-enclosed monastic community of

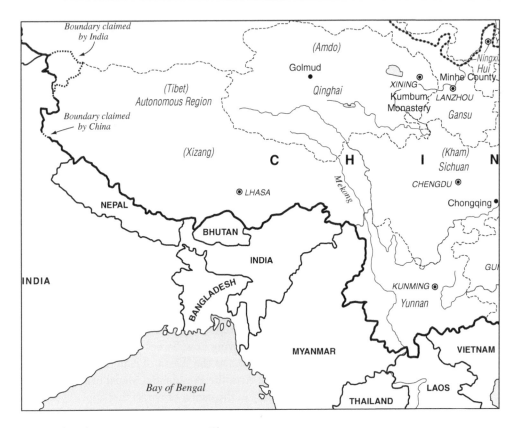

MAP 7.3 The Tibetan region in western China

Source: Garland Encyclopedia of World Music, Vol. 7, East Asia: China, Japan, and Korea

Kumbum, originally built in 1436, Choedrag lives in this traditional world of meditation and ritual as well as the modern world of cell phones, jeans, and digital media production. His recordings combine original songs based on religious and folk materials with video images of the regional landscape and ritual life, both monastic and popular. This artist has managed to walk an incredibly thin line between religion and celebrity, representing traditional Tibetan identity through modern technology. Choedrag produces songs that affirm Tibetan unity for a society encroached upon by the modern world (Figure 7.12, Map 7.3).

Two selections from Acko Choedrag's 2006 album *Tibetans* (7.12) exemplify his conflation of religion and identity. The first song, "Praying," is an unaccompanied invocation based on Buddhist chant. The highly ornamented style of singing would be recognized immediately by a Tibetan listener as deeply traditional. The video imagery shows the artist in his monk's robe meditating by one of the important sacred landmarks of the region, Qinghai Lake. The first two lines of the text come from a meditation treatise by a famous lama (Buddhist high priest); the second two lines were added by the singer.

> Never leaving the side of true gurus [teachers]
> And benefiting from the glory of the Dharma [Buddha's Teaching] in all the lifetimes.
> After finishing "the good qualities of the levels and paths"
> Achieve Buddha-hood quickly!
>> [English translation by Tsering Samdrup and Dawa Torbert]

FIGURE 7.12 Labrang Monastery, Gansu Province, People's Republic of China

The second song, *"Tibetans,"* from which the album takes its name, is in a contemporary musical idiom with synthesizer accompaniment. The music combines folk melodies, religious chanting, and pop rhythms. It also carries traces of Tibetan identity in the language as well as in the ornamented vocal style. The recording juxtaposes a contemporary musical style with images important to Tibetan identity such as the Potala palace (the Dalai Lama's former residence in Lhasa), pilgrims practicing forms of walking meditation, other forms of ritual worship, prayer flags, prayer wheels, religious paintings that decorate the landscape, and the Tibetan people themselves. The song *"Tibetans,"* with lyrics by Choedrag himself, suggests that the greatness of the Tibetan people lay in past glories and now lies in preservation of the old ways. Its contemporary musical idiom speaks to a generation familiar with the popular styles they hear on the radio.

> Nephews! Nieces! [as background singing]
> Endless time is forever passing,
> The glorious stories are still told,
> In a radiant age,
> Heroes died with their anxiety.
> Scholars died in their tears,
> From that moment,
> This snowy land
> Became the battlefield of brothers,
> Nephews and nieces left as orphans.
> Ah ha ha ha [sound of grieving]

FIGURE 7.13 Acko Choedrag playing *dranyin* (Tibetan lute) (L), and recording (R)

> That's why we Tibetans
> Had to change our own way of living and admire others,
> Abandoned our own warmth and slowly welcomed the cold.
> > [English translation by Tsering Samdrup and Dawa Torbert]

On a very cold night in December 2007, Acko Choedrag (7.13) sings a newly composed song in a folk idiom, accompanying himself on the *dranyin* with author Jonathan Kramer recording a cello track (Figure 7.13). The video shows the interior of his cell and his recording equipment. From this small room, Acko Choedrag composed, recorded, and produced music that, while modern in its use of technology and popular idioms, expressed the traditional values that he believes Tibetans need to affirm if they are to resist assimilation. In the Summer of 2008, prior to the Beijing Summer Olympics, there was rioting in the region. Many Tibetans came out in protest against Chinese suppression of the Tibetan language, culture, religion, and autonomy. Choedrag's recording equipment was confiscated and for a short time he was placed under house arrest.[8]

A MULTICULTURAL SOCIETY (SURINAME)

In a multicultural nation with diverse ethnic and immigrant communities, music and dance are important ways of celebrating and perpetuating allegiance to ethnic identity, shared ancestry, a distant homeland, or to a way of life that is no longer viable in the modern world. One such nation, Suriname, formerly known as Dutch Guyana, is a country on the northern coast of South America (Map 7.4). It is approximately the size of the state of Wisconsin and has a population of around 630,000 people. Most of its population lives in a narrow strip of low-lying grassland along the Caribbean coast, and in the capital city Paramaribo situated on the west bank of the Suriname River. This and several other rivers have headwaters deep in the rainforest of the Amazon Basin that covers around 80% of Suriname's land, extending south to the Brazilian border.

MAP 7.4 Suriname in northern South America

Source: Garland Encyclopedia of World Music, Vol. 2: South America, Mexico, Central America, and the Caribbean

Because of a unique pattern of colonization, conquest, resistance, slavery, and indentured servitude, the country has one of the most diverse populations in the world. Carib, Trio, Waraka, and Arawak Amerindians—descendants of the region's original inhabitants—live in villages along the coast and deep in the interior, and as an assimilated population in the multicultural capital, Paramaribo. The first European settlers were English farmers who moved down from the Caribbean island of Barbados, and Portuguese Jews who moved up from Brazil. This transplanted Jewish community in Suriname, escaping religious persecution, built the first synagogue in the New World. The English traded Suriname to the Dutch in 1667 in exchange for New Amsterdam, the modern site of New York City. The Dutch created a plantation economy, growing sugar cane and coffee, with imported African slaves providing the backbreaking labor. Suriname is home to the world's largest Maroon population, the descendants of 17th- and 18th-century slaves who escaped from the plantations and fled down river into the nearly impenetrable rainforest (Figure 7.14). From there, for a hundred years, these slaves and their descendants led daring raids against the planters and fought wars of resistance against the Dutch colonial army until treaties were finally signed in the 1760s, granting them territorial homelands in the interior. To this day their descendants maintain the forms of social organization and cultural practice of their West African ancestors in villages deep in the rainforest.

When slavery ended in 1863, the Dutch plantation owners began importing Chinese, East Indian, and Javanese indentured workers to replace the emancipated slaves. Unlike the permanence of slavery, indentured laborers were granted freedom following a period of servitude. The Asian workers were given the option of returning to their homelands or remaining in the colony. **Creoles** (mixed people of African and European descent) who remained on the coastal plantations, and newly, often illegally arrived Brazilian gold miners complete the complex picture.

Most Surinamese speak the local Creole language, *Sranan Tonga* ("Suriname Tongue"), made up of elements from Portuguese, English, Dutch, and several African languages. However, Dutch, a holdover from the colonial period, remains the official language that all school children learn. Many Surinamese also speak the language of their ethnic communities: Hindi, Javanese, Hakka (a Chinese dialect), and Saramaccan (the language of the largest group of Maroons). Each individual shares an *ethnic* identity with others of common ancestry, as well as a *national* identity with all fellow Surinamese.

In such an ethnically and linguistically complex society, music is an important expression and symbol of identity. All children learn the Surinamese national anthem in school, and sing it with their parents at sporting events and civic ceremonies. In a performance the words are sung twice, in Dutch and in Sranan Tonga. With the line "Wherever our ancestors came from," the song celebrates collective allegiance to their shared country despite the diversity of their ancestral origins.

Beyond this musical expression of shared identity, some children study the traditional songs and dances of their ancestral homelands. Deep in the forest, a group of Maroon boys practice the drumming patterns (7.14) that their fathers perform at rituals and festivals. A few will eventually travel upriver to the capital and become leaders in the popular music industry. This popular music is driven by the vital African "**roots rhythms**" that have been preserved for hundreds of years in the forest.

FIGURE 7.14 Maroon village scene (L), and Maroon drummer (R)

A Carib cultural society, Paramuru (7.15), in the capital of Paramaribo, holds classes for children in dances that will be performed at annual Native American celebrations. They are taught dances that imitate the movements of the eagle and the panther even though they live in town and never see the animals that once populated their ancestors' forest home.

Similarly, the Afro-Surinamese cultural society (*Na Afrikan Kulturu fu Sranan* or NAKS, founded in 1947) holds classes in which teenage Creole girls (7.16) practice songs and dances that derive from the African-based religion called **Winti**. These dances represent deities of the sky and earth through special drum patterns and dance steps. The call-and-response singing invokes Mama Issa (Mother Earth), Legba, the guardian of the doorway, and Adome (snake deity).

Girls from the East Indian community (7.17) rehearse dances based on the **Bollywood** movies that keep them connected culturally to their ancestral home. Before the dance class begins, the teacher offers a prayer to Mother Earth, asking for forgiveness, since "we are going to stamp on her now." The Hindustani community maintains strong cultural connections to the motherland through music, dance, and Hindu religious practices.

Children of Javanese descent learn traditional dances including the *jaran kepang* (7.18) (hobby horse dance). The video shows a team of teenage dancers performing at the annual "Arrival Day" Festival on August 9. On that date in 1900, the first contract laborers from the Dutch East Indies, as Indonesia was then called, disembarked to replace the British East Indian indentured laborers who themselves replaced the freed African slaves. The Javanese community in Paramaribo and the surrounding farming towns gather at the Indonesian Cultural Center for a day of football, food, music, and dancing. The highlight of the afternoon is a performance of the ***jaran kepang***. The children on hobby horses, along with "clown" sidekicks, dance in unison to an orderly choreography imitating stylized horse movements. Like the original version in Java, here replicated halfway around the world, the dance is accompanied by the *gamelan* (Figure 7.15).

FIGURE 7.15 Javanese Surinamese *gamelan* musician

Members of this society take pride in a uniquely Surinamese identity, shaped both by ethnic diversity and by the particular environment of the Caribbean Sea, the rainforest, and the rivers that connect them. In Paramaribo, a multiethnic dance troupe performs dances that showcase Surinamese culture and identity at international cultural events like the pan-Caribbean festival, Carifesta. The amateur dancers of the Folkloristisch Ensemble Paramaribo (7.19), shown in this video, express the various ethnic identities of Suriname through characteristic dance movements. Each member learns all the various dance styles in preparation for a performance at an international dance festival. A musical score was prepared, based on a Surinamese folk song, with each section in a style that reflects a different ethnicity. For the choreography to communicate the diverse nature of Surinamese identity—whereby each member embodies through social proximity a bit of all the other identities—the dance roles are mixed up. For example, the Javanese dancer performs with the maraca rattle of the Carib, the Chinese woman dances to polyrhythmic drumming of the Maroons, while the Maroon dancer twirls a Chinese paper parasol. At the end the dancers huddle together in a circle to represent that the various communities together make up a unified society.

The leading spokesperson and creative visionary of Suriname's multicultural identity was the playwright Henk Tjon (1948–2009), who wrote more than eighty stage plays built upon the unique complexities of his native Suriname. For Carifesta, Henk Tjon organized the percussion ensemble, *Ala Kondre* ("All Colors"), consisting of performers from each of Suriname's ethnic groups. At Henk Tjon's funeral (7.20), *Ala Kondre* performed in a state ceremony honoring his enormous contributions to the cultural life of his country. Those present witnessed a multicultural expression of group identity in which each strand was honored, no strand dominated, and the overall impact was that of unity in diversity.

CONCLUSION

Music is no longer exclusively defined by impermeable geographical and political borders, as was believed in the early years of Ethnomusicology. One is as likely to hear Beyoncé's music in Tokyo, Buenos Aires, or Johannesburg as in Los Angeles. Genres of popular music like rap, techno, EDM, K-Pop, Bollywood, and Salsa reach audiences worldwide. These popular musics are able to carry local meanings that reinforce local group identities while at the same time giving listeners a sense that they share a broader, cosmopolitan identity. Music itself is universal, practiced in every human society. However, music is not a universal *language*. Local musical expressions convey meanings that may not be fully understandable beyond their local context. Instrumentalists, singers, and composers create the soundscapes for ways of life uniquely shaped by history and environment. Thus, performance is one of the important activities through which group identity is projected. Part III examines two further aspects of human identity. Because music is such a flexible form of communication, it can express multiple identities simultaneously in hybrid and fusion styles, the topic of Chapter 8. Chapter 9 demonstrates through a number of case studies how music can express power relationships and divisions between opposing groups.

KEY TERMS AND CONCEPTS

19th-Century Nationalist Movement

Culture Bearer

Ethnic Community

Eurovision Song Contest

Glocalization

Group Identity

Mass Media

Multicultural Society

National and Ethnic Identity

"Roots Rhythms"

Slavery/Indentureship

Superstar

Tone Poem

Urban Music

THINKING ABOUT MUSIC

1 In this chapter, you encountered several singers who expressed through their voices different collective identities: Carlos Gardel, "The Voice of Argentina"; Amália Rodrigues of Portugal; Bob Marley of Jamaica, Acko Choedrag of Tibet. Can you think of a singer who shares and expresses an aspect of your identity? If one of your parents or grandparents was asked the same question, how do you think they would answer?

2 Listen again to the two songs from Acko Choedrag's *Tibetans* recording. They are in very different styles. How do they both express aspects of contemporary Tibetan identity as you understand it from the case study?

3 Is multicultural Surinamese society and musical life like America in miniature? If so, how? If not, how are they different?

4 Think of a group of people you are connected with that shares a common bond (cultural, ethnic, geographic, racial, social, etc.) and describe what music expresses the identity of that group. How does the music express this identity? Through lyrics? Musical instruments? Elements of music (e.g., melody, harmony, rhythm)? What are the markers that put the "identity" into the music?

5 In Chapter 6, you read about a Madagascan vocal trio, Salala, and watched the band's 2005 concert in a soccer stadium in Antananarivo. Which "group" identities does the vocal trio express in its performance, and in what ways do these singers and their song mobilize, inspire, and celebrate group identity?

6 Former American Secretary of State Mike Pompeo stated of multiculturalism: "This is not what America is." What do you think America is in terms of cultural expressions, and how do you think music in America expresses American identity? Does America's motto, "*e pluribus unum*" ("out of many, one") support or deny Pompeo's claim?

7 What does this quote mean: "Music itself is universal, practiced in every human society. However, music is not a universal *language*" (p. 190)? Do you think internet technologies are changing this condition, making music MORE universally understandable? Why, or why not?

NOTES

1 Anthony Seeger, "Foreword," in Laurent Albert, *The Music of the Other: New Challenges for Ethnomusicology in a Global Age*, trans. Carla Ribeiro (Aldershot: Ashgate, 2007), vii.

2 Teddy Peiro and Jan Fairley, "Tango," in *The Rough Guide to World Music*, ed. Simon Broughton and Mark Ellingham, Vol. 2 (London: Rough Guides Ltd., 2000), 304.

3 "One Love," produced by Playing for Change, https://www.youtube.com/watch?v=4xjPODksI08.

4 Eurovision Song Contest, Rotterdam 2021, https://eurovision.tv/event/rotterdam-2021.

5 Marilyn Berger, "Irving Berlin, Nation's Songwriter, Dies," *New York Times*, September 23, 1989, http://www.nytimes.com/1989/09/23/obituaries/irving-berlin-nation-s-songwriter-dies.html.

6 Letters from Florence B. Price to Serge Koussevitzky, 1943, as quoted in Rae Linda Brown, *The Heart of A Woman: The Life and Music of Florence B. Price* (Urbana: University of Illinois Press, 2020), 186–187.

7 Alex Ross, "The Rediscovery of Florence Price," *New Yorker Magazine*, February 5, 2018.

8 Tsering Samdrup assisted in the biographical writing on Acko Choedrag.

CHAPTER 8

Music and Hybrid Identity

Introduction
Cajuns and Creoles in Rural Louisiana (USA)
Montagnards in North Carolina (USA/Vietnam)
Black Atlantic (Africa/Americas)
Indo-Trinidadians (Trinidad/India)
May 4th Movement (China)
Conclusion

INTRODUCTION

The term "hybrid" refers generally to a blending of two or more different components, such as a hybrid plant bred from two diverse species, a mythological creature that is part human and part animal, or a hybrid car powered by both electric batteries and a gasoline engine. This chapter explores the concept of "**hybridity**" as it applies to social and musical identity.

Throughout human history, populations have moved from one geographical location to another either by choice or by force. People have taken with them not only their material possessions but also cultural traits and practices. The retention of culture, language, religion, and music varies widely depending on the particular circumstances of migration and on the social and political situation in the new homeland. Africans brought to North America as slaves, for instance, were forbidden to use drums that were so important in African social and religious life. Yet from their field hollers and spirituals new forms of African American musical expression developed such as blues and gospel. The nomadic Roma, known variously as Tzigane or Gypsies, spread throughout Europe and northern Africa in their long migration from northwest India beginning over a 1,000 years ago. In each country that they passed through or settled in, they integrated local musical styles and instruments with their own traditions. Deprived of land for farming and excluded from many other occupations, they found work as professional musicians, mastering the genres and styles of the dominant society. Long before digital technologies and international travel routes facilitated contemporary musical fusions, the primary reasons for cross-cultural contact and interaction were conquest, migration, and trade.

Hybridity in *music* refers to the blending of two or more different musical styles or traditions. Individuals or groups perform music that contains markers of multiple identities to project their own mixed cultural heritage. Today, creative artists on all continents are blending musical styles and compositions in novel ways. An imaginative advertisement for a Korean construction company seeking to update its image is a hybrid version of German composer Johann Pachelbel's *Canon in D* (8.1) (ca. 1680), here presented in its original form. The next video shows the hybrid *Canon in D* (8.2) from 2013, played by the Sookmyung Gayageum Orchestra on traditional Korean board zithers with beatboxing, DJ scratching, and break dancing. The layers of identities include sophisticated cosmopolitan culture (the original Pachelbel's *Canon*), the expression of traditional Korean culture (through the sound of the *gayageums*), and hip-hop and urban youth culture (beatboxing, scratching, and break dancing) in an imaginative musical stew of references and stylings! The Korean construction company Daelim's new public relations message was: "Novelty and Newness = Amazement."

Another form of modern musical hybridity occurs when musicians from different parts of the world work together. Throughout the last decades of the 20th century, there was a fashion throughout the global music industry for hybrid joint ventures, often referred to as "fusion music." American country, pop, and bluegrass band "Bela Fleck and the Flecktones" performed with Tuvan throat singer Kongar-ol Ondar and Indian *tabla* drummer Sandip Burman on the fusion song "A Moment So Close" (8.3) (*Outbound* album, 2000). The stylistic juxtapositions in the video are striking. The variety of dress, hair, and nationality seen on the stage contrasts with the surprising level of coherence expressed between vastly divergent musical styles.

CAJUNS AND CREOLES IN RURAL LOUISIANA (USA)

The term "Cajun" derives from the word Acadian, the original name for the French settlers of Acadia, a region of modern-day eastern Canada. The early settlers in this part of the French colonial empire were builders, soldiers, sailors, and farmworkers who came from Poitou and surrounding regions in west-central France. They thrived in their new Acadian homeland from their arrival in 1604 until the British took control in 1713 and renamed the colony Nova Scotia (Figure 8.1). The French-speaking Roman Catholic Acadians refused to swear allegiance to the British Crown and were deported in 1755. Several thousand eventually made their way down the Mississippi River to colonial Louisiana where they were welcomed by the French and Spanish inhabitants, also Catholics. They settled in the bayous and prairies of the region, re-established their farming communities, and retained their language and culture.

The first generation of Acadians in Louisiana, isolated in their rural parishes on the bayous, preserved their French musical heritage. They sang long unaccompanied narrative songs in French (*complaintes*). Families entertained themselves in the evenings with both old and new songs reflecting their migrant experience. To this day, Cajun farming communities celebrate Mardi Gras (8.4) with old French traditions. These include begging songs (8.5), which are part of neighborhood dress-up parties. The revelers, wearing costumes similar to those worn in rural France, travel from farmhouse to farmhouse acting out skits. In the past there was a group collection of food ingredients for a communal gumbo, but nowadays they go to the supermarket and make the gumbo in advance.

Musical instruments among the first settlers were rare, but by the end of the 18th century the Acadian exiles had the means to acquire violins, common to their lives in Acadia as well as those of their ancestors in France. Fiddlers and singers accompanied traditional house dances

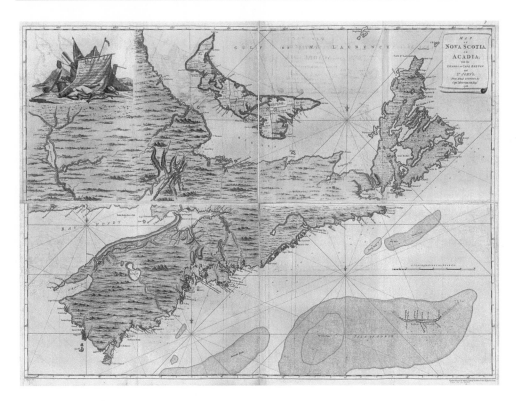

FIGURE 8.1 Map of Acadia, Nova Scotia, 1754

(*bals de maison*), playing waltzes, mazurkas, polkas, and *contredanses* as well as Virginia reels, jigs, and hoedowns learned from their Anglo-American neighbors. A style of twin fiddling (8.6) also developed that has continued to this day, with the second fiddle playing a percussive bass or harmony beneath the melody line. Video 8.6 features fiddling partners Michael Doucet and Mitch Reed. By the mid-19th century, Cajun dance bands had adopted the button accordion, brought into Louisiana by German settlers in Texas. The button accordion could easily be heard in noisy dance parties and was a much sturdier instrument than the fiddle. The accordion, cheap and readily available, was also picked up by recently freed African slaves who played such a dominant and creative role in shaping the musical life of the region.

Over time, the surrounding ethnic groups—Creoles, Afro-Caribbeans, Anglo-Americans, Spanish, Germans, and Native Americans—began to adopt the cultural traditions and language of the Acadians, who in turn absorbed cultural traits of their neighbors. From this cross-cultural exchange, brought about by proximity and to a lesser extent intermarriage, there emerged a new hybrid "Cajun" society. In the early 20th century, black Creole accordion player Amédé Ardoin (1898–1942), together with white Cajun fiddler Dennis McGee (1893–1989), introduced a new hybrid form of Cajun-Creole expression. McGee and Ardoin formed a bi-racial duo, and while not permitted to play in public venues they performed for local house parties. In the early 1930s, they were among the first artists to make recordings of Cajun-Creole music, which became popular throughout southern Louisiana. "Ardoin personified this cultural blend [of European song forms and African rhythms] and enhanced its development through his deft technique and his ability to improvise. Ardoin was a lively, inventive accordionist who could keep a crowd dancing."[1] As folklorist and musicologist Alan Lomax demonstrates in his documentary film *Cajun Country* (8.7), Ardoin's new "active, pulsing" accompaniments contained elements of traditional African rhythms creating "a hot, syncopated accordion style [that] put the heat into" earlier Cajun dance forms and harmonies.[2]

Several factors hastened the Cajun transformation from an isolated rural population into participation in the American mainstream: the discovery of oil in the Gulf of Mexico in 1901, the participation of Cajuns and Creoles in World War I, the development of highways and transportation, and the advent of mass media and national broadcasting.[3] The end of isolation for many rural Cajuns brought about a dilution of Cajun identity and longstanding musical traditions. The Cajun fiddle and accordion sound declined from the 1930s to 1950s as many dance bands introduced electric guitars, drum sets, and amplification. Cajun musicians adopted national music styles such as country, bluegrass, western swing, and rock and roll, and commercial Cajun recordings began sounding unmistakably Americanized.

State and local school boards in Louisiana had made English-language education compulsory in 1916. The French language became stigmatized, and Cajun culture became associated with poverty and ignorance. Not until the late 1960s did state laws re-establish French-language education and officially endorse a Louisiana French renaissance movement, which institutionalized pride in the French language and Cajun identity.

In 1948, a blind Cajun accordionist and singer, Iry Lejeune (8.8), played in the old style of Amédé Ardoin, launching a **revitalization** movement with his hit recording, "*La Valse du Pont d'Amour*" ("Love Bridge Waltz"). He drew enthusiastic crowds wherever he performed. Lejeune's success revived interest in the traditional hybrid Cajun-Creole sound and the French language, especially among the soldiers returning from the battlefields of World War II. Other button accordion players picked up their instruments again, and local music stores and recording companies once again supported regional Cajun music.

In the 1950s, a new Creole popular genre emerged called *zydeco*. Its characteristic sound derived from the combination of Cajun dance music with African American jazz, blues, and R&B. A local Louisiana flavor was retained by adding triangles, spoons, and most notably washboards—implements of the rural life of Creole sharecroppers—to the traditional fiddles and accordions. One of the early *zydeco* hits was "*Zydeco Sont Pas Sale*" (8.9) ("The Snap Beans Aren't Salty"). It features the driving percussive sounds of Clifton Chenier on his piano accordion. A popular *zydeco* bandleader in the 1970s was "Queen Ida" (Ida Lewis Guillory), a Creole button accordion player from Lake Charles, Louisiana. She formed Queen Ida and the Bon Temps ("Good Times"), and sang in English and French (her mother tongue), as well as bilingual songs. The song "C'est Moi" (8.10) from the album *Cookin' with Queen Ida and her Zydeco Band* (1989) has verses in English and the chorus in French (Figure 8.2).

Further impetus to the revitalization of Cajun music came in 1964 when a Cajun band consisting of Gladius Thibodeaux, Louis Lejeune (Iry's cousin), and Dewey Balfa was invited to perform at the Newport Folk Festival in Rhode Island, and unexpectedly received thunderous applause. Such huge success brought national attention to traditional Cajun music and spawned many efforts to preserve and promote this music culture, including the establishment of the Louisiana Folk Foundation, the Council for the Development of French in Louisiana (CODOFIL), the Center for Acadian and Creole Folklore, and Cajun music festivals around the state. In the following decades, this resurgence of Cajun music continued. Musicians play in dance halls and at festivals, and popular dance bands such as Steve Riley and the Mamou Playboys (8.11), featuring the washboard and driving rhythms of *zydeco*, carry Cajun music forward into the 21st century (Figure 8.3). This hybrid roots music remains an important way in which Cajuns and Creoles express and celebrate their mixed cultural heritage. From its origins as dancehall music of southwestern Louisiana, *zydeco* has become an internationally celebrated musical form, performed from Scandinavia to Japan. In 2007, a separate category for *zydeco* and Cajun music was created for the Grammy Music Awards. Creole and Cajun musicians continue to combine musical resources.

FIGURE 8.2 Clifton Chenier (1925–1987) on piano accordion, with his brother Cleveland on saxophone and John Hart on washboard, 1975 (L), and Queen Ida (1929–) on button accordion, from the album cover of *Queen Ida and the Bon Temps Zydeco Band: On Tour* (1982) (R)

FIGURE 8.3 Steve Riley and the Mamou Playboys at the 2012 Rhythm and Roots Festival in Charlestown, Rhode Island

MONTAGNARDS IN NORTH CAROLINA (USA/VIETNAM)

The term **Montagnard** refers to a number of indigenous tribal peoples of the Central Highlands of Vietnam (Map 8.1) who arrived in the United States as political refugees beginning in the mid-1980s. The time period and circumstances of their migration and settlement differ significantly from those of the Cajuns, yet like the Cajuns they retain native cultural and musical traditions while adapting to and adopting aspects of American life. Their ethnicity, culture, and languages clearly set them apart from the lowland Vietnamese in their former Southeast Asian homeland. Until the mid-19th century in Vietnam, these tribal peoples lived in isolation as farmers and hunter-gatherers. In the mid-1800s, French Catholic missionaries arrived in the highlands; and from 1885 France ruled Vietnam until the end of the French Indochina War (1945–1954).

In the war between North and South Vietnam (1959–1975), United States Special Forces recruited Montagnards to fight alongside them against the North Vietnamese Communists. With the defeat of the American military in 1975, thousands of Montagnards fled their villages and many others were imprisoned, executed, or eventually died in re-education camps.

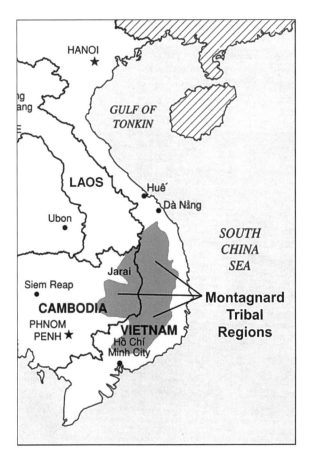

MAP 8.1 Vietnam, Laos, and Cambodia showing Montagnard Tribal Regions

Source: Garland Encyclopedia of World Music, Vol. 4, Southeast Asia

Because of their allegiance to the American military and their connection with the South Vietnamese government, many Montagnard soldiers and their families sought political asylum in the United States. Some were resettled as refugees in North Carolina, a state that offered plentiful entry-level jobs and was home to many American Special Forces veterans willing to serve as sponsors. Since the 1980s the U.S. government has resettled thousands of Montagnard refugees including over 8,000 in North Carolina, a population that represents the largest concentration of Montagnard peoples outside of Vietnam.

In North Carolina, Montagnards reside primarily in Raleigh, Greensboro, and Charlotte. The older community members who grew up in the Central Highlands play an important role in organizing community-wide events that include music and dance, both Montagnard and American. They remember the summer and harvest celebrations from their youth, when the men played gongs and drums and the women danced, and they now plan such communal music-making activities in gatherings that celebrate their collective heritage.

At the 2008 Montagnard Day festival in Greensboro, individuals and groups sang songs on stage in their native tribal languages, teen girls in native dress performed traditional dances, and young girls in American outfits sang American songs. The performance of both Montagnard and American music, like the mixture of language and dress, clearly expresses their dual allegiance to their old and new homelands, and their resulting hybrid identity in America. The day started out with the singing of the American national anthem along with a patriotic Montagnard song, and culminated in a traditional community dance (8.12). The next video shows a rehearsal of the dance accompaniment on hanging gongs and barrel drum (8.13) in the driveway of a Raleigh resident some weeks earlier.

In the privacy of their homes, Montagnards listen to both American music and Southeast Asian music. Some of the older generation play native Montagnard musical instruments brought over from Vietnam, such as the *trung* (8.14) (bamboo xylophone) and *goong* (8.15) (tube zither) played by Dock Rmah, and the *ding nam* (8.16) (mouth organ) played by Y Dha Eban. Others, mostly young people, have taken up the guitar and drum set. American-born Montagnard children and youth are learning Montagnard songs as well as American ones, and some musically talented individuals are composing their own songs either in their native tongue or in English, or both. In Raleigh, community leader and musician Hip Ksor writes his own songs in **Jarai**, his mother tongue, and plays them on guitar adding chordal harmony (Figure 8.4). His song lyrics often refer to the separation of his people, including his own family, divided between North Carolina and the Vietnamese Central Highlands. Hip spent over ten years in Vietnamese jails, persecuted under the Communist government for his political beliefs, before gaining freedom and sanctuary in the U.S. as a refugee. His song *"Char Dega"* (8.17) ("Dega Country") reveals his hopes and dreams, now remote, of one day returning to Vietnam and reuniting with his relatives. In the video, Hip Ksor sings the first verse and chorus of his song (lyrics below translated by Hip Ksor).

> This year, the star is divided in many parts,
> This year, the moon is blooming like a flower,
> This year, look over the country, it is green,
> This year, all the streams gather together
> Chorus:
> Stand up, we go together, (repeat)

O look over there, the Dega country,
There are flowers blooming everywhere in the jungle
This year, the water plant in the stone is blooming,
This year, the leaf comes up at the wrong season,
Everywhere on the road the bird with the red beak (pak k'tra) flies around to ask for something,
In every river valley the bird is looking for something
Chorus:
Stand up, we have to reach, (also: we have to dream)
O look over there, the Dega country,
The mountain is green and the water is good.

An aspiring musician in the Raleigh Montagnard community is Bom Siu, a.k.a. Mondega, who fled Vietnam in 1996 at the age of nine with his father and other family members. After

FIGURE 8.4 Raleigh musician and Montagnard community leader, Hip Ksor

surviving his troubled teenage years living in a refugee housing complex in Raleigh, Bom Siu was introduced to music by his older brother, and soon after, discovered hip-hop artists Tupac Shakur, Wu Tang Clan, and DMX. Both the art form and these artists became his inspiration. Mondega began singing and composing his own rap songs. In 2010, he released his debut album *For The People* that presents his journey from warfare and chaos in Vietnam to immigration and culture shock in the United States In the title track "For the People" (8.18), he raps in English and also in Jarai (at 2'21"). He became a respected Asian American hip-hop artist and producer performing locally and regionally. For Mondega, rapping and hip-hop culture are his way of speaking out for the rights of his people and expressing his own hybrid Montagnard American identity, as clearly articulated in his single, "Stand My Ground" (8.19) (2010):

> …Enemies don't deserve a space in my conscience,
> My culture, my people, I hope for
> Peace back home as our kids grow hopeful,
> For equal rights and a leader they can vote for,
> Instead of communist dictators and vultures,
> We are the future that can change it all,
> But it starts with accepting the person that you are…
> Turn up my song,
> I've been waitin' so long,
> But now that I'm here I ain't goin' nowhere,
> Well I gotta stay strong.
> I tell the people "Rise Up,"
> But they try to put me down,
> Then let it be clear, this is my year,
> I'll stand my ground.

Upon arrival from Vietnam, members of this community encountered American music all around them in the larger cultural environment of their adopted home. Hip Ksor and Mondega represent two responses to the refugee experience, characteristic of the generation to which each belongs. For Hip Ksor, America represents freedom and safety, but also separation and alienation from the life, language, land, and people he once knew. In his musical creativity, he gives expression to his nostalgia for the lost homeland, while also serving his community as a link to Montagnard music and cultural forms now transplanted in North Carolina. Mondega adopts an identity of American urban youth and "uses hip-hop as a tool to speak on behalf of the Asian youths living in America, and for his people suffering back home in South East Asia."[4] While Hip Ksor is suspended between two worlds, Mondega is in many ways as American as his neighbors, in dress, dialect, and musical taste. Yet Mondega too reveals his Montagnard heritage in the stories he communicates to other Montagnard youth. His hip-hop name itself is derived from a combination of "Mon" ("Montagnard") and "Dega" ("Sons of the Mountains"), a term Montagnards use to refer to themselves. Thus, as a rapper, he speaks for his people.

Will the teenage girls who swap tank tops and jeans for the long traditional wrap-arounds of their parents and grandparents at Montagnard celebrations learn and perpetuate the gongs, tube zithers, and dances taught by Hip Ksor and other members of his generation? Will they teach the traditional songs and dances to their children? Or will third-generation Montagnards totally assimilate? Only time will tell.

BLACK ATLANTIC (AFRICA/AMERICAS)

Between the 16th and 19th centuries, more than twelve million Africans were transported as cargo to North and South America and the Caribbean. Those who survived the trans-Atlantic passage labored under extremely harsh conditions in the New World, primarily in agriculture growing coffee, sugar, tobacco, rice, and other commodities. They were frequently and systematically stripped of their African names, their religions, languages, and ways of life. The enslaved Africans and their descendants created new hybrid ways of living, developing Creole languages, syncretic religions, and musical forms that combined the rhythms and melodies of Africa with elements of the European transplants among whom they lived. With emancipation came both the opportunities of freedom and the hardships of poverty, prejudice, and discrimination.

The term "**Black Atlantic**" was first coined in 1983 by Robert Ferris Thompson (1932–2021),[5] and expounded upon in the study by sociologist Paul Gilroy, *Black Atlantic: Modernity and Double Consciousness* (1993). The premise of Gilroy's study is that there is a shared cultural experience for people of African descent in Europe, North and South America, and the Caribbean that transcends national borders. The basis of the shared culture is the collective memory of the brutality of slavery that their ancestors endured. The phrase "double consciousness" derives from W.E.B. Dubois' 1903 essay, "The Souls of Black Folks," in which the author comments:

> [For Black people] one ever feels his two-ness, —an American, a Negro [sic]; two souls, two thoughts, two unreconciled strivings; two warring ideals in one dark body, whose dogged strength alone keeps it from being torn asunder. The history of the American Negro is the history of this strife – this longing to attain self-conscious manhood, to merge his double self into a better and truer self.[6]

The citizens of the Black Atlantic have this shared **double identity** in common. It is not so much a racial or African identity as an experiential identity. It is not only the heritage of slavery, but the continuing legacy of living in societies, on either side of the Atlantic, haunted by attitudes of white supremacy. In 2021, *New York Times* columnist Charles Blow acknowledged this double consciousness and shared identity first articulated by DuBois more than a hundred years ago. Following the deportation of desperate Haitian refugees at the American southern border,

Blow writes,

> Yes, there were the outrageous images of agents on horseback herding the migrants like cattle, and there was also the administration aggressively deporting the migrants back to Haiti.
>
> When I see those Black bodies at the border, I am unable to separate them from myself, or my family, or my friends. They are us. There is a collective consciousness in blackness, born of the white supremacist erasure of our individuality.
>
> Your accomplishment is never your own, but a credit to the race. Your sins are never your own, but a stain on the race. In America, and throughout the diaspora, all Black people are linked together like a chain of paper dolls.[7]

The many hybrid forms of Black music and dance that have come out of the far-flung African diasporic community—blues, jazz, soul, reggae, samba, hip-hop, etc.—have disproportionately influenced musics throughout the world. Gilroy makes the point that it is the enormous vitality of Black creative culture that held this community together with the will to survive during slavery and its aftermath; and the struggle continues.

The 20th-century recording industry contributed greatly to the spread and cross-fertilization of Black musical resources globally. To take one example, from the 1920s through the 1950s, the city of Havana, Cuba attracted thousands of wealthy Americans and others to its nightclubs and gaming tables. Dance bands accompanied the popular dance crazes of the time—rumba, mambo, and cha-cha-cha. Dense polyrhythms played on congas and cowbells, and driving brass arrangements influenced by North American jazz made the music of Havana among the most dynamic and popular in the world. This Afro-Cuban dance music was itself hybrid; it combined the African rhythms brought to the New World during the slave trade with Spanish music of the colonizers. Recordings of this music then found their way back to Africa. In the mid-20th century, the recording industry in Africa was based in Leopoldville, Belgian Congo (known after Independence in 1960 as Kinshasa, Democratic Republic of Congo). Urban musicians there imitated the Afro-Cuban sound they heard on recordings and the radio, but singing in their local languages. Congolese musicians in particular created their own form of rumba and a local style known as *soukous*, further hybridizing an already hybridized form of dance music. Thus, musical forms originating in Africa, brought to Cuba during the slave trade, returned to Africa transformed for further hybridization.

Carifesta is a pan-Caribbean arts festival that has been held every two or three years since 1972 in different Caribbean capital cities. More than thirty countries participate in what has been called "the cultural Olympics of the region,"[8] celebrating over ten days the unity, diversity, and creativity of the Caribbean peoples. The festival began in the small South American country of Guyana, and was the fruition of an idea that came from a Caribbean writers' convention there in 1970. There were simultaneous developments in the economic and political domains under the heading CARICOM (Caribbean Community), modeled after the European Union. The goals of CARICOM were to integrate the various republics of the Caribbean region, many of them newly liberated from colonial rule. Fifteen full members and five associate member states in the Caribbean formed a single market with treaties affecting trade, immigration, health and safety standards, etc. According to UNESCO's Diversity of Cultural Expressions Program, the Carifesta arts festival, "represents the coming together of CARICOM to see and experience the best of the region, culturally"[9] (Figure 8.5).

Reporting from Carifesta X in 2009, Bernice Akuamoah of UNICEF Radio wrote:

> After enduring centuries of colonialism, slavery, and indentured servitude, the people of Latin America and the Caribbean emerged with one of the richest blends of cultures in the world. Throughout the region, Africans, Europeans, east and south Asians, and indigenous Americans are mixing the old ways with the new, creating a dynamic incubator for artists, dancers and musicians.[10]

Carifesta is an expression of the musical, theatrical, artistic, and literary achievements coming out of this "dynamic incubator." It became the cultural voice of CARICOM, demonstrating through the arts the Caribbean community's vision of unity and diversity. Throughout the years, the opening ceremony at Carifesta has provided an opportunity for the host country to showcase its most impressive star performers. A scene from the Carifesta opening ceremony (8.20) held August 15–25, 2019 in Trinidad and Tobago features several of Trinidad and Tobago's most dynamic performers, including superstar calypsonian David Rudder.

FIGURE 8.5 Carifesta XIII poster, Barbados, 2017

Also featured on the sound stage are stilt performers, singers and dancers in native costumes, and a steel band, iconic throughout the region of pan-Caribbean identity. The lyrics of David Rudder's calypso speak to his fervent love for his island home "T & T."

> Sweet sweet T&T, Oh how I love up this country
> Sweet sweet T&T, No place in this world I'd rather be
> Sweet sweet T&T, Oh how I love up meh country
> Sweet sweet T&T, All dis sugar can't be good for me
> All these years I spent abroad in the cold, longing to be home
> Trini to bone, trini to de bone
> God I pray that some sweet day, I will no longer have to roam

What makes these lyrics so poignant is that from a population of nearly 1.5 million people, more than 350,000 have emigrated to the United States and Canada. The song is a call to Rudder's fellow Trinidadians to come home.

INDO-TRINIDADIANS (TRINIDAD/INDIA)

Trinidad is the southernmost island in the West Indies and the larger of the two islands of the Republic of Trinidad and Tobago (Map 8.2). In this former British colony, the largest ethnic group is now the Trinidadian population of Asian Indian descent, which numbers slightly more than Trinidadians of African heritage, known as Creoles. Trinidad was a plantation economy

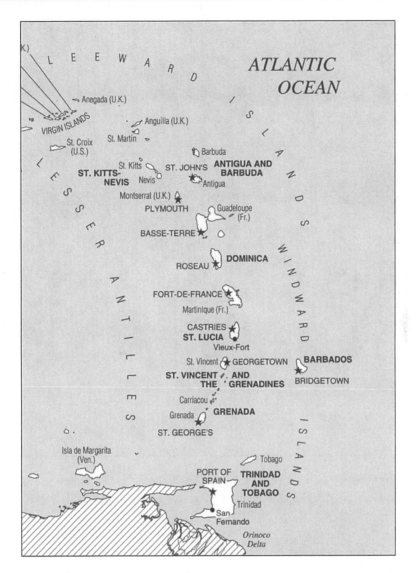

MAP 8.2 Trinidad and Tobago in the West Indies

Source: Garland Encyclopedia of World Music, Vol. 2, South America, Mexico, Central America, and the Caribbean

based on sugar cultivation that required a large population of slave laborers, as in Suriname. After emancipation of the slaves of African descent in 1838, the British brought East Indians from colonial India to work on the sugar cane plantations between 1845 and 1917. Most came from the Indian states of Bihar and Uttar Pradesh as indentured workers, free to return to India by contract after five years or to receive a parcel of land of their own (Map 8.3). Over 75% chose not to return to India. The descendants of African and East Indian populations both preserved and developed music that their ancestors had brought to the island; and living side by side, they created new hybrid musical genres combining aspects of each.

MAP 8.3 North India showing the states of Bihar, Uttar Pradesh, and Rajasthan

Source: Garland Encyclopedia of World Music, Vol. 5, South Asia: The Indian Subcontinent

Until the 1970s, the music and dance styles of the Creoles and East Indian communities had little influence on each other. Trinidad Creoles created a distinct and dynamic music culture from which steel drums, calypso, and the limbo dance originated. The calypso song form in particular, with roots going back to West Africa, was closely connected to Trinidadian Creole identity. Prior to Trinidad's independence from Britain in 1962, calypso lyrics often provided the most reliable source of local news, with clever calypsonians using word play to get around the colonial censors.

The East Indian population sang songs that their ancestors brought with them several generations before, comprising a rich repertoire of vocal and instrumental music associated with life-cycle celebrations, religious festivals, and daily activities. In addition, Bollywood film songs introduced through Hindi films shown on the island became part of their repertoire.

Around the time of Independence, a popular modern genre emerged from the East Indian population called "***chutney***," aptly named after a spicy Indian condiment. *Chutney*'s origins lie in India, in songs and dances that women performed at weddings and other life-cycle events. These wedding songs were sung at gender-segregated gatherings and typically had lewd lyrics and erotic dance movements. The fast tempos, often suggestive love lyrics sung in Hindi, and the sensuous dancing and "wining" (pelvic rotation) of modern *chutney* reflect this Indian heritage.

In the past in both India and Trinidad, Indian men and women typically did not dance together on public occasions such as weddings. "A man who danced with women," writes ethnomusicologist Peter Manuel, "would have been considered effeminate, while a woman who danced with men … would be assumed to be of loose morals."[11] Gradually, however, there was relaxation of social inhibitions in the East Indian community due to the influence of Creole culture, in which intimate male–female dancing was the norm. As *chutney* became more popular and more influenced by Creole dance music, its performers added electric guitars, drum sets, and amplified voices to the traditional Indian *tabla* drums and *dhantal* to give it a more modern and hybrid sound. The hip swiveling of young *chutney* dancers provoked public outcry from conservative and ultra-religious members of the Indo-Trinidadian community. They denounced *chutney* wining as vulgar and obscene. Yet as is evident in this video of an Indo-Trinidadian wedding celebration with singer Sally Sagram and her musicians, *chutney* and *chutney* wining (8.21) remained popular despite these objections (Figure 8.6).

In the mid-1980s another new crossover style emerged from the Indo-Trinidadian community when singer Drupatee Ramgoonai released her first album titled *Chatnee Soca*. The term "*so-ca*" had already been applied to a Creole blend of calypso with soul, R&B, and funk. These genres were introduced from North America. **Chutney soca** is a combination blending *chutney* melodies, **soca** rhythms, and songs sung in both Hindi and English language versions. By the mid-1990s, both **Indo-Trinidadian** and Creole artists were singing English language *chutney socas* and performing them in the enormously popular calypso/*soca* competitions held annually during Carnival time. These events remain hugely popular in Trinidad, attracting hundreds of singers and thousands of listeners. Winners, called "Monarchs," earn large

FIGURE 8.6 Sally Sagram performs at the *Chutney Soca* Monarch finals in San Fernando, Trinidad, 2011

cash prizes and star status. One of the most successful *chutney soca* performers is Sharlene Boodram, whose cover of a French hit song *"Joe Le Taxi"* (8.22) in 1997 became an international hit. One can hear Hindi film song, techno, Afro-Caribbean beats layered beneath clever wordplay, and rapping by the hip-hop artist Mista Vybe. *Chutney* has indeed come a long way from its original context in Hindu weddings. Since the late 1990s, *chutney* and its offshoot *chutney soca* have become internationally popular music and dance genres. Songs by Indo-Trinidadian and Creole singers circulate around the world via the internet and satellite radio, and *chutney* singers perform live concerts in New York, Toronto, and other major cities with sizeable Caribbean immigrant populations

Another expression of musical hybridity in the Indo-Trinidadian community may be heard in the fusion band Pantar, led by sitarist and composer Mungal Patasar (Figure 8.7). Mungal was born in Trinidad in 1948, of parents who emigrated from India. He learned to play a number of musical instruments in his youth including the Indian harmonium and *dholak* drum, the Western clarinet and mandolin, and the Indo-Trinidadian *dhantal*. In his early twenties he took Indian *sitar* lessons with Professor H.S. Adesh in Trinidad and later traveled to India to study *sitar* at Banaras Hindu University. In addition to this interest in Indian classical music, Mungal began experimenting with musical fusion, mixing Indian music with calypso and jazz. He formed his band Pantar in 1994, naming it after the two lead instruments, the steelpan ("pan-") and the *sitar* ("-tar"). His vision was to embrace the diverse cultures of the Caribbean in his band, and the result was a collaboration of Indo- and Afro-Trinidadian musicians and a fusion of musical styles. Pantar's band members play electric guitar, electric bass, drum set, *tablas*, tenor steel pan, second pan, keyboards, flute, saxophone, wind synthesizer,

FIGURE 8.7 Mungal Patasar and his band Pantar perform at Lincoln Center's Caribbean Roots Festival, New York City, July 2000

and *sitar*. The band released its first album *Nirvana* in 1997, followed by *Dreadlocks* in 2000. Mungal continued his creative collaborations on his third album, *Calabasse Café* (8.23) (2006), described in the disc notes as "the place where all the beautiful streams of the different cultures of the Caribbean meet ... the convergence of Europe, Africa, the Americas and the Orient." In a rehearsal of "Awake" (8.24) (on *Dreadlocks*, track 4) at Mungal Patasar's home in 2008, the band creatively adapts the original version of "Awake" (8.25) adding new harmonies, solos on guitar and wind synthesizer (including a quote from The Beatles' "Norwegian Wood"), and North Indian classical music patterns such as the rapid alternation of *sitar* and drum set. Mungal Patasar and Pantar have gained international recognition at performances in the United States and Europe. In reviewing the 2006 WOMEX World Music festival in Seville, Spain, Banning Eyre writes,

> For Sean Barlow and I, the standouts this year were Afel Bocoum of Mali, Alfonso of Cuba, El Tanbura of Egypt, ... and—a surprise—an eclectic band from Trinidad and Tobago, Mungal Patasar and Pantar, who combine steel pans and Caribbean pop beats with Mungal's own Indian *sitar*.[12]

These examples of *chutney, chutney soca,* and Indo-jazz fusion show how this Indo-Trinidadian community has maintained links with its cultural homeland of India. As an immigrant population it continues to face choices on the degree to which it assimilates with the Creole population and simultaneously fosters the culture of its ancestral roots. What emerges is a vigorous hybrid culture in which Indo-Trinidadians preserve, adapt, and negotiate an identity that expresses complex and shifting allegiances to both the distant homeland and their New World home.[13] At the same time the Indo-Trinidadians share an island with the Creole population, whose diet, language, music, dance, and customs have enriched Indo-Trinidadian life, and who in turn have been enriched by the proximity of their Asiatic neighbors.

MAY 4TH MOVEMENT (CHINA)

Another example of hybridity deals with musical reforms proposed by Chinese intellectuals following World War I. The **May 4th Movement** was a call for the re-examination of all aspects of Chinese culture and society: art, literature, education, language, and music. During the 19th century, China suffered a number of defeats at the hands of Western armies with their superior weapons technologies. The industrial powers of the West and Japan had by coercion opened foreign-ruled districts within Chinese port cities, and had taken areas of the Chinese coast and placed them under colonial rule: Hong Kong for Britain, Macau for Portugal, Taiwan for Japan, and Qingdao on the Shandong Peninsula for Germany. The emperors of the Qing Dynasty (1644–1911) and the populace at large considered these conquests deeply humiliating but were powerless to reclaim these territories.

In 1911, a popular uprising overthrew the Qing Dynasty, and a republican form of government was established for the first time in China's 4,000-year history. The new Republic of China supported the Allied Powers against Germany in World War I, sending more than 100,000 laborers to France for the war effort. When Germany was defeated in 1918, the Chinese assumed that the Shandong Peninsula would revert to Chinese control, since the Treaty of Versailles divested Germany of all overseas colonial holdings (Map 8.4). Yet Japan, now the most powerful industrialized nation in Asia, pressured and won over the Allied negotiators and took control of the Shandong Peninsula. On May 4th, 1919, more than 5,000 university students took to the streets of Beijing to protest the weak response by their government to what became known as the "Shandong Problem." There followed a period of social unrest marked by intense cultural re-evaluation. Urban intellectuals sought to account for China's weakness and technological backwardness, and to find a way forward that would lead to the building of a strong and united country.

A small, college-educated urban population of technocrats deemed the music of the old feudal order unscientific, backward, and regressive. These reformers complained that Chinese music was distinct for what it lacked, relative to Western music. An American-educated Chinese journalist wrote in 1919: "So, in one word, Chinese music lacks a standard in every respect. It has no standard scale, no standard pitch, no standard instruments, no standard music compositions."[14] Western instruments like the piano and violin became extremely popular among the urban elites. Several eminent European composers and educators taught in China and encouraged local composers. Russian musicians in particular, fleeing the chaos

MAP 8.4 Eastern and central China showing Shandong Peninsula, Shanghai, Wuxi, and northern Shaanxi Province (Shaanbei)

Source: Garland Encyclopedia of World Music, Vol. 7, East Asia: China, Japan, and Korea

FIGURE 8.8 Ma Sicong (1912–1987) on Chinese stamp, ca. 2012

in their own country following the 1917 Bolshevik Revolution, took active roles in bringing symphonic music to China. Young musicians, eager to take part in the modern world that Europe represented, embraced these innovations. A number furthered their education with study in Europe, and many became highly accomplished artists. Western notation was adapted for use in music education, and Chinese instruments were modified to produce timbres and intonation more like Western instruments. Traditional pentatonic folk songs were provided with chordal harmonies and Western-style accompaniments. A new kind of Chinese national music emerged.

Among the most important of these accomplished Chinese musicians was violinist Ma Sicong (Figure 8.8). Born into a family of scholars, Ma showed great early talent and was sent to Paris for musical study twice: at the age of eleven for the violin, and again at twenty for composition. He was known as "China's King of the Violin," and his compositions for orchestra and violin were extremely popular. Following the Communist victory in 1949, Ma became the Founding President of the Central Music Conservatory in Beijing. Among his compositions for Western instruments are symphonies, concertos, operas, and ballets: genres associated with the European classical tradition. Yet most are based upon Chinese folk melodies, pentatonic scales, and recognizable musical gestures associated with Chinese performance practices, like frequent sliding between pitches. His compositions feature chordal accompaniment and structural principles developed from his studies in the West. Among his most popular works is "Nostalgia" for violin and piano (1937). It was heard all over China in the 1950s via phonograph records and radio broadcasts. Millions responded enthusiastically to its sentimental mood. By mid-century, such harmonies and instrumental timbres had been completely absorbed and accepted as the musical language of the "new" China. A performance of "Nostalgia" (8.26) by Hsiao-mei Ku and the late Dr. Benjamin Ward of Duke University shows why the piece inspired longing for a simpler time in the face of rapid social change. Professor Ku performed for Ma Sicong as a child prodigy in China when she was nine years old.

CONCLUSION

The power of music often lies in its ability to project multiple identities simultaneously, expressing various cultural strands through audible markers. The listener can hear these markers and, while recognizing each as a component of hybrid identity, experiences the expressive whole as greater than the sum of its parts. In Cajun music, the sounds of a cumulative history can be heard. The history of Cajuns and Creoles includes migration, encounters with others, and new technologies and ways of life. This hybrid music, meaningful, enjoyable, and danceable in the present, is at the same time rooted in the combined expressions of past generations. Among the Montagnards, music is a way for an immigrant community to express feelings about both a distant and lost homeland and an adopted country that offers freedom and protection. Music is also a contested area for cultural negotiations across generational lines. Grandparents watch their grandchildren, born in America, seek identities more closely resembling American youth than their family members back in the Central Highlands. Descendants of the twelve million slaves brought to the New World as chattel continue two centuries following emancipation to seek full equality and economic justice. Their forms of music and dance developed throughout the Black Atlantic, both enriching and challenging expressive culture throughout the New World.

In Trinidad, an island nation shared almost equally by two ethnic groups of quite distinct heritage, the Indo-Trinidadian population negotiates between identification with the rich cultural traditions of India, and the popular contemporary styles of their Creole neighbors. Added to the hybrid mix is North American popular music, with its domineering genres of jazz, R&B, soul, and hip-hop. Following the May 4th, 1919 protest in Beijing, Chinese intellectuals and reformers intentionally hybridized traditional music with Western compositional techniques in order to project to themselves and to the world China's entry into the modern age. Music not only expresses the blending and mixing of identities, it can also communicate and convey antagonistic relationships. The next chapter considers music when it serves as a catalyst for protest and resistance in a time of conflict.

KEY TERMS AND CONCEPTS

Ancestral Culture

Assimilation

Black Atlantic

Carifesta

Chinese National Music

Collective Heritage

Creole

Double Identity

Hybrid Culture

Hybrid Identity

Indigenous

Musical Fusion

Old Feudal Order

Refugee

Revitalization

Shandong Problem

THINKING ABOUT MUSIC

1   Video 8.2 showing traditional Korean zithers (*gayageum*) playing Pachelbel's *Canon in D* accompanied by beatboxing, DJ scratching, and break dancing (Chapter 8 Introduction) is an advertisement for a construction company that builds apartment complexes in Seoul, South Korea (ROK). Considering the various identities expressed in the performance, what kind of tenants do you think this advertisement was meant to attract?

2   Define "hybridity" in your own words. Then, think of a hybridized genre of popular music in America such as rockabilly, hip-hop, country-western, K-pop, etc. What musical elements contribute to its defining sound?

3   Many Americans have a "hyphenated" identity—Chinese American, African American, Latin American, for example. Talk to a member of your family, a classmate, or a neighbor for whom this applies. How do they use music to express the different parts of their identity? How do the different generations of their family relate to music of the ancestral homeland in contrast to mainstream American music?

4   Why did Cajun music in Louisiana nearly disappear in the mid-20th century, and why did it make a comeback? How do people in America (the land of immigrants) negotiate their identities between the local and the mainstream? Which of these metaphors do you think better describes America: as a "melting pot" or as a "colorful mosaic"? Why?

5   Considering the Montagnard community, how does the passage of time affect the musical preferences of the Vietnam-born generation and the first generation born in America? Then, how do these two generations relate to each other musically?

6   The music reforms in China that began with the May 4th Movement created a fusion of Western harmonies and Chinese melodies. How did this hybridized form of expression contribute to creating a "modern" Chinese identity? When you listen to the performance of "Nostalgia" (Video 8.26), played on the piano and violin, what makes it sound "Chinese" to you?

7   Is DJ "sampling" a form of hybridity? Explain.

NOTES

1   Ben Sandmel, "Amédé Ardoin," *64 Parishes*, April 20, 2016, updated 2019, https://64parishes.org/entry/amede-ardoin/.

2   Alan Lomax, producer and narrator, *Cajun Country: Don't Drop the Potato*, American Patchwork film series, 1990.

3   Barry J. Ancelet, *Cajun and Creole Music Makers: Musiciens Cadiens et Créoles* (Jackson, MS: University Press of Mississippi, 1999).

4   "Mondega–I Have a Dream," notes on YouTube page, video uploaded by mylifeandrhymes, 2010, https://www.youtube.com/watch?v=3as1kIMJ5gw.

5   Robert Ferris Thompson, *Flash of the Spirit* (New York: Knopf Doubleday Publishing Group, 1983).

6 W.E.B. Du Bois, *The Souls of Black Folk: Essays and Sketches* (Chicago, IL: A. C. McClurg and Co., 1903).

7 From an opinion piece by Charles Blow, *New York Times*, Sept. 26, 2021.

8 Michelle Nurse, "Barbados Gets Ready for Carifesta," *Caricom Today*, Jan. 22, 2017, https://today.caricom.org/2017/01/20/barbados-gets-ready-for-carifesta/.

9 *The Caribbean Festival of the Arts*, UNESCO Diversity of Cultural Expressions, https://en.unesco.org/creativity/policy-monitoring-platform/caribbean-festival-arts-carifesta.

10 Bernice Akuamoah, UNICEF report on Carifesta 1972, no longer available online, formerly at, http://www.unicef.org/infobycountry/guyana_50002.html.

11 Peter Manuel, *East Indian Music in the West Indies: Tan-singing, Chutney, and the Making of Indo-Caribbean Culture* (Philadelphia: Temple University Press, 2000), 172.

12 Banning Eyre, "WOMAD 2006: Report and Photo Essay" (photos by Banning Eyre and Sean Barlow), *Afropop Worldwide*, no longer available online, formerly at, http://www.afropop.orgmulti/feature/ID/660/.

13 Helen Myers, "Indian, East Indian, and West Indian Music in Felicity, Trinidad," in *Ethnomusicology and Modern Music History*, ed. Stephen Blum, et al. (Champaign, IL: University of Indiana Press, 1991), 231–241.

14 Lieu Da-kun, "Chinese Music," in *Peking Leader Special Anniversary Supplement—China in 1918*, Peking [Beijing], February 12, 1919, cited in Kuo-huang Han and Lindy Li Mark, "Evolution and Revolution in Chinese Music," in *Musics of Many Cultures: An Introduction*, ed. Elizabeth May (Berkeley: University of California Press, 1980), 22.

CHAPTER 9

Music and Oppositional Identity

INTRODUCTION

Music is involved in the projection of identity through advertising, tourism, popular media, and collective rituals like sporting events, festivals, and religious ceremonies. However, aspects of identity may derive not from belonging but from opposing. One can describe oneself as anti-Communist, anti-corporate, anti-monarchy. Athletic teams and their fight songs exemplify the concept of oppositional identity. The home team's identity is constructed in opposition to that of the visiting team without whom mascots and fight songs become unnecessary. Oppositional relationships are power relationships, and music is often involved in the expression of power. Some power is institutional and some is subversive of institutions.

Throughout history, music has served as a potent marker of power and prestige. For more than 3,000 years, Chinese emperors sponsored elaborate rituals of state that validated the legitimacy of the rulers. These rituals featured magnificent music and dance performances that were meticulously prepared and choreographed. Emperor Akbar the Great (1542–1605) of the Indian **Mughal Empire** invited the finest musicians of the realm to perform at court as a display of his magnificence. Among them was the legendary Mian Tansen (ca. 1493–ca. 1586), an important composer and singer whom Akbar honored as one of his *Navaratnas* ("nine jewels"), so great was Tansen's esteem. The *Navaratnas* were a distinguished group of powerful courtiers that included generals, ministers, and poets. Tansen led the court music ensemble, called the *naubat*, which served a variety of imperial functions, and was frequently depicted in Mughal paintings of court life, as seen in the illustration in Figure 9.1.

> They played when the emperor made his daily presence before his subjects, they heralded processions, were used for signaling in battle, provided accompaniment for female dancers in the harem and were an indispensable part of celebrations which marked the birth of an heir, marriages, the new year and other festivals.[1]

Like the royal robes, the lavish furnishings of the palace, the royal insignias, and uniformed palace guards, the *naubat* and its music were continuous reminders of the emperor's authority and power.

FIGURE 9.1 Naubat drummers and lute and frame drum players accompanying dancers at the court of Emperor Akbar the Great, 16th-century Persian miniature

For several centuries the kings of Buganda maintained the largest and most powerful state in central Africa, and their palaces resounded throughout each day with music. The musical richness at court featured xylophone ensembles, the royal flute band, the songs of the king's harpist and lyre players, as well as praise drumming and dancing.

Not only political power but also military power has for millennia been symbolized and projected through music. In the Old Testament Book of Joshua, the armed men of Israel went forth "led by the priests who blew trumpets" and brought down the walls of Jericho. Roman legions marched across Europe to the sound of brass trumpets and horns. These instruments signaled instructions such as "advance" or "retreat" to soldiers in battle. They also signified the authority of the general and were blown when an action was carried out under his command, as when a soldier was executed for treason or cowardice. The **janissary** bands of the Ottoman Empire (1299–1922) proclaimed the military superiority of the ruling Sultan with double-reed pipes (*zurna*), natural trumpets (*boru*), bass drums (*davul*), small kettledrums (*nakkara*), large kettledrums (*kos*), cymbals (*zil*), and the jingling bells of the Turkish crescent (*çevgan*). By the 16th century, the Janissaries became a model for military marching bands throughout Europe. Napoleon Bonaparte, rising to power in the aftermath of the French Revolution (1789–1799), placed enormous importance on military bands, both for ceremonial occasions such as the review of the troops, and for coordinating his army's marching and drill. In the 19th century, with European powers colonizing much of the world, the military band became a standard presence in colonial territories. Now in the post-colonial era virtually every military establishment around the globe supports a military band (Figures 9.2 and 9.3).

FIGURE 9.2 Turkish Janissary band playing (L to R) the Turkish crescent (*çevgan*), bass double-reed pipe (*kaba zurna*), and natural trumpets (*boru*) in Bucharest, Romania, 2007

FIGURE 9.3 Roman horns on Trajan's Column in Rome

Music has also frequently served as an expression of oppositional identity. Members of the Irish Republican Army, trade unionists in Korea, and Chinese students in Tiananmen Square similarly used songs, drums, and guitars as weapons against the power of the state. Aware of the subversive power of music to unite people for collective action, governments have frequently resorted to censorship, suppression, and even murder to silence the musical voices of protest.

This chapter begins with a discussion of protest music in the United States. During the 1950s and 1960s, musicians were on the front line of resistance during both the Civil Rights and anti-Vietnam War movements. Singers such as Bob Dylan, Harry Belafonte, Pete Seeger, Odetta, and Joan Baez were public voices articulating the anger and frustration of millions seeking social justice and peace. The chapter presents an additional six case studies that explore oppositional music from various parts of the world in the 20th and 21st centuries.

PETE SEEGER AND PROTEST SONGS (USA)

Pete Seeger (1919–2014) was an American musician and activist who composed, recorded, and popularized some of the most important and influential protest songs of the mid-twentieth century. His father Charles Seeger was a Harvard professor and one of the founders of the field of Ethnomusicology. Pete dropped out of Harvard, taught himself the banjo, and spearheaded a popular folk song revival. He bought his first banjo in 1936 at a pawn shop in New York for $5 and broke it when he jumped from a fast-moving freight train. He had learned to hop freight trains from his folk song mentor Woody Guthrie, composer of "This Land is Your Land, This Land Is My Land," a song with obvious Socialist implications. Indeed, Seeger had joined the Young Communist League at age seventeen (Figure 9.4).

Following World War II, during which Seeger served in an army entertainment unit, he resumed his performing career, focusing on reviving songs from the early 20th-century American labor movement. These songs had galvanized attempts by the IWW (International Workers of the World) and other organizations to unionize workers and collectively shake up the economic status quo. For the labor movement to succeed, solidarity among workers was required, since strikes were often violently suppressed. Union meetings and rallies included much singing of songs and raising of fists. Banjo in hand, Seeger joined the ongoing struggle for unified and collective protest in factories, farms, mills, and mines. Seeger joined rallies, singing songs like "Roll the Union On," "Black Lung," and "I Am Union and I Am Proud."

FIGURE 9.4 Pete Seeger

These songs mobilized the strikers on picket lines and gave them courage to stand up to strike breakers and police baton charges. With his vocal quartet "The Weavers," he popularized such labor anthems as the miner's complaint by Merle Travis, "16 Tons."

> Sixteen Tons and What Do You Get? Another Day Older and Deeper in Debt
> Saint Peter don't'cha call me cause I can't go, I owe my soul to the company store.

In 1956, during Senator Joseph McCarthy's House Un-American Activities hearings, Seeger was found in contempt for refusing to name names of Communist sympathizers he had known before World War II. He was sentenced to a year in prison. His sentence was overturned on a technicality, although he was blacklisted from giving public concerts and making recordings. During the turbulent 1960s, Seeger wrote several of the most powerful and popular Civil Rights and Anti-War protest songs, including "If I Had a Hammer" (9.1) and "Waist Deep in the Big Muddy" (9.2). The latter song gained national notoriety when it was censored from a popular television show, The Smothers Brothers Comedy Hour, in 1967. He adapted what was to become the anthem of the Civil Rights movement, "We Shall Overcome," from an African-American hymn. He sang this song on the fifty-mile Civil Rights walk from Selma to Montgomery, Alabama, along with Dr. Martin Luther King, Jr. and 1,000 other marchers.

In 1969, he began a decades-long campaign to clean up the Hudson River in New York, and he continued into his eighties singing songs of protest against powerful corporate interests. Although his support of left-wing causes, particularly in his youth, continued to haunt him throughout his life, he received many honors in his final years. These included his induction into the Rock and Roll Hall of Fame (in the "Early Influence" category), the Recording Academy Lifetime Achievement Award, the National Medal of the Arts, and among his three Grammy Awards, one in 2009 for the album "At 89." On the head of his banjo were written the words, "This Machine Surrounds Hate and Forces It to Surrender." Pete Seeger died before the Global Warming and Green Movements, Black Lives Matter, #MeToo, and a host of other causes he would have fought for with his banjo and his songs.

The American Civil Rights Movement was a campaign to end Jim Crow discriminatory laws in the South, and a fight for equal rights and protections under the law for African Americans. For more than a hundred years, the struggles produced many powerful songs. None, however, were as dramatic or as effective as the 1939 Billie Holiday classic, "Strange Fruit." The text and tune were written by a Jewish New York City school teacher named Abel Meeropol. He was inspired by the horror of seeing a 1930 photograph of two young African-American men hanging from a tree. Thomas Shipp and Abram Smith had been pulled out of a prison cell in Marion, Indiana by a mob of 4,000 and lynched. Haunted by the image, Meeropol published his 1937 poem in a teacher's union newspaper. It begins,

> Southern trees bear a strange fruit,
> Blood on the leaves and blood at the root,
> Black body swinging in the Southern breeze,
> Strange fruit hanging from the poplar trees...[2]

In 1939, the song was given to Billie Holiday, who was singing nightly at the Café Society on 4th Street, the sole integrated music club in New York City. She made the song her own. The first night she sang it at the end of her set, she requested that the lights be turned out except for a spotlight on her face. Also, she asked that all food and drink service be stopped, and her performance followed by silence. For the next twenty years, until her death, she doggedly repeated the performance nightly, but without pleasure. The song reminded her of her father, who had died at age 39 of lung disease after being denied entrance to a whites-only hospital. In her autobiography, *Lady Sings the Blues* (1956), she wrote, "But I have to keep singing it, not only because people ask for it, but because 20 years after Pop died, the things that killed him are still happening in the South."[3] Her 1939 recording of "Strange Fruit" (9.3) sold more than a million copies. When anti-lynching legislation came before congress, which had repeatedly been blocked by Southern senators' filibusters, thousands of activists mailed copies of the recording to their legislators. In 1999, *Time Magazine* named "Strange Fruit" as "Best Song of the Century."

The murder of a black man, George Floyd, by a white Minneapolis police officer in May 2019 triggered nationwide street protests, among the largest in American history. For more than a decade, the **Black Lives Matter** Movement had actively and publicly expressed dissent against an epidemic of police violence. The BLM protest movement came to a head when millions of Americans saw on video police officer Derick Chauvin kneeling on the neck of Mr. Floyd as he pleaded, "I can't breathe" for nine minutes until his death. These events and their aftermath inspired a song by the artist Gabby Wilson (H.E.R.) called, simply, "I Can't Breathe" (9.4). Named "Song of the Year" by the 2020 **Grammys**, "I Can't Breathe" bore eerie echoes of "Strange Fruit" (in the line "the strange fruit hanging from my family tree") composed nearly a century earlier:

> Is too hard for your trust-fund pockets to swallow
> To swallow the strange fruit hanging from my family tree
> Because of your audacity
> To say all men are created equal in the eyes of God
> But disparage a man based on the color of his skin
> Do not say you do not see color
> When you see us, see us
> We can't breathe…

MARIA STOYANOVA (BULGARIA)

Maria Stoyanova (b. 1953) is a professional performer and teacher of the Bulgarian *gaida* (bagpipe) (Figure 9.5). Bulgaria is a small country in Eastern Europe that, during the time of Stoyanova's childhood, was isolated, agrarian, and part of the Soviet bloc of communist countries. She grew up in a rural, traditional society where only men played musical instruments in public. Maria Stoyanova's story is that of one woman's struggle to assert her identity in a "man's world" (Map 9.1).

Ethnomusicologist Timothy Rice writes that in this society,

> Men and women had, and to a certain extent still have, their distinct spheres of activity, including musical activity. Men, for example, had primary responsibility for taking care of animals, plowing fields, building houses, making wine and spirits, and representing the family in the public arena. Women had primary responsibility for cooking food, cleaning the house and yard, making clothes, and caring for children. Music making was linked to these patterns of work. Men and boys spent long hours alone in pastures and forests with their animals; they made musical instruments from animal skins and wood;

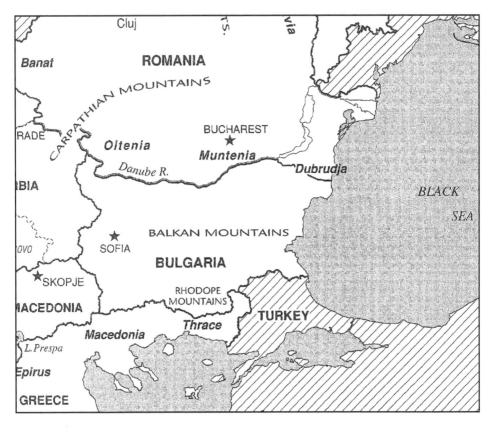

MAP 9.1 Bulgaria in southeastern Europe

Source: Garland Encyclopedia of World Music, Vol. 8, Europe

FIGURE 9.5 Maria Stoyanova

and played them as a way to while away the long hours of solitude. Women's and girls' hands, in contrast, were always busy with housework, and thus not free to play instruments. Thus they learned to sing songs as they learned to embroider, knit, and cook in the social environment of the home among their grandmothers, mothers, aunts, older sisters, and cousins … [but] with the rarest exceptions, never learned to play musical instruments. With all their domestic responsibilities, when would they have had time to practice?

As a child, Maria was fascinated by the sound of the gaida that her father and uncles played. When no one was home, she would take her father's out from under the bed where it was stored and try to play it. When her family discovered this, she was forbidden to continue, but persisted anyway. When she heard that the government was inviting students her age to audition for a newly formed high school for traditional Bulgarian music, she appeared before the admissions panel with her father's gaida and caused an uproar. In the first place, a girl playing the gaida went against the traditions the school was trying to preserve; and in the second, the jury found the thought of a girl blowing into the instrument unseemly and suggestive. However, the communist ideology of the 1960s called for equal opportunity of the sexes, and the constitution put into law "the full emancipation of women."[4]

Maria went on to study *gaida* at a conservatory for traditional music and later became the principal teacher there, as well as a distinguished performer and leader of one of the country's most prestigious wedding ensembles. She came of age after World War II, at a time when gender roles were being redefined and renegotiated. The unusual tenacity she exhibited as a girl learning to play the forbidden instrument met with ultimate success because of shifts in her society at that time, expanding the possible roles a woman could play. This would allow the identities of a woman and an instrumental musician to co-exist in the same person.

In the linked video, Maria Stoyanova (9.5) plays at a wedding in 1998. As in many cultures, weddings in Bulgaria constitute one of the most important venues for musical performance. They are also occasions for the enactment of a society's most conservative forms of communal expression. Although the accordion, electric keyboard, and drum set are fairly recent additions to the wedding band, replacing more traditional instruments, the *gaida* is so ancient and expressive of Bulgarian core values that a proverb states, "a wedding without a *gaida* is impossible." When Stoyanova performs, as she often does with the famous wedding band Kanarite ("The Canaries"; not shown in this video), her presence "always cause[s] quite a stir and provoke[s] lots of audience comments."[5] The irony that the *gaida*, most traditional of all wedding band instruments in her community, is most untraditionally played here by a woman, is not lost on the audience. As the 20th century came to a close, the roles and status of women were being reconsidered in many parts of the world. Maria Stoyanova challenged the limitations historically placed on women in her society, and through her music, *as* a woman, she projected an oppositional identity.

NUEVA CANCIÓN (CHILE/LATIN AMERICA)

The second half of the 20th century saw tumultuous uprisings throughout Latin America by those seeking a more just distribution of resources (Map 9.2). Entrenched oligarchs controlled a large percentage of each country's economy, and powerful militaries were established to defend oligarchic privilege and suppress social unrest. In many Latin American countries, military dictatorships overthrew democratically-elected governments, often with the support of the United States. The American CIA and military regularly intervened to protect American corporate interests in the region and to curb socialist and communist influence during the **Cold War**. To the guns and batons of military repression, musicians throughout Latin America responded with song. From Nicaragua to Argentina and Chile, singers took up the cause of the poor, the imprisoned, and the oppressed rural ***camposinos*** in the "New Song

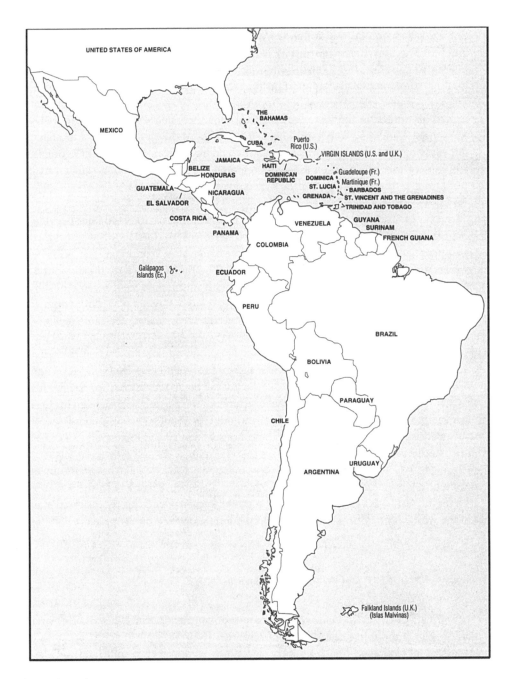

MAP 9.2 Latin America

Source: Garland Encyclopedia of World Music, Vol. 2, South America, Mexico, Central America, and Caribbean

Movement" or **Nueva Canción**. Most of the singers in this movement were college-educated members of the urban middle class. However, they drew their inspiration from the musical traditions of the poor farmers and indigenous peoples of the Andes, traditions that date back to the pre-Columbian period and early Spanish settlement. Their songs and recordings established an internationally recognized Latin American style marked by evocative poetry often accompanied by Andean flutes, panpipes, and the small armadillo-backed *charango*.

> The groups Quilapayún, Inti Illimani and singers such as Victor Jara, Patricio Manns, and Ángel and Isabel Parra epitomise a generation of musicians across the continent and beyond whose formative years in the 1950s and 60s were rooted in ideals of social justice and equality.[6]

In 1970, a popular election in Chile brought to power the socialist Salvadore Allende. Under Allende's leftist coalition government, Victor Jara (1932–1973) and other songwriters and singers enjoyed widespread popularity, performing regularly at a small nightclub in the capital Santiago (Figure 9.6). Jara had been politically active in the period leading up to Allende's election, singing frequently at political rallies. On September 11, 1973, a U.S.-backed military coup brought down the government. Allende was killed and thousands of his supporters, including Victor Jara, were rounded up and imprisoned in a downtown football stadium. There, his captors broke his wrists so that he could not play his guitar, and then, according to eyewitness accounts, taunted him with song requests as he lay on the ground. Defiantly, he sang part of the song of Allende's political party, after which he was executed by machine gun.

Victor Jara became a symbol throughout the world of the oppositional musician martyred for the cause he championed. Pete Seeger created a performance piece around Jara's final poem, *"Estadio Chile"* (9.6), written on a scrap of paper and smuggled out of the stadium after his murder. Seeger's moving narration memorializes Jara and his struggle for the cause of human freedom and dignity.

FIGURE 9.6 Victor Jara

His most famous song, *"Te Recuerdo Amanda"* (9.7), has no shaking fist, but the memory of a lovely young woman going to meet her boyfriend at the factory where he works: a simple acknowledgment of life's surprising beauty. As the Colombian writer Gabriel García Márquez explained, most of the songs of Violetta Parra of Argentina and Victor Jara of Chile, two of the most famous members of the *Nueva Canción* Movement, were not overtly political but rather were profoundly life-affirming.

> I remember you, Amanda,
> the wet street,
> running to the factory where Manuel worked
> The wide smile, rain in your hair,
> nothing mattered,
> you were going to meet with him
> with him, with him, with him, with him
> Five minutes,
> life is eternal
> in five minutes
> The alarm sounds
> for returning to work
> and you, walking, light up everything,
> the five minutes make you blossom.
>
> [English translation by Susan Navey-Davis]

The sports stadium in Santiago where Victor Jara died now bears his name (Figure 9.7).

FIGURE 9.7 Victor Jara Stadium

In his acceptance speech for the 1982 Nobel Prize for Literature, Márquez enumerated for his European audience the collective woes and violent crimes that Latin Americans had endured over the previous several decades.

> We have not had a moment's rest. A promethean president [Salvador Allende of Chile], entrenched in his burning palace, died fighting an entire army, alone…There have been five wars and seventeen military coups … twenty million Latin American children died before the age of one—more than have been born in Europe since 1970. Those missing because of repression number nearly one hundred and twenty thousand. Numerous women arrested while pregnant have given birth in Argentine prisons, yet nobody knows the whereabouts and identity of their children who were furtively adopted or sent to an orphanage by order of the military authorities. Because they tried to change this state of things, nearly two hundred thousand men and women have died throughout the continent, and over one hundred thousand have lost their lives in three small and ill-fated countries of Central America: Nicaragua, El Salvador and Guatemala…. One million people have fled Chile, a country with a tradition of hospitality—that is, ten percent of its population. Uruguay, a tiny nation of two and a half million inhabitants which considered itself the continent's most civilized country, has lost to exile one out of every five citizens. Since 1979, the civil war in El Salvador has produced almost one refugee every twenty minutes. The country that could be formed of all the exiles and forced emigrants of Latin America would have a population larger than that of Norway.
>
> © The Nobel Foundation 1982

Yet he concludes by stating,

> In spite of this, to oppression, plundering and abandonment, we respond with life. Neither floods nor plagues, famines nor cataclysms, nor even the eternal wars of century upon century, have been able to subdue the persistent advantage of life over death. An advantage that grows and quickens.[7]

MUSIC DURING APARTHEID (SOUTH AFRICA)

South Africa is the southernmost country on the continent of Africa, with a population of more than sixty million. Successive waves of European immigrants arrived, beginning in 1652. The first wave consisted of the Dutch *Trek Boers*, meaning "White farmers," who spread north and east into the interior. There they encountered native African populations who frequently engaged them in violent clashes of resistance. The Boers were guided by a pioneering myth similar to the "manifest destiny" of the American West. The British landed at Cape Town in 1795 and likewise moved north and east, annexing land for the Crown. Throughout the next 200 years, thousands of settlers from Great Britain, the Netherlands, and elsewhere arrived and spread through the hinterlands waging wars against each other and the native populations. Europeans controlled nearly the entire region that is today's South Africa by the middle of the 19th century. Only the far northeast remained out of their control. The last holdouts were the descendants of Shaka's great Zulu empire, who resisted the European invasion until 1887 when they finally gave in to superior British firepower.

The British army then took on the descendants of the original Dutch settlers in the two Boer Wars of 1881–1882 and 1899–1902. The strategic location of South Africa, coupled with a temperate climate more like Europe than anywhere else in Africa, led to this wide-scale settlement. Furthermore, the discovery of gold and diamonds in the interior hastened the conquest of the region (Map 9.3).

The Union of South Africa came into being on May 31, 1910 with the incorporation by the British of all the lands previously claimed by **Afrikaners**, ancestors of Dutch, German, and French settlers. Afrikaners were speakers of the Afrikaans language derived from Old Dutch. Immediately the White population, including the British, established harsh policies that segregated most Black South Africans. The Black population itself consisted of a number of ethnic groups before the arrival of the Europeans, including Zulu, Xhosa, Ndebele, Venda, and Lesotho. In 1948 after winning the Whites-only general election, the National Party legalized its racial policies in a system known as **Apartheid**. The entire population was classified into racial groups—Black, White, Colored or Mixed Race, and South Asian—and each group was assigned to separate and segregated lands, areas, and facilities. Black South Africans were denied citizenship and forced to live either in "homelands," economically unproductive regions of the countryside, or in "townships," urban living areas on the edge of "White-only" cities and towns. Only Blacks with approved jobs were allowed into White areas, and then only if they carried an identification pass. Transportation, education, civil institutions such as hospitals, and public facilities such as swimming pools and beaches were all segregated. Such harsh racial discrimination sparked popular uprisings, protests, and in some cases armed insurrection, but the police met all opposition with suppression and brutality. The period of Late Apartheid (1960–1994) was marked by worldwide pressure for its dismantling in the form of economic boycotts and censure. A particularly violent incident occurred in 1960 that brought international attention

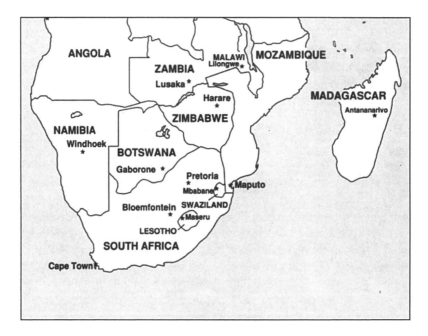

MAP 9.3 Southern Africa and the Republic of Madagascar

Source: Garland Encyclopedia of World Music, Vol. 1, Africa

to this racial strife. A crowd of several thousand Black South Africans staged a peaceful demonstration in the town of Sharpeville against new passbook laws, requiring all non-Whites to show an internal passport to any White person who requested to see it. Police opened fire on the unarmed group, leaving sixty protesters, including women and children, dead in the street. Photographs of the dead appeared in newspapers around the world. The event came to be known as the **Sharpeville Massacre.**

A number of South African musicians emigrated during this period rather than face censorship and possible imprisonment under the Apartheid regime. They used the status they acquired abroad as internationally famous artists to rally support for the economic boycott in Europe and North America. Singer Miriam Makeba (1932–2008), pianist Abdullah Ibrahim (born Adolph Johannes Brand, b. 1934), and jazz trumpet virtuoso Hugh Masekela (1939–2018) all spread the message of racial oppression in their home-land (Figure 9.8). They used their music and celebrity to keep the plight of Black South Africans in the international public eye. One of Masekela's most famous compositions, *"Stimela* (Coal Train)" (9.8), dramatically describes the tragic conditions under which the miners of Johannesburg lived out their lives. Hugh Masekela grew up in the mining camps of Johannesburg in the 1940s and 1950s where his grandmother owned a *shebeen* (tavern) catering to the mineworkers. He was not a miner himself, but as a boy he worked in the tavern. An anti-Apartheid Anglican chaplain, Archbishop Trevor Huddleson, gave him his first trumpet when he was fourteen. Huddleson was a friend of American jazz leg-end Louis Armstrong who, at the recommendation of Huddleson, sent the young prodigy

FIGURE 9.8 Hugh Masekela performing at the 35th Anniversary Playboy Jazz Festival, Hollywood Bowl, June 2013

Masekela one of his own trumpets. By the age of twenty, Masekela was performing with the premier South African band, the Jazz Epistles. Following the Sharpeville Massacre, he left the country to live in political exile for the next thirty years, enjoying a brilliant music career and serving as a spokesperson for the movement to end Apartheid.

American singer-songwriter Paul Simon collaborated with the South African a cappella vocal group Ladysmith Black Mambazo on the song "Diamonds on the Soles of Her Shoes" (9.9) for Simon's *Graceland* album released in 1986. The venture was controversial at the time. There was an international boycott against South Africa in the 1980s due to the system of Apartheid that mandated racial separation and legalized institutional discrimination. Yet, *Graceland's* popularity created a fashion throughout the global music industry for such hybrid joint ventures, often referred to as "fusion."

During the chaotic decades of the 1970s and 1980s, music became a central site for public negotiations in the complex multicultural, multilingual, and multiracial society of South Africa. Musical developments and interactions came to play a significant role in the long and painful process of conflict, resistance, and resolution. Interaction and understanding among the various groups were severely impeded by government repression and censorship. One critical role that music played during the last two decades of Apartheid was to provide opportunities for interracial and intercultural collaborations that symbolized opposition to the government's racist and segregationist policies. The first racially mixed band in South Africa was formed in 1969 when Johnny Clegg (1953–2019), a sixteen-year old White, middle-class student in Johannesburg, met Sipho Mchunu (b. 1951), an eighteen-year old Zulu gardener, and the two began playing music together. They found few locations where a bi-racial group could perform, which forced Johnny and Sipho to play either on the streets or in a few select, unofficial venues.[8] The duo blended Zulu music and dance styles with rock and Celtic music. They sang in both English and Zulu, and their song lyrics were frequently political in nature. In *"Akanaki Nokunaka"* (9.10), for example, Johnny and Sipho sang about the government's removal and destruction of a rural community under its forced relocation program. A website biography of Johnny Clegg states,

> In 1979, the duo changed their name to *Juluka* and released their critically-acclaimed debut album *Universal Men*. Although it was heralded by the press as the wave of the future, it did not receive any airplay in South Africa due to the cultural segregationist laws that prevailed.[9]

In 1981, South African radio banned their song *"Impi"* (9.11), which celebrated a defeat of the colonial British army by Zulu warriors. The song nevertheless became an underground hit, bringing the duo both national and international recognition. This led to tours of Europe and North America in 1982 and 1983. As the first multiracial band in South Africa, *Juluka* used music making as a means to transcend social, cultural, and racial differences. They sang of the social realities of life in South Africa, while simultaneously exploring musical fusions that drew together modern and traditional styles and urban and rural genres. Johnny and Sipho opened the door for other South African interracial and intercultural musical collaborations (Figure 9.9).

One particularly powerful collaborative strategy was the juxtaposition of the two national anthems: "*Die Stem Van Suid-Afrika*" ("The Voice of South Africa"), the South African national anthem before the end of Apartheid, and *"Nkosi Sikelel' iAfrika"* ("Lord, Bless Africa"), the

FIGURE 9.9 Multiracial band *Juluka*, with Johnny Clegg (rear left) and Sipho Mchunu (next to Clegg), London, 1983

anthem of the outlawed political party, the African National Congress. The anthem itself was outlawed and singing it could lead to incarceration. Some composers blended the two anthems to suggest and symbolize social fusion and ideological harmony, as in the popular radio announcer Dan Moyane's recording in which he superimposed the lyrics to "*Nkosi Sikelel' iAfrika*" over the tune of "*Die Stem*." Others employed the anthems' melodies and/ or lyrics to make cynical, satirical, or subversive commentaries on the political and social situation. The group Bright Blue used the banned South African anthem as an inconspicuous theme in the bass of its song "Weeping" on the album *Bright Blue* (1984).[10] To astute listeners, the hidden melody was obvious, and the song circulated widely in the underground world of clubs and bars. "It was a long time before the message was received by the authorities," writes anthropologist Ingrid Byerly, "and the song was banned immediately when the subversive content was recognized."[11] These fusions allowed individuals to express not only their opposition to the repressive and racist government policies, but their vision for a new, democratic South Africa in which all members of society would have full and equal rights and opportunities.

In 1990, a newly elected president, F.W. de Klerk, under intense pressure both from within the country and abroad, put an end to the policies of Apartheid, and held elections in 1994 with universal suffrage. Nelson Mandela emerged from prison as the new President of South Africa. He had been incarcerated for twenty-seven years for subversion, and had led the African National Congress from his prison cell. Victory was finally achieved for the long disenfranchised Black South Africans. The transition to democracy had taken place over many decades, with the participation of millions of South Africans of all races, and without the bloody civil war that many at the time thought was inevitable. As a compromise gesture, a new post-Apartheid South African national anthem (9.12) combined the two previous anthems using five languages, to represent inclusiveness.

Verse 1: first two lines in Xhosa
Nkosi Sikelel' iAfrika Lord, bless Africa
Maluphakanyisw' uphondo lwayo, May her glory be lifted high,
Verse 1: last two lines in Zulu
Yizwa imithandazo yethu, Hear our prayers,
Nkosi sikelela, thina lusapho lwayo. Lord, bless us, your children.
Verse 2 in Sesotho
Morena boloka setjhaba sa heso, Lord, we ask You to protect our nation,
O fedise dintwa le matshwenyeho, Intervene and end all conflicts,
O se boloke, O se boloke setjhaba sa heso, Protect us, protect our nation,
Setjhaba sa, South Afrika, South Afrika. Protect South Africa, South Africa.
Verse 3 in Afrikaans
Uit die blou van onse hemel, From the blue of our skies,
Uit die diepte van ons see, From the depth of our seas,
Oor ons ewige gebergtes, Over our everlasting mountains,
Waar die kranse antwoord gee, Where the echoing crags resound,
Verse 4 in English
Sounds the call to come together,
And united we shall stand,
Let us live and strive for freedom
In South Africa our land.

The powerful have many ways to express their power; the powerless have few. Music is one of the most potent weapons to wield for those who oppose institutional power. Musicians in late Apartheid South Africa were on the front lines of political struggle, as were musicians during the early 20th-century American Labor Movement, the Civil Rights Movement of the 1950s and 1960s, the anti-Vietnam War Movement of the 1970s, and Black Lives Matter in 2020. Ordinary people faced police dogs, batons, fire hoses, and tear gas singing songs of defiance.

GLOBAL HIP-HOP (USA, TUNISIA, UGANDA, GREENLAND)

Hip-hop has become a global phenomenon that includes rap music, break dancing, graffiti art, tattoos, and other forms of identity expression. It began in the Bronx, New York City, during the early 1970s. One of the first hip-hop artists was an immigrant Jamaican disc jockey, DJ Kool Herc (b. 1955). Using two turntables, he developed a technique for extending instrumental breaks in popular music genres like funk, soul, and R&B, and talking over those extended breaks (Figure 9.10). This technique developed into a new genre called "rap" that became especially important to young people in the Bronx who had no specific musical training. Through vocal wordsmithing and rhythmically spoken rhyming poetry, rappers could vent their frustrations against poverty, unemployment, crime, and interracial violence, while at the same time participating in a new art form that had its own virtuosic skill set.

FIGURE 9.10 DJ Kool Herc performing in Grand Army Plaza, New York City, 2008

However, the roots of rap as an oppositional genre go much deeper than a single individual and a single locale.

> Rap's forebears stretch back through disco, street funk, radio DJs, Bo Diddley, the bebop singers ... all the way to the griots of Nigeria and the Gambia. No matter how far it penetrates into the twilight maze of Japanese video games and cool European electronics, its roots are still the deepest in all contemporary Afro-American music.[12]

What started out as local street party music became a national media phenomenon in the 1980s, with competing East Coast and West Coast styles. In 1988, after years of neglect by mainstream media, the first hip-hop show appeared on MTV. By the late 1990s, hip-hop had become the dominant artistic expression of opposition to the White middle-class status quo. Hip-hop came to be associated with various forms of criminality including drug dealing and violence aimed at the police and women. It was the subject of governmental investigations, with campaigns to clean it up and to restrict adolescents' access to it. However, images of African American hip-hop culture, including break dancing and inner-city fashion—expensive sneakers, gold jewelry ("bling"), and low-slung pants—were circulated on a national scale as the reach of American popular culture became more and more pervasive globally.

A headline on the English language website of the international news network *Al Jazeera* from January 7, 2011 reads: "Tunisia arrests bloggers and rapper." The article, from the North African country Tunisia, tells of twenty-two-year-old rapper Hamada Ben-Amor, known to his fans as El Général, who had just posted on the internet a song called *"Rais Lebled"* (Figure 9.11). The title is a rap distortion of *Rais el-Bled*, meaning "President of the Republic." The song is often referred to in the press by its refrain, "Mr. President, Your People Are Dying." The lyrics, sung in Arabic, focused on the absence of employment opportunities for urban youth in the country. His brother was quoted in the article, saying:

> Some 30 plainclothes policemen came to our house to arrest Hamada and took him away without ever telling us where to. When we asked why they were arresting him, they said "he knows why."[13]

The arrest of El Général came in the wake of several weeks of violent public protest following the suicide by fire of a young fruit seller whose cart had been confiscated by the police. In an already volatile situation, the arrest of Ben-Amor sparked days of intense rioting that ultimately contributed to the overthrow of President Zine al-Abidine Ben Ali. This was the beginning of the so-called Arab Spring that swept across North Africa and the Arab Middle East between 2010 and 2014. With the internet providing an easy and instantaneous outlet for rappers and hip-hop artists and their political messages, government crackdowns through censorship and arrests became increasingly common.

FIGURE 9.11 Hamada Ben-Amor performs at a Tunisian opposition party meeting in Tunis, 2011, following the ousting of President Zine al-Abidine Ben Ali

Ironically, politicians occasionally co-opt the hip-hop style to reach younger constituencies. On the same day in 2011 that the BBC and Public Radio International posted the rap video that landed Tunisian rapper El Général in jail, these media organizations posted a video produced by the president of the East African country of Uganda asking an imagined public, "Do You Want Another Rap?" (9.13). The Ugandan President Museveni delivered two verses of traditional African political speech loaded with proverbs and metaphor over a breakbeat. The elder statesman in Western formal attire mixes the traditional imagery of African discourse with the visual cues of the rap music video. He makes himself, the establishment figure, appear oppositional and therefore on the side of those who oppose the establishment.

The global hip-hop phenomenon is an example of the cultural pattern called "glocalization," referring to the adaptation of global processes to local circumstances. In his introduction to *Global Noise: Rap and Hip-Hop Outside the USA*, ethnomusicologist Tony Mitchell writes:

> In the pages that follow, we will encounter Japanese b-boys [breakdancers] struggling with the hyperconsumerism of Tokyo youth culture, Italian posses promoting hardcore Marxist politics and alternative youth culture circuits, and Basque rappers using a punk rock—hip-hop syncretic to espouse their nationalist cause and promote the rights of ethnic minorities globally. Rappers in war-torn Bosnia declare their allegiance with the violent lives of gangsta rappers in South Central Los Angeles, and a rap group in Greenland protests that country's domination by the Danish language.[14]

Because of mass media and worldwide trade and communications, local communities are now infused with goods, services, images, and cultural artifacts from the rest of the world, particularly from the most technologically advanced societies. In Greenland, a protectorate of Denmark, the Inuit ride across the frozen landscape on Japanese skidoos (snowmobiles) wearing sneakers manufactured by American companies in Vietnamese sweatshops. While this is an example of globalization, in Greenland these goods from the outside world are adapted to the local context, and local meanings are attached. The sounds and images of hip-hop culture also traverse the world via the internet and other communication media, and become adapted to local use. In the case of hip-hop, a music genre and a fashion that carries general oppositional connotations, local media producers use it to challenge perceived local injustices. In this video by the Greenland Inuit hip-hop group Nuuk Posse (9.14), the rapper is challenging the imposition of the Danish language on his native culture. This issue is only of local concern, but the band adopts images that have become associated worldwide with oppositional identity, like skateboarding and graffiti.

PLATEAU MUSIC PROJECT (TIBET)

On the high plateau of Central Asia, as in many parts of the world, traditional life, sacred and secular, is rapidly changing beyond recognition. Like endangered species under threat from changes in habitat and climate, cultural forms of expression are also disappearing because of transformations in the human environment. Songs intimately tied to such day-to-day activities as herding, farming, and other forms of labor, which had been handed down for generations, are rapidly being forgotten. In the face of industrialization, economic development, modernization, and globalization, lifeways that form the basis of traditional music are being eroded.

The Tibetan region in western China is the highest inhabited area of the world with an average altitude of 16,000 feet. The Tibetan people are the indigenous inhabitants of the high plateau of Central Asia, the so-called "Roof of the World." Under King Songtsän Gampo in the 7th century CE, Buddhism became the state religion. Throughout its subsequent history, Tibet's political borders fluctuated greatly; at times the Tibetans enjoyed peace and stability, at times the empire fragmented due to internal feuds among the rulers or invasions by the Mongols or Chinese. From the mid-17th century, Tibet was ruled by a succession of monastic kings who held the title of Dalai Lama. Although isolated for much of their history yet living at the crossroads of the great Indian and Chinese civilizations, the Tibetans developed profound, complex, and unique artistic, architectural, musical, literary, and philosophical traditions. In 1724, China absorbed the two eastern provinces of Tibet, Amdo and Kham. In 1950, the army of the People's Republic of China annexed the western province of U-Tsan, traditional heartland of the Tibetan region and site of its capital Lhasa and the Dalai Lama's palace, the Potala. The 14th Dalai Lama, along with thousands of refugees, fled across the Himalayas into India in 1959, following the Chinese military's brutal suppression of a popular uprising. There in the Himalayan town of Dharamshala His Holiness the Dalai Lama formed a government-in-exile.

During the Cultural Revolution (1966–1976) there was a state-sponsored campaign against "**local nationalism**." The term, used by the Chinese government, refers to allegiance by minority groups to their ethnic identities, rather than to the Communist State. Students from the large cities of eastern China traveled throughout the country at that time, destroying markers of minority ethnic identity. In the Tibetan region, they closed monasteries and defaced buildings and works of art. Since the Cultural Revolution, the effacement of Tibetan identity has continued, as the central government relocates millions of Han Chinese into the Tibetan territories. This policy seeks to alleviate overcrowded cities in the east and exploit the mineral wealth of the sparsely inhabited hinterland. With this new population has come Chinese-language mass media: newspapers, radio, CDs, DVDs, and the (highly censored) internet.

By government decree, languages other than Mandarin are forbidden in the mass media, and Mandarin is gradually replacing Tibetan in primary school education. On the Central Plateau, the modern world itself threatens to engulf the region's fragile rural ways of life (see Map 7.3). Young Tibetans are losing interest in traditional forms of expression that were passed down orally in families and communities. They are more likely to sing songs learned from radio and the internet than from older family members or local villagers. Wedding songs, for instance, are particularly affected in this way.

> With a shift to a consumer culture, people are more likely to consume culture than to produce it. As highways, power lines, and satellite dishes bring to the Plateau more and more music from inner China, Hong Kong, Taiwan, India, and the West, people have become creatively less self-sufficient and more dependent on external sources of music.[15]

Thousands of songs may vanish. To combat this trend, the Tibetan Endangered Music Project was founded in 2005 by Australian anthropologist Gerald Roche and his students at Qinghai Normal University in Xining, the provincial capital (Figure 9.12). The project was an extra-curricular activity for the students. With digital tape recorders in hand, they returned to their remote home villages to collect and preserve traditional songs in opposition to the encroachment of time and inevitable cultural change. In 2007, the students posted an "Infomercial" (9.15) on YouTube describing their project and soliciting further financial contributions.

FIGURE 9.12 Plateau Music Project student song collector, Tserang Tso (second from left), with (left to right) her mother, grandmother, brother, and sister

They received training from the older students both in the use of digital technologies and in soliciting songs from older, skeptical villagers and relatives. More than 700 songs have been archived, and some have been posted on YouTube, such as this Tibetan nomadic song (9.16). On return trips to the villages, the students presented the elders with CD recordings of their singing. Together they listened to the songs that had seemed old fashioned and obsolete, thereby validating their worth. In April 2014 the Plateau Music Project, along with a number of other NGOs (Non-Governmental Organizations) operating in Qinghai province, were shut down "for reasons unknown."

ROCK MUSIC IN CHINA

Cui Jian (b. 1961) is a popular artist who made historic contributions to modern Chinese culture (Figure 9.13). He performed his own unique style of rock music and thereby challenged the authority of the Chinese government. The Communist Party, which came to power in 1949 led by Mao Zedong, took over all channels of public media and placed them at the service of the government's various agendas. In his book *China's New Voices*, author Nimrod Baranovitch writes:

> For close to three decades in China after 1949, one could hear in public a single voice, that of the party-state. The government dictated much of culture and imposed unity

in almost every domain. The new revolutionary trend extended from suppression of political views that did not agree with those of Chairman Mao Zedong as far as the attempt to eliminate regional, ethnic, class, and even gender differences.... During the decade of the Cultural Revolution (1966–76) in particular, only militant revolutionary songs that praised the leadership and a handful of revolutionary operas and ballets were allowed to be performed in public.[16]

Following the death of Mao in 1976 and the rise of his successor, Deng Xiaoping, there was a decided liberalization of state control in areas of public culture. Previously forbidden forms of popular entertainment from outside the country provided an appropriate soundtrack to new forms of free-market economic activity and cultural expression. Popular songs, called *tongsu*, were gradually introduced to the airwaves, with styles influenced by such Western forms as jazz and disco, and yet the government still exerted tight control. Songwriters and performers had to belong to separate government work units, and any "sexual songs, nihilistic songs, morbid songs, violent songs" or songs critical of state policies were censored.[17] Typical *tongsu* songs had strongly patriotic themes with song titles such as "China, China I love you" and "The Communist Party Brings Good Times."

Cui Jian, of Korean ancestry, had been a child-prodigy trumpeter who joined the Beijing Symphony Orchestra at the age of fourteen. However, he was captivated by American pop singers like Simon and Garfunkel, whose recordings were just making their way into newly opened China, and in his spare time took up the electric guitar and songwriting. He burst

FIGURE 9.13 Cui Jian performing at the Capital Gymnasium, Beijing, 2005 in his first fully approved concert in twelve years

onto the public stage at a government-sanctioned *tongsu* pop concert in Beijing in 1986. At this televised event, he was one of a hundred invited singers. His standout performance challenged the status quo in a number of ways: his dress was casual in the manner associated with Western rock musicians, and the strong insistent beat and his rough vocal style had a "direct, unrestrained, and liberating quality." The song he sang, "Nothing to My Name" (9.17), was "a celebration of lack of control. It was the antithesis of both the traditional Confucian aesthetics of moderation and restraint … as well as the antithesis of the official communist aesthetic of polished and disciplined professionalism."[18] What was perhaps most radical about the song was that Cui Jian had written it himself. It was unheard of for a singer to publicly sing his or her own song, and "Nothing to My Name" was about Cui Jian's own subjective experience and identity. The personal pronoun in the lyrics is "I," not "we." The song introduced to a generation of Chinese youth the free and nonconformist values associated in the West with rock and roll.

> "Nothing to My Name"
> I've asked tirelessly, when will you go with me?
> But you just always laugh at my having nothing
> I've given you my dreams, given you my freedom
> But you always just laugh at my having nothing
> Oh! When will you go with me?
> Oh! When will you go with me?
>
> [English translation by Andrew Jones]

Of course, the song's implication that after forty years of Communist Party control one should find oneself "having nothing" was seen as a strong indictment of failed policies. There was a period of social unrest due to the frustrated aspirations of people throughout China for greater freedoms. This unrest led to a **Pro-Democracy Movement** in Beijing in 1989. The situation came to a head with thousands of students gathering in **Tiananmen Square** for a peaceful protest. The government responded with a violent crackdown by the military in which a large number of students lost their lives. "Nothing to My Name" was the anthem of the Pro-Democracy students and was sung in Tiananmen Square. Following these events, the government tried to calm political tensions, although Cui Jian himself was banned from public stage performances. In early 1990, Cui Jian was surprisingly allowed to give a concert tour as a fundraiser for the Asian Games. He performed his song "A Piece of Red Cloth" with a red bandana covering his eyes.[19] The implication, hardly missed by the audience, was that the red bandana symbolized the Communist Party, which was preventing him from experiencing freedom and fulfillment. However, after the first few concerts, the song's thinly veiled condemnation of the Chinese Communist Party led to the tour's early termination.

> That day you tied my eyes with red cloth
> You covered up the sky
> You asked what I was looking at
> I said I saw happiness.
> This feeling comforts me
> It lets me forget that I have nowhere to go.
>
> [English translation by Nimrod Baranovitch]

As Baranovitch writes,

> After half a century in which the power of music to mobilize the masses was utilized in China exclusively by the Communist Party to establish its hegemony and control, rock music introduced into the country an alternative way to use music politically.[20]

The popularity of subversive rock music was nevertheless short-lived. By the mid-1990s, the Chinese government banned it from state-controlled television and restricted public performances. Following the government's imposition of repressive policies in response to the Tiananmen Square protests, young people turned away from resistance and rebellion. The opportunity to make money and improve their standard of living appealed to many, including rock musicians. While some musicians continued to uphold their individualism and idealism performing in an underground music scene, the majority toned down their political criticism in order to hold public concerts and appear on state-run media. For these musicians, rock music no longer expressed an oppositional identity.

At the time of the Beijing Summer Olympics in 2008, rock music had become rehabilitated. The city's rock scene was flourishing once again. Rock clubs attracted sizeable crowds and the prominent indie rock label Modern Sky staged the first rock festival. Even Cui Jian was allowed to return to the public stage. On New Year's Eve 2010 and New Year's Day 2011, he hired the Beijing Symphony Orchestra, which he had officially left in 1987, to back his own band for two concerts.[21] Jian has since headlined at major festivals in China and has performed throughout the world, appearing on stage with top rock bands such as The Rolling Stones and Deep Purple. Cui Jian is now considered the grandfather of Chinese rock; no other popular musician from China has had such an impact on the international stage.

In the 2020s, Chinese rock has changed. "Some Chinese rock artists have enjoyed mainstream popularity for years," writes Stacey Anderson in *Rolling Stone*, and "the concept of rock itself has proven media-friendly."[22] This popular style, however, is not the subversive rock music of past years. It is a sanitized form of indie rock with catchy melodies and harmless love lyrics. "The Chinese government wants to control the speech and ideas of people who want to be independent," claims Yaqiu Wang of Human Rights Watch. "The government considers anybody who wants autonomy, wants agency, wants to explain their own ideas as a threat to its rule."[23] For album releases and concert performances,

> "Everything goes through a censorship process now, but there's no one censor, and no clear list of what's allowed and what's not," explains Nevin Domer, a metal musician… "To release albums, you need to submit all your materials to a publisher, which is a partly government-owned company that [a label] has to pay. If the label doesn't get their approval, the factory can't print the album." The materials include all song lyrics, information about band members, their government IDs, the recorded songs, and everything to be printed in the liner notes. These publishers can be capricious in their verdicts, and if an album is denied – as it often is – a label will usually reapply with another company and begin the entire process again. "It's a fundamental strategy of censorship, jumping through bureaucratic hoops," says Human Rights Watch's Wang. "The control is from the very root."[24]

In order to survive and thrive in a repressive authoritarian state, most rock musicians in China today have reinvented rock for mainstream Chinese audiences.

CONCLUSION

Musicians have worked on both sides of oppositional divides, lending their talents and charisma to uphold repressive power structures as well as to undermine them, through reform and revolution. The Czech novelist Milan Kundera, in his historical novel *The Book of Laughter and Forgetting*, describes the paranoia of Communist dictator Gustáv Husák when a popular entertainer goes abroad:

> When Karel Gott, the Czech pop singer, went abroad in 1972, Husák got scared. He sat right down and wrote him a personal letter.... The following is a verbatim quote from it. I have invented nothing.
>
> Dear Karel, We are not angry with you. Please come back. We will do everything you ask. We will help you if you help us...
>
> Think it over. Without batting an eyelid, Husák let doctors, scholars, astronomers, athletes, directors, cameramen, workers, engineers, architects, historians, journalists, writers, and painters go into emigration, but he could not stand the thought of Karel Gott leaving the country.[25]

Some musicians attempt to survive in authoritarian and dangerous regimes, pursuing their careers while still attempting to resist tyranny from within. In the Soviet Union, composers lived in fear of writing music that Stalin and his bureaucrats would find insufficiently "**proletarian**." The composer Dmitri Shostakovich (1906–1975) relates how in 1948, after being officially denounced by the Soviet government, he waited at night in the corridor by the elevator for the police to come and take him away—as they had many other artists and musicians—so that his family would not be disturbed. The Catalan cellist Pau Casals (1876–1973) famously denounced the Fascist dictator Francisco Franco and went into exile following the Spanish Civil War in 1936, never to return to his home. He had been warned that he would be murdered if he ever came back. Casals spent the rest of his life campaigning for various anti-fascist and humanitarian causes. In 1971, at the age of 96, he was presented with the United Nations Peace Medal (Figure 9.14).

Music can serve as a unifying force among human groups as well as a marker of division between them. The case studies in this chapter have examined contexts in which power is distributed unequally between opposing factions. In *Nueva Canción*, for example, musicians served as the spokespersons for those who opposed repressive regimes and sought to redress injustices. The same is true in the anti-Apartheid struggle, where control of the government, the economy, the media, and the police was held by the Apartheid regime. On the other side, musicians used their artistry to mobilize, to inspire acts of resistance, and to catalyze a vision of a more just reality. Hip-hop provides a musical and linguistic style for young people to express opposition to any number of social ills, and to voice discontent with their limited opportunities. The style, encompassing rap, breakdance, graffiti, tattoos, and "bling," spread

FIGURE 9.14 Pau Casals (L), and Dmitri Shostakovich (R)

from the South Bronx around the world. While Part III has discussed the use of music as a means to express group, hybrid, and oppositional identities, the next part explores the near universal relationship between music and religion.

KEY TERMS AND CONCEPTS

Apartheid

American Civil Rights Movement

Black Lives Matter Movement

Censorship

Consumer Culture

Cultural Revolution

Economic Boycott

Eroding Lifeways

Interracial/Intercultural Collaboration

Local Nationalism

Military Band

Oppositional Identity

Political Exile

Power Relationships

Pro-Democracy Movement

Protest Songs

Rap/Rapper

Subversion

Tiananmen Square

THINKING ABOUT MUSIC

1 Describe a case of music supporting a power structure or status quo, and a case in which music is used to oppose a power structure or status quo. In what ways does the music communicate support in the first case, and opposition and resistance in the second?

2 In your own experience, are there particular gender divisions in your society such as Maria Stoyanova encountered in hers? Are there particular gender roles and expectations in the musical life of your community?

3 Why do you think the *Nueva Canción* musicians chose to use simple folk and indigenous instruments and styles to express their opposition to totalitarian regimes?

4 Read again the quote from Gabriel García Márquez' 1982 Nobel Prize acceptance speech describing the plight of Latin America's poor. In the face of so much oppression and sorrow, what roles can music and musicians serve? Correlate your response with some of the ten functions in Chapter 6.

5 In South Africa, Johnny and Sipho created a hybrid musical style, blending Johnny's rock and Celtic styles with Sipho's traditional Zulu style. Why was their music a potent sonic weapon against the assumptions of racial separation?

6 In his song "*Stimela* (Coal Train)," South African jazz trumpeter Hugh Masekela sang of the hardships suffered by his fellow Black South Africans during Apartheid. How did Hugh Masekela use music and lyrics in this song to express his oppositional identity?

7 Why do you think the Chinese government is so cautious about allowing rock music to flourish? Do *you* think rock is inherently destabilizing? If so, why? If not, why not?

NOTES

1 Shalini Saran, "Agra's Musical Past," *The Hindu*, December 3, 2000, reprinted in *Music* (Chennai: Kasturi and Sons Ltd., 2003), 20, http://www.ocf.berkeley.edu/~aathavan/libraire/carnatic/carnaticmusic.pdf.

2 Poem by Abel Meeropol, first published as "Bitter Fruit" under the pseudonym Lewis Allen, in *The New York Teacher*, 1937.

3 Billie Holiday, *Lady Sings the Blues* (New York: Doubleday, 1956), 95.

4 Timothy Rice, *Music in Bulgaria: Experiencing Music, Expressing Culture* (New York: Oxford University Press, 2004), 14–15.

5 Timothy Rice, *Music in Bulgaria*, 4.

6 Jan Fairley, "Nueva Canción," *Grove Music Online* (Oxford University Press, 2010).

7 Gabriel García Márquez, "The Solitude of Latin America" (Eng. trans.), Nobel Lecture, December 8, 1982, Nobel Prize for Literature 1982, cited with permission, © The Nobel Foundation 1982. http://www.nobelprize.org/nobel_prizes/literature/laureates/1982/marquez-lecture.html

8 *Rhythm of Resistance* (Harcourt Films, 1979), Beats of the Heart series, written and directed by Jeremy Marre.

9 "1990+," Johnny Clegg, https://johnnyclegg.lima-city.de/biografie/1990.htm.

10 "Weeping, the South African Anti-Apartheid Protest Song," Dan Heymann, songwriter and band member, includes link to the original "Weeping" video, recorded by Bright Blue, www.weeping.info.

11 Ingrid Byerly, "'Mirror, Mediator, and Prophet': The Music Indaba of Late-Apartheid South Africa," *Ethnomusicology* 42/1 (1998): 33–34.

12 David Toop, *Rap Attack 2: African Rap to Global Hip-Hop* (London: Serpent's Tail, 1991), 19, cited in Tony Mitchell, ed. *Global Noise: Rap and Hip-Hop Outside the USA* (Middletown, CT: Wesleyan University Press, 2001), 4.

13 Yasmine Ryan, "Tunisia Arrests Bloggers and Rapper," *Al Jazeera*, January 7, 2011, accessed November 24, 2021, https://www.aljazeera.com/news/2011/1/7/tunisia-arrests-bloggers-and-rapper. See also, Joshasen, "The Rap That Sparked a Revolution: El General (Tunisia)," *Hip-Hop Diplomacy*, January 21, 2011, http://hiphopdiplomacy.org/2011/01/31/the-rap-that-sparked-a-revolution-el-general-tunisia/.

14 Tony Mitchell, ed., *Global Noise: Rap and Hip-Hop Outside the USA* (Middletown, CT: Wesleyan University Press, 2001), 1.

15 Tsering Bum and Gerald Roche, "The Plateau Music Project: Grass-roots Cultural Preservation on the Tibetan Plateau" (2008). Report circulated among donors and potential supporters of the Plateau Music Project, describing the music group's activities.

16 Nimrod Baranovitch, *China's New Voices: Popular Music, Ethnicity, Gender, and Politics, 1978–1997* (Los Angeles: University of California Press, 2003), 1.

17 Andrew Jones, *Like a Knife: Ideology and Genre in Contemporary Chinese Popular Music* (Ithaca, NY: Cornell University East Asian Program, 1992), 48.

18 Nimrod Baranovitch, *China's New Voices*, 33.

19 Cui Jian, "A Piece of Red Cloth," https://www.youtube.com/watch?v=GZwYX6s55H0&ab_channel=ChenWang.

20 Nimrod Baranovitch, *China's New Voices*, 35.

21 Jonathan Campbell, email with author, December 20, 2013; Campbell, Jonathan, *Red Rock: The Long, Strange March of Chinese Rock and Roll* (Hong Kong: Earnshaw Books Ltd., 2011).

22 Stacey Anderson, "Beijing Calling: Suspicion, Hope, and Resistance in the Chinese Rock Underground," *Rolling Stone*, June 24, 2021, https://www.rollingstone.com/music/music-features/beijing-calling-chinese-rock-underground-1186928/.

23 Stacey Anderson, "Beijing Calling."

24 Stacey Anderson, "Beijing Calling."

25 Milan Kundera, *The Book of Laughter and Forgetting* (New York: Penguin Books, 1980), 181.

PART IV

Music and the Sacred

Introduction
Chapter 10 Sacred Chant and Devotional Singing
Chapter 11 Sacred Embodiment and Sacred Enactment
Chapter 12 Sacred Space and Sacred Time

INTRODUCTION

It is a near-universal phenomenon that music has deep and complex relationships with religions throughout the world. In virtually every society some forms of religious expression are encoded in musical sound. Trying to understand why this is so and what it reveals about the nature of music is the goal of this part. However, just as "music" was difficult to define, the word "religion" is also highly problematic, especially when using this term that derives from a Western worldview as a global concept. Indeed, finding a single defining essence shared by all of the world's religions is probably impossible; it is certainly beyond the scope of this textbook. Nevertheless, throughout the world, systems of belief, moral codes, explanatory narratives, sacred texts, communication and communion with unseen powers and beings, calendrical and life-cycle rituals, together constitute powerful frameworks by which people find order, meaning, and control over their lives. These collectively held ethical systems and worldviews bind families, communities, and societies together with shared values and emotional connections.

Music in religious contexts has many uses. It provides a vehicle for the expression of religious emotions: awe, joy, and wonder. Worshipers respond to its beauty as being akin to the beauties of celestial realms. Music has served as a tool for attracting converts, for drawing people to religious rituals and sustaining their interest once there. Through music, humans communicate with ancestor spirits, supernatural beings, and divine powers, and adults communicate religious teachings to children. Music is often used as a powerful symbol of other realms and beings that religions hold sacred. Throughout Africa and the African diaspora in the New World, drums provide a sonic connection to gods and ancestors, representing their abiding presence in the community. Musical instruments are symbolic of sacred beings: Lord

Krishna's flute, King David's harp, and Gabriel's trumpet. Music is used throughout the world to stimulate physical states of repose and contemplation as well as ecstasy and trance. In some religious communities, dance is an appropriate response to divine presence and an expression of embodied joy and devotion.

Music is widely incorporated in religious ritual, but the *kind* of music considered appropriate varies considerably. People match their music to the responses to the sacred that their religion cultivates. Within Christianity today, there is enormous diversity of religious musical practice. The United House of Prayer for All People employs gospel brass "shout bands" consisting primarily of trombones, bass drum, and cymbals to provide the central component of religious worship. In contrast, many Primitive Baptist congregations use vocal music in worship but exclude all musical instruments. Both denominations find support for their positions in scripture, but come to an opposite conclusion. The United House of Prayer uses Psalm 150 as clear justification for the use of instruments in worship: "Praise Him with the sound of the trumpet; praise Him with the psaltery and harp." **Primitive Baptists**, however, cite the absence of any mention of musical instruments in the New Testament as evidence that, like animal sacrifice, musical instruments are no longer warranted following the coming of Christ.

In the religion of Islam, the use of music is controversial. Musicologist Amnon Shiloah (1928–2014) described the "interminable debate" surrounding the practice of listening to music (*sama*) as a religious act.[1] This controversy derives from the lack of a position one way or another taken in the Qur'an, the holy book of Islam. "Both those in favour of music and those opposed had recourse to it, which is perplexing because nothing in the Qur'an concerns music explicitly." Those in favor of music often cite the saying of Muhammad, "Allah has not sent a prophet except with a beautiful voice, and Allah listens more intently to a man with a beautiful voice reading the Qur'an than does the master of a singing-girl to her singing." Those against music will tell the myth of how Satan, jealous of King David's beautiful voice singing divine praise, "summoned his hordes and ordered them to devise something equally powerful. They then invented the reed-pipes and lutes...."[2]

> Pagan, Judeo-Christian, and Islamic believers all recognize the overwhelming power of music, which exerts an irresistibly strong influence on the listener's soul. Acting as a kind of charm, music produces either sensual pleasure or extreme excitement, and its maximal effect can send the listener into an emotional, even violent paroxysm. As a result of this untamed power, or spontaneous effect, the listener loses control over his reason and behaviour and is consequently governed by his passions.[3]

This unresolved question and controversy over whether or not music is permissible hinges on whether the heightened experiences that it inspires are divinely sanctioned or are distractions from the spiritual life.

Many religions of Africa and the Indian subcontinent consider music in ritual practices to be essential. In sub-Saharan Africa, drumming is used to evoke deities and ancestor spirits, and dancing provides evidence of their spiritual presence in human bodies. Descendants of African slaves continue many of the practices brought to the New World by their forebears. In parts of the Caribbean and South America, slave owners were fairly permissive in allowing religious drumming to continue. Over time, these traditions developed into the dance rhythms and forms found in the region such as *samba* and *merengue*. In North America, the drumming was suppressed to a greater degree, but not entirely eliminated.

Today, African-American Christianity has been invigorated with these African rhythms, re-contextualized as gospel music.

In Hinduism, singing, dancing, drumming, and playing musical instruments are powerful expressions of the sacred. Indeed, musical sound itself is revered as a manifestation of the Divine, hence the concept **Nad Brahman** ("God as sound"). In most forms of Buddhism, music is more subdued, but nevertheless present as the setting for the recitation of religious texts (**sutras**), or to accompany rituals celebrating Buddha's life and teachings. As Islam in the form of Sufism spread throughout the Hindu heartland of northern India in the 15th century, a musical form called **qawwali** developed. The Hindu population, accustomed to experiencing and celebrating the divine through music, was able to continue singing and dancing following conversion, now in the name of Allah.

Part IV examines religious music from a variety of perspectives. Chapter 10 explores the use of music in liturgical chant and devotional singing. The word "liturgy" refers to the words that are always repeated in a specific religious ritual. Chapter 11 examines sacred contexts in which music goes beyond words ... music expressing what words cannot. This chapter focuses on musically inspired states of heightened emotion, ecstasy, and trance; and sacred narratives presented through dance and theater. Chapter 12 deals with the power of music to differentiate sacred spaces and times from secular, everyday experience; and to shape the structure of religious rituals.

NOTES

1 Amnon Shiloah, *Music in the World of Islam: A Socio-cultural Study* (Detroit, MI: Wayne State University Press, 1995), 31.
2 Amnon Shiloah, *Music in the World of Islam*, 33.
3 Amnon Shiloah, *Music in the World of Islam*, 34.

Sacred Chant and Devotional Singing

Introduction
Sacred Chant
Devotional Singing
Conclusion

INTRODUCTION

This chapter describes relationships between sacred music and the words that the music conveys. Music has served as a suitable envelope or delivery system for conveying sacred texts, verbal doctrines, and avowals of faith. However, there was also anxiety in some traditions that music might obscure the words, or redirect the attention of the listener away from the texts toward the sensual and aesthetic beauty of music. In Western Christianity as practiced in America today, even within a single congregation there is often a lack of consensus as to what kind of music to use for a given ritual or context. Other controversies may run along sectarian lines: some people feeling, for instance, that only the most gifted musicians within the community should perform—their gifts considered of divine origin. Others believe that musical participation should be egalitarian and communal—fervor of faith and not quality of voice makes one worthy to participate. Communities may become divided along generational lines, with older congregants wanting to maintain musical traditions while younger members of the community seek contemporary expressions that more closely match their experience and taste. Elsewhere, the very inclusion of music in worship is subject to highly ambivalent attitudes.

The Church Fathers of early Christianity sermonized on both sides of the music debate. The 4th-century Christian theologian St. Basil praised congregational psalm singing in the highest terms, but he condemned all forms of instrumental music. He and other evangelists sought to eradicate the use of instruments because they were held to be sacred to the Pagan gods like Apollo and Dionysus, and their efforts were successful. Only vocal music was performed in Christian practice until around 900 CE when the organ made its way into the church. In one of the most eloquent and influential passages on music, St. Augustine (354–430) states his belief that he is lost in sin when he finds himself paying more attention to the melody of the song than the sacred text to which it is set (Figure 10.1). "Yet," he writes in his Confessions (ca. 398), "when I find the singing itself more moving than the truth which

FIGURE 10.1 *St. Augustine in his Study*, Sandro Botticelli, 1494, Uffizi Gallery, Florence

it conveys, I confess that this is a grievous sin, and at those times I would prefer not to hear the singer." Indeed, at those times he felt inclined, as bishop, to "exclude from my ears, and from those of the Church as well … those lovely chants to which the Psalms of David are habitually sung." In the end, however, he was "inclined to approve of the custom of singing in church, in order that by indulging the ears weaker spirits may be inspired with feelings of devotion."[1] He recounts in the same passage how it was the beautiful singing of his teacher St. Ambrose, Bishop of Milan, that first turned his heart toward the teachings of the church.

Chapter 10 presents forms of sacred chant and devotional singing from a number of world religions including Hinduism, Judaism, Buddhism, Christianity, and Islam.

SACRED CHANT

The term "chant" (or "**cantillation**") refers generally to the recitation of religious narratives, doctrines, and texts on melodic tones in ritual and liturgical contexts. Sacred chant traditions are among the most conservative practices in many religions. Texts often date from the origins of a religious system and form the basis of, and authority for, belief. What these words have in common is that believers consider them to be divinely inspired. They are recited by ritual specialists such as priests, cantors, monks, and imams. Chant texts are preserved in ancient languages, most of them incomprehensible to lay believers: the Vedas of India in Sanskrit; the Psalms of Jewish and Christian traditions in Hebrew, ancient Greek, and Latin; the Buddhist *sutras* (scriptures) in Pali; and the Qur'an in classical Arabic. All are performed using melodic contours and metrical patterns. The widespread practice of chant suggests that music is a special form of heightened speech—a mode of expression worthy of the words it carries in a way that ordinary speech is not. Sacred chant has served as a vehicle for the expression of faith for millennia. In the history of Western music, for example, chanting the Psalms "is surely the oldest continuous musical tradition,"[2] dating from early Judaic times (1000 BCE and earlier).

In many forms of cantillation, the words are the primary focus of the musical expression; the melody, rhythm, and instrumental accompaniment, if any, play a supportive and secondary role. However, in some forms of chant, *musical* aspects are paramount. Two forms of Buddhist chant from Korea exemplify this contrast. This video shows a Korean Buddhist monk (10.1) reciting a sacred text based on the teachings of the Buddha. He punctuates his own chanting with gong strokes. Each syllable of the text gets just one or two notes of the chant. The recitation follows the natural flow of speech rhythms, set to a simple melodic contour, and the text is clearly articulated. In this audio recording, another form of Korean Buddhist chant called *pompae* (10.2) takes a single line of text from one of the *sutras* and greatly expands it by sustaining a single syllable over many notes, thereby emphasizing the musical aspects. A scriptural verse that can be spoken in a few seconds is stretched out in this manner for twenty minutes or more, thus rendering the text incomprehensible. The contrasting emphasis either on words or on melody may represent a distinction in the way the chants are used: syllabic chant may be a form of communication among humans by which religious narratives or sermons are conveyed; melismatic chant may be an aesthetically beautiful musical offering for unseen divine listeners.[3]

In some cultures, the sounds of religious chant are as different from the secular music of the region as are the musics of foreign countries. Perhaps this is because monastic traditions preserve musical practices over generations. Isolation in monasteries and strict adherence to tradition prevent the kinds of fluid adaptations to changing social and technological factors and outside influences that shape secular music. In general, chant elevates the status of the *spoken* word in the same way that the beautiful **calligraphy** of illuminated manuscripts elevates the *written* word. In both cases, these special modes of presenting sacred words acknowledge their sacredness (Figure 10.2).

Vedic Chant (India)

Arguably the oldest unbroken tradition of chant in existence is that of **Vedic chant** in India. **Veda** literally means "knowledge" and the Vedas are the sacred hymns and prayers that were revealed to seers (*rishis*) in ancient India at least 3,500 years ago. The Vedas have been passed down orally since that time by members of a hereditary priestly caste called **Brahmins**, from father to son and from teacher to student. The recitation of appropriate verses accompanied virtually every aspect of ritual life, from the lighting of sacred fires (10.3) and pouring of sacrificial oils to weddings, funerals, and other rites of passage (Figure 10.3). The musical elements—melody and rhythm—were inseparable from the texts and were also considered sacred and immutable. Brahmin priests chanted the ancient Sanskrit verses

FIGURE 10.2 Calligraphy in sacred texts: Christian—the *Book of Kells*, ca. 800 (L); Islamic—gold-illuminated Qur'an from Morocco, 17th century (C); and Buddhist—Japanese Zen, by Muso Kokushi, 14th century (R)

FIGURE 10.3 Nambudiri Brahmin priests performing Athirathram, a 12-day-long Vedic ritual to Agni, God of Fire, in Thrissur, Kerala, 2011

unaccompanied and with great precision. "Particular care had to be taken to preserve these," writes ethnomusicologist Charles Capwell, "because their very sounds were considered to be the necessary means for coercing the gods to provide for the needs of the people."[4] Young students of Vedic chant (10.4) learn the correct chant pitches and rhythms orally. They are memorizing the melodic formulas of the Rigveda, consisting of three pitches. Hand and head movements ensure that no recitation is incorrect.

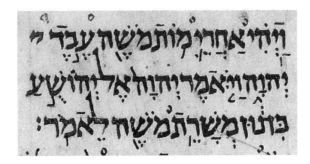

FIGURE 10.4 Judaic chant notation, Joshua 1.1, Aleppo Codex, 10th century

Judaic Cantillation (USA)

The term cantillation was first used by scholars to identify the manner in which the Torah (the first five books of the Hebrew Bible) and other Hebrew scriptures were recited by Jews in synagogue services, led by a cantor or **hazzan**. While there are historical differences between Jews who settled in central and northern Europe (*Ashkanazi*), those originating from Spain and Portugal (*Sephardic*), and those in Western Asia and North Africa (*Mizrahi*), all groups use the same standard text in Biblical Hebrew. The three communities also recite the text orally using principles of cantillation. The text that is recited today is based on several ancient Torah scrolls that have survived from antiquity (Figure 10.4). An authoritative version was compiled by an assembly of rabbis around 900 CE. It was meticulously copied and re-copied down through the ages. The text consists of Hebrew consonants, signs indicating correct vowel sounds, and "trope" marks indicating inflections for recitation. From the earliest times, the Hebrew scriptures were meant to be recited aloud. In the synagogue, cantors still recite from the **Tanakh** scroll containing the collection of Hebrew scriptures (including the Torah) according to these trope marks, and their interpretation of the tropes gives the recitation a sing-song quality. Learning to pronounce the Hebrew letters correctly and to interpret the inflection signs are a significant part of a Jewish boy's and girl's education. This study prepares them for the ritual of initiation into adulthood at age thirteen, known as **bar mitzvah** and bat mitzvah, respectively.

Video 10.5 shows Mizrahi Rabbi Joshua Maroof teaching his seven-year-old son Netanel correct recitation from the Torah Scroll, at Magen David Sephardic Congregation in Rockville, MD. Netanel is learning Judaic Sephardic cantillation (10.5) known as "*Sephardi-Yerushalmi*." This musical tradition was originally based on the Syrian style of "reading" the Torah, which adheres to the Arabic musical system of *maqamat*. The trope symbols, Hebrew vowels, and punctuation used in the *Ashkenazi* tradition are absent from the *Sephardi-Yerushalmi* Torah scroll. Therefore, cantors must memorize the pronunciation, punctuation, and proper melody in advance. In the video, Netanel keeps his place using a ritual pointer or *yad* as he recites a passage from the Book of Exodus, Chapter 18, which is the Torah portion associated with Purim holiday morning.

Buddhist Chant (Laos, China, Tibet)

The sacred texts of the Buddhist traditions consist primarily of sermons that the historic Buddha, Siddhartha Gautama (563–485 BCE), delivered orally to his disciples. These provided instructions for how to live in the world free from pain and suffering, how to establish monastic communities for mutual support, and how to realize the ultimate goal of life: *nirvana* (enlightenment). Generations of his followers repeated these teachings from memory and codified them by topic into the **Tripitaka** ("Three Baskets"). Around 450 years after the Buddha's death, they were finally written down. In the most orthodox branch of Buddhism, **Theravada** ("the Ancient Teaching"), which continues to flourish in Sri Lanka, Myanmar, Thailand, and Laos, Buddhist monks (10.6) chant these teachings in Pali, the original language of the Buddha. Within *Theravada* Buddhist monasteries and temples, these sacred texts are recited using simple melodic patterns in preparation for long hours of meditation.

As Buddhism traveled from its original home in India north and northeast into Central Asia and China, it combined with indigenous religions like Daoism, and became more eclectic, devotional, and ritualistic. The historic Buddha came to be seen as an earthly manifestation of a celestial emanation, having many non-material forms and powers. The Buddhist tradition that developed from this later interpretation became known as **Mahayana** ("Great Vehicle"). This video from Shanxi Province in the People's Republic of China presents monks gathered in a **gompa** (prayer hall) to honor the Enlightened One with collective chanting and walking meditation (10.7). The monks recite a repeating *mantra* or sacred phrase beginning "*Namo Amitabha*," invoking the name and blessings of the Buddha of Compassion.

All Tibetan Buddhist monks learn vocal music because of its importance both in meditation and in rituals involving the recitation of the *sutras*. Of the many types of chant used within the Tibetan monastic tradition, **dbyangs** (pronounced "yung") is the most complex and highly valued. In *dbyangs* (10.8), Tibetan monks chant the texts of the *sutras* on an extremely low fundamental tone. They occasionally sustain one syllable, most notably the sacred word "**aum**" that signifies the sum of all sacred sounds. The monks shape their vocal cavities in such a way that they make audible the upper overtones, which are normally inaudible. This phenomenon can be heard at 0'20" in audio 10.8. Within the forms of Buddhism that developed in Tibet, monks use music to "hear the truth" of the Buddha's teachings, to deepen their understanding, and increase their awareness of the world and the nature of existence. Truths that are normally inaccessible to everyday consciousness become accessible through this practice.[5]

Plainchant (Europe)

The oldest continuous musical tradition of the Western world is the singing of psalms, as documented in Judaic tradition. Psalm verses exhorted the faithful to praise the Lord with voices, instruments, and dance: "Sing unto the Lord with the harp … and the voice of a psalm. With trumpets and the sound of the cornet" (Psalm 98). In the temple at Jerusalem, rituals were elaborate and ceremonial. However, worship in the synagogues (study houses for prayer) employed simpler, purely vocal music. The early Christian church drew on this latter tradition for its rituals and music. The first Christians gathered together for the singing of psalms and prayers, because Jesus had proclaimed, "For where two or three are gathered together in my name, I am in the midst of them" (Matthew 18:20). The singing of psalms was incorporated into the central ritual of the early Church—the Mass. The Church Father, St. Basil wrote of the important benefits of chanting for these congregations: "Psalmody, bringing about choral singing, a bond, as it were, toward unity, and joining the people into a harmonious union of one choir, produces also the greatest blessings, charity"; and "a psalm calls forth a tear even from a heart of stone. A psalm is the work of angels ... a spiritual incense."[6] Melodic formulas from earlier Jewish practices, and newly composed melodies were gradually collected and standardized during the first millennium of Christianity. The composition of these melodies was attributed to Pope Gregory I (ca. 540–604), acting under the influence of the Holy Spirit. This attribution gave the collected melodies authority and stature as "**Gregorian Chant.**" This term was used interchangeably with plainchant and plainsong, referring to the unadorned nature of these melodies. Preservation and standardization of the ritual melodies across Western Europe that began during the reign of Charlemagne (742–814) led to the development of music notation. This body of notated melodies, numbering in the thousands, accompanied all the rituals of the Church Year. In monasteries, convents, and parishes, choirs sang the sacred texts and teachings of the early Roman Church to these unaccompanied plainchant melodies, transmitting Christian teachings in a simple yet appealing manner. The recitation of Gregorian chant (10.9) by the Benedictine nuns of Notre-Dame-l'Annonciation in France demonstrates the continuity of the practice into the present.

Notation and the rise of music "literacy" not only aided preservation and standardization, but notation also encouraged a new form of musical creativity in the adding of multiple parts to the chant melodies. From unison singing to two then three then four and more vocal parts, polyphony developed, mirroring changes in architecture and church organization in the late Middle Ages. As church music became increasingly complex, emphasis shifted from the clarity of the words to the glorious sound of musical harmony. By the beginning of the 17th century, music for worship had become quite elaborate, with the addition of multiple choirs, soloists, and instruments. While composers still used the ancient Gregorian melodies, the melodies became increasingly hidden within multi-part textures.

Islamic Cantillation (Egypt)

The Qur'an is the central revelation on which Islam is based. It is experienced by Muslims throughout the world as an auditory phenomenon, recited in classical Arabic. The use of music in Islam has long been a matter of debate. Orthodox Muslims prohibit from mosque observances all forms of "music" except Qur'anic recitation and the Call to Prayer (**adhan**), delivered at five prescribed daily prayer times. These two forms of religious expression are *not* considered music in Islam, although they sound like music to non-Muslims. Western scholars use the term "cantillation" with reference to Islamic chant in order to differentiate this category from forms of musical expression that have secular content and fulfill secular purposes. According to generally held beliefs, the principles of recitation are based upon the manner in which Archangel Gabriel transmitted the sacred words to the Prophet Mohammad. He then repeated them to his companions exactly as he heard them. They in turn recited the words to their followers, and so on across the generations until the present day. Qur'anic study and memorization are primary components of religious education for Muslim children. The Qur'an is recited according to a system of articulation that children study meticulously so that every letter of the sacred text is clearly enunciated and free of error. Every year, thousands of school children throughout the Islamic world memorize the entire Qur'an, and, passing a recitation exam, attain the title of **Hafiz** (*Hafiza* for girls). This achievement grants them high status within their communities. Perhaps no other book in human history has been memorized by more people.[7]

The practice of Qur'anic recitation (10.10), called **tarteel**, follows strict rules for pronouncing the Arabic syllables, shaping melodic contours, and pausing and breathing during the recitation. In the video, teenage Nusaiba Mohammad demonstrates the excellence of her *tarteel* on a BBC television show in 2009. While Qur'anic recitation is not considered music, the principles of melody that are associated with this practice are based on *maqamat*, the same modal system as classical Arabic music. The purpose of adding melody to the sacred words is to render them with a beautiful voice. A more elaborate practice called **tajweed**, literally "betterment," is learned by specialists (**qari**) who are identified both for the beauty of their voice and for being particularly skillful in their recitation. *Tajweed* is also characterized by intricate vocal ornaments similar to those in classical music styles. Sheikh Abdul Basit (10.11) (1927–1988), one of the finest and most renowned *qari* of 20th-century Egypt, recites Qur'anic verses. In the video, one can hear the ecstatic adulation of his audience.

DEVOTIONAL SINGING

Religions provide opportunities for ordinary people to participate in communal worship practices where they express religious emotions, make requests of the divine, and share devotional experiences with others in their communities. In a small, remote village in eastern Tibet, for example, Buddhist women too old for agricultural and child-rearing duties gather most days for chatting, socializing, spinning the **mani kang** (great prayer wheel), and chanting the *Tara Sutra* (10.12). The **Tara Sutra** is a sacred text in praise of Tara, the feminine manifestation of Avalokiteshvara, the **Bodhisattva** of Compassion. This is fundamentally a communal exercise, as it takes the participation and effort of all the women to turn the wheel, which rings a bell at each rotation. Every turn of the wheel releases a prayer, and with each prayer the women acquire merit for themselves, their families, and their community (Figure 10.5).

FIGURE 10.5 Tibetan women spinning a giant prayer wheel

Hindu Devotional Music (India)

In Hinduism, there are many opportunities for devotional singing by religious congregations. *Kirtan*, the repetitive singing of divine names such as Krishna and his consort Radha, is one of the primary forms of worship. Krishna and Radha are believed to be male and female aspects of the unitary divinity, Vishnu. Among many Hindus throughout the world, repeating divine names is considered the highest form of prayer. An example is the renowned religious figure (guru), Jagadguru Kripaluji Maharaj (1922–2013), shown in this video leading a session of *kirtan* singing (10.13). The guru is seated among his followers on a throne, men on his right, women on his left. The *kirtan* has a call-and-response structure, with a woman caller (not seen in the video) alternating with the guru himself as leader. Bells, cymbals, and drums provide rhythmic accompaniment. Alternate names Radey (Radha) and Govinda (Krishna) are repeated over and over. In this spiritual practice, a form of *bhakti* yoga, the names of the deities are believed to be synonymous with the deity Vishnu, and to pronounce the divine names is to evoke the divine. Repetition leads to oneness and a profound sense of bliss for the devotees.

The practice of repeating the names of divine beings dates back at least to the 15th century and the teachings of a Bengali saint, Chaitanya Mahaprabhu (1486–1534). He traveled throughout India, leading his followers in public sessions of ecstatic singing and dancing. He taught that the singing of *kirtan* bypassed the need for serious scholarship and strenuous exercise to achieve spiritual fulfillment. The teachings of Chaitanya Mahaprabhu are followed to this day.

Jewish Devotional Music (Israel)

Devotional music has an important place in the lives of Jews, both within formal worship services of the synagogue and in domestic life. Prayers are often sung, some with wordless improvised melodies known as *nigun*. Particularly in Hasidic communities, song is a deep expression of religious fervor. The **Hasidim** (as members of these communities are known) trace their origins to the 18th-century religious mystic and healer Israel ben Eliezar, known as the Bal Shem Tov. He taught his followers that access to the divine is more a matter of emotional connection through song and dance than study and learning. The Hasidim wear clothing in the manner of that worn by the original followers of the Bal Shem, Eastern European Jews of several centuries ago. Some Hasidic men grow their beards and sidelocks (*payot*) throughout their lives, and always keep their heads covered with a skull cap or *yarmulke*. When out in public, a black fedora hat is worn over the *yarmulke*. However, married men on the Sabbath and other festive occasions wear a special hat called a "*shtreimel*."

At a Hasidic wedding that took place in Netanya, Israel on November 31, 2017, a *mitzvah tantz* (10.14) was performed. The wedding was between the grandson of an important religious leader, the Rabbi of Sanz Shlita, and the daughter of Rabbi Sternbuch Viznitz, another important leader of a religious community. The event attracted thousands of Hasidim, men and boys, who sang exuberantly throughout the ceremony. Women have traditionally held a celebration equally vital but separate from men. The only woman present at the *mitzvah tantz* is the bride, dressed in her white bridal gown, who stands at one end of the wedding hall impassively as the rabbi and relatives dance before her.

Christian Hymnody (Europe, USA, Australia, Uganda)

As noted in the Introduction to Part IV, the early Church Fathers were cautiously permissive about the inclusion of music in worship services. Within the central rituals of Christianity—the Mass in particular—prayers and Biblical texts were sung, following the pre-Christian practices of the synagogue. From the earliest days of Christianity, believers were encouraged most eloquently by St. Basil to participate in the congregational singing of the Psalms. In addition to these poetic texts from the Old Testament, non-Biblical religious poetry was continuously added to the **liturgy**. These songs of devotion and praise were known as "hymns," from the Greek *hymnos* ("an ode to a god or hero").

Over the next 2,000 years, music developed as a fundamental and indispensable component of Christian religious life. For many Christians, hymn singing became the ultimate outward expression of their faith. Both the Roman Catholic and Eastern Orthodox churches developed rich repertoires of music, some highly sophisticated and performed by specially trained choirs, some more simple for congregational participation.

During the Reformation in the 16th century, led by Martin Luther, John Calvin, and other reform-minded leaders, a number of Protestant sects split from the Roman Catholic Church, and each developed its own ideas for employing music in religious rituals. In the sects that grew from John Calvin's austere interpretation of Christian life and worship, music practices were closely controlled. Simple four-part hymns sung by congregations without instrumental accompaniment became the only musical worship permitted. In contrast, Martin Luther was himself a musician, as was King Henry VIII of England, founders of the Lutheran and Anglican/Episcopal Churches, respectively. The rich musical traditions of these denominations may be directly related to the strong musical preferences of their founders.

Lutheran Churches in 18th-century Germany maintained elaborate musical establishments, including full orchestras, professional choirs, and soloists for Sunday worship. Also, Lutheran churches as well as those of other denominations installed organs in the choir lofts, and music ministers were expert organists. A great body of Christian sacred music was penned by these composer-organists, the greatest of which was Johann Sebastian Bach (1685–1750). Over his lifetime, he composed hundreds of works for the organ that were played during Sunday worship as preludes to the service or for intervals of reflection. When French composer Hector Berlioz (1803–1869) visited northern Germany, he was astounded by the adoration in which Bach was still held, one hundred years after his death. Berlioz wrote in his autobiography:

> They adore Bach, and believe in him, without supposing for a moment that his divinity could ever be called into question … God is God and Bach is Bach.[8]

Polish organist Maria Magdalena Kaczor plays Johann Sebastian Bach's chorale prelude (10.15) "*An Wasserflussen Babylon*" ("By the Waters of Babylon") in this video. The chorale prelude was an organ solo played at the beginning of Sunday worship based on a hymn with a Biblical text that was familiar to the congregation. Bach uses the melody of the hymn, which will be sung later in the service, as the basis for this elaborate polyphonic composition.

One of the most prolific composers of Protestant hymns was the 18th-century English poet and composer Isaac Watts, whose more than 750 hymns spread throughout the

English-speaking world. They became so popular that in 1872, the American preacher and abolitionist Henry Ward Beecher wrote,

> When believers analyze their religious emotions, it is [as] common to trace them back to the early hymns of childhood as to the Bible itself. At least until very recently, most English-speaking Protestants who thought about heaven did so more in terms of Dr. Watts than of the Revelation of St. John.[9]

Today, there is enormous diversity in Protestant hymn singing during communal worship. Styles range from the simple SATB harmony of hymnals from a hundred years ago to "praise and worship" bands using electronic amplification and popular music forms. In the first example of four, a Mennonite choir (10.16) at a funeral sings an unaccompanied hymn, "I Will Meet You in the Morning," composed in 1956 by Albert Edward Brumley Sr. (1905–1977). This style of song has deep traditional roots extending back to the early 19th century, and is unaffected by contemporary popular trends.

The second example is the most famous anthem by the father of the modern gospel tradition, Thomas A. Dorsey (1899–1993), "Precious Lord, Take My Hand" (10.17). Dorsey typifies one of the leading trends in African-American Christian worship: the setting of devotional texts to music drawn from popular idioms. Dorsey himself had a career as a leading pianist in the 1920s, playing behind the popular blues singer Ma Rainey (1886–1939). He was also a prolific composer and arranger of blues and jazz songs. His father had been an evangelical minister and Dorsey began a music ministry in Chicago in the 1930s. At the time, he was still working in blues clubs and touring under the name "Georgia Tom." However, in 1932, while he was playing at a revival prayer meeting, he received word that his wife Nettie had died in childbirth. The child died two days later. Stricken with grief and inconsolable, he tried to pray with some friends and to find answers for the tragedy that had befallen him. By his own account, Dorsey said aloud, "Lord?" and his friend said, "'No! That's not His name! Say, 'Precious Lord!' And ladies and gentlemen, believe it or not, I started singing right then and there…."[10] The effect of Thomas A. Dorsey's musical revolution, combining simple heartfelt words of faith with the harmonies and rhythms of secular blues and jazz, was one of the most significant developments in the history of Protestant church music and has had a global influence.

A third example presents a style of hymn singing known as lining out (10.18), associated with Primitive Baptists in the Southeastern United States, particularly in the Appalachian Mountains. A precentor sings the opening line of a hymn, and when the congregants recognize the melody they repeat it slowly, freely ornamenting and harmonizing it. The precentor then "lines out" the rest of the hymn in the same manner, alternating with the congregation. The congregations that use this technique have religious restrictions against the use of musical instruments in worship. The practice originated in Scotland in the 17th century for the benefit of illiterate parishioners so that they could participate in hymn singing. Scottish immigrants brought the technique to the New World and the technique of **lining out** spread to both White and Black congregations in the segregated South. Video 10.18 shows the technique being used in two southern churches: the Old Regular Baptist Church in Louisville, Kentucky, and Fairfield Baptist Church in Lithonia, Georgia.

A fourth example of modern **hymnody** is the evangelical praise and worship song, "Here in My Life," by Australian pastor and singer-songwriter Darlene Zschech (b. 1965). She was a worship pastor at the Australian megachurch Hillsong from 1996 to 2007. The church was founded by Brian and Bobbie Houston in 1983 in the western suburbs of Sydney, Australia, and today Hillsong has churches in thirty countries around the world with an average weekly attendance of 150,000. Zschech's compositions, including "Here in My Life" (10.19), closely resemble contemporary popular songs in terms of their musical and performance style, with electronic instruments, drums, light show, and amplified voices. The upbeat music serves to attract younger worshipers and to elicit strong emotions of commitment and self-surrender. Evangelical and Pentecostal Christians worldwide sing her songs every Sunday, and her song recordings have sold millions of copies for home devotion. From Seoul to São Paulo, praise and worship hymns have had an enormous influence on forms of Christian music and worship.

In Kampala, the capital city of Uganda (Map 10.1), young urban Christians, often dislocated from traditional home villages and ways of life, find solidarity and community in large, modern mega churches. This typical Sunday morning service at Kampala's Watoto Church (10.20) exemplifies the globalizing impact of missionary work in the digital age. With its video projections, light show, and ear-splitting amplification of the band, it is surprisingly similar to Zschech's service in Melbourne, Australia, 7,500 miles away. This kind of Sunday morning spectacle is now a global phenomenon among evangelical Protestants and charismatic Roman Catholics.

The Roman Catholic Church has remained a vital force in the world despite the schisms of the Reformation that gave rise to the many Protestant denominations. Catholic countries Spain, Portugal, and France led the exploration and conquest of much of Latin America and large parts of Africa and Asia. Missionaries seeking converts followed in the wake of these military conquests imposing alien forms of music and worship. Governing authorities in Rome mandated uniformity of language (Latin) and liturgical music based on Gregorian chant. In Africa, generations-old traditions of drumming and dancing had provided and affirmed links between the living, the familial ancestors, and deities. Missionaries, arriving in Uganda and elsewhere in East Africa in the 1880s, suppressed these practices as rooted in superstition.

The Second Vatican Council (1962–1965) was an attempt to integrate more fully Roman Catholic church practices with the modern world, and to provide opportunities for greater participation by worshipers in church rituals. One modification was the change from Latin to vernacular languages in the celebration of the Mass. Another was to permit local and more contemporary musical forms in worship. These changes in the rituals of the church coincided with the breakup of the British, French, and Portuguese colonial empires. With independence from colonial rule came a new sense of African identity and assertiveness. For many African Catholics, retaining allegiance to the Church while rejecting the degrading effects of the colonizing powers in whose wake Christianity arrived, created a delicate balancing act. How could one be both devoutly Catholic and proudly African? In Uganda, resolving this tension produced novel forms of musical worship.

Ethnomusicologist Nicholas Sempijja describes this religious-musical situation in Uganda as an example of glocalization.[11] The videos linked below show secondary school choir students at a Catholic boarding school preparing to compete with other schools in an annual song and dance competition. Two categories in the competition feature unaccompanied hymns sung in four-part harmony. The first category requires two hymns in English, Uganda's official (former colonial) language; the second requires one hymn in the local African language, Luganda. When the festivals were first instituted in the 1970s, songs by such European composers as Schubert and Mozart were featured. But by the early 2000s all hymns, including those in

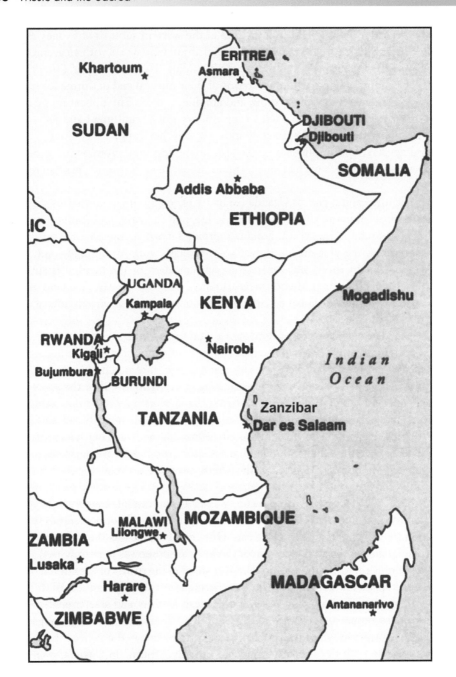

MAP 10.1 East Africa showing Uganda, Ethiopia, and Zanzibar

Source: *Garland Encyclopedia of World Music*, Vol. 1, Africa

Western-style, were written by African composers. In this first video, members of the choir of Archbishop Kiwanuka Secondary School rehearse their first English language hymn "I Believe" (10.21) written by Reverend Father James Kabuye. In the second video, the students rehearse their Luganda-language hymn, *"Tutende Ddunda"* (10.22) ("Let Us Praise the Lord").

The third and final category consists of a performance in pre-Christian Luganda style, replicating East African forms of traditional expression. It combines singing, dancing, and dramatic narrative. The stories behind these dramas are Biblical—the fall of the Tower of Babel, or Christ entering Jerusalem on Palm Sunday, for example. The exuberant performances feature native Lugandan forms of song and dance. The traditional instruments include xylophone (*endongo*), harp (*enanga*), fiddle (*endingidi*), panpipes (*enkwanzi*), and drums (*engoma*). Students at Mbuye Farm and Vocational High School rehearse their "traditional" offering, *"Ngenda Yeruzalemu"* (10.23), showing Christ entering Jerusalem, riding on a donkey.

The final video, taken at the festival itself, shows brief excerpts from the traditional entries of four schools (10.24) performing before judges and audience members. Each performance begins after a judge rings a bell. From then on, every aspect of the performance is evaluated: the deportment of the students, the competence of the actors, the enthusiasm of the instrumentalists, the quality of the choreography, and the skill of the dancers. The song contest serves as an arena for negotiating issues of cultural identity and religious affiliation, resulting in creative compromises between the local (Lugandan) and the global (the Roman Catholic Church). The traditional forms of ritual expression—music and dance—that had been suppressed with the introduction of Christianity have now become vehicles through which young people negotiate an identity that is *both* devoutly Catholic and proudly African.

Islamic (Sufi) Zikr, Sama, and Qawwali (Azerbaijan, Turkey, India)

Within Islam since nearly the beginning of the religion in the 7th century, there were groups who sought a direct experience of the divine. Members of these groups have collectively been known as Sufis. Among Sufi orders throughout Central Asia and elsewhere, believers gather regularly to perform **zikr**. This practice can take many forms, from silent reflection on the "99 Names of Allah," to group ceremonies with a strongly rhythmic form of fervent vocalizing, aimed at inducing a state of ecstasy. For example, Sufi women in Azerbaijan perform a strenuous form of *zikr* (10.25). The group repeats one of the Divine Names accompanied by rhythmic bodily movements while a solo voice intones a devotional poem. Throughout the Islamic world, the public face of men worshiping together in the mosque hides the more private practices of women, who carry out their religious obligations and express their religious devotions in separate spaces within the mosque, or in the home. Repetitive practices such as these, which often combine rhythm with melody, are found in many religious traditions, from the *mantras* of Hinduism and Buddhism to the saying of the Rosary of Roman Catholicism.

In the 7th and 8th centuries, early Sufi groups created a body of sacred poetry and song drawing on the poetic and musical forms of classical Arabic and Persian (Farsi). As Islam spread beyond Arabia through conquest and mass conversions, poetic and musical forms were developed by Sufis in local **vernacular** languages. Throughout the long history of Sufism, the term **sama** (literally "attentive listening") has been used to describe occasions for experiencing and performing devotional poetry, music, and dance. Ethnomusicologist Jonathan Shannon writes, "Poetry is the supreme art of the Arab peoples with a rich history and vibrant contemporary presence… Music has been closely allied with poetry from pre-Islamic times to the present."[12]

One of the greatest Sufi poets was Mevlana Jalaluddin Rumi (1207–1273) (Figure 10.6). Rumi was born in Balkh in what is now Afghanistan, into a Persian-speaking community. His family settled in Konya, Turkey (see Map 2.5), after traveling west to escape the ravages of Genghis Khan's Mongol hordes. The son of a great Islamic scholar and a great scholar

FIGURE 10.6 Statue of Mevlana Jalaluddin Rumi (1207–1273) in Buca, İzmir, Turkey

himself, Rumi came under the influence of a wandering dervish, or mystic, named Shams of Tabriz. Following the death of his teacher Shams and inspired by the intensity of their relationship, he began composing one of the longest religious poems in the history of literature, the *Masnavi*, consisting of 22,000 couplets. These devotional verses, along with the life and teachings of their author, became the basis of the **Mevlevi** Sufi order, founded in Konya by Rumi's followers after his death. These verses have been sung to instrumental accompaniment since the 14th century, and in them, references to music form powerful metaphors for spiritual love, beauty, and ecstasy. For instance:

> Today, like every other day, we wake up empty and frightened.
> Don't open the door to the study and begin reading.
> Take down a musical instrument.
> Let the beauty we love be what we do.
> There are hundreds of ways to kneel and kiss the ground.
> And:
> Don't worry about saving these songs!
> And if one of our instruments breaks,
> it doesn't matter.
> We have fallen into the place
> where everything is music.
> The strumming and the flute notes
> rise into the atmosphere,
> and even if the whole world's harp
> should burn up, there will still be
> hidden instruments playing[13]

Much of the criticism against music and dance in the Islamic world has been directed against the Sufis, who come "from all levels of society," and who seek "to escape from the dullness of everyday life in a heartfelt emotional religion."[14] A highly refined Sufi tradition of sung poetry known as *qawwali* emerged in India and Pakistan. Ethnomusicologist Regula Qureshi writes:

> All over South Asia there is Qawwali, for all over South Asia there are Muslims; where there are Muslims, there are Sufis; and where there are Sufis there is Qawwali, … the authentic spiritual song that transports the mystic toward union with God.… Through the act of listening—sama—the Sufi … in opening himself to the powerful message of Qawwali, hopes for a spiritual experience of intensity and immediacy that transcends his conscious striving. The music serves to kindle the flame of his mystical love, to intensify his longing for mystical union, and even to transport him to a state of ecstasy and to sustain him there to the limit of his spiritual capacity.[15]

Qawwali typically takes place at a Sufi shrine (*dargah*) that houses the tomb of a saint. A shrine is a sacred place that Sufis believe to be charged with spiritual energy (**baraka**). The Nizamuddin Shrine in Old Delhi, India, is the burial site of the saint it is named for, Nizamuddin Auliya (1238–1325) of the Chishti order of Sufis. The shrine also houses the tomb of his great musician-disciple Amir Khusrau (1253–1325), "the father of *qawwali*." At the Nizamuddin shrine, Thursday night is *qawwali* night (10.26). Professional singers (*qawwals*) perform sacred songs, creating an environment of religious enthusiasm and inspiring profound religious feelings in those who congregate there. These singers are members of hereditary professional clans and are employed by the shrine administration. A typical *qawwali* "party," as the performing ensemble is called, consists of between five and ten musicians, often members of the same family or *biradari* ("brotherhood"). In Video 10.26, a lead singer and several secondary soloists sing alternate lines of text, with the supporting members joining them on the choruses and providing rhythmic clapping. The lead singer plays the harmonium, and another musician plays the double-headed *dholak* drum. The atmosphere at the shrine is informal compared with that of the mosque. Tourists brandish their video cameras

FIGURE 10.7 Nusrat Fateh Ali Khan (1949–1997) performs on the British TV show "Big World Cafe," February 1989

and women sit right beside the musicians. A small boy gives money from his family to the *qawwals*, as is the custom.

The greatest modern exponent of *qawwali* was Pakistani singer Nusrat Fateh Ali Khan (10.27) (1949–1997) (Figure 10.7). He belonged to the Delhi *gharana*, also known as the *Qawwal Bachhon gharana*, a lineage of musicians dating back 700 years to Amir Khusrau. Khan performed in over forty countries, and earned the Guinness World Record for the "Most *Qawwali* Recordings," with over 125 albums. He also became one of the most recognizable superstars of World Music, writing film scores and collaborating with several rock musicians including Peter Gabriel and Eddie Vedder, and Indian film composer and producer A.R. Rahman. On October 13, 2015, in celebration of Khan's birth date, Google created a doodle on its homepage, stating "Thanks to his legendary voice, Khan helped bring 'world music' to the world."[16]

CONCLUSION

The beginning of this chapter has discussed music as the setting for sacred words—the foundational verses and texts of five world religions: Hinduism, Judaism, Buddhism, Christianity, and Islam. The chant melodies to which these ancient verses were set are among the oldest surviving musical expressions in the world. Sacred chant has been performed in ritual contexts for millennia. The second part of the chapter has discussed the congregational singing of devotional songs in more contemporary styles. Group singing inspires synchronized expressions of profound emotion as in Hindu *kirtan*, Jewish wedding songs, Darlene Zschech's Hillsong hymns, and Azeri Sufi *zikr*. Indeed, group singing brings about the same "**temporary physiological synchrony**" that primatologist Bruce Richman found among the gelada baboons (Chapter 5). The next two chapters continue exploring world sacred music. Chapter 11 focuses on religious expressions that transcend language and inspire states of ecstasy. These expressions include trance, dance, and dramatic performance. Chapter 12 concerns manifestations of the sacred in terms of space and time.

KEY TERMS AND CONCEPTS

Bar Mitzvah	Gompa
Bhakti Yoga	Hasidim
Brahmin	Hazzan
Buddhist Chant	Hymnody
Cantillation	Islamic Cantillation
Cantor or Hazzan	Kirtan
Chant	Lining Out
Christian Hymnody	Liturgy
Church Fathers	Mani Kang (Great Prayer Wheel)
Devotional Singing	Missionary
Divine Names	Plainchant

Qawwali

Sacred Chant

Sama

Second Vatican Council

Sufism

Vedic Chant

Vernacular Languages

Vocal vs Instrumental Sacred Music

Zikr

THINKING ABOUT MUSIC

1 What do the five forms of chant or cantillation discussed in this chapter have in common?

2 Musicologist Amnon Shiloah describes the "interminable debate" surrounding music in religious contexts. What are the terms of the debate? Why might music support a religious life, and why might it detract from it? Why was St. Augustine tormented by this question?

3 Why are the *adhan* and Qur'anic recitation (*tajweed* and *tarteel*) not considered "music" even though they sound like music?

4 How do generational and racial differences affect the kinds of music used in American Christian churches?

5 Ethnomusicologist Ter Ellingson wrote: "[Music] enhances, intensifies, and ... transforms almost any experience into something felt not only as different but also as somehow better" (Ch. 6, p. 152). How do you think this quote applies to music in religious contexts? Think of an example from your own experience, or from the chapter, and explain how it relates to Ellingson's view.

6 How did the Second Vatican Council affect Roman Catholic church music in Uganda?

7 Consider how music derived from traditional African rituals came to be used in Christian worship. Are there parallels between this and the phenomenon of "Christian rock"? Incorporate in your response a definition, in your own words, of the concept of "re-contextualization"?

NOTES

1 St. Augustine's Confessions (398 CE), cited in Piero Weiss and Richard Taruskin, *Music in the Western World: A History in Documents* (New York: Schirmer, 1984), 32.

2 Piero Weiss and Richard Taruskin, *Music in the Western World: A History in Documents* (New York: Schirmer, 1984), 15.

3 Several of the ideas and examples in this Introduction come from Ter Ellingson's article "Music and Religion," in *The Encyclopedia of Religion* (New York: Collier Macmillan, 1987).

4 Charles Capwell, "The Music of India," in Bruno Nettl et al., ed., *Excursions in World Music*, 6th ed. (Upper Saddle River, NJ: Pearson Prentice Hall, 2012), 37.

5 Information in this paragraph draws on Huston Smith, *Requiem for a Faith: Tibetan Buddhism*. Hartley Film Foundation. VHS video, 1979; https://www.youtube.com/watch?v=40yRXr5WIhE&t=12s.

6 St. Basil, Exegetic Homilies, trans. S. Agnes Clare Way, cited in Weiss and Taruskin, *Music in the Western World*, 26.

7 William Graham, *Beyond the Written Word* (Cambridge: Cambridge University Press, 1993), 80.

8 Hector Berlioz, "On Bach," in *The Memoirs of Hector Berlioz*, trans. David Cairns (London: Everyman Library/Random House, 1865). Cited in C.D. Warner, et al., comp. *The Library of the World's Best Literature: An Anthology in Thirty Volumes*, 1917, https://www.bartleby.com/library/prose/692.html.

9 Esther Rothenbusch Crookshank, "'We're Marching to Zion': Isaac Watts in Early America," in *Wonderful Words of Life: Hymns in American Protestant History and Theology* (Grand Rapids, MI: Wm. B. Eerdmans Publishing Co. 2004), 17.

10 *Say Amen, Somebody*, DVD re-release, 1982, Rykodisc, Inc.

11 Nicholas Ssempijja, "Glocalizing Catholicism through Musical Performance: Kampala Archdiocese Post-Secondary Schools Music Festivals" (PhD diss., University of Bergen, 2012).

12 Jonathan Shannon, *Among the Jasmine Trees: Music and Modernity in Contemporary Syria* (Middletown, CT: Wesleyan University Press, 2009), xviii.

13 Coleman Barks, *The Essential Rumi* (San Francisco, CA: HarperOne, 1995), 34–36.

14 Amnon Shiloah, *Music in the World of Islam*, 42.

15 Regula Qureshi, *Sufi Music of India and Pakistan: Sound, Context and Meaning in Qawwali* (Cambridge: Cambridge University Press, 1986), 1.

16 "Nusrat Fateh Ali Khan's 67th Birthday," Google "doodles" website, October 13, 2015, https://www.google.com/doodles/nusrat-fateh-ali-khans-67th-birthday.

CHAPTER 11

Sacred Embodiment and Sacred Enactment

INTRODUCTION

There are occasions in which religious truths are experienced *within* the body and are enacted *through* the body of the believer. Indeed, for some believers the truths experienced within the body transcend verbal meanings and are believed to validate what the words proclaim. At the United House of Prayer for All People, music plays a central role in ecstatic Sunday morning worship services. The United House of Prayer is an evangelical Christian sect founded in 1919 by a charismatic preacher known as "Daddy" Grace (Marcelino Manuel da Graça, 1884–1960). Instrumental music, and the dancing it inspires, can elevate a ritual beyond the power of words. The trombone shout band (11.1), hallmark of this sect, invites members of the congregation collectively to "catch the spirit" in a manner that sometimes makes preaching unnecessary. This chapter examines ways in which music acts as a vehicle for accessing and physically experiencing the sacred. It begins with a discussion of ecstasy and trance, and goes on to present examples of sacred dance and sacred drama.

ECSTASY AND TRANCE

In popular music terminology, "trance" refers to a style of electronic dance music (EDM) that dates from the 1990s, but in a religious context the term is used to describe various altered states of consciousness. The outward manifestations of trance encompass a broad range of physical responses. These may include uncontrolled emotions, a hypnotic meditative state, hyperventilation, involuntary movement or loss of control of limbs, fainting, the capacity for superhuman feats of endurance, and convulsions. While Western medical science has inadequate explanations for this widespread phenomenon, it may be described by various symptoms observable in entranced individuals. The term "spirit possession" refers to the belief that one's body has been temporarily accessed by a divine or demonic entity.

Many cultures have developed practices and conditions conducive to trance in the context of ceremonial events. Anthropologist David Roche describes a celebration at a Hindu temple as follows:

> The sensory overload common to celebrations in the typical urban Hindu temple [includes] the din of brass bells and large drums, the reflected flashes from oil lamps and sputtering fluorescent lights, the overpowering clouds of incense smoke, the crush of devotees to view the central icon at the auspicious moment, the taste of blessed offerings, and the wafting of flower garlands. When the soundscape also involves ritually encoded music … it can represent both a contributing factor to and evocative symbol of transcendence…. Ritual music … [is] a widespread means by which South Asians access or initiate deep levels of spiritual communication … and trance remains an enduring sign of successful connection to a macrocosmic reality.[1]

Trance and spirit possession phenomena are widely distributed throughout the world. A shaman—a term of Central Asian origin—is a ritual practitioner or healer who may self-induce a trance state. From the South Korean *manshin*, female shamans who transmit messages from the dead and demonstrate the depth of their trance by dancing on knife blades, to the priestesses of Brazilian Candomblé, who become possessed by the gods and goddesses of their West African ancestors, ritual participants consider spirit possession to be proof of successful access to the spirit world.

Although such experiences are less common in Western Jewish and Christian practices, some Pentecostal and charismatic congregations promote occasions in which congregants "speak in tongues," "catch the spirit," or otherwise achieve transcendence and ecstasy. Music in these churches often plays an indispensable role in inducing and sustaining an atmosphere of heightened emotion.

Nadun (China)

A dramatic example of spirit possession may be found among the mountain villagers in a remote region of north central China. The majority Han ethnic group, which comprises approximately 90% of China's population, shares its territory with fifty-five ethnic minority groups. One of these, the Tu minority has a population of around 200,000, occupying mountainous territory known as the Sanchuan region in northeast Qinghai Province, on the northern bank of the Yellow River. Although most members of this ethnic group, who call themselves Monguor, are nominally Buddhist, they also practice devotional rituals dedicated to local deities. These deities are believed to reside in their midst rather than in distant heavenly realms. Here, as in many parts of rural China, people rely on these local deities for protection. In Minhe County on the Qinghai-Gansu border (see Map 7.3), a sub-group of Monguor has a distinct language and customs, and calls its branch of the ethnic group Mangghuer. Fifteen Mangghuer farming villages share the protection of the **local deity**, Erlang Ye (Figure 11.1). While accounts differ among villagers as to who Erlang Ye was, there is agreement that in life he was a high government official. He performed deeds that were beneficial to the people of the region, and after his death, his benevolent influence continues to affect their lives.

Nadun is a two-month long festival dedicated to Erlang Ye that coincides with the harvest season. Like religious festivals elsewhere in rural China, *Nadun* is "performed to thank deities for their protection and to ensure a good harvest, and to avoid incurring the deities' wrath."[2]

FIGURE 11.1 The local deity Erlang Ye housed in a portable shrine, Mangghuer village, Qinghai province, People's Republic of China

For most of the year, the image of the deity resides in his main temple in a central village. During the harvest season, the image is placed in a portable shrine (palanquin) that men carry from one village to the next in a cycle of visitations over the two-month period. In each village there is a small temple that houses the deity during his two-day visit. On the second day a ritual is held, after which the deity moves on to the next village. In this remote region, *Nadun* is the most elaborate annual ritual, and each village begins planning for the following year's event the day after the ritual ends.

Australian anthropologist Gerald Roche, on whose research this case study is based, writes: "The noun *nadun* is derived from the verb *nadu*, meaning to play, joke, or to perform or dance, and the term adequately summarizes the basic content of *nadun*: a series of danced performances."[3] The festival has four stages: the image of the deity is carried from the neighboring village and installed in the temple; the deity is entertained with dances and dramatic displays; he makes his presence known through possession; and he is finally bidden farewell as his image is carried to the next village. Throughout the entertainment portion of *Nadun*, drums, gongs, and singing are used to accompany a military-style dance and the masked dance dramas that follow. When these entertainments are over, villagers invite the deity to reveal himself by possessing the body of one of the farmers who temporarily becomes a vessel for the god. At the moment of possession, this medium, known as *huala* or *fala*, pierces his cheek with a metal skewer (*qianzi*) to indicate success and demonstrate the god's power.

This is the dramatic climax of the event, and if the village *huala* does not attain a state of possession, the participants consider the event a failure (Figure 11.2).

In the body of the entranced *huala*, the deity dances, accepts paper-streamer offerings that the villagers hang on poles, and delivers prophecies for the coming year. During the entire period of entrancement, except while the *huala* is prophesying, the sonic environment is saturated by the deafening sound of gongs and firecrackers. The crashing of the gongs continues as the deity's palanquin is removed from the temple and the deity is escorted out of the village and across the valley. During the journey to the next village, the gongs create a cacophony similar to that produced by firecrackers, which also add to the general commotion. Video 11.2 shows a *Nadun* celebration (11.2) from October 2010.

Gerald Roche writes:

> The number of *huala* is decreasing. *Huala* were once the center of religious life in Sanchuan. But now most *huala* are old … and few new *huala* are appearing. When the last *huala* dies, the gods will have left Sanchuan forever. Reflecting on the fate of the *huala* in Sanchuan, one *huala* said: "There won't be any *huala* in the future. Nobody replaces old *huala* when they die. Now many villages don't have a *huala*. Young people don't believe in the gods. So the gods no longer incarnate here."[4]

When the gods no longer visit, what happens to all the songs, dances, dramas, and traditions by which they were entertained? And what will hold together the communities that once spent a year planning for the god's annual visit? The future of the *huala* tradition is uncertain, but for now, the *Nadun* festival continues as a noisy, joyous celebration of the harvest and of the spirits who protect the communities under their watchful care.

FIGURE 11.2 Villagers playing gongs and drums to entertain the visiting deity (L), and Mangghuer village *huala* dancing with his pierced cheek, Qinghai Province, People's Republic of China (R)

Bira (Zimbabwe)

Among the Shona people of Zimbabwe in southeast Africa, a ritual called **Bira** is performed to unite communities with their ancestors, who are believed to mediate between the living and divine sources of power and protection. (See Map 9.3.) "We don't go straight to God," explains Zimbabwean musician Thomas Mapfumo. "We have to go through our ancestors, because they are the ones who died long time ago and are the nearest to God. We are not near to God. We are the living ones."[5] In the *Bira*, music serves to call the ancestor spirits to possess a medium (*svikiro*) who is the central figure of the ritual. *Mbira dzavadzimu* ("lamellophone of the ancestors") and *hosho* (rattle) players perform music throughout the night to attract the desired ancestor spirit to the gathering, made up of family and community members. A *Bira* is held at times of illness, drought, or social disharmony, when individuals or whole communities feel vulnerable or under some threat. The ritual instills "a feeling of solidarity [among] the community as villagers ritually unite with their ancestors."[6] The evening ceremony begins with the sharing of ritual beer and progresses to singing, dancing, and handclapping as the musicians perform with ever-greater exuberance. Possession occurs at the climax of the ritual. The *svikiro* calls for the musicians to stop playing and then initiates communication with the spirit world. As explained by ethnomusicologist Paul Berliner,

> When possession does take place at the *bira*, it is often sudden and startling to the uninitiated. The prospective host may be sitting quietly with a glazed look in the eyes; without warning he or she is shaken as if by an epileptic fit, filling the *bira* with cries of anguish. Different spirit mediums have different styles of evidencing their possession by spirits. One medium I have observed shot from his seat with a loud exclamation and the dancers jumped out of his way as his body hit the ground…. As he tossed and turned, participants continued to dance around him, careful to stay out of the way of his kicking feet. After fifteen minutes he ceased his cries and his body quieted. Eventually he rose and left the house. He returned shortly after, wearing black cloth in place of his European clothes, and from that point on was the spirit who possessed him…. Once the spirit seizes his or her host, the musical proceedings of the *bira* revolve around the medium.[7]

At this point in the ceremony, the musicians must play with greatest intensity so that the spirit doesn't leave the host before speaking words of guidance to the community through the host's mouth.

Three *mbira* musicians (11.3) in Chaonza village, Zimbabwe play their *mbira dzavadzimu* near the graves of their ancestors. One of the musicians says that they play *mbira*, "to honor our grandfathers or grandmothers who passed away long back, so that they can keep us and they can look after us."[8] The music communicates directly with the ancestors and sustains their interest and care for the living. In the *Bira* ceremony, it is the sound of the *mbira dzavadzimu* that calls the ancestors to possess the medium.

The *Nadun* and *Bira* trance rituals represent phenomena—shamanism and spirit possession—that demonstrate for a community that divine power is both real and accessible. In the two case studies, music serves important ritual functions: structuring the events, communicating between worlds, and sustaining both a heightened sense of anticipation before possession and catharsis afterwards. Music also inspires powerful emotional states that are different from those of daily existence. Ritual music moves many people to experience the extraordinary nature of the divine; such experiences strengthen expressions of faith and render ordinary existence endurable, meaningful, and hopeful.

Winti (Suriname)

Afro-Caribbean religious practitioners perform sacred dances as a form of worship and preparation for spirit possession. In the *Winti* religion (11.4) of Surinamese Creoles, drummers play specific rhythms in ceremonies that invoke the West African deities of their ancestors. In the video, women circle the ritual ground in the back courtyard of a **Winti** leader's home in Paramaribo, singing songs that evoke the goddess Legba who guards doorways. One dancer becomes possessed by the goddess, and in trance begins to ritually sweep the courtyard with a broom, Legba's sacred symbol.

Jaran Kepang (Suriname, Java)

The *jaran kepang* hobby horse dance is performed by young men of the Javanese community in Suriname during "Arrival Day" celebrations (see Video 7.18). At a certain point in the dance-ritual, specially chosen adult dancers take over the hobby horses from the young men and become entranced by horse spirits. In trance for more than an hour, the dancers buck and tumble, eat grass and unhulled rice, and drink enormous quantities of water. Suddenly one or two drop their hobby horses and become possessed by the spirits of birds, in acts of controlled mayhem. They then become possessed by lions, monkeys, eagles, and finally snakes. The dancers are overseen by elders who carefully watch over them to prevent injury, and to bring out of trance a dancer whose behavior has become too extreme. The *jaran kepang* trance dance (11.5) provides a connection with relatives and ancestors from the home island of Java, where *jaran kepang* is also performed. It connects the dancers and audience to a spirit world with which they readily commune. Part religious ritual and part entertainment, the *jaran kepang* is a powerful and durable expression of Javanese-Surinamese identity.

Both *Winti* and *jaran kepang* have roots in distant ancestral societies: West Africa and Java respectively. Both rituals rely on the participants' capacity to enter deep trance states; indeed, without the trance experience there is no ritual. Surinamese society accepts and embraces the validity of trance, and this acceptance creates a public space for the practices. From Brazil to Siberia to Zimbabwe, spirit possession and other psycho-spiritual phenomena are common and viewed not as psychosis but, to the contrary, as signs of spiritual health; and are nearly always accompanied by special music. Why public manifestations of trance are more rare in North America and Europe may have to do with a social and cultural environment that finds these uncontrolled behaviors unacceptable.

SACRED DANCE

Perhaps for as long as humans have sought to connect and communicate with sacred beings, people have used movement and dance as a form of worship, and to achieve spiritual experiences. The Pueblo Native Americans of Arizona and New Mexico dance their sacred stories, beliefs, and healing rituals in numerous and diverse ceremonies, following a cycle that covers a full calendar year. *New York Times* journalist Robert Schultheis writes,

[The dances] mark every important aspect of Pueblo Indian life: birth, procreation, death; farming, hunting, the earth and everything that lives on it; the past, present and future of the tribe.[9]

The most important of these rituals is the mid-summer Corn Dance (Figure 11.3). The dance is believed to invoke rain in this parched land. The Pueblos of the village rehearse intensively for months before the complex ritual. The dance harmonizes the realm of humankind with that of the natural world.

If they did not dance, they say, the tribe would disintegrate, the sky would not rain, the earth would not grow crops, children would not be born, the seasons and stars would not turn.[10]

In Tibetan Buddhist monasteries, monks often stage dance performances in courtyards for the local lay people. These performances convey moral teachings and channel spiritual energies. Attending them provides religious merit both for the dancers and the spectators. In Video 11.6, taken at the Dutsi Til monastery, Tibetan Buddhist monks of the Karma Kagyu ("Black Hat") school portray the battle between the *dharma* (Buddha's teachings) and the demon of selfishness, symbolized by a small black clay effigy. The Buddhist black hat dance (11.6) is accompanied by *gyaling* (double reed instruments) and cymbals.

FIGURE 11.3 Zuni Pueblo corn dance

Sufi Mevlevi Whirling (Turkey)

In Turkey, Sufi dervishes of the Mevlevi Order, founded by followers of Jalaluddin Rumi in the late 13th century, perform a whirling dance during their sacred *sema* ceremony (Figure 11.4). The Mevlevi dervishes (11.7) remove their black cloaks, symbolically leaving behind their attachment to this world, and seek direct communion with God by turning with arms extended. The word "dervish" literally means "doorway," and for the Mevlevi, the *sema* is "the doorway into the spiritual world" where "the soul is freed from earthly ties and can commune joyfully with the divine."[11] Musicians accompany the whirling dance on *qanun* (plucked zither), *ud* (plucked lute), *rebab* (fiddle), *ney* (flute), *bendir* (frame drum), and *kudum* (small kettledrums), and the ceremony ends with chanting from the Qur'an. When the Ottoman Empire broke apart following its defeat at the end of World War I (1918), Kemal Ataturk became the first president of the modern, secular Republic of Turkey. Among his modernization reforms was the banning of the *sema* in 1925. Members of the Mevlevi Order continued the practice in private until, in 1955, it was given official recognition as a "cultural" rather than a religious practice. Since that time the Mevlevi *sema* has been accepted as an important expression of Turkish identity.

Bharatanatyam (India)

Sacred dance may be a form of communal religious worship, as in the examples above. It may also be a form of individual devotion. Furthermore, dance may serve sacred or secular functions, or both simultaneously. In the solo *bharatanatyam* dance (11.8) of South India, for example, the dancer interprets through expressive postures (*asanas*) and elaborate hand

FIGURE 11.4 Mevlevi whirling dervishes during the *sema* in Istanbul, 2007

gestures (*mudras*) religious narratives concerning the deeds of Hindu gods and goddesses, heroes and heroines. Often the theme is the all-consuming love of a woman for the god-man Krishna, symbolic of the yearning of the individual for union with the divine. ***Bharatanatyam*** is rooted in the sacred temple dancing of women, known as *devadasis*, employed by Hindu temples to worship and serve the residing deities. The origin of the ***devadasi*** tradition is unknown, but at least since the 3rd century CE, there have been literary references to female artists dedicated to temples in South India. Today, *bharatanatyam* is one of the primary Indian classical dance forms learned by students in India and elsewhere throughout the South Asian diaspora. While it is a form of artistic expression, it is also a form of worship. Video 11.8 shows dancer Savitha Sastry.

Like music, dance is controversial in some sacred contexts. It is embraced by those who view it as a physical manifestation of divine presence and an emotionally powerful form of expression and communication, yet it is disapproved of by those who find dancing worldly or provocative.

Côte D'Ivoire Masked Dance (West Africa)

Côte d'Ivoire (Ivory Coast) "is the origin of several of the most important and interesting masking traditions in Africa," writes dance scholar Juliana Azoubel.[12] (See Map 2.4.) These masks serve important ritual functions within their native African communities, while they are prized as art objects by museum curators and private collectors in the West. Azoubel continues, "Through their embodiment in dance … masks are the way many Ivorians communicate with supernatural forces and bring power to the community."[13] Masked dancers are overtaken by the deities and ancestors that the masks depict. In the dance, parallel worlds become visible and manifest to audience members.

In the West-Central region of Côte d'Ivoire, adolescent boys of the Guro communities participate in intense seven-day initiation rites. Masked male elders embody powerful beings that provide instruction in the secrets of adult social membership. Some masks are considered dangerous and powerful, and girls and women are forbidden from viewing them. The dancers are usually members of "mask families" that pass down the ritual secrets from generation to generation, although a child from a non-masked family may be "chosen by the ancestors to become a mask." During the initiation rites, the spirit of the mask, Djoanigbe, "is the teacher for the initiates, their spirit guide; and the primary source of enlightenment in their young lives."

Some masks have a more social, entertainment function, as does the Zaouli mask, whose dance is characterized by "rapid-fire movement of the feet." The Zaouli dancer is always male, although the spirit is female (Figure 11.5). "The cross-gender mask performs on many different occasions to amuse people: during holidays, for entertainment of visitors to the community, to collect food from the community members during the initiation process, and also in some funeral ceremonies."[14] Zaouli masks are associated with villages, and in the Zaouli masked dance (11.9) of the Gohitafla region of central Côte d'Ivoire, the mask is decorated with snakes and a warthog. The music that accompanies and drives the dance is melodically simple and repetitive. Three wooden flutes, referred to as father, mother, and child, each play only a single pitch, together producing a three-note melody. A metal bell keeps the time, and six drummers accompany the dancer, playing hand-beaten cylindrical and goblet drums, and stick-beaten hourglass, barrel, and slit drums. The drummers' repeating patterns of interlocking phrases complement the intricate footwork made audible by the

FIGURE 11.5 Zaouli masked dancer from Guro Village, central Côte d'Ivoire

bells on the dancer's feet. As villagers young and old form a wide circle to watch the masked dancing, one audience member shows his great appreciation of the spectacle (at 1'38" in the video) by showering money over the Zaouli dancer.

Juliana Azoubel concludes:

> More than figures used to decorate walls, masks embodied by a performer can express emotions, feelings, and ideas that serve to orient society; and often use the hand of the spirit to control, discipline, and to order lives. This process is facilitated by the fact that the audience, composed of fellow villagers, has been brought up in this tradition and believes in its history and its power. The mask communicates advice, order, and feelings in a dynamic language of motions and real-life presence.... As masked dance paves the way for spiritual guides to protect society, it is also a critical strategy to preserve, practice, and project cultural meaning into the future.[15]

Bon Odori (Japan)

In Japan, the major Buddhist festival of **Obon** (or simply *Bon*) has been held annually since at least the mid-7th century (Map 11.1). It is a midsummer festival, although the exact dates vary from region to region since some follow the lunar calendar and some the solar. At this time,

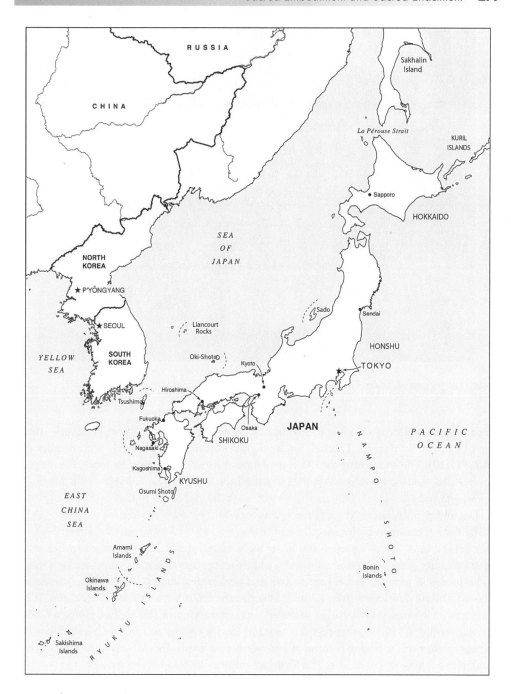

MAP 11.1 Japan

Source: Garland Encyclopedia of World Music, Vol. 7, East Asia: China, Japan, and Korea

people hang lanterns outside their homes and temples to welcome the spirits of their ancestors. In temple courtyards and elsewhere, a raised wooden platform (*yagura*) is built specially for the festival (Figure 11.6). At evening time, musicians and singers perform traditional *Obon* music on the platform while community members and visitors dance around it. In some locations,

FIGURE 11.6 *Yagura* platform for *Obon* festival at Tsukiji Hongwanji Temple, Tokyo

dance troupes perform choreographed dances on or around the *yagura*; in others, dances take place in street parades. Throughout Japan, *taiko* drumming frequently accompanies *bon odori* (11.10). The songs sung for *Obon* may have spiritual lyrics, may be local folk songs, or may even be modern popular songs. People attend the celebrations and join in the dancing to express gratitude toward their ancestors. People mark the end of the festival by floating lanterns on lakes and rivers in order to guide the spirits back to their own world.

The festival commemorates ancestor spirits that are believed to return to earth at this time. Over several days, many Japanese return to their ancestral family hometowns to honor the departed spirits of their ancestors by visiting and cleaning their ancestors' graves, making special food offerings in temples and at home altars, and performing sacred dances. The observance is believed to have developed from a Buddhist scripture about a monk named Mokuren. While meditating, Mokuren visualized his deceased mother starving in the Hell of Hungry Ghosts. She was unable to eat, for whenever she touched food it caught on fire. The monk discovered that his mother was suffering because of her selfish past deeds, and he prayed to the Supreme Buddha to ask how he could help. The Shakyamuni Buddha told him he should:

> make offerings of food from land and sea to his fellow monks at the end of their 90-day retreat which ended in mid-July. Upon following Shakyamuni's instructions, Mokuren danced for joy when his mother and seven generations of his ancestors were freed from their suffering.[16]

Rokusai Nembutsu Odori is a music and dance tradition performed during the *Obon* celebrations in the city of Kyoto. A ritual dance, *Rokusai*, is believed to date back to the 10th century when a Buddhist monk and teacher, Kuya Shonin, traveled through the streets of Kyoto (then the capital of Japan) with a bell hung around his neck, spreading the faith by dancing, beating a drum, and chanting the name of the Buddha. In recent times, *Rokusai* groups have formed to preserve and develop this traditional Kyoto performing art. Troupes consist of up to thirty or more musicians and dancers, ranging in age from young to old. They play a variety of drums, gongs, bells, and flutes, and perform dances at temples and shrines to enact sacred myths and secular tales in a popular regional folk style.

A typical performance of *Rokusai Nembutsu Odori* lasts sixty to ninety minutes. It begins and ends with the chanting of Buddhist prayers (11.11) (*nembutsu*), and includes a sequence of five or more music and dance pieces. In one of the pieces, *yotsu taiko* (11.12) ("Four Drums"), children, starting with the youngest, take turns performing on the four drums accompanied by flutes and gongs. A faster drumming piece concludes with ritual pole spinning (11.13), to ward off evil. Young children participate in dances such as the Circle Monkey Dance (*saru mawashi*), in which the young "monkeys" each play their own small drum as they dance around an adult playing a large drum. The culmination of a *Rokusai Nembutsu Odori* performance is typically the acrobatic lion and spider dance (11.14) (*shishi mai* and *tsuchi gumo*). This enacts a battle between the easy-going, carefree lion, symbolizing Righteousness, and the evil spider that spins numerous webs around his prey. Inevitably the lion, played by two dancers, celebrates victory over the spider (Figure 11.7).

In Japan and throughout the world, the division between the sacred and the secular is growing increasingly blurred. For example, the *Obon* festival incorporates both sacred and ritualistic practices like Buddhist chanting, and new, popular music styles during the dancing around the *yagura*. These styles communicate more directly and more meaningfully with today's audiences. Furthermore, *Obon* represents a blurring of the boundary between the sacred and the political; preparations for the festival are financed through municipal governments that raise funds through taxation. In the United States, with a population that is diverse both ethnically and religiously, the financing of such things as urban Christmas decorations is sponsored by private business associations like the chamber of commerce. In Japan, however, where the population is remarkably homogeneous, the government is able to sponsor religious events such as Obon, which projects a further blurring of boundaries separating expressions of the sacred and of the state.

FIGURE 11.7 *Chudoji Rokusai* group performing at Kiyomizu temple, Kyoto, 2009: the Lion and Spider dance (L), and young *Rokusai* members take turns beating four drums (R)

SACRED DRAMA

Sacred dramas are ritual performances of myths or religious stories that frequently include music and dance. They often take place within or outside churches and temples, and are presented in front of an audience or congregation. In medieval Europe, "mystery plays" enacted episodes from the Bible or from the lives of saints or church leaders. These **liturgical dramas** were first created and performed by monks and priests inside church sanctuaries, and were later performed by amateur actors in village squares or on traveling carts. They served to entertain, educate, and inspire their audiences. The music for several of these has survived in Gregorian chant notation.

In India, Indonesia, and sub-Saharan Africa, ritual ceremonies are often fused with dramatic performances. Texts are often minimal or non-existent, placing central importance on spectacle: gestures, dance movements, shouts and other vocalizations, music, acrobatics, lighting, and sound effects. Sacred dramas don't reveal ordinary everyday reality. Rather, they reveal the "True Reality" of the belief system, which is invisible in daily life. Sacred dramas represent for their audiences the deep past or the beginning times of mythical or celestial realms. Performances are believed to be occasions for visitations by supernatural beings and ancestors, and the suspension of everyday modes of behavior and feeling. Often, there is the expectation of magic, trance, and close encounters with sacred reality. Actors play the roles of gods, goddesses, and archetypal characters. In some dramatic traditions, actors wear decorated masks that depict the nature of the sacred beings they are portraying, and in some cases the masks themselves are believed to embody the power of the deities. Sacred drama is symbolic on many levels and can be a deeply transformational process for both actors and audiences.

MAP 11.2 Java and Bali in Indonesia, Southeast Asia

Source: Garland Encyclopedia of World Music, Vol. 4, Southeast Asia

Calonarang (Bali)

The island of Bali is predominantly Hindu in contrast to the largely Muslim populations of most other Indonesian islands (Map 11.2). On Bali, Hindu temple ceremonies take place on a daily basis, and frequently include masked dance drama. Such events function as religious ritual and as entertainment for their audiences. On sacred occasions, local drama troupes perform longer, more ceremonial versions in temple courtyards and other sacred locations. One such masked dance drama is the *calonarang* or "*Barong* dance," whose mythological origins date back at least a thousand years.

The two principal characters in the drama are the *Barong* and *Rangda*, who represent the forces of good and evil, respectively (Figure 11.8). The *Barong* is a large, shaggy, four-legged creature with the head of a lion or other animal. His striking face has bulging eyes, fangs, and a beard of human hair. Rangda is a hideous witch-like woman (played by a man) also with bulging eyes and fangs, a long tongue, long spiky hair, pendulous breasts, and long tubes representing her victims' intestines attached to her costume.

The **calonarang** performance dramatizes the Balinese worldview of powerful and opposing forces in the universe. It takes place outdoors in an open stage area with a *gamelan* ensemble seated to one side. The demonic character of *Rangda* can inflict great harm, and is simultaneously feared and respected. The *Barong* is believed to have magical and healing powers, and his actions help maintain harmonious balance in the world of human beings. The action centers around the confrontation, direct or indirect, between these two supernatural antagonists. At this *calonarang* performance (11.15) at Camphuan Temple in Ubud, *Rangda* and the *Barong* emerge at the outset. During the ritual, the *gamelan* plays continuously, adding an otherworldly sound to the supernatural proceedings. Followers of the *Barong* appear and attack Rangda with their daggers (*kris*). *Rangda* places a spell on the attendants, causing them to turn their daggers on themselves. At the drama's end, *Rangda* is temporarily held in check by the power of the *Barong* though she is free to cause further damage and destruction in the future.

For the Balinese, masks both possess and are visible representations of extreme spiritual and magical power. Those who carve them, from wood grown in a spiritually powerful place (such as temple grounds or a cemetery), perform purification rituals to ensure protection from supernatural forces. The masked dancers must likewise become spiritually pure, through a period of fasting and sexual abstinence, before putting on their masks and their

FIGURE 11.8 Characters in the Balinese *calonarang* dance drama: the *Barong* (L), and *Rangda* (R)

FIGURE 11.9 Balinese dancer showing protective white spot on forehead

costumes. Unmasked dancers in the drama paint a single white spot on their foreheads to protect themselves from possible attack by harmful spiritual forces (Figure 11.9). Before a *calonarang* performance begins, a priest ceremonially purifies the masks to protect them from any negative energies or defiling pollutants.

In extended, ceremonial *calonarang* performances, the *Rangda* dancer invariably goes into trance, while the two *Barong* dancers are less likely to become entranced because of the concentration needed to manipulate the mask and costume. Occasionally, however, *Barong* dancers do fall into trance. Trance-inducing techniques such as inhaling incense, making ritual offerings, and meditating are typically carried out as the *calonarang* dancer prepares for the performance. During the performance, audience members may also go into trance, overcome with emotion. Performers believe the force that drives them resides in the mask. Revived with holy water, they come out of trance and the spiritual forces remain in the mask. This entrancement and the capacity to fall into trance are viewed positively by the Balinese, and thus *calonarang* provides society with an acceptable outlet for extreme behavior. The *calonarang* sacred drama brings together the enactment of religious and mythological beliefs with the rich artistic traditions of this small Indonesian island. The cosmic stories of good versus evil are vividly depicted in colorful dramatic presentation, by brilliantly costumed dancers wearing exquisitely carved masks, accompanied by experienced *gamelan* musicians (Figure 11.10). The *calonarang* is simultaneously an expression of Balinese identity, a continuation of cultural tradition, a performance of sacred ritual and ceremony, and a primary tourist attraction.

FIGURE 11.10 Balinese *gamelan* ensemble

Kathakali (India)

The subcontinent of India has diverse regional traditions of dance drama that involve troupes of dancers and musicians, and one of the most well-known is *kathakali* from the southwestern state of Kerala (Map 11.3).

Like *calonarang*, **kathakali** is a complete performing art involving music, dance, mime, acting, costumes, and face painting (Figure 11.11). The dramas are based on scenes from the great Hindu epics, the **Ramayana** and *Mahabharata*. *Kathakali* traditionally was performed outdoors in staging areas attached to temples. The performance of a complete *kathakali* play lasts an entire night, beginning at sundown with a recital by the percussionists whose collective din announces the performance. All the characters, both male and female, are played by male actors. Costumes and makeup distinguish the male and female roles. The flaring skirts, elaborate face paint, and paper face-enlargers (***chutti***) all serve to make the actors and the action more visible to the audience from a distance. The makeup color and type help the audience identify each character's role and status—royal or common, human or divine, good or evil. The thick makeup gives the appearance of a mask, but unlike a mask it allows the actor to express emotion through face and eye movements. The makeup process takes from two to three hours. The actor applies his own outline and preliminary colors. He then lies on his back as a specially trained artist adds the details and applies the elaborate *chutti*, white ridges forming a frame from cheeks to chin traditionally made of rice paste but nowadays often of paper (Figure 11.12).

Two male singers present the narrative songs from the back of the stage, accompanying themselves on a small gong (*chengila*) struck with a stick, and a small pair of cymbals (*ilathalam*), that serve to keep time. They are joined by a drumming ensemble consisting of a large cylindrical drum (*chenda*) played with sticks, and a double-headed barrel drum (*maddalam*).

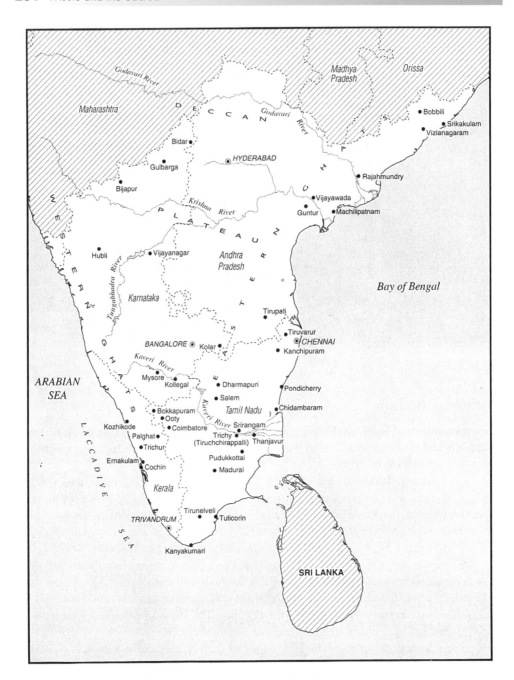

MAP 11.3 South India showing the southwestern state of Kerala

Source: Garland Encyclopedia of World Music, Vol. 5: South Asia: The Indian Subcontinent

The singing is highly ornamented, and lines of text are often repeated, giving the actors time to express the meanings fully. The actors use a highly developed language of hand gestures called **mudras** to interpret the meaning of the lyrics. *Kathakali* actors usually come from acting families and begin their arduous years of training in childhood. The training includes a strenuous

FIGURE 11.11 *Kathakali* actors and musicians on stage in the Sri Vallabha temple, Thiruvalla, Kerala, 2012

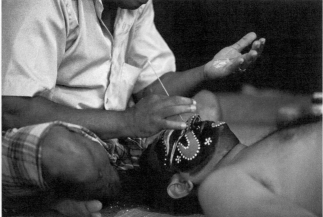

FIGURE 11.12 Green face paint and golden headdresses identify heroes, gods, and kings in *kathakali* (L), and a makeup artist applies designs onto black face paint, portraying evil characters (R)

form of martial art known as *kalaripayattu*. While the stories are of a religious nature and performances are supported by temple administrations, *kathakali* is also a form of entertainment that brings the community together to enjoy the music, artistry, drama, and poetry. It is believed by some that the gods also enjoy *kathakali* and are present at performances.

This eight-minute video clip of *kathakali* dancers (11.16) begins with narration by Ravi Shankar. Then follows several scenes from a famous *kathakali* play, *Kalyana Sougandhikam*

("The Auspicious Water Lilies"), based on a story from the *Mahabharata*. Queen Draupadi asks her husband Bhima, son of Vayu the wind god and a hero of enormous strength, to fetch some sacred flowers from a mountaintop grove from which humans are banned. The proud Bhima brags that he can go anywhere and nothing can stop him. He sets out boldly through the forest, frightening animals and knocking down trees. Bhima's half-brother, the divine monkey-god Hanuman, hears his destructive thrashing and decides to teach him a lesson in humility. Hanuman transforms himself into an old, decrepit monkey and lies down with his tail across the road, blocking the hero-king's way. Bhima demands that the old monkey move aside, and when the monkey refuses, Bhima attempts to push the tail out of the road with his cudgel. Yet with all his superhuman strength, he can't move the tail. Hanuman then rises from the ground and reveals to Bhima his divinity.

Over the past decades, *kathakali* dance dramas are often presented in highly abbreviated form in school auditoriums and tourist hotels. Fewer and fewer all-night performances take place in the temples of Kerala. Former Indian audience members now go to the cinema or stay home and watch soap operas on television. The children of the actors, instead of inheriting the art as their parents did, prefer the steady employment of banking or engineering to the arduous training required for *kathakali*. In her Booker Prize-winning novel, *The God of Small Things*, author Arundhati Roy poetically describes this situation. In order to make a living and survive, many *kathakali* actors are now forced to appear in these truncated performances for tourists who know nothing of the great tales that the actors have been trained since childhood to tell.

> The Kathakali Man is the most beautiful of men. Because his body is his soul. His only instrument. From the age of three it has been planed and polished, pared down, harnessed wholly to the task of story-telling. He has magic in him, this man within the painted mask and swirling skirts.
>
> But these days he has become unviable. Unfeasible. Condemned goods. His children deride him. They long to be everything that he is not. He has watched them grow up to become clerks and bus conductors. Class IV non-gazetted officers. With unions of their own.
>
> But he himself, left dangling somewhere between heaven and earth, cannot do what they do. He cannot slide down the aisles of buses, counting change and selling tickets. He cannot answer bells that summon him. He cannot stoop behind trays of tea and Marie biscuits.
>
> In despair he turns to tourism. He enters the market. He hawks the only thing he owns. The stories his body can tell.[17]

The *kathakali* actor in his distinctive makeup has become a symbol of the region. Traveling through Kerala, one cannot avoid seeing the painted face of the *kathakali* dancer on billboards, advertisements, and tourist brochures.

Epic of Pabuji (India)

In the northwest Indian state of Rajasthan, itinerant hereditary storyteller-priests (*bhopas*) present tales from the Epic of Pabuji—a 14th-century hero and folk deity of the region. (See Map 8.3.) In this pastoral, desert region of India, Pabuji is the protector of animals. According to the epic, it was Pabuji who first brought camels to Rajasthan, having defeated the

demon Ravana and stolen his animals. Later he was martyred while rescuing a herd of cattle on his wedding day. The epic takes thirty-six hours to recite in its entirety, and complete performances—traditionally carried out over five consecutive nights—are rare. A large hand-painted scroll (*par*) of the epic story forms the backdrop to the performance (Figure 11.13). This large painted cloth is treated as a sacred object, and **bhopa** families make daily offerings to it. The storyteller typically performs at the homes of worshipers of Pabuji who seek his mystical powers in times of misfortune or sickness. The *bhopa* dances and sings the narrative while accompanying himself on a bowed fiddle called a *ravanhatta* ("demon-slayer"). Jingle-bells around his ankles, and also attached to the end of his bow, provide rhythmic accompaniment. His veiled wife (*bhopi*) holds an oil lamp and illuminates the pictures on the scroll of the scene her husband is narrating. The *bhopi*, and sometimes their children, join in singing the refrains that punctuate the narrative. During his performance, the *bhopa* frequently interrupts the **epic narrative**, and tea is served as he tells topical stories and jokes, and leads the audience singing devotional songs (*bhajans*) and film songs. Thus, the evening is part religious ritual, part entertainment. The linked video shows an excerpt of an Epic of Pabuji (11.17) performance.

As with *kathakali*, changing economic circumstances have required many traditional artists in India and elsewhere to seek opportunities to supplement their incomes by performing for tourists. On a bus trip through Rajasthan in the first decade of the 21st century, foreign travelers might have seen a *bhopa* and *bhopi* waiting by the entrance of a highway tourist restaurant. The *bhopa* offers his services to the tour guide, to sing a tale to the tourists while they eat their lunch.

Author John D. Smith, who spent five decades chronicling the Pabuji tradition in Rajasthan, writes in his book *The Epic of Pabuji* (2005),

> In the 1970's, when I carried out the fieldwork on which this book is based, the tradition it describes appeared to be in robust health. There were many performers of the epic of Pabuji active in different regions of Rajasthan...By the time the first edition of *The Epic of Pabuji* appeared in 1991, things were already very different. A few months after publication I travelled back to Rajasthan with a film crew...We found that most of the bhopos [sic] whom we met had given up performing and instead had taken up work such as pedaling cycle-rikshas or sweeping out temples...Even Bhopos who were still active were turning increasingly to the tourist trade for their income...It is clear that the tradition of epic performances is rapidly dying.

FIGURE 11.13 Pabuji cloth painting (*par*) from 1938, by Jaravcand Josi of Bhilwara, Rajasthan. Tropenmuseum, Amsterdam

Thus, a performance tradition that was still flourishing in the 1970s ... has, by the beginning of the twenty-first century almost completely lapsed, and a book that was intended as a description of present-day practice has become a work of history.[18]

CONCLUSION

This chapter has demonstrated that religious beliefs, values, and understandings are not only expressed through words; they are enacted, performed, and felt at deep physical and psychological levels. In the *Nadun* harvest ritual in China, the *fala* shows through his trance the abiding presence of *Erlang Ye*. In Zimbabwe, the *bira* ceremony reveals the nearness of the ancestors to the living. In both cases, it is music that calls the spirits to possess the medium and creates a conduit for communication between worlds. Music may also be the very manifestation of the sacred, inspiring emotional states of joy, awe, tranquility, and ecstasy. Some religious traditions embrace the body as an appropriate means of expressing sacred experience, like Mevlevi Whirling Dervishes, *bharatanatyam*, and trombone shout bands of the United House of Prayer for All People. In sacred dance dramas like *kathakali*, stories of gods and goddesses, mythical heroes and heroines, come alive through specially trained actors with elaborate costumes and special music to reveal the otherworldly realms of the belief system. Indeed, it is the power of music to evoke this "otherness." According to Robin Sylvan, a professor of Religious Studies,

> In most cultures of the world, throughout the history of humankind, this spiritual power of music has been acknowledged, cultivated, and celebrated. It is an important part of our common heritage, one of the great expressions of the human endeavor.[19] [Sylvan concludes by quoting ethnomusicologist David McAllester:] We are not all practicing mystics and most of us do not experience God easily. But when we hear music, something like that is happening to us.[20]

This chapter has also called attention to the fragility of sacred theatrical practices, some of which are centuries old, at this time of rapid technological change and social disruption. The final chapter in Part IV examines the concepts of sacred space and time, and the various roles music plays in establishing the contexts for ritual practices.

KEY TERMS AND CONCEPTS

Ancestor Spirit	Sacred Dance
Mevlevi Whirling Dervish	Sacred Drama
Harvest Ritual	Shaman
Huala (or Fala)	Spirit Medium
Initiation Rite	Spirit Possession
Liturgical Drama	Trance
Local Deity	Worldview
Masked Dance Drama	

THINKING ABOUT MUSIC

1 Consider these sentences from the beginning of Chapter 11,

> There are occasions in which the truths proclaimed by religious systems are experienced *within* the body and are enacted *through* the body of the believer. Indeed, for some believers the truths experienced within the body transcend verbal meanings and are believed to validate the meanings that the words proclaim.

Explain this in your own words. How does it apply to: (a) United House of Prayer trombone shout bands; (b) *Nadun*; and (c) Mevlevi dervishes?

2 The relationship between religion (the sacred) and social entertainment (the secular) is in some cases very close, as in *Bon Odori* and *Calonarang*. Does the existence of the secular in a sacred ritual dilute its power? Why or why not? Refer to *Bon Odori* and *Calonarang* in your response.

3 How do you account for the phenomenon of trance, given your own worldview and experience? Have you experienced or encountered similar phenomena? Is there a relationship between the trance states and music encountered in this chapter and the "trance" of popular nightclubs?

4 Individuals and communities respond emotionally and physically to sacred music in a variety of ways. Think of a particularly intense experience that you or someone you know has had, which was triggered or enhanced by music. How did you or your acquaintance respond to the musical sounds, and was the response individual or part of a collective emotional expression?

5 Many religious belief systems are concerned with the relationship between everyday human experience and invisible sacred worlds, beings, and powers that are contacted through prayer and rituals. Music often provides a vehicle or bridge by which people access "the sacred." Consider these three examples: *Nadun, Bira,* and shout bands. What is the music like and what responses does it elicit?

6 What do *calonarang* and *kathakali* have in common as "complete performing arts"?

7 Regarding the *Epic of Pabuji*, what does author John Smith mean by "a book that was intended as a description of present-day practice has become a work of history" (Ch. 11, p. 288)?

NOTES

1 David Roche, "Music and Trance," in *The Garland Encyclopedia of World Music*, Vol. 5: *South Asia*, ed. Alison Arnold (New York: Taylor and Francis, 2000), 288.

2 Gerald Roche, "Nadun: Ritual and the Dynamics of Cultural Diversity in Northwest China's Hehuang Region," PhD diss. (Griffith University, Queensland, Australia, 2010), 64.

3 Gerald Roche, "Nadun," 33.

4 Gerald Roche, "The Gods Incarnate – The Huala of China's Sanchuan Region," 9-minute video documentary, 2013, https://www.youtube.com/watch?v=QUjLwtix2_U&list=UUdljWglGBn0P0XIbTJteTpQ.

5 Interview with Thomas Mapfumo in the documentary film *Mbira Music: Spirit of the People*, directed by Simon Bright and others (Zimmedia, 1990).

6 Paul Berliner, "Music and Spirit Possession at a Shona Bira," *The Soul of Mbira* (Chicago, IL: University of Chicago Press, 1981), 200–201.

7 Paul Berliner, "Music and Spirit Possession," 204–205.

8 "Mbira Maestros," a film by Antonio Lino on three Mbira musicians—Chikomborero, Prince, and William—in Chaonza village, Zimbabwe, uploaded August 21, 2010, https://www.youtube.com/watch?v=qja5kJ37lYA.

9 Robert Schultheis, "Corn Dance: Complex, Hypnotic," *New York Times*, July 11, 1976, 254.

10 Robert Schultheis, "Corn Dance," 254.

11 Narration from "Whirling Dervishes," video by Omar's Travels, uploaded August 25, 2009, https://www.youtube.com/watch?v=DnvSqHDJAnc.

12 Juliana Azoubel, "The Côte d'Ivoire Mask Tradition from the Viewpoint of Dance Ethnology: Dancing the Gap between Spirit and Human Worlds," *Journal of Undergraduate Research*, I/6 (2000), http://ufdc.ufl.edu/UF00091523/00030.

13 Juliana Azoubel, "Côte d'Ivoire Mask Tradition."

14 Juliana Azoubel, "Côte d'Ivoire Mask Tradition."

15 Juliana Azoubel, "Côte d'Ivoire Mask Tradition."

16 "History of Bon Odori," accessed January 6, 2012, webpage no longer available, http://www.angelfire.com/celeb2/obon/page/History.htm.

17 Arundhati Roy, *God of Small Things* (New York: Random House, 1997), 230.

18 John D. Smith, "Preface," *The Epic of Pabuji* (New Delhi: Katha Publishing House, 2005).

19 Robin Sylvan, *Traces of the Spirit: The Religious Dimensions of Popular Music* (New York: New York University Press, 2002), 44.

20 David McAllester, "Some Thoughts on 'Universals' in World Music," *Ethnomusicology* 15/3 (1971), 380.

Sacred Space and Sacred Time

INTRODUCTION

Chapter 12 explores the ways in which music marks the boundary between the sacred and the secular. The term "sacred" derives from the Latin "*sacrare*," meaning to consecrate or to set apart, in contrast to "secular," meaning "worldly, of the world." Special times and places are set aside from the rest of life and are dedicated to sacred moods that may be cultivated, and to sacred actions that may be performed. Many believe that in these places and times set aside, the invisible forces, deities, ancestors, or angelic influences that are central to religious experience are present. Music often provides a sonic bridge between the secular and the sacred, and to those invisible realms that many religions acknowledge and affirm.

Religious practices take place in *sacred spaces*: churches, synagogues, temples, shrines, and pilgrimage sites, which often have special music associated with them. Some religions recognize and celebrate a single, most holy site—the Ka'aba in Mecca (Islam), St. Peter's Basilica in Rome (Roman Catholicism), Bodh Gaya in North India (Buddhism)—and in these singular locations, sacred sounds, chants, and music can reach their highest level of expression. Holy days are *sacred times* that are distinguished from ordinary days by their own distinctive music. Music not only symbolizes the sacred events; it structures them and shapes people's experience of them in a number of ways. Music can also serve as a channel by which prayers are transmitted upward and blessings flow downward. Where there is the belief that sacred places and sacred times are openings between the human world of mundane reality and the divine realms that religions often acknowledge and celebrate, music may connect the two.

SACRED SPACE

Throughout the world, musical sound is used to mark off sacred places; it contributes to creating an environment conducive to worship and it enriches religiously inspired states of mind. Special buildings are designed for ritual purposes and are immediately recognizable as such: churches with steeples, mosques with minarets, etc. For the ancient Celts, Greeks, and Hindus, natural groves, streams, and caves were associated with deities and considered sacred. On a grander scale, the Greeks believed Mt. Olympus to be the abode of the gods and the place where earth and heaven meet—the *axis mundi*. Tibetan Buddhists spend months in walking meditation around Mt. Kailasa and Qinghai Lake, continuously chanting "*Aum, Mani Padme Hum*" ("God is the jewel in the center of the heart-lotus," the mantra of the Buddha of Compassion, Avalokiteshvara). The pilgrims thereby receive the merit that these places and practices bestow. Some sacred places are associated with historical events and serve as pilgrimage destinations: Mecca, Jerusalem, and Sarnath, the site of the Buddha's first sermon that lies near the Ganges River at Banaras (Varanasi), North India.

Ganga Puja (India)

The Ganges is one of the most sacred rivers in the world for millions of Hindus. For millennia, Hindus have made pilgrimages to the banks of this river, to bathe in its waters. Indeed, the river itself is understood to be a divinity—*Ganga Ma* (Mother Ganges). It is believed that the waters flow to Earth from a hole in the heavens, down onto the head of Lord Shiva who meditates in a cave in the Himalayas. From there it streams from his hair and beard onto the Gangetic plain and across India to the Bay of Bengal. The sacred city of Banaras, the "City of 1,000 Temples," lies on its banks. There is a Hindu saying, "To die in Banaras is to live forever." Cremation grounds line the banks of the river, and ashes of the dead are sprinkled on the water's surface. Devotees sing hymns to the river goddess and praise her power of purification. They drink and bathe in its waters to prepare for a favorable rebirth after death.

Today, however, the river itself is seriously polluted by industrial and agricultural run-off. A ritual of purification, *Ganga puja* (12.1), is performed nightly at sundown on the steps (*ghats*) that lead down to the water. This video from 2011 depicts seven priests offering Vedic chants to the sacred river. Each priest involved in the ritual (*puja*) holds a lighted oil lamp (*aarti*) and circles it to the rhythm of *bhajans* sung by the worshippers, while the sonic environment is saturated with the ringing of bells. As one attendee stated to author Jonathan Kramer in 2011, "Our Mother Ganga saved us from harm over many generations; now it is our turn to save her."

Golden Rock of Kyaiktiyo (Myanmar)

One of the most sacred sites in Myanmar is the Golden Rock in Kyaiktiyo (Map 12.1). According to one legend, before the Buddha died, he gave a hair from his head to a hermit who tied the hair into his own topknot and wandered for years seeking an appropriate place to enshrine it. When the hermit saw the rock perched on the edge of a cliff in Kyaiktiyo where it rests today, he realized that it had the same shape as his own head. There he built a pagoda to contain the hair. The enormous rock rests on less than 1% of its surface and seems to be on the verge of rolling off the cliff at any moment into the valley 3,000 feet below. During the seven-mile climb that takes pilgrims and monks to the summit, the sounds of devotion drift down and draw travelers to the center of the sacred space. The entire hilltop is paved with white marble, and positioned around the grounds are white and gold pavilions, shrines, and statues of the Buddha. Worshippers announce their presence before these

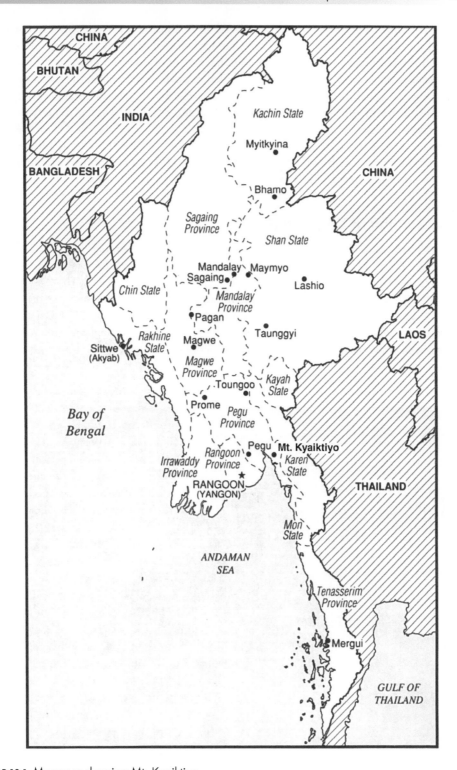

MAP 12.1 Myanmar showing Mt. Kyaiktiyo

Source: Garland Encyclopedia of World Music, Vol. 4, Southeast Asia

images by striking large gongs three times, placed for that purpose in front of the statues. The sound of the gongs (12.2), audible in the video, are believed to purify the air and declare to the world the teachings (*dharma*) of the Buddha. Parties of visiting monks recite Buddhist scriptures in a prayer hall (*gompa*) that are broadcast over loudspeakers. The combination of chanting and gongs, resounding at random intervals, fill the area with an awe-inspiring cacophony that tells the steady stream of approaching pilgrims that the mountain top is sacred. The worshipers, both men and women, light incense, bow, pray, and meditate. Men are allowed to walk down to the rock itself and rub gold leaf directly onto its surface, with the expectation that a wish will be granted (Figure 12.1). Vending booths surrounding the rock have small sheets of gold leaf for sale.

Grand Buddha at Lingshan (China)

A very different kind of sound awaits the visitor to the Great Standing Buddha of Wuxi in China, three hours by train from Shanghai. (See Map 8.4.) The cast bronze statue was constructed from 1994 to 1997. It is 100 feet taller than the Statue of Liberty. The Great Standing Buddha is the centerpiece of a government-supported Buddhist theme park on the site of a 1,000-year-old monastery. Ransacked during the Cultural Revolution (1966–1976), the monastery was rebuilt during a period of relative tolerance for traditional religious practices that had been suppressed under Chairman Mao Zedong.

FIGURE 12.1 The Golden Rock in Kyaiktiyo, Myanmar (L), and monks rubbing gold leaf onto the Golden Rock (R)

As visitors enter the gates of the park, they confront a huge bronze lotus bud atop a column in the middle of a fountain. Banks of loudspeakers stand at the four corners. Several times a day, a computerized mechanism within the column causes the bud to open slowly, accompanied by music coordinated with a "dancing water" display in the fountain. The music begins with deep, mystical chanting of monks digitally mixed with the unearthly sound of Tuvan throat singing. As the lotus bud opens, the chanting gives way to an East-West hybrid orchestral score fit for a Hollywood movie. Within the bud the infant Buddha appears, as harps, trumpets, and kettledrums announce the birth of the child who will become "The Enlightened One." When the music and the mechanized reenactment of the birth reach their climax, water shoots from the mouths of bronze dragons to wash and anoint the figure, which turns slowly to the four directions with a hand gesture of benediction (Figure 12.2). The whole Lingshan Buddha show (12.3) takes almost twenty minutes. The emotional contours of the musical performance, which combines both Asian and Western instruments and elements, engage and guide the viewers through the miracle portrayed in the spectacle. As the bud closes and the music subsides, the water that doused the statue streams out from decorative spigots allowing people to wash, drink, and thereby receive blessings.

These examples demonstrate the power of musical sound to permeate sacred space, thus creating a sonic environment in which people carry out sacred activities—lighting incense, saying prayers, and performing acts of devotion.

FIGURE 12.2 The Great Standing Lingshan Buddha at Wuxi, Jiangsu Province, People's Republic of China (L), and water washing and anointing the infant Buddha statue in the bronze lotus bud fountain at Wuxi (R)

SACRED TIME

In many religious traditions, music demarcates the division between sacred and secular time. In Judaism, the High Holy Days of Rosh Hashanah (Jewish New Year) and Yom Kippur (Day of Atonement) begin with the blowing of the *shofar* (12.4) (ram's horn) (Figure 12.3L). Five times a day in Islamic countries the Call to Prayer (**adhan**) is heard across towns and cities as the *muezzin* announces from the mosque the singular divinity of Allah and bids the faithful to prayer (Figure 12.3R). The *adhan* validates for the faithful the belief that life in this world is continuously interpenetrated by the divine. Sacred seasons are marked around the world by music unheard at other times of the year. In Chinese villages, amateur and semi-professional guild musicians practice all year long for performances at the February **Lunar New Year** celebrations. After Thanksgiving in North America, the radio waves, shopping malls, and churches are filled with songs of the Christmas season. During the four days leading up to Ash Wednesday and the beginning of Lent, Christians in Latin America and elsewhere celebrate Carnival with festivities and dancing that will not be enjoyed during the next forty days of the penitential season.

Often sacred times commemorate an occasion when the higher planes of spiritual reality and the secular plane of earth come into close contact. Solstices and equinoxes, planting and harvest times are also marked in many places by religious festivals. In ancient Ireland, the festival of *Samhain* (pronounced "SAH-win") celebrated the beginning of the Celtic year and the start of Winter. This festival of the dead, the roots of present-day Halloween, was "an 'eerie' time when … the division between the worlds of the living and the dead [was] thin."[1] Spirits easily crossed the thin veil between the spiritual and physical worlds, and the ancient Celts appeased them with food, drink, singing, and playing of musical instruments, to ensure their protection through the harsh winter.

The anniversary of the birth or death of a holy personage or saint is often designated a feast day and time for celebration that may include special music. The two most important holy days for Christians are Christmas and Easter, celebrating the birth and resurrection of Christ, respectively. Through song, Christians of the English-speaking world ask the question at Christmas, "What Child is this who laid to rest in Mary's arms is sleeping?" and make the statement at Easter, "Christ the Lord is risen today…Sing, ye heav'ns, and earth reply,

FIGURE 12.3 Rabbi blows the *shofar* (L), and the *muezzin* calls the *adhan* (R)

Alleluia!" At Sufi shrines in South Asia, devotees gather to celebrate the anniversary of their saint's death. Known as the *urs* ("wedding"), this is the day the saint was united (as in marriage) with the divine. At each shrine, the *urs* celebration is the most important time of the year for the singing of *qawwali*.

Islamic Call to Prayer

The Call to Prayer, *adhan*, is a recognizable sonic feature of Islam worldwide. It announces the time of prayer (*salat*), which is one of the Five Pillars of Islam, along with the profession of faith (*shahada*), giving alms (*zakat*), fasting during Ramadan (*sawm*), and pilgrimage (*hajj*). The continuous tradition of *adhan* dates from the life of the Prophet Mohammed (570–632 CE). Inspired by a dream, he began the practice of having a caller (**muezzin**) announce the time of daily prayer with the simple statement of belief at the core of the religion: "God is great, there is one God only, and Mohammed is His prophet." The first *muezzin*, according to legend, was an African slave named Bilal, chosen by the Prophet because of the beauty and power of his voice and the depth of his faith. Traditionally the *muezzin* stood on a platform at the top of one of the minarets (slender towers) that form an essential architectural feature of a mosque. From there, the *muezzin* called the faithful to prayer at the five prescribed daily prayer times: at dawn, just after noon, in the afternoon, just after sunset, and around nightfall. Throughout the Islamic world, the *muezzin* recites the *adhan* in Arabic from the mosque, and his voice is amplified over loudspeakers (Figure 12.4). A second call (*iqama*), faster, briefer, much less elaborate, is recited in the mosque proper immediately before the communal prayer takes place.

There is a clearly defined manner in which the Call to Prayer is delivered. The *adhan* is never accompanied by instruments. Rhythmic aspects are de-emphasized and the recitation of the text follows the natural flow of classical Arabic speech. The pauses between lines are extended to eliminate all sense of a regular pulse and to contemplate the meaning of the words. In this way, the *adhan* is not experienced bodily but spiritually. While local variations exist, a common melodic form is recognized throughout the Muslim world. In this video, the *muezzin* in a mosque in Kampala, Uganda recites the *adhan* (12.5) into the microphone of a public address system, otherwise stored in a cabinet behind the *minbar* (raised seat of the *imam*).

FIGURE 12.4 Mosque in western China showing two of its minarets (L), and detail of loudspeaker on the minaret to the right (R)

His voice is broadcast across the neighborhood through the loudspeaker mounted on one of the minarets, visible in Figure 12.4. Men from the vicinity leave their work and gather inside the mosque for mid-afternoon prayers. Women gather in a separate section of the mosque, or perform their prayers in the home or elsewhere. In Kampala, the *muezzin* is an employee of the mosque and performs his duty five times every day, as his father did before him.

The Call to Prayer (*adhan*)

> *Allahu Akbar* Allah is most great [four times]
> *Ashhadu alla ilaha illallah* I testify that there is no god but Allah [twice]
> *Ashhadu anna Muhammadar rasulullah* I testify that Muhammad is the Prophet of Allah [twice]
> *Hayya 'alas-salah* Come to prayer [twice]
> *Hayya 'alal-falah* Come to salvation [twice]
> *Allahu Akbar* Allah is most great [twice]
> *La ilaha illallah* There is no god but Allah [once]

With few exceptions, the words of the *adhan* have remained unchanged since the 7th century.

> There was ... a temporary change to the words recited in the *adhan* following the emergence of the Covid-19 pandemic in 2020. In Kuwait, the words "come to prayer" were replaced with "pray in your homes" in the call, to deter people from praying communally at mosques.[2]

Orthodox Festival of St. Michael (Ethiopia)

In the Ethiopian Tewahedo Orthodox Church, Mass on the 12th day of each month is dedicated to the Archangel Saint Michael. Especially on the 12th day of June, special Masses are performed. At Lalibela, the site of eleven 12th-century churches hollowed from a rock escarpment and one of the most sacred places in Ethiopia, 8,000 white-robed worshipers congregate each year to celebrate St. Michael's feast day (12.6). Chanting of the Liturgy begins at 6:00 am in **Ge'ez**, a language that is now only used for ritual purposes. The treasures of the church—paintings, icons, and crosses—are then removed from the inner sanctum by priests and monks and paraded before the worshipers. A replica of the Ark of the Covenant that is housed in every Tewahedo Orthodox Church is brought out as well to much joyous ululation from the crowd. Viewing it provides the climax of the occasion. The celebration continues as priests sway ritualistically, with some holding in their hands one of the world's most ancient musical instruments, the *sistrum* (Video 12.6 at 1'50"). Pictures of the *sistrum* have been found on the walls of Egyptian pyramids dating back some 5,000 years (Figure 12.5). Festivals like these are called "calendrical" because they return each year when their time on the solar or lunar calendar rolls around.

Rites of Passage (Democratic Republic of the Congo, USA)

While **calendrical rituals** occur with the regularity of the seasons, **life-cycle rituals** occur at the transition points in people's lives. When an individual moves from one state of being to

FIGURE 12.5 Queen Nefertari playing a *sistrum*, Abu Simbel, Egypt

another—childhood to adulthood or being single to being married, for instance—rituals are performed to affirm and validate the transition. Rites of passage such as birthdays, adolescent initiations, graduations, weddings, and funerals all have appropriate music. Among the Mbuti pygmies of the Democratic Republic of the Congo, for example, adolescent girls celebrate puberty with the Elima ceremony in which older women teach songs that instruct them in the responsibilities and privileges of womanhood. (While the term *pygmy* is used, it is considered pejorative, and yet there is no other replacement term in common use.) Each girl learns a short phrase that, when sung together with the interlocking phrases of the other girls in her cohort, contributes to a dense polyphonic and harmonious texture. Their Elima song (12.7) is not complete unless each part is sung, and each part only has meaning when joined to the whole. Thus the act of singing both represents and activates the social bonds that assure the cohesion of the group.

In Judaism, when a boy reaches thirteen, he celebrates his coming of age with a special ritual: the bar mitzvah. Since the late 19th century, many Jewish communities also celebrate a girl's coming of age with the bat mitzvah ceremony. In synagogue services, one of the two officiating leaders is the *hazzan* or cantor, a specially trained ritual singer who leads the congregation in prayer services that contain a number of sung portions. Among the cantor's most important duties is the training of a bar mitzvah or bat mitzvah candidate in the recitation of selected passages from the Torah (the five Books of Moses) and the Haftarah (the Books of the Prophets). During the bar mitzvah (12.8) ceremony, the young boy reads Hebrew verses using the traditional chant melodies learned from the cantor over many months of preparation. After the ceremony, he is considered a full member of his community and will be held accountable for his actions.

Funerals (China, Laos)

Anthropologists refer to "in-between" states as "liminal," from the Latin word *"limen"* meaning "threshold." Individuals, societies, and even deities can be in liminal states, and special music is often involved in rituals of liminality. In the Nadun festival, for example, the time between the end of the dances and dramas but before the possession of the medium is **liminal**. This is a period of great intensity and anxiety, as the community waits to see if it will be favored by the visitation of the deity. At no other time are the gongs beaten with such force. In sacred contexts, these times create openings during which the divine or the eternal intersects with the mundane, human world. Perhaps funerals are the ultimate rite of passage, and the time between death and burial is often seen as a highly significant liminal period for a community.

In Shaanxi province, China, near the border of Inner Mongolia, the funeral rituals (12.9) for an eighty-nine-year-old farmer were a noisy, two-day affair. The occasion was mostly a joyous one, since the old man had lived a good life, long and prosperous. His wife had died two years earlier, and the local Daoist priest (**yinyang**) had selected an auspicious gravesite in the high fields that they would ultimately share. The two days between the farmer's death and his burial next to his wife was a liminal time, filled with music, chanting, and noise from gongs and firecrackers. There were formal rituals, prayers, and processions; but also, food and conversation among family and friends brought together by the event. While his body had already been carried to the gravesite before the ritual commenced, his soul had been captured by the priest and placed in a portable cardboard shrine. The soul would be released with the burning of the shrine and other paper offerings at the gravesite on the second day of the ritual. The music was celebratory and went on all afternoon of the first day. The family and all the villagers then gathered for a midnight procession led by the musicians blowing shawms (*suona*), clanging cymbals, and beating drums. The darkness was punctuated by strings of firecrackers and illuminated by a thousand candles placed along the roadway. Bonfires and lanterns burned high up in the hills above the roadway, tended by the neighboring farmers who had known the man their whole lives. At dawn, a smaller procession set off into the mountains to the burial plot. Two brothers played *suona*, as they did for all such events in the area when they weren't farming themselves, and showed extraordinary stamina throughout the ritual. Using a technique known as circular breathing, they were able to maintain a continuous stream of music, even on the long hike to the gravesite. The priest chanted, and the *suona* brothers played on in celebration of life's continuity and cyclical processes.

Funerals are essential among the Laotian Hmong to prevent the deceased's soul from roaming for eternity and to ensure a beneficial reincarnation on earth. Shamans work with ceremonial musicians who play the mouth organ (*qeej*, pronounced *"gaeng"*) (Figure 12.6). Their function is "to guide a dead person's soul back through the twelve heavens with his hauntingly resonant cluster of six steamed bamboo tubes." The shaman's rituals last three days and nights, and music is played on the *qeej* as food is offered three times a day to the deceased body, lest the soul be hungry in the afterlife. The *qeej* player accompanies sacred songs sung both during the rituals and in the funeral procession to the burial site, to help the soul journey to the spirit world. At the burial, family members and friends burn incense and symbolic paper money. The smoke follows the soul into the heavenly realms.

Following the 1975 takeover of Laos by the Communist Pathet Lao, over 200,000 Hmong fled the country. Many came to the United States as refugees and were settled in Minnesota,

FIGURE 12.6 Hmong young men playing *qeej* at a traditional funeral

California, and elsewhere. Hmong families continue to hold traditional funerals and other life-cycle rituals, with several convenient adaptations to their new home. Within the Hmong refugee community in Merced, California, "where bamboo is hard to come by, *qeejs* are sometimes made of PVC plumbing pipe. It is said that if the *qeej* player is good, the soul will have no trouble following directions from the plastic."[3]

Saramaccan Ritual (Suriname)

A final example of a liminal ritual takes place in a Saramaccan Maroon community deep in the Amazonian rainforest in Suriname. Maroons are the descendants of escaped African slaves.

A three-day ceremony will determine the fate of two widows who were married to the same man. He had died exactly one year before, and his widows had been living in forced seclusion, a liminal state, ever since. Because they were originally from a different village, the elders had to determine whether they could remain in the home of their husband, or must return to their birth village now that their status had changed. For three days, the Saramaccan Maroon ceremony (12.10) was an utter disruption of the ordinary routines of life. The two widows were led out each morning to the ritual space at the center of the village, draped in veils and attended by family members. There they sat motionless, awaiting their fate as relatives and neighbors danced around them. Various deities inhabited a pair of shamans, dressed in blue, who both presided over the activities and contributed to the mayhem. Guns

FIGURE 12.7 Young Maroon masked dancers, Amazonian rainforest, Suriname

were discharged, children wearing masks danced in a frenzy (Figure 12.7). At one point, one of the family members charged through the village with a chainsaw. At another point young men went into each home, led by the shamans, and threw everything out into the central clearing. Finally, before the elders met, two large river turtles were slaughtered with machetes as blood sacrifices. It was determined the next day that the widows would return to their native village. Order was restored. During the entire three-day ritual, the drummers almost never stopped playing.

Structuring Sacred Time (Zimbabwe, USA)

As mentioned in the opening of this chapter, not only does music symbolize and frame sacred times, it also shapes sacred events and people's experience of them in several ways. In the *Bira* ceremony of Zimbabwe, music structures the sequence of ritual events. The *mbira* musicians begin playing as an unobtrusive background to the socializing that precedes the event. Gradually, the music grows in volume and intensity as the participants become more focused on dancing, singing, and engaging in the ritual activities that will culminate in the possession of the medium (*svikiro*). The music reaches its greatest intensity at the moment of the medium's possession by the ancestral spirit. At this point in the ritual the music stops and the medium prophesizes and advises the community. Following this climactic event, the musicians resume their playing. Then gradually their music fades away into the background as the ritual draws to a close. The intensity of the ritual action is thus controlled by the waxing and waning of the music.

Many Christian worship services begin with a prelude and end with a recessional or postlude; thus, music provides a sonic frame that separates the events of the service from the rest of the day's activities. Music not only frames Sunday services but organizes the flow of events within the frame. During the service, along with readings and preaching, worship time is punctuated by a variety of musical practices: congregational hymn-singing, anthems from the choir, a solo on organ or piano while the collection plate is passed. In the worship services of many African American Protestant denominations, music is nearly continuous. It underscores and inspires emotional intensity as demonstrated by a 1978 sermon (12.11) by Pastor Audrey F. Bronson at the Sanctuary Church of the Open Door in Philadelphia. In this sermon, the pastor describes God's plan for Jesus, part talking, part singing, part shouting. With greater and greater volume and intensity, she builds to a climax of energy as each Old Testament Prophet fails to meet the challenge of redeeming mankind. Only Jesus, the Bright and Morning Star, is worthy of taking on this mission. Pastor Bronson is accompanied throughout by Hammond electric organ, which punctuates each sentence with a chordal exclamation point. The profound experience of hearing Pastor Bronson preach sends a number of the congregants into trance.

Closer to home, a typical wedding ceremony in North Carolina often begins with a hired string quartet playing unobtrusively off to the side of the sanctuary. Relatives and guests enter the church, greet each other, get caught up on news and gossip, and settle into the pews. A signal to the musicians from the back of the church by a designated guest or professional wedding planner directs a change in the music. A **processional piece** chosen by the couple, like Pachelbel's *Canon* or Bach's *"Jesu, Joy of Man's Desiring,"* accompanies the seating of special family members: grandparents and parents. A second processional piece brings the wedding party—bridesmaids, groomsmen, flower girls, and ring bearers—down the aisle to the altar. Again a signal, and the famous Wedding March begins. At this musical cue, all the guests rise and face the back of the sanctuary to watch the veiled bride march to the front of the church in step with the familiar tune. The officiating clergy speaks the appropriate texts, "Dearly Beloved, We are gathered here today, etc." Toward the middle of the ceremony, the string quartet plays a meditative piece or a ballad chosen by the couple as they light a "Unity Candle"; or a friend comes down to the altar area and sings a popular love song, accompanying herself on the guitar. Finally, when the pastor pronounces the couple "Man and Wife" and they kiss, the string quartet strikes up the **recessional** march and the happy couple heads for the rear doorway. After they leave, the quartet plays celebratory music as the guests move toward the exit. At this point, no one is really listening; each is engaged in a private conversation about how beautiful the bride looked, or about directions to the reception. The quartet's playing again becomes unobtrusive, but its sonic presence closes the frame. A wedding band or DJ at the reception takes the couple back to the secular world of eating, drinking, and dancing, their status now changed in the eyes of the church and community.

SACRED JOURNEYS AND PROCESSIONS

As music serves to set apart sacred spaces, so too does it mark the sacred paths and journeys of religious worshipers. Processions and pilgrimages from one sacred place to another are often accompanied by special music, and on such occasions the music sanctifies the roads and highways of the ordinary, secular world and makes the way suitable for sacred purposes. Group devotional singing transforms a journey into a pilgrimage, and distinguishes the time of pilgrimage from that of ordinary travel.

Christian Processions (Cape Verde)

On Palm Sunday throughout the Christian world, congregations sing hymns and play instruments as they process behind the Cross, re-enacting Jesus' joyous entry into Jerusalem at the beginning of Holy Week. Two Roman Catholic processions (12.12) from the Cape Verde Islands, a former Portuguese colony off the northwest coast of Africa, typify the way, in pilgrimage, people come together as a community. In the first, townspeople process to Our Lady of the Rosary Church for a Roman Catholic Mass celebrating the installation of a new statue of Saint Sebastian. The statue had arrived from Portugal following the destruction of the old one by vandals. The ringing of the church bell accompanies the procession and announces the arrival of the statue at the church. Video 12.12 also documents a procession on Palm Sunday accompanied by the singing of hymns.

Daoist Processions (China)

Video 12.13 also shows two processions. The ceremonial and devotional aspects of Daoism are depicted in the first procession from Hong Kong. Priests, processing from one altar to another, celebrate the *Luo Tian Da Jiao* ceremony dedicated to world peace. In the second, Daoist priests and officials consecrate and celebrate a new temple in Xian. The ceremonial procession includes Chinese instruments such as *erhu, ruan, dizi, sheng, pipa*, and *suona*. Daoism in its original form was based on simplicity and life lived in harmony with the natural processes of existence: the Way (*Dao*). For its founder, Lao Tse (6th century BCE), this ideology, based on the "Three Treasures" of compassion, frugality, and humility, was a reaction against the complex and formal rituals of Confucianism. But as seen in these two Daoist processions (12.13), Daoism itself has become highly ritualized.

Hindu Processions (India)

In Agra, North India, a Hindu wedding procession (12.14) parades through a neighborhood (see Map 8.3). A brass band in full uniform accompanies the groom astride his horse. However, in front of the band is a float on which a portable generator powers a speaker system, and a DJ plays recordings of Bollywood film music at a deafening volume. The brass band

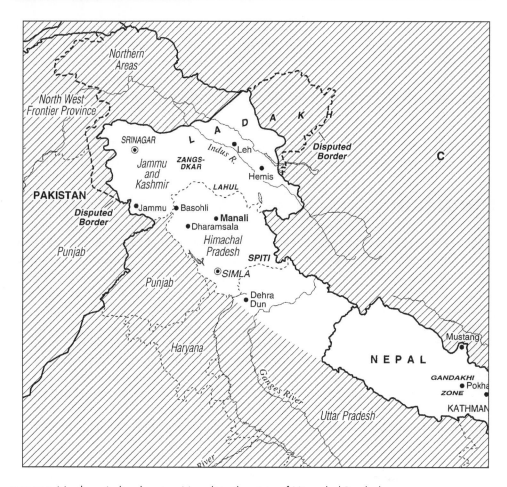

MAP 12.2 Northern India showing Manali in the state of Himachal Pradesh

Source: Garland Encyclopedia of World Music, Vol. 5, South Asia: The Indian Subcontinent

musicians try to play along, but with their traditional role usurped by the new technology, their playing is half-hearted and futile. They seem only to be participating for their flashy instruments and crisp uniforms.

The patrons of the wedding reach an uncomfortable compromise. They have hired a traditional brass band, whose presence in Hindu wedding processions dates back to the time of the British. Yet the prestige of having a DJ, a sound system, and pop music overwhelms the band's contribution. Amidst the din, the bridal "chariot" brings up the rear.

In Manali, a town in the Himalaya Mountains in Himachal Pradesh, North India (Map 12.2), the image (*murti*) of sage Vashistha, one of the mythical authors of the Vedas, resides in a small temple. The sage is worshiped by the townspeople and villagers scattered along the mountain passes. When a wedding is held in a remote village, the *murti* is carried out of the temple to the wedding site so the sage can lend his sacred energy (*shakti*) to the party. But removing the *murti* from the sanctuary of the temple risks compromising its purity as it travels out into the marketplace and along the profane roadway. When the *murti* is neither in the temple nor at the wedding but is in transition between the two locations, it is at its most vulnerable.

So, the environment is purified with prayers and offerings made by a presiding priest, while horns and drums create a sonic envelope through which the deity will travel outside the temple walls and into the town and beyond. Video 12.15 shows the initial purification rites (***puja***) that lasted three days. These included the prayers of the priest, the entry of the *murti* into the temple courtyard, the blessing of flowers and food (*prasad*) on a stone altar, and the sharing of the ritually blessed food among the participants. The video ends with the Hindu procession (12.15) moving from the temple courtyard out into the street, where a participant fell into trance, and on to the wedding village. Because this is a region popular with tourists, many cell phones and digital cameras created a stark juxtaposition with the ancient forms of the ritual.

CONCLUSION

Music and musicians form an essential and integral component of sacred rituals throughout the world. In each of the examples in Chapter 12, music serves as a **demarcator**, creating and sustaining a border between ritual time and space, and ordinary everyday experience. Music is a symbol of the sacred occasions, places, actions, and powers with which religious beliefs and practices are associated. As pilgrims approach the Golden Rock of Kyaiktiyo after a seven-mile climb, the sounds of ritual activity become louder and louder until they envelop the new arrivals at the sacred space. Music also symbolizes sacred time: the *shofar* signifies High Holy Days, organ music signifies Sunday worship, the bridal march signifies matrimony, and the call of the *muezzin* signifies the practice of daily prayer. Music separates sacred events from ordinary times, as in the Feast of St. Michael in Ethiopia. On this special day, people gather to witness the Arc of the Covenant and other relics being carried out of the church. The sounds of ululation, chanting of scriptures, and the playing of sistrums and drums by the priests accompany the ritual procession. Finally, music coordinates ritual activities such as at the wedding in North Carolina and the *Bira* in Zimbabwe. While music may be the central focus or the unobtrusive background in ritual contexts, its presence frames and structures the events. Indeed, many sacred rituals "could not be performed as well, or at all, without music," as stated in Chapter 6. The final chapter of the textbook deals with music associated with secular events and profane times, from Saturday nights "on the town" to presidential inaugurations and Olympic ceremonies.

KEY TERMS AND CONCEPTS

Adhan

Calendrical Rituals

Demarcator of the Sacred

Funeral Ritual

Life-Cycle Rituals

Liminal/Liminality

Muezzin

Pilgrimage

Processional/Recessional Music

Puja

Rites of Passage

Sacred Journeys and Processions

Sacred Space and Time

Sacred/Profane

Sonic Envelope

Wedding Procession

THINKING ABOUT MUSIC

1   Think of two calendrical rituals and two life-cycle rituals and describe the music associated with each. How does music serve to differentiate these times from ordinary profane times?

2   Why do you think the Chinese Communist government, for whom religion is officially anathema, would construct a Buddha of such commanding size as the Lingshan Buddha?

3   Listen again to the sermon of Pastor Audrey Bronson of Philadelphia (Audio 12.11). Consider the role of music in her manner of delivery. How does music structure the emotional trajectory of her sermon? Compare this with the description of the music at the *Bira* ritual of Zimbabwe.

4   Explain in your own words the concept of "liminality." Consider the Surinamese Maroon ritual described in this chapter. If liminal time occurs between the end of one state of being and the beginning of another, how does this concept of liminality relate to the Surinamese Maroon ritual?

5   Think of two examples of sacred musical performance and consider how one relates to sacred space and how the other relates to sacred time. How does the music mark "the sacred" and separate it from ordinary secular space and time? How does music shape and enhance the sacred event or experience?

6   Pretend you are a tourist who has happened upon the procession in Manali, northern India. What roles might music be playing in this ritual, and how would you explain them in a letter to a music teacher, family member, or friend back home?

7   Why do you think the wedding in Agra has a DJ blasting Bollywood music and a military-style brass band, the two competing with each other?

NOTES

1   Nigel Pennick, *The Sacred World of the Celts* (Rochester, VT: Inner Traditions International, 1997), 105.

2   Indlieb Farazi Saber, "The Art of the Adhan: the Multiple Melodies of the Islamic Call to Prayer." *Middle East Eye*, May 5, 2021, https://www.middleeasteye.net/discover/adhan-muslim-call-prayer-melodies-maqams.

3   Anne Fadiman, *The Spirit Catches You and You Fall Down: A Hmong Child, Her American Doctors, and the Collision of Two Cultures* (New York: Farrar, Straus and Giroux, 1997), 227–228.

PART V

Music and Social Life

INTRODUCTION

If music plays important roles in the formation and projection of human identity and in the expression of the core beliefs and values of religions, music is equally important in enhancing social life. Part V focuses on music's relationships to those occasions in which people tell stories, communicate through mass media, and gather socially. Alan Merriam makes the point that because music is incorporated as an integral component of so many social situations, its importance in human life cannot be overestimated. As cited in the introduction to Chapter 6, Merriam writes, "There is probably no other human cultural activity which is so all pervasive, and which reaches into, shapes, and often controls so much of human behavior."

Music in some social situations is the primary element and object of people's attention and the reason why they gather. People attend public concert halls and music theaters, and even fill vast sports stadiums to hear music played out to the crowds over loudspeakers, as at the *Salala* concert in Madagascar (Chapter 6). In South Korea, young people go on dates to the **norebang** ("sound room"). In these store-front enterprises, often located in the basement of shopping centers, couples rent rooms by the hour and spend the evening singing songs to each other. Their voices, processed with reverb through a karaoke machine, sound like pop stars. Nightclubs and dance halls from Buenos Aires to Bangkok provide evening entertainment for locals and tourists alike, and offer employment to musicians and DJs. In some countries, public social life is more restrained. In Iran, the Islamic government tightly controls live public music performance, particularly by women. Traditional Persian classical music has long thrived in the context of private concerts in people's homes. These restrictions in Iran also pertain to Western-style pop music; rock musicians perform "underground" in urban basements and parking garages, and seek audiences on the internet. In each of these cases, music is the primary element that brings people together, even if the gathering is virtual.

Music in other social situations is not the central feature or catalyst for social gathering, yet is an essential component of the sonic environment and in many cases is indispensable. Sporting events often involve group singing of patriotic songs, though fans attend them to watch the games. Popular musicians often perform at political rallies where the speeches of the politicians are the main event. Shopping malls pipe in recorded music to keep shoppers pleasantly engaged in browsing and buying. At outdoor public celebrations like Carnival in Brazil and the Caribbean, Lunar New Year in China, and the Fourth of July in the United States, live musicians play special music that creates and sustains the festive mood, propelling dancers and marchers in parades and street parties.

That is, until the time of COVID-19. Many of the traditions discussed in this textbook have been adversely affected by the global pandemic. It remains to be seen how live music and dancing will recover and what forms they will take in the future. From major symphony orchestras to club bands in local bars, all have been disrupted. For musicians, singers, producers, and audience members, this has been a challenging time.

Many forms of storytelling and theater employ music to enhance the impact of the dramatic situation. Narrative is the subject of Chapter 13, exploring the complex roles music plays in storytelling traditions including Theater and Opera. Chapter 14 discusses music associated with Nightlife, Sporting Events, Public Ceremonies, and Festivals. The subjects of Chapter 15 are Cultural Tourism, Sound Recording Technology, and Film.

CHAPTER 13

Narrative Singing, Theater, and Opera

INTRODUCTION

To participate in storytelling, either as narrator or audience, is to be in at least two worlds simultaneously: the here and now of bodily existence, and the parallel worlds created by the imagination. Anthropologist Clifford Geertz calls the human capacity for abstract thought, "the distinctive characteristic of our mentality."[1] It is because of this capacity that a story can lift us out of the bonds of the immediate into the imagined worlds of the long ago, the make-believe, the far away: the realms that stories create. Stories also reflect back on the reality of the here and now, portraying archetypes, moral teachings, justifications for social hierarchies, and narratives that explain symbolically why things are the way they are. Just as music can create boundaries between secular and sacred space and time, so music provides a vehicle for conveying the spiritual, psychological, and emotional dimensions of a story. This chapter examines ways in which stories are told through music in partnership with other art forms: poetry, dance, theater, and spectacle.

NARRATIVE SINGING

Throughout much of human history, the core beliefs of a society have been transmitted orally within and across generations through stories that were sung. These stories often included creation myths, explanatory fables, and tales of the origins of dynasties and their founding heroes. Because remembering and passing on these narratives accurately and compellingly was so important to maintaining the fabric of a society, specially trained and adept story-tellers served as a people's collective memory. Particularly before the spread of literacy, epic narrators held important positions, often closely associated with powerful ruling families whose authority these tellers of tales helped to legitimize. In pre-Christian Celtic societies, hereditary poets known as "bards" kept and transmitted the oral histories and genealogies of ruling families in poetic verse. The term "**bard**" later acquired a broader, generic meaning comparable to the medieval European **minstrel**, the West African *griot*, the Turkish *asik*, and the Ethiopian *azmari*.

In Video 13.1, Azmari Gezate performs at a traditional coffeehouse in Lalibela, Ethiopia. Accompanying himself on the one-string *masenko*, he sings and improvises satirical verses about the guests, half complimentary, half insulting. Often his wordplay makes the meaning ambiguous and the guest isn't sure whether to be flattered or insulted. In the video, the Ethiopian *azmari* (13.1) first sings a religious song praising Jesus and the Virgin Mary. A sample verse is,

> I couldn't find Holy Mary, when I go to her place
> Her son will call me and I will find her tomorrow
> My mother, Holy Mary, would you like to have *tej* (honey wine)?
> Tell your son you need honey…
> Oh come to me my dear friend
> Oh come to me my Savior
> I'm begging God.

The second song has word play and dark humor. A few lines are:

> Denbera (a woman's name), drag yourself to the backdoor like a chicken who has a broken leg
> Glad you have legs, come through the backdoor
> Denbera, drag yourself to the backdoor like a chicken who has a broken leg
> I would like to buy you shoes…
> [English translation by Emebet Hailu and Caleb Kebede]

Over centuries, collections of stories, legends, histories, and myths were passed on in oral tradition from one poet-singer to another. They later coalesced into great epic narratives that became central to their societies, and many were eventually written down: the *Mahabharata* and *Ramayana* of India, the Malian *Epic of Sunjata*, the Tibetan *Epic of King Gesar*, the Japanese *Tale of the Heike*, the *Kalevala* of Finland, and the ancient Greek epics the *Iliad* and *Odyssey* attributed to Homer. In some cases, the epic was first written as a literary text and subsequently moved into oral tradition. A famous example is the 10th-century CE *Shahnameh* ("Book of Kings") of Firdausi, which recounts the entire history of Persia up to the Islamic conquest in the 7th century CE. It is the national epic of Iran (Figure 13.1).

Epic narration relied upon the vivid imagination of the audience. The singers of tales were skillful at holding the attention of the listeners through many hours of musically weaving their stories. Contexts in which bards transmitted these epic poems have ranged widely from royal courts to teahouses, and from village squares to performance stages. Most singers of tales were illiterate, as were their audience members. Therefore, oral virtuosity was a very important social skill, as was the vivid imaginations of their listeners. The rapid social and technological changes of the 20th and 21st centuries, as well as the rise of literacy, have hastened the decline of many of these traditions. Indeed, some have completely disappeared. The art of oral epic performance offers little competition in today's high-tech world of cinema, YouTube, and videogames, which leave much less to the imagination of their audience.

FIGURE 13.1 Illustration from a 17th-century manuscript of the Persian *Shahnameh*

There are nevertheless communities and cultures in which the singing of oral epics still survives. This chapter begins with the highly influential research of Albert B. Lord and his mentor and teacher Milman Parry on Balkan epics, and then explores other traditions of sung narrative.

Balkan Bards (Bosnia and Herzegovina)

In 1960, Harvard University professor of Slavic Languages, Albert B. Lord (1912–1991), published a study of oral epic poetry based on his own research in Yugoslavia (now divided into seven independent countries) and on that of his teacher, Milman Parry (1902–1935).[2] In his study, *The Singer of Tales*, Lord developed a comprehensive theory of epic recitation that has greatly influenced the way bardic traditions have been studied since then. His theory also applies to the study of ancient oral traditions from which came such milestones of world literature as the *Iliad* and *Odyssey*. Lord describes a process of **oral transmission** that is flexible and creative; the opposite of Vedic transmission. In the case of Vedic recitation, the transmission across generations was strictly controlled so that in ritual performance neither a single syllable nor the manner of its expression would change. Sacred words and actions were repeated with fidelity to a pre-existing template, replicated precisely each time the ritual was performed. By contrast, what Lord and Parry discovered with the Balkan bards was that the gist of a story might remain fairly stable over time, but the telling was never the same twice. Social occasions for storytelling tended to be informal and of varying time intervals, and stories were skillfully tailored to fit the situation. Balkan storytellers were often raised in storyteller families and they grew up hearing the stories over and over, each time embellished or altered. From these multiple retellings, each storyteller developed an individual style based partly on rote learning and partly on imaginative improvisation. From the inherited storehouse of learned and remembered tales, melodies, and rhymes, storytellers would add, delete, and alter as much as their creativity and audiences allowed. Then in turn, the altered versions were passed on to the next generation and became the tradition. In cultures in which literacy was rare or non-existent, sung stories, performed in a manner part memorized and part improvised, constituted the ancient oral wisdom and collective memory of the people.

Albert B. Lord describes in detail a learning process by which the Balkan storytellers acquired their extraordinary skill, as exemplified by the following quote from one of his research subjects:

> When I was a shepherd boy, they used to come for an evening to my house, or sometimes we would go to someone else's for the evening, somewhere in the village. Then a singer would pick up the *gusle* [one-string fiddle], and I would listen to the song. The next day when I was with the flock, I would put the song together, word for word, without the *gusle*, but I would sing it from memory, word for word, just as the singer had sung it.... Then I learned gradually to finger the instrument, and to fit the fingering to the words, and my fingers obeyed better and better...I didn't sing among the men until I had perfected the song, but only among the young fellows in my circle [*družina*] not in front of my elders and betters.[3]

The young singer thus begins his training by listening to accomplished storytellers and repeating, as accurately as he can, what he hears. He then attempts to work out story narratives on his own or among his peers, fitting the lines of narration into the fairly rigid grid of meter, melody, and rhyme; and of course, learning how to accompany himself on the *gusle* as he recites. When he can recite an entire story, he tries out his skill before a critical adult audience. From then on, throughout his life, he will add to his stock of tales, and improve his manner of delivery and rapport with his audiences. Competition among rivals continuously raises the stakes. The most accomplished storytellers perform creative feats of imagination and artistry akin to Homer's.

Milman Parry recorded over 3,500 disks of South Slavic epic singing in the mid-1930s, including almost 500 disks from a single singer Avdo Međedović of eastern Montenegro (Figure 13.2). Parry was also able to record a short film of Avdo Međedović, reciting part of a 12,000-line narrative while accompanying himself on the *gusle*.[4]

Fig. 29 Avdo Medjedovitch, peasant
farmer, is the finest singer the expedition
encountered. His poems reached as many as
fifteen thousand lines. A veritable Yugoslav
Homer!

FIGURE 13.2 Avdo Međedović of Montenegro, accompanying himself on the *gusle*

Avdo Međedović (1875–1953) was raised in a Muslim family in the village of Obrov, east-ern Montenegro, then part of the Ottoman Empire (Map 13.1). He became a butcher, like his father and grandfather before him, and he never learned to read or write. From a young age, Avdo learned the art of singing through listening to his father and other skilled singers. While his singing voice and *gusle* playing were not virtuosic, he was remarkably creative in singing epic tales of the Ottoman Empire and its heroes. He embellished the tales with detailed descriptions, making his versions far longer than those of other epic singers of the time. When once invited by Milman Parry to listen to another epic singer performing a tale he did not know, Avdo sang the epic himself with three times as many verse lines. His own epic song repertoire was extensive, amounting to fifty-eight tales. Parry recorded over 78,000 lines of epic poetry from Avdo, and some fifty-three hours of singing. By all standards, Avdo's

MAP 13.1 The Balkan region in southeastern Europe showing the village of Obrov in Montenegro

Source: Garland Encyclopedia of World Music, Vol. 8, Europe

abilities as an oral epic singer and poet were indeed extraordinary. For people living in rural towns and isolated villages with few other forms of entertainment, listening to the bard sing stories of kings and battles was an event not to be missed. His performances captured the listeners' attention, fired their imagination, and vividly brought to life the characters and heroes of the past.

Yet, the extraordinary narrative and musical accomplishments of the Balkan epic narrators did not occur in a vacuum. The singers and their listeners were part of the same community and all members would have listened to storytellers from early childhood.

Furthermore, they would have grown up in communities in which the tradition of epic narration had been passed on from generation to generation. The telling of and listening to stories in social settings would have been deeply ingrained in community practices. Lord writes:

> The circumstances will be different to some extent in each traditional culture, but speaking for the one that I know best, that of the Slavic Balkans, I would find one of the most normal places for singing to be the house in a small village where neighbors gather for an evening and sit and talk and listen to a singer. Epics are sung also at weddings and to help celebrate the Slava, the family feast for its patron saint. Another informal setting is the coffeehouse in Moslem communities, where men gather, especially during Ramadan, and listen, after a day of fasting, to epic songs that may continue for a whole night. The singers and the listeners are all "insiders;" that is, they are part of the same tradition.[5]

Epic singing in the Balkans continues today largely in Serbia and in the mountainous regions along the Adriatic coast. Singers still accompany themselves on the *gusle*, and professional singers perform at folk music festivals and fairs, on public stages, and in competitions. Modern **guslari**, as the Balkan epic singers are known, sing occasionally from the traditional repertoire, and also perform songs based on more recent events, such as the Yugoslav and Kosovo Wars of the 1990s. Through the 20th century, this geographic region underwent enormous political and social upheavals, from the establishment of the Kingdom of Yugoslavia (1918–1941) to the formation of the Socialist Federal Republic of Yugoslavia (1943–1992), and to its eventual breakup into independent nations accompanied by much bloodshed. Through it all, the ten-syllable epic song remained an important medium for the transmission of culture as well as news and political views. "The **decasyllabic** epic song," writes language professor Ivo Žanić in 2007,

> is even today for a large part of the population not only a source of aesthetic pleasure but also an important, sometimes the main, medium through which information about current events is conveyed, on which they build their value system, form political judgments and model their general social conduct.[6]

Epic singing has remained relevant to Balkan society for several reasons. One is its value as a symbol of traditional culture for a population uprooted under socialism; between 1948 and 1981, 6.5 million people migrated from the countryside to the city and left their agrarian lifestyle to become industrial workers. A second reason is the involvement of epic singers in election campaigns. Political leaders have invited *guslari* to perform at political rallies where the singers both glorify past heroes and promote political messages. Politicians benefit from the singing of epic songs that support their ideology. They also benefit from the epic singers' reinforcement, for their audiences, of a traditional worldview and value system. This engagement of *guslaris* led to the formation of *gusle* associations, a third reason for the continued vibrancy of epic singing. These *gusle* organizations promote regular performances of epic songs at festivals, on the radio and television, and in competitions. Epic singers also play important roles in the private lives of Balkan families, performing for weddings, anniversaries, and the annual celebration of the *slava*.

Until the 1980s epic singers were largely male performers. This video shows Croatian epic singer and *guslar* Dane Jurić (13.2) performing on a public stage. Nowadays women, such as Croatian epic singer and *guslarica* Ruža Jolić (13.3), also perform professionally, reflecting social changes in the Balkans. As the oral epic performance tradition changes it takes on new meanings for its performers and audiences, yet continues to serve as a powerful symbol of cultural identity in this deeply conservative society.

Jalolu (West Africa, USA)

In several countries of West Africa including Mali, Senegal, Guinea, and The Gambia, singers called *jalolu* (in Manding languages) or griots (the term used by the French colonizers) serve as oral historians, genealogists, and praise singers. (See Map 2.4.) *Jalolu* (singular, *jali*) are members of a hereditary profession, born into families that have passed on their inherited knowledge for generations. They are identified within their societies by surnames such as Diabate, Kouyate, Jobarteh, Cissokho, and Suso. Aristocrats employed *jalolu* to chronicle the deeds and lineages of their families at least since the establishment of the great Malian Empire under the Mandinka king Sunjata Keita (reigned 1235–1255). "The Griots are walking libraries, with knowledge of the past, present and future of our people," writes Foday Musa Suso, a 20th-century griot from The Gambia, in his memoir *Jali Kunda*.

> When a Griot arrives in a village he is given great respect, because he is the keeper of tradition. He is welcomed, fed, and given a place to stay. It's very important to have a Griot visit your village. Everyone wants to know about their family history. The Griot sings about ancestors of the village, about kings and wars between the kings, and also about living friends and neighbors.[7]

The **praise songs** of the *jali*, sung on public occasions such as birthdays, anniversaries, and ceremonies of state, celebrated and legitimized the claims of their wealthy patrons to high social position. They also, writes Foday Musa Suso,

> gave … kings the courage to fight battles. Indeed, battles could be won or lost by the sheer power of the *jali's* word. Nowadays, they may sing for politicians or businessmen instead of kings, but they function in very similar ways. Their gift of speech has made them ideal 'go-betweens'; they patch up quarrels and feuds, arrange marriages, and negotiate the most delicate economic and political matters. In the words of Toumani Diabaté, one of Mali's most brilliant young *kora* players: 'They are the needle that sews'.[8]

Griots in some regions are also called upon to sing "songs of ritual necessary to summon spirits and gain the sympathy of the ancestors."[9] Their role as "go-betweens" extends to connections with spiritual powers.

> Even today, you see Griots travelling with their *koras*, moving between cities and towns…If you want to buy some cloth, go to the weaver. If you want a hoe, ax or knife, then go to the blacksmith. But if you want to know the history of the people, you must go to the Griots.[10]

The *jali* typically employs a "fluid set of descriptive phrases, praise names, proverbs, songs, and instrumental patterns, which all feed into a story line or collection of deeds, actions, events, attributes, and social mores. It can be expanded, embellished, or condensed."[11] Both the instrumental and vocal components of a performance contain fixed, repeating patterns and improvisational sections. This is similar to the creative, flexible process that Lord and Parry described in their studies of Balkan bards. Musical instruments associated with the West African *jali* tradition include the *kora* (21-string harp-lute), the *balo* (xylophone), and the *kontingo* (plucked, long-necked lute). *Jalolu* specialize in playing one of these instruments, their choice often dictated by region. In some places they accompany their own singing, while in others, singers and instrumentalists are separate. Women *jalolu* (griottes in French) are also often singers, and in some cases have become highly respected artists. A superior woman singer, according to *jali* Nyulo Jebateh,

> is not afraid of crowds, not afraid of anything, except God. She can stand before a crowd with all eyes upon her and not become confused (*kijo faro*). She can shout (*feteng*), literally 'split' the air with her voice, but do it with feeling (*wasu*) and sentiment (*balafa*), so that people will sympathize with her.[12]

In the West African regions associated with griots, music and musicians are among the most profitable "export products." Many *jalolu* have settled in the United States, Europe, and elsewhere, and pursue careers as concert artists. In the spirit of musical globalization, some join rock and fusion groups creating exciting new hybrid forms. An example is Senegalese musician Diali Cissokho, who now lives in Pittsboro, North Carolina. Diali's lineage stems from two important *jali* clans: his father is Cissokho and his mother is Diabate. Diali met his American wife Hilary Stewart when she was spending a semester abroad in Senegal studying music of the *jali* tradition. She found a *kora* teacher, who became her husband in 2009. Diali emigrated to North Carolina with his new wife in 2010. When he consulted with his family whether to stay within his home community or leave for America, he was told: "Diali, you know what? Music is music. Life is life. But wife is wife. You have to go help your wife."[13] In America, he continues to perform the traditional *kora* songs of his ancestors and also explores new avenues for contemporary expression. In *"Lu Mu Mety Mety"* (13.4), Diali sings an autobiographical song in the traditional style. He tells of his early music education, his family, meeting his wife, and coming to America. This narrative is interspersed with proverbs and pithy metaphors like "Everything is in front of us," and "The instruments give us courage."

In 2011, Diali Cissokho formed the band Kaira Ba with a group of North Carolina roots musicians (Figure 13.3). Kaira Ba (13.5) (pronounced "KAI rah bah") is a Mandinka word meaning "the great peace" or "peace and love." Their hybrid sound is "at once unique and universal," writes National Public Radio correspondent Frank Stasio.[14] That Diali and his collaborators can fit their styles together like hand and glove is really no miracle. The North Carolinians grew up with jazz, R&B, gospel, and blues. Because these styles derived from music brought to North Carolina 400 years ago by West Africans on slave ships, the band members all speak a common musical language. Diali continues to maintain close family relationships in Senegal, and Kaira Ba has toured there finding rapport with their African audiences.

The band's album *Routes* (2018) is truly a bridge across the Atlantic. Kaira Ba recorded the original tracks in M'bour, Senegal, Diali's hometown, with many of his musician friends and relatives contributing to the mix. On returning to North Carolina, the band overdubbed both instrumental and vocal tracks. In the song *"Salsa Xalel"* (13.6), for example, they blend Latin

FIGURE 13.3 Kaira Ba with (L to R) Will Ridenour (*djembe*), Diali Cissokho (*kora*), John Westmore-land (guitar), Austin McCall (percussion), and Jonathan Henderson (upright bass)

American salsa, popular in Senegal, with the Senegalese national popular dance music *mbalax*, and the West African xylophone *balafon*.

> The tie-in to the American South comes by way of the track's funky horn section and gospel singers Shana Tucker and Tamisha Waden, who join Cissokho on vocals as they ponder what kind of world are we leaving for our children.[15]

Diali believes his music is more than entertainment; it is a means to communicate across cultural boundaries about the richness of his African heritage as well as the plight of Africa's poor.

Blind Storytellers (Ancient Greece, Ireland, China, Japan)

In many parts of the world, storytellers are professional entertainers who sing fables, myths, legends, and tales of ordinary people in extraordinary, often amusing situations. Music and storytelling have been among the relatively few professions available to the blind, as farm work and other traditional forms of labor were not practical. This tradition dates back at least as far as the legendary Homer, creator of the epic tales the *Iliad* and the *Odyssey* (Figure 13.4). In 17th- and 18th-century Ireland, itinerant harp players and storytellers traveled around the country entertaining nobles in their castles and great houses, and blind musicians were common among them. Turlough O'Carolan (1670–1738), who was left blind after contracting smallpox at the age of eighteen, composed over 200 songs and tunes for his patrons. He was the only Irish harper-composer of that time period

FIGURE 13.4 *Homer and His Guide* (1874), William-Adolphe Bouguereau (1825–1905)

whose works survive, written down after his death and still played today by traditional Irish musicians and others. Here, Irish harper Mark Harmer plays O'Carolan's piece, "Carolan's Dream" (13.7).

In China and Japan as elsewhere, blind itinerant musicians have eked out a living with their stories and songs. Stephen Jones writes of the *shuoshude* (13.8), blind storytellers of north-central China (northern Shaanxi Province):

> As … the **shuoshude** arrives in a village, a family in the midst of misfortune, perhaps with a handicapped son or ailing livestock, asks him to set up his altar. He invokes the gods to bless the family as he performs a long historical story of romance and suspense, to the rhythmic clicking of clappers tied to his leg, the rustling of slim strips of wood tied to his wrist, and his strumming of the sanxian [a three-string fretless plucked lute]. In return, the family gives him a few coins, a bowl or two of noodles, and a bed for the night.[16]

During the Communist Revolution of the 1930s and under the government of Chairman Mao Zedong, these singers were protected, supported, and encouraged to tell new revolutionary stories. One blind storyteller in particular, Han Qixiang (1915–1989), became famous

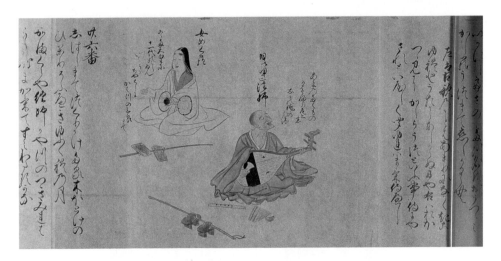

FIGURE 13.5 Blind *biwa hoshi* (story singer), from a scroll housed at the Tokyo National Museum

throughout China as the perfect spokesperson for a storytelling propaganda campaign. "He was an illiterate, impoverished peasant (thus socially and economically oppressed), physically handicapped (thus unfortunate and deprived), and extremely talented at his craft (thus potentially a convincing advocate of Communist ideals)," writes Professor Chiang-tai Hung.[17] However, since 1982 the post-Maoist age, the once revolutionary storytellers again reverted to the old tales of love and adventure.

In Japan since the 8th century, blind Buddhist priests (**moso**) have performed in religious rituals on lutes (*biwa*) (Figure 13.5). Between 1156 and 1185, the country was torn apart by a great civil war between two powerful clans, the Heike and the Genji, which culminated in the end of the glorious Heian period and the establishment of the Kamakura Shogunate. The period of the civil war became the subject of great epic narratives like *The Tale of the Heike*. According to a 14th-century account, the courageous deeds of the warriors from both sides were written down, and set to music by a blind Buddhist monk named Syobutu. For the next several hundred years, storytellers throughout Japan recounted these historical deeds. A powerful guild for blind men (*Todoza*) was responsible for maintaining the integrity of the tradition and for granting performing licenses exclusively to itinerant blind musicians. This practice reached its peak of popularity in the 16th century. It has been in decline ever since, and now there are teachers taking on sighted students in order to perpetuate the art form. The linked video shows a present-day storyteller and *biwa* player, Kikuo Yuji, giving a stage performance of a battle scene from *The Tale of the Heike* (13.9). It begins: "On the third of the second month, Yoshitsune left the capital with the intention of assembling boats at Watanabe in Settsu for an attack on Yashima." The narrative then continues, describing the fierce water battle that ensued.

Pansori (Korea)

A unique form of musical storytelling in Korea is *pansori*. The word "*pansori*" comes from two terms: "*pan*," an area for activity such as a public square or marketplace, and "*sori*" meaning sound, indicating that performances often took place outdoors. The performer (*kwangdae*) tells stories (**madang**) through an alternation of spoken narration and song. The *kwangdae* sings the songs, takes the parts of the various characters in spoken dialogue, and provides poetic descriptions of locales and action scenes. While the narration is spontaneously improvised and may include topical references and jokes, the songs are pre-composed and passed down from teacher to pupil. Traditionally the *pansori* singer was male; however, since the 20th century a number of women have excelled in the art.

A complete narrative can take up to six hours, but the stories are frequently excerpted for shorter performances and the songs are sung independently of the tales in restaurants and teahouses. With only a fan and a handkerchief as props, and staging limited to the dimensions of a straw mat, the *kwangdae* can hold an audience enthralled for hours (Figure 13.6). A drummer (*gosu*) accompanies the sung portions on barrel drum (*buk*) with rhythm patterns (*jangdan*) that are characteristic of much of Korea's traditional music. The **gosu** periodically calls out words of praise and encouragement (**chuimsae**) to the singer, provides sound effects, and acts as a straight man or foil during spoken portions. There is also a great deal of interaction between the storyteller and the audience.

Of particular importance to this tradition is the *pansori* "voice" that is cultivated over many years by apprentice singers. Through arduous training and practice, the singer's voice becomes deeply expressive of the great emotional range the stories demand. The *kwangdae* is a highly cultivated and sophisticated artist. Though traditionally from the very bottom of the social hierarchy and often practicing his trade for commoners, he was occasionally called upon to perform for the nobility.

The origins of this art form are obscure. Literary references exist since at least the 18th century. The first *pansori* narrative, and to this day the most popular, is based on an 18th-century

FIGURE 13.6 *Pansori* performance on a straw mat, at the Busan Cultural Center in Busan, South Korea

story *Chunhyang-ga* (or "Song of Chunhyang") by the aristocrat Yu Jinha (1711–1791): the tale of a wife's devotion to her husband. By the end of the 18th century there were twelve stories in the repertoire of which five survive today. Each exemplifies one of the cardinal social relationships upheld by Confucian ethics: king and subject, father and son, elder brother and younger brother, husband and wife, friend and friend. By the mid-20th century this storytelling tradition was in decline, after decades of colonial occupation by Japan followed by World War II and a bitter civil war that divided the peninsula.

In the 1990s a film titled *Sopyonje* (13.10), directed by Im Kwon Taek, created great popular interest and brought about a renaissance of the art form. The film deals primarily with the training of a girl by her father Yubon to become a *kwangdae*, and her coming to artistic maturity through suffering. Later in the film, with Yubon's two children grown to adulthood, the wandering family of singer-storytellers has come upon hard times. In the scene shown in Video 13.10, the three family members are performing in a winter marketplace to attract a crowd for a medicine dealer. Their narration is interrupted by a modern brass band playing Western music, with which they cannot compete.

In 1966, the South Korean government designated *pansori* "Important Intangible Cultural Property Number 5." This was done as part of a program to preserve the cultural legacies of the country. Important performers of several genres were designated as "Living Cultural Assets" and were provided with a small stipend for passing on their art to new generations. In 2003, UNESCO proclaimed *"Pansori* epic chant" (13.11) one of the Masterpieces of the Oral and Intangible Heritage of Humanity. Today, students of the art study in Korean music conservatories and perform in auditoriums and on television.

THEATER

Stories around the world are not only told and sung, they are also danced and dramatized in performance by actors with costumes, masks, and puppets. In many performance traditions, actors do not attempt to imitate or portray everyday human life in a realistic manner. Rather, they attempt to reveal supernatural powers that are believed to lie behind and control human experience. Performances often depict the deeds of deities, kings, and heroes, and enact great battles in which the forces of Good and Evil are locked in endless struggle. The worlds of myth and the sacred are evoked by actors who are highly trained in forms of physical movement and dance. Often these actors reveal, through their performances, beings that are more than, or other than, human. Many of them belong to theatrical families and are trained from childhood in these specialized forms. Other theatrical traditions have more to do with worldly affairs, exploring concerns that are more social and political. While even in Shakespeare's plays the supernatural is not far from the realm of the living, the stories reveal more about human motives than divine ones.

Bunraku (Japan)

Many parts of the world have highly developed traditions of puppet theater. Japanese *bunraku* arose in the 17th century as an urban middle-class popular entertainment form. It developed from the fusing of itinerant folk puppet theater with the tradition of blind epic

FIGURE 13.7 Puppeteers operate *bunraku* puppet on stage, in Osaka, Japan (L), and *tayu* singer-narrator and *shamisen* player (R)

singers who accompanied themselves on the *biwa*. The roles of narrator, accompanist, and puppeteer were separate and distinct. The louder and more versatile *shamisen* (three-string lute) from Okinawa eventually replaced the *biwa*. *Bunraku* developed in parallel with a theatrical genre performed by human actors called **kabuki**. The two genres competed for audience members and imitated each other as the *kabuki* actors borrowed movements from the puppets, and the puppet designers and puppeteers strove for ever more realistic effects. *Bunraku* and *kabuki* also shared stories. The main categories were historical plays focusing on the samurai class (*jidaimono*), especially set in the 12th to 14th centuries; and contemporary plays about commoners (*sewamono*), including family dramas and love suicides. The puppet theater reached its greatest level of development and popularity in the 18th century, when the half-lifesize puppets came to be manipulated by three puppeteers instead of one. The master puppeteer controls the puppet's right arm and elaborately carved head, while the other two puppeteers, wearing black hoods, manipulate the left arm, and the feet and legs, respectively. Unlike any other puppet tradition in the world, in *bunraku* the puppeteers are on stage with the puppets, fully visible to the audience. Spectators remark that over time they become accustomed to this convention, and the three puppeteers seem to disappear as the audience concentrates on the realistic puppets. Connoisseurs of the art shift their attention back and forth between the puppet itself and the virtuosity of the master puppeteer. A *tayu* (singer-narrator) and a *shamisen* player sit on a revolving side stage and provide all the dialogue and musical accompaniment for the *bunraku* play (Figure 13.7). The *shamisen* closely follows the vocal line, and the singer performs in three different styles: lyrical, declamatory, and most commonly in a half spoken, half sung style. In 2008, Ningyo Johruri *Bunraku* puppet theatre (13.12) was inscribed on the UNESCO Representative List of Intangible Cultural Heritage of Humanity.

Japanese *bunraku*, like Indian *kathakali*, has faced considerable challenges in its long history, and both now might be considered endangered cultural species. Although *bunraku* has had something of a revival since the 1980s, the traditional skilled crafts of the puppet-head carver, costume designer, and backstage technician are not being passed on to the next generation.

Wayang Kulit (Java)

One of the world's most dynamic, highly developed, musically elaborate, and dramatically complex theatrical traditions is the **wayang kulit** shadow puppet theater of Java, Indonesia. (See Map 11.1.) The role of the **dalang** (puppeteer) is similar to the Korean *pansori* singer and the Japanese *tayu* in that he takes on the different voices of all the characters. He, and recently she, is entirely responsible for the narrative and dramatic success of the performance. Yet in addition to telling the story, the *dalang* manipulates leather puppets against a shadow screen, fulfilling the responsibilities of choreographer, director, actor, and producer. As in *kathakali* dance drama in India, many of the stories derive from the Hindu epics **Ramayana** and **Mahabharata**, brought to the Indonesian islands centuries ago and fused with indigenous Javanese mythology. An oil lamp or electric light suspended behind and above the *dalang* projects shadows of the puppets on a screen. Seated on the *dalang*'s side of the screen are musicians accompanying the play on a *gamelan* (Figure 13.8). The *dalang* cues the musicians by striking metal plates (*kepyak*) that hang from the puppet storage box (*keprak*) with his foot, signaling when to begin and end pieces, and to change tempo. Music appropriate to the various stages of the unfolding drama—courtly music, meditative music, and battle music—enhances the power of the narrative. The audience is free to watch the show from either side of the screen, viewing the musicians and the *dalang*'s intricate manipulations, or the shadow drama itself (Figure 13.9L). As with *bunraku*, UNESCO placed *wayang kulit* puppet theatre (13.13) on the Representative List of the Intangible Cultural Heritage of Humanity in 2008.

FIGURE 13.8 Javanese *gamelan* instruments

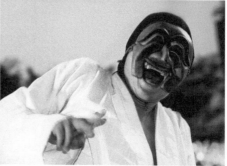

FIGURE 13.9 Leather puppets cast their shadows on the screen in Javanese *wayang kulit* (L), and South Korean *talchum* masked dancer (R)

Talchum (Korea)

Masks are used in secular forms of theater and dance drama throughout the world. Korean masked dance dramas (***talchum***) have been performed outdoors for centuries (Figure 13.9R). These dramas, traditionally enacted by peasant farmers, poked fun at the decadent aristocracy, corrupt monks, and licentious shamans. The performances consist of a series of disconnected vignettes accompanied by native string, wind, and percussion instruments, and can last from a few hours to a full night. The actors improvise much of the dialogue and convey their characters through costumes, appropriate gestures, and dance movements. All the parts were once played by men, but more recently women play the parts of **courtesan** and shamaness. As the dance drama progresses, the boundary between actor and audience becomes more and more ambiguous, and by the end of the evening all present are dancing together. In many parts of the world, masks lend anonymity to members of lower classes, allowing them to mock and satirize the upper class in public without fear of reprisal. This video is a short documentary on *talchum* (13.14).

La Virgen Del Carmen Fiesta (Peru)

High in the Andes Mountains near Cuzco, Peru, a five-day masked pageant and street festival takes place every year starting on July 15 in the remote town of Paucartambo (Map 13.2). The town's population consists primarily of **mestizos** (peoples of mixed Spanish and Native American ancestry) who speak the indigenous language of **Quechua**. The various music groups that perform in the festival include semi-professional musicians hired from other towns, although the people of Paucartambo form the various costumed and masked dance groups of the fiesta.

The festival is held in honor of the town's patron saint, *La Virgen del Carmen* (Our Lady of Mount Carmel), the provider of good health and prosperity. In the mid-18th century, King Charles III of Spain gave two statues of the Virgin to the northern city of Cuzco and the southern city of Puno. The more beautiful of the two was taken to Paucartambo by mistake, instead of Cuzco. The street festival reenacts the legendary struggle between the indigenous people of the lowland jungle (Qhapaq Chunchos) and the people of the high Andes mountains (Qhapaq Qollas) over possession of the precious *Virgen del Carmen* statue. The Qhapaq

MAP 13.2 Paucartambo and Cuzco in southern Peru

Source: Garland Encyclopedia of World Music, Vol. 2, South America, Mexico, Central America, and the Caribbean

Chunchos wear distinctive headdresses made of colorful bird feathers representing the indigenous peoples; the *Qhapaq Qollas*, representing highland merchants, wear white woollen face masks depicting a mythological half-human, half-llama figure. In the drama, the *Qapaq Qollas* steal the statue and the *Qapaq Chunchos* stage various skirmishes in their attempts to retrieve it. The fighting involves tests of valor such as jumping over flames that represent the burning fires of hell. After three days of fighting, the *Qapaq Chunchos* recapture the statue and restore order as well as guarantee spiritual protection for the community.

In addition to the protagonists, the *Qapaq Chunchos* and *Qollas*, groups of townspeople also portray the colonial Spanish, Black slaves, liquor traders, lawyers, government officials, and clowns. Each group plays its role in the drama with its own accompanying band. These bands have their own distinctive instruments, musical styles, and dance pieces that reflect the mixed ancestry of the population. This video shows several of the dance and music groups

FIGURE 13.10 Masked *Saqra* devil dancer in Peru

in the *Virgen del Carmen* fiesta (13.15) procession when the statue is carried through the streets. Walking on guard beside the statue of the *Virgen del Carmen* are the *Qhapaq Chunchos*, wearing their feathered headdresses and carrying spears, to the accompaniment of indigenous flutes and drums. In front of the statue are the Black slaves (*Qhapaq Negros*), in whose accompanying band can be heard a ratchet (*metraca*), bass drum, accordion, and *quena* flutes (0'19"). The *Saqras* devil dancers (at 0'39"), accompanied by another mixed band of European accordions and Andean flutes and drums, wear monster or animal masks (Figure 13.10), and blond wigs that represent the evil European colonizers. Then follow the lawyer and government official characters (*Doctores*), who exploited the rural population (0'56"). Finally come the liquor traders (*Majeños*), who were notorious for swindling the native population. They perform a staggering drunken dance to the accompaniment of a brass band, also symbolic of the former Spanish colonial rulers (at 1'03").

During the five days of the fiesta the entire town is taken over by visitors from all over the region and beyond. On the third day, dance groups, musicians, and visitors alike go to the cemetery to visit the graves of former troupe members and to honor the dead (1'20").

FIGURE 13.11 Ancient Greek masks representing tragedy and comedy

Dancers place their masks and props on the gravestones, and music, songs, and dances follow moments of silence and prayer. The festivities continue throughout the day and night, and the video clip ends with the nighttime antics of the *Qhapaq Qollas* sporting white cloth head masks and jumping over street bonfires, twirling fireworks, and riding on flaming carts (1'50"). "For four days a year," writes ethnomusicologist Thomas Turino, "the plaza and cobblestone streets are transformed into a stage for a music drama that turns the normal order of daily life upside down."[18] The Paucartambo festival provides an opportunity for townspeople to honor their beloved saint, but also for the socially powerless to imagine, celebrate, and dwell at least for a short time in a world in which they have the upper hand.

Masked Drama (Ancient Greece)

In ancient Greece, dramas were spectacles involving masks, mime, dance, musical instruments, and sung or chanted poetry. They were performed as integral parts of the rites celebrating Dionysus, the God of wine and intoxication. Both leading actors and chorus members wore masks that changed their identities into the mythic characters of the dramas, and altered and amplified their voices (Figure 13.11). The philosopher Aristotle (384–322 BCE) developed the concept of catharsis from the powerful impact this theater had on its audience members. According to this theory, the purpose of theater was for the spectators to purify their emotions by experiencing pity and fear intensely yet vicariously, separate from their individual life circumstances. During the Renaissance, nearly 2,500 years later, intellectuals were reviving the forgotten wisdom of ancient civilizations. It was known that the theater of the ancient Greeks involved music, but what exactly that music sounded like was unknown. An attempt to recreate music drama in the ancient Greek manner led to the development of European opera, a sung theater.

OPERA

Opera, defined as music drama involving stagecraft (scenery, lighting, props, costumes, makeup) and dialogue that is usually sung throughout, is one of the great art forms of world culture. In the 19th century, the German opera composer Richard Wagner (1813–1883) coined the phrase **Gesamtkunstwerk** ("total art work") to describe an artistic medium that encompasses all others: literature, poetry, music, dance, drama, visual arts, and architecture. Chinese opera has a very different history and context from Western opera; but like Western opera, it is a composite art form that includes acting, instrumental music, accompanied singing, elaborate costumes, dance, acrobatics, and stagecraft. Like Western opera, sung drama in China is a complete work of art, a *Gesamtkunstwerk*.

Western Opera

As a distinct genre, Western opera's origins lie with a group of aristocratic intellectuals living in Florence, Italy, at the end of the 16th century. They met not in public but in the private home of Count Giovanni de' Bardi, and were thus known collectively as the **Camerata** (from *camera*, the Italian word for "room"). This group of philosophers and artists was concerned with the applicability of classical Greek aesthetic ideals to the culture of their own time. They noted that in poetry, sculpture, architecture, and painting, the Florentines of the Renaissance had surpassed their Greek models. Only in one area of artistic production was the current state of art woefully inadequate when compared with the purported accomplishments of their classical forebears. Nothing in their theater could compare with the great 6th- and 5th-century BCE Athenian playwrights Aeschylus, Sophocles, and Euripides. It was believed at that time, though doubted by some later scholars, that ancient Greek drama was sung, not spoken. Certainly there was music and dance involved; the portion of the stage where the actors sang and danced was known as the "orchestra." However, no music of ancient Greece survived, and the music of Renaissance Italy used for setting texts—masses, motets, and madrigals—was polyphonic and therefore unsuitable for presenting dramatic speech. How, indeed, could music that combined many voices be used to declaim the speech of a single character?

The solution to the problem of writing music that convincingly projected dramatic speech was a device called **monody**, developed by the *Camerata* members themselves. The most important melodic line was sung by the character, and the other parts that filled out the harmony were simplified and performed by instruments. The dramatic narrative unfolded by means of sung dialogue (**recitative**) and songs (**arias**), which stopped the action, allowing characters to reflect on their situation and show off to the audience their vocal prowess. The mandatory chorus, as in ancient Greek theater, provided occasional commentary and played the roles of soldiers, townspeople, furies of Hades, etc. The famous aria, *"Tu sei morte"* ("You are dead") from one of the earliest operas, *Orfeo* (13.16) (1607) by Claudio Monteverdi (1567–1643) (Figure 13.12), demonstrates how, in a single generation, composers were able to combine music and dramatic speech to convey powerfully to the audience both

FIGURE 13.12 Claudio Monteverdi

a dramatic situation and the feelings and motives of the characters. Since the earliest operas were attempts to recreate ancient Greek theater, the stories were taken primarily from Greek mythology. The myth of Orpheus was dramatized numerous times in early opera. The story involves a great musician, Orpheus, whose bride Euridice has died on their wedding day, bitten by a snake. The myth served as a perfect vehicle for a singing actor in emotionally charged circumstances. In the aria *"Tu sei morte,"* Orpheus declares that he will travel to the land of the dead and use his divinely inspired singing voice to persuade Hades, God of the Underworld, to return his wife to the living world. As Monteverdi was perfecting a new form of theater in Venice with his *Orfeo*, William Shakespeare was perfecting the Elizabethan theater in London and writing this immortal sonnet about Orpheus and the enchanting magic of his music:

> "Orpheus with his Lute"
> Orpheus with his lute made trees,
> And the mountain tops that freeze,
> Bow themselves, when he did sing:
> To his music plants and flowers
> Ever sprung; as sun and showers
> There had made a lasting spring.
> Everything that heard him play,
> Even the billows of the sea,
> Hung their heads, and then lay by.

FIGURE 13.13 Wolfgang Amadeus Mozart (L), and the masked ball scene from Mozart's opera *Don Giovanni* (1787) (R)

> In sweet music is such art,
> Killing care and grief of heart
> Fall asleep, or hearing, die.

Shakespeare's Globe Theatre employed musicians who played before, during, and after the spoken plays he wrote and produced. They also provided fanfares, dancing accompaniments, and other music that the play's action required.

The first public opera house opened in Venice in 1637, and by the middle of the 17th century, opera had become the most important form of aristocratic entertainment in much of Europe. In France, a Florentine composer, Jean-Baptiste Lully, adapted the opera to the tastes of the French court. He combined the mythological and pastoral themes of Italian opera with the *ballet de cour* ("ballet of the royal court"). Dance and pageantry in addition to opera were indispensable features of court life during the reign of Louis XIV, the Sun King (1638–1713). A century earlier, Florentine Catherine de' Medici had introduced the tradition of ballet to the French court when she became Queen of France in 1547, and there it received lavish patronage. As Paris became the center of ballet, Italian composers had to insert appropriate scenes into their operatic works if they wanted them performed on a Parisian stage.

The stories of French operas by Lully and his contemporaries were derived from Greek and Roman mythology and history. These were themes fit for a king and queen, and their court. During the latter half of the 18th century, opera stories diversified to include comedies on contemporary themes. The most notable composer of comic opera was the Austrian, Wolfgang Amadeus Mozart (1756–1791) (Figure 13.13). The plots included tensions between members of the aristocracy and their subjects, tensions that would explode toward the end of the century in the French Revolution.

The 19th century was the period of greatest development in opera, as national schools arose and public opera houses opened in major cities of Germany, Russia, Bohemia, and Spain (where opera was called *zarzuela*). In Italy, France, and Austria, opera was already well established as a middle-class entertainment. Two great figures emerged—Richard Wagner and Giuseppe Verdi, both born in 1813—who would polarize the opera-going public and produce works that to this day form the core of operatic literature. Richard Wagner saw music as

FIGURE 13.14 Richard Wagner (L), and a scene from Wagner's opera *Das Rheingold* (1869) (R)

an equal component of a composite art form through which a modern mythology would be ritually presented (Figure 13.14). He wrote both words and music for his operas, unlike most other opera composers who worked with playwrights for the text (called **libretto** in Italian). He also designed the scenery and staging effects, and even designed the theater in Bayreuth in which his works would be ideally presented. The orchestra was as important as the singers and presented a complex musical mirror to the action on stage. For Giuseppe Verdi (1813–1901), opera was fundamentally about the art of singing, the lyrical and dramatic potential of the human voice (Figure 13.15). At the end of the 19th century in Italy and elsewhere, a new type of opera emerged called **verismo** ("realism"), in which opera plots were drawn from real life situations, particularly involving the violence and high passions of the underclass. Sailors, clowns, adulterous peasants, and bohemian artists all sang their distressing tales for upper- and middle-class audiences alike who wept vicariously, in sympathy with their plight.

It would seem that today opera is an anachronism. Few operas have been added to the permanent standard repertoire since the first decades of the 20th century, and opera companies are notoriously conservative. The average age for subscribers to the Metropolitan Opera in New York, North America's oldest and largest company, is sixty. Opera is the most expensive form of live theater, with labor costs for orchestra instrumentalists, stagehands, set designers, etc., in addition to the lead singers who command astronomical fees. Yet composers continue to write them, and young people continue to enroll in opera departments in music conservatories and universities to receive the specialized and arduous vocal training the genre demands. It must be remembered that the form of singing that characterizes opera developed long before the invention of electronic amplification, and since the late 19th century the unaided voice has had to project over an eighty-piece orchestra into a 2,000-seat auditorium. New York, San Francisco, Chicago, Houston, and Los Angeles have world-class resident opera companies, and there are over a hundred smaller regional companies in North America. In Europe, even middle-sized cities have permanent resident companies performing full-season repertoires. Worldwide, there are around seventy fully professional opera companies active in some thirty countries. These artistic institutions are sources of great civic pride. Often resident ballet companies and symphony orchestras share the centrally located opera house, serving as a focal point for social rituals, and a destination for visiting dignitaries much as the medieval cathedral once served.

FIGURE 13.15 Giuseppe Verdi

In East Asia, Western opera has become extremely popular, with opera houses in Malaysia, Singapore, Thailand, South Korea, Japan, and China. In December 2006, New York's Metropolitan Opera Company premiered an opera, *The First Emperor*, by the Chinese composer Tan Dun, who made his reputation in the West with his musical score to the Oscar-winning movie *Crouching Tiger, Hidden Dragon* (2000). As with many performing art forms in the 21st century, opera companies in Europe and North America have sought to open up their repertoires to works by more diverse composers, performers, and audiences. In 2016, the Metropolitan Opera House in New York presented *L'Amour de loin*, an opera by a woman composer, Kaija Saariaho of Finland. It was the first opera by a woman staged there since 1903 when English composer Ethel Smyth's *Der Wald* ("The Forest") was performed. After being closed because of the COVID-19 pandemic from March 2020 until October 2021, the Metropolitan Opera House season opened with Terrance Blanchard's *Fire Shut Up in My Bones*, the first opera by an African American in its nearly 150-year history.

Jingju, Daifanxi, and Yangbanxi (China)

Beijing opera, known as *jingju*, is a spectacular and colorful musical theater now considered the predominant form of opera in China. It combines singing, instrumental music, speech,

FIGURE 13.16 Beijing opera actress

mime, stylized dance, acrobatics, mock battles, elaborate costumes, makeup, and sparse scenery. *Jingju* developed in the late-18th century, drawing on musical and dramatic elements of various older regional theaters. It was initially performed for the imperial court, but the lively productions soon became popular among the lower classes in Beijing. With support and patronage of rulers and the educated upper classes, *jingju* became a more sophisticated and stylized performance art and spread beyond the capital.

Jingju performances typically present scenes from several different plays rather than a single narrative. Many stories are based on Chinese history and folklore, and are classified into martial and civil plays. Actors play character types—male (*sheng*), female (*dan*), painted face (*jing*), and comic (*chou*)—each of which has several subcategories. Actors specialize in one stock character, and the intensive training takes many years. *Jingju* artists learn the acting style, movements, gestures, acrobatic skills, face make-up, and vocal style of their single

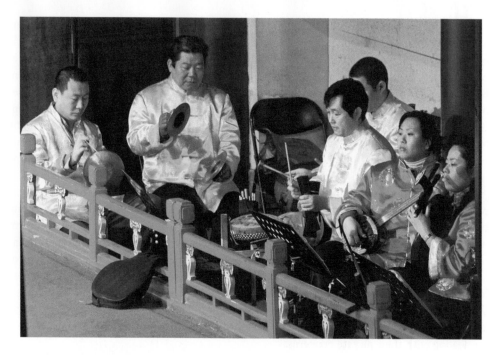

FIGURE 13.17 Beijing opera instrumental ensemble

role. Until 1912 when a ban on female performers was lifted, only male actors appeared on stage, playing both male and female roles (Figure 13.16). In the past, several notable male opera artists such as Mei Lanfang (1894–1961) gained international fame as performers of exclusively female roles.

Instrumental music is continuous throughout a performance, played by two ensembles seated on one side of the opera stage (Figure 13.17). The percussion section (*wuchang*, "military ensemble") consists of large and small gongs, drums, and cymbals, and is led by the drum and clapper player. The *jingju* gongs are distinctive, for the small gong rises in pitch when struck, while the pitch of the large gong falls. This percussion section provides sound effects, conveys moods, and accompanies actors' entrances, exits, and other movements. The ensemble draws from a repertoire of some sixty conventional rhythmic patterns, each named and played by various combinations of the instruments. The melodic section (*wenchang*, "civic ensemble") consists of strings, wind instruments, and a gong-chime. It accompanies arias, dances, and some stage actions, and draws on a large repertoire of precomposed melodies.

Jingju singing, as with all actors' movements, gestures, and dancing, is highly stylized. In comparison with Western opera, the vocal style is nasal and has no vibrato. Beijing opera characters perform arias and short melodic phrases. Those of high social standing also use heightened speech, a form of sung dialogue highly exaggerating the tones of the Mandarin language. Lower class characters use normal Beijing dialect speech.

Various scenes from a *jingju* performance (13.17) at the Huguang Guild Hall, one of Beijing's most renowned opera houses, are shown in this video. The opera, "Meeting of the Elite," is set during the Three Kingdoms Period of ancient China, 220–280 CE. One of the major characters is Huang Gai, a senior general of Wu, one of the three major states then competing for supremacy.[19] The loyal general is an "old male" role with a predominantly red face, enhanced white eyebrows, and a long white beard. After an introductory scene showing a civilian official, Huang Gu appears with his guards and sings an aria. The melodic ensemble plays an introduction and interludes, and the high-pitched *jinghu* (small two-string fiddle) prominently doubles the vocal line. The percussion ensemble starts up in accompaniment to the general's journey, symbolized by his walking in a circle on stage. He then continues his aria, shedding tears as he stands in front of the deceased emperor's tomb. The scene continues with a "young female" character performing heightened speech, followed by a "young female warrior" dancing to various percussion patterns. The video ends with a fight scene between the female warrior and a "young military officer" dressed in a flamboyant costume with four small flags on his back, pheasant feathers in his headdress, and high-soled boots.

While *jingju* is considered the national opera style of China, there are well over 100 forms of folk and regional opera performed throughout the country. These tend to be less elaborate than the urban *jingju*, and differ from it by dialect, repertoire of stories, instrumental accompaniment, and other performance aspects. More significantly, however, is the context of these regional opera styles. Known as **daifanxi**, folk operas are performed by itinerant groups of actors and musicians who travel throughout their region presenting at temple fairs. These festive occasions are held at temples devoted to regional deities such as the Dragon King, the Jade Emperor, and fertility goddesses. The local population considers these entities to be closer to Earth and more accessible than Buddhist, Daoist, Islamic, or Confucianist powers for dealing with their private concerns.

During China's Cultural Revolution (1966–1976) more than a million rural temples were destroyed in the Maoist attempt to eradicate religion. The folk opera tradition went underground. With the death of Mao and China's opening to the world in the early 1980s, religious institutions were restored and temples rebuilt. This video depicts a *daifanxi* performance (13.18) at a temple fair in Shanxi province, north central China. The rural farmers gather twice a year to honor their ancestors and the local deity who assures a sufficient amount of rainfall in this drought-prone region. During these temple fairs, itinerant troupes of actors and musicians together present their stories of kings, ministers, and concubines. The performances are as much to entertain the deities as the people who come and go during the three-day affair. At times people visit the sacred altar, pray, and burn ritual incense. At other times they socialize, eat noodles, and enjoy the operas. The overall atmosphere is informal and festive. As folk religion is ingrained in rural China, so regional opera continues as a unique and vital cultural practice.

All traditional opera performances were suspended during the Cultural Revolution as the Communist government attempted to eradicate the "Four Olds: Old Ideas, Old Culture, Old Habits, and Old Customs." Mao Zedong considered all forms of traditional opera to be reactionary, feudal, and representative of old China, its corruption and superstition. In place of the enormous repertoire of *jingju* and regional operas performed throughout the country, only eight newly composed works (**yangbanxi**) were permitted to be seen during that tumultuous decade (Figure 13.18). Opera reform was spearheaded by Jiang Qing, Mao's wife, who had been a film actress before taking a leading role in the Revolution. She ordered no more stories of emperors, ministers, concubines, and ghosts; the eight model operas told of the oppressed masses, the people's rising against Japanese invaders, the exemplary courage of the soldiers of the Red Army, and other patriotic themes. The small instrumental ensembles of *jingju* and regional operas were supplemented by Western instruments, and formulaic drum patterns and aria melodies were replaced by full scores written by Western-trained composers. For Mao and Qing, the function of the arts in society was to

FIGURE 13.18 Scene from the *Red Detachment of Women*, 1972 *yangbanxi* production

serve the state as propaganda. For ten years, 800 million people watched nothing but eight operas, staged on factory floors, in schools, government buildings, and on outdoor stages. In *jingju*, as a general rule,

> … no script was prepared in advance, and no single person played the role of director. This practice reflects Beijing opera's roots in folk opera, and it worked well as long as new works were based on traditional stories. In the new socialist order, however, opera needed to reflect the lives of workers, peasants, and soldiers, particularly showcasing their heroic efforts at helping to create a communist state. As vehicles of propaganda, the model operas had important messages to convey, and so every word had to be precisely crafted. For this reason, scripts were painstakingly crafted by playwrights, and the action on stage was meticulously honed by directors. Furthermore, performers who had been trained in traditional Beijing opera techniques had to learn a new style of acting in line with the tenets of social realism.[20]

The production values—sets, costumes, choreography—were extremely sophisticated, and while the stories and political philosophy of *yangbanxi* are now outdated, they continue to be watched on television, the songs sung in karaoke bars, and favorite scenes acted out by amateur groups.

Since the end of the Cultural Revolution, significant efforts have been made to revive the *jingju* performance tradition. Modern plays have been written, financial incentives given to star actors, and radio and television have broadcast special productions of opera performances. In 2001, the Communist Party's China Central Television launched a Chinese Opera channel, and in 2010 UNESCO inscribed *jingju* on its Representative List of Intangible Cultural

Heritage of Humanity. Beijing opera has not regained the popularity it once enjoyed, yet it remains one of the major cultural treasures of China.

CONCLUSION

One of the ways people make sense of their lives—the succession of days and years—is by creating episodes that have beginnings, middles, and endings for the re-telling. People carry into adulthood stories rescued from all that has been forgotten of childhood. Often these are stories of extraordinary events like birthdays, trips, victories, injuries, or surprising adventures. Remembering these episodes and sharing them as narratives give a sense of continuity, self-knowledge, and connection with family and home. Groups also have stories, the telling and retelling of which bind the group together with a shared sense of history and destiny. Why is music so universally incorporated in the telling of these collectively meaningful stories? In the case of the epics studied in this chapter, music serves as a mnemonic device, aiding bards in memorizing long passages of text. In storytelling, theatrical, and operatic traditions, melody, rhythm, and instrumental accompaniment provide additional levels of entertainment, symbolism, and psychological depth. Music lifts the experience of narrative out of the ordinary. It makes the telling of the story extraordinary. The next chapter, Music in Public Spaces, ranges from street busking to large public festivals like Carnival in Brazil and Trinidad. The final chapter deals primarily with music and technology, but it also considers the importance of global tourism in the preservation of traditional cultural practices.

KEY TERMS AND CONCEPTS

Aria	Music and Storytelling
Aristotelian Catharsis	Musical Globalization
Blind Storytellers	Opera
Chorus	Oral and Written Texts
Complete Work of Art (*Gesamtkunstwerk*)	Oral Transmission
Daifanxi	Praise Song
Epic Narratives	Public Opera House
Epic Narrator/Bard	Recitative
Griot	*Shuoshude*
Hereditary Profession	Singer-Narrator
"Important Intangible Cultural Property"	Social Satire
Jali (pl. *Jalolu*)	*Talchum*
Jingju	*Verismo*
Libretto	*Wayang Kulit*
Minstrel	*Yangbanxi*

THINKING ABOUT MUSIC

1   Discuss similarities between epic narration and rap. In this response, consider the skill sets that epic narrators and rappers bring to a performance. How are they similar and how are they different?

2   Consider the art of the epic narrator in terms of the composition/improvisation convergence described in Chapter 4 (p. 100). How does Milman Parry's analysis of the bardic process reflect this dichotomy?

3   Both the Balkan bards and the West African *jalolu* are described as occasionally singing for politicians or businessmen. Why and how do traditional artists sometimes serve powerful interests? Are there musicians in American society serving similar functions?

4   Think of musical storytelling in your own experience, in films, theater, songs. What does music add to the telling of a story? Describe an example.

5   Explain in your own words Wagner's concept of opera, *Gesamtkunstwerk*. In Chapter 11, *calonarang* and *kathakali* have been described as "complete works of art." In what ways do these dramatic traditions relate to Wagner's concept of opera?

6   Why do you think wearing theatrical masks is popular in folk theater like *talchum* and Paucartambo?

7   A late 19th-century operatic style was known as "*verismo,*" meaning "realism." Yet, what could be more *unrealistic* than a drama where characters sing their lines? How do you explain this phenomenon?

NOTES

1   Clifford Geertz, *The Interpretation of Cultures*, new ed. (New York: Basic Books, 2000), 95.

2   Albert Lord, *The Singer of Tales*, ed. Stephen Mitchell and Gregory Nagyby, 2nd ed. (Cambridge, MA: Harvard University Press, 2000).

3   Albert Lord, *The Singer of Tales*, 21.

4   "Avdo Međedović, guslar," https://www.youtube.com/watch?v=UhBq_DOEgbM.

5   Albert Lord, *The Singer Resumes the Tale*, ed. Mary Louise Lord (Ithaca, NY: Cornell University Press, 1995), 2.

6   Ivo Žanić, *Flag on the Mountain: A Political Anthropology of War in Croatia and Bosnia* (London: Saqi Books, 2007), 47.

7   Foday Musa Suso, "Jali Kunda: A Memoir," in *Jali Kunda: Griots of West Africa & Beyond*, ed. Matthew Kopa and Iris Brooks (Roslyn, NY: Ellipsis Arts, 1996).

8   Lucy Duran, "Mali-Guinea—Mande Music: West Africa's Musical Powerhouse," in *World Music: The Rough Guide*, ed. Simon Broughton and Mark Ellingham, Vol.1, *Africa, Europe and the Middle East* (London: Rough Guides Ltd., 2000), 542.

9   Paul Oliver, "Music in West Africa," in *Yonder Come the Blues: The Evolution of a Genre*, 2nd ed. (Cambridge: Cambridge University Press, 2001), 53.

10 Foday Musa Suso, "*Jali Kunda: A Memoir,*" 1.

11 Laura Arntson, "Praise Singing in Northern Sierra Leone," in *The Garland Encyclopedia of World Music*, Vol. 1, *Africa*, ed. Ruth Stone (New York: Garland, 1997), 490.

12 Roderic Knight, "The Style of Mandinka Music: A Study in Extracting Theory from Practice," *Selected Reports in Ethnomusicology*, v (1984), 3–66.

13 Sylvia Pfeiffenberger, "Diali Cissokho's Move from Senegal to Pittsboro Sprouted the Music of Kairaba," *Indy Week*, September 11, 2014, http://www.indyweek.com/ indyweek/diali-cissokhos-move-from-senegal-topittsboro-sprouted-the-music-of- kairaba/Content?oid=2655461.

14 Frank Stasio, *Press Review*, accessed November 24, 2021, http://www.kairabamusic.com/ press/.

15 Nelson-Strauss, Brenda. "Review of *Diali Cissokho and Kaira Ba - Routes*," *Black Grooves*, July 3, 2018, https://blackgrooves.org/diali-cissokho-kaira-ba-routes/.

16 Stephen Jones, "Snapshot: Yellow Earth," in *The Garland Encyclopedia of World Music*, Vol. 7, *East Asia: China, Japan, and Korea*, ed. Robert Provine, Yosihiko Tokumaru, and J. Lawrence Witzleben (New York: Routledge, 2002), 258.

17 Chang-tai Hung, "Reeducating a Blind Storyteller: Han Qixiang and the Chinese Communist Storytelling Campaign," *Modern China*, 19/4 (Oct. 1993), 395.

18 Thomas Turino, "The Music of Latin America," in *Excursions in World Music*, ed. Bruno Nettl et al., 5th ed. (Upper Saddle River, NJ: Pearson Prentice Hall, 2008), 271.

19 Paul Noll, "183 Beijing Operas – Huang Gai – Number 33," http://www.paulnoll.com/ China/Opera/list-opera-033.html.

20 Yawen Ludden, Review of *Staging Revolution: Artistry and Aesthetics in Model Beijing Opera during the Cultural Revolution* by Xing Fan, *China Review*, 24/1 (2017), 18–21.

Music in Public Spaces

INTRODUCTION

It is a relatively recent phenomenon that people walking along the street or riding on public transportation listen privately, through earbuds, to music on their mobile phones. In the past, however, private music in public spaces was technologically impossible. Humans are not naturally equipped with the means to close their ears, as they can their eyes, and thus the sounds of vendors calling out their wares, military fanfares, and street entertainers were all inescapable components of the sonic environment. Totalitarian regimes have taken advantage of this by filling public spaces with the sounds of propaganda. The rallies of Adolf Hitler and his Nazi Youth were always accompanied by the martial music of military bands, played at a deafening level. In China after the 1949 establishment of the People's Republic under Chairman Mao, and especially during the Cultural Revolution (1966–1976), more than a million loudspeakers were deployed around the country. They were used to saturate the environment with the incessant sound of political slogans and patriotic songs. Earbuds were not available and there was no way to avoid the omnipresent broadcasts from the central government with their insistent message to conform. These totalitarian tactics represent extreme examples of the way music can be used to fill public spaces, adding its meanings and pervasive presence to the overall "soundscape." Ethnomusicologists use this term to refer to the composite environmental sound of a particular locale. This chapter presents a variety of soundscapes, and the roles music plays in shaping experiences of social space.

In suburban shopping malls in North America, recorded music pervades the corridors with pleasant but non-descript tunes, and draws the public into the individual shops with songs pitched to the particular type of clientele each hopes to attract. Just after Thanksgiving, the soundtrack of the mall switches to Christmas holiday music, symbolically and obsessively repeating the message: "'Tis the Season ... to shop!" At harvest time, North Carolina and other states of America put on a great celebration of agriculture, the State Fair. Throughout the fairgrounds sound stages are set up for concerts by local and regional artists, including some of national repute. The Ferris wheels, roller coasters, and merry-go-rounds each have their own pre-recorded soundtrack. Standing at any location in the midst of all this activity, fairgoers hear these sounds and navigate toward their sources to find the various attractions, just as the cooking smells draw them to the fried dough, hot dogs, and turkey legs. Wherever people gather in numbers, music is usually present serving a variety of functions—entertainment, symbolism, communication—and permeating the environment with its sonic power. At some of these occasions such as concerts and festivals, music is the central focus of the event; at others, music is a significant part of a larger overall public spectacle or celebration, and at still others, it is merely there in the background. At times, it is the musicians themselves who draw the crowds, as when a popular band attracts thousands to a sports arena for a concert. At other times, it is the crowds that draw the musicians, as in the case of buskers and street entertainers performing along the thoroughfares of urban centers and on market day in provincial towns.

BUSKING (ITALY, FRANCE, BENGAL)

Busking musicians in popular tourist locations, in subways, and along downtown city streets hope for donations from passersby for their musical efforts. These public entertainers have been part of the urban landscape at least since ancient Roman times. In 1904, English poet Alfred Noyes wrote a long tribute to the pleasures of hearing the sound of a barrel organ—a mechanical, crank-operated instrument popular at the turn of the 20th century (Figure 14.1). The poem opens:

> There's a barrel-organ carolling across a golden street
> In the City as the sun sinks low;

FIGURE 14.1 Barrel organ player in Bruges, Belgium

And the music's not immortal; but the world has made it sweet
And fulfilled it with the sunset glow;
And it pulses through the pleasures of the City and the pain
That surround the singing organ like a large eternal light;
And they've given it a glory and a part to play again
In the Symphony that rules the day and night.

Buskers continue to be a common sight in many cities and towns throughout the world. Seen as little more than beggars by some, busking musicians (14.1) hope that they are heard and understood as important contributors to the public environment. The video first shows an accordion player from Moldova in the former Soviet Union. Having emigrated to Italy after the collapse of the Soviet state, she tries her luck performing for tourists in a square in central Rome. Stalwart in the terrible cold that day, she played "Lady of Spain" for anyone who

FIGURE 14.2 Baul singer playing *dotara* at annual fair in 2012, Shantiniketan, West Bengal

would listen and perhaps spare her a Euro or two. The video then shows a band of six musicians busking in a busy Saturday morning market in Sainte-Foy-La-Grande, southwestern France. An upright bass, guitar, piano accordion, and two saxophones accompany the singer as she entertains the crowd with a comic song. The singer's tambourine and the saxophone honks serve both to punctuate the song and to thank listeners who kindly put a few coins in their hat.

Among the most renowned buskers in the world are the Bauls of Bengal (14.2), a religious sect for whom song is a direct path to divine union. Freely traveling across the border between Bangladesh and India, this sect of wandering minstrel/mystics has preached human divinity and the unity of humanity for more than 600 years. Their livelihood comes from singing and dancing in villages throughout the region (Figure 14.2), and, famously, busking on trains (they call it "gathering honey"). The **Bauls** attained a degree of fame and notoriety in the latter 20th century, recognized by such popular luminaries as Mick Jagger and Bob Dylan who claimed to be "America's Baul." While a few Baul celebrities have signed recording contracts and made international festival appearances, the majority continue to ply their trade on the railways. Video 14.2 shows two Bauls on the Shantiniketan Express in West Bengal, playing their signature instruments. These are the *dotara*, a two-string fretless lute, and the *ektara*, consisting of a single string stretched through a skin-covered gourd resonator and strummed with a finger. It is literally a plucked drum. The Bauls' songs are mystical sermons, and whether or not they receive a few rupees from the tired passengers, their ecstatic songs will be heard.

CONCERTS (USA, BEIJING)

In cities large and small, there are auditoriums designed exclusively or primarily for public concerts. These structures are some of the grandest architectural achievements in the world, and represent the civic importance of and pride in music performance spaces. In San Francisco there are two such buildings situated across the street from each other: The War Memorial Opera House on one side and the Louise M. Davies Symphony Hall on the other. The War Memorial Opera House was built in 1932 in a luxurious neo-classical style. It was there in 1945 that the delegates to the newly formed United Nations first gathered, following World War II. The Louise M. Davies Symphony Hall on the opposite corner was completed in 1980 at a cost of $28 million (Figure 14.3). Its modernist architecture befits the prestige of the city's symphony orchestra. In Sydney, Australia, the Opera House is one of the world's most iconic structures (Figure 14.4). The facility has eight performance spaces ranging from a symphony hall with more than 2,500 seats and an opera house with approximately 1,500 seats, to an outdoor amphitheater and playhouse. Approximately 1,400 performances take place there each year. The building also houses restaurants, bars, cafes, and other amenities for the nearly 1.2 million annual visitors it hosts.

Auditoriums are venues where the wealthy and not so wealthy gather to socialize, see and be seen in a fashionable locale, and attend high-status concerts. From the late 20th century, international celebrity superstars have drawn crowds of considerably greater size than would fit in even the largest symphony halls, and urban sporting arenas have often been refitted to accommodate these concert crowds.

FIGURE 14.3 Louise M. Davies Symphony Hall, San Francisco

An early example was the 1971 Concert for Bangladesh (14.3) held in New York City's Madison Square Garden, which was designed to host basketball games and boxing matches. Former Beatle George Harrison and Indian *sitar* virtuoso Ravi Shankar (1920–2012) together promoted the concert to raise money for one of the major humanitarian catastrophes of the 20th century. A devastating cyclone in Bangladesh followed by a civil war led to the death of half a million civilians and a mass exodus into India of tens of millions. Shankar and his brother-in-law, the great *sarod* master Ali Akbar Khan (1922–2009), both with ancestral roots in Bangladesh, teamed up with virtuoso *tabla* player Alla Rakha (1919–2000) and Shankar's sister-in-law, singer Lakshmi Shankar (1926–2013) on the drone lute (*tambura*). They started off the concert with a performance of North Indian classical music, as seen in the video. The two soloists play a brief introduction in free rhythm (*alap*) before the *tabla* joins in and the speed and intensity of their playing gradually increases. The rapid alternation of *sitar* and *sarod* improvisations leads to a fast, exhilarating question-answer section (*sawal-jawab*) that ends this landmark performance. Also in the concert were Bob Dylan, former Beatle Ringo Starr, Eric Clapton, and other major rock stars of the time. Forty thousand fans were in attendance, and between the concert itself and the movie and recordings that came out of the event, more than $200,000 was raised for the relief effort.

The concert was followed by a number of similar fundraising events in which celebrity musicians raised money to alleviate suffering after major catastrophes. On July 18, 1985, the "Live Aid" concert took place at London's Wembley Stadium in order to raise funds for Ethiopian famine relief. It was hosted by the British royal family and featured bands such as U2, Wham!, Culture Club, and Duran Duran. The concert was simultaneously broadcast via satellite to 110 countries around the world; more than a billion people saw the sixteen-hour broadcast and the concert raised some $127 million.

FIGURE 14.4 Sydney Opera House, Sydney, Australia

On a much smaller scale, in 2010 an enterprising promoter in Beijing organized a concert by a touring company (14.4) of blind storytellers and street performers. The concert featured two famous *shuoshude*, one of whom plays the traditional *sanxian* with clappers and cymbal. The other performs with the *jinghu*, the small two-string fiddle traditionally used to accompany Chinese opera performances. The remaining members of the ensemble would be out begging on the street without this opportunity to perform with the troupe.

NIGHTLIFE

Nightlife refers to the public activities that people engage in between the hours of work and the hours of sleep. Regimented work schedules dictated by industrial and mercantile economies have affected the life patterns of many people around the world, substituting the agricultural rhythms that follow the sun and the weather with the mechanized time clock. This has created predictable pockets of leisure time—evenings, weekends, vacations—that people can devote to entertainment, socializing, and courtship. Consider Friday nights in particular, when workers have a weekly paycheck in their pockets and an evening and week-end ahead. Urban centers have become the settings for establishments devoted to filling these hours with companionship, alcohol, a relaxation of moral strictures, and music. These establishments include public houses, nightclubs, bars, dance halls, cabarets, movie theaters, playhouses, and restaurants; and in places where alcohol is forbidden, tea and coffee houses serve this function. Many use music, either live or pre-recorded, to attract and entertain their clientele. At restaurants the music is often in the background of the dining experience and enhances the ambience of the place and the character of the cuisine. At discos and dance halls, live musicians or DJs invite people to the dance floor for what is often a prelude to more serious courtship later on. In Xining, a city in central China with a substantial Tibetan minority population, young Tibetans gather in the large central plaza every Wednesday evening for traditional circle dancing (14.5) accompanied by recorded and electronically amplified music. Here, Tibetans who have left the countryside–their farms and herds–and are adjusting to the alien world of the city, find comfort in socializing with other relocated Tibetans. They make new acquaintances and social connections, find dating partners, and reunite with distant family members.

Sonidero Bailes (Mexico/USA)

In the New York City area, DJ dance parties called ***sonidero bailes*** (DJ dances) are held in clubs, community centers, bingo halls, and restaurants (Figure 14.5). They provide a social space where young Mexican immigrants can, in a virtual sense, travel home to Mexico through music, their imagination, and the charismatic person of the DJ or *sonidero*. The *sonideros* spin discs of Columbian-produced *cumbia* dance music amplified and distorted by the high-tech sound systems in which they take "fetishistic pride." The *sonidero* acts "as the voice of a displaced community whose emotions and attentions are constantly shifting between a fragmented reality of 'here' and 'there'— ... the US [and] Mexico," writes ethnomusicologist Cathy Ragland. "The *sonidero* acts as a virtual navigator of the sound experience at the *baile*."[1] With a voice amplified to superhuman proportions, he presides over the evening's events,

FIGURE 14.5 *Sonidero bailes* poster

speaking over the dance music in a running narration of greetings, information, advertising, and self-promotion.

> However as the *baile* progresses, [his] most important and clearly more taxing job is to read into the microphone the personal dedications and salutations which members of the audience and dancers are now giving to him … written … on napkins, scraps of notebook paper … or whatever is handy,[2]

including mobile phones. These he reads through the sound system "with creative flair, personality, and conviction." At the end of a half-hour set, the *sonidero's* crew produce recordings of the show that are purchased by the audience members who submitted the dedications. These are then texted to their relatives in Mexico and elsewhere in the United States. The *sonideros* then travel to Mexico to organize dance parties in which families and friends there record reciprocal greetings and dedications that are sent back to New York.

> The *sonidero's* constant travel to and from Mexico for performances helps keep Mexico alive in the immigrants' collective imaginations. This sensation is enhanced by the physical presence of the *sonidero*, who acts as a conduit for communication between individuals on both sides of the border.[3]

The *sonidero baile* is far more than an evening's entertainment or an opportunity to drink, meet friends, and make liaisons. It binds a community fragmented by poverty, immigration, and cultural displacement. The deafening sounds emanating from the amplifiers constitute "the noise of a community that is determined to maintain family and community cohesion despite being geographically scattered, socially marginalized, and politically powerless."[4]

Courtesans

"All over the world, the sensual pleasure of music has made it the natural accompaniment to the other sensual pleasures of life—particularly the very basic ones—food and sex," writes composer and musicologist Gregory Youtz.[5] Many urban areas have designated "pleasure quarters" and "red-light districts," where evening diversions may include the services of women engaged in prostitution. Shakespeare's original Globe Theatre was located on the south bank of the Thames River in London, an area associated with illicit, as well as theatrical, entertainments. The brothels and whorehouses of the past often employed musicians to entertain clients waiting to be shown a room upstairs. World famous musicians Johannes Brahms and Louis Armstrong began their performance careers in such establishments, the former in Hamburg, the latter in New Orleans.

A strong connection between women, the performing arts, and nocturnal entertainment has existed from ancient to modern times in the role of the courtesan. As "women [who] engage in relatively exclusive exchanges of artistic graces, elevated conversation, and sexual favors with male patrons,"[6] courtesans have differed from prostitutes through their high level of education and their skills as singers, dancers, and instrumentalists. Courtesans have typically belonged to the lower social classes and have been patronized by male members of the upper classes, in some instances using "clothes and makeup to create images of themselves as alluring upper-class women."[7] Referring to the Chinese *min ji*, but applicable broadly, Gregory Youtz writes, "These women ranged from fabulously wealthy and respected queens of urban society, to impoverished and abused victims of the common brothel."[8] The institution of the courtesan flourished in many parts of the world, from ancient Greece to imperial China, and from Renaissance Italy to Edo Japan (17th–19th centuries). The courtesan was known by many names: the Greek **hetaira**, the Italian **cortigiana**, the Chinese *min ji*, the Korean **gisaeng**, the Japanese **oiran**, the Indian *tawaif*. They maintained a high standard of creativity and artistry in music and dance. In some cultural contexts, older members of the profession taught the younger ones the various skills required of them; in others, male music and dance masters taught the girls, sometimes performing with them as accompanists.

> In the pleasure districts of Xian, the ancient capital city of Tang Dynasty China (7th–10th centuries), courtesans in their houses were organized into guilds, and regulated and taxed as businesses…. [The women in these enterprises] were brought into the profession at the age of eight or nine and trained in the arts of serving food and drink, singing, playing instruments, and dancing. They were also given a basic education in reading, writing, history, and literature because these were necessary to participate in the conversations and the literary-poetic games which were the popular pastimes at gentlemen's gatherings.[9]

In northern India in the late 18th and early 19th centuries, the *tawaif* was responsible for a number of innovations in the music and dance of the region. They made available in their salons levels of musical sophistication previously heard only in the royal courts. Their establishments, the *kotha*, were meeting places for wealthy patrons, poets, artists, and intellectuals. First the British colonial authorities and then, after independence, the nationalist bourgeois reform movements suppressed and nearly eradicated all trace of this once vibrant social institution. The descendants of the *tawaif*, a hereditary occupation, are now seeking to revitalize and legitimize their performing arts with the help of non-governmental organizations.

In Japan in the late 18th century, a new kind of artist-entertainer appeared. The **geisha** (Figure 14.6), serving the merchants and craftspeople of the urban middle class, competed with the existing institution of the *oiran* who catered to the aristocracy. While highly educated in music and dance, the *geisha* did not study the erotic arts, like the *oiran* who did. Author and journalist Lesley Downer writes:

> The traditional roles of the courtesan as understood in the West were divided. In Japan, courtesans [*oiran*] provided sexual fantasy and also sexual favors when they chose to do so, while the geisha took the role of entertainer. But the division was never totally clear-cut.[10]

Geishas were at the very pinnacle of the creative arts, and were highly accomplished singers, dancers, *shamisen* players, and conversationalists.

In many cultures of the world, the courtesan appeared importantly as a poetic and literary figure and, unlike most other women, her thoughts and words have come down to us, for she was taught to read and write.

> Courtesans are the elite of prostitutes. Their lives have been lauded by writers of many times and places. In societies where wives were not allowed to interact socially with

FIGURE 14.6 *A Winter Party* depicting *geishas,* silk painting by Utagawa Toyoharu (1735–1814)

men, courtesans have been used to fill the gap. They are the only prostitutes to leave their names in histories, and at times they have had a profound effect on politics and the arts.[11]

While the courtesan is often depicted in literature and film as a vibrant and provocative character, changing sexual mores worldwide have made the cultivated female entertainer almost obsolete. The sex-trade worker has been driven underground, and is now often uneducated, trafficked, abused, and from the poorest of the poor.

SPORTING EVENTS

Sporting events are significant and popular social occasions in many parts of the world. Musicians often take part, entertaining the crowds, stirring emotions in support of athletes, and inspiring group solidarity with songs of unity. In the United States, the half-time show at the National Football League Super Bowl is one of the most anticipated cultural events of the year. These extravagant affairs feature celebrity performers, dancers, elaborate sets, props, and high-tech audio and lighting effects. They cost millions of dollars to stage, while reaping hundreds of millions in advertising revenue for supporting corporations. On a more modest scale, high school and college sporting events, especially football games, feature performances by marching bands often staging highly choreographed, quasi-military drills on the playing field.

Varzesh Bastani (Iran)

The traditional Iranian sport of **varzesh bastani** ("ancient sport") combines martial arts, strength training, calisthenics, a code of ethics, spirituality, and music. Men train in a **zurkhaneh** ("house of strength"), a specially constructed, domed building with a sunken, octagonal pit for exercising. Some 500 *zurkhanehs* exist throughout Iran today.[12] The *zurkhaneh* is considered a sacred structure, and athletes must bow to enter through the low door before descending to the pit, symbolizing their honor code of humility and modesty. Women are not allowed in the *zurkhaneh*. On a raised platform above the pit sits the *morshed*, who leads the ritual exercises with rhythmic drumming on a *zarb* (goblet drum) and singing epic and didactic poetry (Figure 14.7). The music provides energy, coordinates exercises, and reminds the athletes of the importance of religion and ethics. Ancient poetry from the Iranian epic by Ferdowsi, *The Shahnameh* ("Book of Kings," 977–1010 CE), is commonly chanted, telling of battles and fierce hand-to-hand combat. Other ancient poetry, in addition to contemporary verse, include sacred songs honoring Imam Ali, a central figure in Shia Islam, whose image hangs in every *zurkhaneh* in Iran. The *morshed* at the Zurkhaneh Ali Khayat (14.6) in Tehran begins the ritual event with drumming, then leads the various exercises beginning with push-ups (*shena*). The athletes each hold a wooden board that represents the sword used by ancient warriors on the battlefield. They then swing clubs (*meels*), symbolic of ancient war maces, to improve stamina and build strength, as the *morshed* punctuates his singing with drum strokes. In the portions of the ceremony known as *charkh* and *pazadan*, the men take turns whirling in the center, as practice for fighting multiple attackers, and stomp to practice their kicks. The video ends with one athlete gripping a bow and chain (*kabadesh*) that resembles an ancient war bow. He shakes it above his head in perfect time with the rhythm of the *zarb* and the singing of the *morshed*. However, in contemporary Iran, the sport must now compete with modern gyms where the emphasis is on sculpted bodies as well as fitness, and for some, "the soundtrack is all pounding DJ mixes and dirty basslines imported from Europe."[13] In 2004, the International Zurkhaneh Sport Federation (IZSF) was established to promote the sport globally and standardize rules. Seventy-two countries currently participate in the annual competitions.

FIGURE 14.7 Shir Afkan Zurkhaneh ("House of Strength"), Tehran, 2016

Nigerian Boxing

Musicians perform at boxing matches (***dambe***) in the Hausa region of northern Nigeria. *Dambe* has been practiced for hundreds of years, and is now recognized as a legitimate sport with a national federation and leagues. A characteristic feature of the sport is the binding of the "strong arm" fist with cloth and tightly knotted cord that is called the "spear." The other arm, with an open palm, is called the "shield." The fighters go for three rounds and the fight ends when one of the boxers touches the ground with any part of his body except his feet. This is called a "killing." In this video of a boxing match (14.7), a singer, amplifying his voice with an aluminum cup, announces to the townspeople that the matches are about to begin. Five side-blown *sarewa* flutes accompany him. During the matches themselves, talking drums (*jauje*) play throughout. The drummers inspire the boxers and arouse the enthusiasm of the spectators, adding their complex rhythmic patterns to the tumult of the crowd noise. At the end of the video, the voice of a praise singer celebrating the victors can be heard. While the event is a blood sport, music is incorporated, not as the "main event" but almost subliminally, adding its power to the overall excitement of the fight.

World Cup Soccer (South Africa)

Music served similar functions at the 2010 World Cup Football Tournament in Johannesburg, South Africa. (What everyone else in the world calls "football," Americans call "soccer.") This major international event began with an inaugural World Cup "Kick-off Celebration Concert" in Orlando Stadium in Soweto. The FIFA (Fédération Internationale de Football Association) promotional website stated:

> Billed as the greatest entertainment event to date in Africa, the concert will ... feature musical performances by international superstars in collaboration with major African artists... This three-hour celebratory extravaganza, [combining] the two universal passions of football and music before a capacity stadium audience of 30,000, will be broadcast to millions more worldwide.[14]

Producer of the concert, Kevin Wall, stated, "We believe sports and music transcend cultural, language and geographic barriers, and through the official FIFA World Cup Kick–off Celebration Concert [we will present] the sights and sounds of unity and celebration for an unforgettable, must-see experience."[15] During the games themselves, *vuvuzelas* (14.8) (plastic trumpets) that have been popular in South Africa for decades were blown by thousands of fans, creating such a deafening din that international sports commentators discussed banning them (Figure 14.8). Like the talking drums of Nigeria, the ***vuvuzelas*** at the World Cup created a sound environment that was part of the overall experience of the games.

Olympic Games (Korea)

Since the inception of the modern Olympic Games in 1896, opening and closing ceremonies have featured music and dance of the host countries in a display of national identity and collective celebration. At the core of these ceremonies are several mandatory rituals including the opening fanfare, the lighting of the Olympic torch, the Parade of the Athletes, and the performance of national anthems, all of which require the participation of musicians. As the

FIGURE 14.8 Fans blowing *vuvuzelas* at the 2010 World Cup in Johannesburg, South Africa

ceremonies evolved over the subsequent century, they became elaborate affairs that allowed considerable creative freedom for the organizing committees to develop performances fit for a world stage. These rituals of sport set the tone of the Games themselves in the spirit of friendly competition, providing a model for international cooperation and world peace. The ceremonies of the 1936 Olympics in Berlin, however, were a skillfully deployed propaganda showcase for Hitler's Third Reich, with stirring militaristic music accompanying persistent straight-arm salutes and cries of "*Sieg Heil*" from the crowds. In 2008, the opening ceremonies of the Summer Olympic Games in Beijing included a performance by 2008 drummers, a perfectly synchronized visual and audible spectacle. The impact of the performance was overwhelming, as it announced the arrival of China at the center of world events with its newly acquired economic and military might.

Among the most artistically inspired ceremonies in the modern history of the Games were those of the 1988 Summer Olympics in Seoul, Republic of Korea (Map 14.1). Seoul was an unlikely selection for hosting the Games. Korea had been annexed by Japan in 1910 and at the end of World War II, when it was liberated by the U.S. military and the Soviet Union's armies, the Korean peninsula was divided at the 38th parallel. As the Cold War developed, the division became entrenched, with rival and hostile governments established in Seoul (in the South) and Pyongyang (in the North), each proxy to the competing world powers. In 1952, the armies of North Korea invaded the South, triggering a war that would end three years later in a stalemate with nearly three million civilian and military casualties. The city of Seoul, capital of the Kingdom of Korea prior to the Japanese annexation, was in ruins, having changed hands four times during the course of the war through fierce street fighting and aerial and artillery bombardment. Yet Seoul was rebuilt, in part through American investment, and by the 1980s was known as "The Miracle on the Han River." When Seoul was selected by the International Olympic Committee in September 1981 over Nagoya, Japan, its former colonial ruler, there was great celebration. A committee was formed consisting of representatives from the government, sports, the military, and the arts to plan the Opening and Closing Ceremonies. These would glorify both Korean identity and the international values represented by the Olympic Games.[16]

During the initial stages, the committee agreed upon three goals that they wished to achieve in the Opening and Closing Ceremonies: first, the presentation should be sufficiently global in scope to appeal to an international audience; second, it should be sufficiently Korean to appeal to the home audience and to communicate to the outside world something essential of Korean identity; and third, it should be fresh and original, embodying "the shock of the new." Three types of music were identified to capture and project these three goals respectively: Western symphonic; traditional Korean (from aristocratic, folk, and religious sources); and electro-disco (internationally popular at the time). Hundreds of composers, writers, choreographers, costume designers, lighting and sound engineers, and stage directors lent their talents to the productions. There was disagreement among the planners as to how to achieve a balance between projecting serious themes of world harmony and reconciliation while providing entertainment for thousands of visitors and millions watching on television. The scenarios and musical scores went through many revisions, accommodating the competing interests and visions of various factions.

While the planners were developing the script for what was becoming a hugely ambitious project, an individual, on his own initiative far from the capital, was hard at work producing what would become the most memorable symbol of the Ceremonies. American ethnomusicologist Margaret Dilling tells "The Story of the World's Biggest Drum" (Figure 14.9):

> There was a man named Kim Kwan-shik who was skilled in the art of drum making. He came from a family of drummakers … that managed a factory for making traditional instruments. One day in September 1981, a year after his father's death, Kim was watching the news on TV in Baden-Baden, Germany: Korea had been selected to host the 1988 Olympics. He was ecstatic. He clapped his hands, shouting, "Yes, that's it." On the spot, he decided to make the biggest drum in the world, one that could be heard the farthest away, and to dedicate it to the Seoul Olympics. His brothers tried to talk him out of it but he had made up his mind. So began a seven-year saga.[17]

The arrival of the great Dragon Drum of Kim Kwan-shik at the Olympic Stadium signaled the start of the two-week-long international event. According to the explanation developed by the organizing committee and read in the program by the stadium audience:

> The Seoul Olympics opens like the dawn of genesis in empty space. Poised in the universe between Heaven and Earth, Humans greet the sun in an act of homage to harmonize the forces of Heaven and Earth, an echo of the role of the king; but the royal seat is filled not by the king but by an enormous drum marked on either head with a swirl of red, blue, and yellow, symbolizing forces which hold the universe in dynamic and delicate balance. The Dragon Drum (*yonggo*) and splendid retinue cut a diagonal across the open space in the morning of the world to the pulse of folk drums and melodies of court music until they reach the foot of the cosmic tree, the link between Heaven and

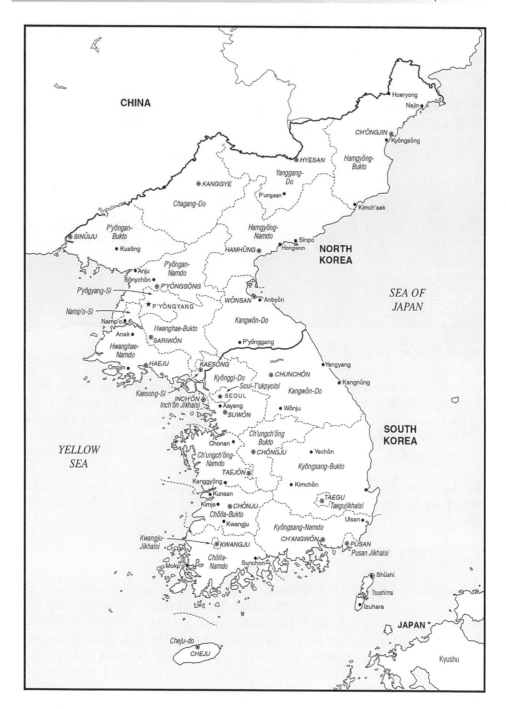

MAP 14.1 Korea

Source: Garland Encyclopedia of World Music, Vol. 7, East Asia: China, Japan, and Korea

FIGURE 14.9 The world's biggest drum, 1988 Opening Ceremony, Seoul Olympics

Earth as well as nest for the sun. At the third stroke of the great drum, the sun rises and the cosmic tree reveals itself as the Olympic torch holder. Soon the tree will burn with fire from Olympus and the Games of the XXIVth Olympiad will open a new era of harmony and progress for humanity from the momentary center of the universe—the city of Seoul.[18]

A popular Korean soap opera, "Reply 1988," was built around nostalgia for these Summer Olympics and for that important year, when Seoul was for a time the center of the world.

CEREMONIES AND CORONATIONS

Worldwide, music is incorporated in rituals of government like royal coronations and presidential inaugurations, serving to confirm and reinforce the established social order. In the United States, the ceremonial march "Hail to the Chief" (14.9) is played by military bands upon the arrival of the president at a formal occasion of state. The melody was composed by English songwriter James Sanderson (1769–1841), and was first played at a patriotic ceremony in Washington DC to honor the end of the War of 1812. For more than 200 years, the song continues as a symbol of the stability of America's democracy. However, ironically, the march was also played for Jefferson Davis, president of the Confederacy during the Civil War.

Presidential Inauguration (USA)

The inauguration of Barack Obama as the first African-American President of the United States on January 20th, 2009 drew one of the largest gatherings in recent American history;

nearly two million people were present to witness this solemn ritual. Along with the speeches, the parade, and the pageantry was music that heralded, honored, and celebrated the event. The day before the swearing-in ceremony, performances on the National Mall by such renowned artists as Bruce Springsteen, Shakira, and will.i.am (of Black Eyed Peas) were projected onto huge screens and transmitted to televisions across America and around the world. Also shown on these screens, and of great symbolic value, was a film of the late African-American singer Marian Anderson (14.10) (1897–1993) in a landmark 1939 performance of "My Country, Tis of Thee" on the steps of the Lincoln Memorial (Figure 14.10). A biographical website devoted to her extraordinary life and career gives the following account of the event:

> Throughout her life, Marian had experienced racism, but the most famous event occurred in 1939. Saul Hurok [her concert manager] tried to rent Washington, D.C.'s Constitution Hall, the city's foremost center, but was told no dates were available. Washington was segregated and even the hall had segregated seating. In 1935, [the contract for renting the hall was re-written to include] a new clause: "concert by white artists only." Hurok would have walked away with the response he'd received, but a rival manager asked about renting the hall for the same dates and was told they were open. The hall's director told Hurok the truth, even yelling before slamming down the phone, "No Negro will ever appear in this hall while I am manager."
>
> The public was outraged, famous musicians protested, and First Lady Eleanor Roosevelt resigned from the Daughters of the American Revolution (DAR), who owned the hall. Roosevelt, along with Hurok and Walter White of the National Association for the Advancement of Colored People (NAACP), encouraged Secretary of the Interior Harold Ickes to arrange a free open-air concert on the steps of the Lincoln Memorial for Easter Sunday. On April 9, Marian sang before 75,000 people and millions of radio listeners. About her trepidation before the event, she said:
>
> "I said yes, but the yes did not come easily or quickly. I don't like a lot of show, and one could not tell in advance what direction the affair would take. I studied my conscience.... As I thought further, I could see that my significance as an individual was small in this affair. I had become, whether I liked it or not, a symbol, representing my people."
>
> Several weeks later, Marian gave a private concert at the White House, where President Franklin D. Roosevelt was entertaining King George VI and Queen Elizabeth (mother of Elizabeth II) of Britain.[19]

Seventy years later on the Capitol steps on the opposite side of the Mall, Barack Obama was sworn into office. R&B singer Aretha Franklin reprised Anderson's performance. Violinist Itzhak Perlman and cellist Yo Yo Ma, two of the most important representatives of the Western Classical tradition, played a commissioned work by John Williams, Hollywood's most successful film score composer. Or rather, because of the cold weather, they soundlessly mimed their performance to a pre-recorded rendition. The pre-inauguration concert juxtaposed multiple musical genres, from rock to gospel to classical. Publicly performed in that singular space resonant with the history of the nation, it served as a powerful sonic enactment of America's motto, "*E pluribus unum*" ("From the many, one"). The music was much more than sound and context. At the time it was a powerful symbol of national reconciliation, heritage, and shared values.

FIGURE 14.10 Marian Anderson

Royal Coronation Anniversaries (Uganda)

In 1862, explorer John Speake arrived at the court of the **kabaka** (king) of Buganda while on his quest for the source of the Nile. He was greeted by the king's royal ensemble of musicians and made the sketch reproduced in Figure 14.11. Royal music was a daily event at court. The *kabaka* himself played the *mujaguzo*, the large drum in the center of the drawing. Its loud sound was said to represent the roaring of a lion, an earthquake, and the king's power. The drawing represented each instrument of the royal household: a gourd trumpet (*amakon-dere*), bow harp (*enanga*), flute (*endere*), a set of drums (*entamivu*), and a small xylophone (*embaire*). Musicians would generally have played in ensembles of like instruments, but it may be that on the occasion of Speake's visit, the *kabaka* had all his musicians play together, to impress the explorer with the mighty din.

On the opposite side of the Nile River was the kingdom of Busoga whose king, the **kyabazinga**, maintained an equally sophisticated royal music establishment. The pride of

FIGURE 14.11 19th-century picture of Buganda court ensemble drawn by John Hanning Speake, first European to visit the source of the White Nile River

the Busoga court was the *bigwala* ensemble of five or more long gourd trumpets. Each instrument produced a single pitch, the ensemble thus creating a five-tone scale. The trumpeters would dance in a circle and play elaborate patterns of alternating blasts that produced pentatonic melodies and polyrhythms.

The British claimed the entire region of present-day Uganda as a protectorate in 1894. However, they allowed the rulers of Buganda, Busoga, and other kingdoms to maintain their royal privileges and ceremonial status until independence in 1963. This arrangement continued under the federal government of the new republic until 1969, when, during a time of great instability and violence, the kingdoms and their courts were forcibly disbanded. On May 23, 1969, the Buganda palace was attacked by federal troops, the king fled, and the royal musicians who were not killed ran for their lives, returning to their farms in the countryside. Similarly, the *kyabazinga* of Busoga was dethroned that year, and went into exile.

In 1996, nearly thirty years after the royal ensembles were disbanded, the central government of Uganda reinstated the kingdoms and their courts as cultural and ceremonial institutions. Most of the royal musicians who knew the protocols of ceremony had died during their period of exile. One drummer, Musisi, who had been sixteen years old at the time of the attack on the Buganda palace, still held in his memory how to reconstitute the instruments, the music, and the rituals of state. Beginning in 2016, ethnomusicologist and educator Dr. James Isabirye undertook, with the help of Musisi and a few other aging survivors, the rebuilding of instruments that had disappeared or fallen into disrepair, and the training of young musicians to play them. The first ensembles of newly trained *entenga* drummers and *amakondere* trumpeters of Buganda, and *bigwala* trumpeters of Busoga, revived the court traditions that had been all but lost.[20] The *entenga* ensemble consisted of six drummers, each playing two or more tuned cylindrical drums. Together, the drummers performed dense, complex polyrhythms. The *entenga* sound had so delighted the *kabaka* of old that every morning at 3 am, he had the royal musicians play for him. That was the only time of day when it was quiet enough for the *kabaka* to hear their intricate drumming patterns. Restoration of the gourd trumpet ensembles was a much larger and more complex process than reviving the drum ensemble. Since the use of gourds for trumpet production had dwindled, seeds for gourd plants were rare and had to be obtained from distant villages. Furthermore, farmers had to be found to resume their cultivation. Carving, fitting, and tuning the trumpets

FIGURE 14.12 Villagers in Busoga, Uganda, playing *bigwala* trumpets

were lost arts that had to be revived, and a new generation of musician-dancers had to be trained. This was achieved by the end of 2016, and the work that James Isabirye did to revive these near-extinct musical traditions has been recognized by UNESCO on its List of Intangible Cultural Heritage in Need of Urgent Safeguarding. The royal courts are at the heart of Bugandan and Busogan identity; the royal music ensembles are at the heart of the kingdoms. Videos of the *entenga* and *amakondere* ensembles (14.11) and *bigwala* trumpet ensemble (14.12) show the results of Dr. Isabirye's revival efforts in the 2016 ceremonies commemorating the anniversaries of the reinstatement of the Buganda and Busoga monarchies (Figure 14.12).

CULTURAL FESTIVALS

In many parts of the world, cultural festivals serve to reinforce local, regional, and global identities and communally shared values. They reinvigorate local musical communities and provide employment for artists who are helping to preserve older and more marginal forms of expression. They also encourage young people and neophytes to explore traditions that might otherwise be forgotten, lost to the commercial mainstream. Some festivals feature regional forms of music and dance that draw the attention of locals and tourists alike to the particular cultural character of a place and population. In the mountains of North Carolina, the annual Highland Games honor the Scottish heritage of many of the region's inhabitants, while to the east, the Bull Durham Blues Festival honors African American roots. Each summer in the historic and picturesque city of Salzburg, the birthplace of Mozart, classical music lovers from all over Europe and elsewhere attend symphony concerts and operas performed by celebrity musicians.

Larger festivals often project a global identity such as the annual Fes Festival of World Sacred Music in Morocco and the World of Music, Arts and Dance (WOMAD) festival held internationally. The Fes Festival juxtaposes musical traditions from a number of religions, such as an American gospel choir and a Sufi *qawwali* group. The festival website states, "The aim of this festival is to harness the arts and spirituality in the service of human and social development, and the relationship between peoples and cultures."[21] In 1980, British progressive rock musician Peter Gabriel laid the groundwork for WOMAD, featuring renowned popular musicians. Every July, the festival is held over four days in England, with "satellite" festivals held in Australia, New Zealand, Spain, Abu Dhabi, and elsewhere. The WOMAD website states:

> Already one of the longest established cultural events in the world, we have hosted festivals in more than 30 countries, with the WOMAD experience enjoyed by a collective audience of millions. Over the years, our aims have remained strong and true: whether at festivals or other performance events, through recorded releases or educational projects, we aim to excite, to create, to inform and to highlight awareness of the worth and potential of a multicultural society.[22]

The Smithsonian Folklife Festival takes place on the National Mall in Washington D.C. Every summer hundreds of thousands of visitors gather there to attend the two-week long event. As explained on the festival website:

> Initiated in 1967 … it has brought more than twenty-three thousand musicians, artists, performers, craftspeople, workers, cooks, storytellers, and others … to demonstrate the skills, knowledge, and aesthetics that embody the creative vitality of community-based traditions.… The Festival has featured exemplary tradition bearers from more than ninety nations, every region of the United States, scores of ethnic communities, [and] more than a hundred American Indian groups.… In many cases, the Festival has energized local and regional tradition bearers and their communities and, thus, helped to conserve and create cultural resources.[23]

Celtic Colours (Canada)

Cape Breton Island, in the Canadian province of Nova Scotia (Map 14.2), hosts the "Celtic Colours International Festival" every October in celebration of its Celtic heritage and culture. Over 60% of Cape Breton's population claims Scottish or Irish ethnicity, some being descendants of the island's earliest settlers. While Cape Breton is also home to Mi'kmaq First Nations (Native American) people and to French-speaking communities whose early 17th-century ancestors named the region L'Acadie (Acadia), in 1621 British settlers began

MAP 14.2 Eastern Canada showing Cape Breton in Nova Scotia

Source: Garland Encyclopedia of World Music, Vol. 3, The United States and Canada

serious efforts to colonize the land they renamed "New Scotland" (Nova Scotia). Many Scots-Irish arrived from New England after the Treaty of Utrecht (1713) gave control of the Acadian peninsula to the British. From the late 18th to mid-19th centuries some 50,000 Highland Scots arrived in Cape Breton. They had been expelled from Scotland during the Highland Clearances, an agricultural program that forced many smallholding farmers off their land to make way for sheep farming. These immigrants established the Scottish Gaelic language and culture that remain a strong part of Cape Breton society today. Since the 1950s, the provincial government has promoted Scottish culture, introduced Gaelic language into schools, and helped fund the Gaelic College of Celtic Arts and Crafts in St. Ann's. The first "Celtic Colours International Festival" took place in 1997, and since then has attracted tens of thousands of visitors to the island.

FIGURE 14.13 Welcome sign for festival visitors at Gaelic College, St. Ann's, Cape Breton (L), and spontaneous step dancing during music jam session at Whycocomagh Waterfront Center, October 2012 (R)

FIGURE 14.14 Celtic Colours square dance at Boisdale Volunteer Fire Department, October 2012 (L), and Boisdale dance musicians playing piano accordion, fiddle, and keyboard (R)

The nine-day festival includes more than fifty concert performances, *ceilidhs* ("gatherings" with songs, tunes, and dancing), and lectures by renowned musicians, dancers, and storytellers from Cape Breton as well as Scotland, Ireland, Brittany (France), Scandinavia, the United States, and elsewhere. Festival goers can participate in a wide variety of cultural events, from music sessions, square dances, and song circles, to community meals, Gaelic teas, and guided "Celtic" walks and hikes. For some, the festival is an opportunity to celebrate their Scottish or Irish cultural heritage. Open Celtic music sessions such as those at the Baddeck Yacht Club (14.13) and the Whycocomagh Waterfront Centre (14.14) allow visiting amateur musicians to play tunes alongside some of the finest Cape Breton musicians and dancers (Figure 14.13R). For other visitors, the festival is a time to enjoy and experience the diversity of Celtic music traditions; to socialize and network with singers, instrumentalists, and dancers (Figure 14.14); or simply to explore the island's spectacular scenery as tourists. For festival organizers, the event requires extensive planning, arranging many simultaneous events in communities spread out all over the island, which is larger than Puerto Rico. The multiple locations of Celtic Colours events distinguish this international music festival from most others of its kind. The festival's mission statement is: "To promote, celebrate and develop Cape Breton's living Celtic culture and hospitality by producing an international festival during the fall colours that builds relationships across Cape Breton Island and beyond."[24]

CARNIVAL

While the musical performances that take place at the ceremonies and festivals described above are entertaining and aesthetically pleasing, in each case they especially serve to promote social order, stability, and integration. Music also accompanies oppositional rallies and celebrations that invert the social order and border on anarchy. The archetypal example of the anarchic and hedonistic festival took place in Bethel, New York, between August 15 and 18, 1969. About 400,000 people gathered in the fields of farmer Max Yasgur for "The Woodstock Festival," now considered the world's most famous rock concert. At this event, although music was the focus and magnet that drew the crowds, it also served as a catalyst for uniting a large portion of a generation with a set of values—peace, freedom, love, and hope—as the Vietnam War raged and divided the country.

According to anthropologist Victor Turner, a healthy, stable society depends on rituals that reinforce structure (like presidential inaugurations) and rituals that provide opportunities for "anti-structure" (like Woodstock). He defines the latter as events in which the hierarchies of the rulers and the ruled as well as class structures are temporarily abandoned.[25] In ancient Rome, the festival honoring the god Saturn, the Saturnalia, embodied the essential spirit of Turner's **anti-structural rituals**. They were characterized by drunkenness, licentiousness, and the inversion of social hierarchies, overturning ordinary conventions of orderly daily life.

> Slaves banqueted together with their masters, whom they insulted and admonished. From among them was elected a King of Chaos who, for the period of Saturnalia only, enjoyed full rights to his master's concubines, and gave ridiculous orders that had to be obeyed by everyone.[26]

At the end of these rituals the King of Chaos returned once again to being a lowly slave. Indeed, in the earliest form of the Saturnalia, he was slain as a sacrifice to the god Saturn. According to Victor Turner, anti-structural rituals like the Roman Saturnalia contribute to a deep feeling of belonging to a group that transcends one's identification with one's social status. This is also true of the Korean masked dance tradition *talchum*.

The roots of Carnival lie in the ancient Greek springtime festival celebrating Dionysus, the god of wine, and in the Roman feasts of Bacchanalia and Saturnalia. These festivals honored the gods of wine and agriculture respectively. In medieval Europe, similar festivities took place during the "Feast of Fools" (also called the Feast of Innocents), celebrated between Christmas and Easter in the Christian church calendar. Revelers wearing masks and costumes paraded through towns dancing and singing, while parodying the holy Mass and making fun of the ecclesiastical hierarchy. As in ancient Rome, the inversion of social and in this case religious roles was a central feature of medieval springtime festivals. The Catholic Church unsuccessfully attempted to control or ban such festivities for nearly a millennium. In 16th-century Italy, "carnivalesque" rebelliousness transformed into masked balls, tournaments, and parades of floats, while in Portugal the rebelliousness continued in the form of the *entrudo*, when people threw flour, eggs, mud, oranges, and lemons at each other; hurled pots and pans out of windows; waged street battles with brooms and spoons; and held gluttonous feasts. These Carnival festivities allowed individuals and communities to engage in unrestrained amusement and boisterous activities in the week before the Christian Lenten season of prayerful reflection and fasting. The term "Carnival" most likely derives from the Latin words *carne vale* meaning "farewell to the flesh," referring to the abstinence from sex and from eating meat during the forty days of Lent that precede Holy Week and Easter Sunday.

Exploration and colonization of the Americas by European powers brought Carnival traditions to the New World. When enslaved Africans were transported to the colonies to provide labor for sugar cane, coffee, and other plantation crops, they brought their own rituals and festivals. In Brazil, Trinidad, Barbados, and other former Spanish, Portuguese, and French colonies, the Roman Catholic colonists held pre-Lenten parades and masked balls. At these grand events, celebrants dressed up as pre-Christian mythical characters and historical heroes like Apollo and Aphrodite, or Caesar, Cleopatra, and Nero. Slave orchestras provided the music. In the slave quarters, they staged their own Carnival celebrations that included drum rhythms, stilt dancers, stick fighters, and large puppets. They employed masks and costumes made out of beads, shells, feathers, and other natural materials, "with each object or combination of objects representing a certain idea or spiritual force."[27] Elements of these African festivals gradually blended with and transformed those of the European colonists. New World Carnival traditions of European landowners, African slaves, and their descendants came to embody and express these multiple meanings.[28]

Most North Americans are familiar with the Mardi Gras (literally, "Fat Tuesday") festivities in New Orleans, but the world's largest and most extravagant celebrations of Carnival take place each year in Brazil and on the Caribbean island nation of Trinidad and Tobago.

Carnival in Rio de Janeiro

In the week ending on Shrove Tuesday, followed by the beginning of Lent on Ash Wednesday, tens of thousands of people participate in the spectacular parades, masked balls, street parties, music, and dancing in Rio de Janeiro, São Paulo, and Salvador de Bahia in Brazil (Map 14.3).

Immigrants from the Portuguese islands of the Azores, Cape Verde, and Madeira first introduced the pre-Lenten *entrudo* to Brazil, a former Portuguese colony, in the early 18th century. People of all social strata doused each other with buckets of water and threw limes. The authorities eventually outlawed these practices. By the mid-19th-century, *cordões* (pageant groups) marched through the streets playing musical instruments, and costumed and masked participants danced in parades. It was from the *cordões* that Carnival groups of musicians and dancers known as **blocos** arose. Today these popular neighborhood groups parade through the streets of Rio de Janeiro and other Brazilian cities for several weeks before the beginning of Lent. While the *blocos* were at first looked down upon by Brazil's social elite for their drunken rowdiness, they paved the way in Rio de Janeiro for samba schools and the official **sambadrome** experience. The sambadrome is the permanent half-mile avenue near downtown Rio built in 1984, which is the scene of one of the world's most extravagant street parties.

The quintessential music and dance associated with Brazilian Carnival is the samba, which originated in the dance parties of freed slaves who left the rural plantations and migrated to

MAP 14.3 Brazil

Source: Garland Encyclopedia of World Music, Vol. 2, South America, Mexico, Central America, and the Caribbean

Rio in the late 19th century. The term is believed to derive from the Angolan word *"semba,"* meaning "invitation to dance." Samba is a solo display characterized by gyrating hip movements (***umbigada***) and outstretched arms. The accompanying music has a regular duple meter with syncopated rhythms played by guitars, *cavaquinhos* (small four-string guitars), and a percussion ensemble (***baterìa***) consisting of bass drums (*surdos*), friction drums (*cuicas*), small tambourines (*pandeiros*), and shakers. At the turn of the 20th century, the samba adopted influences from other music and dance genres in Rio including the Afro-Brazilian *maxixe* and *lundu,* the Cuban *habañera,* and the German polka, reflecting the various strands of an immigrant culture. The result was a highly popular musical form that spread to the middle and upper classes. Through recordings and radio broadcasts in the 1920s and 1930s, the samba quickly gained an international reputation as an icon of Brazilian national identity.

FIGURE 14.15 Queen of the Drums, Imperatriz Leopoldinense Samba School, Rio Carnival 2008

The largest performing groups in the Rio Carnival are associated with the samba schools, which first appeared in the 1920s. These music and dance clubs are located in particular neighborhoods, often poorer shanty-towns (*favelas*), although club membership is open to anyone. Samba schools, whose membership can number in the thousands, work throughout the year to prepare and rehearse for the annual Carnival parade and competition. Every year each samba school selects its own Carnival theme, such as a tribute to a historical figure or event. Members spend thousands of hours making all the respective floats, props, and costumes (Figure 14.15). The schools' music composers create new samba music, the choreographers design the dance sequences, and the performers rehearse at length to perfect their spectacular shows. During the Carnival parade samba school groups march down the sambadrome, performing in front of the judges and up to 90,000 spectators who fill the bleachers on both sides of the parade route. From 8:00 pm until the morning hours on the four days before Shrove Tuesday, samba bands process in turn, each allowed ninety minutes to parade from one end to the other.

A samba school procession begins with costumed individuals who salute the crowds, often followed by a group dressed as early 20th-century Bahian (Afro-Brazilian) women wearing large circular dresses. Marching and dancing on or between the samba school's floats are its various themed groups: vocalists who sing the school's theme song accompanying themselves on the *cavaquinho*; the *bateria* drums and percussion (14.15) led by the "band godmother"; the female flag-holder and her male partner; and the "old guard" of elderly *sambistas* symbolizing the school's history. This video of the Mocidade Samba School (14.16), one of the oldest in Rio, shows its more than 4,000 costumed dancers and musicians on the parade ground. In this fierce samba school competition, the participants await the judges' announcement of the winners on Ash Wednesday, and the five winning samba schools perform once more in a Parade of Champions the following Saturday.

Carnival in Trinidad

As the samba schools signify the Rio Carnival in Brazil, three distinctive elements character-ize Trinidad's pre-Lenten festival—the steel pan, "**playing *mas***" (masquerade), and **calypso**—all of which are rooted in the island's colonial history. (See Map 8.2.) Trinidad was first claimed by Spain in 1498. The initial conquistadors were more interested in gold than in permanent settlement. However, in the mid-1700s the Spanish rulers invited Caribbean French Catholics to settle on the island to establish a plantation economy and to maintain a majority Catholic population. The French colonists established tobacco, coffee, sugar, and cotton plantations, and brought their African slaves with them. In 1802 the Spanish ceded Trinidad to Protestant Great Britain, which didn't celebrate Carnival. Yet "the French com-munity remained in control of the island's economic core and, thus, were able to stamp their cultural characteristics on its ensuing festive developments."[29] By "cultural characteristics," the quote by author John Cowley refers to the Roman Catholicism of the French planters and the continuation of Carnival celebrations.

After emancipation on Trinidad in 1833, freed slaves and other members of the lower classes held pre-Lenten parties called ***canboulay*** in Creole. The term referred to procedures involving the post-harvest burning of sugarcane fields. These festivities included nighttime torch-lit processions with drumming, dancing, singing, and sexually explicit masquerading. The White community considered this immoral and obscene, calling it the ***jamette*** carni-val from the French term "*diamètre*" meaning below the diameter of respectability. Yet the *canboulay* celebration continues to this day. A pre-dawn ritual called ***J'Ouvert*** (from "*jour ouvert*" or daybreak; pronounced "jouvay") takes place on Carnival Monday. Thousands of revelers cover themselves with mud or oil and parade in the streets to deafening steel band or *soca* music. Musician Wendell Manwarren of the Trinidadian *rapso* band 3Canal performs and explains a *J'Ouvert* song (14.17), believed to date from the late 19th century that com-memorates and celebrates freedom.

As Carnival celebrations became more out of control in the late 19th century, tensions between landowners and laborers increased. This led the British authorities to ban all drum-ming. The Black community responded by creating **tamboo-bamboo bands** consisting of tunable bamboo sticks, struck on the ground, and bottle and spoon percussion. Black youths later experimented with making musical instruments from metal hubcaps, brake drums, and biscuit tins. By the late 1930s, ensembles of improvised metal instruments of all sorts pro-vided the characteristic musical accompaniment to the Carnival celebrations of the Black community. This led to the creation of steel pans. A surfeit of oil drums from American bases on Trinidad during World War II allowed further experimentation, resulting in steel pans capable of producing complete musical scales. The steel pan is now the national instrument of Trinidad and Tobago, and the most iconic feature of Trinidad's Carnival. Indeed, the instru-ment has spread to the entire Caribbean region.

The sophisticated, multi-part steel bands (14.18) of today are the legacy of these early struggles. Band members practice year-round for the fierce competitions that begin weeks before Carnival with initial eliminations and semi-finals. Each steel band chooses or com-poses a "Road March" tune months in advance, and seeks to gain popularity through record-ings played in shops, restaurants, taxis, and other public places. The bands, each comprising

up to 100 members, spend months rehearsing longer versions of their Road March in preparation for the Panorama competitions (Figure 14.16). The Grand Finals take place on the
Saturday before Carnival Tuesday in Queens Park Savannah in the capital Port-of-Spain,
when the twelve finalists perform before the judges and huge crowds watch the competition
for prestigious titles and prizes.

The second defining feature of Trinidad's Carnival is *mas*, which refers to the numerous
masquerade groups that parade and dance through the streets. *Mas* groups are open to any
Trinidadians or visitors who wish to buy a costume and join in the parade to "play *mas*."
Some of the largest groups such as Barbarossa, Legend, and Poison, number up to 6,000
or more masqueraders. These groups wear distinctive costumes created around a theme by
a designer, and fashioned by volunteers in *mas* camps over the weeks and months preced-
ing the festival. Each is led by a King and Queen wearing huge costumes that often need
the support of wheels (Figure 14.17). They compete for the "King and Queen of the Festival" title. These costume parades are sometimes referred to as "pretty *mas*" in contrast to the
rowdy, dirty, muddy *mas* celebrations of *J'Ouvert* that precede them on Carnival Monday
morning.

The third defining feature of Carnival is calypso, a song genre native to Trinidad. Calypso
developed from the singing of the "chantwell," a cultural descendant of the West African *griot*
or praise singer. On the plantations, chantwells had served as oral historians and commentators on current events. Prior to the 1920s, descendants of former slaves gathered to hear
the chantwell lead them in call-and-response singing. Their songs concerned topical subjects
and shared grievances as a way to vent their feelings. Gradually over time, the chantwells
became calypsonians. Today they compose their own ballad-style songs, usually consisting of
humorous, witty lyrics often with pointed social and political commentary. Mighty Sparrow,
eight-time winner of Trinidad's Calypso King/Monarch competition, sings his song "Sparrow
Dead" (14.19) in this recording after reading his own premature obituary in the Jamaica
Observer.

In both Brazil and Trinidad, Carnival is perhaps the most culturally significant event of
the year. For outsiders and tourists, it provides highly visible and dramatic visual and sonic
representations of these places that are used by marketers and travel agents to promote them
as vacation destinations. At the very heart of these annual celebrations are music and dance,

FIGURE 14.16 Petrotrin Katzenjammers steel band performs in Panorama semi-final competition,
Trinidad, 2013 (L), and indentations marking pitches on steel pan's concave playing
surface (R)

FIGURE 14.17 Queen of Carnival, Trinidad, 2011 (L), and masqueraders competing in Red Cross Children's Carnival, Trinidad, 2011 (R)

without which the events would not be merely diminished, they would be inconceivable. The saturation of the environment with the special music of Carnival sets this time of year apart from the rest, the din of the *blocos, baterías,* and steel bands provides the sonic cover for the extravagant displays and outrageous behaviors that would not be tolerated in public without this cacophony.

CONCLUSION

This chapter has examined the roles music plays on occasions when people gather publicly. For often, when people congregate, music is somewhere on the scene. On street corners, in train stations, and even on the trains themselves as in India, buskers ply their trade. People attend concerts, theatrical and narrative performances as significant aspects of human social life, for "musicking" brings people together. Sporting events provide opportunities for both spectators and featured musicians to cheer on the competitors. Crowds chant, fans sing, pep bands pump up athletes, and marching bands blare. In Nigerian boxing matches, music accompanies the mayhem. And what would a street party like Carnival be without music propelling people along the roadways dancing. The next and final Chapter 15 discusses cultural tourism and the 20th- and 21st-century developments of sound recording technology and film.

KEY TERMS AND CONCEPTS

Anti-Structural Rituals

Bateria

Baul

Busking

Calypso

Carnival

Ceilidh

Community-Based Traditions

Costume Parades

Courtesans

Cultural Resource

Culture Festivals

DJ Dance Parties

Morshed

Music and Sporting Events

Music in Public Spaces

Music in Shopping Malls

Nightlife

Olympic Games

Opening and Closing Ceremonies

Presidential Inauguration

Rites of Dionysus

Royal Coronations

Samba School

Saturnalia

Sonidero baile

Soundscape

Tradition Bearer

WOMAD (World of Music, Arts and Dance) Festival

Zurkhaneh

THINKING ABOUT MUSIC

1   For the *Bauls* of Bengal, performances on trains are both a sacred duty (preaching to the passengers) and a means of livelihood (busking). Are these two aspects of their activity contradictory? Can you think of another musical tradition that is both a spiritual and economic enterprise?

2   Many students exercise to music. Consider the roles of music in the *zurkhaneh* in Iran. How are they similar to, and how are they different from, your own experience of music and exercise?

3   Attend an opera or ballet, or watch a video of one. Think of how the music affects the overall experience. Of the first six functions in Chapter 6—Emotional Expression, Aesthetic Enjoyment, Entertainment, Communication, Symbolic Representation, Physical Response—which ones do you find the music serving? Choose three of the functions and describe in detail how the music fulfills each one.

4   In the case studies discussed here in Chapter 14—*sonidero bailes*, sporting events, presidential inaugurations, folk festivals, Carnival—music serves to *affirm* membership in a collective by contributing to the experience of *communitas* (concept introduced in Chapter 6). Describe an experience you have had when your individuality was submerged in identification with a group. In what ways did music help to initiate or sustain the experience?

5   Think of a public event you have attended in which music played a part. What was the music like (its musical elements and functions)? How would you describe the music in terms of "context" and "semiotics," two of the four approaches to musical inquiry in Chapter 1?

6   How does the Great Dragon Drum at the Seoul Olympics compare with the drum of the large *mujaguzo* drum of the *kabaka* (king) of Buganda in terms of their symbolic value?

7   According to anthropologist Victor Turner, "a healthy, stable society depends on rituals that reinforce structure (like presidential inaugurations) and rituals that provide opportunities for 'anti-structure' (like Woodstock)." On January 6, 2021, the orderly transfer of the presidency at the Capitol in Washington DC was disrupted by an angry mob. Did this event serve to promote a "healthy, stable society"? Why or why not?

NOTES

1 Cathy Ragland, "Mexican Deejays and the Transnational Space of Youth Dances in New York and New Jersey," *Ethnomusicology* 47/3 (2003), 343.

2 Ragland, "Mexican Deejays," 346.

3 Ragland, "Mexican Deejays," 348.

4 Ragland, "Mexican Deejays," 352.

5 Gregory Youtz, *Silk and Bamboo: An Introduction to Chinese Musical Culture*, unpublished manuscript (2000), 156.

6 Martha Feldman and Bonnie Gordon, "Introduction," *The Courtesan's Arts: Cross-Cultural Perspectives* (Oxford: Oxford University Press, 2006), 5.

7 Feldman and Gordon, *The Courtesan's Arts*, 8–9.

8 Youtz, *Silk and Bamboo*, 158.

9 Youtz, *Silk and Bamboo*, 168.

10 Lesley Downer, "The City Geisha and Their Role in Modern Japan: Anomaly or Artistes?" in Feldman and Gordon, *The Courtesan's Arts: Cross-Cultural Perspectives* (Oxford: Oxford University Press, 2006), 223.

11 Magistra Rosemounde of Mercia, "The History of Prostitution through the Renaissance," accessed November 20, 2021, https://pdfcoffee.com/the-history-of-prostitution-through-the-renaissance-pdf-free.html.

12 Devlin Nestor Daneshforouz, "House of Strength: The History and Traditions of The Zurkhaneh," last modified January 26, 2018, https://medium.com/@dforouznv/house-of-strength-the-history-and-traditions-of-the-zurkhaneh-4c41c58d569a.

13 AFP, "Iran's Gyms, a Clash of the Ancient and the Modern," *The Hindu*, March 24, 2018, https://www.thehindu.com/news/international/irans-gyms-a-clash-of-the-ancient-and-the-modern/article23343715.ece.

14 "About the Concert," 2010 FIFA World Cup South Africa, http://www.fifa.com/worldcup/archive/southafrica2010/organisation/concert/about.html (website no longer available).

15 "About the Concert," 2010 FIFA World Cup South Africa.

16 American ethnomusicologist Margaret Walker Dilling sat in on the seven years of planning that preceded the 1988 Games. Her book has provided source material for much of the case study on the Olympic Ceremonies. Margaret W. Dilling, *Stories Inside Stories: Music in the Making of the Korean Olympic Ceremonies* (Berkeley, CA: Institute of East Asian Studies, 2007).

17 Dilling, *Stories Inside Stories*, 1.

18 Dilling, *Stories Inside Stories*, 1.

19 "Marian Anderson, 'A Dream, A Life, A Legacy'," Marian Anderson Historical Society, accessed November 24, 2021, http://marianandersonhistoricalsociety.weebly.com/biography.html.

20 James Isabirye, email messages to authors, 2021–2022.

21 Fes Festival of World Sacred Music, http://www.fesfestival.com/2013/indexen.php (website is no longer available).

22 "Our WOMAD Story," *World of Music, Arts and Dance Festival*, accessed November 24, 2021, http://womad.org/about/.

23 Smithsonian Folklife Festival, Mission and History, accessed November 24, 2021, https://festival.si.edu/about-us/mission-and-history/smithsonian.

24 "About Celtic Colours," Celtic Colours Festival website, accessed November 24, 2021, http://www.celtic-colours.com/about-celtic-colours/.

25 Victor Turner, *The Ritual Process: Structure and Anti-Structure*, new ed. (New York: Routledge, 2017).

26 Maria Julia Goldwasser, "Carnival," in *Encyclopedia of Religion*, Vol. 3, ed. Lindsay Jones, 2nd ed. (Detroit: Macmillan Reference USA, 2005), 1440–1445.

27 "The History of Carnival," accessed July 25, 2014, http://www.allahwe.org/History.html (website no longer available).

28 "History of Carnival"

29 John Cowley, "Carnival in Trinidad…. Evolution and Cultural Meaning," *Musical Traditions* 4 (1985), updated January 10, 2002, http://www.mustrad.org.uk/articles/trinidad.htm.

Music and Tourism, Sound Recording, and Film

Introduction
Music and Tourism
Sound Recording
Film
Conclusion

INTRODUCTION

This final chapter concerns two aspects of musical experience and music preservation that have shaped the 20th and 21st centuries. The first is cultural tourism; the second is electronic media, and the technologies that made them possible. Both of these 20th- and 21st-century phenomena have played important roles in supporting and maintaining forms of cultural expression. Generations-old artistic genres that were barely, or even no longer practiced within their native social contexts, are renewed and repackaged for tourists who find them to be beautiful, meaningful, and "authentic." Revolutions in sound recording and electronic media such as the gramophone, microphone, cassette tape, and compact disc have led to new forms of entertainment, culminating in what may be the defining art form of the 20th century, the cinema. The role that music played for millennia as an essential vehicle for storytelling continues on screen into the 21st century, accompanying films, videos, and computer games.

MUSIC AND TOURISM

Many countries of the world promote international tourism as one of their most important sources of revenue. National boards of tourism promote their country's natural scenic beauty, sites of archeological and historic significance, and intangible cultural forms of expression. There is strong competition in the global tourism market for attracting international visitors and their hard currency. Prior to the 2020/2022 COVID-19 pandemic curtailing temporarily much of this activity, tourism generated nearly a trillion dollars annually to the global economy.[1] Unlike scenic beauty and archeological heritage, intangible cultural assets like music, dance, and theater are transient. Performance arts are living arts, and they must be taught, one generation to the next, or they are forgotten. As noted elsewhere in this textbook, many art forms that have been preserved and passed on for centuries are now in peril of disappearing. **Cultural tourism** has provided incentives to preserve music, dance, and theatrical traditions by encouraging and promoting master artists to pass on their skills and knowledge to the next generation. Presenting cultural assets for tourists' consumption creates conditions of economic viability and sustainability for traditional artists. However, this practice threatens the authenticity of once vital forms of local expression, turning them into commodities. Tourism provides a means of preserving traditional cultural forms for future generations. Yet it is a double-edged sword. It may corrupt these practices by standardizing them and dumbing them down for easy consumption by visitors who know little about the history or significance of what they are consuming.

Kecak Monkey Chant (Bali)

Kecak is a dance drama based on the ancient Hindu epic, the Ramayana. Also known as the "Monkey Chant," it is one of the highlights of a tourist's visit to the small Indonesian island of Bali. (See Map 11.2.) Performances are held regularly in temples and villages throughout the island, and daily at the 11th-century Uluwatu Temple perched on the edge of a 230-foot high cliff overlooking the ocean (Figure 15.1). As stated on the official website of Indonesia's Ministry of Tourism,

> A visit to the dramatic island of Bali will not be complete without watching some of the most captivating traditional performances the island has to offer … another dazzling performance you definitely don't want to miss is the traditional Kecak Dance.[2]

The *kecak* performance (15.1) presents a shortened version of the Ramayana epic: the demon King Ravana abducts Rama's wife Sita and holds her captive in his palace in Sri Lanka. With the help of his brother Lakshman, the Monkey King Sugriva, the Monkey General Hanuman, and his monkey army, Rama travels to Sri Lanka and fights a fierce battle. The evil Ravana is finally defeated and Rama reunites with Sita. The drama takes place outdoors at night. From fifty to one hundred or more men wearing checkered loincloths enact the army of monkeys, seated in concentric circles, swaying, and voicing interlocking "chak" and "ke-chak" sounds (Figure 15.2). Both male and female costumed dancers play the principal characters. Video 15.1 shows the white costumed Hanuman, Ravana dressed in red, and Rama fighting the demon king. Unlike other Balinese dance drama forms such as *calonarang*, *kecak* is not accompanied by a *gamelan* percussion orchestra.

While *kecak* has the appearance of a "traditional" dance drama, it was developed in the 1930s by Balinese dancer Wayan Limbak (1897–2003) in collaboration with German painter and musician Walter Spies (1895–1942) as a cultural show that would attract foreign tourists. Limbak and Spies based the performance on an indigenous sacred dance tradition, *sanghyang*. In this temple ritual, young girls became possessed by *hyang* spirits, and in a state of trance they danced for the gods to ward off disease and maintain harmony between the sacred and secular worlds. The two artists combined elements of this sacred ritual with episodes of the Ramayana epic and created a new public performance "tradition." Wayan Limbak then popularized the dance drama by touring internationally with Balinese performing groups. The tours proved highly successful, and today the modern, secular *kecak* presents a thoroughly enchanting and captivating cultural performance for its earthly spectators.

FIGURE 15.1 *Kecak* dancers at Uluwatu Temple, Bali

FIGURE 15.2 *Kecak* monkey army seated in concentric circles

Cambodian Orchestras

In Cambodia, tourism is the country's second largest industry after textiles, and the primary destination is the vast, 400-acre temple complex of Angkor Wat near the town of Siem Reap, built in the 12th century (see Map 8.1). As the center of the once powerful Khmer Empire (9th–15th centuries), Angkor Wat now attracts some 2.6 million international visitors annually.[3] Classical Khmer architecture, stone sculptures, and decorative Hindu and

Buddhist wall carvings greet the many foreign tourists that arrive in cars, buses, and motorized three-wheel taxis called *tuk-tuks*. Likewise, welcoming temple goers and visitors are the many musicians who play at the gates and interiors of the various temple sites. Daily musical performance for these artists is their livelihood; it is also an essential means to their survival. Most are victims of landmines laid during the late 20th-century decades of war, genocide, and repression: the Cambodian Civil War (1970–1975), the Khmer Regime (1975–1979), and the Vietnamese Occupation (1978–1992). During this period of war in Southeast Asia, some 10 million landmines and cluster bombs were planted in the ground by opposing forces, and some 4–6 million unexploded landmines are still there. Despite international efforts, they are still maiming and killing innocent people who inadvertently step on them in their backyards and their fields.

In 2008, ethnomusicologist Gavin Douglas encountered many disabled musicians at the various temple ruins of Angkor Wat, the Khmer Empire's last capital. One in particular was a disabled flute player, whose story Douglas relates:

> There before me is a legless man leaning against the wall. He stops playing, looks at me, smiles and waves me towards him. In broken English and French he shares his story of stepping on a landmine in the late 1970s during the devastating Khmer Rouge occupation (1975–79)… Twenty-five years later this flute player rides each day on the back of his friend's bicycle to one of many spots around the Angkor Wat area to play for temple visitors, tourists primarily, who have traveled long distances to see this magnificent wonder of the ancient world.[4]

FIGURE 15.3 Cambodian Musicians at Banteay Srei Temple

Some 40,000 amputees—one of the highest rates of physical disability in the world—now struggle to survive in modern-day Cambodia. One of the few opportunities for them to earn a living is musical performance.

In Video 15.2, an ensemble of landmine victims performs traditional Cambodian music at Banteay Srei (Citadel of Women). This 10th-century temple dedicated to the Hindu god Shiva is located in the area of Angkor, some sixteen miles northeast of the main temple group. Thirteen musicians play a variety of instruments including a crocodile-shaped, fretted zither (*takhe*), a hammered dulcimer (*khim*), a plucked "banjo," two-string bowed fiddles (*tro*), an end-blown flute (*khloy*), xylophone (*roneat*), goblet drums, and small finger cymbals. The lead musician in the center plays melodies on a leaf (Figure 15.3). At the end of each piece, the performers clap, encouraging the small audience seated and standing nearby to place a few coins in their basket and purchase their CDs. With little support from the Cambodian government, disabled artists rely on the generosity of foreign tourists. These Cambodian musicians (15.2) are providing a musical soundscape for visitors to soak in the ambiance and atmosphere of the ancient temple ruins, and are furthermore continuing a musical tradition that might otherwise die out.

Tourist Restaurants (Turkey, Ethiopia)

This video from Istanbul, Turkey, shows a Mevlevi dervish (15.3) whirling to the accompaniment of plucked zither (*qanun*) and frame drum (*bendir*) at an outdoor restaurant. Family groups and tourists wait for food service to begin in order to break the sunup-to-sundown Muslim fast of Ramadan. While the lone Mevlevi dervish at the restaurant is providing a distraction for hungry customers, whirling remains a profound sacred practice for him and for the accompanying musicians. The performance at the restaurant provides guests a "taste" of authentic culture, although exactly how to interpret the dance—as a sacred encounter with the divine or secular entertainment—is ambiguous. For the government tourism board, the whirling dervish dance is one of the most recognized intangible cultural expressions of Turkish identity, and is promoted as such. The sacred *sema* whirling ceremony was identified in 2008 as one of Turkey's contributions to UNESCO's Intangible Cultural Heritage of Humanity list. However, "many *sema* ceremonies are no longer performed in their traditional context but for tourist audiences, and have been shortened and simplified to meet commercial requirements."[5]

Totot Restaurant opened in 2001 in the Ethiopian capital, Addis Ababa. Although it caters to a local clientele, the restaurant showcases traditional Ethiopian cuisine, decor, and entertainment for visitors to the capital. Its motto is "The Future of Tradition" and its mission statement on its website reads, "Our mission is to portray the beauty of Ethiopian culture at its best to those who already know it and to those who are new to it, by offering quality services based on the customer's expectations and beyond."[6] The implication is that foreign guests are accustomed to a high level of hospitality, and may not expect to find it in an African city. In addition to native gourmet dishes and locally brewed fermented beverages, the nightly entertainment (15.4) features folk music and dances of Ethiopia's various ethnicities. The house band consists of highly skilled musicians playing the traditional instruments of the country: lyre (*krar*), the *azmari* storyteller's one-string fiddle (*masenqo*), end-blown flute (*washint*), and various small hand drums played by the dancers, along with Western drum kit. The painted backdrop for the stage is a traditional farming village of grass huts, all juxtaposed ironically with a high-tech sound system. The beauty of the performance, the savory food, and the professional ambiance all contribute to forgetting for a time that one is visiting one of the world's poorest countries.

SOUND RECORDING

Developments in music have always been inexorably linked to developments in technology. The smelting of metals, the drawing of wire, the invention of paper and printing, the design of acoustical spaces have all influenced the ways in which music is created, performed, stored, transmitted, and experienced in incalculable ways. However, technological developments over the past 150 years have had more of an impact on the way music is created and consumed than at any other time in the history of humanity. In 1877, American inventor Thomas Edison (1847–1931) created the first functional phonograph (Figure 15.4). Prior to that year, all music was heard, *and only heard*, in live musical performances. For the first time in history, Edison's machine made possible the separation of the singer from the song.

The earliest models that Edison developed and patented used a stylus to etch sound first onto tin foil then wax cylinders. There were a number of drawbacks to Edison's prototype. Only one cylinder could be recorded at a time and it held no more than two minutes of recorded sound. The playback quality was poor, and the grooves did not hold up over time. The playback devices were hand-cranked, and maintaining a constant speed was a problem. By 1900, Edison's invention had competition from a German American inventor named Emile Berliner (1851–1929). Berliner's device used flat discs of zinc coated with wax to etch sound vibrations into a spiral groove, called a "sound line" (Figure 15.5). The result was a cleaner sound and a more durable, portable, and replicable product than Edison's cylinders. From the initial recording on zinc, multiple copies could be pressed. Several technological breakthroughs happened in rapid succession that made Berliner's invention practical and marketable. By 1920, a clockwork motor was added to steady the turntable. A new material,

FIGURE 15.4 Thomas Edison and his phonograph, 1889

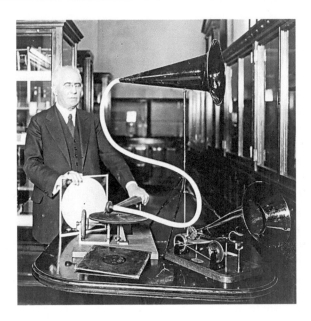

FIGURE 15.5 Emile Berliner with his original gramophone

a mixture of shellac and clay with boot black added for color, was developed by a New Jersey button manufacturer. This material would be the industry standard until the development of long-playing vinyl discs (LPs), after World War II. Berliner's flat disc had completely eclipsed Edison's wax disc technology.

Two decades of patent disputes pitted the two inventors against each other. Ironically, neither man at first realized their invention's potential for an entertainment device: recording songs for sale. Edison thought his invention had a primarily business application as a dictating machine, while Berliner imagined the machine being used to record the last words of the dying. Berliner wrote in an advertising brochure for his invention, patented as "the gramophone":

> Future generations will be able to condense into the brief space of twenty minutes the tone pictures of a lifetime – five minutes of childish prattle, five moments embalming the last feeble utterances from the death-bed. Will this not seem like holding veritable communion with immortality?[7]

In 1901, Berliner's Gramophone Company, which produced both record players and the records to play on them, changed the name of its British subsidiary to "His Master's Voice." The famous image of the dog (called Nipper) in front of a gramophone horn came from an 1898 painting by Francis Barraud that became the company's trademark (Figure 15.6). A scene from the movie *Two Sisters from Boston*, directed by Henry Koster, shows a pre-1926 acoustic recording session and uses a stand-in for Nipper to dramatize the meaning of the logo.[8]

A fortuitous meeting between Berliner and an enterprising twenty-one-year-old piano player named Fred Gaisberg (1873–1951) put the recording and marketing of songs at the forefront of a new global industry. Gaisberg (Figure 15.7) had a talent for locating singers whose voices would work with the new technology. In the first decade of the 20th century, Gaisberg traveled throughout the world recording local artists. The business model was to send the master discs back to facilities in the United States and Europe for pressing, then

FIGURE 15.6 "His Master's Voice" logo

FIGURE 15.7 Fred Gaisberg with Edward Elgar (center) and Yehudi Menuhin (right), 1932

marketing the records back to the singers' home countries. The playback devices, Berliner's gramophones, were manufactured in Europe and North America, and exported to India, China, Russia, Southeast Asia, and Latin America; indeed, worldwide.

Music thereafter became preservable and portable, and it could be bought and sold as a commodity like a pair of shoes. In 1903, an entire Verdi opera was recorded on forty discs, and by the end of the first decade of the 20th century, the music recording industry was a going concern worldwide. Phonographs and records became common household items by World War I, at least for the upper classes.

By the mid-20th century, these devices were in living rooms throughout the world. The term "gramophone" became obsolete, replaced by "record player." Technological advances such as preamps, amplifiers, and internal speakers accommodating both lower and higher frequencies (known respectively as woofer and tweeter) greatly increased signal-to-noise ratio and general fidelity. "Audiophile" hobbyists invested large sums of money in home systems that sought to capture the ambience of concert halls. Just as the playback systems became more and more sophisticated, recording stars of every possible genre provided musical material. The recording engineer became a crucial arbiter for the industry, making artistic decisions that were once made by the artists themselves.

Along with these developments, two other parallel technologies would have an enormous impact shaping musical experiences in the 20th century: radio and cinema. In 1910, Lee de Forest, the American inventor of the vacuum tube, broadcast the Italian tenor Enrico Caruso from the stage of the Metropolitan Opera House in New York City to demonstrate the possibility of using radio for entertainment purposes. The history of modern commercial radio began with the broadcast of the 1920 presidential election results over a Pittsburgh HAM (amateur) radio network. Music from phonograph records was played into the microphone between announcements.

Since the early 20th century, the use of electronic amplification in performance, radio broadcast, and recording playback has radically changed the way singers project their voices. Before sound amplification, popular singers employed vocal techniques much like those of opera singers to project their voices in theaters, and they then used these same voices for singing over the radio. Al Jolson (15.5) (1886–1950), the first to sing in a sound feature film, and Ethel Merman (15.6) (1908–1984), who made a career in the Broadway theater, retained this style of singing. But a few early pioneers of broadcasting, like Bing Crosby (15.7) (1903–1977) and Frank Sinatra (1915–1998), learned how to use the microphone to produce a soft, intimate style of singing that made millions of Americans feel that the

FIGURE 15.8 Bing Crosby in 1942

"**crooners**," as they were called, were singing directly to them in the intimacy of their homes (Figure 15.8). Singers no longer had to fill acoustical spaces with their voices; the microphone and loudspeaker did the job for them.

Through the history of recording technology, recording and playback devices have steadily decreased in size and increased in storage capacity and portability. A typical MP3 player like the iPod or mobile phone can hold an entire library of thousands of songs, and audio files (MP3, M4A, wav, etc.) can be sent almost instantaneously around the world via the internet. Large online music stores like Amazon Music, Bandcamp, eMusic, HDtracks, and iTunes Store carry downloadable recordings from every continent in the world, and music streaming services such as Spotify and Pandora deliver and recommend audio tracks to millions of users on multiple media devices. The amount and variety of music available to the average music consumer is simply unimaginable compared to a generation ago. Most of these musical experiences, however, involve consumption rather than creation; and most are mediated, that is, an electronic technology separates and stands between the music maker and the listener. Many young people have had limited experience with the excitement and immediacy of live music performance; and while music accompanies many of their daily activities—driving, walking, eating, studying, exercising—they do not enjoy the satisfaction of playing an instrument, singing in a choir, or attending a live concert.

FILM

A new form of mass entertainment grew from the invention of the movie camera, which was as revolutionary as the invention of the printing press in the 1450s. From the beginning of the history of motion pictures in the 1890s, music has formed an integral part of the film medium and its history. During the silent film era, live musicians improvised or performed written music to accompany the action, cuing the audience's emotional responses and providing continuity to the succession of images. By the 1920s, musicians were routinely employed by movie theaters, and the music became a sophisticated blend of classical and popular styles interspersed with newly composed and improvised interludes all coordinated with the action on screen. When a studio released a feature film, it sometimes included sheet music notation for musicians to provide a soundtrack. For example, the great American comedian of the silent film era, Charlie Chaplin (1889–1977), composed music scores to accompany all of his silent comedies.

Hollywood (USA)

The first "talkie" with synchronized dialogue was the Warner Brothers' film *The Jazz Singer*, released in 1927, starring Al Jolson (Figure 15.9). Since then, film music composition, sound technology, and cinematic development have been intimately linked. Lavish Hollywood movie musicals date from the late 1930s following the success of *The Wizard of Oz* (1939), with music and lyrics by Harold Arlen (1905–1986). At around the same time, the Walt Disney studios were making full-length animated feature films such as *Snow White and the Seven Dwarfs* (1937) and *Pinocchio* (1940), which incorporated songs that became immensely popular. From the 1950s, cinema versions of Broadway musicals brought this distinctly urban form of entertainment out to rural communities, with such successful movies as *South Pacific*

FIGURE 15.9 Poster for the first sound feature film, *The Jazz Singer* (1927)

(1958), *West Side Story* (1961), and *My Fair Lady* (1964); and more recently *Chicago* (2002), *Phantom of the Opera* (2004), and *Hamilton* (2020). The large motion picture studios of southern California employed symphony orchestras and European-trained composers who often wrote in the style of grand opera to accompany sweeping sagas like *Gone with the Wind* (1939) and Biblical epics like *The Ten Commandments* (1956) and *Ben Hur* (1959). The 1981 sports drama *Chariots of Fire* sent shock waves through the film music industry when the composer Vangelis created the complete score on a synthesizer, bypassing the entire musical establishment. Since that historic milestone, many film scores have been produced digitally, although the symphony orchestra has continued to be a mainstay. Indeed, the most successful film composer of our time is John Williams (b. 1932) who wrote fully orchestrated scores in the Hollywood epic tradition for *Star Wars*, *Superman*, *Jaws*, *Schindler's List*, and the first three *Harry Potter* movies. Popular music styles have also been well represented in film music, including jazz (*Pink Panther*), rock and roll (*Jailhouse Rock*, *School of Rock*, and *Hard Day's Night*), disco (*Saturday Night Fever*), country (*Coal Miner's Daughter*), old timey (*O Brother, Where Art Thou?*), and hip-hop (*Do the Right Thing*), to name a few.

Because music carries and conveys broad and powerful meanings, is richly associative, and evokes deep emotional responses, film viewers have come to rely on musical soundtracks in complex ways to make sense out of the cinematic experience. The producer, director, and film score composer must work together to coordinate the cinematic, narrative, and musical elements of a film. They use several musical strategies to enhance audience engagement with the story. These include:

Diegetic and non-diegetic music
Marker of locale
Establishment of mood
Leitmotif
Sheer entertainment value
Quotation
Foreshadowing

These strategies are discussed below along with examples from the Hollywood film industry.

Film music is categorized as either ***diegetic***, in which the music and musicians are part of the narrative itself, or ***non-diegetic***, in which the audience understands that the characters neither see the musicians nor hear the music. The purpose of non-diegetic music is clearly supplemental to the narrative, like the score for *Harry Potter* films or music that runs during a film's title and credits. Sometimes background music has an ambiguous source and function. Mira Nair's film *Mississippi Masala* (1991), with music directed by L. Subramaniam, tells the story of an East Indian immigrant family living in Greenwood, Mississippi. Before moving to the American South, they lived in Uganda, East Africa, where the husband Jay had been a successful lawyer and businessman. The family was caught up in a historical event in 1971, when the ruling tyrant, Idi Amin, gave all Indian and Pakistani residents ninety days to leave the country. Jay's family lost nearly everything, and had to start over again as proprietors of a liquor store. At the end of the film, Jay has returned to Uganda alone fifteen years later to pursue a lawsuit, unsuccessfully as it happens. As film viewers see him sadly inspecting the ruins of his African home, they hear a blues harmonica in the soundtrack. The scene cuts to his wife in their liquor store in Mississippi reading a letter from him. The camera pans around the store and we see that one of the locals in the shop is actually playing the music. The scene switches back to Africa while the blues music continues, thus having the status of both diegetic music in Mississippi and non-diegetic in Uganda. The scene ends with Jay turning his back on the ruined past and walking into the center of Kampala where a street party is going on. In the soundtrack, the African dance music replaces the Mississippi harmonica. The diegetic music in this scene is thus both part of the narrative and part of the means by which the narrative is conveyed to the audience. The blues symbolizes Jay's feelings of nostalgia for his adopted home, and the Ugandan dance music symbolizes the beautiful but now alien land he must leave forever. The music serves both as a *marker of locale* (the blues identifying Mississippi and the dance music, Uganda), and as an emotional cue (the blues expressing Jay's resignation and acceptance, the African dance music a festive joy that doesn't include him).

In Steven Spielberg's *Jaws* (1975), composer John Williams (Figure 15.10) created the "Shark Theme," an alternating two-note pattern that performs several functions simultaneously. It is used in the film to evoke terror, to *establish the mood* of horror and suspense, and to propel the sense of dramatic time accelerating. It also functions as a ***leitmotif***, a musical/dramatic technique associated with German opera composer Richard Wagner. This technique involves a short musical theme or phrase that consistently represents or symbolizes a character, place, object, or recurring idea in the plot. Throughout the movie, the theme's recurrence coincides with the presence of hidden danger. When the audience hears the repeating two-note theme it knows the killer shark is in the vicinity, even when the on-screen characters do not. The accelerating rhythm and increase in volume both heighten the dramatic tension and locate the characters and situation in relationship to the imminent danger: the louder and faster the music, the nearer the characters are to calamity. The musical build-up, which

FIGURE 15.10 John Williams conducts at the Hollywood Bowl, 2009

parallels the dramatic build-up, also triggers increasing tension, dread, and excitement in the viewers, and the musical and dramatic climax occur simultaneously. Composers of horror movie music are masterful at evoking suspense and terror in a scene that would otherwise be experienced as neutral. Perhaps the most famous example of this is in Alfred Hitchcock's *Psycho* (1960) in which screaming violins accompany the horrific "shower scene."

John Williams also composed the music for the first six films in the *Star Wars* series. In the bar scene in George Lucas' first *Star Wars* film (1977), a decidedly non-human quartet plays an almost recognizable version of Dixieland jazz. The bar "musicians" create and sustain the tawdry honky-tonk atmosphere of the space saloon where Ben (Obi-Wan) Kenobi and Luke Skywalker are meeting smuggler Han Solo for the first time to discuss their spaceship mission to the planet Alderaan. The music is diegetic; it does not underscore for the theater audience the emotional charge of the drama unfolding at the bar in the manner of non-diegetic music (like the Jaws example). In fact, the musical score only responds to the action when Obi-Wan, defending his charge Luke Skywalker, severs the arm of an attacker. At this climactic moment, the music stops because the musicians are temporarily distracted from their music making. But only momentarily, for soon they strike up the tune again, the violent exchange being nothing terribly out of the ordinary in this corner of the galaxy! Despite its grizzly ending, the scene serves as comic relief and the music in the saloon provides *sheer entertainment value* not only for the space travelers but for the cinema audience as well.

Perhaps the most poignant scene in *The Shawshank Redemption* (1994, directed by Frank Darabont) occurs when Andy Dufresne, serving two life sentences at a state prison in Maine for murders he did not commit, locks himself in the warden's office. There, he plays a recording of a duet from Mozart's opera *The Marriage of Figaro* over the public address system. The soaring women's voices coming from the loudspeakers bring the entire Shawshank Prison population to a standstill, stunned by this sudden interruption of intense musical expression. This *quotation* of previously composed music in Thomas Newman's film score is the cinematic equivalent of quoted text or literary allusion in a book. For a brief moment, the sublime music allows the prisoners to experience an inner escape, a freedom from the pain and suffering of their incarceration, which is only later articulated verbally by Andy's friend Red in a voiceover:

> I have no idea to this day what those two Italian ladies were singing about. Truth is, I don't want to know. Some things are best left unsaid. I'd like to think they were singing about something so beautiful, it can't be expressed in words, and makes your heart ache because of it. I tell you, those voices soared higher and farther than anybody in a gray place dares to dream. It was like some beautiful bird flapped into our drab little cage and made those walls dissolve away, and for the briefest of moments, every last man in Shawshank felt free.

The musical quotation enhances the emotional drama, *foreshadowing* both for the audience and for Andy himself, Andy's own eventual escape from Shawshank. Music often serves this function in cinema, telegraphing to the audience information not available to the characters on the screen, such as impending danger or the resolution of a conflict. It also plays a significant non-diegetic role in deepening the audience's understanding of the prisoners' psychological state through the startling juxtaposition of their bleak prospects and surroundings with Mozart's transcendent melody, symbolizing freedom.

There have been many movies made about musicians such as *Amadeus* (Mozart), *Immortal Beloved* (Beethoven), *Coal Miner's Daughter* (Loretta Lynn), *Sweet Dreams* (Patsy Cline), *Bird* (Charlie Parker), *The Last Waltz* (The Band), *Ray* (Ray Charles), *Walk the Line* (Johnny Cash), *Bohemian Rhapsody* (Freddie Mercury), and *Yesterday* (The Beatles), as well as documentaries on music festivals like Monterey Pop and Woodstock. The relationship between music and film has been one of intense interaction and parallel development. Many of the greatest composers of the 20th century composed for films, including Leonard Bernstein, Aaron Copland, Dmitri Shostakovich, Sergei Prokofiev, Johnny Mercer, and Lennon and McCartney. Recently symphony orchestras have given concert performances of film scores, seeking to broaden their audience base. Film songs enjoy radio play, often score highly on the "charts," and are put on playlists. The Academy of Motion Picture Arts and Sciences has given annual awards (Oscars) for Best Original Score and Best Original Song since 1934.

Bollywood (India)

The first motion picture was filmed by the Lumière Brothers of France in 1894, and within twenty years the technology of cinema had spread throughout the world. By the first decades of the 20th century, film studios and theaters had opened on every continent. Pioneering filmmakers adapted the new medium to different cultures and social contexts with unique conventions and trajectories of development. India is one of the largest film industries in the world, producing movies in multiple regional languages such as Tamil, Telugu, Bengali, Marathi, and Hindi. Bollywood refers to the Hindi film industry, a portmanteau of the words "Bombay" (the industry's center, now called Mumbai) and "Hollywood," and India's regional cinemas have followed suit: Kollywood (Tamil), Mollywood (Marathi), and Tollywood (both Telugu and West Bengali), for example (see Map 8.3). While Hindi-language films account for less than 15% of India's total, they are enormously popular and influential both in India and abroad, especially in the Indian diaspora and increasingly among non-Indian audiences. Bollywood films are typically three-hour-long musical extravaganzas that blend melodrama, comedy, violence, action, and romance. Into this eclectic mix are woven at least five or six songs and two or more choreographed dance numbers. A Bollywood film without songs and dances is as rare as a Hollywood film without a music soundtrack. The inclusion of songs and dances dates from the very first Hindi sound film in 1931, *Alam Ara* ("Light of the World"). This practice is rooted in the musical character of Indian theater itself, from the ancient Sanskrit dramas of the early centuries CE to the performances of India's epic tales (the *Mahabharata* and *Ramayana*), as well as regional folk theaters.

With few exceptions, Indian film songs are recorded by professional **playback singers** (ghost singers). These playback artists pre-record the songs in sound studios, and film actors and actresses lip-synch the song lyrics during filming. Throughout the history of Indian sound cinema, a relatively small number of playback singers have dominated the scene, each recording up to five or more songs per day. Indian audiences from the 1940s and 1950s onwards came to love the singing voices of Lata Mangeshkar, Asha Bhosle, Mohammed Rafi, Mukesh, Kishore Kumar, and others, which they heard time and again from the mouths of their favorite actors and actresses on-screen. Both Lata Mangeshkar and her sister Asha Bhosle have been recognized in the Guinness Book of World Records at different times for having recorded more songs than any other artist in music history.

Film songs have not only played an essential role in the film narrative, developing or commenting on the plot, but they became India's pop music, reaching audiences beyond the cinema via recordings, radio, and television. In the "golden age" of Hindi cinema (1950s–1960s), films such as *Awara* ("Tramp"), *Sri 420* ("Mr. 420"), *Jhanak Jhanak Pyal Baje* ("The Ankle Bells Jingle"), *Pyaasa* ("Thirst"), *Mother India*, and *Mughal-e-Azam* ("Mughal Emperor") were enormously successful in large part due to the popularity of their songs. These had simple, memorable melodies, catchy rhythms, and were accompanied by large studio orchestras mixing Indian and Western instruments. In the 1970s and 1980s, the trend for historical and romantic dramas of earlier decades gave way to action thrillers and social dramas, such as *Zanjeer* ("Chains"), *Sholay* ("Flames"), and *Pakeezah* ("Pure"). These films continued the practice of including mandatory songs and dance numbers. A notable, award-winning film, *Amar, Akbar, Anthony* (1977), represents a common theme in Hindi cinema of religious and ethnic harmony in an often fractious society. The narrative, concerning three brothers separated in childhood and raised as a Hindu, a Muslim, and a Christian respectively, provided the music director team Laxmikant-Pyarelal with the opportunity for a diverse musical score referencing the three religious traditions. In general, however, popular music styles such as disco pervaded Bollywood film songs and dances of these two decades. Blockbuster films of more recent years have likewise drawn on new music and dance forms, from hip-hop and rap to breakdancing. Among the most successful movies of the 1990s and 2000s were *Hum Aapke Hain Koun!* ("Who am I to You!" 1994), *Dilwale Dulhania Le Jayenge* ("The Brave-hearted will Take Away the Bride," 1995), *Lagaan* ("Land Tax," 2001), *Devdas* (2002), and *3 Idiots* (2009). Bollywood producers release film songs into the music market prior to a movie's

FIGURE 15.11 Bollywood actor Hrithik Roshan dancing at the 15th International Indian Film Academy Awards, Tampa, Florida, 2014

release as promotional material, and music sales serve to enhance box-office sales. In turn, a successful film will guarantee increased sales of its popular songs (Figure 15.11).

A majority of Hindi film songs over the decades have followed a formulaic structure consisting of a vocal or instrumental introduction, alternating refrain and verses, and instrumental breaks. For variety and to serve the needs of the film narrative, composers have occasionally produced film versions of traditional Indian vocal genres such as film *qawwalis* and film *ghazals*. These subgenres reference the traditional forms but bear only minimal resemblance to them in terms of musical style or context. *Mughal-E-Azam* ("Emperor of the Mughals," 1960) and *Daulat* ("Wealth," 1982), for example, feature female *qawwali* groups, whereas Sufi *qawwali* parties are traditionally all-male. The late, renowned *qawwali* singer Ustad Nusrat Fateh Ali Khan composed for and acted in several Bollywood productions. In the film *Aur Pyaar Ho Gaya* ("And Love Happened," 1997), Khan performs in a wedding scene that incorporates exuberant Bollywood-style dance choreography. Surrounded by a seated male *qawwali* group playing harmoniums and hand-clapping, Khan's ornamented solo vocal lines alternate not with the expected *qawwali* chorus but with playback singers who ghost sing for the film hero and heroine.[9] The scene gives the impression of a *qawwali* performance, for the secular wedding celebration and the Bollywood-style playback singing bely its traditional character. Yet the cinematic adaptation stamps this film music as creative, inventive, and thoroughly Indian. Film music composers have continued to develop new forms of film *qawwali*, including techno and club qawwali.[10]

Bollywood songs and films provide entertainment for hundreds of millions of Indian viewers and listeners, both rural and urban. A parallel cinema arose in India in the mid-20th century, producing small-budget, serious art films for a more discerning audience. Satyajit

Ray (1921–1992) was a leading filmmaker in this movement, who explored in his films and documentaries such topics as India's Hindu society and its colonial history. Unlike Bollywood productions for mass audiences, these art films employed more classical soundtracks, generally without songs. For Satyajit Ray's highly acclaimed Bengali films, the *Apu Trilogy* (1955–1959), the director worked closely with Pandit Ravi Shankar who composed the scores based on classical ragas and Bengali folk melodies. In 1958 Ray worked with another great Indian sitar player, Ustad Vilayat Khan (1928–2004), on the classical score for his film *Jalsagar* (The Music Room).

Many countries have multiple film industries, since they have multilingual societies. Nigeria now has the largest film industry in the world (called Nollywood) in terms of movies produced. Films are made in Yoruba, Hausa, Igbo, and Edo languages for regional audiences. Yet the majority of Nollywood films are produced in English, and their popularity has spread throughout Africa. Besides the government, the Nigerian motion picture industry is the largest employer in the country. It provides, as elsewhere in the world, employment for many musicians, as the hundreds of movies made each year require musical soundtracks to support the narrative.

Already by the end of the 20th century, more than a hundred countries had established motion picture industries, and since the initiation of the American Academy Awards "Foreign Language Film" category in 1956 (now known as the International Feature Film Oscar), submissions from sixty-one countries have been nominated. In the 2022 Oscar competition, eighty-nine countries from every part of the world have submitted entries.[11] While COVID-19 created severe hardships for the traditional movie theater industry, the digital revolution in streaming media arrived globally just in time to maintain the viability of cinema until the pandemic is under control.

CONCLUSION

The musical soundscape of human life has been radically altered since the beginning of the 20th century by technological innovations and urbanization. Rapid social change continues into the 21st century. Attending a movie, for example, was once a public, social event, like going to the opera, ballet, theater, or even attending a religious ritual. The phenomenon of watching a movie in solitude on a tablet or smartphone is quite recent. While music has never been more available, it has become as never before a consumer good rather than a participatory activity. Forms of musical expression passed down through generations are being forgotten in favor of popular music ephemera that are mass-produced in urban studios. Unprecedented disruptions in the world's population have jeopardized many previously thriving musical practices. A September 2021 headline in the Associated Press News reads, "Under Taliban, thriving Afghan music scene heads to silence." Instruments are being smashed by soldiers guarding checkpoints there, wedding musicians are selling their furniture to survive, while seeking ways to leave the country.[12] Since early 2020, the COVID-19 pandemic has further eroded genres of live music and artistic traditions that date back generations. The livelihood of professional musicians as well as actors, dancers, and other performing artists throughout the world has been severely diminished. The long-term impacts of cultural transformation and the global pandemic are unknown. It may be that the spiritual health of the planet depends in no small part on its musical health.

Bo Nyed (Figure 15.12) is a middle-aged Tibetan farmer and herder who, in a 2009 interview with a member of the Plateau Music Project, described these radical changes in patterns of musical behavior as follows:

> At that time (1940–1960s) we sang almost constantly as we harvested. We had different songs for every kind of work, and sang songs from morning to night. Even if someone wanted to chase a girl, they needed to sing a love song to show their emotion and never told someone they loved them directly. For example, if you had a boyfriend who was very far away from you, he would send a song to tell you he was missing you or something. He would sing that song to a messenger and the messenger would relay that song to someone else. Eventually the girl would get the message and reply in the same way. They used song messages to keep in touch. But now, you cannot see anyone singing these songs to each other. People like pop songs most. Young people prefer to sing modern songs. No one sings local songs anymore; instead they imitate everything they see on TV and in movies. In the past, we were so happy to sing those songs. We didn't get tired when we sang them as we worked. We worked from morning to evening and we sang from morning to evening. Some years ago, a local priest asked people if there was anyone who could sing *mgur ma* [a long threshing song]. [I said,] "I sing *mgur ma* the whole day while I cut grass. I'm the only one left who can sing it. Not even my own daughter wants to learn *mgur ma* from me. I never forced her to learn. I never sing modern songs. I have never tried and I never want to. I don't like them at all. My mother really liked to sing. Now everyone is silent; they don't like to sing regardless of where they are and what they are doing. In the past we sang songs wherever we went.[13]

FIGURE 15.12 Bo Nyed, Tibetan singer-farmer, in 2009

The situation she describes is true throughout the world. Few places have been left untouched by the digital revolution in musical sound. This poignant account is indicative of a rapidly transforming world, impoverished by cultural loss while intoxicated with the expanding possibilities for music innovation that the new technologies promise.

In December 1968, when an American astronaut first photographed the planet Earth from outer space and the photo appeared on the cover of LIFE magazine, humans were suddenly able to envision the world as a single unified whole (Figure 15.13). This image became a symbol of unity and interdependence among all people. The subsequent period of history saw the development of the internet giving the symbolic power of the image an experiential framework as millions and then billions of people connected to each other through social media sites. Never before have people been more aware of the forces, beliefs, and institutions that both unite us and divide us, providing hope in a self-sustaining future world at peace, or threatening mutual destruction. Music, a mode of expression and communication common to all peoples, can be a source of understanding and communion across the great divides.

This text has demonstrated how music is integral to all aspects of our lives as an indispensable means of expressing who we are, where we are, what we are, what we believe, what we feel, and sharing these expressions with others. The text explores the functions, exalted and mundane, that music serves. It presents different musical styles that are intimately connected with the ways people project their identities and values. In religious contexts, we

FIGURE 15.13 Earth from 22,000 miles in space, with moon visible

have examined how music serves as a way of marking out the sacred from the everyday, celebrating and accessing higher powers, and binding individuals and groups together in shared experiences of heightened emotion. Music is the soundtrack of our social lives as we dine, shop, court, and seek entertainment and companionship. Living at a time when technological, economic, and cultural systems are integrated across the globe, we each have a responsibility to learn more about the world we share. Perhaps through understanding each other's music we can better understand each other. It was, after all, to a musical metaphor that Abraham Lincoln turned when closing his First Inaugural Address in 1861 at another perilous turning point, the outset of the American Civil War:

> We are not enemies, but friends. We must not be enemies. Though passion may have strained, it must not break our bonds of affection. The mystic chords of memory, stretching from every battlefield and patriot grave to every living heart and hearthstone all over this broad land, will yet swell the chorus of the Union when again touched, as surely they will be, by the better angels of our nature.

KEY TERMS AND CONCEPTS

Bollywood	Leitmotif
Commodification of Music	Marker of Locale
Crooners	Mass Entertainment
Cultural Tourism	Mediated Musical Experience
Diegetic and Non-Diegetic Music	Nollywood
Digital Sound Technology	Playback Singer
Establishment of Mood	Quotation
Foreshadowing	Sheer Entertainment Value
Gramophone	Sound Recording
"His Master's Voice"	"Talkie"
Hollywood	World Cinema

THINKING ABOUT MUSIC

1   Consider the *kecak* dance and the ensemble of Cambodian amputees. To what extent are these "authentic" cultural expressions, and to what extent are they not? What is at stake and to whom does this matter?

2   Explain in your own words the sentence: "For the first time in history, Edison's machine made possible the separation of the singer from the song." How do you think this impacts the ways people experience music today as compared with several generations ago? What are the advantages brought about by the technologies that derive from Edison's original invention? What are the disadvantages?

3   Compare your own experience of live music (either as participant or audience) with your experience of mediated music (via radio, smartphone, etc.). How are they similar? How are they different? What have the musical technologies of the 20th and 21st centuries added to the experience of music, and what might they have taken away from it?

4   Define in your own words the strategies used by film music composers: diegetic and non-diegetic music, marker of locale, establishment of mood, leitmotif, sheer entertainment value, quotation, and foreshadowing. Then watch one of your favorite films. Choose three strategies used in the film score. How does your chosen movie's soundtrack fulfill them? Describe a specific scene that exemplifies each strategy.

5   Imagine you are writing the screenplay for a movie about your own life, and you have been asked to suggest specific songs for the soundtrack. Choose a total of at least three songs. Why does each song you have chosen fit a particular stage of your life (infant, child, teenager, college student, etc.)? What information about you will each song reveal to the film audience that the script alone would not provide?

6   There are many Bollywood movies on YouTube and other streaming sources. Find one mentioned here in Chapter 15 and watch it. Describe the song and dance numbers. What, if anything, does each add to the narrative?

7   Consider Friedrich Nietzsche's words, "Without music, life would be a mistake." How do these words relate to your own life? What does music contribute to your wellbeing, to your social and/or spiritual life, and to the ways you bond with others?

NOTES

1   Soojung Kim, Michelle Whitford, and Charles Arcodia, "Development of Intangible Cultural Heritage as a Sustainable Tourism Resource: The Intangible Cultural Heritage Practitioners' Perspectives," *Journal of Heritage Tourism*, 14/5–6 (2019), 422–435.

2   "The Dramatic Kecak Dance: Episode taken from the Ramayana Epic Poem," *Wonderful Indonesia*, official website of the Ministry of Tourism, Republic of Indonesia, https://www.indonesia.travel/sa/en/destinations/bali-nusa-tenggara/ubud/kecak-dance.

3   "Angkor Hosts 2.6M Visitors," *The Phnom Penh Post*, January 2, 2019. During the COVID-19 pandemic, however, tourism in Cambodia was severely impacted and the number of visitors to Angkor Wat dropped sharply.

4   Gavin Douglas, *Music in Mainland Southeast Asia: Experiencing Music, Expressing Culture* (New York: Oxford University Press, 2010), 3–4.

5   Mevlevi Sema Ceremony, UNESCO Intangible Cultural Heritage, https://ich.unesco.org/en/RL/mevlevi-sema-ceremony-00100.

6   Totot Restaurant, Addis Ababa, Mission Statement, http://www.totottraditionalrestaurant.com/about.

7   Library of Congress "Emile Berliner Collection," https://www.loc.gov/item/berl0190/.

8   Scene from *Two Sisters from Boston*, directed by Henry Koster (RCA Victor: HMV, 1946), https://www.youtube.com/watch?v=-cqnATSWX6I&t=1s&ab_channel=GracevilleMN.

9 Nusrat Fateh Ali Khan Singing *"Koi Jaane Koi Na Jaane"* from *Aur Pyaar Ho Gaya* (1997), in a Bollywood version of *qawwali*, with playback singers Anuradha Paudwal and Udit Narayan recording for the film heroine and hero, Aishwarya Rai and Bobby Deol, https://www.youtube.com/watch?v=tnrgt3wWZ6Q&ab_channel=saraialamgirPRINCE.

10 The Bollywood film songs referenced in this case study are all available and easily accessible online at video sites such as YouTube.

11 Ben Dalton and Mona Tabbara, "Oscars Best International Feature 2022: All the Films Submitted So Far," *ScreenDaily.com*, November 11, 2021, https://www.screendaily.com/news/oscars-2022-china-selects-zhang-yimous-cliff-walkers/5163079.article.

12 Bernat Armangue, "Under Taliban Thriving Afghan Music Scene Heads to Silence," *AP News*, September 25, 2021, https://apnews.com/article/entertainment-middle-east-music-arts-and-entertainment-afghanistan-a2ac1095df0568387d6cee15eb82a3b5.

13 Interview transcript, written and translated by interviewer Dawa Torbert.

Glossary

A cappella: (Literally, "in the style of the chapel.") The term refers to a choir performing without instrumental accompaniment.

***Adhan*:**   Muslim "Call to Prayer." Heard five times a day in Islamic countries of the Middle East and elsewhere.

Aerophone: Sachs-Hornbostel category of musical instruments comprising those that produce sound primarily from a vibrating body of air, usually in a tube.

Aesthetic: The comprehension of a phenomenon based upon perception or appreciation of its sensual form and characteristics. Often used in association with the contemplation of beauty or works of art.

Afrikaner: South African of Dutch, French, or German descent.

Afropop: African popular music as it is presented and marketed in Europe and North America. Term popularized by the National Public Radio program "Afropop World-wide," produced by Sean Barlow and launched in 1988.

Amateur: Musicians who practice their art for the love of it.

Analysis: Mode of understanding based on dividing a whole phenomenon into its component parts.

Anti-structural ritual: Type of ritual event that celebrates the temporary suspension of rules of decorum and the overthrow of social categories and hierarchies in favor of egalitarianism and anarchy.

Apartheid: System of legalized separation of races in the Republic of South Africa from 1948 to 1994.

Aria: In European opera, a sustained vocal solo for a single character.

***Asik*:**   Turkish storyteller-singer.

Assimilation: Process by which immigrants give up the cultural identity of their native country and adopt the language, dress, customs, etc. of their new homeland.

***Aum*:**   Sacred syllable repeated in Hindu and Buddhist meditation practices, said to represent the original vibration of sound in the creation of the universe. Sometimes used as an equivalent term for "God."

***Aum, mani padme hum*:**   Tibetan Buddhist prayer (*mantra*) that invokes the Buddha of compassion, Avalokiteshvara.

Avant-garde: (Literally, "forward guard.") Most innovative artistic movement, usually associated with 20th-century Modernism.

***Avaz*:**   Persian (Iranian) classical vocal form in free rhythm.

***Axis mundi*:**   (Literally, "axis of the world.") World center or connection between earth and heaven.

Azmari: Ethiopian traditional storyteller, praise singer, or musician-entertainer.

Bagpipes: Type of aerophone in which single- or double-reed pipes are connected to a bladder or bag in order to produce a continuous airflow. Instruments are outfitted with both a melody chanter and one or more drone pipes. The bag is inflated either with a mouth pipe or with bellows.

Baile: Dance party in a Spanish-speaking country or community.

Baithak gana: (Literally, "seated music.") Song genre of the Hindustani (Asian Indian) community in Suriname, South America.

Ballad opera: 18th-century theatrical entertainment in England that appealed to the middle classes, with familiar tunes and spoken dialogue. Distinguished from grand opera with its sophisticated, newly composed melodies and sung dialogue.

Bandoneon: Button accordion; primary instrument in the Argentine tango orchestra. Player of the instrument is known as a *bandoneonista*.

Bar mitzvah: Coming-of-age ritual for Jewish boys. Comparable ritual for Jewish girls called bat mitzvah.

Baraka: Sufi term for "blessing"; a beneficent emanation of blessings and grace from God.

Bard: General term in English for epic narrator, storyteller, or poet-singer.

Bateria: The rhythm or percussion section of a Brazilian samba school ensemble.

Baul: Religious sect from Bengal, NE India, for whom song is a direct path to divine union.

Bell: Subcategory of idiophone consisting of a resonant, cup-shaped body struck either by an internal, suspended clapper or external striker or hammer.

Bhajan: Hindu devotional song.

Bhakti: Sanskrit concept of devotion in Hinduism, often expressed through song and dance.

Bharatanatyam: South Indian classical dance genre, perhaps the oldest form of dance in India, that provided a model for later genres such as Odissi and Kuchipudi.

Bhava: Sanskrit term for feeling or emotion; transmitted through the gestures and facial expressions of Indian artists.

Bhopa: Narrator-priest of Rajasthan who performs the Epic of Pabuji—a regional deity—and its associated rituals.

Biomusicology: The study of music in relationship to the natural world, particularly concerned with the ways animals and birds make and use sound.

Bira: Ritual of the Shona people of Zimbabwe involving music, dance, and spirit possession.

Black Atlantic: Shared cultural experience for people of African descent in Europe, North America, and the Caribbean that transcends national borders.

Black Lives Matter: Social movement from 2016 seeking social justice for African Americans; in response to police brutality.

Blocos: Street bands in cities and towns of Brazil associated with Carnival celebrations.

Bodhisattva: In Tibetan Buddhism, beings who have postponed enlightenment in order to help others reach this state through the bodhisattva's compassion. A famous example is Avalokiteshvara, known as Guanyin in China.

Bollywood: Hindi-language film industry based in Mumbai, India—the largest film-producing nation in the world. The term is a combination of Bombay (former name of Mumbai) and Hollywood, center of the American film industry.

Brahmin: Member of hereditary Hindu priestly caste.

Bunraku: Japanese puppet theater originating in 16th-century Edo (Tokyo).

Busker: Street musician who performs and entertains for donations.

Calendrical rituals: Sacred or secular celebrations that recur each year on the same date. Often associated with agricultural cycles or religious feast days.

Call and response: Mode of group singing in which parts alternate between a solo leader and a group response. Used in many ritual circumstances, and characteristic of much sub-Saharan African vocal music.

Calligraphy: Art of decorative writing, as in illuminated sacred manuscripts.

Calonarang: Ritual drama in Bali, Indonesia, that pits the forces of light, personified by the sacred lion Barong, against the witch Rangda, personification of darkness. Their battles, staged in temple courtyards and accompanied by a *gamelan* ensemble, are always fought to an inconclusive end.

Calypso: Afro-Caribbean song genre of Trinidad and Tobago originating in the early 20th century, with roots in West Africa and brought to the New World by slaves imported by French planters. Calypsonians were the most reliable source of news and commentary, through their topical and satirical song lyrics. Hybridized forms include *soca* (soul calypso), *rapso* (rap and calypso), and *chutney soca* (Indo-Trinidadian soul calypso).

Camerata: Group of Florentine intellectuals who met in the home of Count Giovanni de' Bardi to discuss philosophical and aesthetic issues in the late 16th century that led to reforms of contemporary Italian theater, based on their understanding of Classical Greek theater, and in turn to the invention of Italian opera.

Camposino: Spanish for "rural peasant." During the *Nueva Canción* movement in Latin America (1960s–1980s), musicians sang in support of oppressed and marginalized agricultural laborers.

Canboulay: Nighttime festivities during Trinidadian Carnival involving the rowdy and satirical re-enactment of sugarcane field fire brigade procedures.

Candomblé: Afro-Brazilian religion based on worship of Yoruba (West African) deities and frequently involving spirit possession.

Cantillation: Ritual chanting or vocalization of sacred texts using musical elements like melodic contour and meter.

Capoeira: Martial art originating in southwestern Africa and brought to Brazil by slaves from Angola. Part dance, part fighting strategy, *capoeira* is accompanied by a musical bow called *berimbau*.

Carnatic: South Indian classical music tradition based on the elaboration of a repertoire of Hindu religious songs primarily composed by three musicians in the early 19th century: Tyagaraja, Shyama Shastri, and Muthuswami Dikshitar.

Castrato: Adult male soprano from mid 16th- to 19th-century Europe whose voice remained in the treble register after the onset of puberty because of surgical castration.

Ceilidh: Scottish Gaelic term for a social gathering centered around the live performance of traditional music and dance. The equivalent Irish term is *ceili*.

Chordophone: Sachs-Hornbostel category of musical instruments comprising those that produce sound from a vibrating string set in motion by striking, plucking, bowing, or rubbing.

Chuimse: Vocalized shouts and calls of encouragement performed by the drummer (*gosu*) in Korean *pansori* storytelling.

Chutney: Indo-Caribbean popular music and dance genre based on traditional Indian wedding songs.

Chutney soca: Indo-Trinidadian popular fusion song and dance genre combining chutney with Afro-Trinidadian "soul calypso."

Chutti: Paper ridges attached, like a beard, to the chin of a *kathakali* actor using thick rice paste. This face makeup signifies royalty or divinity in the South Indian dance drama.

Circular breathing: Technique practiced by performers of various aerophones allowing for continuous sound production by exhaling air stored in the cheeks while inhaling through the nose.

Clarinet: Subcategory of aerophone employing a single vibrating reed.

Cold War: Standoff between the Western bloc and the Soviet bloc including China following World War II, and lasting from approximately 1947 to 1989. The Cold War was a period of hostility exacerbated by the possession of nuclear arms by both sides.

Communitas: Subjective experience of group solidarity, and the transcendence of social, economic, and political divisions during anti-structural rituals. Associated with theories of anthropologist Victor Turner (1920–1983).

Complainte: French-language long song associated with the first generation of displaced Acadian settlers in Louisiana.

Composition: Term for music created prior to performance and fixed by notation or other form of preservation. Contrasts with improvisation, the act of spontaneous creation at the time of performance. In many traditions, the two processes are combined.

Conjunct motion: Melodic contour in which successive pitches are arranged more or less in stepwise order, using consecutive notes of a musical scale.

Context: Approach to musical inquiry concerned with the natural and human environment in which music occurs.

Cordões: Groups of outdoor masked revelers in 19th-century Brazilian Carnival festivities; precursors of *blocos*.

Cortigiana: Courtesan in Italy, 14th–17th centuries.

Courtesan: Educated female artist-musician and companion of upper-class men. Equivalent term found in many languages suggesting widespread social practice.

Creole: Term for a person of mixed ancestry living in a current or former colonial society; also, for a primary language formed by the fusion of two or more parent languages, usually one European and the other that of a colonized or enslaved population.

Crooner: American male singer whose voice was characterized by an intimate, conversational tone made possible by the invention of sound amplification. In 1929, Bing Crosby (1903–1977) was awarded the title, "America's Crooner."

Cultural Revolution: Decade-long social upheaval in the People's Republic of China (1966–1976) when young adults, mobilized under the instigation of aging Communist leader Mao Zedong, attempted to purge society of the "Four Olds": old customs, culture, habits, and ideas. Mass destruction of property and lives took place until the death of Mao in 1976.

Cultural tourism: Type of tourism in which visitors experience and learn about cultural attractions.

Cumbia: Colombian music and dance genre popular throughout Latin America, also among Mexicans living in the United States.

Daifanxi: Chinese regional folk opera traditions.

Dalang: Javanese shadow puppeteer and storyteller in the *wayang kulit* tradition.

Dambe: Northern Nigerian boxing sport.

Dbyangs: Form of multiphonic vocal chant practiced by Tibetan Buddhist monks, in which extremely low pitches are sustained while manipulation of the oral cavity produces audible upper overtones.

Decasyllabic: Ten-syllable line structure used in Balkan oral epic narration.

Decibel: Unit of measurement (dB) for the amplitude or volume of sound.

Demarcator: A marker of division or boundary between two categories. Music often serves as a demarcator between secular and sacred space, and secular and sacred time.

Devadasi: Female dancer dedicated to the service of a deity in traditional South Indian Hindu temples; institution outlawed in 1988.

Diegetic/Non-diegetic: Music in theater or film whose source is visible to the audience, and is presumed to be audible to characters in the narrative. Non-diegetic refers to music whose source is invisible to the audience and presumed inaudible to the characters in the narrative.

Disjunct motion: Melodic contour in which successive pitches are arranged with leaps, using non-consecutive notes of a musical scale.

Double Identity: An experiential identity shared by the descendants of African slavery based on the legacy of past hardships and present discrimination.

Drone: A single pitch or combination of pitches that sounds continuously through an entire performance, providing a reference or sonic environment for melodic and rhythmic music. Some instruments are equipped with extra strings or pipes to provide this harmonic feature.

Duration: Duration can be described subjectively as in a long or short sound; and objectively as a sonic event measured in minutes and seconds.

Electrophone: Sachs-Hornbostel category of musical instruments comprising those that produce sound primarily electronically, either by amplifying a sound produced mechanically (as with the electric guitar) or entirely by electronic or digital means (as with the synthesizer).

Enculturation: Process by which an individual acquires the norms, characteristics, customs, language, and communicative codes of a culture or group, usually associated with early childhood conditioning but also referring to adaptations made by colonized or immigrant groups.

Entrudo: 16th-century Portuguese form of Carnival mayhem in which people threw flour, eggs, mud, oranges, and lemons at each other; hurled pots and pans out of windows; waged street battles with brooms and spoons; and held gluttonous feasts.

Epic narrative: Recitation of extended oral narrative poems (epics) based on memorization and improvisation. Performances of epic narratives were particularly important in preliterate societies, since they concern issues central to the identity of a tribe, nation, or similar group. These issues include the lives of gods and heroes, creation myths, and other foundational stories that communicated core beliefs and values across generations.

Ethnomusicology: Academic discipline concerned with the study of music as a component of human culture, emphasizing music's social, environmental, semiotic, and material dimensions, as opposed to its isolated sound components. The field developed from 19th-century attempts by Western scholars to account for non-Western musical practices and repertoires—frequently those encountered through colonial expansion—as well as oral tradition and vernacular repertoires of Western music.

Fado: Portuguese urban song genre associated with the city of Lisbon conveying feelings of loss, regret, and the hardships of the poor. Dating from the early 19th century, the genre reached an international audience in the 1950s through the success of superstar Amália Rodrigues (1920–1999).

Falsetto: Upper extension of the adult male singing voice reaching the treble female vocal range. Early rock vocalist Frankie Valli of the Four Seasons made falsetto singing his signature sound.

Fiddle: Subcategory of chordophone consisting of instruments with strings stretched over a body and neck and played with a bow, thus capable of sustaining a pitch.

Film score: Music composed specifically to accompany a movie. The musical soundtrack enhances the emotional impact, provides continuity between scenes, establishes the locale, and foreshadows narrative events. It is a near universal component of feature film production.

Fipple flute: Subcategory of flutes in which a duct at the mouth end directs the air current against a sharp edge.

Flute: Subcategory of aerophone in which the flow of air is split over an opening in a tube or chamber, causing the air inside to vibrate.

Four-part harmony: Practice dating from the 14th century and possibly earlier of arranging music in four vocal parts: soprano, alto, tenor, and bass.

Free aerophone: Subcategory of aerophone, such as the bullroarer, that produces sound by vibrating air not enclosed in a tube or chamber.

Free reed: Subcategory of aerophone that produces sound when air passes over a reed set in a frame. This technology, used in East Asia from ancient times, was unknown in Europe until the early 19th century when free reed instruments imported from China became the basis for the accordion, harmonica, and reed organ (harmonium).

Gagaku: Ancient Japanese court music based on models imported from China and Korea. The *gagaku* ensemble, maintained by the Japanese Imperial Household Agency, is one of the oldest continuous music traditions in the world.

Gamak: Term for melodic ornament in the classical music of South Asia (Hindustani and Carnatic).

Gamelan: Traditional instrumental ensemble of Indonesia, consisting mainly of tuned bronze or iron idiophones and drums. Also played in mainland Southeast Asia, Suriname, and elsewhere.

Ge'ez: Semitic language from the Horn of Africa (Ethiopia and Eritrea), extinct in its spoken vernacular forms and used today only as the liturgical (ritual) language of the Ethiopian Orthodox Tewahedo Church and other Christian denominations of that region.

Geisha: Japanese professional female artist-entertainer.

Gesamtkunstwerk: (Literally, "complete work of art.") Term coined by German composer Richard Wagner (1813–1883) to describe music drama as a combination of music, poetry, drama, stagecraft, and architecture.

Gharana: In North India, the social organization of musicians by hereditary lineage or apprenticeship whereby the purity of a musical style is protected, maintained, and passed on across generations.

Ghazal: Poetic form of South Asia, rooted in Arabic poetry that consists of a number of rhyming couplets, frequently set to music.

Gisaeng: Korean hereditary profession of courtesan artist-entertainer.

Globalization: Process of progressive integration of the world's political, economic, transportation, communication, and information systems and networks, having profound effect on both cosmopolitan and remote regions, leaving few places unaffected.

Glocalization: Term for the processes by which globally distributed goods, services, and forms of expression have been adapted and transformed to meet specific local requirements.

Gompa: Prayer hall in a Tibetan Buddhist temple or monastery.

Gong: Subcategory of idiophone consisting of round, flat, metal discs that are struck with a mallet or beater.

Gosu: Drummer in Korean *pansori* who accompanies storyteller on barrel drum (*buk*) and provides shouts of encouragement (*chuimse*) during performance.

Grammys: Annual awards presented by the American Recording Academy recognizing major achievements in the music recording industry.

Gregorian Chant: Repertoire of notated chant melodies, compiled primarily during the 9th and 10th centuries for use in the Roman Catholic Mass Liturgy. Named for Pope Gregory the Great (ca. 540–604) to whom the melodies were attributed. Also known as plainsong or plainchant.

Griot (f. *griotte*): French term for West African praise singer/musician.

Grooves: Term coined by ethnomusicologists in the 1990s for repetitive and propulsive dance rhythms. Term comes from the channels cut into a phonograph record in which the needle rides.

Gugak: Korean traditional music.

Guru-shishya: Formal relationship between teacher (*guru*) and student (*shishya*) in South Asia through which a spiritual or musical tradition is transmitted and maintained.

Guslari (f. *guslarica*): Balkan bard or epic narrator; named for the single string fiddle (*gusle*) Balkan storytellers use to accompany their performances.

Hafiz (f. *hafiza*): In Islam, one who has memorized the entire Qur'an.

Harmonic progression: A series of chords that seem to be directed forward in time toward a resolution or goal. Also called chord progression.

Harp: Subcategory of chordophone in which strings suspended in a frame lie perpendicular to the resonating chamber.

Harvest celebration: Calendrical ritual celebrating the harvest, especially in agricultural communities.

Hasidim: Members of 18th-century East European Jewish sect and their descendants.

Hazzan: Jewish liturgical singer or cantor.

Hetaira: Courtesan in ancient Greece.

Heterophony: Musical texture in which multiple instrumental and/or vocal parts perform the same melody simultaneously, but using different ornaments or variations.

Hindustani: North Indian classical music tradition derived from the merging of aristocratic styles developed during the Mughal Empire (1526–1857) and Hindu devotional practices. Characterized by extreme melodic and rhythmic virtuosity, and fusion of Hindu and Islamic aesthetic principles. Term also used to identify the South Asian community in Suriname.

Hocket: Technique for producing a melody by alternating the pitches of two or more instruments or voices.

Homophony: Musical texture in which a single melody is supported by a harmonizing accompaniment.

Hybridity: In music, the blending of two or more styles or traditions that may reflect a mixed cultural heritage, or the collaboration of performers of different cultural backgrounds.

Hymnody: The practice of singing hymns—songs of praise or devotion—primarily in a religious context.

Iqa':   Rhythmic mode or pattern in Arabic music that repeats, with or without variations, throughout all or part of a performance. Patterns may range from as few as two beats to as many as forty-eight.

Idiophone: Sachs-Hornbostel category of musical instruments comprising those that produce sound from vibrations of the body of the instrument itself when struck, shaken, rubbed, etc.

Imam: Worship leader in a mosque and Muslim community.

Improvisation: Spontaneous musical creation at the time of performance, usually based on conventions within a musical tradition.

Indenture: Form of servitude in which a servant was bound to a master for a specific time period. On completion of the term, laborers imported from abroad were granted freedom and either return fare home or land in the place of indentureship.

Indigenous: Native to a particular region or environment.

Indo-Trinidadian: Trinidadian whose ancestors came from India, usually as indentured laborers.

Interval: The distance between two pitches, described as melodic if the two pitches are in succession, and harmonic if they are sounded together. Usually measured in terms of scale degrees.

Inuktitut: Language spoken by the Inuit of Canada's northwest province, Nunivut.

Irish session: Musical gathering of amateur musicians who share an ever-expanding repertoire of memorized Celtic dance tunes.

Jali (pl. *jalolu*):   Mande language term for hereditary praise singer, poet, and oral historian in the Mande region of northwest Africa.

Jamette Carnival: Originally a derisive term applied by white planters to the unruly Carnival celebrations of the Afro-Trinidadian population that involved street parades, drumming, dancing, and sexually explicit masquerading.

jangdan: Korean rhythmic mode and drum pattern performed in many aristocratic and folk genres as well as in the *pansori* storytelling tradition.

Janissary band: Military band of the Ottoman Turks, believed to be the oldest such ensemble in the world.

Jarai: Tribal language of the Montagnards in the Central Highlands of Vietnam.

Jaran kepang: Traditional dance by Javanese males on stylized hobbyhorses that involves spirit possession and acrobatics. Practiced also by members of the Javanese diasporic community in Suriname.

Jingju: Beijing opera that developed in the late 18th century.

J'Ouvert: Carnival Monday pre-dawn celebration of Afro-Trinidadians in which revelers cover themselves in mud or oil and parade in the streets, accompanied by loud steel band or soca music.

Kabaka: Title of the kings of Buganda, a kingdom bordered by Lake Victoria and the west bank of the Nile River, now in modern Uganda.

Kabuki: Theatrical tradition that developed in Edo (Tokyo), Japan in the early 17th century.

Katajjaq: Vocal technique and entertainment genre of Inuit women, almost always performed as a duet. Also known as Inuit throat singing.

Kathakali: Elaborate dance drama tradition of the South Indian state of Kerala.

Kecak: Modern Balinese dance drama based on the ancient Hindu epic, *Ramayana*.

Khoomei: Vocal style of north central Asia involving production of a low fundamental pitch combined with audible upper overtones such that several pitches are sounded at once.

Kirtan: In Hinduism, the repetitive singing of divine names such as Krishna and his consort Radha.

Klezmer: Genre of instrumental ensemble music associated with Jews of Eastern Europe, known for lively dance rhythms and expressive ornamentation.

Kotha: The first floor of a salon where South Asian courtesans (*tawaif*) entertained upper-class men with song and dance.

Kriti: Form of South Indian sung poetry that is the basis for Carnatic vocal and instrumental performance.

Kwangdae: Storyteller in the Korean *pansori* tradition.

Kyabazinga: Title of the kings of Busoga, now in modern Uganda.

Lamellophone: Subcategory of idiophone consisting of thin strips of metal fastened at one end to a frame and plucked with the thumbs at the unattached end. Instruments of this type include the *mbira, sanza, kalimba*, and *endongo*, and are widely distributed throughout sub-Saharan Africa.

Leitmotif: A repeating melodic or rhythmic theme associated with a character, situation, or other aspect of the narrative, in opera, music drama, and film music. Term originally associated with Richard Wagner's compositional practice.

Libretto: In opera, the playbook or script.

Life-cycle rituals: Rituals that mark transition points in a person's life, like coming-of-age initiations, weddings, and funerals.

Lilting: Genre of Irish performance art utilizing non-lexical vocables.

Liminal: (From Latin *limen*, "threshold.") In-between phase or transition from one state of affairs to another.

Lining Out: Style of hymn singing in which a leader sings each hymn line slowly, followed by the congregation repeating the line, without instrumental accompaniment.

Liturgical drama: A sacred narrative performed in the context of a religious ritual. The medieval Christian morality play is an example.

Liturgy: Fixed set of spoken or sung texts that are repeated in a ritual setting.

Local deity: A deity associated with a particular environment or group, often seen as a protector or intercessor for higher, more powerful spiritual forces.

Local nationalism: Allegiance to one's ethnic group rather than to the nation state, as with Kurds in eastern Turkey.

Lunar New Year: The first day of the New Year in cultures basing their calendar on the lunar cycle. In East Asia, New Year celebrations fall in late January or February, and in China they are the most extravagant of the year involving fifteen days of music, dance, fireworks, and festivities.

Lute: (From Arabic *al-'ud*, "wood.") Subcategory of chordophone in which strings are stretched across a resonating body and neck, and plucked in contrast to the bowed fiddle.

Lyre: Subcategory of chordophone related to the harp, in which strings are suspended from a crossbar and fastened perpendicular to the resonating chamber.

Madang: Tales told by the Korean *pansori* storyteller.

Mahabharata: Sanskrit epic of ancient India and the source material for various artistic traditions in South and Southeast Asia. The story concerns two families—the Pandavas and the Kauravas—in a battle for succession to the throne of the Kuru kingdom. Composed by the legendary sage Vyasa, it is ten times longer than the Greek epics *The Iliad* and *The Odyssey* combined.

Mahayana: (Literally, "The Great Vehicle.") Branch of Buddhism that developed in East Asia when teachings of Shakyamuni Buddha spread east from India and combined with the indigenous religions of China. Central to its tenets is veneration of otherworldly Buddhas and Bodhisattvas, beings dedicated to the liberation of others.

Mani kang: Giant Tibetan Buddhist prayer wheel used in devotional practices. Each turning of the wheel is believed to utter a prayer, thus bestowing merit upon the practitioner.

Maqam: Modal system for melodic invention in use from northwest Africa through the Middle East and Central Asia to western China.

Maroon: Descendant of escaped African slaves in the New World. Suriname has the greatest Maroon population in the world because of the inaccessibility of settlements in the Amazonian Rainforest.

Mass media: Technologies like radio, television, cinema, audio and video recordings, newspapers, and the internet designed to reach a mass audience.

May 4th Movement: In China, student-led social turmoil and subsequent reform movements following Japan's annexation of the Shandong Peninsula in 1919.

Mediated Music: As the term is used in ethnomusicology, music distributed and accessed through electronic media.

Melismatic: In sacred chant and other vocal genres like Irish *sean-nós*, a single syllable stretched over a number of melodic pitches.

Melodic contour: The shape of a melodic phrase described in terms of the rise and fall of successive pitches.

Melodic mode: System containing the pitch material used to generate melodies in a music tradition. Examples include *raga* (India) and *mugam* (Azerbaijan).

Membranophone: Sachs-Hornbostel category of musical instruments comprising those that produce sound from a vibrating membrane. Most membranophones are drums of various shapes and sizes.

Mestizo: In Latin America, a person of mixed race, especially of Native American and European ancestry.

Meter: The organization of beats and accents in music into regular patterns.

Mevlevi: Sufi religious order founded in Konya, Turkey in the 13th century by followers of Mevlana Jalaluddin Rumi (1207–1273). Members of the order are known as "whirling dervishes" after their practice of whirling in the sacred *sema* ceremony.

Minaret: Tall, slender tower with a balcony near the top, affixed or adjacent to a mosque, from which, historically, the *muezzin* delivered the Call to Prayer (*adhan*) five times a day. Today, most minarets broadcast the Call to Prayer through loudspeakers.

Min ji: Chinese courtesan.

Minstrel: Itinerant European musician-storyteller.

Mnemonic: A learning technique that aids information retention. The word is related to the Greek goddess of memory, Mnemosyne, the mother of the nine Muses.

Monody: Technique invented by members of the Florentine Camerata in the late 16th to early 17th centuries for the melodic delivery of dramatic speech with simple instrumental accompaniment. The invention was crucial to the development of Italian opera.

Monophony: Musical texture comprising a single, unaccompanied melody.

Montagnard: Member of one of several tribal groups indigenous to the Central Highlands of Vietnam.

Moso: Blind Buddhist priests who developed the Japanese tradition of epic narration.

Mudra: A symbolic hand gesture in South Asian dance and religious traditions.

Muezzin: Appointee of a mosque responsible for performing the Call to Prayer (*adhan*) five times a day.

Mughal Empire: South Asian dynastic empire established by Babur in 1526 and brought to an end in 1857 when the last Mughal emperor, Bahadur Shah II, was deposed by the British and exiled to Burma. Arts and learning flourished under several Mughal rulers, most notably Akbar the Great (1542–1605).

Murti: Image of a deity housed in a Hindu temple.

Music therapy: Branch of medicine dealing with the application of music in therapeutic treatments.

Musical bow: Subcategory of chordophone consisting of a single string attached at both ends to a bent, flexible stick. The stick, in turn, is often attached to a resonator, which in some cases is the mouth of the performer.

Musical fusion: The blending of musics from several styles or traditions. The term is usually applied to popular music genres.

Musicking: Term coined by musicologist Christopher Small in 1998 to refer to music not as an object but as a process ("to music"), including any activities connected with the performance of music.

Musicology: The academic study of music, usually from an historical or analytical perspective and primarily focusing on Western art music.

Musiki: Classical Greek term for the arts that fall under the influence of the nine muses.

Muzak: American company founded in 1934 for delivery of background music to commercial clients. The term has been used to refer to any piped-in environmental music or the system that delivers it.

Nad Brahman: In Hinduism, the reverence for god as sound. Also, in Indian classical music, an understanding that the universe was created from sound.

Nadun: Harvest ritual involving spirit possession among the Mangghuer ethnic group in western China.

Natya Shastra: Indian treatise on music, dance, and drama first compiled between 200 BCE and 200 CE. Source of Sachs-Hornbostel instrument classification system.

Naubat: Royal music ensemble of the Mughal emperors of northern India.

Non-lexical vocables: Meaningless syllables used in singing, associated with such genres as American swing and Irish lilting.

Norebang: Korean "song room," a private, intimate form of karaoke.

Notational systems: Symbol systems for preserving and performing music based on visual signs. At least two kinds have been invented, those that represent pitch and note duration, and those that represent execution on an instrument.

Nueva Canción: Folk-inspired and politically motivated song movement in Latin America from the 1960s and 1970s.

Oboe: Subcategory of aerophone in which air enclosed in a tube is set in motion by the vibration of two reeds.

Obon: A major midsummer festival in Japan commemorating the return to earth of ancestor spirits.

Ocarina: Subcategory of aerophone in which air is blown into a chamber or vessel with several finger holes for changing the pitch. Ancient forms have been found in prehistoric China and Mesoamerica.

Oiran: Japanese courtesan, catering to urban aristocracy.

Opera: Dramatic work for vocalists and orchestra that includes acting, costumes, and scenery. This secular genre began in late 16th-century Italy.

Oral transmission: Transmission of cultural information—including narratives, histories, genealogies, sacred verses, and music—across generations without the use of writing.

Organologist: Scholar engaged with the academic study of musical instruments.

Ornamentation: Embellishment of pitches using techniques characteristic of a particular style or genre. These include vibrato, trills, shakes, slides, *gamak*, and *tahrir*.

Overtones: Inaudible pitches produced along with an audible fundamental tone that are related to the frequency of the fundamental by simple ratio. These determine the timbre of the audible tone by their relative prevalence.

Panpipes: Subcategory of aerophone consisting of a set of connected hollow tubes or pipes, closed at one end, and arranged in order of length. Blowing across the open end of each pipe produces its respective pitch.

***Pansori*:** Musical storytelling tradition from Korea.

***Par*:** Large, hand-painted scroll used in the Epic of Pabuji narrative tradition of Rajasthan, North India.

Patronage system: European economic system whereby artists and musicians worked for, and were supported by, church institutions or wealthy aristocratic patrons who controlled their creative output.

***Pelog*:** Seven-tone scale used in Javanese *gamelan* music.

Pentatonic: Five-note scale or mode, used in musical systems of East Asia, sub-Saharan Africa, and folk traditions of the British Isles among others.

Periodicity: As used in music, the term describes the regular recurrence of rhythmic and melodic patterns that gives stability to musical structures and experiences.

***Phi Faa*:** Healing ritual of Thailand and Laos.

Pitch: Pitch is a tone of measurable frequency. It can be described subjectively with terms such as "high" and "low"; and measured objectively by calculating how many times per second an object vibrates through a complete wave cycle.

Plainchant: Alternate term for Gregorian chant.

Playback singer: Singer in the Indian film industry who pre-records songs for actors to lip-synch on screen.

Playing *Mas*: (*Mas*, "masquerades.") Participating in Trinidad's Carnival costume parades.

Polyphony: Musical texture of multiple simultaneous melodies.

Polyrhythm: Two or more independent rhythmic patterns played simultaneously (such as 2s against 3s), creating a complex rhythmic texture that often serves as the underpinning for solo improvisation by a lead drummer. Characteristic of sub-Saharan rhythmic structures.

Praise song: Improvised song text in praise of a patron. Associated with the *griot* tradition of West Africa.

Processional Music: Special music, such as a wedding march, to accompany a line of participants entering a ritual space.

Program Music: Musical depiction of non-music situations, objects, or states of being.

Proletarian: Member of the working class; a term associated with Marxist ideology.

Primitive Baptist: Conservative Christian denomination that adheres to Calvinist doctrine forbidding the use of musical instruments in worship services.

Pro-Democracy Movement: After the death of Mao Zedong in 1976, student-led protests in the People's Republic of China that culminated in massive public demonstrations at Tiananmen Square in Beijing, and subsequent government crackdown and reprisals.

Psalm: One of 150 sacred and devotional song texts in the Old Testament of the Bible.

***Puja*:** A Hindu ritual of devotion and purification, performed either publicly or privately.

Qari: An expert in Qur'anic recitation.

Qawwali: Genre of sacred sung poetry in Sufi traditions of northern India and Pakistan performed by professional hereditary musicians primarily at Sufi shrines. *Qawwali* performing ensemble called "party."

Quechua: Native peoples of the Central Andean region of South America including Peru and Bolivia, and the languages they speak.

Radif: The basis for the traditional music of Iran; a collection of melodies organized by melodic mode (*dastgah*) and transmitted orally from teacher to student.

Raga: Melodic system used in the music of North and South India, as well as parts of Pakistan, Afghanistan, and Bangladesh. Also, an individual melodic mode consisting of five to seven pitches arranged in ascending and descending order, and associated with a time of day, season of the year, particular deity, and/or a mood.

Ramayana: Sanskrit epic of ancient India composed, according to legend, by the sage Valmiki. The story concerns the defeat of demon Ravana by god-king Rama and his loyal general, the monkey king Hanuman. It provides the source material for a number of artistic traditions in South and Southeast Asia.

Raqs sharqi: Classical Egyptian style of belly dance.

Rasa: (Literally, "juice" or "taste.") In classical Indian aesthetics, the dominant emotional content of a work of art or musical performance.

Recessional Music: Special music to accompany a line or group of participants leaving a ritual space.

Recitative: Sung dialogue in Italian opera, using the inflections and rhythms of spoken language.

Recorder: European family of wooden duct flutes. Sizes range from sopranino to contra bass.

Reggae: Song and dance genre from Jamaica.

Revitalization: Process by which obsolete or neglected musical traditions gain renewed interest among practitioners and audiences.

Rhythmic mode: Rhythmic pattern repeated, with or without variations, throughout a performance. Rhythmic modal systems include *tala* (India), *iqa'* (Middle East), and *jangdan* (Korea).

Rishi: (Sanskrit, "seer; conduit for revelation.") Mystics to whom it is believed the Vedas were divinely revealed at least 3,500 years ago.

Rokusai Nembutsu Odori: Japanese music and dance tradition associated with *Obon* celebrations in the city of Kyoto.

Roots Rhythms: Rhythmic patterns used in popular dance music genres that derive from earlier forms of sacred ritual music.

Sachs-Hornbostel system: Musical instrument classification system developed in 1914 by ethnomusicologists Erich Moritz von Hornbostel (1877–1935) and Curt Sachs (1881–1959).

Salsa: Form of dance music originating in the Bronx, New York City. It is rooted in dance music of Puerto Rico and Cuba, and is now danced worldwide.

Sama: See *sema*.

Sambadrome: Exhibition venue for samba parades during Brazilian Carnival where teams from samba schools compete before judges.

Samba School: Brazilian neighborhood-based social clubs in which teams develop themes, songs, and choreography; create costumes and props; and rehearse for Carnival parades at the sambadrome exhibition venue.

Sambista: Experienced participants of Brazil's Carnival samba music and dance traditions.

Sangat: Melodic technique used in Hindustani classical music in which the primary soloist (vocal or instrumental) is "followed" by a secondary line at a time interval of one to several seconds.

Sangita: Sanskrit term for music that includes melody, rhythm, and bodily movement or dance.

Sanskrit: Liturgical language of Hinduism and ancient literary language of India. It is the original language in which the Vedas were revealed.

Saturnalia: Ancient Roman festival dedicated to the god Saturn and celebrating the harvest that included the overturning of daily conventions, drunkenness, licentiousness, and the inversion of social hierarchies.

Scale: Stepwise sequence of ascending and descending pitches that form the basis for melodic composition and improvisation.

Scat singing: Vocal jazz improvisation in which non-lexical vocables replace song texts; associated with the careers of Louis Armstrong and Ella Fitzgerald.

Sean-nós: (Literally, "in the old way," Irish Gaelic.) Genre of unaccompanied Irish singing in free rhythm.

Sema: (Turkish; *sama*, Arabic. Literally, "listening" and "that which is heard.") Term refers to sacred ceremonies of various Sufi orders from North Africa to the Indian Subcontinent. In Turkey, refers to the ritual of the Mevlevi whirling dervishes.

Semiotic: The study of meaning and how it is communicated through signs and symbols.

Shakti: Sanskrit for the sacred energy generated by yoga practices and radiating from holy objects such as images of a deity housed in Hindu temples.

Shaman: Spiritual healer and guide capable of making direct contact with spirits and supernatural forces through self-induced trance. The term was originally applied to Central Asian practitioners; now applied generally.

Shape notes: Notation system designed to facilitate congregational and social singing developed in late 18th-century England.

Sharpeville Massacre: Civil disturbance in South Africa on March 21, 1960 resulting in the shooting death of 69 black African protesters by police officers. The event gained worldwide media coverage and initiated international condemnation of the Apartheid regime.

Shuoshude: Blind itinerant musician-storyteller of China.

Singspiel: German musical theater genre for middle-class audiences that flourished in the 18th and 19th centuries, in which spoken dialogue alternated with songs and ballads.

Slendro: Five-tone scale used in Javanese *gamelan* music and associated with nighttime *wayang kulit* performances.

Soca: Popular song genre of Trinidad combining indigenous calypso with elements of Indo-Trinidadian music including fast tempos and heavy percussion accompaniment.

Solkattu: Recitation of syllables that represent drum strokes in Carnatic music.

Songlines: Long melodies, memorized by Aboriginal Australians, whose contours correspond to pathways through trackless Australian hinterlands.

Sonidero bailes: DJ-led Mexican and Mexican-American dance parties.

"Stimela":   (Literally, "steam train," Nguni language.) Title of a song by South African jazz trumpeter Hugh Masekela, released in 1974 during the period of Apartheid. The song describes the hated train that carried Black laborers from all parts of southern Africa to work in the gold and diamond mines around Johannesburg.

Sufi: Member of an Islamic mystical order.

Sutra: Sanskrit term for a written collection of spiritual sayings or aphorisms in Hinduism or Buddhism.

Sympathetic string: One of a set of secondary strings, on South Asian chordophones like *sitar*, *sarod*, and *sarangi*, that vibrate when the primary melody strings are played, to increase the resonance of the instrument.

Sympathetic vibration: Acoustical phenomenon whereby a vibrating object of a specific frequency will cause another object of the same size to vibrate at the same frequency.

Symphony: Composition for Western orchestra in several sections (movements), originating in 18th-century court entertainments. By the early 19th century, principally due to Beethoven's influence, it had become the most ambitious, complex, and profound form of instrumental music of the Western classical tradition.

Syncopation: Displacement of expected accentuation pattern, commonly used in American jazz and elsewhere.

Taarab: Genre of East African popular music that inspires ecstasy in the listener, developed in the 1920s.

Tablature: Symbol system for representing how music is physically executed on an instrument.

Talchum: Korean genre of masked dance.

Tahrir: A vocal ornament characteristic of Persian (Iranian) vocal music.

Tajweed: Rules for correct pronunciation of the Qur'an during recitation.

Tala: Rhythmic system in South Asian music; and also a single rhythmic mode identified by the number of beats, pattern of accents, and rests per cycle.

Tamboo-bamboo band: Ensemble of idiophones including large tuned bamboo sticks and bottles struck with spoons that developed in Trinidad and Tobago when British authorities outlawed drums in the Afro-Trinidadian community in the 1880s.

Tanakh: The Hebrew Bible; an acronym for its three sections, the Torah (five books of Moses), the Nevi'im (the Prophets), and the Ketuvim (miscellaneous writings including the books of Job, Psalms, Proverbs, and Ecclesiastes).

Taqsim: Melodic improvisation in Arabic and Turkish instrumental music based on maqam and usually in free meter. May be an introductory or internal section of a performance.

Tara sutra: Short prayer or mantra addressed to Tara, a female *bodhisattva* (liberated being) who embodies perfect compassion, repeated by Tibetan Buddhists as a devotional practice while turning a prayer wheel.

Tarab: (Arabic term for "enchantment.") Ecstatic feeling associated with playing and listening to music.

Tarteel: Recitation of the Qur'an with clarity and understanding, according to exact rules of pronunciation.

Tassa drumming: In Trinidad, an Indo-Caribbean tradition of playing the *tassa* drum (of Indian origin) with sticks, in street parades on the Muslim holiday of Hosay as well as at Hindu weddings and other celebrations.

Tawaif: North Indian courtesan/entertainer who catered to the aristocracy, particularly during the Mughal period.

Techno music: Electronic instrumental dance party music, developed during the late 1980s.

Tempo: The speed or pace at which music is performed.

Temporary physiological synchrony: Social phenomenon described by primatologist Bruce Richmond in which gelada baboons achieve a state of metabolic and emotional coordination through group vocalizations. Richmond theorized that the same effect might be experienced by primitive or modern humans through collective or choral singing or chanting.

Texture: Element of music defining the relationship between simultaneous, coordinated parts, such as melody and accompaniment (homophony), and multiple melodic lines (polyphony).

Theravada: (Literally, "teaching of the elders.") Branch of Buddhism that took root in Sri Lanka and Southeast Asia. Most conservative form of Buddhism and least modified by contact with other religions, Theravada puts emphasis on acquisition of merit through individual effort, including service to monastic communities.

Throat singing: Term used to describe various vocal techniques of Central Asia and the Arctic regions of North America. Techniques in Central Asia involve production of audible whistle-like overtones above a fundamental pitch, while Inuit women of North America produce unique sounds in the neck below the larynx, and in the oral cavity.

Tiananmen Square: Large, open public space in central Beijing, site of the 1989 student protests of the Pro-Democracy Movement.

Timbre: Technical term for the quality of a vocal or instrumental sound, also described as tone color.

Tone poem: Single-movement composition for symphony orchestra with a descriptive title.

Tongsu: Officially sanctioned popular song genre in the People's Republic of China.

Trance: Any of a number of psychological states that differ from normal waking consciousness. These range from deep meditation to hyperactive ecstatic states in which the subject is capable of extreme feats of strength or endurance. Music usually aids the initiating or sustaining of trance states, which in a religious context are often understood as evidence of contact with invisible realms or beings.

Trek Boer: Native Dutch, French, or German livestock farmers who migrated to the interior of South Africa in the 17th and 18th centuries.

Tripitaka: (Literally, "three baskets.") The collected Buddhist scriptures, divided into three categories: sermons of the Buddha, laws for organizing monastic communities, and Buddhist philosophy.

Trumpet: Subcategory of aerophone in which the air enclosed in a straight, curved, or folded tube is set in motion by the player's vibrating or buzzing lips.

Ululation: High-pitched warble involving the rapid flicking of the tongue back and forth, usually associated with women producing celebratory vocalization.

Umbigada: Gyrating hip movements characteristic of Brazilian samba dance.

Urs: Annual festival at a South Asian Sufi shrine, commemorating the death anniversary of the saint entombed there. *Sama* or sacred rituals include the singing of *qawwali*.

Varzesh bastani: Traditional Iranian sport practiced in a *zurkhaneh*, combining martial arts, strength training, calisthenics, a code of ethics, spirituality, and music.

Veda: One of four collections of sacred prayers and invocations in ancient India, dating from the 2nd millennium BCE and transmitted to the present through oral tradition. The four Vedas constitute the oldest hymns and revelations of Hinduism: Rigveda, Samaveda, Yajurveda, and Atharvaveda.

Vedic chant: World's oldest unbroken tradition of sacred chant, from India.

Verismo: Late 19th-century style of Italian opera with plots based on real life situations involving the violence and passions of the underclass.

Vernacular language: Spoken language of a community or population, in contrast to a liturgical language used only in ritual circumstances.

Vibrato: Vocal or instrumental ornament involving the production of microtonal pitch fluctuations that increase resonance and projection of musical sound.

Virtuosity: Great technical skill displayed by a musician.

Vodun: West African traditional religion also practiced by descendants of the African slave trade in Haiti, Puerto Rico, and elsewhere. In the New World, African religious practices blended or syncretized with aspects of Christianity.

Volume: Volume (amplitude) can be described subjectively using terms such as "loud" and "soft"; and measured objectively by calculating the physical pressure of the sound waves.

Vuvuzela: South African plastic trumpet that gained notoriety when played incessantly by audience members at the 2010 FIFA World Cup Football Tournament games.

Waulking song: Scottish folk songs, traditionally sung in the Scottish Gaelic language by women while fulling (waulking) cloth.

Wayang kulit: Indonesian shadow puppet theater accompanied by a *gamelan* ensemble.

Winti: Afro-Surinamese religion based upon ancestor worship, spirit possession, and belief in a pantheon of gods (also called *winti*) derived from West Africa.

World Music: The term has a double meaning. The first is the academic study of musics of the world as defined by ethnomusicologists. The second meaning is a genre of recorded popular music by non-Western artists marketed to Western audiences.

Xylophone: Instrument made from tuned wooden bars or keys that are struck with a mallet.

Yangbanxi: Chinese Model operas based on revolutionary or patriotic themes; the only performance works permitted during the Cultural Revolution (1966–1976).

Yaogun yinyue: Genre of Chinese rock music with subversive and individualistic lyrics banned from the radio and not supported by the state.

Yin yang: In Chinese philosophy, terms referring to opposing forces, such as heat and cold, light and dark, heaven and earth. As a single word, *yinyang*, a Daoist ritual leader and priest.

Yodeling: Vocal style featuring rapid alternation between low-pitched and high-pitched registers. Associated with herders in the Swiss and Austrian Alps, as well as American country singers in the early 20th century, most notably Jimmie Rodgers.

Zikr: In Islam, a devotional practice for being mindful of the will of God; forms range from silent recitation of Qur'anic verses to the music and dance of Sufis.

Zither: Subcategory of chordophone in which strings are stretched across a flat soundboard and typically plucked or strummed.

Zurkhaneh: (Literally, "House of Strength.") Iranian traditional gymnasium or exercise hall.

Zydeco: Popular dance music genre of Louisiana Creoles combining elements of Cajun, jazz, blues, and R&B.

Further Resources

"Further Resources" are organized by relevance to specific chapters, except for those listed under Chapter 1. The Chapter 1 resources are of general relevance to the study of World Music. Chapter 1 presents twenty-five sources, while Chapters 2–15 each include between six and eleven.

Chapter 1

Blacking, John. *How Musical Is Man?* Seattle: University of Washington Press, 1974.

Broughton, Simon, and others, eds. *The Rough Guide to World Music: Africa & Middle East.* London: Rough Guides, 2006.

———. *The Rough Guide to World Music: Europe, Asia & Pacific.* London: Rough Guides, 2009.

Cook, Nicholas. *Music: A Very Short Introduction.* 2nd ed. New York: Oxford University Press, 2021.

Exploring the World of Music. 12-vol. instructional video series. Annenberg Learner. https://www.learner.org/series/exploring-the-world-of-music/melody/.

Feld, Steven. *Sound and Sentiment: Birds, Weeping, Poetics, and Song in Kaluli Expression.* 3rd ed. Durham, NC: Duke University Press, 2012.

JVC Video Anthology of World Music and Dance, produced by Katsumori Ichikawa. 30-vol. DVD set. Tokyo: Japanese Video Corporation, 2005.

Levitin, Daniel J. *This Is Your Brain on Music: The Science of a Human Obsession.* New York: Plume, 2007.

Marre, Jeremy, producer/director. *Beats of the Heart.* Harcourt Films. DVD documentary series on world music, 2006. Original 14-part VHS series, 1977–1989.

———. *The Nature of Music.* 3-part video documentary series, 1988.

Myers, Helen, ed. *Ethnomusicology: An Introduction.* New York: W.W. Norton, 1992.

———. *Ethnomusicology: Historical and Regional Studies.* New York: W.W. Norton, 1992.

Nettl, Bruno. *The Study of Ethnomusicology: Thirty-Three Discussions.* 3rd ed. Urbana-Champaign: University of Illinois Press, 2015.

Nettl, Bruno, and others, eds. *The Garland Encyclopedia of World Music.* 10 vols. New York: Routledge, 1997–2002.

Post, Jennifer. *Ethnomusicology: A Research and Information Guide.* 2nd ed. New York: Routledge, 2011.

———, ed. *Ethnomusicology: A Contemporary Reader.* New York: Routledge, 2006; Vol.2, 2017.

Rice, Timothy. *Ethnomusicology: A Very Short Introduction.* New York: Oxford University Press, 2013.

Sacks, Oliver. *Musicophilia: Tales of Music and the Brain.* Rev. ed. New York: Alfred A. Knopf, 2008.

Sadie, Stanley, and John Tyrrell, eds. *The New Grove Dictionary of Music and Musicians.* 2nd ed. 29 vols. Oxford: Oxford University Press, 2004. Also available as *Grove Music Online.* https://www.oxfordmusiconline.com/grovemusic/.

Schafer, R. Murray. *The Soundscape: Our Sonic Environment and the Tuning of the World.* New ed. Rochester, VT: Destiny Books, 1994.

Seaton, Douglass. *Ideas and Styles in the Western Musical Tradition.* 4th ed. Oxford: Oxford University Press. 2016.

Small, Christopher. *Musicking: The Meanings of Performing and Listening.* Middletown, CT: Wesleyan University Press, 1998.

Smithsonian Folkways Recordings. https://folkways.si.edu/.

UNESCO Multimedia Video & Sound Collections. *Intangible Heritage: Arts and Traditions of the World.* www.unesco.org/archives/multimedia/index.php?pg=13&sj=Intangible+heritage.

Wade, Bonnie. *Thinking Musically: Experiencing Music, Expressing Culture.* 3rd ed. Oxford: Oxford University Press, 2012. The central volume in a Global Music Series; each individual volume is written by a different author and focuses on a single area of the world.

Chapter 2

Danielson, Virginia. *The Voice of Egypt: Umm Kulthum, Arabic Song, and Egyptian Society in the Twentieth Century.* Chicago, IL: University of Chicago Press, 1997.

Eidsheim, Nina Sun. *The Race of Sound: Listening, Timbre, and Vocality in African American Music.* Durham, NC: Duke University Press, 2019.

Farinelli. Gérard Corbiau, director. Stéphan Films, 1994. Distributed by Sony. Biographical film on the life of Carlo Broschi (1705–1782), known as Farinelli, considered the greatest castrato singer of all time.

Folkstreams. *Preserving the Stories of America.* A national archive of documentary films about American Roots Cultures. www.folkstreams.net.

Harkness, Nicholas. *Songs of Seoul: An Ethnography of Voice and Voicing in Christian South Korea.* Berkeley: University of California Press, 2014.

Keita, Cheick M. Chérif. *Outcast to Ambassador: The Musical Odyssey of Salif Keita.* Saint Paul, MN: Mogoya Books, 2011.

Meizel, Katherine. "Two Voices: Singing and Signing in the Hearing/Deaf Borderlands." *Multivocality: An Ethnography of Singing on the Borders of Identity.* New York: Oxford University Press, 2017.

Norton, Kay. *Singing and Wellbeing: Ancient Wisdom, Modern Proof.* New York: Routledge, 2016.

Zemp, Hugo, ed. *Voix du Monde - Voices of the World.* 3 CD set. Paris: Centre National de la Recherche Scientifique et Musée de l'Homme, 1995. Includes 187-page booklet in French and English. https://archives.crem-cnrs.fr/archives/collections/CNRSMH_E_1996_013_001/.

Chapter 3

Abrashev, Bozhidar, and Vladimir Gadjev. *The Illustrated Encyclopedia of Musical Instruments: From All Eras and Regions of the World.* Potsdam: H.F. Ullmann, 2008.

Hesselink, Nathan. *P'ungmul: South Korean Drumming and Dance.* Chicago, IL: University of Chicago Press, 2006.

Kartomi, Margaret. *On Concepts and Classifications of Musical Instruments.* Chicago, IL: University of Chicago Press, 1990.

Libin, Lawrence, ed. *The Grove Dictionary of Musical Instruments.* 2nd ed. Oxford: Oxford University Press, 2014.

The Diagram Group. *Musical Instruments of the World: An Illustrated Encyclopedia with More Than 4000 Original Drawings.* New York: Sterling Publishing, 2002.

418 Further Resources

Zemp, Hugo, ed. *Instruments de Musique du Monde – Musical Instruments of the World.* CD. Paris: Centre National de la Recherche Scientifique et Musée de l'Homme, 1990. Includes 118-page booklet in French and English. https://archives.crem-cnrs.fr/archives/collections/CNRSMH_E_1990_014_001/.

Chapter 4

Bohlman, Philip. *World Music: A Very Short Introduction.* 2nd ed. New York: Oxford University Press, 2020.

Kelly, Lynne. *The Memory Code: The Traditional Aboriginal Memory Technique that Unlocks the Secrets of Stonehenge, Easter Island, and Ancient Monuments the World Over.* Victoria: Allen & Unwin, 2016.

Khan, Ali Akbar. *The Classical Music of North India: The Music of the Baba Allauddin Gharana as Taught by Ali Akbar Khan at the Ali Akbar College of Music.* Edited by George Ruckert. New Delhi: Munshiram Manoharlal Publishers Pvt. Ltd., 2013.

Lavezzoli, Peter. *The Dawn of Indian Music in the West.* London: Continuum, 2007.

Stock, Jonathan. *Musical Creativity in Twentieth-Century China: Abing, His Music and Its Changing Meanings.* Rochester, NY: University of Rochester Press, 1996.

Tenzer, Michael, and John Roeder, eds. *Analytical and Cross-Cultural Studies in World Music.* New York: Oxford University Press, 2011.

Williams, Sean, and Lillis Ó Laoire. *Bright Star of the West: Joe Heaney, Irish Song Man.* New York: Oxford University Press, 2011.

Chapter 5

D'Amico, Leonardo, and Francesco Mizzau, eds. *Africa: Folk Music Atlas.* Book, CD-Rom, 3 Audio CDs. Florence: Amharsi Edizioni Multimediali, 1997.

Dissanayake, Ellen. *Art and Intimacy: How the Arts Began.* Seattle: University of Washington Press, 2012.

Killin, Anton. "The Origins of Music: Evidence, Theory, and Prospects," *Music and Science,* 1 (2018), 1–23. https://doi.org/10.1177/2059204317751971.

Mâche, François-Bernard. *Music, Myth, and Nature, or, The Dolphins of Arion.* Rev. ed. Chur: Harwood Academic Publishers, 1992.

Marett, Allan. *Songs, Dreamings, and Ghosts: The Wangga of North Australia.* Middletown, CT: Wesleyan University Press, 2005.

Storr, Anthony. *Music and the Mind.* New York: Ballantine Books, 1992.

Wallin, Nils L., Björn Merker, and Steven Brown, eds. *The Origins of Music.* Cambridge: MIT Press, 2000.

Chapter 6

Barz, Gregory. *Music in East Africa: Experiencing Music, Expressing Culture.* Oxford: Oxford University Press, 2004.

Chernoff, John Miller. *African Rhythm and African Sensibility: Aesthetics and Social Action in African Musical Idioms.* New ed. Chicago, IL: University of Chicago Press, 1981.

Crafts, Susan D., Daniel Cavicchi, and Charles Keil. *My Music: Explorations of Music in Daily Life.* Middletown, CT: Wesleyan University Press, 1993.

Merriam, Alan. *The Anthropology of Music.* Evanston, IL: Northwestern University Press, 1964.

Pedersen, Morten Axel. *Not Quite Shamans: Spirit Worlds and Political Lives in Northern Mongolia.* Ithaca, NY: Cornell University Press, 2011.

Turner, Victor. *The Ritual Process: Structure and Anti-Structure.* New ed. New York: Routledge, 2017.

Chapter 7

Brown, Rae Linda. *The Heart of a Woman: The Life and Music of Florence B. Price.* Urbana: University of Illinois Press, 2020.

Connell, John, and Chris Gibson. *Sound Tracks: Popular Music, Identity, and Place.* Hove: Psychology Press, 2003.

Copland, Aaron. *What to Listen For in Music.* New York: Penguin Group, 2011.

Hutchinson, Earl Ofari. *It's Our Music Too: The Black Experience of Classical Music.* Los Angeles, CA: Middle Passage Press, 2016.

Margolick, David. *Strange Fruit: Billie Holiday and the Biography of a Song.* New York: HarperCollins, 2001.

Pollack, Howard. *Aaron Copland: The Life and Work of an Uncommon Man.* New York: Henry Holt and Company, 1999.

Seaton, Douglass. *Ideas and Styles in the Western Musical Tradition.* 4th ed. Oxford: Oxford University Press, 2016.

Turino, Thomas, and James Lea, eds. *Identity and the Arts in Diaspora Communities.* Sterling Heights, MI: Harmonie Park Press, 2004.

Walker-Hill, Helen. *From Spirituals to Symphonies: African-American Women Composers and Their Music.* Urbana: University of Illinois Press, 2007.

Chapter 8

Ancelet, Barry Jean. *Cajun and Creole Music Makers: Musiciens Cadiens et Créoles.* Oxford: University Press of Mississippi, 1999.

Brinner, Benjamin. *Playing Across a Divide: Israeli-Palestinian Musical Encounters.* New York: Oxford University Press, 2009.

Dudley, Shannon. *Carnival Music in Trinidad: Experiencing Music, Expressing Culture.* New York: Oxford University Press, 2003.

Gilroy, Paul. *The Black Atlantic: Modernity and Double Consciousness.* Cambridge, MA: Harvard University Press, 1993.

Jones, Leroy. *Black Music.* New York: Akashy Classics, 2010.

Manuel, Peter. *Caribbean Currents: Caribbean Music from Rumba to Reggae.* Philadelphia, PA: Temple University Press, 2006.

Chapter 9

Flaes, Rob Boonzajer. *Brass Unbound: Secret Children of the Colonial Brass Band.* Amsterdam: Royal Tropical Institute, 2000.

Jones, Andrew F. *Like a Knife: Ideology and Genre in Contemporary Chinese Popular Music.* Ithaca, NY: East Asia Program, Cornell University, 1992.

Larkin, Colin, ed. *Encyclopedia of Popular Music.* 4th ed. 10 vols. New York: Oxford University Press, 2006.

Meintjes, Louise. *Dust of the Zulu: Ngoma Aesthetics after Apartheid.* Durham, NC: Duke University Press, 2017.

Moskowitz, Marc L. *Cries of Joy, Songs of Sorrow: Chinese Pop Music and Its Cultural Connotations.* Honolulu: University of Hawaii Press, 2009.

Rice, Timothy. *Music in Bulgaria: Experiencing Music, Expressing Culture.* New York: Oxford University Press, 2004.

Schechter, John M., ed. *Music in Latin American Culture: Regional Traditions.* New York: Schirmer Books, 1999.

Shepherd, John, ed. *Continuum Encyclopedia of Popular Music of the World*. London and New York: Continuum, 2003.

Tenaille, Frank. *Music Is the Weapon of the Future: Fifty Years of African Music*. Chicago, IL: Lawrence Hill Books, 2002.

Chapter 10

Beck, Guy L., ed. *Sacred Sound: Experiencing Music in World Religions*. Waterloo, ON: Wilfrid Laurier University Press, 2006.

Cutsinger, James S., ed. *Paths to the Heart: Sufism and the Christian East*. Bloomington, IN: World Wisdom, Inc., 2002.

Eliade, Mircea, ed. *Encyclopedia of Religion*, 16 vols. London: Macmillan Co., 1987.

Ellingson, Ter. "Music and Religion." In *Encyclopedia of Religion*, edited by Mircea Eliade. Vol. 10, 163–172. New York: Collier Macmillan, 1987.

Hartley, Elda, dir. *Requiem for a Faith,* DVD, Hartley Film Foundation, 2009. Available at https://www.youtube.com/watch?v=40yRXr5WlhE.

Mouw, Richard J., and Marc Noll. *Wonderful Words of Life: Hymns in American Protestant History and Theology*. Grand Rapids, MI: W.B. Eerdmans Publishing Co., 2004.

Norton, Barley. *Songs for the Spirits: Music and Mediums in Modern Vietnam*. Urbana: University of Illinois Press, 2009.

Patterson, Beverly Bush. *The Sound of the Dove: Singing in Appalachian Primitive Baptist Churches*. Urbana: University of Illinois Press, 2001.

Shiloah, Amnon. *Music in the World of Islam: A Socio-Cultural Study*. Repr. ed. Detroit, IL: Wayne State University Press, 2001.

Summit, Jeffrey. *The Lord's Song in a Strange Land: Music and Identity in Contemporary Jewish Worship*. London: Oxford University Press, 2000.

Weiss, Piero, and Richard Taruskin. *Music in the Western World: A History in Documents*. 2nd ed. Boston, MA: Cengage Learning, 2007.

Chapter 11

Barks, Coleman, trans. *The Essential Rumi*. Expanded ed. New York: HarperCollins, 2004.

Beaman, Patricia. *World Dance Cultures: From Ritual to Spectacle*. New York: Routledge, 2018.

Becker, Judith. *Deep Listeners: Music, Emotion, and Trancing*. Bloomington: Indiana University Press, 2004.

Berliner, Paul. *The Soul of Mbira: Music and Traditions of the Shona People of Zimbabwe*. Chicago, IL: University of Chicago Press, 1993.

Dorsey, Lilith. *Voodoo and African Traditional Religion*. New Orleans, LA: Warlock Press, 2021.

Emoff, Ron. *Recollecting from the Past: Musical Practice and Spiritual Possession on the East Coast of Madagascar*. Middletown, CT: Wesleyan University Press, 2002.

Smith, John D. *The Epic of Pabuji*. New Delhi: Katha, 2012.

Chapter 12

"Great Ritual Offerings to the Overarching Heaven," *The Daoist Encyclopedia*, last updated Oct. 17, 2009. https://en.daoinfo.org/wiki/Great_Ritual_Offerings_to_the_Overarching_Heaven.

Hall, Susan Elizabeth. *Sacred Space, Sacred Sound: The Acoustic Mysteries of Holy Places*. Wheaton, IL: Theosophical Publishing House, 2007.

Lee, Tong Soon. "Technology and the Production of Islamic Space: The Call to Prayer in Singapore." In *Eth-nomusicology: A Contemporary Reader*, edited by Jennifer Post, 199–208. New York: Routledge, 2006.

Qureshi, Regula Burckhardt. *Sufi Music of India and Pakistan: Sound, Context and Meaning in Qawwali*. New ed. Chicago, IL: University of Chicago Press, 2006.

Sarangrel. *Riding Windhorses: A Journey into the Heart of Mongolian Shamanism*. Detroit: Simon & Schuster, 2000.

Turnbull, Colin. *The Forest People*. Illustrated ed. New York: Touchstone, 1987.

Chapter 13

Abbate, Carolyn. *A History of Opera*. New York: W.W. Norton, 2015.

Brandon, James R., ed. *No and Kyogen in the Contemporary World*. Honolulu: University of Hawaii Press, 1997.

Charry, Eric. *Mande Music: Traditional and Modern Music of the Maninka and Mandinka of Western Africa*. Chicago, IL: University of Chicago Press, 2000.

Chau, Adam Yuet. *Miraculous Response: Doing Popular Religion in Contemporary China*. Stanford, CA: Stanford University Press, 2006.

Lau, Frederick. *Music in China: Experiencing Music, Expressing Culture*. Oxford: Oxford University Press, 2008.

Lord, Albert. *The Singer of Tales*. 2nd ed. Edited by Stephen Mitchell and Gregory Nagy. Cambridge, MA: Harvard University Press, 2000.

Okpewho, Isidore. *The Epic in Africa: Towards a Poetics of Oral Performance*. New York: Columbia University Press, 1991.

Park, Chan E. *Voices from the Straw Mat: Toward an Ethnography of Korean Story Singing*. Honolulu: University of Hawaii Press, 2003.

Pihl, Marshall L. *The Korean Singer of Tales*. New ed. Cambridge: Harvard University Press, 2003.

Silverberg, Ann L. "A Brief Introduction to Beijing Opera." *Education about Asia, Online Archive*, 17/1 (Asian Visual and Performing Arts, Part 1), Spring 2012. https://www.asianstudies.org/publications/eaa/archives/a-brief-introduction-to-beijing-opera/.

Chapter 14

Ali, Ahmed. *Twilight in Delhi*. Reprint ed. New Delhi: New Directions, 1994.

Anderson, Marian. *My Lord, What a Morning: An Autobiography*. Reprint ed. Urbana: University of Illinois Press, 2002.

Barmé, Geremie R. *In the Red: On Contemporary Chinese Culture*. New York: Columbia University Press, 1999.

Bernstein, Arthur, Naoki Sekine, and Dick Weissman. *The Global Music Industry: Three Perspectives*. New York: Routledge, 2007.

Dilling, Margaret Walker. *Stories inside Stories: Music and the Making of the Korean Olympic Ceremonies*. Berkeley: University of California Press, 1997.

Jeal, Tim. *Explorers of the Nile: The Triumph and Tragedy of a Great Victorian Adventure*. New Haven, CT: Yale University Press, 2011.

Jones, Stephen. *Plucking the Winds: Lives of Village Musicians in Old and New China*. Leiden: CHIME Foundation, 2004.

———. *Ritual and Music of North China: Shawm Bands in Shanxi*. With accompanying DVD. New York: Routledge, 2017.

Morcom, Anna. *Illicit Worlds of Indian Dance: Cultures of Exclusion*. Oxford: Oxford University Press, 2013.

Taylor, Timothy. *Global Pop: World Music, World Markets*. New York: Routledge. 1997.

Turino, Thomas. *Music as Social Life: The Politics of Participation*. Chicago, IL: University of Chicago Press, 2008.

Chapter 15

Booth, Gregory D., and Bradley Shope, eds. *More than Bollywood: Studies in Indian Popular Music*. Oxford: Oxford University Press, 2014.
Gaisberg, Fred W. *The Music Goes Round*. New York: Arno Press, 1977.
Jones, Andrew F. *Yellow Music: Media Culture and Colonial Modernity in the Chinese Jazz Age*. Durham, NC: Duke University Press, 2001.
Morcom, Anna. *Hindi Film Songs and the Cinema*. Aldershot: Ashgate, 2007.
Ritter, Jonathan, and J. Michael Daughtry, eds. *Music in the Post-9/11 World*. New York: Routledge, 2007.
Slobin, Mark, ed. *Global Soundtracks: Worlds of Film Music*. Middletown, CT: Wesleyan University Press, 2008.
Sterne, Jonathan, ed. *The Sound Studies Reader*. New York: Routledge, 2012.

Credits

IMAGE CREDITS

0.1 Courtesy of Jonathan C. Kramer; 1.1 Erich Auerbach/Getty Images; 1.2 https://en.wikipedia.org/wiki/Vajtim#/media/File:Gjama.jpg; 1.3 Marco Saracco/Shutterstock.com; 1.4 https://en.wikipedia.org/wiki/B%C3%A9la_Bart%C3%B3k#/media/File:Bartok_recording_folk_music.jpg; 1.5 https://en.wikipedia.org/wiki/Frances_Densmore#/media/File:Frances_Densmore_recording_Mountain%20_%20Chief2.jpg; 1.6L Alila Medical Media/Shutterstock.com; 1.6R Courtesy of Dr. Michael Y. Parker; 1.7L https://en.wikipedia.org/wiki/Hurrian_songs#/media/File:Hurritische_hymne; 1.7R https://en.wikipedia.org/wiki/Musical_notation#/media/File:Bachlut1.png; 1.8L https://en.wikipedia.org/wiki/Znamenny_chant#/media/; 1.8R https://en.wikipedia.org/wiki/Musical_notation#/media/File:Bhat_notation1.jpg; 1.9L https://en.wikipedia.org/wiki/Tablature#/media/File:Guitar_tablature_sample.svg; 1.9R https://en.wikipedia.org/wiki/Guitar_chord#/media/File:FifthsCSevenths.svg; 1.10 https://upload.wikimedia.org/wikipedia/commons/1/1d/Frontispiece_Libro_de_m%C3%BAsica_de_vihuela_de_mano_intitulado_El_maestro_by_Luis_Milan.jpg; 1.11L https://en.wikipedia.org/wiki/Tablature#/media/File:Vihuela-Tab_Fuenllana_1554.jpg; 1.11R https://en.wikipedia.org/wiki/File:Tempyo_Biwa_Fu.jpg; 2.1 Courtesy of Jonathan C. Kramer; 2.2 snapgalleria/Shutterstock.com; 2.3 https://en.wikipedia.org/wiki/Enrico_Caruso#/media/File:Enrico_Caruso_VIII.png; 2.4 https://commons.wikimedia.org/wiki/File:Jimmie_Rodgers_in_1931.jpg; 2.5 Jean-Claude Deutsch/Paris Match via Getty Images; 2.6 Victoria Hazou/AFP/Getty Images; 2.7 https://commons.wikimedia.org/wiki/File:Salif_Keita.JPG; 2.8 Jack Vartoogian/Getty images 1279212223; 3.1 Peter Bischoff/Getty Images; 3.2L https://en.wikipedia.org/wiki/Bianzhong_of_Marquis_Yi_of_Zeng#/media/File:%E6%B9%96%E5%8C%97%E5%8D%9A%E7%89%A9%E9%A4%A8%E6%9B%BE%E4%BE%AF%E4%B9%99%E7%B7%A8%E9%90%98.jpg; 3.2R Religious Images/UIG; 3.3 https://www.wikiart.org/en/ancient-egyptian-painting/a-mural-of-a-blind-musician-playing-a-harp-from-the-tomb-of-the-ancient-egyptian-scribe-called-nakht--1390; 3.4L Mario Andrioll/Shutterstock; 3.4R Three Lions/Getty Images; 3.5 Independent Picture Service/UIG via Getty Images; 3.6 Michel Renaudeau/Gettyimages; 3.7 Courtesy of Alison E. Arnold; 3.8 Andy Sheppard/Redferns via Getty Images; 3.9 Courtesy of Alison E. Arnold; 3.10L https://en.wikipedia.org/wiki/Pipa#/media/File:Female_figure_as_Venus%20_T'ang_dynasty.jpg; 3.10R https://www.metmuseum.org/art/collection/search/54052; 3.11 Courtesy of Heiko Spallek; 3.12L Courtesy of Ulf Jagfors; 3.12R https://en.wikipedia.org/wiki/Ngoni_(instrument)#/media/File:Bassekou_Kouyate_photo.jpg; 3.13L Courtesy of Jonathan C. Kramer; 3.13R DeAgostini/Getty Images; 3.14 Courtesy of Jonathan C. Kramer; 3.15L

Alison E. Arnold; 5.2R Courtesy of Alison E. Arnold; 5.3 Dario Lo Presti/Shutterstock.com; 5.4 https://en.wikipedia.org/wiki/Narada#/media/File:Narad_-_Vintage_Print.jpg; 5.5 12_ Tribes/Shutterstock.com; 5.6 Danita Delimont; 5.7 ChameleonsEye/Shutterstock.com; 5.8 Courtesy of Alison E. Arnold; 6.1 Paul Bernhardt; 6.2 https://en.wikipedia.org/wiki/Nadia_ Boulanger#/media/File:Nadia_Boulanger_1925.jpg; 6.3 Alamy 2D2NH0C; 6.4 basel101658/ Shutterstock.com; 6.5 http://en.wikipedia.org/wiki/File:Minuet_(PSF).png; 6.6 Alamy EH6NAA.jpg; 6.7 Patrice Hauser; 6.8 http://en.wikipedia.org/wiki/File:Henry_Ossawa_ Tanner_-_The_Banjo_Lesson.jpg; 7.0 JJ van Zyl/Wikimedia Commons/CC-BY-SA-30/ GFDL; 7.1L http://en.wikipedia.org/wiki/File:2002_TN_Proof.png; 7.1R http://en.wikipedia.org/wiki/File:2002_LA_Proof.png; 7.2L Sergei Svetlitsky/Newsmakers; 7.2R Jeffrey Holsen/Wikimedia Commons/CC-BY-SA-30/GFDL; 7.3 Courtesy of Alison E. Arnold; 7.4L elnavegante/Shutterstock.com; 7.4R ALEJANDRO PAGNI/AFP/Getty Images; 7.5 Dasha Petrenko/Shutterstock.com; 7.6 Roger Viollet Collection/Getty Images; 7.7 Michael Ochs Archives/Getty Image; 7.8 https://en.wikipedia.org/wiki/Irving_Berlin#/media/File:Irving_ Berlin_-_Ragtime.JPG; 7.9 APIC/Getty Images; 7.10 Pix Inc/Pix Inc/The LIFE Picture Collection/Getty Images; 7.11 Florence Price portrait by G. Nelidoff in Chicago, Illinois, Special Collections, University of Arkansas Libraries, Fayetteville. MC988Box1Folder12Item 1FlorencePrice.jpeg; 7.12 Courtesy of Alison E. Arnold; 7.13L Courtesy of Jonathan C. Kramer; 7.13R Courtesy of Jonathan C. Kramer; 7.14L Courtesy of Jonathan C. Kramer; 7.14R Courtesy of Jonathan C. Kramer; 7.15 Courtesy of Jonathan C. Kramer; 8.1 Buyenlarge/Getty Images; 8.2L User:Bozotextino/Wikimedia Commons/CC-BY-SA-30; 8.2R George Rose/ Getty Images; 8.3 Douglas Mason/Getty Images; 8.4 Courtesy of Hip Ksor; 8.5 Rodney Legall / Alamy Stock Photo; 8.6 Sean Drakes/LatinContent/Getty Images; 8.7 Hiroyuki Ito/ Getty Images; 8.8 Joinmepic/Shutterstock.com; 9.1 Werner Forman/Universal Images Group/Getty Images; 9.2 Photosebia/Shutterstock.com; 9.3 Art Media/Print Collector/ Getty Images; 9.4 https://en.wikipedia.org/wiki/Pete_Seeger#/media/File:Pete_Seeger_ NYWTS.jpg; 9.5 Maria Stoyanova. Courtesy of Timothy Rice; 9.6 Gems/Redferns; 9.7 https://en.wikipedia.org/wiki/V%C3%ADctor_Jara_Stadium#/media/File:Estadio_V%C3%ADctor_Jara_(calle).PNG; 9.8 Rodrigo Vaz/Getty Images; 9.9 Fin Costello/ Redferns; 9.10 Al Pereira/WireImage; 9.11 FETHI BELAID/AFP/Getty Images; 9.12 Courtesy of Jonathan Kramer; 9.13 FREDERIC J BROWN/AFP/Getty Images; 9.14L http:// en.wikipedia.org/wiki/File:Pablocasals.jpg; 9.14R http://en.wikipedia.org/wiki/File:Dmitri1. jpg; 10.1 https://en.wikipedia.org/wiki/Augustine_of_Hippo#/media/File:Sandro_Botticelli_-_St_Augustin_dans_son_cabinet_de_travail.jpg; 10.2L The Print Collector/Print Collector/Getty Images; 10.2C Xavier ROSSI/Gamma-Rapho via Getty Images; 10.2R http:// en.wikipedia.org/wiki/File:Muso_Soseki_3.jpg; 10.3 AJP/Shutterstock.com; 10.4 https:// en.wikipedia.org/wiki/Aleppo_Codex#/media/File:Aleppo_Codex_Joshua_1_1.jpg;10.5 Courtesy of Jonathan Kramer; 10.6 https://commons.wikimedia.org/wiki/File:Mevlana_ Statue,_Buca.jpg; 10.7 Tim Hall/Redferns; 11.1 Courtesy of Jonathan C. Kramer; 11.2L Courtesy of Jonathan C. Kramer; 11.2R Courtesy of Jonathan C. Kramer; 11.3 Shiiko Alexander/Alamy stock photo 2A76B5E; 11.4 GALI TIBBON/AFP/Getty Images; 11.5 MyLoupe/UIG via Getty Images; 11.6 Courtesy of Alison E. Arnold; 11.7L Courtesy of Alison E. Arnold; 11.7R Courtesy of Alison E. Arnold; 11.8L magicinfoto/Shutterstock.com; 11.8R magicinfoto/Shutterstock.com; 11.9 Agung Parameswara/Getty Images; 11.10 Sylvain Grandadam; 11.11 AJP/Shutterstock.com; 11.12L Travelstock44-Juergen Held; 11.12R Zzvet/Shutterstock.com; 11.13 User:MicheleLovesArt/Wikimedia Commons/CC-BY-SA 20; 12.1L happystock/Shutterstock.com; 12.1R topten22photo/Shutterstock.com; 12.2L

VIDEO CREDITS

Chapter 1

1.5: Competing Amazonian songbirds, Paramaribo, Suriname, 2008. Courtesy of Jonathan C. Kramer.

1.8: Buzzing beetle, Kaulong area, southwest New Britain, Papua New Guinea. Birgit Drüppel, *Re-counting Knowledge in Song: Change Reflected in Kaulong Music* (Boroko: Institute of Papua New Guinea Studies, 2009). Courtesy of Birgit Drüppel.

1.9: Albanian funeral ritual, *gjama*. Courtesy of Fran Kodra.

1.10: Shape note singing. Courtesy of Great Smoky Mountains Association; Valerie Polk.

1.11: *Biwa* notation. Demonstration courtesy of Silvain Guignard.

Chapter 2

2.1: Kajod Wangmo singing a "sky song" in Yulin, PRC, 2006. Courtesy of Jonathan C. Kramer.

2.2: Vocal folds. Courtesy of Michael Y. Parker, www.wilmingtonhealth.com; Seth M. Cohen, MD, MPH, and Leda Scearce, MM, MS, CCC-SLP, and Duke Voice Care Center, www.dukevoicecare.org.

2.3: Young voices: 1. Lalibela, Ethiopia, 2012; 2. Yulin, Shaanxi province, PRC, 2006. Courtesy of Jonathan C. Kramer.

2.4: Quechua traditional ensemble, Cuzco, Peru. Courtesy of Jorge Choquehuillca Huallpa and Familia Choquehuillca.

2.7: *Katajjaq* throat singing by Karen Panigoniak and Ida Kolola, recorded in Arviat, Nunavut, Canada, 2021. Courtesy of Karen Panigoniak.

2.8: Bengali wedding ululation. Courtesy of Rupin Dang, Wilderness Films India, Ltd., WildfilmsIndia.

2.9: Unidentified farmer/folk singer, Yulin, Shaanxi province, PRC, 2006. Courtesy of Jonathan C. Kramer.

2.10: Tibetan love song. Courtesy of Tsering Samdrup and the Plateau Music Project.

2.11: Whisper singing. Courtesy of Olympe Niragira and Joseph Torobeka.

2.12: Gospel singing in Malawi, Limbe Mvano Choir. Blantyre Synod, Church of Central Africa Presbyterian, Malawi. Courtesy of Karen Plater, associate secretary for stewardship, the Presbyterian Church in Canada, www.presbyterian.ca.

2.13: London Bulgarian Choir. Courtesy of Dessi Stefanova and the London Bulgarian Choir and Wellcome Institute.

2.14: Estonian Song Festival XXVI, Tallinn, 2014. Courtesy of Toomas Luhats, Estonian national television channel (ETV).

2.15: Old Time Camp Meeting song. Courtesy of Mount Carmel Baptist Church, Atlanta, GA, Pastor Timothy Flemming Sr., www.mtcarmelbaptistchurch.org.

2.17: Throat singing, Bao Narisu, Mongolia. Courtesy of Bao Narisu.

2.19: Irish lilting. Courtesy of Eimear Arkins, with bodhrán accompaniment by Shane Farrell.

2.20: Jimmie Rodgers. Courtesy of Jimmie Rodgers Foundation and Museum, Meridian, MS, www.jimmierodgers.com; and the Folklore Alliance International, Kansas City, MO, www.folkalliance.org.

2.21: Umm Kulthum. From *Umm Kulthum, A Voice Like Egypt*, Michal Goldman, producer. Courtesy of Michal Goldman. © 1998. All rights reserved.

2.24: Mohammad Reza Shajarian, Iranian vocalist. Courtesy of Shabnam Ataei, IT manager of Maestro Mohammad Reza Shajarian, www.mohammadrezashajarian.com.

Chapter 3

3.1: Korean court ensemble, National Gugak orchestra. From *Gugak: The Korean Traditional Music and Dance*, DVD publication of the National Gugak Center, Seoul, Republic of Korea. Courtesy of the National Gugak Center, www.gugak.go.kr:9001/eng/. © 2011. All rights reserved.

3.2: *Kalumbu* (musical bow) played by Chris Haambwiila, Zambia Roadside 2, CD, SWP 041. Courtesy of Michael Baird, founder, SWP Records, www.swprecords.com.

3.3: *Berimbau*. Acervo da capoeira Angola YouTube Channel by Mestre Fábio Melo, Courtesy of Fábio Melo.

3.4: Celtic harp. Julie Gorka playing Scottish traditional tune, "Lochaber No More," recorded by Alison E. Arnold, 2014. Courtesy of Alison E. Arnold.

3.5: *Arpa*, Paraguayan harp played by Silvio Solis, recorded in Providence, RI, 2011. Courtesy of Jonathan C. Kramer.

3.6: Burmese *saung gauk* (arched harp), played by Zaw Win Maung in Kyaukpadaung, Myanmar, 1998. Courtesy of Gavin Douglas, University of North Carolina, Greensboro.

3.7: *Seperewa* (harp-lute) played at the Center for Cultural and African Studies, Nkruma University, Kumasi, Ghana, 2006. Courtesy of Ulf Jägfors.

3.8: Lyre documentary. Courtesy of Michael Levy, www.ancientlyre.com.

3.9: Ethiopian *krar* (lyre), Totot Traditional Restaurant, Addis Ababa, 2013. Courtesy of Jonathan C. Kramer.

3.10: Arabic *ud* (lute) played by Naji Hilal, www.najihilal.com, recorded by Alison E. Arnold, 2021. Courtesy of Alison E. Arnold.

3.11: *Tar* (Iranian lute) played by Sahba Motallebi. Courtesy of Sahba Motallebi, www.sahbamusic.com.

3.12: *Dotar.* The late Uzbeki *dotar* master, Abdurahim Hamidov, recorded in 2001. Courtesy of Jean During.

3.13: *Setar* (Iranian lute) played by Sahba Motallebi. Courtesy of Sahba Motallebi, www.sahbamusic.com.

3.14: *Sitar* (North Indian lute) played by Harihar Sharan Bhatt at Jawahar Kala Kendra, Jaipur, Rajasthan, India, 2007. Courtesy of Harihar Sharan Bhatt, www.trivet.org.

3.15: *Pipa* (Chinese lute). "Collage 2000" played by Wu Man, www.wumanpipa.org. Courtesy of Brandon Ahlstrom and Shuman Associates, New York, NY.

3.16: *Charango.* Courtesy of Jhonathan "PUKA" Simon.

3.17: Ukulele. Herb Ohta, Sr. playing "Hawaii" on Oahu, HI. Courtesy of Herb Ohta, Sr.

3.18: *Akonting* (Senegalese lute). Remi Diatta playing and singing *"Alinom de Caraba."* Appreciation to Remi Diatta and Laemouahuma (Daniel) Jatta. Courtesy of Chuck Levy, videographer and publisher, Gainesville, FL. © 2008. All rights reserved.

3.19: Banjo. Chuck Levy playing clawhammer banjo in Gainesville, FL. Courtesy of Chuck Levy, www.banjourneys.com. © 2013. All rights reserved.

3.20: Sergio and Odair Assad playing Astor Piazzolla's "Tango Suite" for two guitars, 1997. Courtesy of Sergio and Odair Assad, www.assadbrothers.com.

3.21: *Kamanche* (spike fiddle). Imamyar Hasanov playing Azerbaijani Mugham Bayati-Shiraz. Courtesy of Imamyar Hasanov, www.kamancha.com.

3.22: Ciompi String Quartet. Eric Pritchard and Hsiao-mei Ku (violins), Jonathan Bagg (viola), Fred Raimi (cello), playing Haydn String Quartet Op. 76, 3rd movement. Courtesy of Hsiao-mei Ku and the Ciompi Quartet, www.ciompi.org.

3.23: *Kamanja* (Moroccan viola). Ouled Ben Aguida ensemble performing at a wedding celebration in Safi: Hafida Hasnaouia, lead vocals; Aicha Nousmi, co-lead vocals; Bouch'aib Benshlih, *kamanja*; Boujm'a Benshlih, *darbuka* (goblet drum) and vocals; Miloud Hilali, *ud* (lute); Mustapha Hokaki, *bendir* (frame drum); Hassan Zatani, *bendir*. Courtesy of Alessandra Ciucci.

3.24: *Sarangi* (North Indian fiddle) demonstration by Dhruva Ghosh, 2012. Courtesy of Jasper Berben, Stichting Nieuw Ensemble & Atlas Ensemble, www.nieuw-ensemble.nl/en/.

3.25: *Morin khuur*, played by Mongolian musician Daxi Jiapu, at Heavenly Lake, Xinjiang, PRC. Courtesy of Alison E. Arnold.

3.26: *Santouri* (Greek hammered dulcimer). Areti Ketime singing and playing "Nanourisma" (traditional lullaby) at the "Tribute to Asia Minor" concert, the Odeon of Herodes Artticus, Greece. Courtesy of Areti Ketime, aretiketime.com.

3.27: *Qanun* (Arabic zither) played by George Sawa. Courtesy of George Dimitri Sawa, georgedimitrisawa.com.

3.28: Harpsichord. The late Rafael Puyana playing Domenico Scarlatti's Sonata K119. Courtesy of Canal de Hauptwerkian.

3.29: *Guqin* (Chinese long zither) played by Dai Xiaolian, Shanghai Conservatory. Courtesy of Dai Xiaolian.

3.30: *Guzheng* (Chinese long zither) played at a teahouse northwest of Beijing, 2007. Courtesy of Alison E. Arnold.

3.31: *Gayageum* (long zither) played by Yi Ji-Young. From *Gugak: The Korean Traditional Music and Dance*, DVD publication of the National Gugak Center, Seoul, Republic of Korea. Courtesy of the National Gugak Center, www.gugak.go. Kr:9001/eng/ © 2011. All rights reserved. Courtesy of Yi Ji-Young, www.yijiyoung.org.

3.32: *Dan bau*, in accompanying ensemble for water puppet show, Hanoi, Vietnam. Courtesy of Alison E. Arnold.

3.33: Bullroarer played by Wirruungga Dunnggiirr. Courtesy of Michael Ney, Eagle Spirit Media.

3.34: Arabic *ney* improvisation, played by Bassam Saba. Courtesy of April Centrone, info@nyarabicorchestra.org.

3.35: Native American fipple flute played by Wolfs Robe. Courtesy of Wolfs Robe, akaflutemanent.com.

3.36: Pennywhistle played by Nelson Makoka, and Solomon Sibiya, guitar, of the Sophia Town Stars. Courtesy of Nikki Wanting, African Frenzy.

3.37: *Dvoyanka* (double flute). Courtesy of Zdravko Beshendzhiev.

3.39: *Enkwanzi* (Ugandan panpipes) played by Haruna Walusimbi of the Nile Beat Artists Traditional Ensemble, www.nilebeatartists.org, 2013. Courtesy of Jonathan C. Kramer.

3.40: Ocarina. Courtesy of Durian Songbird, Songbird Ocarinas, songbirdocarina.com.

3.41: *Nplooj* (leaf) played by a Hmong woman. Courtesy of Mikkel Hornnes.

3.42: *Suona* (Chinese oboe) played in a public park in Urumqi, Xinjiang, 2007. Courtesy of Alison E. Arnold.

3.43: *Taepyeongso* (Korean oboe). From *Gugak: The Korean Traditional Music and Dance*, DVD publication of the National Gugak Center, Seoul, Republic of Korea. Courtesy of the National Gugak Center, www.gugak.go.kr:9001/eng/. © 2011. All rights reserved.

3.44: *Duduk*. Performer Arsen Petrosyan; video documentary by Robert Louis Baghdasaryan.

3.45: Uilleann pipes. Courtesy of Darragh O Heiligh.

3.46: *Cornamusa* (Italian bagpipe). Courtesy of Luca Paciaroni, bagpipes and wind instruments maker, www.varropipemaker.com.

3.47: Royal Military Tattoo, Edinburgh Castle, Scotland. Courtesy of Barry Ferguson.

3.48: *Pungi*. Alexandra Sfintesco, filmed in Kochi, Kerala, Southwest India.

3.49: *Launeddas* (Sardinian triple-pipe clarinet). Courtesy of Pitano Perra, www.pitano.it.

3.50: European clarinet. Mauricio Murcia Bedoya playing Jean Françaix, Clarinet Concerto, 4th movement (1967), with the Orquesta Filarmónica de Bogotá, Colombia, 2007. Courtesy of Mauricio Murcia Bedoya.

3.51: Klezmer. Courtesy of Ahnes Horovitz Binder, manager, Budapest Klezmer Band, budapestklezmerband.webnode.hu.

3.52: Wanamaker Organ. The Virgil Fox Legacy, virgilfoxlegacy.com. Courtesy of Len Levasseur.

3.53: *Khaen* (mouth organ) played by Sombat Simlah, Thailand. Courtesy of Mikkel Hornnes.

3.54: English concertina played by Tim Smith, recorded by Alison E. Arnold, 2014. Courtesy of Alison E. Arnold.

3.55: Accordion with Chinese *sheng* (mouth organ), Chen Jun (accordion) and unknown *sheng* player at the American Accordionists' Association Convention, 2008. Courtesy of Linda Soley Reed, President, American Accordionists' Association, www.ameraccord.com.

3.56: Didgeridoo. Courtesy of Michael Ney, Eagle Spirit Media, 2021.

3.57: *Dung-chen* (Tibetan trumpets). Courtesy of Makoto Masaje and Jetokey.

3.58: Bugle. Army Sgt. Keith Clark playing "Taps" at the State Funeral of John F. Kennedy, 1963. Courtesy of Jari Villanueva, www.tapsbugler.com.

3.59: North Carolina Brass Band, Brian Meixner, director. www.ncbrassband.org. Courtesy of Jonathan C. Kramer.

3.60: *Pat waing* (drum circle) played by a senior student group at the Yangon University of Culture, Myanmar. Courtesy of Gavin Douglas.

3.61: *Derbake* (goblet drum) played by Jussef Bichara, director, Escuela Banjara, Chile. Courtesy of Victoria and Jussef Bichara, www.banjara.cl.

3.62: *Seoljanggu*, Korean dance performed by *janggu* drummer. Courtesy of Kim Seong-hoon. Seunggyun

3.63: West African "talking drum" played by Ayan Bisi Adeleke. Louis Jackson, camera, Ade Panko, director/editor. Courtesy of Louis Jackson III, Creative Improv Productions, Inc.

3.64: Powwow drum played by Armour Hill Singers at the Las Vegas powwow. Courtesy of Armour Hill Singers.

3.65: Glen Velez playing the frame drum. Courtesy of Glen Velez, glenvelez.com.

3.66: *Pandeiro* (frame drum) played by Louis-Daniel Joly. Courtesy of Louis-Daniel **Joly**, founder, Baratanga Productions, www.baratanga.com.

3.67: Congas played by Juan Álamo. Courtesy of Juan Álamo, www.juanalamo.com.

3.68: Large hanging bell at Sudeoksa Buddhist temple, Republic of Korea. Courtesy of Donald Belmore (DragonDon).

3.69: Church bells in Seville, Spain. Courtesy of Jennifer Westrom.

3.70: *Agogo* (iron double bell). Courtesy of Chief Yagbe Awolowo Onilu Agba Awo of Ile-Ife, Osun state, Nigeria.

3.71: Castanets played by Barbara Hennerfeind, with Erik Weisenberger, guitar. Courtesy of Barbara Hennerfeind and Duo Agua y Vino, www.guitarbara.de.

3.72: *Baithak gana* ("seated singing"). Rakieb Waggidhossain (vocalist), Roy Raghu (*dholak*), and Narinder Singh (*dhantal*) in Paramaribo, Suriname. Courtesy of Jonathan C. Kramer.

3.73: *Embaire* (Ugandan pit xylophone). Courtesy of Jonathan C. Kramer.

3.74: *Jaltarang* (Indian tuned, water-filled ceramic bowls) played by Ranjana Pradhan, Sydney, Australia, 2006. Courtesy of Damien Reilly, CEO, Blue Pie Productions, www.bluepierecords.com.

3.75: *Endongo* (Ugandan thumb pianos) played by James Isabirye and Haruna Walusimbi of the Nile Beat Artists Traditional Ensemble, www.nilebeatartists.org, 2013. Courtesy of Jonathan C. Kramer.

3.76: *Zil* (finger cymbals) played by belly dancer Christine Dempsey ("Willow"). Courtesy of Christine Dempsey, www.bellydancewillow.com.

3.77: Soultone cymbals played by drummer Brook Alexander. Soultone Cymbals Extreme Demo Video, 2011. Courtesy of Iki Levy, founder, Soultone Cymbals, www.soultonecymbals. com.

3.78: Tibetan *rolmo* (cymbals). Labrang Monastery, Gansu province, PRC. Courtesy of Alison E. Arnold.

3.79: Hand-held gongs, as used in Beijing opera, Jianxi province, PRC. Courtesy of Jonathan C. Kramer.

3.80: Tuned gong performance in Guilguila, Tanudan, Kalinga, Philippines. Courtesy of Glenn Stallsmith.

3.81: Chinese tam tam demonstration. Courtesy of Mark Wessels, director of internet activities, Vic Firth Company, www.vicfirth.com.

3.82: Theremin documentary by Carolina Eyck, www.carolinaeyck.com.

3.84: Korean *shinawi* folk ensemble. From *Gugak: The Korean Traditional Music and Dance*, DVD publication of the National Gugak Center, Seoul, Republic of Korea. Courtesy of the National Gugak Center, www.gugak.go.kr:9001/eng/. © 2011. All rights reserved.

3.85: South Indian Carnatic ensemble, with Aishu Venkataraman (violin), accompanied by *kanjira* (tambourine) and *mridangam* (barrel drum). Courtesy of V.R. Venkataraman, www.divinestrings.com.

3.86: Javanese *gamelan*. Courtesy of Londoireng.

3.87: Surinamese gamelan. Bangun-Utomo Ensemble, Mariënburg, Suriname. Courtesy of Jonathan C. Kramer.

3.88: Starlift Junior Steel Orchestra rehearsal, directed by Barry Mannette, Port of Spain, Trinidad, March 5, 2008. Courtesy of Alison E. Arnold.

3.89: *Sikuri* panpipe band in Aguas Calientes, Peru. Courtesy of M. Jill Barone.

Chapter 4

4.1: University of Michigan Marching Band. Courtesy of John D. Pasquale. All rights administered by the University of Michigan Board of Regents. University of Michigan Marching Band, © 2014. All rights reserved.

4.3: Souhail Kaspar demonstrating Arabic rhythm pattern on *dumbek* (goblet drum), recorded by Jonathan C. Kramer. Courtesy of Jonathan C. Kramer.

4.4: Belly dance. Souhail Kaspar, *Masterclass at Home Series: Rhythm and Movement for Egyptian Raqs Al-Sharqi*, Vol. 3, DVD. Courtesy of Souhail Kaspar, www.neareastmusic.com.

4.5: *Adi talam.* Segment of Carnatic percussion lecture/demonstration by Kapil Ramanarayanan, *mridangam* and Samarth Rao, *kanjira*, recorded at NC Museum of Art, May 16, 2021. Courtesy of Phil Hart, Dataforge.

4.6: *Shakuhachi* (Japanese bamboo flute) played by Koji Matsunobu, University of Washington, Seattle campus, March 2008, recorded by Jonathan C. Kramer and Alison E. Arnold. Courtesy of Jonathan C. Kramer and Alison E. Arnold.

4.7: *Sean-nós* singing session, recorded by Seán Ó Mainnín for the Gaelic Song in Ireland, Scotland, and Canada conference, funded by the Irish Research Council, convened by Lillis Ó Laoire, Roinn na Gaeilge/Discipline of Irish, the National University of Galway. Courtesy of Lillis Ó Laoire.

4.8: Polyrhythm. From FOLI (*There Is No Movement Without Rhythm*) produced by The Rhythm Project Company and A Moving Company, Thomas Roebers and Floris Leeuwenberg, directors. Courtesy of Thomas Roebers and Floris Leeuwenberg. © 2010. All rights reserved.

4.9: *Bateria* rehearsal in the Mocidade Samba School building, 2013. Courtesy of Paul Hodge, SoloAroundWorld, www.genpolicy.com.

4.10: Prison work gangs. From Afro-American Work Songs in a Texas Prison, Folklore Research Films; Pete and Toshi Seeger with Bruce Jackson, producers. Courtesy of Pete Seeger. © 1966. All rights reserved.

4.11: Women hoeing garden rows. Ghanaian Ministry of Food and Agriculture in partnership with Engineers Without Borders Canada. Courtesy of Megan Timmins Putnam, ing. Engineers Without Borders Canada.

4.12: Traditional waulking song sung by Sgioba Luaidh Inbhirchluaidh, learned from Flora McNeil of Barra. Courtesy of Florence M. Dunlop.

4.13: Wedding party in Mali. Courtesy of Jeremy Chevrier, Rootsyrecords.

4.14: Hand and foot drum solo by Nana Kimati Dinizulu, the Dinizulu Center for African Culture and Research, Jamaica, NY. Courtesy of Nana Kimati Dinizulu, Jr., www.dinizulu-center.org.

4.15: *Ghatam* (South Indian clay pot) played by Vikku Vinayakram, with Afro-Swedish band, Mynta. Courtesy of Christian Paulin, www.mynta.net.

4.16: Tito Puente playing *timbales* in "El Sabroso Son," written, composed, and arranged by "La Palabra," aka Rodolfo M. Foster. Courtesy of La Palabra.

4.17: *Slendro* (five-tone scale) and *pelog* (seven-tone scale) *gamelan* tuning systems. Demonstration by Professor John Caldwell, UNC-Chapel Hill. Courtesy of Alison E. Arnold.

4.18: Azerbaijan *mugam.* "Singing at a small mosque" video clip from the bonus DVD to the recording entitled *Music of Central Asia* vol. 6: *Alim and Fargana Qasimov: Spiritual Music of Azerbaijan*, SFW40525, courtesy of Smithsonian Folkways Recordings. *Music of Central Asia* is a co-production of the Aga Khan Music Initiative and Smithsonian Folkways Recordings. (p) © 2007. Used by permission.

4.19: *Muqam* (Uighur modal system). Uighur musicians playing in Kashgar, Xinjiang Province, PRC, 2007. Courtesy of Alison E. Arnold.

4.20: *Ragam.* Demonstration of Carnatic *veena* and South Indian mode by Smriti Sridharan. Courtesy of Alison E. Arnold.

4.21: Demonstration of Chinese pentatonic scale and performance of *Erquan Yingyue* ("Moon Reflected in the Second Spring") by Xiao Chu. Courtesy of Dai Xiaolian.

4.22: Demonstration of Korean modes for both voice and *gayageum* by Jinsook Choi, Dr. Jocelyn Clark, and Seunggyun Kim (buk). Courtesy of Dr. Jocelyn Clark.

4.26: *Sijo* (traditional Korean art song) sung by Hong Changnam, with National Gugak Center Ensemble. From *Gugak: The Korean Traditional Music and Dance*, DVD publication of the National Gugak Center, Seoul, Republic of Korea. Courtesy of the National Gugak Center, www.gugak.go.kr:9001/eng/. © 2011. All rights reserved.

4.27: *Ajaeng* (Korean seven-string bowed zither) played by Kim Young-gil. From *Gugak: The Korean Traditional Music and Dance*, DVD publication of the National Gugak Center, Seoul, Republic of Korea. Courtesy of the National Gugak Center, www.gugak.go.kr:9001/eng/. © 2011. All rights reserved.

4.28: "*Shadanane,*" by Muthuswami Dikshitar, sung by Vijayalakshmy Subramaniam. Accompanists: Akkarai Subhalakshmi (violin), Neyveli Skandasubramaniam (*mridangam*), Dr. S. Karthick (*ghatam*), Harini Ramakrishnan (*tambura*), Shankari Subramaniam (vocal support). Courtesy of Vijayalakshmy Subramaniam, www.vijayalakshmysubramaniam.com.

4.29: Mongolian long song. Courtesy of Adiyabold Namkhai, New Milestone Tours, Mongolia.

4.31: *Taqsim.* Demonstration of Arabic mode and improvisational techniques by Naji Hilal. Courtesy of Alison E. Arnold.

4.32: "*Soeur Monique,*" by François Couperin, played by Pastór de Lasala on a double Flemish harpsichord made by Carey Beebe, in Neutral Bay, New South Wales, Australia, 1998. Courtesy of Pastór de Lasala.

4.33: Irish fiddle. Demonstration of Irish ornamental style by Mairead Brady. Courtesy of Alison E. Arnold.

4.34: *Gaida* (Bulgarian bagpipe) played by the late Dafo Trendafilov in village of Gela, near Shiroka Laka Smolyan, Bulgaria, 2005, filmed by Ivor Davies. Courtesy of Ivor Davies.

4.35: *Tambura* (Indian long-necked lute) played by *dhrupad* singer Shanti Shivani at North Carolina State University, 2011. Courtesy of Shanti Shivani, www.shantishivani.com.

4.40: *Bansuri* (Bangladeshi bamboo flute) played by Jalal Ahmad. Courtesy of Nasim Haider.

4.41: *Gadulka* (Bulgarian fiddle) played by Ivan Iliev Kovachev at Bulgarian folk music workshop in Switzerland. Courtesy of Ivan Iliev Kovachev, www.folkfactory.com, www.audiofactory.com.

4.42: *Rabab* (Afghani plucked lute) played by the late Ustad Rahim Kushnawaz, filmed by John Baily in 1994. From *Ustad Rahim: Herat's Rubab Maestro*, John Baily, producer/director, distributed by Royal Anthropological Institute, London. Courtesy of John Baily. © 2008. All rights reserved.

4.43: "*Samai Nahawand*" by Simon Shaheen, played by Maya Beiser (cello), Simon Shaheen (*ud*), and Glen Velez (frame drum). From the album *Kinship—Maya Beiser*, Koch International Classics. Courtesy of Maya Beiser. © 2000. All rights reserved.

4.44: "*Nhemamusasa*" played on *mbiras* (Shona thumb pianos) by Ambuya Beauler Dyoko and Cosmas Magaya. Courtesy of Cosmas Magaya.

4.48: *Isicathamiya.* "*Inkanyezi Nezazi*" ("The Star and the Wiseman") performed by Joseph Shabalala and Ladysmith Black Mambazo. Courtesy of Ladysmith Black Mambazo. © 1998. All rights reserved.

4.49: *"Shojo No Tsuru," sankyoku* performance by Yamaguchi Goro (*shakuhachi*), Nakanoshima Keiko (*koto*), and Nakanoshima Kinichi (*shamisen*). Recording by NHK, 1979. Courtesy of John Singer.

4.50: Irish session at the Modern Life Deli and Drinks, Pittsboro, NC, January 2020. Courtesy of Alison E. Arnold.

4.51: *Jiangnan sizhu* (Chinese wind and string ensemble) at the Huxinting teahouse in Huangpu district, Shanghai, 2007. Courtesy of Alison E. Arnold.

4.52: *Sangat* (melodic shadowing) in Carnatic performance by vocalist Sanjay Subrahmanyan and violinist S. Varadarajan. Courtesy of Sanjay Subrahmanyan.

4.53: Urdu *ghazal* performance by Talat Aziz. Courtesy of Talat Aziz.

4.55: "Large Hadron Rap," lyrics and video production by Kate McAlpine, music by Will Barras, CERN, Geneva, Switzerland. Courtesy of Katherine McAlpine.

4.56: Ravi Shankar and Ali Akbar Khan, concert performance on New Year's Day, 1973. Courtesy of James DeWeaver.

4.57: San Francisco jazz by Steve and Kate Fowler. Courtesy of Steven H. Fowler.

4.58: Computer music, *"Sonnez la Cloche"* by Karlheinz Essl, performed live during exhibition by Gunter Damisch at Würth Art Room in Böheimkirchen, Austria, on October 3, 2003. Video by Uta Birk. More information at www.essl.at/works/sonnez-la-cloche.html. Courtesy of Karlheinz Essl, Universität für Musik und darstellende Kunst, Wien Institut für Komposition und Elektroakustik.

Chapter 5

5.1: Humpback whales. Courtesy of Rob Knourek.

5.2: Gibbons. Courtesy of Lara Mostert, www.monkeyland.co.za, www.saasa.org.za, www.birdsofeden.co.za, www.jukani.co.za.

5.3: Gelada baboons. Recorded near Debre Birhan, Ethiopia, 2013. Courtesy of Jonathan C. Kramer.

5.4: Mother-infant interactions between Maren Boudra and baby Sophia. Courtesy of Maren Boudra.

Chapter 6

6.1: "Mother." Composed and performed by John Lennon and the Plastic Ono Band. Courtesy of Yoko Ono Lennon. © Yoko Ono Lennon.

6.2: *"Fado Loucura"* performed by Ana Moura. Courtesy of Rita Gouveia, Lisbon, Portugal, www.anamoura.com.pt/indexnm.aspx.

6.3: Tito Puente salsa band. Courtesy of Milton Esteban, www.miltonesteban.com.

6.4: Nadia Boulanger. From documentary *Nadia Boulanger: Mademoiselle*, produced by Bruno Monsaingeon. Courtesy of Bruno Monsaingeon, www.brunomonsaingeon.com. © 1977. All rights reserved.

6.5: *"Kyo no shiki"* ("Four Seasons of Kyoto") performed by Satoyuki (shamisen and vocals) and Naosuzu (dancer). Courtesy of Kiyohito Takenaka, Ritsumeikan University, Kyoto, Japan.

6.6: Bi Kidude of Zanzibar, performing at the Les Orientales festival, France, 2004. Courtesy of François Mauger, director, Editorial de Mondomix, www.mondomix.com.

6.7: Kalulu Ukulele Band, Melbourne, Australia. Courtesy of Helen Lauder.

6.8: Georgian unaccompanied polyphonic singing by Vaja Ujmajuridze and friends. Video acquired with assistance from Marika Mikeladze and AskConselTbilisi.

6.9: Remo talking drum. Courtesy of Ayodapo Oyelana, Iyallu Arts, Culture and Tradition of the Yorubas, Nigeria, www.iyailu.com.

6.10: *Apenti* (Surinamese talking drum), demonstration by Henk Tjon, Paramaribo, 2009. Courtesy of Jonathan C. Kramer.

6.12: "*Sai Ma*" ("Horse Race") by Huang Haihuai, played on *erhu* by Dai Shenghua, Shanghai Conservatory, 2014. Courtesy of Dai Shenghua and Dai Xiaolian.

6.13: *The Lone Ranger.* Opening scene of television series starring Clayton Moore (The Lone Ranger) riding his horse Silver, 1949. Imageways/Getty Images 89132890.

6.14: *Tassa* drumming. From *Tassa Thunder: Folk Music from India to the Caribbean*, Peter Manuel, director. Courtesy of Peter Manuel. © 2010. All rights reserved.

6.15: South African lullaby. From *Rhythm of Resistance: Black South African Music*, Beats of the Heart Series, Jeremy Marre, director, Harcourt Films. Courtesy of Jeremy Marre. ©1979. All rights reserved.

6.16: New Orleans jazz funeral parade. From *Jazz Parades: Feet Don't Fail Me Now*, Alan Lomax, producer, 1990. From the Alan Lomax Collection at the American Folklife Center, Library of Congress.

6.17: Music therapy infomercial. Courtesy of Joanne V. Loewy, DA, LCAT, MT-BC, Director, The Louis Armstrong Center for Music and Medicine Hospital Mount Sinai Beth Israel, Associate Professor, Albert Einstein College of Medicine.

6.18: Mongolian shamaness: Courtesy of Tsoggy, 6/6 trips@mongolianways.com.

6.19: *Phi Faa* healing ritual of northeast Thailand and Laos. Courtesy of Dr. Reinhold Spatz/mickspatz.

6.20: Byzantine hymn of Saint Kassia (ca. 805–ca. 865). Performed by Men's Choir of Kimissis Tis Theotokou Greek Orthodox Church, Brooklyn, New York. Courtesy of Archdeacon Panteleimon, director, Archdiocesan School of Byzantine Music; managing director, Archdiocesan Byzantine Choir, Greek Orthodox Archdiocese of America.

6.21: *Nadaswaram* (South Indian oboe), played by Indian musicians Kasim and Babu Kalaimamani for the annual Brahmotsavam Festival, Sri Venkateshwara Temple, Cary, NC, 2014. Courtesy of Jonathan C. Kramer.

6.22: *Bhajans* in Surinamese temple. Courtesy of Jonathan C. Kramer.

6.24: "*Lanitra Manga Manga*" ("Blue, Blue sky") (1994) performed by Salala in Antananarivo, Madagascar, 2005. Courtesy of Olombelo "Ricky" Olombelona.

6.26: Rakesh Yankarran teaches his daughter, in Freeport, Trinidad, 2008. Courtesy of Alison E. Arnold.

6.27: "Singing at a house party" video clip from the bonus DVD to the recording entitled *Music of Central Asia*, vol. 6: *Alim and Fargana Qasimov: Spiritual Music of Azerbaijan*, SFW40525, courtesy of Smithsonian Folkways Recordings. *Music of Central Asia* is a co-production of the Aga Khan Music Initiative and Smithsonian Folkways Recordings. (p) © 2007. Used by permission.

6.28: Korean rhythmic pattern. From *Sopyonje*, Taehung Pictures, Im Kwon-taek, director. Courtesy of Im Kwon-taek, Im Kwon Taek College of Film and Performing Arts at Dong Seo University, Republic of Korea. © 1993. All rights reserved.

6.29: "A Visit to Kirina's New Music School," filmed and produced by Playing for Change Foundation, Kirina, Mala. Music, "*Soundiata*" by Boubacar Traoré. Courtesy of Playing for

Change Foundation, a multimedia music project started in 2004 by producers Mark Johnson and Whitney Kroenke, www.playingforchange.org. © 2011. All rights reserved.

Chapter 7

7.1: *Bandura* (Ukrainian lute-zither) played by Stepan Shcherbak, **Kyiv**, Ukraine. Courtesy of Leonard (Len) Wicks, www.ody-see.com.

7.2: Argentine dance orchestras. "Bandoneon & Tango, Buenos Aires" video compilation by Stefan Gergely. Courtesy of Stefan Gergely.

7.3: Tango. Courtesy of Paul Hodge, SoloAroundWorld, www.genpolicy.com.

7.10: *Fantasie Nègre.* Courtesy of Elijah Stevens, piano.

7.11: *Five Spirituals in Counterpoint*, Mvt. Five, *"Swing Low Sweet Chariot"* by Florence M. Price. Courtesy of Matthew J. Detrick and the Apollo Chamber Players, info@apollochamberplayers.org.

7.12: *Tibetans* by Acko Choedrag. Courtesy of Acko Choedrag. © 2007. All rights reserved.

7.13: Acko Choedrag at Kumbum Monastery, Qinghai province, PRC, filmed by Tsering Samdrup. Courtesy of Jonathan C. Kramer.

7.14: Afro-Surinamese drumming patterns, in Djoemoe, Suriname. Courtesy of Jonathan C. Kramer.

7.15: Native American dance. Paremuru Native American Culture Organization dance class, Paramaribo, Suriname. Courtesy of Jonathan C. Kramer.

7.16: Teenage Creole girls performing traditional Afro-Surinamese dance. NAKS (*Na Afrikan Kulturu fu Sranan*) Community Organization, Paramaribo, Suriname. Courtesy of Jonathan C. Kramer.

7.17: East Indian dance class in Paramaribo, Suriname. Courtesy of Jonathan C. Kramer.

7.18: *Jaran kepang* (Javanese hobby horse dance). Javanese Arrival Day Celebration, Javanese Cultural Center, Paramaribo, Suriname, 2008. Courtesy of Jonathan C. Kramer.

7.19: The Folkloristisch Ensemble, Marléne Lie A. Ling, director, Paramaribo, Suriname. Courtesy of Jonathan C. Kramer.

7.20: Henk Tjon's funeral, September 18–19, 2009, Paramaribo, Suriname. Courtesy of Jonathan C. Kramer.

Chapter 8

8.1: Johann Pachelbel, *Canon in D* (original instruments version). Courtesy of Voices of Music, www.voicesofmusic.org.

8.2: Korean *gayageums* with DJ, beatboxing, and break dancing, featuring Sookmyung Gayageum Orchestra. Courtesy of Professor Song Hye-jin, Sookmyung Women's University, director.

8.3: "A Moment So Close" by Bela Fleck and the Flecktones, recorded live at the Quick Center for the Arts in Fairfield, Connecticut. Featuring the late Kongar-ol Ondar (Tuvan throat singer), Sandip Burman (*tabla* drums), and Victor Wooten (electric bass). Courtesy of Bela Fleck and the Flecktones.

8.4: Mardi Gras. From *Dance for a Chicken: The Cajun Mardi Gras*, Pat Mire, director. Courtesy of Pat Mire, www.patmire.com. © 1993. All rights reserved.

8.5: Cajun begging songs in Iota, Louisiana. Courtesy of Eric Breaux.

8.6: Cajun twin fiddling with Michael Doucet and Mitch Reed, Louisiana. Courtesy of Eric Breaux.

8.7: Afro-Cajun accordion style. From *Cajun Country: Lache Pas la Patate!* ("Don't Drop the Potato!"), Alan Lomax, producer, 1990. From the Alan Lomax Collection at the American Folklife Center, Library of Congress.

8.11: Steve Riley and the Mamou Playboys. Video by Wilson Savoy. Courtesy of Steve Riley, www.mamouplayboys.com.

8.12: Community dance at the Montagnard Day Celebrations, Greensboro, NC, 2008. Courtesy of Alison E. Arnold.

8.13: Montagnard hanging gongs and barrel drum played at a rehearsal in Raleigh, NC, 2008. Courtesy of Alison E. Arnold.

8.14: *Trung* (Montagnard bamboo xylophone) played by Dock Rmah, Greensboro, NC. Courtesy of Alison E. Arnold.

8.15: *Goong* (Montagnard tube zither) played by Dock Rmah, Greensboro, NC. Courtesy of Alison E. Arnold.

8.16: *Ding nam* (Montagnard mouth organ) played by Y Dha Eban, Raleigh, NC. Courtesy of Alison E. Arnold.

8.17: "*Char Dega*" ("Dega Country") composed and performed by Hip Ksor, Raleigh, NC. Courtesy of Alison E. Arnold.

8.18: "For the People" performed by Montagnard hip-hop artist Mondega (Bom Siu) at NC State University, 2008. Courtesy of Alison E. Arnold.

8.19: "Stand My Ground," written and performed by Bom Siu (aka Mondega), music produced by Aaron McLean. Courtesy of Bom Siu.

8.20: Carifesta opening ceremony, from Carifesta XIV, Nailah David Rudder and Carl Jacobs. Courtesy of Desiree Sampson, Documentary Filmmaker and Content Creator, DSPMediaTT.

8.21: *Chutney* wining at Hindu wedding celebration in Trinidad, 2008, with singer Sally Sagram and musicians. Courtesy of Alison E. Arnold.

8.23: *Calabasse Café*, composed and performed by Mungal Patasar and Pantar. Music video by Aya Vision Ltd., Jason Riley, director. Courtesy of Mungal Patasar. © 2007. All rights reserved.

8.24: "Awake." Rehearsal with Mungal Patasar and his band Pantar, Trinidad, 2008. Courtesy of Alison E. Arnold.

8.26: "Nostalgia." From *Inner Mongolia Suite* (1937) by Ma Sicong, performed by Hsiao-Mei Ku and the late Benjamin Ward. Recorded in the Nelson Room, Duke University, recorded by Jonathan C. Kramer and Alison E. Arnold. Courtesy of Jonathan C. Kramer and Alison E. Arnold.

Chapter 9

9.5: Maria Stoyanova playing *gaida* (Bulgarian bagpipe). Courtesy of Timothy Rice, Professor Emeritus, University of California at Los Angeles.

9.13: "Do You Want Another Rap?" Courtesy of Ronald Mutebi and Afroberliner Enterprises, Kampala, Uganda.

9.14: "Qitik" ("Dance") by Greenland hip-hop group Nuuk Posse. Courtesy of members of Nuuk Posse.

9.15: Infomercial (Tibet). Courtesy of Gerald Roche and the Plateau Music Project.

9.16: Tibetan nomadic song. Courtesy of Tsering Samdrup and the Plateau Music Project.

Chapter 10

10.1: Korean Buddhist monk performing syllabic chant accompanying himself with gong strokes. Courtesy of Dr. Jongmae Park and Korean Buddhist Taego order, Loyola Marymount University, Los Angeles, CA.

10.3: Vedic chant by Brahmin priests seated around a sacred fire. From *Raga: A Film Journey into the Soul of India* (2010), featuring Ravi Shankar, directed by Howard Worth. A presentation of East Meets West Music and the Ravi Shankar Foundation. All rights reserved. (Originally produced as *Raga* (1971) by Ravi Shankar and Gary Haber, edited by Merle Worth.)

10.4: Vedic chant transmitted by Nambudiri Brahmins, Kerala, South India. From *Altar of Fire*, Robert Gardner and J.F. Staal, producers. The Film Study Center at Harvard University. Courtesy of the late Robert Gardner. © 1976. All rights reserved.

10.5: Judaic Sephardic cantillation, performed by Netanel C. Maroof, recorded by Joshua A. Maroof. Courtesy of Joshua A. Maroof.

10.6: Theravada Buddhist monks chanting, Wat Sene monastery, Luang Prabhang, Laos. Courtesy of Laos Essential Artistry, www.gotlaos.com.

10.7: Walking meditation. Buddhist monks in Shanxi province, PRC. Courtesy of Jonathan C. Kramer.

10.9: Benedictine nuns of Notre-Dame-l'Annonciation, Abbaye Sainte-Madeleine du Barroux, France. Gregorian chant, Psalm 59, "Commovisti, Domine." Courtesy of Patrick Robles.

10.10: Qur'anic recitation (*tarteel*) by Nusaiba Mohammad, 2009. Courtesy of Nusaiba Mohammad, Fashion Designer and Qur'anic teacher; featured in *The Guardian* newspaper UK, Islam Channel, and various TV channels. Also known as @iamndora on Instagram.

10.11: Sheikh Abdul Basit 'Abd us-Samad reciting Qur'anic verses. Courtesy of Jazak Allha.

10.12: *Tara Sutra* (Buddhist prayers) chanted by Tibetan women as they spin the giant prayer wheel. Courtesy of Jonathan C. Kramer.

10.13: *Kirtan* singing, *"Radhey Radhey Govinda"* by Jagadguru Shri Kripalu Ji Maharaj. Courtesy of Radha Madhav Society, branch of Jagadguru Kripalu Parishat.

10.14: *Mitzvah tantz, Shiezoli* YouTube Channel. Courtesy of Joshua Weber.

10.15: Chorale Prelude. Maria Magdalena Kaczor plays J. S. Bach *"Ein Wasserfluessen Babylon"* BWV 653 1. Courtesy of Maria Magdalena Kaczor.

10.16: "I Will Meet You in the Morning" sung by a Mennonite choir, 2010. Courtesy of Charles L. Alligood.

10.17: "Precious Lord, Take My Hand" sung by composer Thomas A. Dorsey. From *Say Amen, Somebody* (1982), Rykodisc DVD re-release. Courtesy of George T. Nierenberg, Folk Traditions, Inc.

10.18: Lining out: 1. "What a Friend I Have in Jesus," Fairfield Baptist Church, Lithonia, GA, Cleon Frazier, pastor. Courtesy of Bonni Ware; 2. Filmed at Antioch Old Regular Baptist Church, Betsye Layne, KY. Courtesy of Dan Torigoe, Dolceola Recordings.

10.19: "Here in My Life" sung by Darlene Zschech, Hillsong Church. Written by Mia Fieldes, © 2006 Hillsong Music Publishing (APRA) (adm. In the US and Canada at CapitolCMGPublishing.com. Hillsong Worship appears courtesy of Hillsong Church t/a Hillsong Music Australia © 2010 Hillsong Church. All rights reserved. Used by permission.

10.20: Watoto Church service, Kampala, Uganda, 2013. Courtesy of Jonathan C. Kramer.

10.21: "I Believe" sung by Archbishop Kiwanuka Senior Secondary School choir, Masaka district, Uganda, 2013. Courtesy of Jonathan C. Kramer.

10.22: *"Tutende Ddunda"* ("Let Us Praise the Lord") sung by Archbishop Kiwanuka Senior Secondary School choir, Masaka district, Uganda, 2013. Courtesy of Jonathan C. Kramer.

10.23: *"Ngenda Yeruzalemu"* ("I am Heading to Jerusalem") sung by Mbuye Farm School choir, Rakai district, Uganda, 2013. Courtesy of Jonathan C. Kramer.

10.24: Four school choirs competing in the Secondary School Sacred Song Competition, Masaka district, Uganda, 2013. Courtesy of Jonathan C. Kramer.

10.25: Muslim women performing *zikr* ("remembrance of God") in Azerbaijan. Courtesy of János Sipos.

10.26: Professional *qawwal* perform sacred songs on *Qawwali* night, Nizamuddin Shrine, Delhi, India. Courtesy of Jonathan C. Kramer.

10.27: Nusrat Fateh Ali Khan and party performing *qawwali* on stage in Paris, 1988. Courtesy of Nusrat Online Team, nusratonline.com.

Chapter 11

11.1: Kings of Harmony gospel brass shout band, United House of Prayer, Washington, DC. From *The Music District*, Susan Levitas, producer. Courtesy of Susan Levitas. © 1996. All rights reserved.

11.2: *Nadun* celebration in Mangghuer farming villages, Qinghai province, PRC. Courtesy of Jonathan C. Kramer.

11.3: Three *mbira* (thumb piano) musicians, Chikomborero Dutiro, Prince Mandere, and William Saviriyo, of Chaonza village, Zimbabwe. From *Mbira Maestros*, documentary film by Antonio Lino. Courtesy of Gilbert Mandere and Antonio Lino. © 2010. All rights reserved.

11.4: Women evoke the goddess Legba in a Winti ceremony, an Afro-Surinamese traditional religion, in Paramaribo, Suriname. Courtesy of Jonathan C. Kramer.

11.5: *Jaran kepang* trance dance. Courtesy of Jonathan C. Kramer

11.6: Buddhist monks perform the Black Hat dance at the Dutsi Til monastery, Surmang, Tibet, 2002. Courtesy of Ginny Lipson and Holly Gayley of the Konchock Foundation, www.konchok.org.

11.7: Mevlevi whirling dervishes, video documentary by Omar's Travels, 2009. Courtesy of Omar Farooque, Omar's Travels.

11.8: *Bharatanatyam Margam*, invocatory section of South Indian classical dance performance by Savitha Sastry. Courtesy of Savitha Sastry, www.savithasastry.com and Sai Shree Arts. © 2009. All rights reserved.

11.9: Zaouli masked dance. Courtesy of Nabil Zorkot, Côte d'Ivoire.

11.10: Obon celebrations. Bon Odori dance in Yutenji district, Tokyo, Japan, 2012. Courtesy of Minoru Tanaka.

11.11: Chanting of Buddhist prayers by members of the Chudoji Rokusai group for Obon celebrations, Kiyomizu Temple, Kyoto, 2009. Courtesy of Alison E. Arnold.

11.12: *Yotsu taiko* ("four drums") performed by members of the Chudoji Rokusai group at Kiyomizu Temple, Kyoto, 2009. Courtesy of Alison E. Arnold.

11.13: Ritual pole spinning by members of the Chudoji Rokusai group, Kiyomizu Temple, Kyoto, 2009. Courtesy of Alison E. Arnold.

11.14: Lion and spider dance by members of the Chudoji Rokusai group, Kiyomizu Temple, Kyoto, 2009. Courtesy of Alison E. Arnold.

11.15: *Barong* trance dance at Camphuan Temple, Ubud, Bali. From *Calonarang* video, © Swami Arun. Courtesy of Swami Arun, The Yoga Barn. All rights reserved.

11.16: *Kathakali* compilation: 1. From *Raga: A Film Journey into the Soul of India* (2010), featuring Ravi Shankar; original film written by Ravi Shankar, produced and directed by Howard Worth, 1971. Courtesy of Cat Celebrezze, East Meets West Music, DVD © 2010. All rights reserved; 2. Margi Theater, Thiruvananthapuram in "Kathakali" from *Symphony Celestial: A Unique* Collection, Featuring Ten of India's Fascinating Dance Forms (2003). Courtesy of Hari Madathipparambil, managing director, Invis Multimedia Pvt. Ltd., invis-multimedia.com.

11.17: Epic of Pabuji performance in Rajasthan. Courtesy of Manohar Lalas.

Chapter 12

12.1: *Ganga puja*, ritual purification of the Ganges river, in Benares, 2011. Courtesy of Jonathan C. Kramer.

12.2: Sound of the gongs at the Golden Rock at Kyaiktiyo, Myanmar. Courtesy of Walter Kaspar-Sickermann, www.mp.haw-hamburg.de/pers/Kaspar-Sickermann/mm/emm005.html.

12.3: Great Standing Lingshan Buddha and the musical water fountain display in Wuxi, PRC. Courtesy of Ting Ting Chen.

12.4: *Shofar* (ram's horn) blown at sunrise, Jerusalem. Courtesy of Rabbi Rodriguez Sabino.

12.5: *Adhan* ("Call to Prayer") recited by the *muezzin* in a mosque in Kampala, Uganda. Courtesy of Jonathan C. Kramer.

12.6: St. Michael's Feast in Lalibela, Ethiopia, 2014. Courtesy of Jonathan C. Kramer.

12.8: Bar mitzvah. Courtesy of Gregory Rosner.

12.9: Funeral rituals in Shaanbei, Shaanxi province, PRC. Courtesy of Jonathan C. Kramer.

12.10: Three-day Saramaccan Maroon ceremony in Suriname. Courtesy of Jonathan C. Kramer.

12.12: Two Roman Catholic processions in Cape Verde, 1997. From Viva Cape Verde, Pacheco e Valadares Produções. © 2002. All rights reserved. Courtesy of Marcia Rego and Hermes Illana.

12.13: Two Daoist processions: 1. Luo Tian Da Jiao ritual, Hong Kong, 2007. Courtesy of James E. Miller; 2. Celebration of a new temple in Xian. Courtesy of Robert S. Bonati.

12.14: Hindu wedding procession in Agra, India. Courtesy of Jonathan C. Kramer.

12.15: Hindu ritual procession in Manali, Himachal Pradesh, India. Courtesy of Jonathan C. Kramer.

Chapter 13

13.1: Ethiopian Azmari Gezate accompanying himself on the *masenko* (one-string fiddle), Lalibela, 2014. Courtesy of Jonathan C. Kramer.

13.2: Dane Jurić, Croatian epic singer and *gusle* player. Courtesy of "Brojevni," J. Habrun.

13.3: Ruža Jolić, Croatian epic singer and *gusle* player. Courtesy of "Brojevni," J. Habrun.

13.4: West African praise singer. Diali Cissokho singing *"Lu Mu Mety Mety,"* accompanying himself on *kora* (harp-lute). Boone, NC, 2010. Courtesy of Diali Cissokho, www.kairabamusic.com.

13.5: Kaira Ba performing in Saxapahaw, NC, 2013. Courtesy of Will Ridenour and Kaira Ba, www.kairabamusic.com, and Saheed Adeleye, African Rhythms.

13.7: "Carolan's Dream" by Turlough O'Carolan, played on Celtic harp by Mark Harmer. Courtesy of Mark Harmer.

13.8: *Shuoshude* (blind storytellers) in Suide, Shaanxi province, PRC. Courtesy of Jonathan C. Kramer.

13.9: *The Tale of the Heike*, "Reverse Oars" (*Sakaro*) episode, narrated by *biwa* player Kikuo Yuji. Video used with permission of Todo Music Preservation Association (*Todo Ongaku Hozankai*). Courtesy of Haruko Komoda.

13.10: From *Sopyonje*, Taehung Pictures, Im Kwon-taek, director. Courtesy of Im Kwon-taek, Im Kwon Taek College of Film and Performing Arts at Dong Seo University, Republic of Korea. © 1993. All rights reserved.

13.11: Korean *pansori* performers with barrel drum (*buk*) accompaniment. UNESCO Intangible Cultural Heritage of Humanity.

13.12: *Ningyo Johruri Bunraku Puppet Theatre*, UNESCO Intangible Cultural Heritage of Humanity.

13.13: *Wayang* Theatre, UNESCO Intangible Cultural Heritage of Humanity.

13.14: *Talchum* masked dance drama. Courtesy of Bongsan Mask Dance-Drama Preservation Society of Seoul, Korea, www.bongsantal.com/index_en.html. © 2012. All rights reserved.

13.15: *Virgen del Carmen* festival, Paucartambo, Peru. Courtesy of Chris Forster.

13.17: *Jingju* performance at the Huguang Guild Hall, Beijing, 2007. Courtesy of Alison E. Arnold.

13.18: Chinese regional opera, from "Doing Things," DVD accompanying *Ritual and Music of North China: Shawm Bands of Shanxi* (2007), by Stephen Jones. With permission of Stephen Jones.

Chapter 14

14.1: Busking musicians: 1. Rome, Italy, 2012. Courtesy of Jonathan C. Kramer; 2. Sainte-Foy-La-Grande, France, 2011. Courtesy of Alison E. Arnold.

14.2: Bauls of Bengal, recorded on Shantiniketan Express by Deepa Dutta Chaudhuri for travel blog WheelsOnOurFeet.

14.3: Concert for Bangladesh. Ali Akbar Khan (*sarod*), Ravi Shankar (*sitar*), and Alla Rakha (*tabla*) performing at Madison Square Garden, August 1, 1971. From reissued Apple DVD. © Apple Films Inc.

14.4: Touring company of blind musicians in Beijing, PRC, 2010. Courtesy of Jonathan C. Kramer.

14.5: Traditional circle dancing in Xining, PRC. Courtesy of Xiaofei Song.

14.6: Zurkhaneh Ali Khayat, Tehran, Iran, with *zarb* drumming and narration by *morshed* Amir Hossein, 2014. Courtesy of Esmail Gholamreza.

14.7: *Sarewa* (flutes) and *jauje* (talking drums) played at a Nigerian boxing match. From *Konkombe: Nigerian Music*, Beats of The Heart series, Jeremy Marre, director, Harcourt Films. Courtesy of Jeremy Marre. © 1977. All rights reserved

14.8: *Vuvuzelas* played at the FIFA Confederations Cup, Johannesburg, South Africa, 2009. Courtesy of Jon M. Combs, www.sunlightpeak.com.

14.10: Marian Anderson performs at the Lincoln Memorial, Washington DC on April 9, 1939. Public Domain.

14.11: *Entenga* (drum) and *Amakondere* (gourd trumpet) ensembles. Courtesy of James Isabirye.

14.12: *Bigwala* trumpet ensemble, Bigwala Cultural Group-Magic Moment, The Singing Wells Project. Courtesy of James Allen.

14.13: Open Celtic music session at Bras d'Or Yacht Club, Baddeck, Cape Breton. Celtic Colours International Festival, 2012. Courtesy of Alison E. Arnold.

14.14: Celtic Jam Session at Keltic Quay, Whycocomagh Waterfront Centre, Cape Breton. Celtic Colours International Festival, 2012. Courtesy of Alison E. Arnold.

14.15: *Bateria* rehearsal in the Mocidade Samba School building, 2013. Courtesy of Paul Hodge, SoloAroundWorld, www.genpolicy.com.

14.16: Mocidade Samba School in the Sambadrome parade, Rio de Janeiro, Brazil, 2013. Courtesy of Paul Hodge, SoloAroundWorld, www.genpolicy.com.

14.17: *J'Ouvert* song explained and sung by Wendell Manwarren of 3Canal rapso band, Port of Spain, Trinidad, 2008. Courtesy of Alison E. Arnold.

14.18: Steel bands. From "Oil Barrels, Steel Drums: Pan in Trinidad and Tobago" (1996). Courtesy of Chris Simon, founder, Sageland Media, www.sagelandmedia.com. © 1996. Museum of International Folk Art.

Chapter 15

15.1: *Kecak* performance, Uluwatu Temple, Bali. Courtesy of Valdas J. Steponavicius.

15.2: Cambodian musicians at Banteay Srei Temple, Angkor, 2010. Courtesy of Alison E. Arnold.

15.3: Mevlevi dervish at an outdoor restaurant in Istanbul, Turkey. Courtesy of Jonathan C. Kramer.

15.4: Nightly entertainment, filmed at Totot Restaurant, Addis Ababa. Courtesy of Jonathan C. Kramer.

Media Index

By Chapter

CHAPTER 4

By Geographical Region

AFRICA

THE AMERICAS

EUROPE

Index

Note: *Italic* page numbers refer to figures.

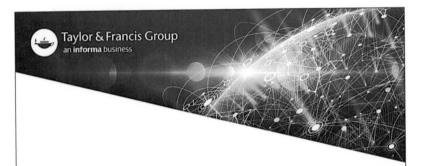